Social Catholicism for the Twenty-First Century?

— Volume 1 —

"This is that rare volume combining scholarly erudition with inspiring visions (and many heroes) of social justice. Each essay in this book serves as a reminder that Catholic social teaching, while solidly principle-based, is never reducible to ideology or abstractions. Rather, it is an adaptable resource capable of nurturing our practice of charity and our commitment to social justice. The reader will emerge from this volume with a thousand ideas for living out a renewed social Catholicism for our times."

—**Thomas Massaro, SJ**, professor of moral theology, Fordham University

"This volume provides essential historical and theological context for an appreciation of the renewed focus on social Catholicism and the controversies that the pontificate of Pope Francis has sparked especially in North America. This book is essential for all those who want to comprehend the potential of social Catholicism in the context of the crisis of the liberal order and the disruption of globalization."

—**Massimo Faggioli**, professor of historical theology, Villanova University

"As strange as it is to call these very current and forward-looking volumes a recovery, the essays compiled in *Social Catholicism for the Twenty-First Century?* in fact do recover some of the priority of practical reason for social questions in the moral tradition. The effort is timely and much needed. Murphy has gathered a splendid group of scholars in these volumes whose essays offer much for students of Catholic social thought to think about."

—**Steven P. Millies**, professor of public theology, Catholic Theological Union

"The antiliberal and antidemocratic drift of some contemporary conservativism has found an unforeseen expression in the re-emergence of Catholic integralism—a tradition that resists the postwar evolution of Catholic social doctrine as the papal and conciliar magisterium moved toward a reconciliation with constitutional democracy and a strong affirmation of human dignity and rights against totalitarian threats. Partly in response to these developments, William Murphy has brought together in these volumes a forceful reaffirmation of social Catholicism that is both timely and welcome. These two volumes will be essential reading not only for scholars and students, but also for bishops, policymakers and advocates."

—J. AUGUSTINE DI NOIA, OP, archbishop

Social Catholicism for the Twenty-First Century?

—— Volume 1 ——

Historical Perspectives and Constitutional Democracy in Peril

Edited with an Introduction by
WILLIAM F. MURPHY JR.

☙PICKWICK *Publications* • Eugene, Oregon

SOCIAL CATHOLICISM FOR THE TWENTY-FIRST CENTURY?— VOLUME 1
Historical Perspectives and Constitutional Democracy in Peril

Copyright © 2024 Wipf and Stock Publishers. All rights reserved. Except for brief quotations in critical publications or reviews, no part of this book may be reproduced in any manner without prior written permission from the publisher. Write: Permissions, Wipf and Stock Publishers, 199 W. 8th Ave., Suite 3, Eugene, OR 97401.

Pickwick Publications
An Imprint of Wipf and Stock Publishers
199 W. 8th Ave., Suite 3
Eugene, OR 97401

www.wipfandstock.com

PAPERBACK ISBN: 978-1-6667-8859-4
HARDCOVER ISBN: 978-1-6667-8860-0
EBOOK ISBN: 978-1-6667-8861-7

Cataloguing-in-Publication data:

Names: Murphy, William F., Jr., editor.

Title: Social Catholicism for the twenty-first century?—volume 1 : historical perspectives and constitutional democracy in peril / edited by William F. Murphy Jr.

Description: Eugene, OR : Pickwick Publications, 2024 | Includes bibliographical references and index(es).

Identifiers: ISBN 978-1-6667-8859-4 (paperback) | ISBN 978-1-6667-8860-0 (hardcover) | ISBN 978-1-6667-8861-7 (ebook)

Subjects: LCSH: Catholic Church—Doctrines. | Church and social problems—Catholic Church. | Christian sociology—Catholic Church—History—20th century. | Capitalism—Religious aspects—Catholic Church. | Economics—Religious aspects—Catholic Church. | Christianity and politics.

Classification: BX1753 .S6250 2024 (paperback) | BX1753 .S6250 (ebook)

VERSION NUMBER 09/06/24

Scripture quotations marked (NRSV) are from the New Revised Standard Version Bible, copyright © 1989 the Division of Christian Education of the National Council of the Churches of Christ in the United States of America. Used by permission. All rights reserved.

Scripture quotations marked (RSV) are taken from Revised Standard Version of the Bible, copyright © 1946, 1952, and 1971 National Council of the Churches of Christ in the United States of America. Used by permission. All rights reserved worldwide.

This book is dedicated to my wife, Dr. Patricia Pintado-Murphy, who has been my best friend for many years, an invaluable collaborator in many projects, and my most effective advocate.

So in the present case, I tell you, keep away from these men and let them alone, because if this plan or this undertaking is of human origin, it will fail; but if it is of God, you will not be able to overthrow them—in that case you may even be found fighting against God!

(Acts 5:38–39)

Contents

Lists of Tables | ix
Contributors to Volume 1 | xi
Preface | xv
Acknowledgments | xxv

1. Introduction | 1
   —William. F. Murphy Jr., Initiative for Social Catholicism

2. The Social Catholicism of Fr. Félix Varela (1788–1853) | 75
   —Peter Casarella, Duke University

3. Wilhelm von Ketteler: Nineteenth-Century Advocate for Catholic Social Thought | 102
   —Martin J. O'Malley, Friedrich Schiller University

4. Johnny versus Tommie: What We Can Learn from a Historical Controversy | 137
   —Martin Schlag, University of St. Thomas

5. The Social Formation of Msgr. John A. Ryan | 161
   —William. F. Murphy Jr., Initiative for Social Catholicism

6. Maurice Blondel's Defense of the Social Catholics and His Enduring Critique of Catholic Integralism | 177
   —Peter J. Bernardi, SJ

Contents

7 The Gospel and Human Dignity: Catholicism
   and Liberalism in Dialogue | 204
   —Drew Christiansen, SJ, Georgetown University (†)

8 Liberalism, Conservatism, and Social Catholicism
   for the Twenty-First Century? | 222
   —William. F. Murphy Jr., Initiative for Social Catholicism

9 Metaphysics, Ethics, Politics, and Theology: Can
   Natural Lawyers Embrace Liberalism? | 270
   —Thomas Howes, Princeton University

10 The Boundaries and Authority of Catholic Social
   Teaching: A Reply to John Finnis | 295
   —Bernard G. Prusak, John Carroll University

11 Integralism, Political Catholicism, and
   Democracy in the Modern West | 320
   —Julian G. Waller, George Washington University

12 The World out of Joint: The Hard Right and Postliberalism
   in Twenty-First Century American Politics | 354
   —Matt McManus, University of Michigan

13 Formation for a New Social Catholicism | 370
   —William. F. Murphy Jr., Initiative for Social Catholicism

Subject Index | 395
Author Index | 415

Lists of Tables

Table 1. The Age of Revolutions and the Americas | 83–84

Contributors to Volume 1

Peter J. Bernardi, SJ, Professor Emeritus of Theology at Loyola University Chicago and of the *Lumen Christi* Institute. He is author of *Maurice Blondel, Social Catholicism, and Action Française: The Clash over the Church's Role in Society during the Modernist Era* and various related articles including "Maurice Blondel: Precursor of the Second Vatican Council" and "Action Française Catholicism and Opposition to Vatican II's *Dignitatis Humanae*."

Peter Casarella, Professor of Theology at the Divinity School of Duke University has published widely and held leadership positions at various institutions while also serving on multiple ecumenical dialogues. A collection of his essays was published as *Reverberations of the Word: Wounded Beauty in Global Catholicism*. Most recently, he edited *The Whole Is Greater Than Its Parts: Ecumenism and Inter-religious Encounters in the Age of Pope Francis*. He is currently working on a book titled *The God of the People: A Latinx Theology*.

Drew Christiansen, SJ (†) was Distinguished Professor of Ethics and Human Development in Georgetown's School of Foreign Service and a senior fellow at the Berkley Center for Religion, Peace, and World Affairs. His areas of research included nuclear disarmament, nonviolence and just peacemaking, Catholic social teaching, and ecumenical public advocacy. He served as a consultant to the Holy See, in the leadership of the Catholic Peacebuilding Network, on the Atlantic Council's Middle East Task Force, and was part of the Holy See delegation that participated in the negotiation of the Treaty on the Prohibition of Nuclear Weapons.

Contributors to Volume 1

Thomas D. Howes is Editor-in-Chief of *The Vital Center*, Research Fellow at the Austrian Institute in Vienna, and a member of the James Madison Society at Princeton University, where he is also a Lecturer in Politics. He is currently working on a book called *Natural Law & Constitutional Democracy* and he has a contract with Acton Institute to co-write a book with the preliminary title *Why Postliberalism Failed*.

Matt McManus, a lecturer in the department of political science at the University of Michigan. He is the author of *The Emergence of Postmodernity* and *Liberalism and Liberal Rights: A Critical Legal Argument* amongst other books. His forthcoming work includes the essay collection *Nietzsche and the Politics of Reaction* and *The Political Right and Equality*.

William F. Murphy Jr., Theologian in Residence at St. Edmund's Retreat and Founder of the Initiative for Social Catholicism and A Better Kind of Politics, while also serving as Adjunct Professor of Theology at University of St. Mary of the Lake/Mundelein Seminary. He was previously a Professor of Moral Theology for over twenty years at various institutions and edited the *Josephinum Journal of Theology* for seventeen years. He has also previously edited four books through Catholic University of America Press and published numerous scholarly essays.

Martin J. O'Malley, Research Scholar and Instructor at the Center for Applied Ethics at the Friedrich Schiller University in Jena, Germany. His recent research has focused on intergroup reconciliation and the moral status of life forms and artifacts related to synthetic biology.

Bernard Prusak, the Raymond and Eleanor Smiley Chair in Business Ethics in John Carroll University's Boler College of Business. His recent publications include *Catholic Moral Philosophy in Practice and Theory*, *Catholic Higher Education and Catholic Social Thought* (edited with Jennifer Reed-Bouley), "Abortion & Democracy in Ohio" and "The Pro-Life Movement: Less Popular Than Ever?"

Martin Schlag, Alan W. Moss Endowed Chair for Catholic Social Thought at the University of St. Thomas in St. Paul, MN and the director of the program in church management at the Pontifical University of the Holy Cross in Rome. He has published widely based on his research that focuses on the tradition of Catholic social thought in political and economic questions, on the promotion of principled business leadership to advance the common good and on overcoming poverty by helping the poor participate in the market economy.

Julian G. Waller, Associate Research Analyst at the Center for Naval Analyses and part-time faculty member at George Washington University where he lectures in the Department of Political Science and on Russian Politics. He has published widely in his research areas of comparative authoritarian politics, strategic decision-making in authoritarian states, political-military affairs in Eurasia, and ideological illiberalism in Europe, Eurasia, and North America.

Preface

THE REMOTE ROOTS OF this project trace back to my seventeen years as Professor of Moral Theology at the Pontifical College Josephinum in Columbus, OH and Editor of the *Josephinum Journal of Theology*. When I began offering a course on Catholic Social Teaching in 2008, my social and political views had been shaped by various factors including my graduate studies during the 1990s when a new generation of "JPII Catholics" was coalescing in an increasing alignment with the conservative era ushered in by the Presidency of Ronald Reagan. These graduate studies had focused on the recovery of Thomistic ethics at the Dominican House of Studies and included a good amount of work in New Testament and Pauline studies, along with an introduction to the rich traditions of *ressourcement* and *Communio* theology from the Pontifical John Paul II Institute for Studies on Marriage and Family. My immersion into these living streams of the Catholic tradition was part of a broader dynamic in which many young Catholics were motivated to learn our tradition after postconciliar decades during which the tradition was deemphasized as engagement with the modern world was prioritized. From the various courses I took at The Catholic University of America, I also came to appreciate the importance of approaching intellectual questions "critically," which required understanding the "state of the question," including historical and comparative perspectives. As I plunged into social ethics, which engages many fields of study, my aspiration to a critical perspective was a constant reminder of the limitations of my own grasp of an inherently complex subject matter.

My social and political views had also been shaped by a quarter century of membership in the Reaganite form of the Republican Party, by my involvement in the pro-life movement, and by an interest in conservative thought tracing back to the mid-1980s when I entered a first career in engineering, business and technology. I was also an avid reader of the journal *First Things*, which was edited by Fr. Richard J. Neuhaus where questions of faith and public life were discussed by a coalition of religious conservatives, commonly known as the (religious) neoconservatives or the theoconservatives. In addition, I also followed the ongoing debate between Neuhaus and David L. Schindler, who was on the faculty of the John Paul II Institute and edited the journal *Communio*. This debate was over the compatibility between Catholicism and American liberal democracy. In this debate, Neuhaus emphasized that Catholics should contest in the "public square" of the political process for the best version of American liberal democracy achievable by informing it with the truths of Catholic faith. Schindler, on the other hand, emphasized that liberalism is radically disordered because it was not founded on a proper metaphysics that reflected the foundations of truth in God and creation.

At the time I began offering a yearly course for seminarians on Catholic Social Teaching, I was in the middle of several years focused on some of the more disputed questions of fundamental and applied morals. This work was rooted in a collaboration with Fr. Martin Rhonheimer through which I acted as editor to bring four volumes of his works into English through the Catholic University of America Press. I had become aware of Rhonheimer's work during graduate school based on his prominent argumentation in support of John Paul II's 1993 moral encyclical *Veritatis Splendor: The Splendor of the Truth*. Compared to the predominant interpretations of Thomistic ethics at the time, his work aligned more closely with the directions encouraged by the encyclical and—it seemed to me—with the texts of Aquinas, while also illuminating the flaws in the alternative approaches. As I was completing my doctoral studies at the John Paul II Institute, I had been encouraged by the senior moralist at the central Roman session of the Institute, Msgr. Livio Melina, to study the work of Rhonheimer. This work was recommended not only on the topic of "action theory," where Rhonheimer showed the way between the flawed alternatives of physicalism on the right and proportionalism on the left, but also for his recovery and articulation of the Thomistic understanding of practical reason.

I will pick up on this apparent tangent below, when I discuss how a renewed emphasis on metaphysics over practical reason among some influential American Catholic scholars led back to the preconciliar

Preface

situation of a more physicalist approach to moral theory that resulted in more stringent positions on some key open questions than the discernment of the Papal magisterium. This debate over the reception of *Veritatis Splendor*—in my opinion—marked a key moment in the opening of a division between American Catholic conservatives and the Papal magisterium that would greatly widen during the Pontificate of Francis. Although I can understand how American "JPII Catholics" after the sexual revolution, amidst the "culture wars," and part of a renewed era of "tradition mindedness" would be more inclined to fight for more rigorous positions on "disputed questions," than to accept less strict ones, I think these complex problems need to be revisited in the much broader context of what some call the global "polycrisis," including the crisis in the Church regarding the long-delayed—or some would say failed—reception of the Second Vatican Council.

During my early years of becoming more familiar with our social tradition through study and teaching while at the Josephinum, we published a thematic issue of the *Josephinum Journal of Theology* on *Catholicism and Liberal Democracy* (2009). This occurred at a time when much of the world was trying to recover from—and make sense of—the financial crisis that began in 2008 and led to the subsequent Great Recession. Unfortunately, the hopeful expectations for the new millennium that St. John Paul II fostered had been seriously diminished by an ong ing plague of sexual abuse scandals that had festered under his w but there was still confidence among my generation that he had Church on a sound path for the future. This confidence was when his long-time collaborator Joseph Cardinal Ratzinger s him in the Chair of Peter in 2005.

To understand magisterial discernment regarding the s opments during the subsequent years that were marked by th cial crisis and the Great Recession that followed it, I took B XVI's 2009 social encyclical *Caritas in Veritate: On Integr in Charity and Truth* as an indispensable point of referen for the present project are at least five points that merit cae, tion to grasp their profound significance, as to do so willcate one toward the whole argument of this collection. Froe five I would argue, it becomes possible to better apprethe liv- of Francis as building on that of his predecessors. T le. Given points was Benedict's presentation of Catholic Soci ing out of charity in the modern world, as was cle the absolute centrality of the virtue of charity to Christian life and morality, the importance of this point must not be overlooked. Second was his reaffirmation that this doctrine entailed a Christian humanism in harmony with the entire postwar social tradition as, for example, had been previously synthesized in the 2003 *Compendium of the Social Doctrine of the Church* under the heading of "an integral and solidary humanism." It is all too common, however, for American Catholics to sneer at humanistic collaboration, although John Paul II's social vision was certainly a Christian humanism. The third was Benedict's insistence that both justice and charity call us to commit ourselves to the common good through being solicitous for and participating in the institutions that shape society. Fourth was his recognition of the need for significant reforms to the predominant economic paradigm that had contributed significantly to the financial crisis. Fifth was Benedict's affirmation of the need to give urgent attention to the rapidly accelerating environmental crisis.

During the years of the Great Recession, I also edited a thematic issue of the *Josephinum Journal of Theology* under the heading of "*Thomism and the Nouvelle Théologie*" (2011). This thematic issue explored not just the twentieth century history between these two schools but also what I saw as a promising renewal of them, including their mutual interaction in different forms of what one might call "*ressourcement* Thomism." In my introductory essay to that journal issue, however, I also discussed what I thought was a problematic dimension of this increasingly influential dialogue. This concerned how both contemporary Thomists and *Communio* thinkers were approaching matters of morality predominantly from the perspective of metaphysics as distinguished from that proper to morality, an area of the post Tridentine moral tradition that required clarification in light of the post conciliar crisis. For Aristotle and Aquinas, moral philosophy concerns the order that reason puts into human acts to direct them to ends. This aligns with what John Paul II called "the perspective of the acting person" that he emphasized in pointing toward a resolution of the crisis. My concern was that the emphasis on metaphysics and over the recovery of Aquinas's approach to properly human action in *Veritatis Splendor*—and from the corresponding recovery of properly practical reason—was undermining the core of the only plausible resolution of the postconciliar crisis of morality that occasioned the encyclical. Absent this resolution, we had influential American Catholic conservatives taking on positions that I would argue were "more Catholic than the Pope" even when that Pope was Benedict XVI and when he was interpreting the legacy of John Paul II's teaching magisterium, of which the former Prefect of the Congregation for the Propagation of the Faith was arguably the most credible voice.

Similarly, to approach questions of constitutional democracy and social ethics from the perspective of metaphysics—instead of practical reason—risks failing to appreciate the fact that our public and international institutions have been established as means to achieve important practical ends—such as living together in peace or protecting human rights, or preventing Russian military expansion across Europe—that share in the common good as the Church understands it. These means are deliberated and established, moreover, within the tumultuous struggles of human history that do not await the speculations of metaphysicians. Aware of the vulnerability of constitutional democracies and international security to nefarious political forces, especially amidst financial crises and subsequent disruptions, Pope Benedict XVI encouraged Catholics to be solicitous for these institutions and to avail ourselves of them, a message of even greater relevance today, but one to which the institutional infrastructure of American Catholicism seems unaware.

During these same years of the Great Recession, I also edited—and wrote a detailed introduction to—a collection of texts by Martin Rhonheimer entitled *The Common Good of Constitutional Democracy: Essays in Political Philosophy and on Catholic Social Teaching* (2013). This text not only aligned nicely with Pope Benedict's emphasis on fostering our public and international institutions but also provided philosophical resources to deepen the postwar rapprochement between Catholic social thought and constitutional democracy. This project helped me to better understand some of the key philosophical and historical questions surrounding Catholic Social Doctrine, at least through the years when there was still a broad consensus in the developed world for neoliberal economics, which had always been difficult to reconcile with the discernment of the magisterium as reflected in the social encyclicals. During the years of the Great Recession, I was becoming increasingly convinced of the need for a profound rethinking of the dominant economic paradigm given the ever more evident unsustainability of the existing one, whether considered politically, environmentally, or otherwise. It also seemed clear that the economic inequality that had grown over recent decades was integral to the broader breakdown in social and international stability that was manifesting itself in tribal polarization, "culture wars," deaths of despair, the proliferation of weapons and violence, populist hostility

Preface

to "elites," nationalism, xenophobia, growing oligarchic power, and autocratic alliances, among other social and global maladies.

Over the subsequent decade, I have tried to deepen my understanding of the "state of the question" regarding these various challenges, and of how Catholic Social Doctrine might relate to them, and especially whether the Catholic Church had something important to offer as the human family faces an increasingly urgent set of crises. As I sought to find a path forward that not only better reflects the fundamental unity of the Church under the guidance of the magisterium, but also the Catholic harmony between faith and reason, I have come to appreciate the history and potential of the model of social Catholicism corresponding to Pope Francis's calls for a "better kind of politics." The reasons for this conviction include that this approach encourages a wide range of citizens to work in solidarity for the common good, in a mode of social friendship and dialogue. They also include that this model draws freely from all relevant fields of knowledge and is guided by a proven set of principles, which is a promising approach to addressing matters of inherent complexity. Without even considering the divine assistance upon which such living out of social charity depends, a renewal of social Catholicism would seem to indeed offer something that is not only unique, but desperately needed in our polarized societies, and that could perhaps be decisive in preventing the dystopia that many fear is inevitable, especially if American democracy—or even the NATO alliance—are lost.

My appointment as the 2020–22 Chester and Margaret Paluch Lecturer at the University of St. Mary of the Lake/Mundelein Seminary gave me the occasion to pull together and present a series of four lectures under the heading of "Social Catholicism for the Twenty-First Century?" My initial plan was that those lectures would become the basis of a monograph on the topic. Given that Catholic social doctrine depends on dialogue with various fields of study which are beyond the ability of any one person to master, the best approach to understanding and addressing the social questions of our day would need to be a dialogical and collaborative one. Although the "study circles" and "social weeks" of European social Catholics since the Industrial Revolution provided a remote inspiration for contemporary imaginations, collaboration on thematic journal issues or edited volumes seemed the most promising way to proceed, especially given the geographic distribution of the potential contributors. I embarked, therefore, on the long process of identifying potential contributors and securing their participation toward a

Preface

collaborative effort that might complement my anticipated monograph. When the journal was subsequently discontinued, that left the edited collection as the venue for publication.

These contributions trickled in over time, with some who had hoped to contribute having to withdraw for various reasons, while others were added. This long process, unfortunately, presented those who had been most timely in delivering their texts with an opportunity to practice the virtue of patience as the project dragged out far longer than I had originally anticipated. After I had received over half of the contributions with others promised in the upcoming months, St. Edmund's Retreat center in Mystic, Connecticut made a significant contribution to the project by providing me with a position as Theologian in Residence and Director of the Edmundite Initiative for Human Dignity. This position gave me the several months that were needed to prepare the manuscript for publication, which were necessary as my contributions became a more significant part of the collection than originally anticipated.

After having corresponded with scores of scholars from a wide spectrum of views, I eventually received contributions from the twenty-five who appear in these two volumes. Upon reviewing them, I was delighted with their quality and how they complemented each other to address most of the subjects I had hoped to cover. With these essays, many of which are quite substantial in both content and length, the collection was growing too large for most potential publishers, but the complexity of the challenges being explored seemed to require a broad set of substantive essays. I was delighted, therefore, that the Pickwick Publications imprint of Wipf and Stock was interested in concurrently publishing the whole collection as two volumes, and that they had an efficient process that could get them into print relatively quickly, which was important given the timeliness of the matters under discussion.

Upon studying the various essays and considering how they might contribute not only to advancing knowledge about their specific topics, but to fostering collegial discussion about—and hopefully action toward—a new social Catholicism, I decided that some of the material from my Paluch lectures would serve better as part of this conversation than as a monograph. I developed, therefore, some of that material into chapters 5, 8, and 13. I also decided that a very robust introductory chapter would best serve the project, which had the downside of further delaying the completed manuscript. This introductory chapter drew upon the whole first volume to make a more integral argument, while also introducing the essays from the rest of the contributors.

Within that introduction, I also bring the thought of some of the most influential contemporary Catholic voices into dialogue with this project. I try to engage them in a collegial way and affirm some of what I think are key insights and emphases in their thought, such as a recovery of some of our richest doctrinal traditions. I also explain where I think their social and evangelical approaches need to be more closely and evidently aligned with Catholic Social Doctrine, with the discernment of the papal magisterium, and with the demands of sound reason given the signs of our times. This engagement with these voices is ordered to the primary short-term goal of forging a consensus and collaboration among especially American Catholics that our social tradition and the signs of our times call us to join in protecting American democracy—and the international order—from the urgent threat from the illiberal right. This presumes, of course, that a Catholic social vision also rejects the excesses of the illiberal left, which have been concentrated at the cultural level (i.e., in higher education and entertainment) but could possibly become a relatively greater threat in the future if the one from the from the illiberal right can be dissipated. Regardless of the signs of a given time, the emergence of the non-partisan, non-ideological and principled voice and movement of social Catholicism merits our shared and intense labors. The broader hope is that the contributions in these volumes can help to foster the growth of a new social Catholicism to renew our democracy and build a future worthy of the human family, thereby demonstrating by our incarnate love that this-worldly goodness is just a foreshadowing of transcendent goodness.

A Brief Explanatory Note on the Epigraph

A few words on the epigraph I chose for this first volume may be in order since at least one early reviewer thought the reason for its selection might be enigmatic to readers. The text is from the fifth chapter of the Acts of the Apostles which narrates a gathering of the elders of Israel with the High Priest to discuss what to do about the apostles who are proclaiming the resurrection of Christ. My epigraph citation is the core of the sage advice that the Pharisee Gamaliel provides to the elders. His counsel reads as follows:

Preface

> So in the present case, I tell you, keep away from these men and let them alone, because if this plan or this undertaking is of human origin, it will fail; but if it is of God, you will not be able to overthrow them—in that case you may even be found fighting against God! (Acts 5:38–39)

The basic idea behind the selection of this text is that if a contemporary renewal of social Catholicism to address the grave challenges of our century is—as Gamaliel says—"of God," then we can legitimately hope in the Divine help to bring it to fruition. This collection strives to offer an argument that it would indeed be "of God," at least in the sense of following from our social doctrine—which develops from God's revelation—and in responding to the signs of the times, while aligning with the best contemporary scholarship. Beyond that, the text serves as an act of hope that God's grace will be operative in bringing it about, within the mysterious drama of Divine Grace and human freedom. This would entail, as I would hope, not merely the remediation of earthly problems but the realization of the long-delayed reception of the Second Vatican Council in its many dimensions, including the apostolate of the laity and the universal call to holiness, with the Church not only bearing witness to truth but rescuing and serving, in ecumenical and interreligious collaboration, and in manifesting herself as an efficacious sign of the unity of the human family.

Acknowledgments

As noted in the preface, these volumes could not have been brought to completion without the support St. Edmund's Retreat in Mystic, CT under the leadership of Fr. Tom Hoar, SSE. Fr. Tom was able to bring me on as Theologian in Residence and Director of the Edmundite Initiative for Human Dignity. Besides the natural beauty of Ender's Island on which it is located, St. Edmund's Retreat is perhaps best known for its recovery ministry, which exemplifies the emphasis on hope and healing that pervades all its programs. This emphasis on healing and hope aligns closely with the goal of these volumes as can be seen in the subtitle to Volume 2, *New Hope for Ecclesial and Societal Renewal*, although this first volume is more focused on dealing straightforwardly with a wide range of exceedingly delicate topics. I especially appreciate the freedom I was given to work on these delicate matters as I saw fit. Of course, any deficiencies in it are solely my responsibility.

Chapter 3 is developed from parts of the author's doctoral dissertation and from his *Wilhelm Ketteler and the Birth of Modern Catholic Social Thought: A Catholic Manifesto in Revolutionary 1848*. Edited by Nikolaus Knoepffler. Munich: Utz, 2009. It is republished with permission.

Chapter 5 is a development of the first half of William F. Murphy Jr. "Formation for Social Catholicism: The Example of Msgr. John A. Ryan (1945†) and The Renewal of Constitutional Democracy," in *Chicago Studies* 61 (2023). It is republished with permission.

An earlier version of Chapter 8 was previously published by William F. Murphy Jr. as "Liberalism, Conservatism, and Social Catholicism for the 21st Century?" in *Chicago Studies* 60 (2021/2022). It is republished with permission.

Acknowledgments

Chapter 13 is a development of the second half of William F. Murphy Jr. "Formation for Social Catholicism: The Example of Msgr. John A. Ryan (1945†) and The Renewal of Constitutional Democracy," in *Chicago Studies* 61 (2023). It is republished with permission.

Scripture quotations are from the New Revised Standard Version Bible, unless otherwise noted.

1

Introduction

WILLIAM. F. MURPHY JR.,
INITIATIVE FOR SOCIAL CATHOLICISM

Abstract: This extended introductory essay, which reflects the editor's efforts to focus and foster a synodal conversation about a contemporary renewal of social Catholicism and not necessarily the consensus of the contributors, is divided into four main parts. The first highlights the need for careful discernment amidst a tumultuous era in which the postwar hopes for the human family and Church[1] have been deeply disappointed, with the secular world failing to realize the postwar hopes for a more just and peaceful world, and with the Church failing to manifest her incarnation of the Gospel ministry of reconciliation, as a light to the nations, as an efficacious sign of unity, and a leaven in society. In the wake of these disappointments, we are faced with a series of interlocking and potentially existential challenges for the human family that has been described as the polycrisis, which coincide with an unprecedented degree of contestation within the Church over the reform agenda of Pope Francis. The second section argues that such discernment should lead to a decisive choice to live out a new social Catholicism—corresponding to what Pope Francis calls "a better kind of

---

1. I will almost always capitalize Church as I am referring primarily as the Catholic Church, although I see the various Christian denominations as part of the one Church that is established by Christ, though participating in this fullness to different degrees.

politics"[2]—to address the polycrisis and build a future worthy of the human family. Although this second section presents serious arguments against what currently seem to be "alternative directions,"[3] it does so in the synodal spirit of inviting Catholics with different views on Catholic Social Teaching (CST)[4] to consider how they might refocus their efforts to build a broad coalition of

---

2. Francis, *Fratelli Tutti*, no. 154.

3. A primary characteristic of these "alternative directions" can be characterized as a "modest adjustment" to the socially conservative and economically neoliberal alignment of influential Catholics with "conservatism" and the Republican Party centered on the issue of abortion but focused more broadly on defending innocent human life from conception to natural death. I affirm the goal of defending innocent life but think public policy toward that end needs to address the complexities of the various cases and proceed by democratic and constitutional means as distinguished from illiberal ones. Following the Supreme Court "Dobbs" decision that effectively overturned the "Roe" precedent, this modest adjustment is to reaffirm to priority of life issues while pointing also to aspects of Catholic social teaching to provide a more robust social vision. It largely ignores, however, the radicalization of the right. As I discuss in part 2, there are various flavors of this modest adjustment, but I will argue that these respected colleagues should take a much more profound turn from alignment with contemporary "conservatism"—especially given the profound threats posed to the common good by its authoritarian orientation—and embrace a more properly Catholic, non-ideological and non-partisan position as expressed in the various magisterial documents that will be cited in this collection. For an example of what I am calling a "modest adjustment" to the recent emphasis of Catholics on abortion as the preeminent social issue, see the recent statement by Fr. Thomas Joseph White, OP and his collaborators, "Life at the Center: A Pro-Life Statement." See also section two below where I will engage some influential American Catholics who would seem to embrace this "alternative direction," inviting them to a synodal dialogue about the reasons for a more robust embrace of social Catholicism.

4. In this introduction and my essays, I will use "Catholic Social Teaching," "Catholic Social Doctrine," "Catholic social tradition," and "social Catholicism" in overlapping ways for both technical and stylistic purposes. By Catholic Social Teaching (and CST), I refer primarily to the documentary heritage of modern magisterial documents, especially those promulgated by Popes, but in the context of the broader tradition out of which these documents arise, starting from Scripture and including the social movements that both led to and flow from these most authoritative of Catholic social documents. By Catholic Social Doctrine (and CSD), I refer to the same realities, but with an allusion to the doctrinal nature of this tradition and to the 2003 synthesis of it during the Pontificate of St. John Paul II by the Pontifical Council for Justice and Peace, namely the *Compendium of the Social Doctrine of the Church*. My use of Catholic social tradition is more self-evident, referring to the broader tradition of writings and action. By social Catholicism, I refer to the living out of CSD, especially as it has been done since the industrial revolution beginning with Bishop Wilhelm E. von Ketteler and the study circles and other social movements that arose most prominently in Europe after his example. I will discuss some of the key characteristics of this social Catholicism below, but for now I will highlight that it aligns with the social friendship and "better kind of politics" highlighted by Pope Francis.

those willing to work in a mode of social friendship for the future of the nation, the world, and the Church. The third part outlines, for ongoing consideration, several convictions about Catholic Social Doctrine (CSD) in support of the decisive choice of the second section. The fourth section offers an introduction to the essays that comprise this first part of a two-volume collection. It does so with a focus on how these contributions can be understood to fit into a narrative that contemporary Catholics are invited to not only appropriate but also to help realize. This is a story in which Catholics rediscover, in the social tradition of the Church, a path toward the realization of the hopes of the Second Vatican Council. This path, which grows out of the heart of the Church and through the living out the universal call to holiness, manifests itself in a "better kind of politics" through which Catholics in an increasingly "synodal" Church of disciples walking with Jesus collaborate with those of good will in a spirit of fraternity and social friendship to stave off the threat of a dystopian future and build a future worthy of the human family.

1. The Need for Discernment amidst the Disappointed Hopes of the Postwar World and Church[5]

IN THE DECADES FOLLOWING the Second World War, there were legitimate grounds for hope that a more peaceful and just future might be achieved through a postwar liberal consensus, and that the Catholic Church might flourish in a more collaborative relation with this order. The secular grounds for hope included the apparent success of constitutional democracies with so called mixed economies,[6] the founding of the United Nations, and the adoption of the Universal Declaration of Human Rights in 1948. By the opening of the Second Vatican Council in 1962, the Catholic Church was well down the path of articulating—through her deepening tradition of social doctrine—a global humanism that entailed a fraternal[7] collaboration for the common good, especially within

---

5. Given the purpose, length, and structure of this introductory essay, I will reiterate several key points for the sake of clarity and ask the indulgence of readers who might find that monotonous.

6. By this, I refer to the balance of market activities and public institutions to provide "public goods" like defense, diplomacy, public safety, a judicial system, infrastructure, education, regulation, and a social safety net. Other terminology for such arrangements includes "imbedded liberalism" and social democracy.

7. Regarding the postwar embrace of a more fraternal participation in democratic

the liberal consensus that seemed to be building, despite the ongoing disruption and risks associated with the Cold War.

The Catholic Church and the Postwar Hopes

The Catholic Church, moreover, had been a perhaps surprisingly influential collaborator in forging this postwar liberal consensus.[8] Drawing on the deepest wellsprings of the Catholic tradition, this more humanistic and collaborative perspective—emphasizing respect for the equal dignity of every human person and working for their integral good—could be seen in the introductory paragraph of the Second Vatican Council's *Dogmatic Constitution of the Church: Lumen Gentium*. Within the framework of Christian humanism that marked postwar Catholicism, it proclaimed the deeply traditional belief that "the Church is in Christ like a sacrament or as a sign and instrument both of a very closely knit union with God and of the unity of the whole human race."[9]

In a similar vein, the *Pastoral Constitution on the Church in the Modern World: Gaudium et Spes* opened with a preface under the heading of

---

society as distinguished from the earlier paternalism that had allied the Church with fascist regimes that had deceptively manipulated the Church based on her concern for areas ranging from education to laws governing marriage, procreation and family, see Chappel, *Catholic Modern*. This postwar Catholic embrace of Christian humanism was deeply indebted to the work of Jacques Maritain, such as his notion of integral humanism. Maritain, *True Humanism*. For a broad discussion of the meaning and importance of Christian humanism—including that of Maritain—to Catholic Social Teaching, with special attention to contemporary thinkers and its importance for a new social Catholicism in our digital age, see chapter 15 in the second volume of this collection: Ossewaarde-Lowtoo, "Social Catholicism and Christian Humanism."

8. The especially Catholic contribution to the postwar consensus on human rights has—in the last several years—become a specialized field of study among historians with considerable relevance for diagnosing the disappointed hopes of the postwar world and Church. See Cajka, "Catholic Church, and Human Rights," which is chapter 16 in the second volume of this collection.

9. Paul VI, *Lumen Gentium*, no. 1. This understanding of the Church as effecting unity within the human family has deep roots in Scripture and Tradition. Consider, for example, the Pauline epistles. In the First Letter of Paul to the Corinthians, the thesis statement in 1 Cor 1:10 centers on unity, and the theme is developed throughout the letter. In the letters to the Galatians and Romans, a central theme is how Christ's redemption unites Jews and Gentiles, representing all people. In the late Pauline letters to the Colossians and Ephesians, the cosmic rule of Christ entails God's plan "to unite all things in him" (Eph 1:10). Within this context, Ephesians chapter 4 begins with the famous seven-fold passage on unity. In the Gospel according to John, the high priestly prayer of Jesus includes a petition "that they may be one. As you father are in me and I in you, may they also be in us" (John 17:21). Much more could be said.

the "Solidarity of the Church with the Whole Human Family,"[10] presenting the church as offering a service to humankind.[11] Within this conciliar teaching, the *Decree on the Apostolate of the Laity: Apostolicam Actuositatem*, spelled out the lay vocation to act as leaven in the world, infusing a Christian spirit into society,[12] which is accomplished—with God's help, of course—through living out our social teaching to advance the justice, peace and unity that follow naturally from the church, at least to the extent she is living the life of charity in truth.[13] There was sufficient optimism about the future in these decades that Pope St. Paul VI included—in his 1971 apostolic letter *Octogesima Adveniens: A Call to Action*—a balanced discussion of how Catholics should relate to the contemporary rebirth of utopian thinking.[14] Building on his warning about the limitations of all ideologies, Paul acknowledges the potential value in employing the imagination to such ends but warns against the possible danger of ne-

---

10. Paul VI, *Gaudium et Spes:*, no. 1.

11. This humble service is, of course, not contrary to but fully consistent with a deep faith that Christ reveals the full meaning of human life—see Paul VI, *Gaudium et Spes*, no. 22—as the Alpha and Omega, the beginning or origin and end or goal of history, as in *Gaudium et Spes*, no. 45. A fundamental stance of humble service in all Christian action reflects the exemplarity of Jesus, who came "not to be served but to serve, and to give his life as a ransom for many" (Matt 10:45). As I will discuss below regarding postliberal *ressourcement* Thomists who emphasize compelling articulations and presentations of the faith, appreciation of the place of such work is also fully compatible with living out the Social Doctrine of the Church.

12. Paul VI, *Apostolicam Actuositatem*, nos. 2, 12.

13. I allude here to the underappreciated 2009 social encyclical of Benedict XVI, *Caritas in Veritate*. For Benedict, who is writing in commemoration of the 1967 encyclical on development, Paul VI, *Populorum Progressio*. Benedict writes that Paul's letter "deserves to be considered 'the *Rerum Novarum* of the present age,' shedding light upon humanity's journey towards unity" (no. 8). This inherently unifying effect of living the truth of social relations is no small matter for Benedict, who traces it to the mysterious unity of the Trinity (*Caritas in Veritate*, no. 54), and the truth "of the unity of the human race" (no. 55). Through our social doctrine, "the unity of the human race, a fraternal communion transcending every barrier, is called into being by the word of God-who-is-Love" (no. 3). As I will discuss later, Benedict's presentation of his own magisterial discernment regarding CSD as a contemporary rereading of Paul's discernment, which was a contemporary rereading of John XXIII's discernment, reflects what he will later a hermeneutic of "reform and renewal" within the life of the one Church.

14. Paul notes how this terminology was current in the search for alternatives to the futility of the ideological thinking of the day, in the forms of "bureaucratic socialism, technocratic capitalism and authoritarian democracy," which seemed to obstruct the realization of justice and equity. The utopian thinking to which he refers instead imagines how to build a just and equitable future. Paul VI, *Octogesima Adveniens*, no. 37.

glecting practical responsibilities.[15] Given that the Council's *Dogmatic Constitution on Divine Revelation: Dei Verbum* had adroitly articulated the Catholic understanding of the interdependence in theology between Scripture, Tradition and the teaching office of the Church,[16] one would hope that Catholic thinkers would have a fundamentally receptive stance toward the discernment of the magisterium regarding our social doctrine, including the warnings about ideologies that I will reiterate below.

The Emerging Failure to Realize the Postwar Hopes: An Earlier Diagnosis

By the time of the 2003 publication of the *Compendium of the Social Doctrine of the Church*[17] during the Pontificate of St. John Paul II, it was already judged appropriate to say something about the failure to realize a social life of civil friendship, with respect for freedom and equality. The reason for this failure should be noted carefully as it is a central presupposition of this project and is reiterated by Pope Francis, namely that the reception of our social doctrine has been obstructed by ideological opposition in which Catholics have too often been entangled. The text puts it as follows: "In large part, this principle [of Civil friendship and fraternity] has not been put into practice in the concrete circumstances of modern political society, above all because of the influence of individualistic and collectivistic ideologies."[18] Although I also reject a col-

---

15. Although it may sound novel, Paul VI's recourse to the imagination has deep roots in Scripture and anthropology and will be echoed later in this introductory essay. The importance of the imagination in reading the Old Testament has been most fully treated by the eminent Protestant Old Testament scholar Walter Brueggemann, whose work I will further discuss and recommend later.

16. Paul VI, *Dei Verbum*, no. 10. This section concludes the second chapter on "The Handing on of Divine Revelation" with the following memorable text. "It is clear, therefore, that sacred tradition, Sacred Scripture and the teaching authority of the Church, in accord with God's most wise design, are so linked and joined together that one cannot stand without the others, and that all together and each in its own way under the action of the one Holy Spirit contribute effectively to the salvation of souls."

17. Pontifical Council for Justice and Peace (PCJP), *Compendium*.

18. PCJP, *Compendium*, no. 390. By this time, the Church's social tradition had articulated various warnings about ideologies beyond the traditional rejection of the extremes of socialism on the left and laissez faire liberalism and individualism on the right. They even went beyond Paul VI's warning about the inadequacies of any ideology to the challenges of the 1970s (no. 100). These broader warnings addressed "any purely intra-worldly ideology of progress" (no. 48), "various reductionist conceptions of the human person" (no. 124) that deny the transcendent origin, destiny and uniqueness

lectivism that denies or overshadows the dignity and rights of human persons, such collectivism was largely discredited after 1989 and did not govern how globalization proceeded.[19] To follow this judgment of the *Compendium*, it makes sense, therefore, to focus below on the need for Catholics in especially the United States to break free from ideological influence of the especially economic individualism that has permeated the Church through the growing alignment with the conservative movement and the Republican Party over the last several decades.[20] For those Catholics who are presumably—I would hope—alarmed by what that party has become, this would entail the more explicit appropriation of a distinctly Catholic identity that subordinates partisan and ideological commitments to the principles and methodology of Catholic Social Doctrine, as will be outlined below.

(no. 131) of each person, and "materialistic and nationalistic ideologies" (no. 433). They also warn against "narrow ruling groups which usurp the power of the State for individual interests or for ideological ends" (no. 390). There is also a warning (no. 416) about the manipulation of media *"by ideology, the desire for profit and political control, rivalry and conflicts between groups, and other social evils,"* and another about "all forms of monopolies and ideological control" of culture and social communication (no. 557), and regarding "political ideologies of an individualistic nature and those of a totalitarian character, which tend to absorb civil society into the sphere of the State" (no. 417). As a remedy, the *Compendium* encourages the building of those relationships which are the core of civil society and doing so "in a climate of cooperation and solidarity to overcome ideological divisions, prompting people to seek out what unites them rather than what divides them" (no. 420).

19. For my attempt at a more detailed and balanced discussion of liberalism and conservatism, see chapter 8, Murphy, "Liberalism, Conservatism." Besides the collectivism of the socialist left, a kind of libertine individualism is also more associated with the left and the right.

20. I write here of my own experience as one who was at least a fellow traveler with those trends for decades, before attempting to appropriate a more explicitly Catholic identity. Individualism permeates American culture and is inseparable from the modern conservative movement as the very word "individualism" was in the forefront of the movement until leaders determined that "conservatism" would be more conducive to building a movement, especially given that Catholics were in the forefront. In 1953, for example, the Catholic individualist William F. Buckley Jr. was the founding President of the Intercollegiate Society of Individualists which was later renamed the Intercollegiate Studies Institute, with a mission of promoting this individualist and conservative thought on college campuses. Buckley went on to become, arguably, the most important figure in the development of the American conservative movement. Although individualism pervades the whole culture, it is difficult to both accuse the American left of socialism—as the right has done consistently over the last century—and claim that individualism is equally prevalent on the left.

Accelerating Crises and Divergent Readings of the Signs of the Times

In our third decade of the twenty-first century, moreover, fears of an emerging dystopia are ubiquitous in certain sectors[21] but largely ignored in others.[22] Such fears follow from various factors including the daily and global evidence of an emerging environmental catastrophe, the threats to especially American constitutional democracy from the manipulation of populist rage by aspiring autocrats, from the worldwide rise of an alliance of autocratic states, from the spread of disinformation and propaganda, from the polarization of societies, and from the breakdown of family and community life, among many others. Indeed, more than a few today speak of an impending civilizational collapse; many others would prefer not to think about the present or future challenges, especially because it is not clear what can be done to address them.

This project on "Social Catholicism for the Twenty-First Century?" seeks to indicate a positive path forward and to foster collaboration along that path, while also critically engaging with what I find deficient in some alternative perspectives among influential Catholics. By deficient, I mean especially from the perspectives of CST, of right reason, and of the discernment of the magisterium. I would argue, for example, that these various grave challenges I have lumped under the heading of the polycrisis are not given a defensible level of attention by the "alternative direction" of mainstream conservative American Catholics, an approach I am describing as a modest adjustment to the decades long strategy of prioritizing the defense of innocent human life over any other concerns.[23]

As previously noted, the November 2023 statement "Life at the Center: A Pro-Life Statement" published in *First Things*, rightly seeks to defend innocent human life, and rightly encourages a broader recovery of Catholic social teaching, but—in my opinion—takes an indefensibly narrow scope given a Catholic understanding of the common good. By this I mean that it fails to alert readers to the grave crises facing the human

---

21. These include international institutions like the United Nations, most UN member states especially those impacted by the climate crisis, most specialties of higher education, a majority of the young, and the Vatican.

22. These include especially conservative Americans and others who benefit from the extraction and burning of fossil fuels.

23. As I noted previously, I agree with defending innocent human lives, but within a framework of Catholic Social Doctrine, sound moral and political philosophy, and the Catholic Church's comprehensive understanding of the common good.

family that should shape our priorities, nor does it alert readers to how the Catholic social tradition provides the resources so Catholics can play a vital role in addressing them. Because so many distinguished Catholic intellectuals, clergy and committed laity have come to hold similar views, however, the present collection is partially an attempt to foster a broader conversation. Such conversation would help well-disposed Catholics to assess such views synodally and critically,[24] to better appreciate and align with the ongoing discernment of the magisterium in union with the Pope, and to live out the Gospel ministry of reconciliation (2 Cor 5:18), thereby showing the church to be the efficacious sign of unity that the Fathers of the Second Vatican Council proclaimed her to be.

Whereas I think contemporary American Catholic scholarship has produced a vibrant renewal of—for example—the *ressourcement* and Thomistic traditions as I will discuss at greater length below, these renewals to date are not integrated with a robust reception of Catholic Social Doctrine, especially one that aligns with the documentary heritage as synthesized in the *Compendium*, and with the social teaching of Pope Francis. This truncated reception of Catholic Social Doctrine among influential Americans, in my opinion, helps to explain the long-running disconnect between much of the Catholic Church in the United States and Pope Francis, which this project in "Social Catholicism" seeks to ameliorate.[25]

---

24. This will require dealing forthrightly with delicate questions, including the need to keep a critical distance from ideologies and political parties, and the need to understand the influence between money, particular agendas of political parties that foster the polycrisis, and the funding of Catholic entities that do not deal forthrightly with the "dark clouds" spoken of by Pope Francis in chapter 1 of *Fratelli Tutti*, nos. 9–55.

25. Although I can understand why American churchmen would want to emphasize a harmonious relation with the Holy Father, the actual degree of agreement needs to be assessed in light of the 2023 publication of the Pope Francis's apostolic letter *Laudate Deum: On the Climate Crisis* and the motu proprio *Ad Theologiam Promovendam: To Advance Theology*, which build upon his social encyclicals *Laudato Si': On Care for Our Common Home* and *Fratelli Tutti: On Fraternity and Social Friendship*. My hope is that the synodal emergence of a "new social Catholicism" and "better kind of politics" will manifest authentically Catholic bonds between American Catholics and the Holy See.

Pope Francis on Theology for a Missionary and Outgoing Church

Much like his predecessors since at least St. John XXIII, Pope Francis puts considerable emphasis on Social Doctrine and has recently published two documents reflecting his ongoing discernment of a deepening set of crises to which the church should be responding, but largely is not. The first of these was his letter *Laudate Deum: On the Climate Crisis* whereas the second was his recently published *motu proprio, Ad Theologiam Promovendam: To Advance Theology* (hereafter, ATP).

Because this introductory essay and collection strive to address some of the needs addressed in ATP, and because they endeavor to do so in a way that is potentially compatible with the best fruits of the renewal of *ressourcement* and Thomistic thought in the United States, I will summarize some of the key points of the motu proprio, which calls for a renewal of theology so it becomes a vital force in addressing the great challenges of our century. Although it seems to me that Social Doctrine is the field where the kind of renewal sought by ATP makes the most direct sense, I invite specialists in other fields to consider how their work might contribute to a new conversation in a more synodal church, eschewing the tendencies to tribalization and siloed media we see in the surrounding culture.

ATP no. 1 opens with the need for theology to especially address the "profound cultural transformations ... [and] 'a change of epoch'"[26] we are witnessing. After a second section that locates ATP within the history of the statutes of the Pontifical Academy of Theology that it is revising, the third section introduces the necessity of a development of theology to meet the needs of a "missionary and 'outgoing' Church," which requires theology to be open "to the world, to man in the concreteness of his existential situation, with its problems, wounds, challenges, and potential."[27] ATP no. 4 calls for theology to read and interpret "the Gospel in the conditions in which men and women daily live ... having as its archetype the Incarnation of the eternal Logos, its entering into the culture, worldview, and religious tradition of a people." This section calls us to foster dialogue and encounter with others, while recognizing more deeply the "web of relationships" and interconnection of all things that reflect the Trinitarian

---

26. Francis, *Ad Theologiam Promovendam*, no. 1.
27. Francis, *Ad Theologiam Promovendam*, no. 3.

imprint.²⁸ Through such dialogue with all sources of knowledge and mindful of the Trinitarian relations at the root of all things, ATP no. 5 calls for theology to adopt a "transdisciplinarity" that leads to a more adequate grasp of the "Wisdom that emanates from God's Revelation."²⁹ In no. 6, ATP calls for broad synodal dialogue within the Church about how theology can speak to the great challenges of the day, with no. 7 reminding us that we ultimately seek wisdom and to live in charity. The ninth paragraph calls for the creation of communities of faith, for study and for building relationships to carry out this mission of a theology renewed to serve a missionary and outgoing church, one that brings our theological tradition to bear in addressing the challenges that confront the human family today. In my opinion, the kind of renewal sought by ATP is perhaps most evident in the field of Catholic Social Teaching and aligns closely with the argument of this introduction and collection.

Pope Francis, *Fratelli Tutti*, and the "Signs of the Times"

Compared to the view among influential American Catholics that our time requires a reaffirmation of the preeminence of abortion, I would argue that Pope Francis offers a far more discerning reading of the "signs of the times," precisely because he considers them in light of a comprehensive, Catholic understanding of the common good. In his tragically underappreciated 2020 social encyclical *Fratelli Tutti: On Fraternity and Social Friendship*, where he devotes his first chapter to a discussion of "Dark Clouds Over a Closed World."³⁰ He begins with a subsection on the "shattered dreams" extending outward from postwar Europe, hopes and dreams for a world of peace, fellowship, and integration.³¹ He proceeds by specifying the dark clouds, which he significantly traces to a failed model of globalization based on individualism and "limitless consumption."³² In this, he echoes not only the above reference to the *Compendium* published during the Pontificate of St. John Paul II, but what is evident from an informed reading of the social encyclicals. Among the many dark clouds, he mentions the following.

---

28. Francis, *Ad Theologiam Promovendam*, no. 4.
29. Francis, *Ad Theologiam Promovendam*, no. 5.
30. Francis, *Fratelli Tutti*, nos. 9–55.
31. Francis, *Fratelli Tutti*, nos. 10–12.
32. Francis, *Fratelli Tutti*, nos. 10–12.

First, a disorientation about our place in history that allows ideologies to "reign unopposed."[33] As will be further developed in this collection, this point reflects Francis's judgment that our failure to understand how the ideologies of individualism and consumerism have displaced the postwar efforts to build a just future have left us at the mercy of these ideologies. A second dark cloud is the undermining of politics through "hyperbole, extremism and polarization."[34] The third is the emergence of a throwaway world following from a forgetfulness of the common good that comes with individualism.[35] Fourth, the insufficient realization of human rights is another dark cloud hanging over humanity.[36] A fifth dark cloud, is the war, violence and fear afflicting the human family.[37] Sixth is a model of globalization that is indifferent to the solidarity of humanity and—as he develops in *Laudato Si'*—the interconnection of all things.[38] Seventh are the pandemics and other calamities with which our time in history has confronted us.[39] The eighth category of dark clouds are the violations of the human dignity of migrants.[40] The ninth is centered in the myriad challenges raised by digital communication, including in Catholic media.[41] A tenth dark cloud is the subjugation of the vulnerable through the cultural domination of "powerful interests" including "financial speculators and raiders," and by prosperous countries.[42] Francis's perspective in solidarity with those suffering from the side effects of an economy rigged for the elites, therefore, provides a stark contrast to the perspective of conservative American venues, for example, enjoying generous funding from such powerful interests. For Francis, these many challenges point to the great need for hope,[43] the grounds for which will be spelled out in the subsequent chapters of the encyclical, but center

33. Francis, *Fratelli Tutti*, no. 13.
34. Francis, *Fratelli Tutti*, no. 15.
35. Francis, *Fratelli Tutti*, nos. 18–21.
36. Francis, *Fratelli Tutti*, nos. 22–24.
37. Francis, *Fratelli Tutti*, nos. 25–28.
38. Francis, *Fratelli Tutti*, nos. 29–31.
39. Francis, *Fratelli Tutti*, nos. 32–36.
40. Francis, *Fratelli Tutti*, nos. 37–41.
41. Francis, *Fratelli Tutti*, nos. 42–50. The contemporary challenges of digital media are further complicated by advances in artificial intelligence and deep fakes as we approach what is arguably the most dangerous election season since the 1860 lead-up to the Civil War.
42. Francis, *Fratelli Tutti*, nos. 51–53.
43. Francis, *Fratelli Tutti*, nos. 54–55.

in the living of Christian love through social friendship in a better kind of politics.[44] I would encourage Catholics who are inclined toward the conservative alternative approach to consider carefully this Papal reading of the signs of the times in light of a properly Catholic disposition toward the repeated teaching of the Holy Father, and in dialogue with the immensity of complementary literature and arguments, towards which this collection strives to provide an introduction.

Global Voices Echo the Priorities of Pope Francis

By the time of the March 2023 World Economic Forum (WEF), the neologism "polycrisis" was catching on among political, economic and intellectual leaders as a particularly apt way to describe the contemporary situation. According to *The Global Risks Report 2023*, published by the WEF,[45] the polycrisis was a situation "where disparate crises interact such that the overall impact far exceeds the sum of each part." The historical background, meaning and appropriateness of this term was further elucidated for the WEF by the esteemed economic historian Adam Tooze.[46] He explains that a polycrisis is a "shared experience" that leaves people feeling unable to cope because disruptions spanning the realms of economics, politics, geopolitics, the natural environment, mental health and social psychology are not reducible to any common denominator or explicable by any single factor. There can be no single rationale or disciplinary logic, therefore, that governs potential interventions. No wonder we are tempted to ignore the problem, busying ourselves with an endless variety of distractions. As I am arguing, however, the principle-based integral and solidary humanism of Catholic Social Doctrine, with its critical openness to all sources of knowledge, and its development through engagement with a wide range of situations, provides an invaluable

---

44. The grounds for hope include rediscovering fraternal love for our vulnerable neighbors (Francis, *Fratelli Tutti*, chapter 2), envisaging and engaging an open world that takes us out of our self-centeredness and into love of others (chapter 3), opening our hearts to the whole world (chapter 4), a "better kind of politics" centered in a social friendship directed to the common good (chapter 5), living out dialogue and friendship in society (chapter 6), learning to encounter our neighbors as persons (chapter 7), and embracing the role of religions in the service of fraternity in the world (chapter 8).

45. World Economic Forum, *Global Risks Report 2023*.

46. World Economic Forum, "Polycrisis." All references to Adam Tooze in the next two paragraphs are from this piece.

resource for responding to the polycrisis, provided it remains free from ideological or partisan distortion.

In a sobering judgment, Tooze advises acceptance of the fact that there is no foreseeable way to reverse the polycrisis that has emerged with the evolution of modernity, especially since the explosion of economic growth following the Second World War. Instead, he compares the situation to a nuclear reactor that is incredibly powerful and dangerous, capable of powering a great city or destroying it. What matters is who's running the reactor. These "complex, entangled problems," he warns, can be "much worse than they need to be as a result of failed political coordination." Skilled management, on the other hand, can allow certain problems to be taken "off the board" so limited political capital can be spent where it is most needed. What is essential is building sufficient political consensus to make the relevant institutions effective in addressing especially the most pressing problems. As psychologically challenging as it is to accept the reality of the polycrisis, Tooze can be summarized as advising that we accept its existence and work toward the renewal of our institutions to best manage the various challenges it entails.[47]

As shorthand for describing an exceedingly complex set of challenges that extend deeply into the life of the contemporary church, I will employ the term polycrisis, but hopefully not to the point of monotony. I do so with, on the one hand, a profound sense of the disproportion between the scope of the problem and my own abilities, and on the other hand, a hope that with God's help I can at least advance the conversation, especially through the collaboration of the many erudite contributors to these volumes, and hopefully through the insights of others who will constructively enrich the dialogue in a broad collaboration in hope for the future.

2. The Crucial Choice between Two Paths for Contemporary Catholics

If it is true that we are facing a polycrisis and that the best hope for managing it depends on competent leaders and strong public institutions and—to borrow the illustration of Tooze—on "who is running the nuclear reactor," this raises a crucial question. What should be the

---

47. For another recent discussion of the notion of polycrisis, see Lawrence et al., "What Is a Global Polycrisis?"

fundamental orientation of Catholics toward this situation, acknowledging the primarily American context of the present discussion, but also thinking globally? Besides the fundamentally Christian orientation toward trusting God, hoping in the divine help, and living a life of love, what fundamental orientation toward the social, political, economic, legal and cultural realms should Catholics adopt?

I will argue that Catholics need to make a decisive choice to live out Catholic Social Doctrine in a new era of social Catholicism and what Pope Francis calls "a better kind of politics," and that this should have an immediate focus on preserving and renewing the institutions of our constitutional democracy, so we are best prepared to deal with the dark clouds of the polycrisis. In so doing, I will argue against the main alternatives being advanced by Catholics in the United States, which are different forms of continuing the "culturally conservative"[48] strategy of recent decades that prioritizes culture war issues like abortion. Among the different versions of this culturally conservative focus that are currently being advanced by American Catholics, I will argue most directly against what I will call postliberal integralism. I will also discuss at some length an influential contemporary school of thought that I will call postliberal *ressourcement* Thomism. Although this school might currently seem to be more inclined toward postliberal integralism, I will argue that such thinkers should instead robustly embrace the living out of Catholic Social Doctrine in social Catholicism. I will further introduce these alternatives in the remaining few paragraphs of this section before treating them at greater length in separate subsections below.

This first fundamental orientation, for which this volume hopes to build momentum, is hardly known among large segments of American Catholicism for reasons I will explain below but is marked by a robust appropriation of the principles and methodology of CSD. Through living this "social Catholicism," this first orientation would seek to addresses the great challenges of our day through a fraternal collaboration with those seeking to renew our tottering democratic institutions under the pressure of an unprecedented internal and external threats.[49] Such

48. For a more detailed discussion of what I mean by "culturally conservative," see chapter 8: Murphy, "Liberalism, Conservatism."

49. The signs of the fragility of American democracy are visible daily. Two international rankings are worthy of note. The first is by Freedom House, "Global Freedom Score," which assesses 210 countries and territories. According to this measure, the 2023 classification for the United States two years into the Biden Administration was, not surprisingly, "free." This reflected a 2023 score of 83 out of a possible 100, with 70

a response would be in complete harmony with not only the deepest biblical roots of the Christian moral life concerning justice and charity, but with the last several decades of magisterial discernment about how to live out justice and charity in the social realm, continuing through the teachings of Pope Francis who calls us to live the life of social friendship in a better kind of politics as the present collection will consider at considerable length. This social doctrine is introduced beautifully in the opening section of the *Compendium* under the heading of "An Integral and Solidary Humanism,"[50] an introduction that is replete with the theological virtues of faith, hope and charity while the whole document should be read as a trustworthy articulation of how to live the Gospel in the contemporary world. Regarding Tooze's image of having the right people operating the nuclear reactor of the polycrisis, this approach would focus Catholics on collaborating to uphold and continually renew the institutions needed to "run the reactor" as safely and effectively as possible. This requires putting virtuous and qualified persons into public office who are seeking to serve the common good.[51] Although I would argue that the Catholic tradition is fundamentally non-ideological and non-partisan and respects the freedom of citizens to follow their judgment of conscience about which candidates can best serve the common good, I will also argue that the institutions of constitutional democracy are integral to that good and that Catholics should protect and renew those institutions against urgent threats.

---

being the cutoff for "partially free." This score resulted in a mediocre ranking of 59 out of 210, with 17 of our peer democracies scoring 95 or better. The second is by the Institute of Political Science and Sociology, the "Democracy Matrix." According to this measure, the United States ranking for 2020, the last year of the Trump Administration, was 36 out of 176 countries measured. This earned us a categorization of "deficient democracy," just above the thirty-fifth rank for Israel. That is not encouraging because the latter had been paralyzed by several months of mass protests over Prime Minister Benjamin Netanyahu's removal of the main institutional check on his political power, apparently increasing the vulnerability of the state to an unprecedented terrorist attack by Hamas. There is a wealth of recent literature on the decline and collapse of democracies. Perhaps the most acclaimed is Levitsky and Ziblatt, *How Democracies Die*.

50. PCJP, *Compendium*, nos. 1–19.

51. Drawing upon Cathleen Kaveny's work and upon the Thomistic tradition, I would argue that voting—for example—should not be understood in terms of issues but in terms of an exercise of political prudence to select candidates who are best qualified to serve the common good by filling particular offices. They should be selected considering their competence for the office, their character, their ability to collaborate, and their connections. Kaveny, *Law's Virtues*.

Introduction—MURPHY

The second orientation is profoundly different in decisive respects, but it is a much more prominent part of the conversation in the United States regarding how Catholicism relates to our social, political and cultural life. It is advanced by prolific Catholic scholars, who present it as the recovery of an authentically Catholic approach from before the Second Vatican Council but it is hard to see how it could be reconciled with the last several decades of magisterial social teaching. In identifying themselves as postliberal, these scholars are at least suggesting the obsolescence of the existing political order and its institutions, implicitly setting themselves against them if not boldly denouncing them as corrupt fruit of the liberal tree. By also catering to contemporary right-wing cultural populism and thus appealing more to the irascible passions like anger than to reason, and by focusing on contested "wedge issues" of sexual and conjugal morality that engage "us versus them" tribalism, it is hard to imagine that a postliberal polity could be trusted with overseeing the nuclear reaction of the polycrisis given the fact that populism is largely driven by emotion. I will refer to this orientation as "postliberal integralism" not because its proponents use this precise formulation but to distinguish it from some other influential thinkers—to be introduced in subsection C below—who affirm a kind of postliberal theology but could either align with the contemporary right that is seeking to overthrow American democracy or they could more fully appropriate Catholic social teaching and renew it.

In this introduction to the project, I largely bypass consideration of a third possibility that has been attractive to many Catholics in recent decades, namely one rooted in "classical liberalism" that embraces both market-oriented or liberal economics and liberal or constitutional democracy. While I greatly value and cite the contributions of classical liberals in cutting through the formidable rhetoric and argumentation of the postliberals to defend constitutional democracy, I think this is a very difficult time to argue for some of the traditional economic priorities of classic liberals, even if one values the power of market mechanisms, personal initiative, and entrepreneurship, and even if one thinks—as I do—that we will need to employ market mechanisms to address the environmental crisis and transition to a sustainable economy.[52] Without claiming expertise in macroeconomics, it seems to me that the lasting

---

52. Doer, *Speed & Scale*. While Doer at recognizes the urgent problem of global warming, our current encroachment of various planetary boundaries must also be addressed.

insights regarding market economics favored by classical liberals will have to find their proper place in a broader context that addresses the challenges of our day. These include the following that have become evident after forty years under a neoliberal paradigm: (1) increased economic and political inequality; (2) democratic backsliding and the threat of a quasi-oligarchic situation degrading into state failure or autocracy; (3) the role of well-funded propaganda campaigns by those seeking to maximize profit and political power; and (4) the need for a sustainable economic paradigm to address the climate crisis.

A. The Renewal of Democratic Institutions through "A Better Kind of Politics"

I think there are several compelling reasons for Catholics to embrace the first orientation of renewing our democratic institutions through a new social Catholicism along the lines of Pope Francis's better kind of politics. These reasons include the magnitude of the polycrisis and the disinclination of postliberalism to address it, the importance of robust institutions to address the many dimensions of it, the social tradition of the church including its understanding of the political community and its unique appreciation for democracy[53] and the importance of its institutions, and the receptivity to the discernment of the magisterium that is traditionally understood to be inherent to the Catholic faith. These reasons to embrace the Social Doctrine of the Church also align with other key teachings of the Second Vatican Council such as the directives for the renewal of moral theology that encourage Catholics to embrace their high calling in Christ to bear the fruit of charity in the world.[54] To address the "dark

---

53. "The Political Community" is treated in chapter 8 (nos. 377–427) of PCJP, *Compendium*, part four of which (nos. 406–16) discusses the Church's judgment regarding "The Democratic System." In particular, the Church uniquely values democracy because of the way it enables the broad participation of citizens, provides means to hold leaders accountable, and fosters the peaceful transition of power, while rejecting the usurpation of such power by narrow groups for personal or ideological ends. Given the contemporary phenomenon of "spin dictators" who present themselves as democratic while being anything but, it is worth emphasizing that the Church values not any democracy but "authentic democracy" which is "ruled by law," and based on a "correct conception of the human person" and "formation in true ideals" (no. 406). Regarding the notion of spin dictators, see Guriev and Treisman, *Spin Dictators*.

54. Paul VI, *Optatam Totius*, no. 16. This call for a renewal of moral theology encourages a robust grounding in Scripture, pointing people to their high calling in Christ, which echoes the Council's *Lumen Gentium*, chapter 5 on the Universal Call to

clouds" spoken of by Pope Francis and to ensure the competent management of the polycrisis, this new social Catholicism would be focused, as already noted, on a renewal of the various institutions of contemporary constitutional democracy, including the international institutions necessary to the global dimensions of the common good.

Despite the precarious state of American democracy, however, within the broader context of the polycrisis, there does not seem to be any broad or prominent discussion among especially conservative American Catholics to respond to these urgent signs of our times. Despite the urgency of Pope Francis in *Fratelli Tutti*, in *Laudato Si': On Care for Our Common Home*, and in his new apostolic exhortation on the environmental crisis *Laudate Deum*, and despite the emphases of global and political and economic leaders at the World Economic Forum, it is difficult to identify any significant responses among Catholics. To be sure, there are many Catholics who admirably live out various aspects of our social teaching, such as advocating for the most vulnerable, or offering direct support to the poor, or working in various other ways for the common good. Such laudable efforts, however, are different from addressing the existential threats emphasized for good reason by the Holy Father and many others.

Why Catholic Social Doctrine Has Been So Poorly Received

If this "Better Kind of Politics" is needed as I contend in support of the discernment of Pope Francis, it would be helpful to understand why Catholic Social Doctrine has been received so partially in the United States, and what has changed since the time of its being marginalized so that we might hope and work anew for its flourishing? In this subsection, I will sketch a partial response for the purposes of this introductory chapter, although subsequent chapters will cover some of the same ground in greater detail.[55]

Perhaps the best way to explain the limited reception of CST is through an economic narrative, although a cultural story centered on

---

Holiness. On this basis, the same section emphasizes the ensuing obligation to bear the fruit of charity for the life of the world. This last point is a clear allusion to living out our social doctrine. I discuss the failure of the Church in especially the United States to receive this conciliar discernment regarding moral theology in Murphy, "Ethics of Life, Synodality, and Untying Knots." This online publication includes a link to Murphy, "Reflections on Fundamental Morality."

55. See chapter 8: Murphy, "Liberalism, Conservatism," which also provides further discussion of the cultural side of the story, including abortion politics.

abortion is, arguably, even more important.[56] The economic narrative builds on our opening remarks about how CST developed significantly in the postwar era alongside the political-economic paradigm of the Keynesian mixed economy as embodied in the United States by the New Deal, which aligned with the social priorities of the Catholic Church, which were advanced especially by Msgr. John A. Ryan in his work for the U.S. Bishops. The key elements of this New Deal consensus were supported by not only Democrats, but by a significant number of Republicans until well into the 1970s. Because the Keynesian economic toolkit was ineffective against the "stagflation" of the 1970s, those who had been advocating a different political-economic paradigm[57] took advantage of the opportunity to campaign upon and implement their alternative. By the 1980s, the Reagan Administration was advancing an economic program emphasizing free markets, small government and tax cuts that would allegedly pay for themselves. Decreased marginal tax rates on the wealthy, moreover, would allegedly result in wealth trickling-down to others through a rising economic tide that lifts all boats.

After inflation cooled under the high interest rates set by the Federal Reserve into the mid-1980s, these rates were subsequently lowered and the country began to emerge from stagflation and enter a period of growth that was also fueled by a massive increase in military spending.[58] By the 1990s, this new conservative economics—which was closely

---

56. The place of abortion at the heart of the socially conservative component of Reagan era "fusion conservatism" is mentioned below and discussed at greater length in chapter 8: Murphy, "Liberalism, Conservatism."

57. Regarding the understanding of a paradigm shift from the neoliberal consensus, see Strickland and Wong, "New Paradigm for Justice and Democracy." Against the earlier neoliberal model that emphasized fostering economic freedom—especially that of the business elites—in the belief that the benefits would trickle-down to others, these contemporary thinkers seek to advance a new paradigm they call "middle-out economics" that focuses on building a broad middle-class. This approach is reflected in the constant refrain of the Biden Administration about building shared prosperity "from the middle out and the bottom up" or equivalently "from the bottom up and the middle out." Rather than focusing on preventing "deadbeats" from free riding on "government handouts" as would follow from accepting *The Big Myth* of Orestes and Conway, this approach starts from the dignity of persons and focuses on providing the resources needed to enable as many of them as possible to flourish in the contemporary world, which aligns nicely with CST.

58. It soon became clear that the tax cuts didn't pay for themselves but were ballooning the deficit, and the deregulation led to a crisis in the savings and loan sector requiring a large federal bailout. Only gradually, however, would it become clear that this new economic paradigm shipped our manufacturing base offshore, undermined the middle class and rigged the economy to the benefit of a new class of billionaires

aligned with libertarianism and is also known, somewhat confusingly, as neoliberalism—was significantly accommodated by the Democratic Administration of Bill Clinton, who famously declared in his 1996 State of the Union speech that "the era of big government is over."[59] As this new political-economic paradigm was gaining broader national support, many Catholics were also aligning with it, and with other aspects of the so-called "fusion conservatism" of the Reagan coalition, which also emphasized a strong national defense against the Soviet threat and a new socially conservative alliance of Catholics and Evangelical Protestants centered on issues at the heart of the growing "culture wars" including abortion and gay rights. Many Catholics felt compelled, moreover, to support the Republicans as the Democratic Party was becoming increasingly extreme on things like partial birth abortion, and by excluding Catholics who felt obliged to speak up for vulnerable unborn lives.

Within this more conservative political-economic, social and geopolitical perspective that many American Catholics of my generation were adopting, the articulations of social ethics in the magisterial documents seemed contrary to the emerging contemporary consensus that promised peace, prosperity and freedom for all. Few of us, therefore, gave serious consideration to CST at the time. An excellent case in point is the 1986 intervention by the United States Catholic Bishops, *Economic Justice for All: Pastoral Letter on Catholic Social Teaching and the U.S. Economy*, which came out just as the neoliberal paradigm was taking hold. Although *Economic Justice for All* received detailed and balanced front-page coverage by *The New York Times*,[60] and although it is grounded in the deepest wellsprings of our tradition and looks prescient considering the economic and political developments since its publication, it was directly and publicly opposed by a large and well-organized group of Catholic conservatives,[61] and was largely ignored by the broader Catholic population that was shifting to the right.

---

who used their wealth to buy more political power and to further shape laws and jurisprudence in their favor.

59. Although Clinton, as a lifelong democrat, would have preferred to build on the legacy of the New Deal and Great Society, he found it politically expedient to "triangulate" to a position that would gain support from the center and right, keeping his Republican opponents off balance under the increasingly radicalized leadership of Newt Gingrich.

60. Regarding the reaction to a substantial 1984 draft of the letter, see Briggs, "Catholic Bishops Seek Vast Changes."

61. See Goldman, "Catholic Bishops Criticized on the Poor."

Through a variety of historical studies published in the last several years, however, we have a much better understanding of how public opinion shifted so strongly toward an extreme form of neoliberalism that can be called "market fundamentalism." This occurred largely through a comprehensive campaign of "persuasion" funded by business interests seeking profit and political power, and often explicitly dismissive of the notion of the common good through the influence of thinkers like Ayn Rand.[62] By all measures, this campaign was an incredible success as literally trillions of dollars of wealth were shifted from the middle to the upper classes over four decades,[63] and the political institutions were largely captured by what is being increasingly spoken of, by voices on the left and right, as a new oligarchy.[64] To summarize this largely economic thread of the story, CST became increasingly unattractive in the United States as the country shifted away from the postwar New Deal paradigm of the Keynesian mixed economy—that is, a model of social democracy or embedded liberalism—that seemed to align with the Catholic social tradition in the decades following the Second Vatican Council. As Americans during the Reagan administration were increasingly persuaded to trust free markets and see government as the problem,[65] CST became

---

62. It would seem indisputable that contemporary American and Catholic discussion of social, political, economic, legal and cultural affairs—regarding which CST provides principles for ethical reflection—needs to include consideration of works such as Oreskes and Conway, *Big Myth*, which shows how much public opinion about questions of political economy is deeply shaped by a campaign by business interests to oppose government, regulation and taxes. This important new book builds on Oreskes and Conway, *Merchants of Doubt*, which showed how the same kind of massive and ongoing propaganda campaigns have mislead the public on everything from the dangers of tobacco smoke to global warning. For an account of how such campaigns depend on massive and secretive political spending, see also Mayer, *Dark Money*. Regarding how such spending is rooted in the attempts by those seeking oligarchic rule to undermine the democratic participation of the broader population, see MacLean, *Democracy in Chains*. Such machinations were well-understood by earlier generations of social Catholics like Msgr. John A. Ryan, but contemporary conservative American Catholics, especially those inclined toward classical liberalism, tend to ignore or downplay them.

63. There are many ways to measure the transfer of wealth to the already wealthy. For one recent example, see Smith and Russell, "Greatest Wealth Transfer in History."

64. There is an abundance of recent work on this problem. A good starting place to put this in historical perspective is Richardson, *How the South Won the Civil War*. Also valuable is Reich, *System*, offers a very accessible overview from the perspective of someone who has worked not only at the cabinet level of presidential administrations, but also at the university, media, and activist levels.

65. Oreskes and Conway, *Big Myth*.

increasingly marginalized and the few who understood and appreciated it called it "the Church's best kept secret."

Circumstances Conducive, or Not, to the Reception of Catholic Social Doctrine?

Besides the successful promotion of an alternative social vision that seemed to address the challenges of the 1980s, another way to understand the failure of Catholics to advance a social vision more aligned with the magisterial documents is that the historical circumstances were not conducive to doing so. By this I mean that the alternative consensus for market fundamentalism had to run its course so its political, social and environmental unsustainability could become more apparent, and a range of potential dialogue partners and collaborators might arise. Since the loss of consensus for the neoliberal paradigm following the 2008 financial crisis and amidst the growing polycrisis, it seems to me that the circumstances are now much more favorable for a broad collaboration among those working for a more just and sustainable future, a situation for which the integral and solidary humanism of Catholic Social Doctrine is well suited. This potential is not well-understood, however, among the institutional infrastructure of the Catholic Church in the United States. This collection of essays is part of an effort to stimulate collegial and synodal discussion about it.

The dependence of the whole human family on addressing the polycrisis indicates another reason why our era is much more conducive to a recovery of the Catholic social tradition. This reason concerns the interdependence that this tradition recognizes between evangelization and social doctrine, an interdependence that has been widely neglected in the United States. Through the pontificates of John Paul II and Benedict XVI, there was much talk about "the new evangelization," but the percentage of Americans identifying as Catholic has continued to decline rapidly, especially among the young.[66] Since the pandemic, the percentage of

---

66. A 2019 Pew survey found a decline from about 24 percent identifying as Catholic in 2007 to 20 percent in 2019, despite most immigrants coming from countries with significant Catholic populations. This decline comes with a corresponding increase in the "nones" or non-affiliated, especially among the youngest cohort of millennials. The percentage of Hispanics identifying as Catholic showed an even more rapid drop from 57 percent to 47 percent between 2009 and 2019. Pew Research Center, "In U.S., Decline of Christianity Continues at Rapid Pace."

Catholics attending mass has declined even further among all cohorts studied, but especially for non-whites under fifty.[67]

The causes for the failed—or hopefully delayed—reception of Catholic Social Teaching in the United States are many and complex,[68] but I would argue that one of the best ways to address them is to realize the delayed reception of the Second Vatican Council, including an appreciation of the Church as an efficacious sign of unity, the Universal Call to Holiness, the apostolate of the laity, the renewal of moral theology, the understanding of the Church in service to the world, and the Social Doctrine of the Church. Understood within the broader Catholic tradition in the wake of the Council, the second chapter of the *Compendium* is entitled "The Church's Mission and Social Doctrine." This chapter elucidates how it is precisely by working in a spirit of social friendship to address social challenges that we demonstrate the divine love for men and women and the beauty of the Catholic faith. If that were true, it is no surprise that this evangelical mission has suffered in an era where the Church allowed the scope of our social doctrine to be greatly truncated and tainted by partisan politics. In my opinion, we need to recover—in a way proper to the challenges of our day—the successful missionary strategy of Archbishop John Ireland as it was taken up by his protégé Msgr. John A. Ryan from the era of early twentieth-century Progressive Reform movement through the New Deal era. Ireland's strategy was "to make America Catholic" precisely by taking the lead in solving the great social challenges of the day.[69] In our more pluralistic context, of course, we might want to restate that as something like "make American a place of solidarity and social friendship where the Church and everyone can flourish," but the basic strategy is sound.

---

67. Witt-Swanson et al., "Faith after the Pandemic." A concise way to summarize its findings is to compare the percentage by which various cohorts attend mass "less or much less often" with those who attend "more or much more often," leaving aside those whose attendance is unchanged. For all cohorts the decline exceeds the increase. For whites, this is by 11 percent, for 65 or older it is 8 percent, for Hispanics it is by 14 percent, for 18–29 years old it is 19 percent, for 30–49 years old it is 15 percent.

68. Among the many causes, I would highlight the shaping of Catholic social opinion less by our social tradition and more by other factors including the political alliance with the Republican party and Evangelical Protestants around culture war issues like abortion, and by the corresponding shaping of opinions through the influence of libertarian think tanks and conservative media.

69. See chapter 5: Murphy, "Social Formation of Msgr. John A. Ryan"; and chapter 13: Murphy, "Formation for a New Social Catholicism."

Introduction—MURPHY

The Dangerous Distraction of Postliberal Integralism: An Extended Introduction

Having outlined some initial reasons for why a new social Catholicism and what Pope Francis calls a "better kind of politics" would be the proper response to the polycrisis understood broadly to include also its ecclesial dimensions (i.e., the Catholic polycrisis), and having sketched key reasons for why our social doctrine has been marginalized for decades, and why contemporary conditions may now be more favorable to a new flourishing of social Catholicism, it remains to discuss in further detail the alternative approach that influential Catholics in the United States are instead advocating, namely postliberalism.[70] In my opinion, what we might call postliberal integralism[71] and allied forms of right-wing illiberalism threaten to divert especially Catholics from their needed contribution to renewing the institutions of contemporary constitutional democracy in a historical context in which there is no time to spare. I will, therefore, comment on this school of thought at some length in this introduction, in a way that I hope will be complementary to the relevant essays included in this volume.[72] In the spirit of hoping that many of those attracted to this postliberal integralism will be persuaded by arguments against aspects of it, especially the tendency toward an illiberalism of the right and the advocacy of integralism, I will also note some of the ways that I think that postliberal scholars have helped to advance the conversation.

---

70. Such tension between American Catholics and the teaching of the magisterium is sadly characteristic of contemporary Catholic life. A primary hope of this volume is that many of these American Catholics, will awaken to the emerging threats and come to a better appreciation of our social tradition and how Pope Francis is wisely encouraging us to recover it. One of the aspects of our social tradition that I would encourage American Catholics to consider is the warnings about ideologies and how that relates to the conservative identity embraced by so many. In a conversation with fellow Jesuits on August 5, 2023, Pope Francis lamented those American Catholics who have let their faith be corrupted by ideology. See White, "Pope Francis Blasts Reactionary American Catholics."

71. This formulation reflects the way the leading Catholic postliberals also advocate a new Catholic integralism through which the coercive power of the state is at the service of the Church.

72. These include especially chapter 11: Waller, "Integralism, Political Catholicism"; and chapter 12: McManus, "Hard Right and Postliberalism."

The Roots and Development of Postliberalism

Although the term postliberal was previously employed by theologians like George Lindbeck to describe an alternative to the theological approach of liberal Protestantism that emphasized experience over doctrine, the new usage indicates a fundamentally critical orientation toward the liberal political order that is reminiscent of the stance of Catholics from earlier centuries—and also of recent decades—who might be described as radically antiliberal, emphasizing that liberalism[73] is disordered from its deepest roots. The word postliberalism refers—provocatively—to what comes after liberalism, assuming that it has already failed even if much of the political order in the developed world has evolved out of the so-called postwar liberal consensus centered in the embrace of constitutional democracy.

This alleged failure of liberalism ultimately traces to its radically flawed foundations, especially its alleged grounding in an ideology of atomistic individuals with unconstrained freedom. Although an individualistic anthropology is certainly a problem in liberal societies like the United States, various critics argue that the postliberal charge is exaggerated and imprecise.[74] Other prominent critics of postliberalism in the United States, including Francis Fukuyama and Yascha Mounk, have objected that the postliberals perform a rhetorical sleight of hand by criticizing certain features that may be present in some of the various forms of liberal society and then claiming they are inherent to liberalism itself and thus to all forms of liberal—or as I prefer to say, constitutional—democracy.

Putting the postliberal critique of liberalism otherwise, they charge liberalism with the fatal flaw of separating nature from *telos*, namely the end or goal of true human flourishing. Against this separation, they want

---

73. Regarding liberalism, I follow Martin Rhonheimer in preferring to speak of constitutional democracy, and tracing its evolution not simply through Enlightenment thought, but more through medieval mixed regimes, English constitutionalism, and the achievements of ancient Greece and Rome.

74. The classical liberal Larry Arnhart, for example, cites various primary sources against this central objection of the postliberals. He summarizes that "what Deneen and Dreher scorn as atomistic individualism—human beings living as completely solitary creatures with no social bonds—is rejected by liberals like Locke, Adam Smith, and Friedrich Hayek as 'false individualism.' Liberal individualism is actually a communal individualism in which human beings as naturally social animals live as family members, as friends, and in voluntary associations such as schools, churches, and other groups." See Arnhart, "Failure of Deneen and Dreher in Their Critique."

to recover a long-discarded Catholic integralism that unites Church and state so that the coercive power of the state can be employed to direct people to what the Catholic Church proclaims to be their fulfillment. This ordering includes especially conformity to traditional norms of sexual, conjugal and life ethics, which are seen as foundational to fulfillment in God. As social conservatives[75] firmly committed to the cultural and political right, the postliberals seek to harness contemporary populist energy against the threat to the common good they see coming from the illiberal left, the clearest example of which is the campus cancel culture that is illiberal in the sense of violating the liberal commitment to free speech. Much more disputable, the postliberals tend to see legislation and policy that fails to uphold traditional sexual and marital ethics as meriting the illiberal imposition of these traditional views, by which I mean imposing them in ways that violate fundamental liberal principles like human rights, equal human dignity and constitutional democracy.[76]

---

75. For our present purposes, it may be helpful to specify how I am using the terms "social conservatism" and "social conservatives." By the latter, for example, I refer to those who prioritize the preservation of goods they perceive to be threatened by social change, a priority that is typically distinguished from a progressive emphasis on building a better future. For early conservatives like Edmund Burke (1729–97), his conservatism included a respectful attitude toward received tradition and efforts to defend threatened institutions like the family and the Church. In the wake of the so-called "sexual revolution" that followed the introduction of the birth control pill, social conservatives—including Catholics—understandably sought to preserve traditional norms of sexual and conjugal ethics. This traditional ethic sought to locate sexual behavior in the context of stable marriages at the service of the responsible transmission of human life, which followed from the understanding that this was conducive to the virtuous integration of our desires for pleasurable goods, an integration that was considered foundational to personal and societal flourishing. I certainly strive to understand, live and foster all the truths mediated through the Catholic Church. That is different, however, from ignoring the complexities in the tradition, from refusing to consider new data, from insisting on positions that are "more Catholic than the Pope" or attempting to impose them through state coercion. These tendencies, however, are not uncommon among those I am describing as social conservatives. With the increased demand for elective abortion that followed from the sexual revolution, the most contested issue of the emerging "culture wars" had come to the forefront. In subsequent years, the primary concerns that social conservatives have prioritized have included euthanasia, gay and transgender rights, wokeism and cancel culture. See chapter 8: Murphy, "Liberalism, Conservatism."

76. This seems to reflect a nostalgia for the Christendom that is long past. For an insightful reflection on coming to accept the diminished cultural authority of the Church—including over moral matters including sex, life and marriage—see chapter 17 of Vol. 2: Bauerschmidt, "Christendom." The postliberals, in my opinion, are repeating the mistake Catholics made in Europe during the interwar decades during which there was widespread support for fascism.

Social Catholicism for the Twenty-First Century?—Volume 1

Key Works and Thinkers of American Catholic Postliberalism

The banner of postliberalism has been increasingly embraced by Catholic social conservatives[77] since the 2018 publication of Patrick J. Deneen's *Why Liberalism Failed*. The fact that the most prominent group of postliberals has named their Substack "Postliberal Order" indicates that they have in mind a particular kind of order after the anticipated collapse—or perhaps the overthrow—of a liberalism, especially the political and economic forms of it.[78] This order is reflected in the name of the postliberal Adrian Vermeule's bestselling 2022, *Common Good Conservatism: Recovering the Classic Legal Tradition*. That is, they want to recover a political order grounded in a legal tradition that finds an objective basis for civil law in the truth about what is just, as reflected in the right reason of natural law. This contrasts with an understanding of posited or civil law that is measured only by authorial intent or original public meaning of the text.

From the perspective of Catholic tradition, this grounding of law in truth makes sense, because we believe the entire cosmos reflects the divine wisdom and goodness, even if we also recognize our limited ability to grasp that truth. There are also important differences to be recognized between—on the one hand—the moral law, grounded in the divine wisdom, that rules and measures human acts regarding their relation to human flourishing and—on the other hand—the civil law that is ordered to the common good and the flourishing of society. The best of the Catholic tradition recognizes, moreover, several factors regarding the moral law and its reflection in civil law. These include the following. First, the more one departs from first principles of morality like do good and avoid evil, the more disagreement there will be about the conclusions about what reflects the moral law; this includes the realms of sexual, marital and life ethics of foremost concern for postliberals. Second, the rationale for civil law is not to reflect the whole moral law, but only what is conducive to the flourishing of the community. Third, civil law needs to be acceptable

---

77. The meaning, forms, history and present state of conservatism—and the Republican party that has championed various forms if it—is of great relevance to the seemingly modest prospects for a significant renewal of social Catholicism, so these will be at least touched upon in various essays in this collection, including my "Liberalism, Conservatism, and Social Catholicism for the Twenty-First Century?"

78. The online home for the postliberals is the Substack "Postliberal Order." The initial four collaborators were Patrick J. Deneen of Notre Dame, Gladden Pappin of the University of Dallas, Chad Pecknold of Catholic University of America, and Adrian Vermeule of Harvard Law School. More recently the philosopher Edward Feser and the Economist Philip Pilkington have joined the Substack.

to the people who are to be governed by it if there is to be respect for and adherence to the rule of law, in civil harmony and stability. Fourth, contemporary Catholic social teaching leads to an approach to civil legislation that centers on broad participation in work for the common good, dialogue, and personal example, not alignment with illiberal right-wing populists to impose a stringent morality on an unwilling public.

Vermeule's work does, however, make valuable contributions to the conversation, especially in its critique of the constitutional originalism that has dominated conservative jurisprudence and politics for decades. This critique is getting considerable attention because it comes from the right, whereas serious criticisms of originalism from the left have been available for some time without getting much traction.[79] More controversial is Vermeule's advocacy for the "integralism" that puts the coercive power of the state under the direction of the Catholic Church; this does not reflect contemporary Catholic teaching, nor is it remotely feasible given the state of the Church, nor does it seem conducive to the common good given the widespread civil disturbance it would be expected to provoke, nor would it be anything short of a disaster for the Church.[80]

The scope of the liberalism that postliberals attack goes beyond the anthropological individualism often present in such societies to include "free market" economics[81] and the political theory and culture that underlies so-called liberal democratic states. The self-described postliberal economist Philip Pilkington surprisingly reflects the consensus of the social, political and economic left that neoliberal economics normalizes rule by an oligarchic economic elite. To counter this plutocracy, he

---

79. Chemerinsky, *Worse Than Nothing*; Fleming, *Fidelity to Our Imperfect Constitution*. The dire state of the conservative legal establishment can be seen in the recent founding of an alternative to the Federalist Society by conservative legal luminary and former Judge, Michael Luttig, together with over three dozen colleagues. The Society for the Rule of Law, "About Us," opens with the following paragraph: "Our mission is to protect the Constitution and rule of law against rising threats posed by illiberal forces in our society. That includes the authoritarian drift of certain elements within the conservative legal movement, which in recent years have come to embrace a series of positions antithetical to the American Constitutional system."

80. For a critique of Vermeule's work leading up to the book, see Blakely, "Integralism of Adrian Vermeule."

81. Deneen rejects the neoliberal economics of what he calls "right-liberals," associating it with a "managerial elite"; he is more sympathetic to the social democratic tradition, although his project that aligns clearly with the right provides no foreseeable hope of enacting social democratic policies because libertarian donors are essentially opposed to this, and they largely fund, and thus decisively control, Republicans in the U.S. Senate, along with decisive blocks of Republicans in the House (e.g., the Freedom Caucus).

argues that there must be "economic support for a public-spirited class" to counter them, a new postliberal Catholic aristocracy.[82] Conservative convert to Catholicism Sohrab Ahmari, who also describes himself as postliberal, goes even further in his new book,[83] calling the polity being shaped by libertarian economic elites tyrannical. With many prominent economists,[84] I think the postliberals make a significant contribution to the conversation by offering a right of center critique of market fundamentalism and the oligarchy it has spawned.

These radical flaws of liberalism are also understood to follow from the fact that liberal regimes were explicitly conceived to be neutral regarding theological and metaphysical truth claims about God, about the world and about human persons. The postliberals reject this neutrality claim as masking a bias against these truths. Defenders of liberalism counter, incontrovertibly I think, that it was conceived as an alternative to absolutism and to allow those with different views to live together in relative peace, and that this was a monumental achievement in ending civil conflict over questions of faith and morals regarding which no consensus is foreseeable. After decades of conservative media attacks have turned the word "liberal" into an epithet, the populist rhetoric of the postliberals has a ready audience. They would better serve the common good and conservative principles, in my opinion, if they focused on reforming our institutions rather than attacking them or taking them over through regime change as I will discuss below.

From a radically antiliberal or postliberal perspective, the crises facing the contemporary world would trace largely to the flaws at the deepest roots of liberalism. Such a charge would merit a more detailed response than can be given here as many recognize that we are in a

---

82. See Pilkington, "Economic Case for Aristocracy," para. 1.

83. Ahmari, *Tyranny, Inc.* Given that prominent postliberal conservatives like Ahmari and Deneen are now taking for granted the seemingly incontrovertible evidence that networks of libertarian business interests, donors, and think tanks have gravely undermined American democracy and the common good, I think they have helped to focus the conversation. I think, however, that Deneen's solution of Catholic integralism through a new Catholic aristocracy is profoundly misguided, and that they should instead embrace the authentic social doctrine of the Church and work to renew the institutions of our constitutional democracy.

84. As Anthony Annett, for example, will argue in his contribution to our symposium on New Economic Thinking after the Neoliberal Consensus, neo-classical economics has created a situation that is both politically and environmentally unsustainable, and we need an approach that serves the broader human family in a sustainable way. Annett, "Toward a New Economics." See also Stiglitz, "After Neoliberalism."

transition between eras, and different approaches to understanding the situation and responding to it should be discussed with deep humility. The grave challenges faced by the Church since the Second Vatican Council, moreover, would also—according to a radically antiliberal or postliberal assessment—follow largely from an overly sanguine accommodation to liberalism during the postwar decades.

Postliberalism, Catholic Social Teaching, and Evangelization

Although the postliberals present their work as reflecting CST, they tend toward preconciliar understandings of it, which locates those who do so in opposition to the ongoing discernment of the magisterium, a red flag regarding the properly Catholic nature of their project. They tend to read conciliar era and subsequent social teaching through what Pope Benedict XVI calls a "hermeneutic of continuity" so that the more recent teachings are read to emphasize continuity with the earlier ones. Benedict XVI rejects this hermeneutic as deficient and advocates a "hermeneutic of reform and renewal" in the life of the one Church, with elements of both continuity and discontinuity. He proposes this hermeneutic of reform as a sort of virtuous mean between the errors of continuity on the one side and "discontinuity and rupture" on the other, and he employs it explicitly to counter the integralism favored by the postliberals.[85]

To the extent that it follows a hermeneutic of continuity, postliberalism has much in common with that of the schismatic Archbishop Marcel Lefebvre (1905–91). For him, the allegedly misguided accommodation of liberalism by the Catholic Church is rooted in the teachings themselves of the Second Vatican Council, especially the acceptance of the secular state and religious freedom in *Dignitatis Humanae: The Declaration on Religious Liberty*.[86] If, on the other hand, one rejects Lefebvre's

---

85. Benedict XVI's teaching is often misrepresented—by those who should, and sometimes do, know better—as embracing the hermeneutic of continuity. For an insightful discussion that critically engages the traditionalist perspective, see Rhonheimer, "Benedict XVI's 'Hermeneutic of Reform.'"

86. A decisive step in the modern Catholic acceptance of the right to religious freedom was its affirmation in no. 14 of John XXIII's 1963 encyclical *Pacem in Terris: Peace on Earth*. This text affirms that "Also among man's rights is that of being able to worship God in accordance with the right dictates of his own conscience, and to profess his religion both in private and in public." This right was later treated at greater length in Paul VI, *Dignitatis Humanae*. The question was so complex and weighty, however, that it was perhaps the most contested topic at the Council, was central to the only schism following from the council and remains at the heart of the contemporary debate that

schismatic path, this allegedly misguided post conciliar accommodation to liberalism is traced to a misinterpretation of the Council, especially the error of accepting the separation of Church and State. Because the rapid decline of Catholic practice in recent decades, there is no possibility of establishing a Catholic state in places like the United States through consensus. Postliberal Catholics still seek, however, to forge or reestablish a privileged relationship between an earlier, antiliberal version of Catholicism and a postliberal state to better align the latter with the truth claims of the former that liberalism failed to uphold. Along these lines, postliberal Chad Pecknold of The Catholic University of America has argued that the remedy to the decline in Catholic faith and practice is a recovery of what he sees as the traditional and preconciliar missionary strategy.[87] According to this approach, the Church should align with political power to form an allegedly "Catholic state" so that state power could be employed to coercively foster what he understands as "evangelization," even if done through the soft coercion of more carrots than sticks. Such views, however, are irreconcilable with the last eighty years of magisterial discernment regarding our social doctrine, which reflects the recovery of an authentically Christian understanding of evangelization and conversion, which was recovered more widely after the disastrous experience of fascism.

Postliberalism and Regime Change for an American Illiberal Democracy?

With many contemporary conservatives, as evident in recent meetings of the Conservative Political Action Committee (CPAC) in Budapest and keynoted by Hungary's Victor Orbán, postliberals increasingly look to his so-called "illiberal democracy" as a promising model for the United States and beyond.[88] Although this Hungarian exemplar appears democratic by maintaining a neutered set of democratic institutions and by holding regular elections, the whole system has been ingeniously rigged

---

I am sketching with many conservatives adopting a position identical with or close to that of the schismatics.

87. See, for example, Pecknold, "Making Disciples of All Nations."

88. See the remarks on Hungary in Pecknold, "Cure for the Nations." He writes of "beautiful Hungary," which "has a true vision of reality," not one based on the "democratic disorder which wrecks the family and the person" but on the "great tradition which is mindful of the truth about God and his eternal law."

to maintain single party rule.[89] Patrick Deneen fleshes out how this postliberal future might be achieved in his new book *Regime Change: Toward a Postliberal Future*.[90] In it, Deneen envisions the replacement of liberal elites with a new aristocracy of Catholic postliberals as the vanguard of an aristopopulism, advancing a political order of Vermeule's common good constitutionalism. Although CST certainly envisions a multitude of Catholics living out their lay apostolates to foster the common good, it presupposes that this is done through witness, dialogue and participation in the public life of a constitutional democracy, not through "riding the tiger"[91] of right-wing populism to establish an illiberal democracy, which would most likely be controlled by oligarchs, or perhaps an autocrat like the mercurial Donald Trump who might or might not turn from the oligarchs he served in his first term to an economic populism.

Whereas Republican economic conservatives have been focused for decades on the libertarian goal of starving, shrinking and deconstructing public institutions and the administrative state, postliberals like Deneen and Vermeule speak favorably of institutions, at least those that could be employed to advance their socially conservative priorities. Under Deneen's postliberal Catholic aristocrats, these political institutions would be redirected to advance common good constitutionalism, centered in a pro-life and pro-family agenda. This might seem attractive to American

---

89. Orbán's systemic rigging requires sustained effort to grasp, let alone defeat. See Scheppele, "How Victor Orbán Wins." Similar efforts to effectively gerrymander and rig American democracy at the state level has been ongoing for years, with Wisconsin struggling to recover from it. For a case study of how this was done in Ohio where I lived the last seventeen years, see Pepper, *Laboratories of Autocracy*. For a discussion of the latest such behavior in Wisconsin, see Bouie, "Breathtaking Contempt." Similar antidemocratic tactics are being employed in other Red States such as Alabama, where the Republican state legislature is defying court orders to remedy gerrymandered districts, an approach that was successful in Ohio. Although Democrats have also recently engaged in gerrymandering in New York and Illinois, the situation is not symmetrical, so we should not fall into the false equivalence of "bothsidesism." For example, the 2021 Freedom to Vote Act introduced by the Democrats would have outlawed voter suppression, partisan sabotage, gerrymandering, and dark money, but was defeated by a Republican filibuster. It was reintroduced in 2023 with universal support from the Senate Democrats and has supermajority support from the American public but has no chance of passage without a Democratic supermajority in the Senate. Brennan Center, "What the Freedom to Vote Act Would Do."

90. Deneen, *Regime Change*.

91. This understanding of "riding the tiger" was popularized on the right by the eclectic Italian traditionalist Julius Evola. Evola, *Ride the Tiger*. To see the disturbing parallels between the postliberal thought among Catholics and earlier forms of the radical right that led to twentieth-century fascism, see Rose, *World after Liberalism*.

pro-life Catholics, until they consider the Orwellian downsides of life in the illiberal autocracy that would implement it. The Catholic postliberals also want to employ public institutions to advance a working-class agenda that overlaps significantly with the political economics of the contemporary Democratic party. There is currently little support for such a thing on the right, even if the postliberal Sohrab Ahmari advocates for a "pro-life New Deal." Instead, if the Catholic postliberal aristocrats were to be part of a coalition of the illiberal right, that coalition has largely embraced the use of the coercive power of government to punish and suppress any voices to their left.

There is a real danger of such aspiring Catholic aristocrats misguiding the American Catholic population to oppose the Social Doctrine of the Church and the discernment of the Magisterium to grant political power to autocratic forces of the contemporary right that are speaking openly of violence and retribution against political enemies, at the time when the world is facing a polycrisis. The postliberals would do well to consider the importance of the institutions of constitutional democracy to the common good in the contemporary world, even if those institutions are not dominated by their postliberal Catholic aristocrats.[92] Although I think the importance of institutions to the common good should be almost self-evident to those with some sense of the modern world, I also think the importance of public institutions has been shown convincingly by not only philosophers in dialogue with the Catholic Social Tradition,[93] but also political scientists surveying the broad experience of the human family.[94]

---

92. To be clear, I'm strongly in favor of virtuous and learned Catholics participating in public life to advance the common good, presuming it is done in a way that reflects our authentic social tradition, which is informed by social friendship, example, respect for human rights, dialogue and the building of relationships and institutions.

93. Rhonheimer, *Common Good of Constitutional Democracy*.

94. Regarding the importance of open and inclusive political institutions as the decisive factor for flourishing societies, see Acemoglu and Robinson, *Why Nations Fail*. This acclaimed work shows that the failure to build and maintain such healthy institutions is the path to state failure, with all the social misery that follows. They deepen their analysis with their subsequent work. Acemoglu and Robinson, *Narrow Corridor*. This work draws upon experience across many cultures and eras to elucidate the delicate balance required to ensure not only human freedom from tyranny but safety and prosperity. They highlight the needed balance between state institutions and society. In my opinion, the renewal of social Catholicism aligns nicely with their thesis, whereas the socially conservative priorities that entail the continued attack on our institutions is the path to dystopia.

Benedict XVI: Taking a Stand for the Common Good through the Institutional Path

Pope Benedict XVI, for example, has a deep appreciation for this centrality of institutions—including public ones—to the common good, and a key emphasis of his 2009 social encyclical *Caritas in Veritate* is that Catholics take the lead in renewing them. In the introductory section, he urges us to "take a stand for the common good, . . . to be solicitous for, and on the other hand to avail oneself of, that complex of institutions that give structure to the life of society, juridically, civilly, politically and culturally."[95] Here Pope Benedict not only presupposes that citizens avail themselves to rely upon and participate in these institutions. He articulates that political participation should be ordered to the common good, but he does so in terms of institutions, namely by being solicitous for their flourishing. Benedict XVI further makes clear the reason why these institutions deserve such care, namely because they "give structure to the life of society, juridically, civilly, politically and culturally." Benedict continues that this is "the institutional path—we might also call it the political path—of charity, no less excellent and effective than the kind of charity which encounters the neighbour directly." Perfectly consistent with sound Catholic theology, Benedict XVI thinks that working to renew our institutions through political participation is no less "excellent and effective" than direct service to our neighbors; we could go even farther than that to say it could be better to the extent that the good of the many that can be fostered through institutions is better than the good of the one or few who we might help directly.

One would hope that the postliberals would agree. These institutions, however, are at the heart of what is understood as liberal democracy, and the broad postliberal attack on liberalism seems to include these institutions thereby harming the common good by doing precisely the opposite of what Benedict encourages. Perhaps most troubling, the broad postliberal attack on liberalism—at a time when American democracy and the postwar liberal order are already facing existential threats—seems to ignore the grave dangers of degrading from a still democratic polity, with strong elements of oligarchy and plutocracy, into a dystopian tyranny of the minority or some kind of failed state.

---

95. Benedict XVI, *Caritas in Veritate*. All citations from this paragraph are from no. 7.

As I have already indicated, however, the postliberals do recognize that the previous consensus for the political-economic paradigm of a market fundamentalist version of neoliberalism has led to a situation in which democratic forces are dominated by oligarchic ones with a threat of deterioration into tyranny or perhaps a failed state. In this recognition they align with prominent thinkers on the left.[96] On the other hand, there are no reasonable grounds to hope that Catholic postliberals will prevail in a Republican Party that is split between those in the grip of libertarian donor networks and an enraged populist right thrilled with Trump's promises to use a second term to punish enemies. To align themselves with right wing populism in the hope of directing it, the postliberals seem to have an explicit strategy of presenting themselves as men of the populist right, which puts them at odds with the donor networks representing the economic right. In our time of tribal polarization, however, this self-identity as men of the (populist) right would seemingly preclude their building coalitions with the economic left to challenge these loci of power and wealth.

If, on the other hand, the Catholic postliberals eschewed ideological and partisan commitments, and followed Pope Benedict XVI's call to take a stand for the common good by working to renew our institutions[97] through what Pope Francis calls a better kind of politics, they could perhaps make a significant contribution to bringing hope and healing to the church, nation and world.[98]

---

96. Levitsky and Ziblatt, *Tyranny of the Minority*. Note how this alarm among scholars at elite institutions like Harvard aligns with that coming from conservatives like Ahmari. Although the challenges of the polycrisis are indeed grave, this project on Social Catholicism for the Twenty-First Century is based on the conviction that—with God's help—it is possible to build a worthy future, and that the new social Catholicism and better kind of politics may be decisive if we are to do so. This could be seen as a contemporary reflection of the insistence on the necessity of the Church in the social realm, not to help illiberal neo-fascists enforce a stringent sexual ethic and punish deviants, but to be the indispensable salt and light within the human family.

97. This positive appreciation of participation in the institutions of liberal democracy also aligns with the recent public remarks of Pope Francis where he "prayed that God would raise up a new generation of 'well-educated and faithful Catholics leaders committed to promoting the church's social and ethical teachings' through public service, especially in politics." Wooden, "World Needs Politicians," para. 1.

98. My point here is that postliberal integralism is perhaps the trendiest contemporary alternative to the social discernment of the post conciliar magisterium regarding liberal/constitutional democracy with significant influence on the institutional infrastructure of the Church in the United States, including clergy and those working in higher education and media. For this reason, their embrace of a more Catholic and defensible perspective on the political community could have significant impact.

C. Postliberal Theology and *"Ressourcement* Thomism"

In this subsection, I will discuss some influential trends in Catholic theology in the United States as they relate to the present argument for a new social Catholicism with an immediate focus on the preservation and renewal of American democracy. I refer to the popular contemporary tendency to combine a kind of postliberal theology with the *ressourcement*[99]—or back to the sources—and Thomistic traditions. I will call this postliberal *ressourcement* Thomism for short. For some decades in the United States, these traditions have appealed to young Catholics, including an increasing majority of seminarians, who are "tradition minded"[100] in the sense that want to become grounded in trusted sources from our tradition.[101] Because my own formation and subsequent work has been grounded in these approaches or traditions, an appreciation for them can be fully compatible with the social Catholicism being proposed through the present project. In my experience, however, formation in these traditions can present obstacles to appreciating our social tradition and how it might apply to the challenges of our day, or it could even lead one toward the postliberal integralism and illiberal democracy that threaten a new authoritarianism and certainly do not reflect the mind of the Church.

---

99. By *ressourcement* with a lower case, I mean to refer to the general approach of going back to the sources in a broad sense, especially to the Scriptures and the fathers of the Church, but also to medieval figures like Aquinas or even twentieth-century sources. This is done in the conviction that the Church will be most successful in engaging the contemporary world when it draws upon the full resources of the tradition. My usage of *ressourcement*, therefore, refers more to an approach to theology than its instantiation by the leading *Ressourcement* thinkers in the decades before and after the Second Vatican Council. Both senses are reflected in the *Communio* school of theology, rooted especially in the American edition of the International Catholic Review of that name, and centered in the Pontifical John Paul II Institute for Studies on Marriage and Family at the Catholic University of America. This school is very robust intellectually and appeals to thoughtful Catholic conservatives. It is perhaps uniquely characterized by a network of friendships, which has the advantage of providing fellowship. Despite my esteem for the persons and many of the intellectual contributions of this school, my concern is that a tendency toward radical antiliberalism has and will discourage American Catholics from contributing to the renewal of democracy that I think follows from our social doctrine. See part 3 of Murphy, "Three Contemporary Alternatives."

100. Regarding the most recent survey of priests, see Vaidyanathan et al, "Polarization."

101. Because of the still unique place of Aquinas's thought as a point of reference and exemplar of the harmony between faith and reason, and because of the richness of *ressourcement* theology and its importance to the Second Vatican Council, I see familiarity with these two schools as an important common ground for Catholic theology.

For this reason, I will engage the thought of one the most prominent examples of this theological approach, Bishop Robert Barron, who has been exemplary in his utilization of the internet to communicate the faith in robust and attractive ways. I will do so under the aspect of explaining how this thought with its current emphases would seem to present obstacles to the argument of this collection, or—as I would hope—could be developed to align with it. I will more indirectly engage the thought of the prolific *ressourcement* Thomist theologian Matthew Levering, primarily through some of his work on Bishop Barron's thought. I will begin with some introductory remarks regarding Barron's theological approach. Then I will review an outline of how Barron's sources and emphases have evolved to a current "Barron 3.0" that reflects a clear alignment with the cultural right, and I will suggest that the Church and world need a "Barron 4.0" that aligns with the argument of this collection. It would therefore better align with the long discernment of the Papal Magisterium regarding our social tradition, through the Pontificate of Francis which—as this collection tries to show—provides a faithful and organic development thereof. I will further introduce Bishop Barron's approach to evangelization, briefly indicating how and why I think it too needs enrichment as part of a "Barron 4.0." This approach would include a robust and imaginative renewal of social Catholicism working in broad collaboration to address a more comprehensive reading of "the signs of our times," thereby building creatively upon the discernment of the Papal Magisterium in what the *Compendium* describes as not just "an integral and solidary humanism" but a "friendly dialogue with all branches of knowledge."[102]

Postliberal Ressourcement *Thomism: Some Introductory Remarks*

I will introduce Barron's thought by drawing largely on a short popular article "Two Visions of Evangelization" published online in *Catholic World Report* by Matthew Levering, who also recently wrote a book on *The Theology of Robert Barron*. Like most of us who came into theology during the Pontificate of St. John Paul II, Levering's work resonates with Barron's dissatisfaction with what he calls the "beige" or "balloons-and-banners Catholicism"[103] of the postconciliar decades, which is usually traced to the views of thinkers like the Jesuit Karl Rahner who thought

---

102. PCJP, *Compendium*, nos. 76–78.
103. Levering, *Theology of Barron*, loc. 186.

an emphasis on doctrine would be unappealing to those formed in the modern world. Barron criticizes much Catholic thought and culture of this era as "without metaphor, charm or beauty."[104]

Whether the blame should be assigned to the erudite Vatican II peritus Karl Rahner or perhaps to well-meaning popularizers at the local level, or whether—as I think—we do better to seek understanding with humility and refrain from assigning "black hats," this tendency to deemphasize doctrine, tradition and rational explanation, was indeed common in the decades following the Council.[105] It gave many of us the impression that Catholicism didn't have a rich doctrinal tradition that merited ongoing study, or that the faith was boring, or vacuous or irrelevant to our lives in the modern world. Among the many of us who came to appreciate that tradition during the pontificate of St. John Paul II, and even enter intellectual apostolates, the consensus seems to be that such approaches were not particularly effective in passing on the faith, especially one that was intellectually engaged.

On the other hand, what some have mocked as the "silly seventies" were also a time when it was very common for parishes to have a thriving justice and peace ministry; this coexistence of a de-emphasis on our doctrinal tradition with those who enthusiastically sought to live out Catholic Social Teaching seems to have resulted in a view that the two were inseparably linked in a chaotic era for the Church. This seems to have fostered the widespread but problematic view—which I think needs to be understood considering wider cultural and political dynamics[106]—that

---

104. Levering, *Theology of Barron*, loc. 501. I do think that Barron's rhetoric gets at a legitimate deficiency in much of the Catholicism of this era and therefore can be helpful. I also think, however, that it entails the danger of fostering an "us versus them" division in the Church between we "conservative/orthodox" Catholics who care about doctrine and those Vatican II "liberals" who disregard doctrine and capitulate to the culture. For a more critical assessment of such rhetoric, see Faggioli, "Barron's 'Beige.'"

105. On the other hand, my experience of active participation in the Church of those decades was that although it was common for religious and clergy to be less appreciative of the intellectual tradition than I would have advised, such postconciliar Catholics also tended to have excellent interpersonal skills and be generous in loving service. I do not recall, moreover, any hint among them of the tribalism that plagues the contemporary Church and culture. Nor was there antagonism toward democracy or the magisterium. In a nutshell, I think we should be humble in assessing the strengths and weaknesses of not only the approaches of the postconciliar decades but also of today's more of heavily intellectual, conservative Catholicism. It seems to me that the properly Catholic approach is captured by the cliché of "both/and" given that none of us can grasp or live the fullness of the faith.

106. See, for example, Oreskes and Conway, *Big Myth*.

treasuring our doctrinal tradition is the mark of conservative/orthodox/faithful Catholics whereas valuing our social tradition characterizes liberal/heterodox Catholics. From two decades of teaching in Catholic seminaries, I can attest that there are more than a few seminarians and clergy ordained in recent decades who are inclined toward this false dichotomy, increasingly identifying with the conservative side of it.[107]

Like many of our generation, the young Barron also came to appreciate the postliberal theology of the American Lutheran George Lindbeck that explicitly eschewed the liberal Protestant emphasis on religious experience over doctrine, tradition and argumentation. This postliberal perspective aligns closely with the combination of *ressourcement* theology and the Thomistic harmony between faith and reason to inform Barron's evangelical approach. This model of evangelization starts with recovering the art of argumentation and is centered in giving compelling and attractive reasons to be Catholic, employing modern media to do so, and engaging in public dialogue with leading cultural figures to show the ongoing relevance and appeal of Catholicism. In my opinion, the work of Bishop Barron to bring an appealing account of Catholicism to a mass audience is a valuable contribution to the life of the Church, as is the work of other *ressourcement* Thomists like Matthew Levering. Such work has special appeal to key audiences including those who are "tradition minded," those who are intellectually inclined, those who come to appreciate that growing in faith helps us to enrich our lives by forming our highest human faculty, and those who make up the institutional infrastructure of the Church.

The Evolution of Bishop Barron's Sources and Emphases

A recent article on Bishop Barron can help us to locate his past and current emphases and provide an opportunity for me to explain how I think these would need to shift to contribute significantly toward the realization of a new social Catholicism which I think would greatly strengthen his work in evangelization. The article in question was published in the London-based international Catholic review *The Tablet* during the Summer of 2023 and is entitled, "The New Evangelisation—In the Shoes of

---

107. Again, I think American Catholics need to understand this shift not simply as something that emerged naturally, or providentially, but in light of the well-documented efforts of those seeking wealth and political power to demonize the social left of the day.

the Fisherman." In it, Madoc Cairns discusses Bishop Barron's thriving ministry of evangelization that draws unprecedented thousands of enthusiastic participants to Church events, and hundreds of thousands of subscribers to his YouTube channel, with a similar magnitude of followers on Twitter or X. In discussing Barron's work, Cairns sketches the development in the evangelist's sources and emphases through the tech idiom of "versions."

Cairns employs the label "Barron 1.0" to describe the gifted young priest-theologian who begins to establish himself after being sent for higher studies in Paris by his Ordinary, the "heavy on social justice, light on culture war"[108] Cardinal Joseph Bernardin. Cairns observes that this Barron 1.0 has strikingly different "emphases and influences" than the current "Barron 3.0," although there is continuity in that he had always appreciated the thought of St. Thomas Aquinas, a touchstone of Catholic orthodoxy. According to Cairns, key sources at this time included "the censured Jesuit Pierre Teilhard de Chardin . . . the dissident Dominican Matthew Fox and another censured Jesuit, Anthony de Mello." Barron himself writes of how the reputed liberal Fr. Andrew Greely was an influential mentor.[109] In addition, Cairns writes that during these years "Barron attends interfaith conferences" and "talks about writing a book reaching out to New Agers." In a text that is reminiscent of the accompanying style of Pope Francis, Cairns tells us how the younger "Barron writes 'The orthodox believer does not want to calm and moderate the New Ager,' 'he wants to join him and push him further.'" Regarding personal style, Cairns observes that "byline pictures show him scruffy and relaxed in shirtsleeves, not a dog collar in sight."[110] Cairns continues that Barron's

> master's dissertation on Karl Marx is sympathetic to the old revolutionary's anti-capitalism; his PhD thesis on the liberal Protestant theologian Paul Tillich admires Tillich's attacks on the Catholic theology of his time. Barron's images of the Christian life are Dorothy Day and Thomas Merton. At this point, he's clearly not a conservative, even if he's not quite a liberal either."[111]

---

108. Cairns, "New Evangelisation," para. 9.

109. See Barron, "Andrew Greely," for excellent insights into Barron's key influences and development.

110. Cairns, "New Evangelisation," para. 10.

111. Cairns, "New Evangelisation," para. 11.

By Cairns' reckoning, we can understand Barron 2.0 as evolving from this Bernardin era Chicago priest-theologian in the decade or so after Francis George takes over the archdiocese in 1996. A decisive step in this evolution was when Cardinal George asked the then Fr. Barron to focus on evangelization after the Cardinal had been scrutinized by Pope John Paul II about what the archdiocese was doing to evangelize the culture. Amidst the sex abuse crisis and ongoing decline of the Church, Barron developed his approach based on a conviction regarding the need to present the faith as attractive and inspiring, a matter of "opening the doors to an ancient cathedral and inviting them inside."[112] Barron soon discovers that YouTube provides a powerful vehicle for reaching a wide audience, and he—as Cairns puts it—"swaps the shirt-sleeves for roman collars, Rahner and Teilhard for Balthasar and Ratzinger. It's not a change of heart so much as a shift in emphasis, intonation, style: less of a voice crying out in the wilderness, more of a man of the Church."[113] Barron's profile continues to rise with the striking success of the video series *Catholicism*, and his appointments, first as Rector of Mundelein Seminary and then as auxiliary bishop of Los Angeles in 2015. During the next several years, polarization—both in the broader culture and online—rose exponentially with the election of Donald Trump, with Brexit, with the online campaigns of the Russian security services to propagate disinformation and division, and with social media becoming siloed between venues serving the left or the right. Whereas Barron had long followed a largely middle or perhaps better "center-right" course on theological and ecclesial matters, Cairns notes that it would have been suicidal to Barron's social media venture to continue to chart a middle course in an age of siloed media, because—to the extent that people are self-selected into tribes—there is no longer a middle. In a 2021 article, moreover, Massimo Faggioli notes how Bishop Barron stakes out a clear defense of the Second Vatican Council against the rad-trads who have been critical of him.[114]

The evolution to the current Barron 3.0 begins, for Cairns, with "a choice" to become what Cairns provocatively describes as

> a semi-detached feature of the so-called "Intellectual Dark Web," a loose coalition of right-wing pundits anxious about an intolerant, extremist left. Barron never quite identifies himself with figures

---

112. Cairns, "New Evangelisation," para. 15.
113. Cairns, "New Evangelisation," para. 19.
114. Faggioli, "Barron's 'Beige,'" para. 7.

like Ben Shapiro or Dave Rubin, but he tries to find common ground with them, stress sympathies, downplay disagreement."[115]

This seeking of common ground with conservative activists while minimizing disagreements with them can also be seen in Barron's ongoing friendly interviews with other luminaries of the right including Jordan Peterson, Sohrab Ahmari and Chris Rufo, a key influence on Ron DeSantis's "war on woke."[116]

Although I can understand potential reasons for the apparent choice in Barron 3.0 to move from a center-right position to one marked by regular friendly discussions with members of the "new right" and "Intellectual Dark Web," I think this comes at a potentially high price, especially regarding Catholic Social Teaching. This downside reflects the "signs of our times" where postliberal integralism is in the air, and the American new right is increasingly antidemocratic—i.e., the "hard right"—and the clear alignment of influential Catholics like Barron with the right will likely be taken as episcopal encouragement to support the right politically.[117] Since this introduction and two volume collection discuss many reasons for charting a path based on a more robust appropriation of Social Catholicism, I will not repeat them here. Instead, I will simply state that I hope to see the emergence of a Bishop Barron 4.0 more aligned with the argument of this collection.

115. Cairns, "New Evangelisation," para. 23.

116. Cairns, "New Evangelisation," para. 30, discusses how the Word on Fire Institute has taken a similar path, citing a course by Matthew Petrusek on "The Idolatry of Identity: Progressive-Wokeist Ideology and the Catholic Response," which includes lectures such as "Wokeism: The Frankenstein of Political Ideologies." To be fair, Petrusek offers a more recent course under the heading of "Catholic Social Ethics: The Antidote to Ideology." I think this is an excellent heading marking what I consider a move in precisely the right direction, although Petrusek largely follows Barron's argumentative/apologetic approach to evangelization and engages Catholic Social Teaching under this aspect, with a reading of the signs of the times that I think is profoundly inadequate. To build upon this modest step in the right direction, I hope that Petrusek, Barron and Word on Fire will engage fruitfully with the arguments of this collection, with the urgency that our times demand.

117. To be fair, Bishop Barron certainly has a broader appreciation of Catholic Social Teaching. For example, he frequently advocates the "See-Judge-Act" methodology articulated in the 1920s by the Belgian Priest Fr. Joseph Cardijn, who later became better known as Cardinal Cardijn. My impression, however, is that Barron's apparent choice to align with the right, results in a reduced scope of CST that would encourage following the example of a Dorothy Day in direct service to the poor, but nothing approaching responses that would follow from the social magisterium of Pope Francis. One should note, however, that Day was one of the few interwar Catholics who wrote clearly about the incompatibility between fascism and Catholicism.

I think, moreover, that such an evolution would make perfect sense for him, and would be very conducive to evangelizing the many youth who have great reason to care deeply about things like the climate crisis, the survival and renewal of American democracy, the fostering of global solidarity to lessen the chance of war, the movement from a rigged neoliberal economy to a more just one that works for everyone, safety from the epidemic of gun violence, racial justice (with particular attention to policing and against widespread efforts to restrict voting access), and finding ways to respect the human dignity of "sexual minorities." If on the other hand, the current American right gains political power with the perhaps indirect help of American Catholics and establishes an illiberal democracy, I fear that future generations of youth will blame Catholics for having helped to usher in a dystopian future in which political action toward all these urgent needs is effectively precluded by one party rule.

Having completed this excursion into a proposed sketch of Bishop Barron's sources and emphases over time, we can now return to the discussion of the approaches to evangelization that follow from the postliberal *ressourcement* Thomism advanced by Bishop Barron, Matthew Levering and many others.

Postliberal Ressourcement Thomism and Evangelization

Whereas Bishop Barron has reached a broad international audience through his media apostolate and Word on Fire ministry, Levering has done complementary work from within the theological community by exemplifying the fecundity of a *ressourcement* Thomism in dialogue with various interlocutors. Overall, I think these resources are a great gift to the Church as far as they go, but I also hope these colleagues would find the arguments of this collection persuasive, not only because I think the stakes are high for the Church and world, but also because I think their influence could be decisive in fostering an apt response by the many Catholics—especially those in the institutional infrastructure of the Church—who have been influenced by their robust and attractive articulations of Catholic teaching. Given that Bishop Barron and Matthew Levering rightly want their work to contribute to evangelization, I will contrast below two ways that evangelization could be understood by those drawing on the strengths of postliberal *ressourcement* Thomism in a way that illustrates why I think these theological colleagues should explicitly eschew the former and robustly embrace the latter.

The first approach would highlight the contrast between the postliberal *ressourcement* Thomist emphasis on strong and attractive articulations of doctrine, on the one hand, and the "liberal" emphasis on respecting the human search for transcendence and building coalitions to work for justice, on the other. It would center evangelization in such articulations and presentations of doctrine and see emphases on respecting the human search for God and working together for the common good and for human rights as reflecting the failed evangelical and social strategies of both liberal Protestantism and the so-called liberal Catholicism of the "silly seventies." It would be generous in its affirmation of conservatism and in outreach to conservatives, while overlooking the contemporary radicalization of the right and the grave threats that poses to humanity. It would present liberalism in the worst possible light, as the "wokeism" that follows from the corrupting influence of Marx, Foucault, and Nietzsche. It would tend to present the Social Doctrine of the Church as an apologetics directed primarily against the excesses of liberalism, such as "wokeism" or "cancel culture." It would emphasize the distinction between evangelization/mission and the exhortations of Pope Francis to go out on mission and build collaborations to address the "dark clouds" he outlines in *Fratelli Tutti*. Instead, it would insist that Catholic political engagement must be centered on a prophetic defense of innocent human life, even after Roe v. Wade has been overturned and the complexity of crafting workable and sustainable civil laws is becoming more evident. In taking a fundamentally critical stance toward a broad understanding of liberalism, and in thereby effectively discouraging humanistic collaboration in the public institutions of liberal democracy to foster the common good, this first approach would incline toward the postliberal integralism discussed in an earlier section of this introductory chapter.

The second approach sees the Church's articulation of her Social Doctrine as rooted in the deepest sources of revelation and indeed doctrine, and as inseparable from what I would argue is a properly Catholic understanding of evangelization as this has evolved through the discernment of the Magisterium. Such an understanding is clearly reflected in the *Compendium of the Social Doctrine of the Church*, especially the second chapter entitled "The Church's Mission and Social Doctrine," which opens with a section on "Evangelization and Social Doctrine."[118] This second approach would, of course, recognize that every human person is created in the image of God, and is inclined toward and fulfilled only in the perfect good who is God. But it would allow that we can both respect "where each person is" in relation to God and make attractive and compelling articulations readily available in various ways, through media, through scholarly literature, through conversation and proclamation. It would also recognize that an exemplary way of manifesting the divine love for humankind and thereby earning the right to speak about the reason for our hope, is for Catholics to live out our Social Doctrine by working in a spirit of "integral and solidary humanism" to collaborate in dispersing the "dark clouds" Pope Francis—with good reason—sees as providing grave threats to the human family. As discussed above, I think this second approach—which could be further articulated[119]—would much better facilitate the evangelization of young people because it would demonstrate that Catholics are in solidarity with them, recognizing and laboring to ameliorate the threats to our shared future.

This introductory essay and the collection that it introduces can be read as an extended argument to eschew the first approach and embrace the second, granted that this might require exemplary virtue as the first path is much easier both culturally and financially.[120]

---

118. PCJP, *Compendium*, nos. 60–104. For an apparent criticism of this, see Bishop Robbert Barron, "My Experience of the Synod," where he writes about what he calls "ambiguity" in the use of the word "mission" at the Synod, including in its *Instrumentum Laboris*. He writes: "Mission seemed, more often than not, to designate the Church's work in favor of social justice and the betterment of the economic and political situation of the poor." He bemoans the "real danger" of failing to mention "sin, grace, redemption, cross, resurrection, eternal life, and salvation," and emphasizes that "point of fact, the primary mission of the Church is to declare the Resurrection of Jesus Christ from the dead and to invite people to place themselves under his Lordship." Barron grants that "discipleship, to be sure, has implications for the way we live in the world, and it certainly should lead us to work for justice, but we must keep our priorities straight." Although there is some truth in his words, I think the argument for a Barron 4.0 is compelling.

119. Patricia Pintado-Murphy, for example, responds to Barron's discussion of evangelizing today's "buffered selves" as Charles Taylor puts it, by pointing out the importance of friendship, community and witness, all of which I think would be fostered by locating evangelization with a more robust social Catholicism. Pintado-Murphy, "Crisis of the Buffered Self."

120. In the interest of speaking what I understand to be the truth in love, let me be clear. By culturally easier, I mean—for example—that focusing on friendly exchange with influential figures on the right will foster dialogue with conservatives and is likely to lessen the attack of right-wing trolls. I would grant that such friendly exchange has

3. Some Guiding Convictions for a New Social Catholicism

Since this project seeks to foster renewed, widespread and zealous commitment to the social apostolate, it seems opportune to outline several of the convictions that are key to understanding social Catholicism. In my opinion, these convictions largely follow from an understanding of the Catholic social tradition, especially as articulated in what is sometimes called the "documentary heritage"[121] and as helpfully synthesized in the previously mentioned *Compendium* published by the Pontifical Council for Justice and Peace under Pope St. John Paul II. As I will discuss below, these largely correspond to the convictions of Bishop Wilhelm E. von Ketteler who is recognized to be the father of modern CST and they align with this whole tradition. These convictions will be supported to a greater or lesser degree by various essays in this collection and are meant to highlight some key points in documents like the *Compendium* that merit emphasis. Among these convictions are the following, some of which I have already touched upon, and all of which could be expressed differently. They should be understood in the context of the way CST considers the ethical dimensions of the social, political, economic, legal and cultural spheres, where ethics is understood not primarily in terms of law but in terms of what is conducive to human flourishing.

The first of these convictions is that Catholic Social Doctrine is part of the deposit of faith, of God's revelation disclosed to us through Scripture, Tradition and the discernment of the magisterium regarding how to

---

its place in efforts to evangelize the right, but if it is not part of a broader presentation along the lines of the *Compendium* as advanced by the present collection, I don't see how that would be faithful to Catholic Social Teaching. It is also culturally easier to identify explicitly with the right in Catholic educational contexts such as seminaries where most—especially American born—students in recent decades have identified as conservative. In this situation, teachers can establish sympathy with the audience by presenting as conservative. In my opinion, however, CST as an expression of the Gospel calls all of us who have been formed in our individualistic culture to conversion. Although doing so is a challenge, teachers and seminary formation faculties, in my opinion, need to be working to foster the appropriate intellectual conversion if they are to be faithful to their vocations and to Christ. By financially easier, I refer to the fact that there are massive sources of funding to present a version of Catholic Social Teaching that ignores—for example—the climate crisis and the grave threats to American democracy posed by the contemporary Republican Party. In accepting such funding, leaders of Catholic institutions need to make sure that they have not compromised the Gospel and God's revelation, which includes the Social Doctrine of the Church.

121. O'Brien and Shannon, *Catholic Social Thought*.

live the life of charity in the modern world. As an integral part of Catholic faith and morals, it is to be received as such and lived, a conviction that seems to be in profound tension with several widespread tendencies in the United States.[122] Continuing with the theological virtues, the second conviction is that social Catholicism is to be lived in a most confident hope of the divine assistance for receiving the good things we need. Given the challenges of the polycrisis and the widespread temptations to despair over the future, or over the Lord's presence in and guidance of his Church and given the technique of contemporary authoritarians to exhaust people with disinformation and chaos, the importance of the virtue of theological hope cannot be overstated, especially if we expect to attract people by our witness. Nobody will be attracted by "doomerism," and the aspiring autocrats and plutocrats will triumph if Catholics fall for the trap of disengaging from work for the common good because it is too messy. Third, as the first chapter of the *Compendium* develops, CSD reflects God's loving plan for humanity. That is, it seeks to illumine the way of living Christian charity in the modern world. The first three convictions, therefore, highlight how social Catholicism, should be understood as following from the three theological virtues.

The fourth conviction is that the Catholic social tradition, although deeply rooted in Scripture, is eminently reasonable and grounded in truth, reflecting the Catholic harmony between faith and reason. This

---

122. Because I think these tendencies are widespread in especially the United States, I will list the most common ones here, which will echo some of the points I made above regarding postliberal *ressourcement* Thomism. The first tendency would be to underestimate our social doctrine as insignificant or lacking practical relevance. I challenge this tendency because the major goal of the present project is to foster a robust recovery of our Social Doctrine to play what I think is the indispensable part of the Church in addressing the polycrisis. This means our social doctrine must be enfleshed in broad movements of social Catholicism reflecting a better kind of politics, which I think is perhaps the best hope for the future of the human family. A second contrary tendency would see our social teaching as reflecting the naïve views of European or Latin American Catholics like Pope Francis, or of outdated Protestant social Gospelers, or of "liberals." Similarly, one might assume that an emphasis on living out our social teaching is for those who neglect the importance of doctrine, of personal conversion and of prayer in favor of mere social activism. My experience, on the contrary, is to be deeply humbled by the authentic Christian witness of those who live out charity by doing the arduous labor of working for justice in the world. Another alternative would be to reduce a Catholic social perspective to voting for politicians who espouse opposition to "intrinsic evils" like abortion, whereas another alternative would transpose CST considering the postliberalism that I just argued against. A final alternative that tempts Americans would be to reduce our social doctrine to a species of apologetics, targeted primarily at attracting conservatives by criticizing the excesses of the left.

can be seen in the way the *Compendium* presents this social doctrine in "friendly dialogue with all branches of knowledge,"[123] where friendly does not exclude a properly critical sense.[124] In our post-truth age of propaganda, media controlled by oligarchs, weaponized disinformation and information silos, and an upcoming proliferation of "deep fakes" generated by artificial intelligence, Catholic social engagement will need to develop more sophisticated ways of being people of truth. Regarding the "signs of the times," for example, I tried to illustrate above—and as the essays in this collection will develop at great length—that Pope Francis's reading of the "signs of the times" aligns with the insights from multiple fields of study, whereas I would argue that the alternative view that insists on the "preeminence of the issue of abortion" tends toward a practical neglect of many grave threats toward which Francis rightly directs our attention.

A fifth guiding conviction is that CSD is grounded in a set of rational principles that have evolved over time and remain open to further elaboration. These principles can be enumerated in different ways but typically center on the following:

- The dignity of every human person, a principle that has been prioritized since the postwar era because it is intuitively attractive and can be seen to imply other principles.

- The ordering of society and social interaction towards the common good, which is a fundamental presupposition tracing to the classical tradition.

- The pursuit of justice, regarding which human rights are a reflection, as are any duties corresponding to those rights. Because justice is the virtue that orders relations between persons and things, the whole of Catholic social ethics has sometimes been organized under this heading.

- The solidarity of the human family, reflecting our shared dignity and interdependence.

---

123. PCJP, *Compendium*, nos. 76–78.

124. Regarding the critical engagement with the findings of social science, see Bevir and Blakely. *Interpretive Social Science*; Blakely, *Alasdair MacIntyre*; Blakely, *Lost in Ideology*.

- The subsidiary distribution of power so decision making takes place at the appropriate level.[125]
- The right to possess private property balanced by a duty to use it in a manner consistent with the common good and the universal destination of goods; this is to say, the ethics of the possession and use of property includes both individual and communal dimensions.
- Integral development that seeks to make available, to every person, the goods conducive to human flourishing.
- Responsible stewardship of creation, corresponding to the need for sustainable development, and reflecting the interdependence of the human family and the interconnection of all things.
- The special concern and care due to the poor and vulnerable, often expressed more narrowly as the preferential option for the poor. This special concern is important not just because they are the most vulnerable, but because it provides an invaluable epistemological insight into questions of justice. In chapter 5, I discuss how John A. Ryan's experience as part of a Catholic community subject to injustice helped him to properly grasp the social challenges of the Gilded Age. In what has been called a new Gilded Age, however, much of the institutional infrastructure of the Catholic Church in the United States tends to identify much differently, largely as middle class, and as conservative, which aligns them with a business class with disproportionate power over the political process at the expense of the less fortunate. This identification, I would argue, is a major obstacle to both understanding the signs of the times and of how our social tradition relates to them.
- The relatively stable, procreative family unit as a natural institution important to the common good.[126]

125. This principle is rooted in the Latin word *subsidium* for help. Against reductionistic understandings, it requires, on the one hand, that lower-level entities not be denied the freedom to act on matters within their competence. It requires, on the other hand, that higher-level entities are established and empowered to perform those tasks that naturally pertain to their broader scope.

126. Recognition of the importance of this institution dates to antiquity, although discussion of it is complicated by historical and contemporary diversities. A less specific statement was articulated in Article 16.3 of the 1948 Universal Declaration of Human Rights: "The family is the natural and fundamental group unit of society and is entitled to protection by society and the State." United Nations General Assembly, *UDHR*. This is perhaps the most contested principle because of differing views in

Sixth, this social tradition includes not only a set of rational principles but also what we might call a methodology. Although it is not often emphasized in discussions of CST, such a methodology is implicit in the heading under which the 2003 *Compendium* presents the whole tradition of social doctrine, namely as "an integral and solidary humanism." This heading implies living out a comprehensive humanism in solidarity with all men and women, which presupposes the centrality of dialogue and participation in working toward the common good.[127] What I am calling the methodology is simply the living out of Christian charity in the modern world, which occurs through building relations with our neighbors, inspiring them through our virtuous example, as well as dialoguing and collaborating with them in pursuit of the good guided by the various principles listed above. Pope Francis captures the same reality with his emphasis on social friendship.

Seventh, out of solicitude for the good of the human family, this tradition is alert to the "signs of the times," especially as they threaten human dignity or present opportunities to rectify injustices or otherwise advance the common good. Such solicitude should naturally—and has often—put Catholics in the forefront of efforts to address the great challenges of the day. This solicitude is, moreover, receptive to the discernment of the magisterium regarding the interpretation of these signs.[128]

---

pluralistic societies regarding sexuality, marriage and family. It is especially contentious given the culture war politics in which illiberals on the right and left attempt to force their views on others rather than working out a *modus vivendi* so that those of diverse views can live together in social friendship. It is further complicated by the global environmental crisis and by anticipated population peaks later this century as we blast beyond boundaries for planetary resilience, after which a precipitous decline in population is expected.

127. Given that CSD entails living out the Divine plan of love in the world, this heading from the PCJP, *Compendium* also suggests the preeminent Christian virtue of charity, which is brilliantly elucidated by Thomas Aquinas as a kind of friendship, drawing on Aristotle's classic treatment of the latter. According to this understanding, charity sees our neighbors as like us and works for their good. In the modern world, this good would include everything from the necessities of life to the eternal embrace of the perfect good in God. The benevolence and beneficence at the heart of charity entail that we not only wish for, but work for, a just social order in which all can flourish.

128. For Benedict XVI in the wake of the 2008 financial crisis, these signs required—as we already saw—that we take "the institutional path" to reform the institutions of presumably constitutional democratic states so they are informed by sound ethical principles. For Benedict, this meant seeking economic models that are not limited to maximizing profits as in the era of market fundamentalism, and he articulated a greatly enhanced emphasis on the need to protect the environment as the results of human activity were presenting an increasingly existential threat.

For Pope Francis, the signs of the times require us to address the impact of economic inequality on the poor and to prioritize the rapidly unfolding climate catastrophe and its impact on the most vulnerable, especially migrants. Indeed, he has recently promulgated *Laudate Deum: On the Climate Crisis*. This, unprecedented, second intervention into the climate crisis builds on his 2015 environmental encyclical *Laudato Si': On Care for Our Common Home*, emphasizing how the situation has become even more acute given the failure to respond in proportion to the problem. Americans bear a special responsibility to act given the proportion of the pollution we have caused, given our disproportionate role in promoting disinformation about the problem, and given the impact we could have in lessening the damage if we would only do what we can and should. Pope Francis also emphasizes the need to cultivate a sense of universal fraternity and social friendship, and—as I have emphasized—to develop a better kind of politics in the wake of an unjust and unsustainable political and economic system dominated by the wealthy at the expense of the rest.

Eighth, and building on this receptivity to the discernment of the magisterium, the Catholic social tradition encourages us to keep a critical distance from ideological and partisan commitments, to subordinate them to principles and a methodology of social friendship. Whereas one could get the impression from aspects of contemporary culture that we must either be of one tribe or the other—of the left or right, liberal or conservative, Republican or Democrat—Catholics should have a higher allegiance to God, to the truth, and to principles like the dignity of every person, justice, the solidarity of the human family, the common good and the responsible stewardship of our common home on earth. Rather than allowing tribal allegiances to political parties and ideologies to forestall dialogue and action, Catholics should be able to discuss—in a spirit of relative detachment—the merits of political parties and their policies as they relate to the common good, and we should be able to readily change our support as conditions merit.

Ninth, although this social tradition includes a complex history marked by an often-contentious relationship with evolving "liberal" states and the philosophical articulations thereof, the postwar discernment of the Catholic magisterium has come to recognize the institutions of what I prefer to call constitutional democracy as integral to the common good. As such, they are something that Catholics should work to maintain and develop, including by informing them with sound principles of social ethics and a spirit of social friendship.

Tenth, since the Industrial Revolution, I would argue that so called modern CST has consistently sought a path between two political-economic extremes, about which I will comment at great length as it is perhaps the most contested of my enumerated principles with considerable relevance to addressing contemporary challenges. On the one hand, CST rejected socialism in the sense of communal ownership of the means of production because this denied the possession of private property that people required for sustenance and security.[129] On the other hand, it rejected the economic liberalism associated with laissez faire, social Darwinism and individualism. In the decades surrounding the Second World War and surrounding the council, the magisterium came to favor the emerging political-economic consensus for what was called a "mixed economy" or social democracy,[130] but as I already mentioned, this seemed obsolete as a consensus developed for the neoliberal economic paradigm through the 1980s.

Since the 2008 financial crisis, however, the consensus for a market fundamentalist version of the neoliberal paradigm has collapsed due not only to its evident role in that crisis, but also to the fact that it has shifted a vast portion of wealth to the economic elites, who have gained at least quasi-oligarchic political power in the United States and much of the developed world, bringing corruption and both destabilizing constitutional democracy and bringing us to the verge of catastrophic environmental tipping points.[131] Although the consensus regarding a new social

129. The Church also rejected the doctrines of socialism including its materialism based on our belief in spiritual realities and its understanding of the class struggle based on our belief in the unity of the human family.

130. Such arrangements sought to balance market activities with institutions designed to lessen the frequency and impact of market failures, to provide for public goods like infrastructure and a social safety net, and to deliver services that help a broad portion of the population to rise from precarity to the security associated with the middle class. Although it seems clear to me that magisterial social teaching has continued to reflect this social democratic perspective, most of the last forty years of global economics have been marked by a consensus for a neoliberal paradigm, especially in a market fundamentalist form, emphasizing economic freedom from government regulation, the reduction of taxes on businesses and the wealthy, and deep cuts in social services.

131. The Stockholm Resilience Centre at Stockholm University has published in 2023 the third major assessment according to the planetary boundaries framework that was introduced in 2009. This 2023 assessment is the first that measures all nine planetary boundaries for the "processes and systems that maintain the stability and resilience of our planet." The finding is that we have already far exceeded seven of them, clearly indicating the urgency of a more sustainable course. Richardson et al., "Earth beyond Six of Nine Planetary Boundaries."

democratic paradigm seems to be forming on the left, with the Biden Administration promoting a "middle out" economics in contrast to an earlier "trickle-down" approach, we have already seen that there are at least some voices on the American right who are also advocating for a more of a mixed economy or social democratic model. This rethinking on the left and right is conducive to a new intellectual and practical engagement of Catholics considering our social tradition so that economic policy is not simply left to the market but becomes part of public discussion regarding the common good and guided by the various principles of our tradition.

My eleventh guiding conviction is that the living out of this Social Doctrine is fundamental to an authentically Catholic approach to evangelization, that this approach to evangelization follows from the magisterial documents, that it corresponds with sound doctrine and pastoral practice, that it has been relatively successful to the extent that it has been employed,[132] that it has not been broadly followed in the United States for at least several decades,[133] and that this failure provides a plausible but largely unnoticed part of the explanation for the rapidly declining share of Catholics in the population in recent decades.

4. Fostering a New Conversation about Social Catholicism and a Better Kind of Politics

In this section I will introduce the contributions that make up this first volume of our two-volume collection, which is subtitled Historical Perspectives and Constitutional Democracy in Peril. Since each essay is already prefaced by an abstract, in what follows I seek primarily to fit the essays into the narrative I am striving to articulate. According to

---

132. See, for example, John Ireland's approach of "making America Catholic" by putting Catholics in the forefront of solving the great social challenges of the day. See chapter 5: "Social Formation of Msgr. John A. Ryan."

133. I would argue that the largely unsuccessful social and evangelical approach employed by American Catholics in the United States over the last several decades was influenced less by our tradition and more by the political alliance with Evangelical Protestants and the Republican Party. According to historian Randall Balmer, "In fact, it wasn't until 1979—a full six years after Roe—that evangelical leaders, at the behest of conservative activist Paul Weyrich, seized on abortion not for moral reasons, but as a rallying-cry to deny President Jimmy Carter a second term. Why? Because the anti-abortion crusade was more palatable than the religious right's real motive: protecting segregated schools." Balmer, "Real Origins of the Religious Right," para. 4.

this narrative of faith, hope and social charity, Catholics—inspired by our broad social tradition—enter a broad coalition to address the grave challenges of our day, starting with the renewal American democracy through a better kind of politics informed by the principles of Catholic Social Doctrine, and by a methodology of social friendship, dialogue, and participation. This is a narrative with deep roots in Scripture and Tradition, starting with the Old Testament story of a God who creates a world that is good, and hands it over for our stewardship. It is a story of a God of justice, in whom his people can trust, and cry out for help, confident in the divine assistance. It is an emerging story that is largely yet to be written, employing the imagination in a way that grows out of the nexus between Scripture, Tradition, the teaching office of the Church and the whole human family to dissipate the storm clouds of the polycrisis and join to build a peaceful, just and sustainable future. It is a story that realizes the vision of the Second Vatican Council for a Church that acts as an efficacious sign of unity in the world, helping to bring hope and healing to the human family.

Locating Modern Catholic Social Doctrine in the Broader Tradition

Although this collection focuses on the modern era of CST that emerges in response to the industrial revolution, I think it is important to further elucidate how this doctrine flows from the deepest wellsprings of divine Revelation in both the Old and New Testaments. As we might expect, the first chapter of the *Compendium* draws primarily from Scripture to introduce CSD under the heading of the "God's Plan of Love for Humanity."[134] For our present purposes, it will suffice to note that there is also a great wealth of scholarship that can help us to build on the biblical foundations in the *Compendium* to enable Catholics and other Christians to trust more deeply in God, to hope more surely in the divine assistance, and to love our neighbors more generously. Although the resources from Catholic authors are perhaps less plentiful than we might hope—reflecting, apparently, the delayed reception of both the Second Vatican Council's directives on the renewal of moral theology and of our social doctrine—there are excellent materials available.[135] If we draw upon the

---

134. PCJP, *Compendium*, ch. 1.
135. Donahue, *Seek Justice That You May Live*. Burghardt, *Preaching the Just Word*.

work of our separated Christian brothers and sisters, there is an even greater abundance of materials to deeply ground our work for justice and the common good in the inspired Word of God.[136]

As an excellent example of the long tradition between this biblical revelation and the era of modern Catholic social teaching, the next essay following this introduction is by Peter Casarella of Duke University on "The Social Catholicism of Fr. Félix Varela (1788–1853)." For our purposes, Fr. Varela serves as an example of those Catholics throughout history who have been attentive to the signs of their times and the implications of the Gospel, and how the properly modern social tradition develops from what precedes it. Like the social Catholics to follow, Varela exemplifies a high level of intellectual engagement with the best thinking of his day, a deep grounding in the Catholic tradition, a firm commitment to the interdependence of truth and virtue, and a strong advocacy for justice. For Varela, this included his early advocacy for Cuba's political independence from colonial domination and for the abolition of the slave trade. Given the contemporary threats to constitutional democracy, Varela's advocacy for a "public spirit"—that he equates with personal freedom, independence, democracy, the rule of law and a critique of ideologies—provides a fitting start to our collection.

Appreciating Modern Social Catholicism within History

Overlapping chronologically with the later years of Varela's ministry but in the context of the industrial revolution in Germany, our third contribution is "Wilhelm von Ketteler: Nineteenth Century Advocate for Catholic Social Thought" by Martin J. O'Malley of Friedrich Schiller University, in Jena, Germany. It treats how this acknowledged father of modern CST sets the trajectory for the subsequent tradition. Analogous to the list of convictions I sketched in section three above, Ketteler sets a lasting example for subsequent social Catholics through the profoundly

---

136. For an example of an ecumenical scholarly collaboration on this topic see Portier-Young and Sterling, *Scripture and Social Justice*. Catholics seeking to appreciate our social tradition can benefit greatly from the abundant works of the previously mentioned Protestant Old Testament scholar Walter E. Brueggemann, who has been especially attentive to social justice throughout his long career with over one hundred books and many essays. Especially valuable from a Catholic perspective are his works addressing the themes of faith, hope, justice, liberation, the common good and solidarity. A listing of these works can be found at https://www.walterbrueggemann.com/resources/books/.

Christian and Catholic standpoint from which he works, through his serious engagement with and appropriation of both secular and Protestant insights, and through his attentiveness to history. He also sets the trajectory for the subsequent tradition through his tireless advocacy for human dignity and the common good, through his acceptance of the structural separation of Church and state while also insisting on the indispensable role of the Church, through his avoidance of the extremes of both the political left and right, and through his prudential discernment of the means that best serve the end of fostering the common good in a given time and place. In the face of different historical challenges, such insights have shaped the social magisterium of the Church and the social movements that have embodied that teaching. Kettler's example also provides key criteria of discernment for those of us today who seek to follow an authentically Catholic path in addressing the polycrisis.

Our fourth contribution is from Rev. Martin Schlag of the University of St. Thomas and considers what we can learn from an early twentieth century controversy between two ethnic communities of Catholic immigrants to America during the industrial revolution. The potential lessons concern how Catholics should relate to two key aspects of liberal modernity. The first concerns what can be called "political liberalism" and is centered in constitutional democracy, religious freedom (the separation of Church and state), human rights and the separation of powers. The second is economic liberalism, which can take different forms.

This controversy included—on the one side—the conservative German American Catholics, who sought to avoid the dangers of a culture marked by secularism, Protestantism and liberal in the sense of the "laissez faire" economics as it existed in America, which they explicitly opposed. On the other side were Irish American Catholics who appreciated their vastly improved situation in the New World. Under the leadership of Msgr. John A. Ryan, they aligned first with the progressive era reforms (roughly 1900-1917) that sought to employ governmental power to remedy the rampant injustices that were being inflicted upon the factory and farm workers who were often Irish. While Ryan was marginalized in the laissez faire era of the "roaring twenties," the collapse of laissez faire into the Great Depression provided the opportunity for him to forge a new partnership with the New Deal reforms of President Franklin Delano Roosevelt. Schlag discusses how the German Catholics accepted an interpretation of American democracy that prioritized the "states' rights"—originally championed by states in the American South to protect their system of racial segregation—against the power of the federal government.[137] Irish Catholics, on the other hand, aligned with the tradition of Abraham Lincoln, Theodore Roosevelt and Franklin Delano Roosevelt that sought to employ federal power to ensure justice for the exploited. Returning to the key question about how Catholics should relate to the institutions of political and economic liberalism that characterize modernity, Schlag also notes the how Pope Benedict XVI strongly endorses the former while criticizing the latter. Considering a "twenty-first century [that] seems to be on the way to becoming a century of anti-humanism," Schlag advocates "a revival of the natural law tradition along the lines of Pope Francis's pastoral hermeneutic of evangelization" and a revival of Christian humanism.[138] Schlag observes that we "now need a hermeneutic of evangelization that struggles for social justice but also shares the faith, as Pope Francis has been pointing out."

I would add that Benedict XVI's previously discussed emphasis on renewing our institutions clearly aligns with the emphasis of this collection on prioritizing the defense of democracy against the contemporary rise of populists and aspiring autocrats. Benedict XVI would also concur with the German American Catholics in their rejection of laissez faire liberalism or its approximation in the market fundamentalism of the neoliberal era. Consistent with especially postwar Catholic social teaching, his emphasis on renewing our institutions would also align with the reformist approach to market economies embraced by John Ryan and the social democratic tradition in Europe. The second volume on *New Hope for Ecclesial and Societal Renewal* can be understood as an extended conversation on how a new era of social Catholics might work for a better future building on the lessons of the past and the best contemporary thinking.

To further explore the embrace of social Catholicism by Catholics in early twentieth century America, the fifth chapter is by William F. Murphy Jr. and is entitled "The Social Formation of Msgr. John A. Ryan." Ryan was the most influential disciple of Archbishop John Ireland and strove to realize Ireland's goal of "making America Catholic" through a strategy of putting the Church into the forefront of addressing the great

---

137. From their experience in Germany with Bismark, they had reason to fear the intrusion of the government. In the United States where the Catholic infrastructure was largely dominated by the Irish who could be tribal and biased, the German Catholics had to establish their own institutions such as seminaries.

138. A renewed Christian humanism is treated in vol. 2, chapter 15: Ossewaarde-Lowtoo, "Social Catholicism and Christian Humanism."

social problems stemming from the Industrial Revolution and Great Depression. This essay sketches the experiences, education and personal study that enabled Ryan to bring a Catholic social perspective into fruitful collaboration with programs of social and economic reform during the Progressive and New Deal eras, setting a model that continued into the turbulent decades following the Second Vatican Council.

Our sixth contribution is from Peter J. Bernardi, SJ, of the *Lumen Christi* Institute of the Loyola University Chicago and is entitled "Maurice Blondel's Defense of Social Catholics and His Enduring Critique of Catholic Integralism." In it, Bernardi introduces us to perhaps the most intellectually sophisticated debates in the decades following the First World War regarding the role of Catholics in modern secular states. In so doing, he outlines a historical analogue to the decisive contemporary choice outlined in part two above between continuing in the trajectory of the social Catholics set by Bishop Ketteler or reverting to the integralist alliance of Church and state that entangled Catholics with the Fascism evolving in Europe and leading to the Second World War. In discussing the support of Blondel for the social Catholics, Bernardi also illumines the contemporary situation in which representatives of the *ressourcement* tradition have been in the forefront of advancing radically antiliberal and postliberal positions, as opposed to decisively supporting social Catholicism like Blondel or by recognizing and opposing the dangers of fascism as did Henri de Lubac, SJ.

Liberalism, Conservatism, and the Rise of Illiberalisms

The next several essays focus on the topic of liberalism and its relation to the Catholic social tradition, including the rise of moderate and then increasingly radicalized forms of conservatism, such as the antiliberalism and postliberalism. The first of these is our seventh chapter, "The Gospel and Human Dignity: Catholicism and Liberalism in Dialogue," by the Rev. Drew Christiansen, SJ (†), of Georgetown University. Reflecting the author's deep mastery of the subject matter, the essay explains how our social doctrine manifests a fruitful dialogue between Catholicism and especially Anglo-American forms of liberalism. It highlights how the social encyclicals of Pope St. John XXIII mark what the author calls "the first ample embrace" by the magisterium of the key tenets of liberalism including human rights, constitutional and democratic government, and the equal dignity of every human person. This sets a trajectory that has continued through the Second Vatican Council to the present day putting our social tradition—as Christiansen tactfully but clearly says—"at odds in recent years with illiberal populist, movements and overly zealous advocates of religious liberty." Notice how Christiansen affirms the institutional achievements of liberalism that the Church accepts rather than, for example, claiming that contemporary liberal democracy is tainted by deficient metaphysical foundations and therefore in fundamental opposition to Catholicism.

Compare Christiansen's sober assessment that aligns with the discernment of the magisterium and the practical need to uphold democracy, on the one hand, with a range of contemporary conservative Catholics, on the other hand, who would instead emphasize that contemporary liberalism is "woke liberalism," thereby discouraging Catholics from the urgent task of taking "the institutional path" as Pope Benedict XVI advises or from participating in collaborative efforts toward social justice.

The eight chapter, entitled "Liberalism, Conservatism and Social Catholicism for the Twenty-First Century?," is by William F. Murphy Jr. It sketches a broad narrative in the hope of fostering a more balanced and sober understanding of how both liberalism and conservativism have evolved, especially in the United States and in relation to CST. Although this narrative recognizes and rejects the excesses of the illiberal left—which are primarily in cultural venues like education and entertainment, but also health care—it sees the threats from the illiberal right—which are largely directed at political power—as posing a much greater threat to contemporary society and therefore to the Catholic Church in the United States, meriting more detailed consideration. Through this narrative, the article seeks to not only illumine the contemporary crises in our Church and world. It also seeks to open a path to recover our social tradition as not only the Catholic way to live the life of charity in the modern world, but also a better kind of politics that can bring renewal and hope to a world already shaken by various manifestations of the polycrisis.

Perhaps most noteworthy is the discussion of developments since Catholics increasingly aligned with the conservatism of the Republican party, starting with the so-called fusionism of the Reagan era. Of decisive importance in this alignment were the efforts of the Republican political operative Paul Weyrich. Although his name is not widely known among contemporary Catholics, Weyrich's influence was profound as he not only fostered the establishment of Jerry Fallwell's Moral Majority, but also helped to forge the alliance between Evangelical Protestants and Catholics centered on the issue of abortion, which he correctly foresaw would bring immense and lasting political power, especially for those who bankrolled the project. This alliance was decisive in the gradual shift of Catholic social engagement from a more general advocacy for justice and human dignity to a narrower focus on culture war issues like abortion.[139]

As the Republican Party has become increasingly radicalized in recent years, to the point of being openly antidemocratic and authoritarian, and as the polycrisis continues to grow, one would hope that Catholics who have come to identify as conservative would be striving to understand how we got here and what can be done. This collection has such Catholics especially in mind. Regarding how we got here, Weyrich was also a key figure in the establishment of conservative think tanks like the Heritage Foundation, that have channeled immense streams of money to shape the national conversation, distracting the public from the key issues of economic and public policy that have significantly caused the polycrisis, primarily for the sake of maximizing the wealth and power of economic elites.[140] Regarding what can be done, the essay advocates—of course—a new social Catholicism and a better kind of politics, with an immediate focus on preserving and then renewing American democracy. As we saw above, however, we have influential American Catholics "doubling down" on the abortion-first strategy, and other prominent

---

139. In pointing out the political origins of the prioritization of abortion, I don't mean to doubt the motives of those who joined in the pro-life movement to protect the innocent lives of the unborn. My own entry into moral theology was influenced by such concerns, I did my graduate studies in two of the most pro-life institutions at the time, and have spent decades studying these matters, teaching and publishing relevant scholarship. As developments in the wake of the 2022 Dobbs decision by the U.S. Supreme Court have shown, however, there is no clear path to a consensus on abortion policy, and rancorous contention over it seems to have metastasized to the states. As we approach an election season where the prospects for political violence would seem to be the highest since the Civil War, one would hope Catholics would be able to step back and critically assess the approaches we have taken to issues like abortion, and to reconsider how to move forward in a way that better aligns with our social tradition that the PCJP, *Compendium*, presents under the heading of an "integral and solidary humanism" and heeds the underappreciated call of Pope Francis for a focus on social friendship and political love.

140. For an excellent recent discussion of how the culture war debates over the threats from the illiberal left and illiberal right have been fostered as a distraction from the true threat to democracy and the common good—namely the economic elites who have been working to achieve plutocratic control—see Stern "Centrist Illusions."

Catholics presenting a view of CST aligned with a generous outreach to key figures of the hard right while focusing criticism on the woke left.

The ninth chapter is entitled "Metaphysics, Ethics, Politics, and Theology: Can Natural Lawyers Embrace Liberalism?" and was written by Thomas Howes, who is Postdoctoral Fellow at the James Madison Program and a Lecturer in Politics at Princeton University. Howes offers a penetrating analysis and critique of a Catholic postliberal "Politics of the Real" that is articulated by the prolific David C. Schindler, building on a radical—meaning from the metaphysical roots—rejection of liberalism that employs largely metaphysical arguments.[141]

Before discussing Howes' contribution, I would like to contextualize it within the argument of this introductory essay. Schindler is professor of metaphysics and theological anthropology at the Pontifical John Paul II Institute for Studies on Marriage and Family at the Catholic University of America and longtime co-editor of the influential journal *Communio: International Catholic Review*.[142] As a leading figure in contemporary *Communio* theology, Schindler's work is of particular interest to the present project because *Communio* theology grows out of the twentieth century *ressourcement* movement, whose central thinkers include Maurice Blondel, Henri de Lubac, SJ, Hans Urs von Balthasar, and Joseph Ratzinger/Pope Benedict XVI. As discussed by Peter Bernardi in chapter 6, Blondel was a strong defender of the French social Catholics whose prioritization of securing justice for industrial workers made them willing to collaborate broadly, even with anti-clerical republicans. Such collaboration opened them to the attacks of proto-fascist, monarchist movement *Action Française*, an early twentieth century form of right-wing integralism. At the risk of redundancy but for the sake of clarity, my contention is that contemporary American social Catholics—which should be all of us—and Catholics in the *ressourcement* tradition should take a similar approach to that defended by Blondel, with a particular focus on the urgent task of defending constitutional democracy against the neo-fascist threats of today, working with those of good will to renew it so

---

141. The second part of the book is described as "rethinking a postliberal sense of politics." Schindler, *Politics of the Real*.

142. I should note that I completed my Doctorate in Sacred Theology (STD) from this institution, and that I have great esteem for David C. Schindler and the rest of the faculty. I do not see, however, how a radical antiliberalism can be reconciled with the discernment of the magisterium reflected in CSD, or with the way that the institutions of constitutional democracy are integral to the common good in our contemporary world.

we can meet the challenges of the polycrisis. Bernardi also discusses how Hans Urs von Balthasar's nephew Peter Henrici, SJ, thought Blondel's "articles were the unsurpassed treatment of the symptoms and diagnosis of the 'integralist' mentality, a recurrent temptation for militant Catholics."

As discussed by Peter Cajka in chapter 16 of this collection, Henri de Lubac, SJ, and his collaborators similarly decried the fascist encroachments against human rights. In a laudable desire to confront rapid secularization, however, de Lubac insisted on combining his opposition to fascism and the violation of human rights with a special concern to uphold the theological conviction that every human person—created in the Image of God—is also ordered to fulfilment in God, and that cooperation with non-believers in earthly struggles for justice should not be taken to imply the acceptance of the view that there is an independent, natural order of fulfillment distinct from the actual divine order of salvation. As noted above, Benedict XVI should be understood as standing in harmony with these earlier *ressourcement* thinkers in his call for Catholics to take the institutional path, together with those of goodwill to renew the institutions of constitutional democracy that—among the many ways they foster human flourishing—defend human rights.

For various reasons, Schindler's intervention into the current debates about liberalism has the potential to have great influence upon what I call the contemporary "institutional infrastructure" of the Church in especially the United States for several reasons. These include not just his erudite and prolific publications, but also that his work is part of a robust school of thought that includes gifted collaborators, that this school has made important contributions in transmitting the *ressourcement* tradition in fruitful dialogue with Thomism, that this school of thought has been widely communicated through education, journals, job placements, and other means, and that it has a particular affiliation with the Pontificates of St. John Paul II and Benedict XVI. It seems to me, however, that being radically opposed to a broad understanding of liberalism has the potential to solidify the alignment of Catholics with contemporary antiliberal and antidemocratic tendencies, the dangers of which are discussed in not just chapter 8, but especially chapters 11, 12, and 13 of this volume.

Despite the erudite scholarly presentation in the book that certainly merits study, I think two provocative texts from it have the potential to be extracted from their more nuanced context to be the primary "takeaways" that could support many Catholics in their alignment with contemporary right-wing illiberals who threaten the constitutional democratic institutions and human rights that people like Blondel, de Lubac, St. John Paul II, Pope Benedict XVI, and the Catholic tradition have been in the forefront of defending for generations. The first provocative extract follows. "The thesis we will propose is the following: at the theological core of liberalism is the most radical rejection of Christianity possible."[143] The second is that "liberalism is evil in political form."[144] While leaving a more detailed discussion of Schindler's book to Tom Howes in chapter 9, I do not see how this radical antiliberalism can be reconciled with the embrace of key tenets of liberalism by our social tradition or by the Christian humanism of the last several decades of CST, and it will do nothing to prevent Catholics from aligning with the contemporary radical right.[145] The first endorser on the book jacket, for example, is Chad Pecknold, who—as I already discussed—is promoting some combination of preconciliar integralism and Victor Orbán's illiberal democracy, which he thinks will help the Church employ a more effective model of "evangelization."

This metaphysical argumentation of Schindler's book is challenging to evaluate critically, however, by those working in social ethics or political philosophy because such scholars are often not prepared to assess how metaphysics should or should not relate to the practical realm. For this reason, Howes's critical engagement with Schindler's text makes a valuable contribution to our collection. For our present purposes, I will simply say that Howes not only articulates several key challenges to Schindler's primarily metaphysical criticism of liberalism, but also offers a lucid articulation of a more helpful way of thinking about the

143. The full sentence reads as follows. "The thesis we will propose is the following: at the theological core of liberalism is the most radical rejection of Christianity possible, because it posits and enacts an undoing of the very thing that defines Christianity, that makes Christianity Christian, namely, the incarnation of the Son of God, which is an "extension" of God, so to speak, into time and space, an extension that aims ultimately to embrace the whole of reality: the cosmic liturgy." Schindler, *Politics of the Real*, 8.

144. The broader context is "to put this in an extreme formulation, understanding evil in the ontological sense of the privation of goodness, we could say that liberalism is evil as a political form. To put it thus is not to exaggerate the problem of liberalism and the threat it poses; quite to the contrary, this formulation trivializes, or at least relativizes it, and in any event allows us to keep things in perspective. As a political form of evil, liberalism only ever exists as a perversion of what is antecedently real, of what is genuinely good, true, and beautiful in itself." Schindler, *Politics of the Real*, 38.

145. I would like to assume that members of this school would encourage Catholics to live out the integral and solidary humanism of the PCJP, *Compendium*, but a radically antiliberal stance does not seem conducive to one centered in—for example—the social friendship of Pope Francis.

relationship between these domains. He does so by drawing on the work of Martin Rhonheimer, while also engaging that of Joseph Ratzinger. In so doing, Howes provides a way of supporting the political theology of the Second Vatican Council and the postconciliar social documents, and a contemporary Catholic understanding of the political community.[146] Radical antiliberalism and postliberalism, on the other hand are not only difficult to reconcile with the social discernment of the magisterium as synthesized in the *Compendium*, but would seem to have the practical result of aligning Catholics with a radical right that is openly threatening to turn public institutions like the Justice Department into weapons for punishing political opponents.[147]

Our tenth contribution is "The Boundaries and Authority of Catholic Social Teaching: A Reply to John Finnis" by Bernard G. Prusak of John Carrol University. It responds to an article by the distinguished Catholic philosopher and legal scholar entitled "A Radical Critique of Catholic Social Teaching" that was published as the concluding essay in the formidable collection *Catholic Social Teaching: A Volume of Scholarly Essays*.[148] The critical engagement with this essay by Prusak is an important contribution to our collection because of the stature of Finnis, because of the role that he and his collaborators have had in Catholic moral theology since the Second Vatican Council, and because of the way Finnis's argument about the state and future of CST goes strongly against the renewal of social Catholicism as a better kind of politics, following the long trajectory of magisterial discernment through Pope Francis.

For our present purposes, it may be helpful to note that Finnis and his collaborators are especially known for articulating the New Natural Law theory, for employing it against "revisionist" moralists in defense of traditional norms of sexual and life ethics, and in support of the idea that some kinds of human acts are "intrinsically evil," that is always contrary to human flourishing.[149] In contrast to postliberals whose broad attack on liberalism does not spare constitutional democracy, they support it, although they also advance a strong sense of the moral law being

---

146. See, for example, chapter 8 of PCJP, *Compendium*, nos. 377–427 on "The Political Community," and part IV of this chapter on "The Democratic System," nos. 406–16.

147. Arnsdorf et al. "Trump and Allies Plot Revenge."

148. Bradley and Brugger, *Catholic Social Teaching*.

149. I should note that I too have worked to uphold the traditional teaching that certain kinds of human acts are always evil.

reflected in civil law, especially in the contested area of sexual and life ethics, which brings them closer to the postliberals. They see this legislative enforcement of sexual and medical ethics as beneficial to society based on the pedagogical function of law. With these emphases, their work has been a resource for Catholics focused on opposing permissive laws regarding elective abortion among other issues. Prior to their recent collection, however, their work has not been a significant resource for those working in CST, as it has always had a different emphasis than the "integral and solidary humanism" we find in the *Compendium* and social encyclicals. I think we can see Finnis's essay as the reflection of post conciliar form of Catholic social conservatism centered on questions like abortion, which he seeks to expand into the field of social ethics so that the scope of Catholic moral theology is effectively truncated to those issues emphasized by social conservatives like himself.

In his "Radical Critique," Finnis basically argues that CST needs to acknowledge that most social questions are matters of prudence and that the Catholic focus regarding public policy should be on advancing authoritative moral teachings, such as those regarding intrinsically evil acts. For Finnis, the magisterium should say and write considerably less about contemporary issues like the climate crisis, the plight of immigrants or inequality. Ecclesial institutions focused on social justice like the Dicastery for the Promotion of Integral Human Development, moreover, should be shuttered. According to this view, Catholics are following CST if they direct their social engagement to opposing intrinsic evils like abortion. Against Finnis's deflationary view of CST, Prusak intervenes by softening the distinction between prudential and authoritative matters, by indicating ways to distinguish different levels of teaching, and by encouraging a more receptive, deliberative and prayerful consideration of Church teaching on social matters.

The next two contributions under our subheading of Liberalism, Conservatism and the Rise of Illiberalisms focus on the ascent of illiberal forms of conservatism with which many Catholics have become aligned in recent years. In the eleventh chapter, entitled "Integralism, Political Catholicism, and Actually-Existing Democracy in the Modern West," Julian G. Waller of George Washington University surveys a wide range of contemporary literature to illumine the phenomenon of Catholic integralism, and allied intellectual trends. He considers the different understandings of what integralism is, where it fits as an "ideational project" in relation to other contemporary forms of postliberal and illiberal political thought, its practical ambitions for advancing what it sees as the common good, and its relation to earlier forms of political Catholicism. Waller also offers insightful remarks regarding the emergence of a new form of conservative Catholicism in which integralism provides an "alternative to breakaway insubordination that is attractive to some elite, conservative Catholics."

These new conservative Catholics then claim orthodoxy by drawing from "Leonine and Neo-Thomistic thought," that is by highlighting preconciliar thought before what Drew Christiansen, SJ, calls the magisterium's "first ample embrace" of liberal principles like constitutional democracy, human rights and equal human dignity. This alleged orthodoxy provides these conservatives with a rationale for illiberal modes of political engagement, through which they seek to recover various hierarchies such as Christian over non-Christian, male over female, or Church over state, regardless of political consensus. Waller also provides a survey of the political orientation that different forms of integralist movements have taken over time and how these forms might relate to actually-existing democracies of today. In addition, he helpfully considers issue-areas around which this movement is likely to find traction, how it might interact with other movements, and how it might relate to possible regime-types.

The twelfth chapter is "The World Out of Joint: The Hard Right and Postliberalism in Twenty-First Century American Politics" by Matt McManus of the University of Michigan. In it, McManus outlines the broad spectrum of "hard right" conservatism in the United States, by which he means "far right" or antidemocratic movements that have achieved mainstream appeal. These include the Nietzschean right, national conservatism, and postliberalism, which gets the most attention. Whereas postliberalism tends to reject the extremes of the Nietzschean right, it has affinities with national conservatism. This suggests these strands could readily coalesce, most likely in a form of Christian nationalism that includes Catholic integralists. McManus sees such an alliance as delivering more of the agenda of socially conservative populism—opposition to abortion, same sex marriage, contraception, reading liberal books—than that of economic populism—increased minimum wages, unions, health care—because the entrenched economic and institutional power behind the Republican Party can allow the former while it opposes the latter. After exposing the frightening alternatives coming out of the antidemocratic right, McManus closes provocatively by introducing the political ideology that he thinks deserves a real shot at the future, namely liberal socialism, which puts together two terms that are not commonly joined in contemporary American discourse because they have been made into almost expletives. This liberal socialism is generally understood, however, as a form of the Keynesian mixed economy. Along these lines, McManus presents it as a form of political economy ordered to fulfilling "the Jeffersonian promise to create a country where all of us who are created equal genuinely have an equal opportunity to lead a good life."

The thirteenth and final chapter in this first volume is by William F. Murphy Jr. and is entitled "Formation for a New Social Catholicism." It builds on chapter 5 which treated "The Social Formation of Msgr. John A. Ryan." Presupposing formation in the theological and moral virtues, it advances ten theses concerning primarily the intellectual formation that would enable contemporary Catholics to understand the challenges of our time and bring an authentically Catholic social vision to bear in the world, one that aligns with the social documents of the Church and the discernment of the magisterium regarding the "signs of the times."

Conclusion

This extended introduction began with a consideration of the disappointed hopes of both the postwar world and postconciliar Church as we confront the polycrisis, proposing the need for a decisive choice to live out the Social Doctrine of the Church through a new social Catholicism with a focus on renewing our democratic institutions through what Pope Francis calls a better kind of politics. It then illumined the multifaceted rationale for this choice by sketching some key episodes from the history of modern social Catholicism as treated in the essays to follow.

The rationale for this decisive choice was further supported through reference to several essays that treated what became a fruitful dialogue between Catholicism and especially Anglo-American forms of liberalism or constitutional democracy in the decades following the Second World War. Against a significant contemporary trend among influential conservative Catholics to promote a postliberalism that would coerce victory in the culture wars through perhaps a blend of Victor Orbán's illiberal democracy and preconciliar integralism, we reviewed some reasons why these moves toward the antidemocratic right are contrary to both the Catholic faith and sound reason, besides undermining the institutional support needed to manage the polycrisis and threatening a future dystopia.

The hope and prayer behind this project is that a multitude of Catholics will recognize the futility of this hard right alternative, appreciate more fully the truth and beauty of our Social Doctrine, and join in a synodal journey social friendship with those of good will to build a future worthy of the human family.

In the second volume of this collection, the essays are organized under the subtitle of *New Hope for Ecclesial and Societal Renewal*. They look less toward the past and more toward key themes and topics that will be important for a new social Catholicism. The include Christian humanism and integral development in the information age, a new surge of scholarship on human rights, a discussion of a new path for the Church after the end of Christendom, a four part symposium on new economic thinking after the neoliberal consensus, the social vision of Pope Francis, the ongoing challenge of racism, the importance of Catholic social movements, the theology of work, the relevance of social media to social Catholicism, pastoral leadership in a time of polarization, the future of CST, and an epilogue about how Francis's better kind of politics is the path forward for the Church after the rise of populism and tribal polarization.

Bibliography

Acemoglu, Daron, and James A. Robinson. *The Narrow Corridor: States, Societies, and the Fate of Liberty*. New York: Penguin, 2019.

———. *Why Nations Fail: The Origins of Power, Prosperity, and Poverty*. New York: Crown, 2012.

Ahmari, Sohrab. *Tyranny, Inc.: How Private Power Crushed American Liberty—and What to Do About It*. New York: Forum, 2023.

Arnhart, Larry. "The Failure of Deneen and Dreher in Their Critique of Liberalism." *Darwinian Conservatism* (blog), February 20, 2019. http://darwinianconservatism.blogspot.com/2019/02/the-failure-of-deneen-and-dreher-in.html.

Arnsdorf, Isaac, et al. "Trump and Allies Plot Revenge, Justice Department Control in Second Term." *Washington Post*, November 6, 2023. https://www.washingtonpost.com/politics/2023/11/05/trump-revenge-second-term/.

Balmer, Randall. "The Real Origins of the Religious Right." *Politico Magazine*, May 27, 2014. https://www.politico.com/magazine/story/2014/05/religious-right-real-origins-107133.

Barron, Robert. "Fr. Andrew Greely, Priest." *Word on Fire*, June 7, 2013. https://www.wordonfire.org/articles/barron/fr-andrew-greeley-priest/.

———. "My Experience of the Synod." *Word on Fire*, November 21, 2023. https://www.wordonfire.org/articles/barron/my-experience-of-the-synod/.

Benedict XVI. *Caritas in Veritate: On Integral Development in Charity and Truth*. Vatican City: Libreria Editrice Vaticana, 2009. https://www.vatican.va/content/benedict-xvi/en/encyclicals/documents/hf_ben-xvi_enc_20090629_caritas-in-veritate.html#_ednref112.

Bevir, Mark, and Jason Blakely. *Interpretive Social Science: An Anti-naturalist Approach*. Oxford: Oxford University Press, 2018.

Blakely, Jason. *Alasdair MacIntyre, Charles Taylor, and the Demise of Naturalism*. Notre Dame: University of Notre Dame Press, 2016.

———. "Does Liberalism Lack Virtue? A Critique of Alasdair MacIntyre's Reactionary Politics." *Interpretation: A Journal of Political Philosophy* 44 (2017) 1–20.

———. "The Integralism of Adrian Vermeule: Not Catholic Enough." *Commonweal*, October 5, 2020. https://www.commonwealmagazine.org/not-catholic-enough.

———. *Lost in Ideology: Interpreting Modern Political Life*. Newcastle upon Tyne: Agenda, 2024.

Bouie, Jamelle. "A Breathtaking Contempt for the People of Wisconsin." *New York Times*, September 8, 2023. https://www.nytimes.com/2023/09/08/opinion/wisconsin-judge-impeachment-democracy.html.

Bradley, Gerard V., and E. Christian Brugger, eds. *Catholic Social Teaching: A Collection of Scholarly Essays*. Cambridge: Cambridge University Press, 2019.

Briggs, Kenneth A. "Catholic Bishops Seek Vast Changes in Economy of U.S." *New York Times*, November 12, 1984. https://timesmachine.nytimes.com/timesmachine/1984/11/12/078469.html.

Brennan Center. "What the Freedom to Vote Act Would Do." July 13, 2023. https://www.brennancenter.org/our-work/research-reports/freedom-vote-act.

Burghardt, Walter J. *Preaching the Just Word*. New Haven: Yale University Press, 1996.

Cairns, Madoc. "The New Evangelisation in the Shoes of the Fisherman." *The Tablet*, June 2023. https://www.thetablet.co.uk/features/2/23181/the-new-evangelisation-in-the-shoes-of-the-fisherman.

Chappel, James. *Catholic Modern: The Challenge of Totalitarianism and the Remaking of the Church*. Cambridge: Harvard University Press, 2018.

Chemerinsky, Erwin. *Worse Than Nothing: The Dangerous Fallacy of Originalism*. New Haven: Yale University Press, 2022.

Deneen, Patrick J. *Regime Change: Toward a Postliberal Future*. New York: Sentinel, 2023.

———. *Why Liberalism Failed*. New Haven: Yale University Press, 2018.

Doer, John. *Speed & Scale: An Action Plan for Solving Our Climate Crisis Now*. New York: Portfolio, 2021.

Donahue, John R. *Seek Justice That You May Live: Reflections and Resources on the Bible and Social Justice*. New York: Paulist, 2014.

Evola, Julius. *Ride the Tiger: A Survival Manual for the Aristocrats of the Soul*. Rochester, VT: Inner Traditions, 2003.

Faggioli, Massimo. "Bishop Robert Barron's 'Beige' Version of Vatican II." *National Catholic Reporter*, May 14, 2021. https://www.ncronline.org/opinion/guest-voices/bishop-robert-barrons-beige-version-vatican-ii.

Fleming, James E. *Fidelity to Our Imperfect Constitution: For Moral Readings and Against Originalisms*. New York: Oxford, 2015.

Francis. *Ad Theologiam Promovendam*. Vatican City: Libreria Editrice Vaticana, 2023.

———. *Fratelli Tutti: On Fraternity and Social Friendship*. Vatican City: Libreria Editrice Vaticana, 2020. https://www.vatican.va/content/francesco/en/encyclicals/documents/papa-francesco_20201003_enciclica-fratelli-tutti.html.

———. *Laudate Deum: On the Climate Crisis*. Vatican City: Libreria Editrice Vaticana, 2023.

———. *Laudato Si': On Care for Our Common Home*. Vatican City: Libreria Editrice Vaticana, 2015. https://www.vatican.va/content/francesco/en/encyclicals/documents/papa-francesco_20150524_enciclica-laudato-si.html.

Freedom House. "Global Freedom Score." https://freedomhouse.org/countries/freedom-world/scores.

Goldman, Ari L. "Catholic Bishops Criticized on the Poor." *New York Times*, November 5, 1986. https://www.nytimes.com/1986/11/05/us/catholic-bishops-criticized-on-poor.html.

Guriev, Sergei, and Daniel Treisman. *Spin Dictators: The Changing Face of Tyranny in the 21st Century*. Princeton: Princeton University Press, 2022.

Institute of Political Science and Sociology. "The Democracy Matrix." https://www.democracymatrix.com/ranking.

John Paul II. *Veritatis Splendor: The Splendor of the Truth*. Vatican City: Libreria Editrice Vaticana, 1993. https://www.vatican.va/content/john-paul-ii/en/encyclicals/documents/hf_jp-ii_enc_06081993_veritatis-splendor.html.

John XXIII. *Pacem in Terris: Peace on Earth*. Vatican City: Libreria Editrice Vaticana, 1963. https://www.vatican.va/content/john-xxiii/en/encyclicals/documents/hf_j-xxiii_enc_11041963_pacem.html.

Kaveny, Cathleen. *Law's Virtues: Fostering Autonomy and Solidarity in American Society*. Moral Traditions. Georgetown: Georgetown University Press, 2012.

Lawrence, Michael, et al. "What Is a Global Polycrisis? And How Is It Different from a Systemic Risk?" *Cascade Institute*, September 16, 2022. https://cascadeinstitute.org/technical-paper/what-is-a-global-polycrisis/.

Levering, Matthew. *The Theology of Robert Barron*. Elk Grove Village, IL: Word on Fire Academic, 2023. Kindle.

———. "Two Visions of Evangelization." *Catholic World Report*, September 20, 2023. https://www.catholicworldreport.com/2023/09/20/two-visions-of-evangelization/.

Levitsky, Steven, and Daniel Ziblatt. *How Democracies Die*. New York: Broadway, 2018.

———. *Tyranny of the Minority: Why American Democracy Reached the Breaking Point*. New York: Crown, 2023.

MacLean, Nancy. *Democracy in Chains: The Deep History of the Radical Right's Stealth Plan for America*. New York: Penguin, 2018.

Maritain, Jacques. *True Humanism*. Translated by M. R. Adamson. New York: Scribner's Sons, 1950.

Mayer, Jane. *Dark Money: The Hidden History of the Billionaires Behind the Rise of the Radical Right*. New York: Doubleday, 2016.

Murphy, William F. Jr. "Ethics of Life, Synodality, and Untying Knots in Moral Theology." *Where Peter Is*, September 26, 2022. https://wherepeteris.com/ethics-of-life-synodality-and-untying-knots-in-moral-theology/.

———. "Reflections on Fundamental Morality, Conscience, Norms, and Discernment (nos. 109–33)." In *Etica Teologica della Vita: Scrittura, tradizione, sfide pratiche: Atti Seminario Studio Promosso Dalla Pontificia Accademia Per La Vita*, edited by Vincenzo Paglia, 217–43. Vatican City: Libreria Editrice Vaticana, 2022.

———. "Three Contemporary Alternatives to Social Catholicism." *Chicago Studies* 61 (2023). Forthcoming.

O'Brien, David J., and Thomas A. Shannon, eds. *Catholic Social Thought: Encyclicals and Documents from Pope Leo XIII to Pope Francis*. 3rd rev. ed. Maryknoll, NY: Orbis, 2016.

Oreskes, Naomi, and Erik M. Conway. *The Big Myth: How Business Taught us to Loath Government and Love the Free Market*. New York: Bloomsbury, 2023.

———. *Merchants of Doubt: How a Handful of Scientists Obscured the Truth on Issues from Tobacco Smoke to Global Warming*. New York: Bloomsbury, 2010.

Pappin, Gladden, et al. "Hungary's Christian Realism." *Postliberal Order*, March 9, 2023. https://www.postliberalorder.com/p/hungarys-christian-realism.

Paul VI. *Apostolicam Actuositatem: Decree on the Apostolate of the Laity*. Vatican City: Libreria Editrice Vaticana, 1965. https://www.vatican.va/archive/hist_councils/ii_vatican_council/documents/vat-ii_decree_19651118_apostolicam-actuositatem_en.html.

———. *Dei Verbum: Dogmatic Constitution on Divine Revelation*. Vatican City: Libreria Editrice Vaticana, 1965. https://www.vatican.va/archive/hist_councils/ii_vatican_council/documents/vat-ii_const_19651118_dei-verbum_en.html.

———. *Dignitatis Humanae: Declaration on Religious Freedom*. Vatican City: Libreria Editrice Vaticana, 1965. https://www.vatican.va/archive/hist_councils/ii_vatican_council/documents/vat-ii_decl_19651207_dignitatis-humanae_en.html.

———. *Humanae Vitae: On the Regulation of Birth*. Rome: Libreria Editrice Vaticana, 1968. https://www.vatican.va/content/paul-vi/en/encyclicals/documents/hf_p-vi_enc_25071968_humanae-vitae.html.

———. *Gaudium et Spes: Pastoral Constitution on the Church in the Modern World*. Vatican City: Libreria Editrice Vaticana, 1965. https://www.vatican.va/archive/hist_councils/ii_vatican_council/documents/vat-ii_const_19651207_gaudium-et-spes_en.html.

———. *Lumen Gentium: Dogmatic Constitution on the Church*. Vatican City: Libreria Editrice Vaticana, 1964. https://www.vatican.va/archive/hist_councils/ii_vatican_council/documents/vat-ii_const_19641121_lumen-gentium_en.html.

———. *Octogesima Adveniens: A Call to Action*. Vatican City: Libreria Editrice Vaticana, 1967. https://www.vatican.va/content/paul-vi/en/apost_letters/documents/hf_p-vi_apl_19710514_octogesima-adveniens.html.

———. *Optatam Totius: Decree of Priestly Training*. Vatican City: Libreria Editrice Vaticana, 1965. https://www.vatican.va/archive/hist_councils/ii_vatican_council/documents/vat-ii_const_19641121_lumen-gentium_en.html.

———. *Populorum Progressio: On the Development of Peoples*. Vatican City: Libreria Editrice Vaticana, 1967.

Pecknold, Chad C. "A Cure for the Nations." *Postliberal Order*, March 9, 2023. https://www.postliberalorder.com/p/hungarys-christian-realism.

———. "Making Disciples of All Nations." *Postliberal Order*, April 3, 2023. https://postliberalorder.substack.com/p/making-disciples-of-all-nations.

Pepper, David. *Laboratories of Autocracy: A Wake-Up Call from Behind the Lines*. Cincinnati: St. Helena Press, 2021.

Pew Research Center. "In U.S., Decline of Christianity Continues at Rapid Pace." *Pew Research Center*, October 17, 2019. https://www.pewresearch.org/religion/2019/10/17/in-u-s-decline-of-christianity-continues-at-rapid-pace/.

Pilkington, Philip. "The Economic Case for Aristocracy." *Postliberal Order*, August 7, 2023. https://www.postliberalorder.com/p/the-economic-case-for-aristocracy.

Pintado-Murphy, Patricia. "The Crisis of the Buffered Self and the Call to Friendship, Community, and Witness: A Response to Bishop Barron." *Chicago Studies* 61 (2022/2023). https://issuu.com/chicagostudies/docs/vol._61.1_fall_2022-winter_2023-the_church_in_the_/32?fr=sZjhjYTY3ODQxMDA.

Pontifical Council for Justice and Peace. *Compendium of the Social Doctrine of the Church*. Washington, DC: USCCB, 2005. https://www.vatican.va/roman_curia/pontifical_councils/justpeace/documents/rc_pc_justpeace_doc_20060526_compendio-dott-soc_en.html.

Portier-Young, Anathea E., and Gregory E. Sterling, eds. *Scripture and Social Justice: Catholic and Ecumenical Essays*. Lantham, MD: Lexington, 2018.

Reich, Robert. *The System: Who Rigged It, How We Fix It*. New York: Knopf, 2021.

Richardson, Heather Cox. *Democracy Awakening: Notes on the State of America*. New York: Viking, 2023.

———. *How the South Won the Civil War: Oligarchy, Democracy, and the Continuing Fight for the Soul of America*. Oxford: Oxford University Press, 2020.

Richardson, Katherine, et al. "Earth beyond Six of Nine Planetary Boundaries" *Science Advances* 9 (2023) 1–16.

Rhonheimer, Martin. "Benedict XVI's 'Hermeneutic of Reform' and Religious Freedom." *Nova et Vetera* 9 (2011) 1029–54.

———. *The Common Good of Constitutional Democracy: Essays in Political Philosophy and on Catholic Social Teaching*. Edited by William F. Murphy Jr. Washington, DC: Catholic University of America Press, 2012.

Rose, Matthew. *A World after Liberalism: The Philosophers of the Radical Right*. New Haven: Yale University Press, 2021.

Scheppele, Kim Lane. "How Viktor Orbán Wins." *Journal of Democracy* 33 (2022) 45–61.

Schindler, David C. *The Politics of the Real: The Church between Liberalism and Integralism*. Steubenville, OH: New Polity, 2023.

Smith, Talmon Joseph, and Kerri Russell. "The Greatest Wealth Transfer in History Is Here, with Familiar (Rich) Winners." *New York Times*, May 14, 2023. https://www.nytimes.com/2023/05/14/business/economy/wealth-generations.html.

Society for the Rule of Law. "About Us." https://societyfortheruleoflaw.org/about/.

Stern, Alexander. "Centrist Illusions: How Not to Defend Liberalism." *Commonweal* 150 (2023) 36–41.

Strickland, Kyle, and Felicia Wong. "A New Paradigm for Justice and Democracy: Moving beyond the Twin Failures of Neoliberalism and Racial Liberalism." *Roosevelt Institute*, November 3, 2021. https://rooseveltinstitute.org/publications/new-paradigm-for-justice-and-democracy-moving-beyond-the-twin-failures-of-neoliberalism-and-racial-liberalism/.

United Nations General Assembly. *Universal Declaration of Human Rights*. New York: United Nations, 1948. https://www.un.org/en/about-us/universal-declaration-of-human-rights.

United States Catholic Bishops. *Economic Justice for All: Pastoral Letter on Catholic Social Teaching and the U.S. Economy*. Washington, DC: United States Conference of Catholic Bishops, 1986. https://www.usccb.org/upload/economic_justice_for_all.pdf.

Vaidyanathan, Brandon, et al. "Polarization, Generational Dynamics, and the Ongoing Impact of the Abuse Crisis: Further Insights from the National Study of Catholic Priests." *Catholic Project*, November 2023. https://catholicproject.catholic.edu/wp-content/uploads/2023/10/Further-Insights-NSCP-Nov-2023-rev.pdf.

Vermeule, Adrian. *Common Good Conservatism: Recovering the Classic Legal Tradition*. New York: Polity, 2022.

White, Christopher. "Pope Francis Blasts Reactionary American Catholics Who Oppose Church Reform." *National Catholic Reporter*, August 28, 2023. https://www.ncronline.org/vatican/vatican-news/pope-francis-blasts-reactionary-american-catholics-who-oppose-church-reform.

White, Thomas Joseph, et al. "Life at the Center: A Pro-Life Statement." *First Things* (2023). https://www.firstthings.com/article/2023/11/life-at-the-center-a-pro-life-statement#print.

Witt-Swanson, Lindsey, et al. "Faith after the Pandemic: How COVID-19 Changed American Religion." *Survey Center on American Life*, January 5, 2023. https://www.americansurveycenter.org/research/faith-after-the-pandemic-how-covid-19-changed-american-religion.

Wooden, Cindy. "World Needs Politicians Who Uphold Catholic Social Teaching, Pope Says." *National Catholic Reporter*, August 26, 2023. https://www.ncronline.org/vatican/vatican-news/world-needs-politicians-who-uphold-catholic-social-teaching-pope-says.

World Economic Forum. *The Global Risks Report 2023*. https://www3.weforum.org/docs/WEF_Global_Risks_Report_2023.pdf.

———. "This Is Why 'Polycrisis' Is a Useful Way of Looking at the World Right Now." March 7, 2023. https://www.weforum.org/agenda/2023/03/polycrisis-adam-tooze-historian-explains/.

2

The Social Catholicism of Fr. Félix Varela (1788–1853)

PETER CASARELLA, DUKE UNIVERSITY

Abstract: Félix Varela was an early advocate for social Catholicism in the United States. He was also ahead of his time in advocating Cuban independence and ending the slave trade. For him these forms of oppression were named idols to be destroyed even though his fierce social and political discourse was not at all in substance like the nativist anti-Catholic tirades of his Protestant opponents. He is, moreover, a moral and ethical thinker who maintains that the relationship between truth and virtue is mutually determinative. He advocated a theology of "public spirit." *L'esprit public* had been used at the end of the French revolution to refer to public opinion. Like Jean-Jacques Rousseau and Baron de Montesquieu, Varela also favors public discourse about social questions. Yet Varela in an essay of 1834 champions his own version of "public spirit," equating it with advocacy for personal freedom, independence, democracy, and a rule of law while interrogating pressing social realities through a critique of ideologies. This essay will show that the defense of social justice in Varela is achieved through his prophetic and still essentially Thomistic theology of the "public spirit."

Social Catholicism for the Twenty-First Century?—Volume 1

Introduction

THE HISTORY OF THE social Catholicism in the United States is a work on progress. It is more than a little myopic to take the present polarizations in U.S. Catholicism as a starting point, even assuming that one could isolate a coherent vision in that controverted mix.[1] At the same time, the history of the Catholic engagement with politics and society from the early colonial period to the present is generally available only in isolated snapshots. This essay aims to focus on just one figure from that early period whose legacy should be better known to all Catholics. Any pretense to add to the total picture will be at best tangential, but this unpeeling of a largely forgotten layer of history will hopefully nonetheless add to the emerging mosaic.

Fr. Félix Varela was the first hemispheric thinker on religion and politics from Latin America to think and publish on U.S. soil. His work foreshadows Pope John Paul II's historic call on January 22, 1999 to develop a new discourse about just one "*Ecclesia in America*."[2] Varela can also be considered the first Latinx theologian writing in the United States although never would have used that particular term.

This chapter makes it possible to think about larger questions, but the focus is nonetheless on the Catholic notions of justice and the public realm that Varela forged after arriving in 1823 in the Archdiocese of New York as a Cuban in exile whose very life was endangered on account of his prophetic stances. While others in Cuba and the United States have tried to grasp the intellectual scope of Varela's legacy on political discourse, his relationship to the broader tradition of Catholic thought has seldom been subjected to detailed scrutiny. His well-earned reputation as an anomaly in his own time makes that task challenging even now. Although Varela eschewed easy labels and the scholastic penchant for formal disputations (preferring the essay style of French writers like Michel de Montaigne), his contribution to social Catholicism still retained a novel Thomistic inflection that has generally gone unnoticed.

---

1. See Wessman, *Church's Mission*.

2. Lamas, *Latino Continuum*, 23–56. On John Paul II and the unity of the Americas as one transcontinental ecclesial reality, see Casarella, "Solidarity," 98–123.

Historical Context

Varela never wrote from an ivory tower; nor was he a mere practitioner who blithely accommodated to the ebbs and flows of his own age. He brought his vast erudition, extensive training in the history of philosophy, and familiarity with the Anglo-American theory of democratic constitutionalism to bear on the pastoral concerns of his flock and the shaping of an emerging civil society. His social thought grew out of the unique and dangerous circumstances of his age and his exceptional journey from colonial Cuba and the iron grip of imperial, post-Napoleonic Spain to the recently liberated United States of America. A quick review of some of the basic facts of this period and his life within this complex milieu will shed much light on his thinking about social Catholicism.

Félix Varela was born in Havana on November 20, 1788, but he spent his childhood in St. Augustine, Florida. He was sent from there to Havana to study at the San Carlos Seminary, and years later he would become its most brilliant professor. In 1811, Varela was named Professor of Philosophy in the Seminary of San Carlos and San Ambrosio of Havana. On this year he also became a priest. In Cuba, Varela was the leading educator, philosopher and patriot of his time, teaching philosophy, chemistry, physics, theology, and music. Many future Cuban leaders were his students. He argued for giving women the same education as men and introduced many teaching innovations. In 1816, a compilation of earlier written works was published under the title *Doctrinas de Lógica, Metafísica y Moral* ("Teachings concerning Logic, Metaphysics, and Morality").

The young Varela emulated Cuban thinkers like Fr. José Augustín Caballero (influential seminary professor), Fr. Juan Bernardo O'Gavan (taught Varela physics and the importance of learning how to replicate scientific experiments), and Juan José Díaz de Espada. Espada was the Bishop in Havana between 1802 and 1832 and taught Varela in seminary.[3] Espada was nurtured in modern critical thinking while studying for a doctorate in theology at Salamanca. Espada was a pivotal influence in the development of Varela's anti-slavery thought.[4] Espada gave Varela

---

3. See Figueroa y Miranda, *Religión y política*.

4. Concerning Espada's own formation in this quickly evolving matrix of new learning, Eduardo Torres-Cuevas writes: "De Salamanca salió nutrido el futuro Obispo de La Habana de 'las luces.' Allí debió conocer las críticas de los padres Feijóo e Isla; las ideas económicas de Ward y Campomanes, entre otros; las concepciones del derecho natural y de gentes y el contrato social, ya por la versión de Rousseau, ya por la de

a chair in constitutional law while he was still in Cuba *even though the latter had no formal training as a lawyer.*

In 1821 at the tender age of thirty-three, Varela was elected by his fellow Cubans to participate in the newly formed Cortes of Cádiz and was sent to Spain with Espada's support. Spain was already in turmoil. The revolution of 1820 brought back to power the liberals of the 1812 who had been persecuted by Ferdinand VII and were recently freed from jail. At that point they reestablished the constitution of 1812 and other reforms. But Varela made his boldest moves just as this intermittent wind of change subsided, and Spain was left with only a few colonies (including Cuba). In 1823 the liberals were purged with the help of the King of France, and a decade of the return of Bourbon King Ferdinand VII ensued.

Varela, undeterred, made the recommendation in the Cortes that the Spanish colonies in Latin America be considered independent. He also asked for Cuban self-rule and an end to slavery. These proposals were quickly deemed subversive. Soon after their return to power, the Spanish Crown dissolved the courts and condemned Varela to death. But Varela escaped and made his way to New York, where he arrived in December of 1823. He lived the rest of his life in the U.S. An assassin was still sent by the Spanish Crown to follow him to New York City but never succeeded in that mission.

He was then assigned to a parish in New York in the Irish section. (Today it's known as Church of the Transfiguration in Chinatown and has a statue recording Varela as its founder.) Even though there were many racial/ethnic problems at the time, he became a defender of immigrant rights and of the poor Irish immigrants. He led his ministry as priest for over twenty-five years. In 1824 he began to publish an independent journal: *El Habanero*. It ran for seven issues and was regularly smuggled into Cuba. In 1837 Varela became Vicar General of the Diocese of New York. At that time, the title of Vicar General also covered the whole state

---

Marín de Mendoza; la filosofía moderna de Descartes, Bacon, Newton, Leibniz, Locke, Condillac y Mably. Allí se nutrió del nuevo espíritu de progreso, de búsqueda científica y racionalista de los tiempos modernos, y allí se consolidaron sus concepciones religiosas, no al viejo estilo del oscuro siglo XVII español, sino al nuevo que intentaba hacerse compatible con la modernidad, condenando la superstición y la ignorancia. La época de su formación ha sido determinante. Díaz de Espada había arribado a los colegios mayores y a las universidades junto con las opacas 'luces' españolas. Amará el progreso, las ciencias y el arte nuevo, y ellos señalarán sus pasos." Torres-Cuevas, *Obispo Espada*, 19.

of New York and New Jersey. The Spanish Crown intervened with Rome to prevent him from ever being installed as a bishop, for which he was eminently qualified.

Varela was well known as a vigorous and engaged pastor and as a promoter of the arts.[5] He exerted some influence in the U.S. as a clergyman and educator on the national level. He attended the First, Third, and Sixth Provincial Councils of Baltimore. In accord with a decree of the First Council and to the consternation of his nativist critics, Varela had reservations about lay trusteeism since it also might allow wealthy elites to control and inhibit the erection of new parishes.[6]

Varela died in St. Augustine, Florida on February 25, 1853. Varela thus began and ended his life in St. Augustine. José Martí, who was very influential in Cuban independence and continues to generate a liberating consciousness across the Americas, was born the same year as Varela's passing.[7] Martí famously said: "Varela is the one who taught us Cubans to think." Varela's remains were moved from St. Augustine to Havana on August 22, 1912 and buried at Aula Magna, near Havana University. In 1998 John Paul II in his historic journey to the island of Cuba gave an invigorating speech about Varela's thoughts on Cuban identity at this site.[8] The Polish Pope underscored the moral exigency that Varela placed on his own people in the pursuit of the new and not yet attained ideal of democratic governance:

> He also spoke of democracy, judging it to be the political project best in keeping with human nature, while at the same time underscoring its demands. Among these demands, he stressed two in particular: first, that *people must be educated for freedom and responsibility*, with a personally assimilated ethical code which includes the best of the heritage of civilization and enduring transcendental values, so that they may be able to undertake decisive tasks in service of the community; and second, that *human relationships, like the form of society as a whole, must give people suitable opportunities to perform*, with proper respect and solidarity, *their historic role giving substance to the rule of*

---

5. See, above all, Estévez, *Perfil pastoral*.

6. The First Provincial Council of Baltimore rejected in 1829 the notion that lay people could govern and dismiss the Catholic clergy. See Navia, *Apostle of the Immigrants*, 102–3.

7. The first Latinx monograph on Martí was published only recently: De La Torre, *José Martí's Liberative Political Theology*.

8. John Paul II, "Address of John Paul II at the University of Havana."

law, which is the essential guarantee of every form of human concourse claiming to be democratic.[9]

Having undergone in his own personal life and sacerdotal ministry the harsh imposition of a ban on freedom of speech and belief, Pope John Paul II highlights with great clarity and personal conviction the dual role proposed by Varela of being free *from* such external restrictions and free *for* political responsibility and the maintenance of a rule of law that generates genuinely democratic participation in society. This insight from a fellow-traveler on the path to freedom brings us to the core of Varela's project.

Félix Varela's Theory of Justice

The definitive study of Varela's theory of justice still needs to be written, particularly as it pertains to the later period of his life. His early writings composed in Havana reflect a sober reception of a Catholic tradition, and the later polemics manifest an engaged priest and controversialist who is willing and able to respond to polemical attacks with vigor. The synthesis of his overall contribution in both theory and practice is thus somewhat elusive, a point to which I return at the end of this chapter.

The best writing on the political thought of Varela in English was written to reflect his defense of Cuban independence and the end of slavery in the Spanish Courts. Much has also been written about his fight for the rights of the recently arrived Irish Catholic immigrants in New York City.[10] He also helped to organize the Latinx immigrants through advocacy of their political agency long before Hispanic Ministry as a form of social justice came to light in New York City through Ivan Illich and his companions in the 1950s.[11]

What inspired Varela's thinking about social concerns? A dissertation written in 1966 by a nun at the University of New Mexico gives the best account in English to date of his political thought through a careful analysis of his defense of a possible constitutional democracy for Cuba as that evolved in his time as a seminary professor in Cuba and later in his writings in New York City that were published in *El Habanero* (literally

---

9. John Paul II, "Address of John Paul II at the University of Havana," no. 4.

10. See, for example, Casarella, "Priestly Ministry," 207–11.

11. See Lamas, "Father Félix Varela," 157–75. On Illich in that period, see Díaz-Stevens, *Oxcart Catholicism*.

entitled "The Man from Havana").[12] Very little, however, has been written since that time or beyond that post-Cold War framework about the myriad and surprisingly diverse sources of his social and political thought.

Not surprisingly, many of the sources of his social philosophy were classical ones. He draws heavily upon both St. Thomas Aquinas and Cicero on natural law but tends to interpret law here as a right. This interpretation is not the same transformation that occurs in the late twentieth century when Thomist theorists like John Finnis favor right to law in their interpretation of Aquinas on reclaiming moral foundations in a secular age.[13] Varela's defense of an immutable law found within the conscience of a rational creature is tied to both democratic principles of governance that are in his time still largely out of favor in both the Spanish-speaking world and some of the English speaking one, at least the small island of an English-speaking Catholic world that he encountered (e.g., James Carroll), and to the struggle of the immigrants and slaves who were being violently oppressed due to the lack of an adequate language of justice to protect their rights against the slave-holding and corruptly enmeshed elites.[14]

True to his age and especially to the French-speaking authors like Rousseau and Montesquieu whom the educated, land-owning elites in Cuba were reading, Varela favors the language of "public spirit." "Public Spirit" (*l'esprit public*) is also a term commonly used at the end of the French revolution to refer to public opinion.[15] The early literary Edmund Burke followed traditions of Irish nationalism in lauding the public spirit as a way to exercise conscience and maintain social harmony.[16] The later Edmund Burke, in his critique of the spirit of the French revolution, argues that the concept should be replaced with "public opinion."[17]

On Feb. 16, 1833, Varela had an essay from his own pen sent to Cuba through his collaborator and fellow exile, the learned layman Tomás Gener (a recipient of an honorary doctorate in law from Columbia University). The piece was received in Cuba by Varela's disciple and collaborator, José Antonio Saco and published on the island in the

12. Del Duca, "Political Portrait."
13. Finnis, *Aquinas*.
14. See Veiga González, *Justicia*.
15. Ozouf, "'Public Opinion,'" 1–21.
16. Crowe, "Public Spirit and Public Order."
17. See Jürgen Habermas's many works on *Öffentlichkeit* (usually rendered as "public reason") and my Latinx critique of that concept in Casarella, "Public Reason and Intercultural Dialogue," 51–84.

influential journal *Revista Bimestre Cubana*.[18] The editors of the twentieth century edition note that this essay was written just prior to the publication of the first tome of the *Letters to Elpidio* and can be read as a first draft of that work. Varela may have been influenced by the same Irish sources that shaped Burke.

What is the public spirit in Varela? Varela starts the essay with a classical vignette drawn from Michel de Montaigne's "Of Democritus and Heraclitus (1686)" in which the Frenchman champions in a manner equally risible (cf. Democritus) and lamentable (cf. Heraclitus) his own skeptical version of "public spirit." For Varela defending the public spirit is also filled with irony and must be carried out with wit, but it still represents, in the end, the social conscience of the patriotic (if often misunderstood) Cuban intellectual who writes for a wider public on pressing social questions. Varela was far ahead of his time in advocating Cuban independence and the end of the slave trade. He advocated for the end of these oppressive systems and their violent tactics and never whitewashed the structural dimension of these evils. He saw them in Biblical terms as idols even though his preferred discourse was not at all like that of North American Puritanism. Despite his prophetic stance no structural change came to Cuba or to Cuban Americans living in exile. The time was clearly not ripe for Cubans to change their political system.[19] Varela also realized the unique role of free thinking in the toppling of unjust regimes. He thus struggled to find a way of thinking that would destroy the idols that propped up these two unjust systems. His thought was concrete and political and in no way like the *Utopia* of Thomas More or 20th century utopian counter-hegemonies. Varela's educational philosophy focused on the growth into self-consciousness of a living, speaking person whose very being remains open to infinitude but who needs real freedom to live virtuously and in the truth. In a decidedly unmodern (but not antimodern) manner, the relationship between truth and virtue is for Varela mutually determinative. This legacy has not died; the torch has been passed in Cuban Catholicism of the present. Today in the Centro Cultural Padre Félix Varela, at the heart of old Havana, one finds Varela's most famous motto inscribed on a panel at the front of the main auditorium: *No hay*

---

18. Varela, "Espíritu Público." Soon afterwards Saco had to flee Cuba for England and then Spain because of the appetite of the Cuban elites for his progressive political thought had been sated.

19. One classic account of Varela's pivotal role in the gradual but decisive development of a modern Cuban consciousness of freedom is Vitier, *Ese sol del mundo moral*.

Patria sin virtud, ni virtud con impiedad ("There is no homeland without virtue, nor virtue where impiety reigns").

Varela was searching for a historical future in which his people could live in freedom. Retired Bishop Felipe Estévez, a leading expert in Varela studies, says that three factors characterized the state of religion in 1820s Cuba: (1) the open atheism of the liberal, anticlerical elites, (2) the failure of the Church to evangelize Black slaves, and (3) the identification of all clergy with Spanish rule.[20] The majority of the population favored independence, but the Church was not seen as a vehicle for such a revolution. Cuban independence followed a very different path from most of countries in Latin America. Consider in the following annotated list the fact that the Cuban independence from Spain and the United States does not even take place in the nineteenth century:

Table 1. The Age of Revolutions and the Americas	
1776	American Revolution. Varela promoted U.S. democratic constitutionalism and translated into Spanish the *Manual of Parliamentary Democracy* by Thomas Jefferson.
1789	French Revolution
1804	Haiti (from France). Haiti is geographically very close to Cuba. The closest point between them is less than four hundred miles. The decision of elites in Cuba not to follow suit provided Spain with a base of operations for the defense of their lands in the New Spain and gave the landowners in Cuba many socioeconomic benefits.
1810	Chile (from Spain)
1810	Colombia (from Spain)
1810	Mexico (from Spain)
1811	Paraguay (from Spain)
1811	Venezuela (from Spain)
1816	Argentina (from Spain)
1821	Costa Rica (from Spain)
1821	El Salvador (from Spain)
1821	Guatemala (from Spain)
1821	Honduras (from Spain)
1821	Nicaragua (from Spain)
1821	Peru (from Spain)
1822	Brazil (from Portugal)

20. Estévez, Introduction to *Letters to Elpidio*, 8.

Table 1. The Age of Revolutions and the Americas	
1822	Ecuador (Spain)
1825	Bolivia (from Spain)
1825	Uruguay (from Brazil)
1844	Dominican Republic (from Haiti)

This delay of an independent Cuba was decisive for the inhabitants of the island and for Varela. Cuban independence arrives only after the Latin American liberations made possible by Simon Bolivar, José de San Martín, and after a full century of independence movements had taken root in truly American soils and begun to form the consciousness of the new nations. The Cuban path to independence was not only belated but fraught with difficulty. This table also illustrates how Varela inherited the legacies of both U.S. independence and Latin American revolutionary thought and was faced with the task of forging a discourse of freedom and nationhood that was specific to the needs of the oppressed people of Cuba.

To be more specific, when the USS Maine sank in Havana's harbor in February 1898 after a mysterious explosion, the United States had an excuse for war, and the Spanish-American War followed. By the time of the American intervention in Cuba in April 1898, Antonio Maceo, the "Bronze Titan" and vice-general of the Cuban military had been killed, but the war proved to be brief and one-sided. It was over by August 12, when the United States and Spain signed a preliminary peace treaty. By the Treaty of Paris of December 10, 1898, Spain withdrew from Cuba. A U.S. occupation force remained for more than three years, leaving only after a new constitutional order was established to protect the U.S. hegemony. In fact, accordingly, the new Republic of Cuba had to incorporate the provisions of the Platt Amendment (1901), which specified the conditions for American withdrawal. Among those conditions were (1) the guarantee that Cuba would not transfer any of its land to any foreign power but the United States, (2) limitations on Cuba's negotiations with other countries, (3) the establishment of a U.S. naval base in Cuba, and (4) the U.S. right to intervene in Cuba to preserve Cuban independence. Thus, the creation of the Republic of Cuba was ratified on May 20, 1902 (almost fifty years after Varela's passing). This is the independence that Varela and later José Martí had struggled so long and so valiantly to achieve but without genuine autonomy or unrestricted freedom for the Cuban people.

These sociopolitical constraints already present in his lifetime underscore that Varela did not have the luxury of philosophizing from an armchair. Nor did he theologize without attending to the field hospital in his midst. He was passionate about the defense of the poor, the plight of the vulnerable, and the injustice done to victims of calumny, but his experience of being viciously maligned both in the Spanish Empire and in the United States also taught him to take a step back from the to-and-fro of daily polemics in order to discern the principles needed to guide action. He advocated justice as a socially engaged moral philosopher.

Varela summarizes his general position on social justice with three maxims:

> 1.) To prefer the common good to the particular good, 2.) To avoid that which can be opposed to the unity of the social body, and 3.) To enact only that which it is possible for the good of own's own society and in accord with its own end. The first two maxims guide those who can realize the common good perfectly. The third one is for the imperfect.[21]

The three maxims need to be considered in their unity. Standing alone, they lose their full effect. The third principle should not be confused with either a self-absorbed nationalism that followed the Enlightenment of the independence movements or self-serving parochialism. On the contrary, Varela supported both the common good of Cuba for the island and of the United States in his new home in New York despite the conflicts already brewing between these two powers. Promoting the good of one's own society is a recognition of the blessings inherent in a local culture, including the culture of Irish migrants that Varela served in his local parish. There is one common good that has its end in God, but this single end is realized in plural ways in diverse settings. In the tradition of modern Catholic social teaching that comes a century later, this principle of unity in diversity and relative non-interference in local governance came to be known as the principle of subsidiarity.[22]

---

21. Varela, *Obras*, I [hereafter FV1], 83: "El principio de las leyes sociales es la recta razón bajo estas máximas: 1o Preferir el bien común al particular; 2o No hacer cosa que puede oponerse a la unidad del cuerpo social; 3o Hacer sólo lo que sea posible en favor de la misma sociedad, y según el fin de ella. Las dos primeras máximas inducen un oficio perfecto, la tercera pertenece a los imperfectos."

22. *Catechism of the Catholic Church*, no. 1883: "Socialization also presents dangers. Excessive intervention by the state can threaten personal freedom and initiative. The teaching of the Church has elaborated the principle of subsidiarity, according to which 'a community of a higher order should not interfere in the internal life of a community

Justice is rooted in a larger, Catholic vision, but the experience of being a Catholic pastor in the United States taught Varela not to imitate the harsh intolerance associated with the Second Great Awakening that was on the rise in early nineteenth century North America.[23] A good example of this concern to avoid religious and political extremism is found in Varela's critique of fanaticism:

> Fanaticism, on the contrary, produces the most baneful consequences, the most prominent being the alienation of the religious and the making of many enemies of religion. The fanatics are responsible for so many of the impious! Mocking religion with their stupidities makes religion look despicable. . . . What resources will fanaticism not seek in order to cover up its cruelty? I am not going to waste time on this point because the injuries produced by this fever are ever apparent, and besides I confess that I have to be very careful in addressing it.[24]

Although his own rhetoric is far from irenic, Varela still makes valid points that maintain their relevance even today. If the marginalized, pilloried, and Romanticized Catholicism of the early nineteenth century were to imitate its Protestant detractors, their still modest numbers would diminish even more so. Varela's passion to denounce intolerance was only surpassed by his worry that the new fundamentalism in Protestant quarters would hurt the fragile community of lower-class, immigrant Catholics even more so given the rise in the wider culture of elite, secular despisers of all forms of Christianity.

---

of a lower order, depriving the latter of its functions, but rather should support it in case of need and help to coordinate its activity with the activities of the rest of society, always with a view to the common good.'" Here the *Catechism* cites *Centesimus Annus* 48§4 and also refers to Pius XI, *Quadragesimo Anno* I, 184–86.

23. The young Varela, for example, was an exact contemporary of Rose Hawthorne Lathrop (1851–1926, later Mother Mary Alphonsa), a descendant of Puritans and the daughter of novelist Nathaniel Hawthorne. In 1899 Hawthorne established with a new community of Dominican nuns St. Rose's Free Home for Incurable Cancer on Cherry Street near the East River in the Lower East Side. Her struggle to find a literary and religious identity after her "shocking" conversion to Catholicism, presages Varela's later experiences in New York. Cf. Cummings, "Making of American Saints," 329–31.

24. Varela, FV1, 295: "El fanatismo, en sentido contrario, produce efectos funestísimos, siendo el más notable separar de la religión a muchas personas y granjearle muchos enemigos. ¡Cuántos impíos han formado los fanáticos! Poniendo la religión en ridículo con sus necedades la hacen despreciable, . . . ¡Qué recursos no busca el fanatismo para cohonestar su crueldad! Yo no me detendré en este punto, porque son bien palpables los daños producidos por esta fiera, y además confieso que me es muy sensible contemplarlos."

A different sort of justice is revealed in Varela's critique of false patriotism. Varela was a defender of patriotism and the idea of national autonomy that was fundamental to the revolution of freedom and democracy the marked the transition from colonies to the United States. He was inspired by Thomas Jefferson's *Manual of Parliamentary Practice* and prepared an annotated translation that was intended for Spanish-speaking residents of the U.S., for the emerging republics of Latin America, and as a goad to independence in colonial Cuba. But the false patriots desecrated this venerable tradition of freedom with self-serving gestures and empty promises. Even those who were not outright frauds were liable to be tempted by some form of false patriotism:

> True patriots wish to contribute with their lights and all their resources to the good of the country. If this is their true goal, then they don't share the ridiculous pretense of holding positions for which they are not qualified to serve. Overall, even the best patriots occasionally fall into a defect that causes great evils, and that consists of imagining that nothing is well managed when it's not in accord with their own opinion. This sentiment is almost natural to human beings, but it must be corrected without losing sight of the fact that judgment in these matters depends upon a multitude of facts that we do not always have; and the general opinion, when it is not patently absurd, produces a better outcome than the particular one even though the latter is more grounded. Sometimes the desire to find the better solution makes us lose all that is good.[25]

There is no easy path to social justice for either the new democracies or those still subject to colonial rule. Human nature, which Varela believes is created as good, can still tarnish the efforts of true patriots. Genuine

25. Varela, FV1, 281–83, 434–40, here at 282: "Otro de los obstáculos que presenta al bien público el falso patriotismo consiste en que muchas personas las más ineptas y a veces las más inmorales se escudan con él, disimulando el espíritu de especulación, y el vano deseo de figurar. No puede haber un mal más grave en el cuerpo político, y en nada debe ponerse mayor empeño que en conocer y despreciar a estos especuladores. Los verdaderos patriotas desean contribuir con sus luces y todos sus recursos al bien de la patria, pero siendo éste su verdadero objeto, no tienen la ridícula pretensión de ocupar puestos que no pueden desempeñar. Con todo, aun los mejores patriotas suelen incurrir en un defecto que causa muchos males, y es figurarse que nada está bien dirigido cuando no está conforme a su opinión. Este sentimiento es casi natural al hombre, pero debe corregirse no perdiendo de vista que el juicio en estas materias depende de una multitud de datos que no siempre tenemos; y la opinión general, cuando no es abiertamente absurda, produce siempre mejor efecto que la particular, aunque ésta sea más fundada. El deseo de encontrar lo mejor nos hace a veces perder todo lo bueno."

self-sacrifice is needed to realize the dream of a patriotism directed to the common good and in accord with the best model of freedom for each distinct people. This admonition is not Rousseau's enlightened submission to the *volonté générale*. It is a free decision of a virtuous moral agent to look beyond one's own self-interest to the authentic common good of the people.

Varela's Social Philosophy: Ripple Effects of the Catholic Enlightenment

Recently, Ulrich Lehner has advocated the use of the term "Catholic Enlightenment" to describe the presence of a religious thought in Catholic soil in the seventeenth and eighteenth centuries, a strand of modern thinking that departs radically from the secularizing strand in Spinoza and the scientizing strand in Descartes.[26] Lehner sees the origins and initial trajectory of this development in the reforms of the Council of Trent and downplays the discontinuity between Tridentine Catholicism and Catholic freedom from self-incurred tutelage. In fact, Varela's sense of seminary education, model of priesthood, and catechetical methods resemble those of the Tridentine reforms. But the comparison of Varela as a Catholic recipient of Enlightenment thought to Lehner's "Catholic Enlightenment" seems to end there.[27]

Who are some of the key thinkers that helped Varela to constitute a new philosophy? Varela has a rightful place in the Catholic Enlightenment but not because he continues the Eurocentric tradition of thought that stems from Trent but because he extends the insights of the then brand-new but still untested Catholic liberalism into the world where peoples have been violently conquered by the Europeans.

One paragon of the Catholic Enlightenment who left a significant mark on Varela was Benito Jerónimo Feijóo y Montenegro, a Spanish monk who lived from 1676–1764. Feijoo was a staunch critic of the formal logic of scholastic philosophy because of its detachment from usage in everyday life, a critique that had left its impact on Bishop Espada.[28] "The erudite and illustrious Fr. Feijoo" introduced Varela to the theory of

26. Lehner, *Catholic Enlightenment*.
27. Lehner rightfully lists Archbishop James Carroll as a model on North American soil of the Catholic Enlightenment but omits mention of Carroll's more enlightened successor in the early nineteenth century, Félix Varela.
28. Benitez, "Benito Jerónimo Feijoo," 39–58.

signs and enabled him to adapt his own presentation of formal logic into a more useable system of lucid and clear thinking that could be deployed in everyday life.[29] Varela aimed to provide an updated and abbreviated version of Feijoo's logic for his new audience outside of Europe. It is reported that these notes on logic by Varela were used in the textbooks of Mexican public schools afterwards.

Felipe Estévez notes that Varela in *Letters to Elpidio* stands closer to Lammenais's *Essai sur l'Indifférence en Matière de Religion* and Lammenais's 1820 work *De la Religion Considerée dans ses Rapports avec l'Ordre Politique* than to Feijoo's *Teatro Crítico* and *Cartas Eruditas*.[30] In *De la Religion* Lammenais took on the twin evils of conservative nationalist Gallicanism and the secularizing tendencies of Liberal thought. This proximity is true about Varela's systematic elaboration of ideas but ignores the similarity of style.

Like Feijoo, and even more so like the sixteenth century sceptic Michel de Montaigne, Varela still employs skepticism in a satirical vein generously and with great wit to unmask the politicians and their pretentious use of religious categories that have no basis in empirical fact. Montaigne's rhetoric has been labeled both conservative in its Pyrrhonian roots as well as in its defense of existing customs and very traditional religion and progressive in its time for its vigorous defense of private belief.[31] Varela's use of satire also makes him surpass the usual binaries that we encounter in the Enlightenment of liberal or conservative, defender

---

29. Varela writes: "En lo absoluto de su necesidad insisten constantemente los escolásticos, hasta el extremo de afirmar que sin ella no puede conseguirse a perfección el dominio de ciencia alguna. Creyendo preferible dar de lado a tal polémica, ya que cuestiones más importantes nos reclaman, trataré de exponer el contenido de la Lógica, no sin invitar antes a que se recuerde lo que tan docta y graciosamente escribió sobre esta materia el erudito e ilustre P. Feijoo. La presentaré, si es que puedo lograrlo, limpia de complicaciones y sedimentos de la escolástica y bien provista de doctrinas depuradas por la crítica, que a la vez considero como las mejores y las más útiles. Los que se han formado al cabo de largos años en las escuelas peripatéticas y se han nutrido y hasta saturado de sus enseñanzas, querrían ver aquí tratadas en toda su amplitud las eternas cuestioncillas de las categorías, de los postpredicamentos, de las cualidades de las proposiciones, de las equivalencias, de las conversiones y de las figuras de los silogismos. En la imposibilidad de atender los deseos de todos bastará complacer a aquéllos que, aspirando a lo mejor, se contentan con lo más simple y fundamental. Yo, por mi parte, creo que sólo pueden avanzar con paso firme por el camino de la verdad quienes, sacudiéndose el polvo de una inveterada ceguera y prescindiendo de las opiniones de los hombres, tienen para sus pesquisas por impulso y guía a la naturaleza, obra brillantísima del divino Hacedor." Varela, FV1, 31.

30. Estévez, introduction to *Letters to Elpidio*, 7.

31. Laursen, *Politics of Skepticism*, 125–44.

of the status quo or advocate of revolutionary change. Varela is prophetic; he does not vacillate in his opinions. At the same time, there is a dynamic ebb and flow to his consideration of starkly opposed opinions that builds upon and surpasses the skeptical model of Montaigne.

Experience for Varela is pivotal and is based upon the empirical data collected by the mind. But the mind still has the task of organizing this data and thus remains much more than a *tabula rasa* merely shaped by sensory percepts.[32] Varela's theory of knowledge has also been compared to that of the commonsense philosophy of the Scottish thinker Thomas Reid (1710–96). Varela nonetheless advocated a sensationism without reserve and attributed his allegiance to this theory of empirical knowledge to both John Locke and Étienne Bonnot de Condillac. Thinking for de Condillac was thinking in translation, akin to the intercultural philosophy defended today by the Argentine/Mexican philosopher Enrique Dussel or the Cuban in exile in Germany, Raúl Fornet-Betancourt.[33]

Influenced by his fellow Frenchman Condorcet, Antoine Destutt de Tracy (1754–1836) coined the term *idéologie* to indicate a new science of ideas, a path of thinking later taken up as a form of critical analysis by Karl Marx and his followers.[34] The original meaning assigned by Destutt de Tracy is bereft of the deterministic materialism of the second half of the nineteenth century even if it paves the way for many of these developments. Louis Dupré in his phenomenal study of this question, *Marx's Social Critique of Culture*, writes that Tracy introduced the term to further the sensationalist theory of knowledge introduced by Condorcet.[35] Tracy was a convert to Catholicism and the Republican cause after the Revolution and was criticized by the defenders of the Enlightenment for these conservative tendencies. Tracy's critics see little more than a defense of the bourgeois thinking of the post-Revolutionary elites in Tracy's idea of ideologies. Marx's famous critique of ideologies is based in part on a wholescale attack on Napoleon's global rejection of philosophical ideas as divorced from empirical reality. Hegel's love for Napoleon, for example, was apparently not reciprocated by Napoleon. Karl Marx too was interested in unveiling a new view of the reality that undergirded ideological

---

32. On the question of experience, Vicente Medina even sees a parallel between Varela and his contemporary North American pragmatist, William James. See Medina, "Félix Varela," 23.

33. See, for example, Dussel, "Transmodernity and Interculturality," 28–59.

34. Cf. Blakeslee, "Félix Varela," 25.

35. Dupré, *Marx's Social Critique*, 219.

superstructures. Marx thus codifies the idea, still dominant in our day, that ideologies are ideologies when they represent only the vested interest of a segment of society and become divorced from empirical realities.

Varela's critique of ideologies is very different from the dialectics that later developed in Hegel and Marx. Like Destutt de Tracy but unlike most Catholic apologists of the early nineteenth century, Varela uncovered ideological distortions of reality that needed to be unmasked and were lurking behind the surface of the supposedly liberal and Enlightened doctrines of his contemporaries in Cuba, Europe, and the United States. Varela develops his own approach to *ideología* as a form of thinking already in his early philosophical work, the *Miscellenea Filosófica* of 1819, which then came into a third, updated edition in New York in 1827.[36] We draw here from the more mature work. *Ideología* is a critical form of learning that cannot dispense with formal logic or "a general grammar" (Varela's scholastic term for a comprehensive theory of signs) but envelops both of those tools of knowing into a more systematic whole.[37]

The fourth and fifth chapters of the third edition of the *Miscellanea* testify to the profound and creative meaning of this new art of knowledge.[38] Varela starts with the elusive facticity of speech. A spoken word in a conventional language is a peculiar semiotic conjunction of sound and spirit, with spirit surpassing that which is expressed in sound:

> To the degree that [ideology] begins to acquire a sign [with] precision, it loses its brevity and clarity, such that this is one of those points in which I judge there to be an insuperable difficulty, namely, between spirit and matter. Our soul breathes out what it hears, and our lips cannot pronounce all that is contained in this breath.[39]

36. Varela, FV1, 315–93.

37. Varela, FV1, 339: "Sin embargo, es preciso confesar que la palabra Ideología lo envuelve todo, y que estas cosas se hallan tan unidas, que es imposible ser ideólogo sin ser lógico, y usar de la Gramática general. Este es el motivo por qué se suele poner indiferentemente Ideología por Lógica, aunque no suele en el uso confundirse con la Gramática general. Podemos concluir que toda la inexactitud consiste en que la palabra Ideología ha llegado a ser equívoca, pues o significa la ciencia que comprende todo el orden de nuestros conocimientos en todas sus relaciones, y entonces no se confunde con la dirección del espíritu humano, que los antiguos llaman Lógica, o se toma en un sentido más riguroso, contrayéndonos solamente a la adquisición de ideas, y le llamaremos Ideología propia o rigurosa."

38. Varela, FV1, 342–45.

39. Varela, FV1, 343: "Al paso que va adquiriendo un signo exactitud, pierde su brevedad y claridad, de modo que éste es uno de aquellos puntos en que yo juzgo que

The ideological component in this form of knowing cannot take recourse to an innate idea since Descartes is credited by Varela with having destroyed once and for all this vestige of Platonism.[40] Innatism and the mind as *tabula rasa* are thus both ruled out; only a theory of signs that looks beyond what can materially be signed will get beyond this impasse.

The solution, such as it is, can be found in a new *arte de saber*, an art of knowing modeled on the epistemology of translation Varela learned from de Condillac.[41] Varela is not interested in a mechanical application of the know-how of being able to translate from one language to another into the domain of epistemology. The intercultural significance of his thought is rooted in a deeper level of reflection on the conjunction of everyday and scientific modes of learning. In fact, he explicitly states that he is interested in knowing in order to translate rather than in translating in order to know.[42] Often the codes that he utilizes to talk about semiotic systems are drawn from the sciences, e.g., algebra as opposed to higher mathematics. As an example, he states that a student beginning to learn algebra may have to practice with algorithms several times to grasp a theorem that someone versed in higher mathematics can understand without practice. At some point in the learning process, the language of algebra and that of mathematics can converge without cancelling out one another. Herein lies the process of achieving a new level of understanding. The mere array of systems by itself does not teach. The switching of systems of knowing, however, can ineluctably yield insights not encapsulated by one of the other system. Varela summarizes: "This doctrine of Condillac lead us to observe the *great* difference between *saber* ("the act of knowing") and having a lot of ideas."[43] *Saber* is genuine knowledge that is groundbreaking, personal, insightful, and unitive without positing one system of knowing that stands above every possible semiotic code or scientific mode of inquiry. One sees foreshadowings here of John Henry Newman's illative sense, Pierre Rousselot's eyes of faith, and Bernard Lonergan's notion of insight.

---

hay una dificultad insuperable, por la diferencia que existe entre el orden mecánico y pausado de los sonidos, y la dignidad y prontitud de los pensamientos; en una palabra, entre el espíritu y la materia. Nuestra alma suple mucho a lo que oye, y nuestros labios no pueden pronunciar todo lo que ella ha suplido."

40. Varela, FV1, 322.
41. Varela, FV1, 343–45.
42. Varela, FV1, 343.
43. Varela, FV1, 345; emphasis added.

As a complement to this immersion in eighteenth century semiotics and pragmatics, Varela also turned to a Roman school of theology. This interface of these two worlds is particularly relevant for understanding the uniqueness of Varela's synthesis. For example, Varela knew and cited Giovanni Battista Piccadori (1766–1829), author of *Ethicæ Seu Moralis Philosophiæ Institutiones* (1828).[44] Piccadori had a reputation as an ascetical priest and was consequently named superior General of the Minorite order by the Pope. As a moral theologian, he offered a Thomistic critique of Rousseau's social contract theory and Hobbes's state of nature in *Leviathan* (1651).[45] In general, both of these modern approaches ignore "the natural mode" that is self-evident and can be known by natural reason as a norm of the will. Varela always carried out his thinking in dialogue with Roman sources of moral thought, but unlike late nineteenth century European Catholic Thomists like Joseph Kleutgen (1811–83), Varela's thinking is not allied with a particular Roman school of moral theology. Eclecticism and the non-adherence to a particular school of philosophy is a Cuban "principle" that Varela defends in his *Miscellanea filosófica*.[46] He believed in the idea of a canon of moral thought guided by the theory of virtue of St. Thomas Aquinas, but not one that was applied rigidly.

As a result, Varela was working out of his own eclectic system and not adhering to a pre-established school. In fact, Varela was not altogether alone for advocating a broadly Thomistic but still democratic approach to social questions in the early nineteenth century, but there are few obvious points of comparison. What kind of Thomism was available in the United States during Varela's period of literary activity, i.e., 1823–40s? Of the major centers of post-secondary Catholic education already in existence, one can point only to the Jesuit foundation of Georgetown University in 1789 (but still had no graduate programs until 1851) and St. Mary's Seminary in Baltimore, which awarded Varela an honorary doctorate in 1841, which occurred just after he was named Vicar General

---

44. Varela, FV1, 258: "¿Pero cuál es la norma de las acciones? Admira leer en el célebre Piccadori, que se han dado doscientas respuestas a esta pregunta, o sean doscientas opiniones sobre esta materia. ¡Lamentemos la miseria humana, cuando un objeto tan claro se ha podido oscurecer en tales términos! La norma es la voluntad divina, pero como el orden filosófico exige que indiquemos el modo natural con que se manifiesta, diremos que la norma es la evidencia de lo que conviene a la naturaleza de los objetos y sus relaciones, para darles el valor que efectivamente tienen y proceder según ellas." Here Varela is citing: *Ethicae et Moralis Philosophiae Inst.*, Tomo 1, 79.

45. Varela, FV1, 258.

46. Medina, "Félix Varela," 24–26.

of New York. Major universities like Fordham and Notre Dame only came into being later in the 1840s. In other words, U.S. Catholic theology as an academic pursuit was still basically a dream during Varela's lifetime.

A more apt comparison of Thomistic approaches to social justice might be Varela's younger contemporary in southern Italy, Luigi Taparelli (1793–1862).[47] Both the drafter (Matteo Liberatore) and author (Leo XIII) of *Rerum Novarum* were his students, but Taparelli's rejection of the liberal notion of popular sovereignty seems to have led to his relegation to relative oblivion in the standard histories of modern Catholic social thought. Taparelli tried through a revival of Thomism to reform the Collegio Romano right after the papal ban on the Jesuits was lifted but was banished to Palermo for holding curricular views that were deemed overly antagonistic to liberal Enlightenment norms. Working in Palermo in the 1840s, Taparelli wrote his multi-volume *Saggio teoretico di dritto naturale appoggiato sul fatto* ("Theoretical Essay on Natural Right based upon an Observance of Historical Realities and Contexts"). Taparelli's Thomism was briefly revived towards the end of his life. In 1850 Pope Pius IX brought him back from exile and asked him to be the founding editor of *La Civiltà Cattolica*.

For both Varela and Taparelli, and for very few other major Catholic authors that were impacted by the Catholic Enlightenment, social justice was a good that must be promoted for the sake of the common good and not as a modern right or the fruit of a social contract. *Social justice merits promotion as a virtue*, a theme that runs consistently from Thomas Aquinas through his modern interpreters, including Luis de Molina. Here we still run into a hermeneutical problem. The modern reader is tempted to interpret this recourse to virtue ethics as an antidote to the focus on distributive justice that developed starting with Oswald von Nell-Breuning (1890–91) and was taken to a certain extreme in contemporary Catholic social theory. William Collinge is careful to note the Thomistic interplay between personal virtue and the social arrangement or state of affairs that leads to the establishment of laws and institutions and how both are preserved in Taparelli's lucid account of the virtue of justice.[48]

---

47. Collinge, "Review of Social Justice and Solidarity," 170–79. See also Schuck, "Early Modern Roman Catholic Social Thought," 99–124.

48. Taparelli writes: "Social justice is first and foremost a personal virtue with regard to the disposition to protect and promote the exercise of the rights and the fulfillment to the duties of others in society. Secondarily, the term can be meaningfully used as a characterization of a socioeconomic and political order, the actual arrangement of institutions, laws and policies that operate to protect and promote the same exercise

The Agon of Religious Tolerance in the *Letters to Elpidio*

The full and mature articulation of Varela's concept of justice can also be found in his *Letters to Elpidio* (1835–38). This work is his *magnum opus* and was projected to be in three books, even though only two were finished. The first book takes on the "monster" of irreligiosity. The second book looks at the "monster" of superstition. The third volume was written but never published because the author was disconsolate about the poor reception of the first two volumes.[49] It was said to address the "monster" of fanaticism. It would undoubtedly have been his most prophetic writing.[50]

If the second book were an application of Trent's teaching on popular piety, then its scope would have been very narrow and in keeping with the kind of superstitious behavior that most moderns or metamoderns would find offensive today.[51] But the scope was very broad, for it included Catholic clergy, including bishops, who did not practice what they preach; anyone in any Christian regime who used religious rhetoric for the sake of usurping temporal power, and Protestants who professed the Gospel as freedom from tyranny and then irrationally turned their modern self-understanding against the Catholic faithful.

The letters reveal Varela to be defending a pro-constitutionalist, anti-monarchical Thomistic rearticulation of the political doctrine of *natural right*. In the second book, he offers a religious foundation for tolerance that is consonant with this view. He was not specifically defending the revolution that took place in the United States nor the one in France even though those reference points were clearly in mind. He was thinking of a Cuban independence but never speaks about it in concrete terms in the *Letters*.

---

of rights and duties of individuals who make up that society." Behr, *Social Justice and Solidarity*, 149–50, as cited in Collinge, "Review of Social Justice and Solidarity," 172.

49. Blakeslee, "Félix Varela," 37.

50. In an interview posthumously published Varela revealed his disappointment at the failure of the first two volumes to gain traction in Cuba. He said that the Cuban elites were incensed that he criticized the lack of religious tolerance in the United States since the U.S. was their model of perfect social harmony. With that prejudice in view, a volume dedicated to the topic of the idol of fanaticism as it existed in supposedly enlightened North America would have been even more poorly received than the first two volumes. See Estévez, Introduction to *Letters to Elpidio*, 12–13.

51. For a provocative and relevant view of Trent forged from within the U.S. Hispanic community, see Espín, "Trinitarian Monotheism," 177–204.

The title is both significant and elusive. The genre of a letter is not unusual for this period. Who is Elpidio, the supposed recipient of these letters? Most commentators agree that Elpidio is a fictional Cuban, whose person and name bear within them the hope (from the Greek *elpis*) for a new and better future. Elpidio is thus much like "Theophilus," the fictional addressee of the Gospel of Luke (1:3) and the Acts of the Apostles (1:1). He is lover of the true God who wants to see a vital message of hope carried across the world. But the message here is not the Gospel of the Second Great Awakening that was spreading through revival meetings across the Northeast and into the U.S. South and unfortunately also generating rabid and xenophobic anti-Catholicism in some quarters. It is rather a public philosophy, open to diverse confessions and traditions, that is both consonant with the free practice of Christian virtue and the political exigencies of democratic constitutionalism.

But this philosophy of hope also emerges from the struggle of the pastor Varela. He says in the preface: "*Estoy como el yunque, siempre bajo el martillo.*"[52] Few commentators have noticed that Varela thinks not only as one who lives in exile but as a thinker who reflects with considerable lament from the generating power of that struggle.[53] Estévez opines that Varela went ahead of European Catholic thinkers in advocating a philosophy of public life precisely because of his Latin American context.[54] Varela wrote to cultivated elites in Latin America and was maligned by them for telling them about a reality in North America that they did not want to accept. The man known universally respected as the father of modern Cuban identity felt homeless because he had no real home. The postmodern condition of exile is likewise the condition of being permanently banished from the promised land, of being neither here nor there.[55] Fernando Segovia likewise is a Cuban exile who teaches Biblical hermeneutics today at Vanderbilt University. He champions the exilic practice of "reading across" cultures in a critical, intercultural fashion.[56] In reading across, Segovia abandons the essentialism underneath liberationist schemes that claim to unmask the veil from the oppressive structure of one culture

---

52. "I am like the anvil, always under the hammer."
53. See, however, McCadden, *Félix Varela*, for a sympathetic but slightly hagiographic reading of what Varela represents to the Cubans in exile in the United States.
54. Estévez, introduction to *Letters to Elpidio*, 7.
55. See Segovia, "In the World and Not of It," 15–42.
56. Segovia, "Reading-Across," 59–83.

while claiming superiority for the rationalist critical perspective that hovers above contexts, languages, and power differentials.

Varela too has suspicions of the intellectuals of his day that shared that pretense in their imitation of the remarkable Voltaire. Nowhere is the agonistic nature of Varela's task apparent than in his subtle but spirited defense of religious tolerance in the *Letters*. He was very wary of recent visitors from Latin America to the United States like the wealthy and literate young Cuban Domingo del Monte, for they naively assumed that the United States had established a paragon of tolerance that could effortlessly be imported to Latin America. These intellectuals knew nothing of the neo-Puritan doctrine of religious tolerance that effectively masked nativist sentiments against Catholics and others.[57] In fact, Varela divided religious tolerance into three levels in his *Letters*: the legal, the theological, and the social. The unanticipated experience of being a Cuban in exile had taught Varela that the first could exist on the books without any semblance in the reality of everyday life of either the second or the third.

Varela's Significance for Social Catholicism Today

Varela's contemporary legacy is vast and significant, both in Cuba and beyond Cuba. The torch of freedom that he lit has already been passed to multiple future generations. In 1988, on the bicentennial of his birth, the U.S. postal service issued a $0.32 stamp in his name. In the same year The Varela Project was started by Oswaldo Payá of the Christian Liberation Movement in Cuba.[58] Dagoberto Valdés from Pinar del Río and his banned journal VITRAL also represent a Catholic legacy of Varela. Many members of these groups were imprisoned during the Black Spring in 2003. Payá died in a mysterious and suspicious car crash in 2012. Payá's daughter Rosa María Payá continues in the face of great opposition to fight in the spirit of her father for democratic reforms for the island of Cuba.

Writing contemporaneously with Alexis de Tocqueville, Varela theorized about the new civil religion emerging plurally in the now liberated colonies of the U.S. and sought to promote the common good in that milieu and elsewhere with a public spirit.[59] The idea of the public spirit in Varela retains vestiges of classical natural law theory deriving from Cicero

---

57. Lamas, *Latino Continuum*, 39.
58. See Hoffman, *Give Me Liberty*, 268–97.
59. See Casarella, "Public Reason and Intercultural Dialogue," 51–84.

and Augustine but is also grounded in a realist fallibilism not characteristic of these pre-modern political theologies.[60] Varela thus stands between the foundationalism of new natural law theory and the "responsible relativism" of Ada-María Isasi-Díaz and Neo-pragmatists like Richard Rorty and Cornell West. This transcending of dichotomies that are neither reasonable nor Catholic should make Varela's thought palatable to both the "progressives" and traditionalists" in contemporary Catholicism. Varela is equally suspicious of the dangerous dogmas of the political absolutists as well as the dogmas of those who refuse to ignore the exigency for individuals and society of relativizing the relativizers.[61] His relevance for contemporary political thought derives from this very displacement.

Varela's life was filled with pathbreaking initiatives and the communication of a promise of reward that was not realized in his lifetime. It would be peremptory, however, to dismiss his contribution to the history of social Catholicism on those grounds. He was a prophet whose decrying of the injustice of his day arguably resounds more loudly in the present than the past.[62] A metaphor from the history of sculpture may be instructive. Michelangelo famously referred to each his sculptures of *Bound Slaves* in an agonistic manner as an *opera non finito*, works that are not yet and will never be complete. Modern sculptors like Auguste Rodin and Ivan Meštrović imitated this technique. In the case of the Pietà and the stone slaves, Michelangelo wished to convey the idea that achievement of freedom can and should be cut into the hard matter of life, but final freedom in nonetheless never fully achieved in this life.

---

60. Writing about probabilism and conscience in a manner very reminiscent of North American pragmatism's approach to the fixation of belief and Newman on the illative sense, Varela states: "Aunque siempre debe el hombre operar según su conciencia, no siempre opera bien conformándose con ella. El hombre está obligado a seguir la opinión que vulgarmente se cree más probable; pero ha de seguir la que él juzga serlo. Inferiremos por tanto que el hombre no se justifica siguiendo una opinión porque sea probable en juicio de muchos, siempre que él crea su contraria más probable. En esta materia nos parece que toda la gran cuestión entre probabilidades y probabilioristas depende sin duda de no haber distinguido lo que es probabilidad de una opinión en sí, por sus fundamentos, y partidarios de lo que es probabilidad respectiva, atendiendo al entendimiento de cada uno, pues la opinión que a Pedro le parece más probable para Juan es menos probable." Varela, FV1, 80.

61. Cf. Berger, *Rumor of Angels*.

62. Catholic film director Martin Scorsese includes a scene in the movie *The Gangs of New York* (2002) that recognizes that Varela may still have a place in today's public imagination. In that scene rival gangs line up in the Five Points neighborhood of the 1820s for a violent conflict, and Fr. Varela emerges from his parish to quell the sudden outburst of rage on both sides.

Michelangelo provides a mournful but still encouraging paradigm for an existence that is much more than solitary and not ultimately constricted by our finitude. This too is the vision that Félix Varela proposed under the pseudonym of "Elpidio," a missive for the sake of the public spirit sent to those in his future audience who today wish to re-imagine in a new key both the epistemological struggle of life in the modern world and the social message of the Catholic Church.

Bibliography

Behr, Thomas C. *Social Justice and Solidarity: Luigi Taparelli and the Origins of Modern Catholic Social Thought*. Washington, DC: The Catholic University of America Press, 2019.

Benitez, Juan Manuel Campos. "La crítica de Benito Jerónimo Feijoo a la lógica." *Revista de Filosofía* 24 (2006) 39–58. http://ve.scielo.org/scielo.php?pid=S0798-11712006000200003&script=sci_abstract.

Berger, Peter. *A Rumor of Angels: Modern Society and the Rediscovery of the Supernatural*. New York: Anchor, 1970.

Blakeslee, William Francis. "Félix Varela—(1788–1853)." *Records of the American Catholic Historical Society of Philadelphia* 38 (1927) 15–46. http://www.jstor.org/stable/44208668.

Casarella, Peter. "Priestly Ministry: Helping the Source for True Life." In *Entering into the Mind of Christ: The True Nature of Theology*, edited by James Keating, 191–224. Omaha, NE: Institute for Priestly Formation Publications, 2014.

———. "Public Reason and Intercultural Dialogue." In *At the Limits of the Secular: Catholic Reflections on Faith and Public Life*, edited by William Barbieri, 51–84. Grand Rapids: Eerdmans, 2014.

———. "Solidarity as the Fruit of Communion: *Ecclesia in America*, 'Post-Liberation Theology,' and the Earth." *Communio: International Catholic Review* 27 (2000) 98–123.

Catechism of the Catholic Church. 2nd ed. Vatican City: Vatican, 1997.

Collinge, William J. "Review of Social Justice and Subsidiarity: Luigi Taparelli and the Origins of Modern Catholic Social Thought." *Journal of Social Encounters* 6 (2022) 170–79. https://digitalcommons.csbsju.edu/social_encounters/vol6/iss2/24.

Crowe, Ian. "Public Spirit and Public Order: Edmund Burke and the Role of the Critic in Mid-Eighteenth-Century Britain." PhD diss., University of North Carolina at Chapel Hill, 2008. https://doi.org/10.17615/5nbb-bs50.

Cummings, Kathleen Sprows. "Samuel Mazzuchelli, Rose Hawthorne Lathrop, and the Making of American Saints." In *Preaching with Their Lives: Dominicans on Mission in the United States after 1850*, edited by Margaret M. McGuinness and Jeffrey M. Burns, 316–44. New York: Fordham University Press, 2020.

De La Torre, Miguel. *José Marti's Liberative Political Theology*. Nashville: Vanderbilt University Press, 2021.

Del Duca, Gemma Marie, Sr. "A Political Portrait: Félix Varela Y Morales, 1788–1853." PhD diss., University of New Mexico, 1966.

Social Catholicism for the Twenty-First Century?—Volume 1

Díaz-Stevens, Ana María. *Oxcart Catholicism on Fifth Avenue: The Impact of the Puerto Rican Migration upon the Archdiocese of New York*. Notre Dame: University of Notre Dame Press, 1993.

Dupré, Louis. *Marx's Social Critique of Culture*. New Haven: Yale University Press, 1983.

Dussel, Enrique. "Transmodernity and Interculturality: An Interpretation from the Perspective of Philosophy of Liberation." *Transmodernity: Journal of Peripheral Cultural Production of the Luso-Hispanic World* 1 (2012) 28–59. http://dx.doi.org/10.5070/T413012881.

Espín, Orlando. "Trinitarian Monotheism and the Birth of Popular Catholicism: The Case of Sixteenth Century Mexico." *Missiology* 20 (1992) 177–204.

Estévez, Felipe. Introduction to *Letters to Elpidio*, by Félix Varela, 1–20. Mahwah, NJ: Paulist, 1989.

———. *El perfil pastoral de Félix Varela*. Miami: Ediciones Universal, 1989.

Figueroa y Miranda, Manuel. *Religión y política en la Cuba del siglo XIX: el obispo Espada visto a la luz de los archivos romanos, 1802–1832*. Miami: Ediciones Universal, 1975.

Finnis, John. *Aquinas: Moral, Political, and Legal Theory*. Oxford: Oxford University Press, 1998.

Hoffman, David E. *Give Me Liberty: The True Story of Oswaldo Payá and His Daring Quest for a Free Cuba*. New York: Simon & Schuster, 2022.

John Paul II. "Address of John Paul II at the University of Havana." https://www.vatican.va/content/john-paul-ii/en/speeches/1998/january/documents/hf_jp-ii_spe_19980123_lahavana-culture.html.

———. *Centesimus Annus*. https://www.vatican.va/content/john-paul-ii/en/encyclicals/documents/hf_jp-ii_enc_01051991_centesimus-annus.html.

Lamas, Carmen E. "Father Félix Varela and the Emergence of an Organized Latina/o Minority in Early Nineteenth-Century New York City." In *The Cambridge History of Latino/a American Literature*, edited by John Morán González and Laura Lomas, 157–75. Cambridge: Cambridge University. Press, 2018. https://www.cambridge.org/core/books/abs/cambridge-history-of-latinao-american-literature/father-Félix-varela-and-the-emergence-of-an-organized-latinao-minority-in-early-nineteenthcentury-new-york-city/2DA88E002943F728081ECDA1F2CD8D0C.

———. *The Latino Continuum and the Nineteenth-Century Americas: Literature, Translation, and Historiography*. Oxford: Oxford University Press, 2021.

Laursen, John Christian. *The Politics of Skepticism in the Ancients, Montaigne, Hume, and Kant*. Leiden: Brill, 1992.

Lehner, Ulrich. *The Catholic Enlightenment: The Forgotten History of a Global Movement*. Oxford: Oxford University Press, 2016.

McCadden, Joseph, and Helen M. McCadden. *Félix Varela: Torchbearer from Cuba*. 3rd ed. San Juan: Ramallos Bros., 1998.

Medina, Vicente. "Félix Varela en la antesala de la modernidad: filosofía, eclecticismo y utilidad." *Inter-American Journal of Philosophy* 11 (2020) 17–34.

Navia, Juan M. *An Apostle for the Immigrants: The Exile Years of Father Félix Varela y Morales (1823–1853)*. Salisbury, MD: Factor, 2002.

Ozouf, Mona. "'Public Opinion' at the End of the Old Regime." *Journal of Modern History* 60 (1988) 1–21. http://www.jstor.org/stable/1880368?seq=3#fndtn-page_thumbnails_tab_contents.

Piccadori, Giovanni Battista. *Ethicae seu moralis philosophiae institutiones exaratae*. Rome: ex typographia Salviucci, 1828.

Pius XI. *Quadragesimo Anno.* https://www.vatican.va/content/pius-xi/en/encyclicals/documents/hf_p-xi_enc_19310515_quadragesimo-anno.html.
Schuck, Michael J. "Early Modern Roman Catholic Social Thought, 1740–890." In *Modern Catholic Social Teaching, Commentaries & Interpretations,* edited by Kenneth R. Himes and Lisa Sowle Cahill, 99–124. Washington, DC: Georgetown University Press, 2005.
Segovia, Fernando. "In the World and Not of It: Exile as a Locus for a Theology of Diaspora." In *Hispanic/Latino Theology: Challenge and Promise,* edited by Ada Maria Isasi-Díaz and Fernando Segovia, 195–217. Minneapolis: Fortress, 1996.
———. "Reading-Across: Intercultural Criticism and Textual Posture." In *Interpreting Beyond Borders,* edited by Fernando F. Segovia, 59–83. Sheffield: Sheffield Academic, 2010.
Torres-Cuevas, Eduardo, ed. *Obispo Espada.* La Habana: Imagen Contemporanea, 1999.
Varela, Félix. *Cartas a Elpidio, sobre la impieded, la superstición y el fanaticismo en sus relaciones con la Sociedad.* Miami: Editorial Cubana, 1996.
———. "El Espíritu Público." *Revista Bimestre Cubana,* January 1, 1834.
———. *Obras.* Vol. 1. Edited by Eduardo Torres-Cuevas et al. Havana: Editorial Cultura Popular y Ediciones Imagen Contemporánea, 1997.
Veiga González, Roberto. *La justicia en el padre Félix Varela.* Cuba: n.p., 2012.
Vitier, Cintio. *Ese sol del mundo moral.* México: Siglo Veintiuno Editores, 1975.
Wessman, Aaron. *The Church's Mission in a Polarized World.* Hyde Park, NY: New City, 2023.

3

Wilhelm von Ketteler

Nineteenth-Century Advocate for Catholic Social Thought

Martin J. O'Malley, Friedrich Schiller University

Abstract: This article examines Bishop Wilhelm Emmanuel von Ketteler's biography, published works, and correspondence to demonstrate his relevance for CST in five points: First, Ketteler's primary identity and loyalty was uncompromisingly Christian, rooted in Thomistic natural law, and thoroughly consistent with the church's scriptural, theological, and ecclesiological commitments. Second, Ketteler's legal education and experience informed his social writings. He respected and often incorporated secular and Protestant intellectual insights, including especially the "historical school" of jurisprudence—a branch of German Romanticism. Third, Ketteler's dignitarian defense of individual human persons is consistent with contemporary discourses of human dignity and human rights. Fourth, Ketteler's practical reasoning was ordered towards a theologically informed conception of human dignity and the common good. He sought prudential paths, which he called corduroy roads, to deal with this period's social challenges. And fifth, Ketteler's resourceful participation with representational forms of government demonstrates the rich potential for the church in public life where religious freedom is constitutionally protected. His social action took place in a context of an increasingly secular public discourse where Roman Catholics were a minority in the national structure formed in 1870 Germany. Ketteler confronted threats from the political left attempting to privatize religion and from the right that tried to nationalize church activities. He identified religion as politically essential while respecting structurally independent public spheres for both church and state.

Introduction: Ketteler's Early Nineteenth-Century Westphalian World

WILHELM EMMANUEL VON KETTELER (1811–77) was a nineteenth-century German bishop whose work to address "the social question" profoundly shaped Roman Catholic social teaching.[1] Ketteler's life as lawyer, priest, and bishop of Mainz (1850–77) spanned a critical time for Europe and the world, from Napolean's defeat and the subsequent Congress of Vienna to the political, social, and economic revolutions of late nineteenth century. His social writings and pragmatic leadership responded to those crises and made him a forerunner of the church's more structured modern tradition of social teaching (CST) launched for the universal church in Pope Leo XIII's *Rerum Novarum* (1891).[2]

As bishop, Ketteler's antagonists in Germany included figures like Otto von Bismarck (1815–98) and Karl Marx (1818–83), social-political-ideological figures who (a) interpreted the signs of the times according to identifiable conceptual or ideological systems, (b) gained wide recognition as much for their political activity as for their ideas, and who (c) dramatically shaped social and political history. We know of Bismarck and Marx, but Ketteler's story is relatively unknown.

The nineteenth century began in Germany with secularization of church properties and public offices; religion was increasingly viewed as a purely private matter.[3] These developments were well established during Ketteler's early life and a priestly career bracketed by the 1848

---

1. O'Malley, *Catholic Rights Discourse*; O'Malley, *Birth of Catholic Social Thought*. Both provide materials for this article, with permissions.

2. Pope Benedict XVI references Ketteler's pioneering role for the church's social teaching in his first encyclical, *Deus Caritas Est*, §27 (2005). Regarding Ketteler's influence on Leo XIII and *Rerum Novarum*, see Misner, "Predecessors of *Rerum Novarum*."

3. Krieger, *German Idea of Freedom*, 11.

revolutions and the 1870s *Kulturkampf*. During this time of nation building in Germany, the liberal banner of reform was used to concentrate and magnify political power using rationalized bureaucracies, centralized governments, and modern armies. Ketteler, well-trained in secular and Catholic intellectual traditions, was both a product of the times and a public critic of movements perceived to be damaging to the Roman Catholic Church. He was able to read the signs of these times and to engage effectively in the expanding public sphere of newspapers, weekly broadsheets, pamphlets, parliamentary forums, and speeches to mass gatherings. In the heat of crises, he pioneered responses to social questions that protected human dignity, justice, and the human community's need for solidarity. His example and social writings influenced Pope Leo XIII's *Rerum Novarum* at the end of the century.

This article presents the case that Ketteler was a righteous pastor with the theological and worldly wisdom to recognize and respond to modern social challenges. His example is probably not worthy of sainthood, but it certainly remains relevant. He vigorously confronted threats to the church and advocated for marginalized persons. His social involvement was courageous and creative in advocating for prudential paths that he called "corduroy roads" to provide guidance during this period of social transformation.[4] This article examines Ketteler's biography, correspondence, and published work to demonstrate his relevance for CST in five points:

First, Ketteler's primary identity and loyalty was uncompromisingly Christian and rigorously embedded in that tradition. His works are rooted in Thomistic natural law and thoroughly consistent with the church's scriptural, theological, and ecclesiological commitments.

Second, Ketteler's legal education and experience informed his social writings. He incorporated insights from secular legal traditions, especially from the "historical school" of jurisprudence that was largely advanced by Protestant scholars.

Third, Ketteler's defense of individual human persons is consistent with contemporary discourses of human rights and human dignity. He used an unqualified language of subjective rights—rights of individual

---

4. Ketteler, *Sämtliche Werke und Briefe (SWB)* I, 3:71. Requiring a massive scholarly effort by editors Erwin Iserloh, Norbert Jäger, and Christoph Stoll, Ketteler's collected works and correspondence were published in eleven volumes from 1977 to 2001, They are referenced below as *SWB* followed by the volume number and page.

persons—in a political context aware of the American and French revolutions with their unequivocal rights catalogues.

Fourth, Ketteler's practical reasoning—prudence—was ordered towards a theologically informed conception of human dignity and the common good. He sought prudential paths—corduroy roads—to deal with this period's social challenges. This prudence was theoretically rooted in a natural law framework informed by Roman law jurisprudence of the historical school and his own reading of Aquinas's *Summa Theologica*.

Fifth, Ketteler's resourceful participation with representational forms of government demonstrates the rich potential for the church in public life where religious freedom is constitutionally protected. His social action took place in a context of an increasingly secular public discourse where Catholics were a minority in the national structure formed in 1870 Germany. Ketteler confronted threats from the political left attempting to privatize religion and from the right that tried to subsume church activities within state supervision. He identified religion as politically essential while respecting structurally independent realms for church and state.

Ketteler's Early Life

As a priest and member of the 1848 Parliament in Frankfurt, Ketteler voted to abolish aristocratic privileges and advocated extending legal protections to all social minorities. Nevertheless, he was the product of German aristocracy, and his political worldview was shaped by pre-Enlightenment values. He was raised in a hierarchical context where sortal differences (such as social class) were considered part of the natural order. This worldview shaped his relationships, his career paths, and informed his understanding and expectations of family, church, society, and political structures. His capacity for prudence served him well as he transformed ecclesial engagement in an emerging democratic public sphere.

He was born on Christmas day in 1811 in Munster, Westphalia, and christened Wilhelm Emmanuel von Ketteler. As a biographer notes, Emmanuel—anointed one—was a fitting name for an exceptional son of minor Westphalian nobility.[5] Personal letters reveal aristocratic ideals of purpose, duty, and order, and they glowingly describe his parents's principles of stewardship, their immaculately run house, the modesty of their

5. Vigener, *Ketteler*, 7.

table, and the works of charity they performed for their own servants as well as local poor. Because young Wilhelm struggled to acquire these virtues for himself, he was sent in 1824 to a Jesuit boarding school in Brig, Canton Wallis, Switzerland.[6] The Jesuit order, re-established in 1814, had preserved their reputation for humanizing youth during the years of suppression and Ketteler himself credited the Jesuits with instilling discipline. He remained loyal to the order during his tenure as bishop.[7]

Correspondence with family demonstrates the strong will and passions of an ambitious man with aristocratic pretensions. Not an academic overachiever, his letters reveal an assumed noble status that required a suitable *Bildung*—the German ideal of a well-rounded intellectual, moral, aesthetic, and physical formation. He enjoyed the benefits offered by his social situation and was an avid hunter.[8] Hunting identified Ketteler with an aristocratic status that distanced him from liberal ideals and manners. For a young nobleman, Catholic or Protestant, it was the activity that signified passage into a politically charged adult society.[9] Ketteler's discernment for the priesthood in Munich was as influenced by his hunting acquaintances and contacts as by the group of Catholic intellectuals striving to revitalize the German church, the Görres circle (*Görreskreis*).

Westphalian nobles, according to Ketteler's critical biographer Vigener, were rooted in their rural districts, their histories, and their minor privileges and dignities. Disinclined to move into the cities, they preferred "to rule a little rather than be ruled."[10] Of Ketteler's biographies, Vigener's (1924) is the most thorough and the most unsympathetic work, arguing over 750 pages that Ketteler's great influence was marred by his misapprehension of liberalism.[11] Vigener mocks Ketteler's traditionalism as archaic and scorns noble privileges as unmerited, yet he argues that Ketteler's life was plainly shaped by his birth. His noble status distinguished him from emerging bourgeois classes despite his family's modest

---

6. Bolten, "Watch, Pray, Fight," 35. Bolton's biographical material builds upon Pfülf, *Ketteler*.
7. Bolten, "Watch, Pray, Fight," 36. See also *SWB II*, 1:135.
8. Berdahl, *Politics of the Prussian Nobility*, 73.
9. Bolten, "Watch, Pray, Fight," 41.
10. Vigener, *Ketteler*, 4.
11. Hogan, "Ketteler's Interpretation," xiii.

estate; more important for social status and career was a twelfth-century family lineage.¹²

While embracing their Westphalian traditions, Ketteler's immediate family were pragmatic in adapting to new circumstances.¹³ Napolean's campaigns brought the French Civil Code, followed by Prussian rule after the treaty of Vienna (1815). Though possessing an estate in Harkotten, the father adapted to the new situation by becoming a civil officer (*Landrat*) for the newly established Prussian government in nearby Warendorf.¹⁴ The key to this family background is that Wilhelm Emmanuel inherited an aristocratic and Catholic identity together with forward-looking prudential capacity.

University: In Göttingen, Berlin, Heidelberg, and Munich (1829–33)

After Brig with the Jesuits, Ketteler began university in 1829 at Göttingen with a goal of entering Prussia's civil service like his father Friedrich¹⁵ and older brother Clemens.¹⁶ For this career path, his Catholic identity was less important than his social status (*Stand*).¹⁷ This section details three aspects of Ketteler's university experience that locate him within the political and intellectual crosscurrents of the broad German-speaking regions.

First, he studied at four advanced German universities with diverse philosophical and religious perspectives. Göttingen had a famous law faculty that included Jacob Grimm and Gustav Hugo. Grimm (who with his brother also assembled folk tales) was a Germanist, a legal historian, and close Savigny associate.¹⁸ Hugo was a nationally recognized legal scholar.¹⁹ Ketteler was well positioned in Göttingen to prepare for an administrative career until a fraternity dueling injury forced a move. Officially forbidden by university and church, dueling was considered

12. Elias et al., *Germans*, 63.
13. *SWB I*, 5:2n1–2.
14. Vigener, *Ketteler*, 8.
15. Bolten, "Watch, Pray, Fight," 26.
16. Bolten, "Watch, Pray, Fight," 41.
17. Berdahl, *Politics of the Prussian Nobility*, 73.
18. Wieacker, *History of Private Law in Europe*, 322–23.
19. Reimann, "Nineteenth Century German Legal Science," 848.

an honorable activity for university men. The risk of punishment posed no obstacle for Ketteler who, like Bismarck, received his Schmiss or scar as a mark of honor at Göttingen.[20] The code of honor trumped the laws of state and religion. The dual that resulted in a lacerated nose was instigated by a modest slight of honor; someone had stepped on his toe.[21]

Ketteler's transgression motivated his move from Göttingen to Prussia's capital Berlin where the renowned Friedrich Carl von Savigny taught jurisprudence.[22] While the brutal graft surgery to repair his nose may have distracted Ketteler, he left no record regarding G. W. F. Hegel, who was also teaching in Berlin at the time. Rather, the two semesters of legal study in Berlin deepened an appreciation for Savigny and the historical philosophy of Romanticism.[23] After Berlin, Ketteler moved to another center of Romantic philosophy, the university in Heidelberg,[24] where he also studied "conceptual jurisprudence" (*Begriffsjurisprudenz*) taught by constitutionalist Anton Thibaut (1774–1840).[25] After having experienced a range of legal approaches, Ketteler moved to the re-established university in Munich for courses in church law with Eduard Joseph von Schmidtlein and George Phillips.[26] Finally, in 1832, Ketteler returned to Berlin and attended the lectures of jurists, including Eichhorn (a legal historian) and Homeyer (a Germanist). Eichhorn was famous for his work in establishing the historical school, and Homeyer earned a name by publishing an edition of the *Sachsenspiegel*—the ancient law source that functioned in German law analogously to the United Kingdom's *Magna Carta*. Thus, Ketteler had firsthand experience of diverse theological, political, and legal movements during this exhilarating German intellectual period.

A second aspect of Ketteler's education worthy of note was the historical focus of his academic work: his legal studies were from the start historically oriented and integrated with theological and ecclesial interests. In Munich, for example, he studied church-state issues and canon law with Schmidtlein and Philips.

---

20. From Elias et al., *Germans*, 65.
21. Bolten, "Watch, Pray, Fight," 42. Bolton quotes Pfülf, *Ketteler*, 1:28.
22. On Savigny, see Sheehan, *German History*, 548–50.
23. Discussed at length in O'Malley, "Currents."
24. O'Meara, *Romantic Idealism and Roman Catholicism*, 56.
25. Pfülf, *Ketteler*, 1:32.
26. Pfülf, *Ketteler*, 1:32.

Thirdly, Ketteler's concluding academic work in law demonstrates his abilities and inclinations to defend minority-groups in terms of individual rights. The work's long title shows Ketteler's preferred topics and methods: "A Survey of the General Principles Followed by the Prussian State in Governing the Jews and Mennonites since the Year 1815 and the Legal Condition of These Religious Groups in the Administrative District of Munster."[27] Here, he precisely addressed the rights of two religious minorities within the legal structure of the Prussian state.

With an education that included three predominantly Protestant universities, Ketteler experienced religious diversity and the most influential legal theorists of the nineteenth century. There wasn't much scholasticism. Instead, the context included Kantian and Hegelian views and, in Munich, Catholic scholars fully engaged in wider continental and specifically German-language scholarship.

From Prussian Bureaucracy to Cologne Conflict (1833–38)

Ketteler's university experience prepared him for an administrative post in the Prussian bureaucracy.[28] The Prussian legal system had undergone reforms, but remained a complex matrix of overlapping legal jurisdictions, detailed codes, and methods.[29] In taking a position in this system, Ketteler's role was to interpret the complex law of the state, and to apply it prudentially in complex and often unique circumstances. Personal letters reveal a continuing skepticism of Prussian political intrusions, but Ketteler recognized the value of a *Rechtsstaat*—the legal framework that insured political and social order in a diverse land.

As with most civil service posts, family ties probably aided the appointment in the Prussian bureaucracy.[30] The historian Sheehan stresses that the transition of German nobility into the bureaucracy marked their conservation of social status and power, while transitioning their loyalty away from the matrix of feudal relations. For young nobles, the bureaucracy required allegiance to the state as represented by the crown.[31] Summing up, Ketteler was a typical university student, was a member of a

---

27. Hogan, "Ketteler's Interpretation," 22–23.
28. Pfülf, *Ketteler*, 1:39; Hogan, "Ketteler's Interpretation," 22.
29. Blackbourn, *Long Nineteenth Century*, 23.
30. Sheehan, *German History*, 520.
31. Sheehan, *German History*, 509.

dueling fraternity, seems to have willingly entered the bureaucracy, and was able to adapt to the social and employment pressures of the early nineteenth century. Where university preparation was theoretical, Prussian bureaucratic work was practical and focused upon applying legal reforms regarding property, taxation, military service, labor, family, and religious minorities. These reforms required legal codification and interpretation, and this was Ketteler's experience as government officer.

On November 20, 1837, the archbishop of Cologne, Clemens August Baron (*Freiherr*) von Droste zu Vischering, was jailed for refusing to recognize Prussian directives regarding mixed marriages and the education of children from such marriages. For Ketteler, this "Cologne Conflict" delegitimized Prussian rule and its Rechtsstaat principles; it revealed an underlying absolutism and enmity to the church.

Mixed marriages were problematic for Roman Catholics in Prussian-controlled regions. Pope Pius VIII's 1830 *Litteris* "granted German priests permission to accept mixed marriages up to the point of, but not including, active participation in the marriage ceremony."[32] Pope Gregory XVI's 1832 encyclical on mixed marriages, *Summo Iugiter Studio*, begins with the claim: "The Apostolic See has always ensured that the canons forbidding the marriages of Catholics with heretics have been observed religiously."[33] Gregory XVI offered the rare possibility of an exception to prevent greater evils, but, like Pius VIII before him, he offered no real path to enter a mixed marriage and remain a practicing Catholic within Prussian jurisdiction.

Droste zu Vischering had been appointed archbishop of Cologne in 1836, representing a hardening of the Vatican's position articulated by Pius VIII and Gregory XVI. Once installed, the archbishop forced a confrontation with the Prussian monarch Fredrick William III and the conflict became one between princes.[34] For German Catholics, the conflict created a wedge in national politics that continued for decades and was institutionalized in the Catholic-dominated Center Party with its struggle against Bismarck's Kulturkampf. The Catholic position, most thoroughly articulated by Görres's *Athanasius* (1838),[35] was championed by Droste zu Vischering who became a martyr and rallying point for religious and political resistance.

32. Bolten, "Watch, Pray, Fight," 71; See Pius VIII, *Litteris*.
33. Gregory XVI, *Summo Iugiter Studio*.
34. Bolten, "Watch, Pray, Fight," 65.
35. Vanden Heuvel, *Joseph Görres*, 329.

Ketteler interpreted Prussia's actions in chivalric terms, an insult to princely dignity requiring satisfaction. Private letters and later reflections link this moment to the stirrings of a religious vocation—a calling rooted in his traditional worldview. For Westphalian aristocrats like Droste zu Vischering and Ketteler, priesthood was a quite acceptable and even conventional life path; ambitions for clerical advancement within the church hierarchy was expected.

Ketteler's Priestly Preparation in Munich (1838–41)

The 1837 Cologne Conflict began Ketteler's vocational discernment, which his letters and personal notes reflect was a sincere spiritual process that continued over three years of study, travel, conversation, hunting, and ceremonial activities. In German, Italian, and Austrian locations, he made retreats, stayed in boarding houses, and was hosted by aristocratic families who shared his extended family and social networks. Correspondence topics include deliberations about property investments, the well-being of other nobles, and politics—especially church-state issues. Ketteler's letters also revel in his significant time hunting. At the end of this period, the decision to become a priest seems both spiritually and politically motivated, as was his decision to build upon his former university disciplines to prepare for the priesthood.

Roman Catholic academic theology in the first half of nineteenth-century Germany was, professionally speaking, not yet equal to the Protestant faculties, but there were encouraging advances during Ketteler's formative years. Catholic theology in German seminaries and universities had been devastated by the suppression of the Jesuits, the Napoleonic Wars, and secularization.[36] First in Tübingen and later Munich, Catholic theologians developed competence and confidence to engage Enlightenment ideas, and specifically Kantian philosophy.[37]

What was not immediately revived was the scholastic theology of the Jesuit-dominated universities of the seventeenth and eighteenth centuries. Instead, what developed was a theology that prioritized Christian Scripture and original reading of patristic and classical sources. New

---

36. O'Meara, *Church and Culture*, 3. O'Meara notes Paul Schantz's determination that German speculative theology was in a "period of decline" from 1760 to 1830. McCool's 1977 judgment is more positive, but stills calls the first few decades "rebuilding" years. McCool, *Catholic Theology*, 30.

37. See Kaplan and Vander Schel, *Modern German Theology*.

scholarship was distinguished by engagement with non-Catholic sources as well as their appreciation of historical and organic development of the church.[38] Catholic scholars emphasized a positive anthropology, human dignity, and the essential role of human reason and freedom in Christian faith. Scripture was relevance for all aspects of Christian life.[39] Catholic scholasticism, or neo-scholasticism, was revived later in the century, including in Mainz, yet Ketteler's theological approach remained close to Möhler's *Symbolik*, which best represents the concerns, interests, and advances of this intellectual period of Catholic theology.

Ketteler's correspondence after his resignation resounds with Romantic themes. For example, in 1839 he visited Cologne with its magnificent cathedral. In awe of its grandeur and size, he meditated upon his own path in terms of such existential topics as infinity, eternity, and the relative smallness of individual humans to all of God's creation.[40] Once in Munich, his focus turned to the pious life of Catholics in their religious, liturgical, and intellectual lives. He happily made acquaintance with the Görreskreis and was as impressed by their character as he had been by their articles and books.[41] Johann Joseph Görres (1775–1848), the center of this circle (*Kreis*), became a leading figure of Catholic political opposition to Prussia's action after the Cologne Conflict with *Athanasius* (1838) and later with *Church and State after the Cologne Crisis* (1842). A lecturer in Munich, he was reconciled with Rome and a recognized Catholic scholar by 1838. As leader of the Görreskreis, derisively and affectionately nicknamed *Congregatio*, he was surrounded by like-minded Catholics in Munich intent to rival the great Protestant intellectual centers.

Ketteler praised Görres's *Church and State*: "Indeed, if our king would only read such a book from cover to cover! It is written in such a way, that the truth of its argument is plainly evident. If the reader is at all open to the truth, they must be impressed by the book's presentation."[42] During Ketteler's time in Munich, he entered the inner circle of the *Congregatio* and became close friends with Guido Görres, Joseph's son and the editor of the influential Catholic journal *Historisch-Politische Blätter*. Together, they participated fully in social and intellectual movements, excitedly reading and discussing the latest important books, journals, and

38. O'Meara, *Romantic Idealism and Roman Catholicism*, 9–10.
39. See Kaplan, *Answering the Enlightenment*.
40. *SWB I*, 4:14.
41. *SWB I*, 4:14.
42. *SWB I*, 4:198.

intellectual tracts and meeting with Catholic public intellectuals such as Clemens Brentano who were drawn to Munich as a center of Catholic thought. Their ire was aimed at both Prussian centralization and liberal rationalism. Munich's Görreskreis became critically important for later political Catholicism at the 1848 Parliament and eventually for forming the Center Party which resisted Bismarck's Kulturkampf.[43]

Transition to Clerical Life (1841–44)

Prior to ordination in 1844, the social question was rarely mentioned in personal letters. Though, this was also before the years of widespread agricultural blights and famines that kindled the 1848 revolutions. What Ketteler did write about was hunting. This is a seemingly trivial point, but one that offers insight into his social class and circumstances. Hunting rights illustrate the mottled nature of Germany's reform and the continuation of feudal vestiges during the *Vormärz* period before the 1848 revolutions. In addition to hunting, Ketteler's travels provided him a privileged opportunity to observe the variety of government interventions and their relative merits. He observed economic conditions of various provinces and continued to review family business concerns and real estate prospects. Many German conservatives opposed the agrarian transition marked by the increased failure of estates and the consequent rise in land turnover.[44] For Ketteler, however, these conditions provided opportunities for his family and social circle.[45] His appraisals also included class relations, the moral state of aristocracy, but little about the conditions of the rural or urban poor.

Ketteler earnestly followed politics by reading the *Historisch-Politische Blätter*, and he sent home lengthy letters recounting new acquaintances. These included theologians, academics, and literary figures, but mostly other aristocrats. Correspondence to his sister Sophie and brother Wilderich show that the decision to become a priest was in no way a rejection of his social standing or aristocratic worldview. The letters do become increasingly pious over time with references to God's care and providence.

---

43. In the difficult internal Catholic discord symbolized by the oppositions regarding the *Syllabus of Errors* (1864) and the doctrine on infallibility (1870), Ketteler never renounced his affiliation with the theology, politics, or his Roman Catholic friends in Munich.

44. Blackbourn, *Long Nineteenth Century*, 110.

45. *SWB II*, 1:13–16.

But as much as they reference entry to a "new world," they do not suggest that priesthood meant separating himself from former activities. His pivotal vocation letter to Wilderich, for example, transitioned without pause from his vocational decision to hunting matters. Ketteler was so pleased with his favorite hunting dog, Pink, that he was taking steps to ensure the hound's progeny would provide many years of talent.[46] Ketteler's most dramatic action was his move to the city Eichstatt in the summer of 1841—yet even that move was not into a seminary, but to be close to Bishop Reisach, a central player in German church-state struggles.

Ketteler's piety was focused on action and not withdrawing from worldly concerns. His self-reported spiritual life was distinctively influenced by the *Spiritual Exercises*, a program and method of prayer written by St. Ignatius of Loyola, a Basque nobleman and Jesuit founder. Ketteler had learned from Jesuits in Brig and his praise of the Jesuits deals primarily with the value of their spiritual guidance and the order's educational competence. The Jesuit order was associated with political intrigue, papal loyalty, and neo-scholasticism, yet references to Jesuits in Ketteler's papers are mostly non-political and free from neo-scholastic language. A letter to his sister Sophie in 1841 describes his experience:

> I was moved by endless blessings by the Spiritual Exercises of St. Ignatius. From beginning to end, they are remarkable in the deep wisdom of their order and the special graces of God that the Exercises help reveal.
>
> I know of no better means than these Exercises to build a sure foundation for the spiritual life—a foundation to protect against the doubts and uncertainties that one constantly encounters in the world.
>
> And they are actually constructed for people in everyday life. They allow a spiritual period of solitude to examine and place in perspective your whole spiritual life. And afterwards, you can draw the experiences together to store up your spiritual resources for the future.[47]

Ketteler's collected works include private notes from a retreat with the Jesuits in Innsbruck in October 1841. The notes adopt St. Ignatius's courtly images and martial language. Christ is a prince/warrior who conquers the enemies of God and establishes a kingdom of justice under his banners

---

46. *SWB II*, 1:109.
47. *SWB II*, 1:184.

of justice.⁴⁸ Ketteler uses martial images even when he is reflecting on the baby Jesus in a manger. Though the retreat begins with the enthusiasm for battle, the notes gradually change focus and tone to Christian virtues of humility and obedience. Late in the retreat, he reflects on an image called "Two Standards," referencing the battle banner of Christ as opposed to that of Lucifer. This clearly martial image elicits rather introspective reflections probing Ketteler's own lack of decisiveness and commitment when choosing Christ's army over the army of the devil.⁴⁹ The grace of his retreat, he writes, is his recognition that Christ works through him, despite his unworthiness.⁵⁰ This theme can be found in his later public sermons. Similarly, the Jesuit virtue of "holy indifference," extolled in the retreat notes, confirmed his family's "noble simplicity" lifestyle virtues that characterized his widely publicized austere private life as a priest and bishop. The retreat notes finish with his conviction to become a priest. He lists his commitments regarding his daily order, including daily meditations and prayerful examinations of his life using Ignatian methods practiced during the retreat.⁵¹ His later pastoral letters to the priests of his Mainz diocese show that he held to this commitment.⁵²

Once his decision was set, Ketteler's method of entering priestly life was strikingly feudal; he sought a sponsor to whom he could swear fealty, his dedication, rather than applying himself to a local seminary or diocese. The sponsor was Karl August Graf von Reisach (1800–1869), bishop of Eichstatt and later archbishop of Munich. Ketteler conscientiously sought an official introduction to Reisach and socialized with him at aristocratic banquets, such as one hosted by Prince Lowenstein with the nuncio also present.⁵³ Once acquaintance had been made, Ketteler revealed his desires and qualifications to be a priest, and then he placed his future in the bishop's hands.⁵⁴ This personal fealty crossed diocese lines and assumed primary importance in Ketteler's priestly formation and career right up until he was elected bishop of Mainz in 1850. Reisach shared Ketteler's aristocratic background and political outlook and was deemed just the right leader during "these troubled times in the German

---

48. *SWB I*, 5:11. Ketteler's notes from *Spiritual Exercises*, October, 1841.
49. *SWB I*, 5:15.
50. *SWB I*, 5:20.
51. *SWB I*, 5:21.
52. *SWB I*, 5:337.
53. *SWB II*, 1:63.
54. *SWB II*, 1:109.

church's history."⁵⁵ Reisach had also studied law in Göttingen before entering the priesthood and, unlike Ketteler, earned a doctorate before moving to Rome for theological training. He then worked in the Vatican curia for some years and was squarely marked as a prominent conservative ultramontane. It was Reisach who delivered Pope Pius VIII's message to Droste zu Vischering in 1837 approving a confrontational path with the Prussian government.⁵⁶ In September 1841, Ketteler was invited into Reisach's personal orbit in Eichstatt, sharing the bishop's table and assisting with episcopal duties.⁵⁷

When the bishop turned his attention to Ketteler's priestly training, however, several complications emerged. Ketteler did not have the standard structured academic preparation for the seminary system. He was older than most seminarians, and his character, talents, and interests required a more personalized arrangement. Reisach first proposed a complete course of seminary studies at the Jesuit-run Roman College.⁵⁸ Ketteler declined this path. Bolton suggests that Reisach, ever the diplomat, probably understood the doubly negative associations that a Roman and Jesuit education would pose for Prussians.⁵⁹ The Passau seminary was also floated as a more local and conventional possibility. That too was rejected and instead Ketteler returned to Munich with the determined ambition for an accelerated priestly preparation.⁶⁰ Bolton suggests that Reisach's support for Munich was influenced by his own imminent move there.⁶¹

Ketteler's return to Munich brought him back to the intellectual and political center of German Catholicism and his close friends. He also returned to Munich as a cleric after years of uncertainty since the Cologne Conflict. With his outward bearing in clerical attire now reflecting his inner identity, Ketteler wrote to his brother that he finally felt himself to be a whole man.⁶² His professors were peers he already knew well. They were Ignaz von Döllinger (1799–1890) for church history, George Phillips (1804–72) for canon law, Max von Stadlbaur (1808–66) for moral

---

55. *SWB II*, 1:62.
56. Bolten, "Watch, Pray, Fight," 73.
57. *SWB II*, 1:63.
58. *SWB II*, 1:143.
59. Bolten, "Watch, Pray, Fight," 102.
60. *SWB II*, 1:187.
61. Bolten, "Watch, Pray, Fight," 102.
62. *SWB II*, 1:181.

and dogmatic theology, and Franz Xaver Reithmayr (1809–72) for Scripture.[63] His spiritual mentor and confessor during these years was exactly Ketteler's age and a professor of canon law and Scripture, Friedrich Windischmann (1811–61).[64]

Ketteler's letters during this period deal less with political topics. They are pious, familiar, and curiously introverted during this time that Sheehan describes as, speaking of political activity, "particularly intense in Prussia's western provinces, where regional loyalties, lingering confessional antagonisms, and popular hostility to official economic policies combined to feed a broad opposition movement."[65] The letters remain focused upon topics of study, contentment with his present life of study, and joy that his brother Richard joined him in priestly studies. Vigener describes Ketteler's developing religious and political worldview as a shift in focus from Westphalia to Rome, citing an unpublished essay from 1841 that bore the influence of Klee's *Dogmatik*.[66] The handwritten document idealizes the medieval world where king and pope were like "twin brothers" wielding the swords of state and church according to a divine plan.[67] The twin pillars supporting the foundation of the Christian German states were shifted by the Protestant Reformation's priority of the ego (*Ich*) as the source of all authority. Once shifted, the pillars have finally fallen and the implications for both society and church are severe, as humanity and not God becomes the measure of all things. This is a classic Romantic critique of Protestantism and the Enlightenment, and the essay's message was to be aware of the signs of the times (*Zeichen der Zeit*) to protect against present storms.[68]

Returning to Westphalia in 1843, Ketteler finally spent some time in a regional seminary, in Munster, and was ordained in 1844. He then began a three-year assignment in nearby Beckum, where his attention was finally drawn to realities of poverty and social injustice, and where he founded a hospital.[69] Subsequently appointed pastor in Hopsten, Ketteler encountered profound deprivation and suffering due to the enduring

---

63. *SWB II*, 1:187n6.
64. *SWB II*, 1:210.
65. Sheehan, *German History*, 627.
66. Vigener, *Ketteler*, 42.
67. *SWB I*, 5:56.
68. *SWB I*, 5:59.
69. *SWB II*, 1:243.

famines and social unrest prior to the 1848 revolutions. The passion and focus of 1848 and later writing show the impact of those years.

Revolutionary 1848 and Ketteler's Sermons on the Social Question

After three years of agricultural disasters and resulting famines, revolutions ignited throughout Europe in 1848—three decades after the Congress of Vienna. For German Catholics, the unrest was met warily and without enthusiasm for popular sovereignty. Nevertheless, the church could no longer see itself as a "perfect society" with its bishops as princes on equal terms with the secular powers. Understanding the advantages of legal recognition of the church as a corporate body with legal protections, Catholics—including priests and bishops—participated in political processes and proceedings of the 1848 Frankfurt Parliament. The wider church had not yet embraced democracy as a public good, yet this participation performatively accepted the elected parliament's legitimacy and the rights that popularly elected body sought to constitutionally anchor.

By the fall of 1848, revolutionaries abandoned the democratic processes lacking the support from Prussia's Frederick William IV and gathered with increasing menace outside the parliament doors. Gathered mobs found encouragement from parliament liberals using threats of popular violence to support reform policies. Tensions boiled over when labor-conditions legislation was voted down and two conservative delegates were killed, one of whom had been a pivotal voice against the bill.[70] This ignited wider unrest that focused nationwide attention upon the public funeral of the two victims. Ketteler was among the speakers who, with open graves before him, addressed both the social problems that had given cause to the rioters's anger, and the violence that he argued could not resolve social injustice.

In stirring words, he praised Enlightenment ideals and contrasted those ideals to radicalism and murderous violence. People ought to desire freedom, equality, unity, fraternity, and wish to raise the condition of the poor, but liberalism's marginalization of religion brought moral slavery, disparities of wealth, social conflict, and violence. The poor are not helped but are reduced to conditions of servitude and idleness by liberal social policies. He argued for the continuing wisdom of the Christian

---

70. Hogan, "Ketteler's Interpretation," 38.

Gospel.⁷¹ Without Christ, the utopian ideals of the Enlightenment are unrealizable in the political and social realms. Published and distributed in pamphlet form, this funeral oration—*Leichenrede*—earned him widespread respect among Catholics and Protestants as a forthright defender of Christian values and political moderation.⁷²

Fourteen days later in an address to assembled Catholic associations, Ketteler balanced the *Leichenrede*'s sometimes ominous fusion of religious, social, and political matters in three ways: First, he defined freedom in a way that removes the church from any official state function. Second, he expressed respect for Protestants and offered a path for reconciliation that implicitly excluded the use of any state office or function for accomplishing that aim. Thirdly, he designated the social question (*Sozialfrage*) as the most important issue for the church. That means that the church's public activities ought to directly benefit the poor—to witness through service. In his organic social model, he envisioned a strong and independent church, a strong and independent state, and constitutionally preserved freedoms for both protected by rights. He stressed the human need for a full social life that required the values, beliefs, and most importantly the sense of meaning provided by religion. Therefore, he rejected the liberal understanding of freedom that radically fenced off religious from political aspects of social life.

First, regarding freedom, Ketteler boldly claimed that religion has nothing to fear from it. In fact, the true power of the church could be best demonstrated in a situation of complete freedom.

> When one has seriously examined the present situation, one must confess, that when the people do not return to religion, then it can bear no freedom. Only the church, Christianity, makes possible humanity's fullest freedom. We need not shrink from any free institution in the state when we are firmly established in religion.⁷³

He rejected institutionalizing the church in any state office. The separation of church and state was preserved insofar as, simply, one rules and the other worships. Notably, he also rejected the strict marginalization of church from political discourse.

---

71. *SWB I*, 1:15.
72. Bolten, "Watch, Pray, Fight," 154.
73. *SWB I*, 1:18.

Secondly, his admittedly triumphalist language is balanced by his respect for Protestant members of the Frankfurt Parliament. And it is balanced by the arena he chooses for churches to demonstrate the truth and strength of their beliefs. He never advocates the use of state power for denominational advantage such as an official state church or a continuation of political power for religious officials such as the prince-bishops exercised before the secularization in 1803. Rather, quoting Scripture, he claims "by their works will you know them." He explicitly advises against doctrinal disputes in favor of tangible demonstrations of love. Only the practical and concrete actions of love will dissolve the causes of Christian divisions.

Thirdly, in a point related to the second, he balances the *Leichenrede*'s potential heavy-handedness of church involvement by specifying just how the church should be involved in politics. It should be involved on the level of analysis and critique, of course, but also on the moral level by advocating policies that help the poor. The Sozialfrage is urgent; that is where churches should demonstrate their worth and their possession of truth.

Ketteler's burgeoning reputation led to an invitation to deliver Advent sermons in Mainz's Cathedral, a short trip from Frankfurt. Titled "The Great Social Questions of the Present," the six sermons outlined his broad social theory based upon Thomistic natural law philosophy.[74] Though philosophical and socially relevant, they were also proper sermons relevant to the diocese's liturgical preparation for Christmas. They each begin with scriptural reflections and then relate the Scripture message to the life of the worshipping community and to the wider church. As Advent sermons, they prepare for the celebration of the Christian mystery of God's incarnation in the birth of Jesus Christ. Each sermon counsels the congregation to recognize God in their lives and to act in accordance with their religious convictions.

Nevertheless, the sermons are unmistakably political in their focus, intent, and structure. Ketteler marshals systematic arguments, gives history lessons, and presses the congregation to defend the church in the political forum. The structure and content of the sermons, individually and as a group, reflect the church's long tradition of natural law theory and moral catechesis. Ketteler seemed to thrive in the atmosphere of conflict, and the *Advent Sermons* are charged with a sense of urgency inspired by the threat of opposition. The *Sermons* set him on a path to

---

74. The *Advent Sermons* had many printed editions in the nineteenth century; *SWB* I, 1:22–87. Ederer prepared an English version in Ketteler, *Social Teachings*, 7–99.

higher ecclesiastical offices, a path smoothed by noble status (*Stand*) and experience as pastor. His election and interventions in the Frankfurt Parliament proved his leadership capacities, and the *Advent Sermons* launched him as a national figure and a defender of Catholic interests. His consecration as bishop of Mainz less than two years later in 1850 confirmed and institutionalized this status.

Ketteler's biographers agree that the *Advent Sermons* are fairly ordinary theologically, sociologically, philosophically, and politically. "Regarding a technical or practical solution to the social question, it is true that Ketteler's sermons in Mainz's cathedral broke no new intellectual grounds, and they offered no new approach for legislation."[75] There is also consensus, however, that when they were delivered, there was no single Catholic approach to the growing social crisis, described by the term Sozialfrage, that had spawned the revolutions in 1848. Marx and Engels seized this revolutionary moment by publishing the *Communist Manifesto*. Analogously, by so succinctly and convincingly summing up a Catholic response to the social question, Ketteler's *Advent Sermons* became a "Catholic Manifesto."[76]

Bishop of Mainz (1850–77)

Secular political approval was necessary for appointment to church offices in Prussian controlled dioceses. This was no problem for Ketteler, who served as rector of Berlin's St. Hedwig's for just a short period before being selected, approved, and installed as bishop of Mainz in 1850. Conservative credentials secured at the Frankfurt Parliament trumped potential misgivings about his defensive Catholic outlook. This 1849 recommendation to Frederick William IV for Berlin's St. Hedwig's parish shows the source and nature of national reputation:

> [Ketteler] has gained an eminent reputation for his work with the poor and suffering as well as for his preaching. He has proved his worthiness during these exceptional times as a man with resolute political character and true loyalty. As a testament to this, he proved his moral integrity and courage by his actions at the Frankfurter National Assembly . . . and especially

---

75. Bachem, *Vorgeschichte*, 2:58.
76. O'Malley, *Birth of Modern Catholic Social Thought*, 7.

at the memorial services for Prince Lichnowsky and General von Auerswald.[77]

Mainz was a relatively small German diocese, but Ketteler's influence as bishop extended well beyond the diocese during his twenty-seven-year tenure. With a defining conviction of the church's essential role for all social life, he was a leading Catholic voice in the German public sphere on social issues. His pioneering example and writings influenced the great social encyclical, *Rerum Novarum*.[78] What follows here are accounts of a select number of his writings as bishop showing his critical voice, as well as his hopes for a robust Christian Church benefiting society by living its faith. One necessary condition for a beneficial church-state relationship is a constitutionally rooted foundation of clear and enforceable rights.

Constructing Corduroy Roads for Unprecedented Social Challenges

Church historian Klaus Schatz describes the Catholic Church in Europe after the 1848 revolutions as increasingly occupied with the Vatican's struggles to maintain papal authority against threats from secular governments and from liberal intellectual movements. Representative of this defensive posture are *Quanta Cura* (1864) with its *Syllabus of Errors*, and the First Vatican Council in 1870 with its definition of papal infallibility. The church was nevertheless quite modern in identifying itself with Europe's poor using media of newspapers, petition drives, and huge gatherings.[79] Schatz notes ironically that the German church even benefited from the oppositions raised during 1848. With Rome distracted, German Catholics were left to be creative in dealing with the Prussian government. As a minority without prospects for secular power, they had no "sword" to wield. Thus, Ketteler's example is critical because, first, church-state separation was viewed positively and church leaders acting in this emerging public sphere were performatively recognizing the legitimacy of democratic discourse and representational government, if not popular sovereignty. Second, Ketteler fought for constitutional protections in the form of rights to protect the church's participation in this emerging

---

77. Vigener, *Ketteler*, 126. Quotation from the "Akten des preuss. Kultusminis." Cited in Hogan, "Ketteler's Interpretation," 43.

78. Craig, *Germany*, 63.

79. Schatz, "Phase Des Ultramontanismus," 69.

political constellation. Critically, he argued for church rights as extensions of individual rights within a legitimate state of law—Rechtsstaat. With his subsidiarity understanding of governance, Ketteler's Mainz appointment was timely in both his fidelity to the universal church and his advocacy for the local German church.

An early work that reflects his concerns is "The Law and the Legal Protection of the Catholic Church in Germany."[80] Published in 1854, it considered the Cologne Conflict still unresolved and the church still legally vulnerable. With the experience of a failed parliament and constitution in 1848, he knew that the free exercise of religion requires concretely promulgated corporate rights for the church.

Using arguments of historical jurisprudence, Ketteler traces continuities and discontinuities in church-state law beginning with the Middle Ages. The Peace of Westphalia (1648) introduced political deference for internal church affairs that lasted until 1803 when secularization broke 250 years of precedent.[81] Then, church buildings, schools, universities, monasteries, and other church properties were transferred to secular authorities. Ketteler outlines the injustice of secularization according to various categories and standards of property possession. His argument includes internal criteria of German laws regarding possession, and external criteria referencing points of universal justice as well as harms to the common good. A half-century of injured rights is charted before the focus shifts to 1850s state encroachment upon the sovereignty of the church, i.e., over the church's properly internal governance, *jura intra sacra*.[82] Ketteler argues that the church's corporate rights are expressions of member's individual rights. The Frankfurt Parliament's constitution was never promulgated, and the church was legally vulnerable to secular encroachment, so he argues using existing German legal principles. Private property was the clearest example of individual rights in German private law, and violation of intra-church independence was demonstrated as analogous to the plunders of secularization.

This may recall contemporaneous Vatican defenses of corporate rights—rights of the church, but Ketteler makes the argument using subjective rights of citizens. The document's fear of liberalism and its continuing vehemence against the French Revolution mirror papal documents. Yet *SWB* editors attribute such ultramontane language to

80. *SWB I*, 1:133.
81. *SWB I*, 1:145.
82. *SWB I*, 1:154.

aides' assistance at the time. Unique among his extant works since he dictated later works, Ketteler personally wrote this manuscript and aides Heinrich and Lennig amended that text to more ultramontane positions. We are privy to Ketteler's first-draft rights language, for example, that under the Protestant government, "the rights (*Rechte*) of Catholics had been violated"[83] by proselytization. Heinrich corrected "rights" with "the laws (*Gesetze*) of the provinces were violated."[84] In another example, Ketteler argues that the history of positive law in Protestant provinces was heavily swayed against the Catholic Church—as is supported by the "historical school of law;" Lennig changed that phrase to "history of law."[85] This is critical because later in the paragraph, Ketteler scorned the "flags of human rights"[86] that accompanied the bullets of revolutionary movements. Out of context, this could be interpreted as a scorn for all subjective rights. Yet Ketteler is pointedly critiquing liberalism while also identifying with historical jurisprudence, which fully recognizes subjective rights as potentially legitimate.

"The Law and the Legal Protection of the Church in Germany" has parallels to ultramontane concerns, and both are concerned with the church's corporate rights. The *Syllabus* (1864), for example, lists 20 paragraphs of errors regarding church rights. Nevertheless, there are differences of context, argument, and expectations in Ketteler's early 1854 work, and it was probably influenced by more ultramontane aides.[87]

A better representation of Ketteler's developed position is "Freedom, Authority, and the Church" (1862) responding to German liberals regarding the nature of freedom in terms of religious belief and practice. Here, he engages liberal thought from a more confident philosophical position in terms of his rights language—specifically referencing the rights of individuals. Ketteler essentially argues that a state which hinders the free work of the church deprives citizens of their freedom. The church, correspondingly, may not hinder the actions of the state or adopt means like physical coercion that are exclusively state measures. When expressing his conception of the proper relationship of the church to the state, he projects a remarkably modern notion of the public sphere and the role of the Catholic press to direct public opinion towards justice.

83. *SWB I*, 1:156.
84. *SWB I*, 1:156.
85. *SWB I*, 1:162.
86. *SWB I*, 1:163.
87. Müller, *Politik Kettelers*.

While the state (*weltlichen Souveränität*) is ordered towards justice, the church has the role to instill the virtues that inform justice. The care of justice in the state is defined practically and juridically.

> A principle duty of the state is to legally protect all rights, as well as the prompt and careful dispensation of justice. We are lacking greatly in this most important aspect of civil life! Under the demands of the time, there is no more important benefit, than the ability to have our rights protected by a court of law. The Catholic press must diligently work towards this end. The protection of denied rights has always been respected as one of the highest moral virtues of Christianity.[88]

This principle is central to the legal principles of the historical school of jurisprudence and Ketteler describes it in a way that would appeal to a liberal-minded public. He rhetorically claims a liberal plank for his own house, and he elevates the state's "lofty" role in creating law.[89] When the state fails in its legislative function to create good and clear laws, confusion abounds. This is compared to the perfect simplicity of the premodern German peoples's "lived" cultural law. "Our German ancestors loved the law; they had a deeply cultivated sense of the law (*Rechtssinn*) and venerable norms for their matrix of legally definable human relations (*Rechtsverhältnisse*)."[90] The rhetorical shift is noteworthy, moving from key terms of liberalism and tying them to key ideas of German historical jurisprudence. He even cites the *Sachsenspiegel*, that ancient and cherished landmark of German law.

Adolf Birke's key insight in *Ketteler und der Deutsche Liberalismus* (1971) is that Ketteler recognized value in liberal arguments concerning freedom; the church could embrace this human good. Ketteler "did not distinguish himself from the liberal Catholics of Western Europe, with whom he shared the difficulties of representing to the church a position favoring tolerance."[91] To his Catholic audience, he supported tolerance on classical theological principles. And to non-Catholics, he fought stereotypes of intolerance intensified by the *Syllabus* in 1864. Ketteler's fulcrum was his Thomistic anthropology; the human person is endowed with a

---

88. *SWB I*, 2:249.
89. *SWB I*, 2:249.
90. *SWB I*, 2:249.
91. Birke, *Bischof Ketteler und Der Deutsche Liberalismus*, 29.

conscience and a capacity for practical reason.[92] Birke argues further that Ketteler's concerns with social questions were generated by sincerely considering liberal criticisms. Contrary to Habermas's argument that religious communities, as pre-rational life-world spheres, would crumble under the scrutiny of reason, liberal scrutiny provided new life and vigor to the German Catholic Church.[93]

Ketteler's achievement was more than a shift to a modern rhetoric, though the language is key. He recognized liberalism's potential in individual rights discourse to protect aspects of human dignity historically undervalued in Catholic traditions. Rights to freedoms and human goods, such as private property, were worth supporting and benefited from Catholic traditions like Thomism and others. Relevant here is the argument Ketteler made in "Liberalism, Socialism, and Christianity" (1871), that the ideas of freedom and equality championed by liberals are not only compatible with Christianity, but are harmed without the contributions from religion.[94] Liberalism and socialism benefit from Christianity's views on justice, human transcendence, and critiques of secular state intrusions on religious and private-conscience matters. The Rechtsstaat, Ketteler argues, requires a bureaucratic structure protecting rights, an independent court of law, and laws authentically participating in justice. Ketteler quoted Aquinas's *Summa Theologica* and utilized Augustine's "Two Kingdoms" framework for these insights.[95]

Ketteler's theory of religious freedom, using a language of rights, foreshadows Vatican II's commitments. First, religious faith can never be forced, and the church can never use violence to achieve its ends. Further, individuals's right to freely choose their religious faith may not be restricted by the state. Only internally, *jura intra sacra*, does the church have rights to exercise processes of membership and leadership.[96] Ketteler applied principles of subsidiarity and rights creatively to church-state relations. Beginning with Jesus Christ, "the first right is the right of Christ,"[97] and every other right in the church is founded on this one. The

---

92. Birke, *Bischof Ketteler und Der Deutsche Liberalismus*, 32.

93. Habermas, *Between Facts and Norms*, 21. Also, Habermas *Structural Transformation*, 141.

94. *SWB I*, 4:21.

95. *SWB I*, 2:286. *Freiheit, Autorität, und Kirche*. Ketteler references Aquinas, *Summa Theologica*, I-II, q. 90, a. 1, "Treatise on Law."

96. *SWB I*, 2:309.

97. *SWB I*, 2:317.

church, without secular force to achieve its aims, is free from the state in carrying out Christ's will, and therefore it has a right to that freedom without state interference. By extension, bishops have rights within their proper spheres, as do pastors and teachers, and finally families and individuals have their rights regarding their faith in Christ. The state has *Patronsrecht*, the right and duty to protect the church, which is important but external from the central element of the church, namely belief.[98]

An example of this subsidiarity argument concerns state opposition to the Jesuit order functioning in his Mainz diocese. Ketteler argues that the Jesuits pose no specific threat to the state and so the state's exclusion of Jesuit institutions from German soil is a violation of established subsidiarity-rights principles. The bishop may exercise rights as teacher, and parents may exercise rights to educate their children in matters of faith.[99]

Similarly, the subsidiarity principle is applied to the property rights of previously secularized church lands and funds in his book *The Workers' Question and Christianity*, published in 1864.[100] His concept of private property is not absolute, but ordered to common good ends—this is a central pillar of *Advent Sermons* as well. The extra-legal acquisition of substantial church property ought not be conceded. Fifty years later, however, the principle guiding restoration is not to simply return the value, but to consider common good priorities and outcomes. The property value should be awarded to that social sphere most in need of it. The church, as impacted party, has a say in this deliberation and a right to fulfill its function, including the care for the poor. And the poor have the right to flourish in their own familial communities. Thus, given that there is already a claim by the church on the secularized property, and given the principle of subsidiarity, the property in question should be extended to the churches for the purpose of caring for the poor.

The practical and pragmatic nature of Ketteler's rights argument allowed him to reach some levels of compromise during his tenure as bishop. He stressed the need for the nation to build community virtues, and the church can aid that effort, especially in education.

Central to Ketteler's argument regarding rights was his conception of true freedom and a robust value for what we would call civil society today. Freedom, as a principle, functions within an organic social model where individuals and institutions foster practices that sustain productive

---

98. *SWB I*, 2:318.
99. *SWB I*, 2:549. From Ketteler's 1864 work "Die Jesuiten In Mainz..."
100. *SWB I*, 2:376.

conventions benefiting the common good. It is a teleological logic. Historical jurisprudence also fits with this model because history proves the worth of conventions—an idea championed earlier by Edmund Burke. In this approach, children's education is critical for civil society and Ketteler used his legal competences to advocate for parents's priority regarding responsibilities and rights. He accused the liberals of essentially colonizing education rights for the state.

The parameters of the debate were demonstrated in an 1848 exchange between Judge Thüssing and Father Ketteler. Thüssing challenged Ketteler and granted the local community (*Gemeinde*) no rights of self-regulation in schools.

> The community is only an institution which has title to existence in virtue of the state and without the state it cannot be so much as thought of. Self-government for a community is a concession from the state. . . . The state alone is the only receptacle of rights; it alone has its legal existence of its own right or from the people as a totality, but not from any community.[101]

This is a classic German liberal jurisprudence and understanding of rights stemming from the state. The state, according to this approach that emerged in late-century legal positivism, is not even subject to critical reason and universal law.[102] Ketteler countered with his own subsidiarity understanding of the state, of rights, and of how those rights emerge from and adhere in the local community; these bottom-up rights are tied to related obligations to foster a good society. Reflecting Thomistic legal principles as well, legislated and promulgated law participates in the eternal law to the extent that it is consistent with the natural law. Reflecting the historical school, tried and true laws survive over time, helping the community thrive, and thus reflect the communities' ideals. Laws may not be introduced from outside the community and especially not in ways that violate cherished values. Parents have rights regarding their children according to their role as parents; this right is holy and inviolable.[103] Ketteler argues this principle already in 1848 in a letter to his parliament constituency—also reflecting his patriarchal worldview:

> It is my leading principle, gentlemen and fathers of families, that you yourselves by divine and natural law are the

---

101. *SWB II*, 1:346.
102. Dietrich, *Goethezeit*, 22–23.
103. Stahl, *Philosophie Des Rechts*, 483.

responsible persons for your children and that you, parents, have the holy and inviolable right to decide how your children are to be educated.[104]

Ketteler's social theory informed his ideals for church-state relations as well as the church's critical voice regarding social problems. Book-length treatises addressed the suffering of low-wage laborers and he developed pragmatic proposals to protect individuals's dignity. This human dignity criteria (*Menschenwürde*) used no Kantian arguments, but rather anticipated the *imago Dei* logic of *Rerum Novarum* (§20) as well as its approvals for labor unions and collective bargaining. Ketteler's titles reflect both his concerns and approach: *The Labor Problem and Christianity* (1864); *The Labor Movement and Its Goals in Terms of Religion and Morality* (1869); *The Charitable Concern for Factory Workers, Journeymen, Apprentices, and Women Domestic Laborers* (1869); *The Sovereignty of the State* (*after 1865*); and *The Separation of the Church and the State* (1875).[105]

The arguments in these works follow a standard pattern. First, he argues for his right to speak on the issue as separate from his religious duties, and then he argues for fundamental rights of all people in terms of their dignity as human beings. For low-wage laborers, being treated as a commodity degrades the worker because the earnings do not satisfy basic human needs. Thus, there is need for minimum-level wages based upon human dignity standards. He critiques deterministic economic theories that leave workers with no practical help. "It is like the supposed friend who has pushed his comrade into the water and now stands on the riverbank concocting various theories as to how the drowning man might be saved."[106] Ketteler, in reasoning a right to a living wage, is building upon his previous writings on private property. Using prudence, he was laying corduroy roads to deal with unprecedented circumstances in real time and in the face of human suffering. Natural law arguments are mostly used when exploring minimum standards—they are based upon basic human needs and principles of human flourishing comprising the

---

104. *SWB II*, 1:325.

105. *Die Arbeiterfrage und das Christenthum* (*SWB I*, 1:367); "Die Arbeiterbewegung und ihr Streben im Verhältniß zu Religion und Sittlichkeit: Eine Ansprache, gehalten auf der Liebfrauen-Haide am 25 Juli 1869" (*SWB I*, 2:407); "Die Fürsorge für Fabrikarbeiter, Gesellen, Lehrlinge und dienstlose weibliche Dienstboten," (*SWB I*, 2:429); "Die Souverainetät des Staats," (*SWB I*, 5:373); "Trennung von Kirche und Staat," (*SWB I*, 5:388).

106. Ketteler, *Social Teachings*, 327.

common good. Private property is a principle practically derived—experience shows that it is an effective convention for achieving personal and social goods. Just as there is no inherent or timeless private property right, a living wage is discovered by prudence—justice reflects fair discernment of families's basic requirements. "It is a requirement of justice and of Christianity that the workingman is entitled to a just wage."[107] Even here he accepts variability in the application of this law: "The particular national character of a people also influences and introduces particular peculiarities into the development of the private property right."[108] The common good and human dignity are best nurtured in a society guided by Christian principles that prohibit exploitation of the working poor.[109] Countering socialist approaches, Ketteler recognized the potential value of private property rights. Countering unfettered liberalism, he embraced worker's participation in political-economic processes through laborer's associations and trade unions. Advocacy in the public sphere required the leverage provided by collective action, such as trade union's right to strike. Workers are otherwise powerless actors compared to the state and business actors. Again, these were corduroy roads of prudence guided by broad principles of justice and human dignity.

The Church's Role in a Modern Public Sphere

Prussian-led military forces decimated the Austrian army in July, 1866, forcing a battlefield retreat and exclusion from the new German nation in 1870. The resulting "small Germany" solution left Catholics as a minority in the Prussian-dominated state formed after the Franco-Prussian war in 1870. Birke describes Roman Catholic reactions as ranging from disappointment to enthusiasm. Bismarck's political reality was achieved through military strength—blood and iron—which also characterized his chancellorship lacking popular, legal, and political accountability. Bolton argues that Ketteler nevertheless achieved significant freedom for the church in his own diocese despite challenges of Prussian absolutism.

Birke notes that the convergence of Prussia's successful bureaucracy, army, and politics inspired religious interpretations of historical events. The defeat of Austria was seen as a victory for Protestantism,

---

107. Ketteler, *Social Teachings*, 444.
108. Ketteler, *Social Teachings*, 361.
109. Ketteler, *Social Teachings*, 398.

which was destined to unite the German nation by sublating—Hegelian idea—the Catholic Church in a new German Church.[110] Prussian rulers had long held wildly unrealistic ideas of a unified German Christian church under the Hohenzollern crown. In an atmosphere of distrust and vulnerability, Ketteler published "Germany after the War of 1866." His recommendation, true to form, was to ensure continued freedom of the Catholic Church in a nation under Prussian leadership, but limited by the insurance of constitutional limitations. Regarding recent wars, Ketteler attributed equal blame to realpolitik Prussians and hubristic Austrians blocking German national hopes. He argued that absolutism was the great threat to justice, absent constitutional and political limits.[111]

The encyclical *Quanta Cura* raised German concerns in 1866, so Ketteler needed to defend the principle of religious freedom and the Catholic Church's rights in the same breath.[112] He argues that German unification was bringing together people of diverse cultures and religious faiths. Yet unification requires rights protecting religious freedoms and supporting toleration as a public good—the freedom to believe.[113] This is a quite modern notion of tolerance and was an attempt to steer a middle path before the First Vatican Council. Ketteler went to the bishop's conference in Fulda to prepare for the council with a letter to Pope Pius IX containing a plan to deal with social problems in Germany and was quickly forced to abandon it.

> The signs of the times, it appears to me, call for me to put forward the principles of justice and love, whereby the different classes in the human community might be able to join in a common life, the rich and poor, the aristocratic and the worker.[114]

The legitimacy of his system required a public face that reflected the reality of the church's deepest claims. Ketteler was concerned with spillover effects from Catholic Rome's ideological and secular struggles addressed at the First Vatican Council, 1870, and epitomized in its doctrine of infallibility.[115] Ketteler defended the essentially theological claim, publicly and privately. Still, the council's difficult reception in Germany underlines the

110. Birke, *Ketteler und Der Deutsche Liberalismus*, 73.
111. Birke, *Ketteler und Der Deutsche Liberalismus*, 73.
112. *SWB I*, 2:75.
113. *SWB I*, 2:36.
114. *SWB I*, 2:113.
115. Bolten, "Watch, Pray, Fight," 302.

interconnected nature of the church and state in Europe. Ketteler's course was one of moderation and compromise, insuring the wrath of zealots on both sides. Ultramontanes thought Ketteler was caving to liberal pressures. German conservatives and liberals (joined together in the period of national consciousness under Bismarck) considered Ketteler a threat to the new nation's full political integration.

Conclusion

Ketteler's writings on political and theological issues represents a significant early Catholic engagement with modern forms of representational and constitutional governments and theories. He was a consummate political pragmatist with a keen awareness of legal practice and political theory. He addressed and respected many liberal critiques of the social, economic, and political order, but he unequivocally rejected the individualistic and atomistic premises of the liberal political theory he encountered in Germany. He acknowledged and learned from the social analyses from the left,[116] but in response to the staunch secularism of liberalism, he argued that religion was necessary to reform the tragic social conditions that plagued Germany as it transitioned to an industrial market economy. His own position was both traditional in holding to natural law conceptions and pioneering in reading Aquinas's text in the original and creatively adopting its prudential methods for social challenges. His approach was influenced by Romantic philosophical insights and the related historical school of jurisprudence. His primary source of inspiration was his Christian faith, and as German jurisprudence shifted to a legal positivism that unreflectively supported absolutist-state policies in the newly formed German nation, Ketteler recognized and condemned the dangers.

His 1848 *Advent Sermons* made his signs-of-the-times analysis widely known. And Ketteler's delivery of these words is probably relevant to its initial enthusiastic reception. He must have been a charismatic public speaker. As for the text itself, it acknowledged Aquinas's authoritative natural law teaching—analogous to the great tomes of Roman law for the jurists. This approach was also analogous to Savigny's historical jurisprudence in that Ketteler put aside the centuries of scholastic gloss to

---

116. Lasalle was the most prominent of the socialists whom Ketteler addressed. For Ketteler's dealings with Lasalle, see Vigener, *Ketteler*, 506, 543–45.

appreciate the original historical texts. In the thirteenth-century *Summa Theologica*, Ketteler found resources to deal with social questions (Sozialfrage) facing the church in the nineteenth century because Aquinas's work contains wisdom that transcends the medieval context. The wisdom is partially theological, concerning God's nature and God's revelation to humanity through Christ. The wisdom is also philosophical, concerning the potentials and limitations of human understanding. Essential for Ketteler were Aquinas's distinctions and relations of theology-to-philosophy, first principles-to-action, and wisdom-to-prudence. Well-trained in Aquinas's system, Ketteler had the confidence to cut corduroy roads for social action.

The liberalism of nineteenth-century Germany that Bishop Ketteler opposed was distinct from other European lands (especially England, France, and Italy), but still shared rationalist presuppositions and a secularizing agenda. Maritain's language to describe liberal rights theory reflects a Catholic suspicion that Ketteler would share:

> A person . . . is subject to no other laws than those which he (either alone or jointly with others) gives to himself.' . . . This philosophy built no solid foundations for the rights of the human person, because nothing can be founded on illusion . . . it led men to conceive them as rights in themselves divine, hence infinite, escaping every objective measure, denying every limitation imposed upon the claims of the ego, and ultimately expressing the absolute independence of the human subject and a so-called absolute right.[117]

Classical natural law, on the other hand, locates its philosophical roots in Aristotelian moral theory, building on its teleological eudaemonistic framework and its reliance upon practical reason for discerning the human good in robust political deliberation. Aquinas is the constant referent for the Catholic version of classical natural law, and his *Summa Theologica* is the single most authoritative textbook of its moral theory.[118] The fact that this is a theological book should not be overlooked, for while St. Thomas maintained the distinction between the natural and the supernatural, human "nature" is most authentically understood in

---

117. Maritain, *Man and the State*, 83. Maritain quotes from Kant's *Introduction to the Metaphysics of Morals*, IV:24.

118. The most relevant passages of Aquinas's *Summa Theologica* for the modern question regarding subjective rights are: I-II, q. 91, a. 1–3; q. 94, a. 1, 4–5; q. 96, a. 1–2; II-II, q. 42, a. 1, 2, 7; q. 66, a. 2.

terms of its divine origin (humans are creature of God), its capacities imaging God's being (the intellect and the will mirror God knowing and loving, if incompletely), and its ultimate purpose (resting in God). That said, the natural law may be summarized as a moral-realist philosophical approach that begins with the ontological and anthropological claim that there is a common and essentially social human nature.

Classical natural law holds that humans are intelligent beings ordered to "the good" with an intrinsic rational capacity to discern their personal goods—including happiness—and in communities to discern the common good. Because the faculty of practical reason is limited, however, by deficient understanding and disordered personal and social wills, social order relies upon civil government to foster the good life and protect society from threats to the common good. In this, the state uses positive law (the promulgated laws of the state) to foster the ends of natural law, though with the obvious caution that "human law does not prescribe concerning all the acts of every virtue,"[119] and the law cannot prohibit every vice.[120]

Ketteler's published works reflect Maritain's insights, and especially the nature and importance of practical reason. The binding principles of natural law are not derived in pure abstraction but are developed in the lived experience of reasonable people in history. In sum, the natural law is essentially historical and thus necessarily dynamic, but it is also inherently rooted in traditions of reasonableness; its principles by participating in truth are abiding.

Bibliography

Aquinas, Thomas. *The Summa Theologica*. Translated by Fathers of the English Dominican Province. New York: Benziger, 1947.

Bachem, Karl. *Vorgeschichte, Geschichte, und Politik Der Deutschen Zentrumspartei: Zugleich Ein Beitrag Zur Geschichte Der Katholischen Bewegung Sowie Zur Allgemeinen Geschichte Des Neueren und Neuesten Deutschland, 1815–1914*. 9 vols. 2nd ed. Aalen: Scientia, 1927.

Berdahl, Robert M. *The Politics of the Prussian Nobility: The Development of a Conservative Ideology, 1770–1848*. Princeton: Princeton University Press, 1988.

Birke, Adolf M. *Bischof Ketteler und Der Deutsche Liberalismus; Eine Untersuchung Über Das Verhältnis Des Liberalen Katholizismus Zum Bürgerlichen Liberalismus in Der Reichsgründungszeit*. Veröffentlichungen Der Kommission Für Zeitgeschichte. Reihe B, Forschungen; Bd. 9. Mainz: Matthias-Grünewald, 1971.

---

119. Aquinas, *Summa Theologica*, I-II, q. 96, a. 3.
120. Aquinas, *Summa Theologica,*. I-II q. 96, a. 2.

Blackbourn, David. *The Long Nineteenth Century: A History of Germany, 1780–1918*. New York: Oxford University Press, 1998.

Bolten, Analouise Clissold. "Watch, Pray, Fight: Wilhelm Emmanuel Ketteler as Priest-Politician." PhD diss., George Washington University, 1983.

Craig, Gordon A. *Germany, 1866–1945*. New York: Oxford University Press, 1978.

Dietrich, Donald J. *The Goethezeit and the Metamorphosis of Catholic Theology in the Age of Idealism*. European University Studies; Series 23: Theology. Berne: Lang, 1979.

Elias, Norbert, et al. *The Germans: Power Struggles and the Development of Habitus in the Nineteenth and Twentieth Centuries*. Translated by Eric Dunning and Stephen Mennell. New York: Columbia University Press, 1996.

Gregory XVI. *Summo Iugiter Studio*. https://www.papalencyclicals.net/greg16/g16summo.htm.

Habermas, Jürgen. *Between Facts and Norms: Contributions to a Discourse Theory of Law and Democracy*. Translated by William Rehg. Studies in Contemporary German Social Thought. Cambridge: MIT Press, 1996.

———. *The Structural Transformation of the Public Sphere: An Inquiry into a Category of Bourgeois Society*. Translated by Thomas Burger and Frederick Lawrence. Studies in Contemporary German Social Thought. Cambridge: MIT Press, 1989.

Hogan, William Edward. "The Development of Bishop Wilhelm Emmanuel von Ketteler's Interpretation of the Social Problem." PhD diss., The Catholic University of America, 1947.

Kaplan, Grant. *Answering the Enlightenment: The Catholic Recovery of Historical Revelation*. New York: Crossroad, 2006.

Kaplan, Grant, and Kevin M. Vander Schel. *Oxford History of Modern German Theology*. Vol 1, *1781–1848*. New York: Oxford University Press, 2023.

Ketteler, Wilhelm Emmanuel. *Sämtliche Werke und Briefe*. Edited by Erwin Iserloh et al. 11 vols. Mainz: von Hase und Koehler, 1977–2001.

———. *The Social Teachings of Wilhelm Emmanuel Von Ketteler: Bishop of Mainz (1811–1877)*. Translated by Rupert J. Ederer. Washington, DC: University Press of America, 1981.

Krieger, Leonard. *The German Idea of Freedom: History of a Political Tradition*. Boston: Beacon, 1972.

Maritain, Jacques. *Man and the State*. Charles R. Walgreen Foundation Lectures. Chicago: University of Chicago Press, 1951.

McCool, Gerald A. *Catholic Theology in the Nineteenth Century: The Quest for a Unitary Method*. New York: Crossroad, 1977.

Misner, Paul. "The Predecessors of *Rerum Novarum* within Catholicism." *Review of Social Economy* 49 (1991) 444–64.

Müller, Klaus. *Die Staatsphilosophischen Grundlagen Der Politik Kettelers*. Munich: University of Munich Press, 1963.

O'Malley, Martin J. "Catholic Rights Discourse in Nineteenth-Century Germany: Bishop Ketteler Protected Religious and Social Freedoms from the Equal Threats of Secularizing Liberalism and Anti-Catholic Absolutism." PhD diss., Boston College, 2007.

———. "Currents in Nineteenth-Century German Law and Subsidiarity's Emergence as a Social Principle in the Writings of Wilhelm Ketteler." *Journal of Law, Philosophy, and Culture* II 1 (2008) 22–52.

Social Catholicism for the Twenty-First Century?—Volume 1

———. *Wilhelm Ketteler and the Birth of Modern Catholic Social Thought: A Catholic Manifesto in Revolutionary 1848*. Edited by Nikolaus Knoepffler. Ta Ethika 7. Munich: Utz, 2009.

O'Meara, Thomas F. *Church and Culture: German Catholic Theology, 1860–1914*. South Bend: University of Notre Dame Press, 1991.

———. *Romantic Idealism and Roman Catholicism: Schelling and the Theologians*. Notre Dame: University of Notre Dame Press, 1982.

Pfülf, Otto. *Bischof von Ketteler (1811–1877): Eine Geschichtliche Darstellung*. 3 vols. Mainz: Kirchheim, 1899.

Pius VIII, *Litteris*. March 30, 1830.

Reimann, Mathias. "Nineteenth Century German Legal Science." *Boston College Law Review* 31 (1990) 837–900.

Schatz, Klaus. "Die Phase Des Ultramontanismus (1850–880)." In *Vorlesungen: Katholische Kirche, Liberalismus und Demokratie*, 69–115. Munich: Munich School of Philosophy, 2001.

Sheehan, James J. *German History, 1770–1866*. Oxford History of Modern Europe. New York: Oxford University Press, 1989.

Stahl, Friedrich Julius. *Die Philosophie Des Rechts*. Vol 2.1, *Rechts- und Staatslehre Auf Der Grundlage Christlicher Weltanschauung, Die Allgemeinen Lehren und Das Privatrecht*. 4th ed. Heidelberg: Mohr, 1870.

Vanden Heuvel, Jon. *A German Life in the Age of Revolution: Joseph Görres, 1776–1848*. Washington, DC: The Catholic University of America Press, 2001.

Vigener, Fritz. *Ketteler: Ein Deutsches Bischofsleben Des 19. Jahrhunderts*. Munich: Oldenbourg, 1924.

Wieacker, Franz. *A History of Private Law in Europe: With Particular Reference to Germany*. Translated by Tony Weir. New York: Oxford University Press, 1995.

4

Johnny versus Tommie
What We Can Learn from a Historical Controversy

Martin Schlag, University of St. Thomas

Abstract: Starting from Joseph Ratzinger's pronouncements on the relationship between the Church and modernity, this chapter takes up the historical controversy between German-American conservative proposals of social reconstruction and Irish-American progressive reformers to shed light on contemporary challenges. The key point of reference is the natural law, which concerns our ability to grasp the right reason that rules and measures human action and thus the social realities shaped by it. The chapter proposes a revival of the natural law tradition along the lines of Pope Francis's pastoral hermeneutic of evangelization. Such a hermeneutic spreads the faith while at the same time struggling for social justice. Natural law, as it is traditionally understood in Catholic social thought, is itself part of the Christian intellectual tradition. Christian humanism, in the past, imbued our culture with the values of human dignity, equality, and freedom. The chapter argues that inserting natural law into an explicitly Christian discourse will preserve the above-mentioned values as secular ones. Every generation has its own "modernity," characterized by social movements that question and challenge the Christian vision of man and woman. Our own twenty-first century seems to be on the way to becoming a century of anti-humanism, in contrast to the twentieth century that was one of atheist humanism. Reviving natural law and thus Christian humanism will provide good answers to the questions of modernity.

Introduction

Critical Reserve

IN 1965, THE SECOND Vatican Council published its Pastoral Constitution *Gaudium et Spes*. Its full Latin title is *De Ecclesia in Mundo Huius Temporis*. In literal translation into English this title means "The Church in the World of 'This Time,'" or, in the official version, "The Church in the Modern World."

Several things are significant and noteworthy in this title. For one, the Pastoral Constitution speaks of the Church *in* the world, not the Church *and* the world, or Church and State, as earlier documents might have done. This is not only a terminological shift. Whereas Leo XIII and the magisterium up to the Second Vatican Council had seen the relationship between the Church and society as a relationship mainly between the popes and the "princes," or legislators—a top-down relationship—the Council sees the relationship as a bottom-up or inside-out operation carried out by all God's People. Christians are leaven in the world which they are called to sanctify by exercising the three offices of Christ (priest, prophet, king, or queen) in their secular activities. By sanctifying the world in their secular activities, Christians themselves are sanctified.

More noteworthy, however, is the question that Joseph Ratzinger asked ten years after the end of the Second Vatican Council: What is meant with "modern world?" What is "world" and what is "this time," what is "modern" about it?[1] Ratzinger notes that the Pastoral Constitution does not define its concept of world but uses the expression in a pre-theological sense. The world is simply something that exists vis-à-vis the Church. It is that with which the Church wishes to enter into dialogue and edify. "World," so Ratzinger, seems to mean the sum of all technical, scientific, social, and political elements that had brought about and were shaping modernity. As a kind of Counter-Syllabus or Anti-Syllabus, *Gaudium et Spes* aimed at replacing the Church's critical reserve against modernity with the conviction that the Church needs to join forces with

---

1. Ratzinger, "Kirche und Welt," 395–411.

it. "Contemporary world" means, so the Bavarian theologian thinks, "the spirit of modernity."[2] "The Church in the contemporary world" meant a Church that had finally razed the bastions of its fortresses and come out of the ghetto to embrace modernity with optimism. What was then an affirmation of today seemed to guarantee a brighter tomorrow. In the West, this opening was received euphorically as the long-awaited acknowledgment of the Enlightenment and of liberalism. However, this was not the exact intention of the council but a one-sided interpretation of its decisions. As Joseph Ratzinger wrote, such a belated embrace of modernity cannot constitute true progress in the Church of the future.

In Latin America, *Gaudium et Spes* was received very differently. The Church there had no reason to aspire to enlightened liberalism as a system of hope. Economic and political liberalism were too closely associated with capitalism and the USA to be attractive. Rather, the reception of *Gaudium et Spes* in Latin America led to the development of the theology of liberation.

Mutual Rapprochement of Church and Modernity

Thirty years later, in 2005, the same Joseph Ratzinger, recently elected Pope Benedict XVI, found more positive words for modernity.[3] The Second Vatican Council brought about a long overdue reconciliation of the Church with modernity, especially with the modern state, modern science, and other religions. This reconciliation was possible thanks to a historical process of mutual rapprochement between the Church and modernity, particularly political liberalism. Benedict XVI picks religious liberty as an example of an apparent discontinuity of church doctrine before and after the Council. In reality, so Benedict XVI thinks, there has been continuity in the principles and discontinuity in their application according to a hermeneutic of reform. In the case of religious liberty, the Church rediscovered her origins by reconciling with modernity.[4]

Some months before this address and his election as pope, Joseph Ratzinger had given a speech in Subiaco,[5] in which he praised some in-

2. Ratzinger, "Kirche und Welt," 400.
3. A more nuanced approach can already be observed in his interview with Vittorio Messori in 1985: Ratzinger and Messori, *Ratzinger Report*, 27–37.
4. Benedict XVI, "Address to Curia Offering Christmas Greetings."
5. Ratzinger, "Europe in the Crisis of Cultures," 355.

dispensable innovations of the Enlightenment: human rights, religious freedom, division of power, popular sovereignty, etc. At the same time, he proposed an enlarged concept of reason that could save the social achievements of the Enlightenment from self-destruction, a concept of reason that remained open to faith and revelation. In an inversion of Hugo Grotius's famous adage, Ratzinger invited his atheist fellow citizens to live "as if God existed." I consider this to be a central point of Ratzinger's intellectual legacy: the wish to preserve the positive achievements of the Enlightenment by opening its concept of reason to faith.

Interestingly, Ratzinger does not include economic liberalism among the movements with which the Church reconciled at the Second Vatican Council, or those that are worth preserving. It took the Church longer to accept economic liberalism than political liberalism, and it seems Ratzinger himself never accepted it. In 1986, e.g., he dismissed the economic "tradition inaugurated by Adam Smith"[6] as irreconcilable with a vision that integrated ethics into business life. The tradition based on Adam Smith is capitalism and political economy, quite an important chunk of modernity.

Capitalism, democracy, the Enlightenment: these are central concepts for the United States of America. Modernity, defined by these three elements, is closely linked to the United States. America was an important place of gestation of the Church's contemporary stance toward modernity. The Church's flourishing in this country under a regime of religious liberty was an important reason for the Council's Declaration *Dignitatis Humanae* on religious freedom, drafted by the American Jesuit John Courtney Murray. So, in a certain way, we could rewrite the title of this chapter as "God and the American political and socioeconomic experiment." The "modern world" in *Gaudium et Spes* is the world after World War II, in which America emerged as the undisputed leader of the free world. In the decades after the Second Vatican Council, we have been cured of any undue optimism that might have inspired the Council Fathers. Nevertheless, without naiveté I think we should maintain the attitude of openness to modernity in a spirit of dialogue. We can find God in modernity, in the hearts and consciences of people. To be precise: we can find God in the questions and challenges—not necessarily in the answers—our culture and its expressions supply. It is up to the community of believers to find and act on answers inspired by Christian

---

6. Ratzinger, "Church and Economy," 200.

humanism. This need is not recognized by certain conservatives who sometimes reject slogans and policies that are not in accordance with Christian anthropology without sufficiently taking into account the underlying questions and providing answers to them.

To give an example, some time ago, I presented a paper on "diversity, equity, and inclusion (DEI) in the Catholic social tradition" at an international conference on business ethics. I was trying to explain how the concept of diversity had been understood over the past decades, the problems it addressed, and which interpretations contradicted Catholic anthropology. I was surprised that the comments during the Q&A session denied the need for anything called DEI because we already had the principle of human dignity. This was disappointing because I had tried to explain that DEI addressed issues that had not been given sufficient attention in the past.[7] Some progressives, in contrast, try to heal diseases with therapies that are actually not solutions for, but symptoms of, the illness. The example that comes to mind here are applications of so-called critical theory to social problems like racism and gender inequalities. I would suggest that we need to replace critical theory with critical thinking. Critical thinking is a specific way of exercising reason. It means distinguishing well, questioning assumptions until we are satisfied that we have come as close as humanly possible to truth. Critical thinking assumes that action is based on truth and measured by it. Critical theory, in contrast, is an aspiration to power. It assumes that all structures of society are hidden oppression that deserve to be destroyed. Truth, for critical theory, is the outcome of action. Truth is created to conform to the will of the group that claims to be oppressed and victimized.[8] Structures of power can indeed be unjust. However, authority and just social structures created over time, when exercised for the good of individuals and communities, are liberating and stabilizing. As Edmund Burke already pointed out, "our liberty becomes a noble freedom" through "conformity to nature" and respect for our institutions.[9] The power of government, but also the seemingly-ominous influence of all other social pressure groups, media, lobbies, etc., is limited by institutions that have withstood

---

7. For unsettling illustrations of some of these issues, see Alexander, *New Jim Crow*; Stevenson, *Just Mercy*; Zimring, *When Police Kill*, 41–73; Bowen and Bok, *Shape of the River*; Boyle, *Tattoos on the Heart*.

8. See Mering, *Awake, Not Woke*, 102–3. See also McWhorter, *Woke Racism*, in particular 71–76.

9. See Burke, *Reflections on the Revolution in France*, 34.

the tide of time, are inherited from our ancestors, and tried by experience to serve the common good. Prime among these institutions is the family. This is why efforts to "liberate" people from the constraints of the family ultimately harm those critical theory purports to help. Unfortunately, many progressives have become true believers in this self-defeating creed.

As someone who grew up and lived most of my adult life in Europe, I find American culture to be a fascinating, churning cauldron of ideas and innovations. People here seem to me to be very receptive for ideas that appeal to them and tend to immediately put them into practice even in quite extreme ways, publicly and at considerable personal expense. People here are educated to express their opinions openly. It comes as no surprise to me that America has also been a place of tension and controversy on God and modernity. In the title, I have tried to capture this tension in a historical example, which I explain in the next section, in a cipher. "Johnny" stands for St. John's University in Collegeville, Minnesota, traditionally an institution of higher education associated with German-American Catholics; "Tommie" for the University of St. Thomas in St. Paul, Minnesota, traditionally linked to its founder Archbishop John Ireland and the Irish Catholics.

A Historical Example

Conservative Reconstruction vs. Progressive Reforms

I have come across a fascinating tension, centered on our topic, between the German-American Catholics, organized in the Central Bureau and the Central Verein, and progressive Americanists, like John A. Ryan, who were mainly of Irish origin. This is sufficiently far behind us so as not to be emotionally charged and can thus help illustrate underlying principles.

German Catholic immigrants to the U.S. formed the German-American Catholic association Central-Verein in 1855, which published its own bilingual German-English journal in St. Louis, *Central-Blatt and Social Justice*.[10] Under the intellectual leadership of Frederick P. Kenkel and Fr. William Engelen, SJ, who was a disciple of Fr. Heinrich Pesch, SJ, and his school of solidarism, these German-American Catholics were both conservative and critical of the American economic system. Usually, we would assume that a conservative social ethicist would endorse

---

10. Gleason, *Conservative Reformers*.

the American economic system. In the case of the editors of *Central-Blatt and Social Justice*, however, conservatism led them to defend and uphold the American Constitution and its founding values, while at the same time strongly criticizing the American economic system and culture of the time, which they considered incompatible with Catholicism.[11] Liberalism was their enemy, and thus so was its economic expression, capitalism. Engelen and Kenkel associated capitalism with individualism and selfishness and dreamt of a return to a medieval society structured by corporations. Corporations united all members of a profession or a state in life in one organization, independently of whether they were owners or mere apprentices, fully professed religious or novices. The classical example is the guild. In the imagination of the social romanticists of the nineteenth and twentieth centuries, the medieval corporations worked together harmoniously under the leadership of the clergy without class struggle or strife. All were building up the body of political society, which was meant to reflect the Church as Mystical Body of Christ. *Central-Blatt and Social Justice* is full of articles that demand both a radical change of heart and a radical reconstruction of the structures of the economy. Reforms to the existing system, like those proposed by Ryan and the National Catholic Welfare Council, seemed to *Central-Blatt and Social Justice* as mere band-aids that did not go to the heart of the matter: the structures.[12] Even though John A. Ryan was an early contributor to the *Central-Blatt and Social Justice* and there was no open conflict, their conservatism brought the authors in the *Central-Blatt and Social Justice* into tension with the reforming John A. Ryan. An example is the Child Labor Amendment to the U.S. Constitution in 1924. It successfully passed both Houses, but to this day was ratified by only six states. It gives the Union the power to regulate, limit, and forbid the labor of persons under eighteen years of age. John A. Ryan forcefully supported the amendment and its ratification. Frederick P. Kenkel, the editor in chief of *Central-Blatt and Social Justice* and its *spiritus rector* for over forty years, opposed the amendment because it would infringe on the rights of the States. Kenkel recognized that the defense of states' rights, in principle, is an essential element of American federalism. Although the principle can be

---

11. See Curran, *American Catholic Social Ethics*, 103, 125.

12. See Engelen's final lengthy series of articles for the *Central-Blatt and Social Justice* (henceforth *CBSJ*) entitled "Social Reconstruction." It starts in *CBSJ* 17 (1924) 184–85 in thirteen installments. Installment number 13 is split into five. So, in all there are seventeen pieces. The last is *CBSJ* 19 (1926) 219–20. See also Curran, *American*, 111.

used to thwart justice—after all, it was invoked to maintain slavery in the Southern States before emancipation—Kenkel rejected the proposed amendment to preserve federalism. He saw that the federalist principle of states' rights is an important part of the division of power built into the Constitution that keeps central power in check. The system may need calibration and balancing to adjust to new challenges, but in light of subsidiarity the principle should not be abandoned. His arguments reveal a profound knowledge and love of the American Constitution and of political philosophy.[13]

What the editors of *Central-Blatt and Social Justice* thought of John A. Ryan becomes apparent in a note on personalia in the very last volume of the bilingual journal in September of 1939. This note must have escaped Charles E. Curran, who qualifies the relationship between *Central-Blatt and Social Justice* and Ryan as "interesting." What follows goes beyond even the Minnesotan semantics of "interesting." The note in *Central-Blatt and Social Justice* copies a paragraph of an editorial in the *Catholic Record* of Toronto covering the dinner held in honor of John Ryan in Washington, DC:

> Msgr. Ryan holds a theory of economics which is highly disputable, that there is too little spending and too much saving, that with less capital there would be more prosperity. With his customary forthrightness Msgr. Ryan reaffirmed his theory at the Washington dinner. American Catholics are not given to debating with each other. Those who disagree with Msgr. Ryan keep silent, just as those who disagree with Father Coughlin keep silent.[14]

Even though the tightly knit group of German-American Catholics was isolated both from non-German Americans and from non-Catholic German immigrants and had little practical impact, Charles E. Curran praises them: "In a very creative way they combined their Catholicity, their conservatism, and their critique of American society. By insisting that social reform involves both a change of heart and a change of structures, they made a lasting contribution to the ongoing dialogue about Christian social ethics in the United States."[15] This movement came to an end during the two World Wars. German-Americans were assimilated.

---

13. *CBSJ* 18 (1925) 114–16; *CBSJ* 18 (1925) 150–52.
14. *CBSJ* 32 (1939) 198–99.
15. Curran, *American*, 129.

Since then, German and American national traditions have been going their own separate ways, and German influence on American Catholic social ethics is small.

The USA, in contrast to Germany and to all other parts of the world, is a unique case for the Catholic Church. Here, she was never either friend or foe. The political regime of religious liberty (First and Fourteenth Amendments) favored the expansion of the Catholic Church throughout the country. Nevertheless, despite the Church's growth, in America Catholics always were and still are a minority. From very early in the history of this country, the Catholic hierarchy and theologians, once they existed, sided with the poor, the marginalized, the workers, and immigrants. The reason is simple: the Catholics, be they German, Irish, Italian, Poles, or from whatever other nationality, were largely poor immigrant workers, not accepted by the WASP majority; a situation that changed in the 1960s. Thus, concern for Catholic faithful meant concern for the workers' plight. The poor then and now need support.

Catholics were excluded, however, from the Protestant institutions of mutual support and education; frequently, this was also in the interest of the Catholic mentality of the time that sought to preserve the Catholic faith of immigrants by denominational segregation. Ecumenism is a later movement. Catholics, therefore, created their own institutions of social concern, education, and mutuality or insurance. Despite this segregation, or perhaps even because of it, Catholics always felt that they had to defend their American identity and their openness to the principles of American political society in the face of the Protestant accusations that they depended on a foreign political power. American Catholics had to prove to the Protestant Americans, the original settlers, that they too were true Americans. The prominent and outspoken Catholics of this bent were called "Americanists" or "liberals." Archbishop Ireland is a well-known representative of this current. Aaron Abell stresses that American Catholic liberalism was not only patriotic, but also "social and ethical in origin and purpose and was not to be confused with the theological movement bearing the same name in the Protestant world."[16] The Americanists increasingly became social reformers, in particular after the financial crisis of 1873. The reforming Catholics, like Ireland and Ryan, because of the social and ethical meaning of the word, did not object to the tag liberal, even though by today's standard their firm

---

16. Abell, *American Catholicism and Social Action*, 97–98.

position for Christian marriage and against contraception would place them in the conservative camp. By the standards of the late nineteenth and early twentieth centuries, they were "progressives." Progressivism at that time meant something very different from what it means today.

According to Abell, progressivism became a middle class—and thus politically effective—movement, when young, industrious men woke up to a country in which success through work had become difficult because of capitalist monopolies and monied privileges. The working class found their way upwards barred by plutocracy. Progressive politicians, in reaction, spoke out against the banking system and for more direct democracy, diffused ownership, trade unions, and farmers' bureaus. On the social side, progressives campaigned for the prohibition of child labor, limited working hours, just wages, and, in general, protection of labor. They found surprising support among the Catholic liberals. The Catholic social reformers of the Progressive Era, like John A. Ryan, "the Right Reverend New Dealer," saw many of these demands realized by the reforms introduced by FDR and the New Deal. In contrast to the conservative reconstructionists, the Catholic liberal social reformers made concrete and practical proposals that were nevertheless audacious and radical, as Msgr. Ryan's demands for workers' rights, unionization, and a living wage through a minimum wage. His demands frequently implied strengthening federal power to implement the reforms but did not reject capitalism as such. The reconstructionists, in contrast, were increasingly detached from reality, dreaming of the Middle Ages as a supposedly Christian ideal, whereas the modern capitalist, liberal, individualistic, and selfish economic system filled them with disgust.

It is interesting to note that the attitude of rejecting capitalism as such seems to be more frequent now in America than it is in Germany. The tables seem to have turned when we consider that distributism, despite its English origin, is mainly an American phenomenon, or the surveys that show that a substantial portion of millennials in the USA are skeptical of capitalism. In the USA, there have been attempts to keep the intellectual legacy of Heinrich Pesch, SJ, solidarism, alive.[17] Solidarism is an attempt to construct an economic theory on principles of Christian philosophy and Catholic social thought. In the words of the late Rupert J. Ederer:

---

17. See Ederer, *Heinrich Pesch on Solidarist Economics*. Rupert J. Ederer also translated other books by Heinrich Pesch and published on "Christian Economics."

Roman Catholic popes are not in a position to devise new economic or social systems; Pesch, as a trained economist, however, was, and that is precisely what he sought to accomplish by his work. On the basis of his social philosophy termed *solidarism*, he went on to develop an economic system called the *solidaristic or social system of human work*. It was designed to alleviate what the Jesuit scholar saw as the devastating effects of economic liberalism in the capitalistic order, and to avert the preposterous alternative suggested by Marx and his followers. Sometimes referred to as a 'third way' since it steers between the excesses and flaws in two alternative systems, the solidarist system nevertheless stands on its own principles and offers a separate and distinct approach to organizing an economic system.[18]

In the eyes of solidarists, striving to reform the "rotten capitalist system" would be nothing but a waste of time. I am not aware of any attempts in Germany to revive solidarism. In that European country, in contrast, social market economy has created a safety net for all that allows people to participate in free (though regulated) markets without questioning the market economy as such.[19] There are hardly calls for complete reconstructionist alternatives, but rather for reforms, mainly to ensure clean energy and other ecological goals, as so many social goals have already been achieved.

What can we learn from the historical tension between reconstructionists and reformers in America for today? Obviously, the lessons to be learned are indirect. Much of what was extremely controversial in the past was accomplished in the sense of the reformers, e.g., through the New Deal legislation of the 1930s. However, the Johnnie vs. Tommie division and what it stands for remains of considerable interest in the contemporary political climate, in which the Democrats hope to usher in a new era of "social democracy" more along the lines of European

---

18. Ederer, *Heinrich Pesch*, viii.

19. After and already during World War II, a group of German economists saw the urgent need to return to a free market economy without, however, leaving social concerns unattended, which could have again led to totalitarianism. They devised a system that created a legal framework ("*Wirtschaftsverfassung*") regulating competition but not interfering with the markets, while at the same time ensuring basic needs of the population. This system was successfully implemented after the War and is associated with the post-war "German economic miracle." The concept of "social market economy" has come to mean different things over the decades. It has been used by social democracy to defend massive redistribution efforts by taxes resembling more a Keynesian mixed economy, or social democracy than the original conception after the Second World War intended. See Koslowski, *Social Market Economy*.

models, whereas the Republicans would repeal much of that legislation, for instance the Affordable Care Act, rather privatizing Social Security and deconstructing the administrative state. Someone like myself, who has moved to the United States from Europe, is startled by the divisiveness and polarization of the American political scene, the eruptions of violence, and the seeming incapability of both parties to talk with each other. The post-war liberal consensus seems to have given way to political sectarianism. Robert D. Putnam and Shaylyn Romney Garrett describe these social developments in their book *Upswing*. The main thesis of this book is that there is a surprising constancy in the graphic representation of the statistical analysis of a series of trends: namely, the rise and fall of economic equality, the move from political tribalism to comity and back again, the escape from isolation to solidarity and the loss of solidarity in society, and the defeat of individualism by community spirit and then its opposite. All of these phenomena can be represented in an inverse U-curve that starts to rise around 1900 with a short inverse blip in the roaring '20s (a return to individualism) right up to its peak in the early 1960s. After that, the curve descends to the low levels of community spirit that characterize our age just as they characterized the Gilded Age. The authors call this the "I-We-I curve." Its continuous assent from the Gilded Age to the progressive era (as mentioned above, with a slight downtick in the 1920s) was suddenly halted around the year 1967, when everything abruptly changed. The authors compare this cultural movement to a flock of birds that unexpectedly and unpredictably changes the direction of its flight without a clear cause. The authors cannot establish a causality for the I-We-I curve but rather propose a narrative. In all data they examine—economic inequality, political comity, cultural attitudes, associationism, religious congregationalism and donations, race and gender advances—economic inequality lags behind the other changes. Thus, while some might be tempted to see the driver of this phenomenon as economic inequality, what seems to be driving change is culture. Culture is a central theme for Catholic social thought.

What could Catholic social thought contribute to a climate of social friendship and neighborliness? Is there anything relevant for today's polarized social climate in the old debate between the conservative reconstructionists and the progressive reformers? I think it is significant that both sides of the debate justified their demands with arguments based on natural law. Natural law was and is an important source for Catholic social teaching and thought as well as for Christian ethics in general. A new, revived form of natural law in social ethics could be the element to be taken from the Tommie vs. Johnny debate. Thus, I now turn to the topic of natural law.

Revival of Which Natural Law Tradition?

Historical Consciousness vs. Historical Hermeneutic

Before the Second Vatican Council, which is the era in which the Johnny vs. Tommie debate took place, Catholic social teaching used natural law in a deductive way. This so-called "neo-scholastic natural law tradition" implied that some premises, which were considered certain either because they were revealed principles or evident to reason, could yield conclusions that were also certain. E.g., the government must protect the truth; the Catholic religion is the only true religion; therefore, the government must protect the Catholic religion. Marie-Dominique Chenu unmasked this kind of reasoning in Catholic social teaching as an ideology aimed at recovering the political power the Church had lost in the course of modernity. Explicitly taking up Chenu's ideas, Charles E. Curran proposes a modified form of natural law, which he attributes to the Second Vatican Council, and which he calls "historical consciousness" or "historical mindedness." Curran invokes Bernard Lonergan as author of this expression. Curran explains that historical consciousness goes beyond historical hermeneutic. As Curran understands it, historical hermeneutic recognizes the fact that, in the development of Church doctrine, unchangeable transtemporal principles are applied differently in varying historical circumstances. Historical consciousness, in contrast, "cannot accept the notion of truth as something that objectively exists 'out there,' apart from history and the subject and expressed in unchangeable propositions."[20] And again he invokes Lonergan who, according to Curran, "regards historical consciousness not only as recognizing historical change but also as involving differentiation of subjective human consciousness. Lonergan saw the teaching on religious liberty as well as the new developments in Vatican II in general precisely in terms of historical consciousness."[21]

---

20. Curran, *Catholic Social Teaching*, 58.
21. Curran, *Catholic Social Teaching*, 59.

This is not the place to investigate Bernard Lonergan's methodological insights and their relevance for Catholic social thought. My overall impression is that Lonergan tells us what must be overcome, what is obsolete, what is deficient in past theological approaches. He opens up theology for a daring new beginning but does not show where this should lead. For him, theology should be more like a riverbed than a dam: "when the natural and human sciences are on the move, when the social order is developing, when the everyday dimensions of culture are changing, what is needed is not a dam to block the stream but control of the river-bed through which the stream must flow."[22] He insists on method and conversion but, honestly, the fruits of this attempt have been bitter. Lonergan in his time could still presuppose the existence of a diffused Christian culture. This no longer is the case. To stay within the image he uses: the water seems to have dried up, the riverbed is empty, there is no water to channel. Might it have been better to build a dam in order to hold some of the water for times of drought? In Germany, the churches are empty but still, at public universities, culturally adapted theologians produce dubious publications that do little to support the faith. We now need a hermeneutic of evangelization that struggles for social justice but also shares the faith, as Pope Francis has been pointing out.[23]

A hermeneutic of evangelization strives to bring the Catholic faith to normal men and women in this world of today, to the "people on the streets."[24] Its aim is not to change the doctrine of the Church but to find new forms and expressions of the faith that address the real questions and sensibilities of the people. It therefore presupposes listening to the people it wishes to help. Pope Francis has described this effort in different ways, "synodality,"[25] "accompaniment,"[26] "dialogue,"[27] all of which express the pastoral approach necessary for sharing the faith with tenderness. Theology has an important role to play in this effort. I agree with Lonergan that we need to distinguish between religion and theology.[28] Religion is necessary for salvation; theology is not. However, theology is thinking and developing the faith in the light of the faith and in the community

22. See Lonergan, "Future of Thomism," 46.
23. See especially Francis, *Evangelii Gaudium*.
24. See Delgado and Sievernich, "Zur Rezeption," 15–32.
25. Francis, "Address of His Holiness Pope Francis for the Opening of the Synod."
26. See Francis, *Amoris Laetitia*, nos. 223–43.
27. See Francis, *Evangelii Gaudium*, nos. 110–29, 238–58.
28. See Lonergan, "Theology in Its New Context," 51.

of the Church. Theology, rather than simply repeating magisterial texts, is an ecclesial service that can and should make religion and faith more intelligible. Of course, the hierarchy teaches religious truth; the theologian faithfully reflects on the religious fact. However, theology is not only the result of religion, but also of culture.[29] Each new cultural context shapes how the faith needs to be communicated and thus shapes theology. In this sense, while there is continuity of faith before and after the Second Vatican Council, there can and perhaps should be discontinuity in theology.

As I have already noted, Benedict XVI's address to the Roman Curia in 2005 contains an interesting hermeneutic of reform. By distinguishing between the continuity of perennial principles and the discontinuity of their application, he cuts a kind of *via media* between continuity and discontinuity. I think we can expand this hermeneutic of reform to a hermeneutic of evangelization that helps us find God in modernity.

The Tradition of the Natural Law Tradition

In the course of this chapter, I have spoken frequently of "hermeneutics." Hermeneutic philosophy is the philosophy of interpretation or understanding. Wilhelm Dilthey distinguished natural sciences (*Naturwissenschaften*) from behavioral or human sciences (*Geisteswissenschaften*). It is the task of natural science to explain (*erklären*) the world. However, in order to understand it (*verstehen*), we need to know how the world is given to us through mediating symbolic practices, like language. Every explanation is received in the horizon of a historically situated consciousness. When we reach the limit of our explanations, we can cross that limit and reach out to new limits. However, we never reach the horizon. The horizon is what defines our world. This horizon is our consciousness determined by tradition or culture. Everything we express and think is in the horizon of our culture. Even when we cross the limits inherent in our culture, we do so inside its horizon. This is because as long as we are growing in understanding, our horizon is ever widening—or even merging with the horizons of others, as Hans-Georg Gadamer has shown is possible. For instance, when I read and understand a text, my horizon merges with that of its author. My judgments are then situated within a new horizon, a new tradition, which has been handed on to

---

29. See Lonergan, "Theology in Its New Context," 51.

me by the author. This also applies to moral judgments, which Alasdair MacIntyre has convincingly argued make sense only when situated in a moral tradition.

Usually, we refer to natural law as the basis of moral judgments and social principles and values. However, I believe that the natural law tradition itself as used by Catholic social teaching and thought is comprehensible only when embedded in a tradition. This larger tradition, which is its horizon, is that of the Catholic faith based on Sacred Scripture. For a modern legal philosopher, the whole point of natural law is that it is not linked to any faith. Rather, it is an instrument to present moral claims as purely rational, and thus universally binding for all people, of all times and places, independently of their faith and independently of whether they accept the authority of the Church as moral legislator or not. In contrast, as Jean Porter has shown, the medieval Scholastics who developed the natural law tradition saw things differently. They did accept pre-Christian elements in natural law, especially from Stoic philosophy and the Roman legal tradition. By definition, these elements were not based on Christian faith but on reason alone. However, the Scholastics understood human nature and reason as something shaped by Scripture. The Scholastics took their basic framework and the contents of natural law from Revelation.[30] Writing specifically on Catholic social thought, Porter affirms:

> Yet at the same time, they [the Scholastics] interpreted reason itself in theological and, ultimately, scriptural terms. That is why they did not hesitate to draw on Scripture as well as rational arguments in order to determine the concrete content of the natural law, and it is also why they did not attempt to derive a system of natural law thinking out of purely natural data or rationally self-evident intuitions.[31]

John Coleman points out that this was precisely what the modern exponents of natural law attempted to do, and their project seems to have failed. The distinctively modern assumption that natural law can only be

---

30. Porter, *Natural and Divine Law*, 123–41. In this chapter, I do not intend to summarize or digest the debates of the last decades on the natural law. I basically agree with Martin Rhonheimer's philosophical proposals on natural law, see, e.g., Rhonheimer, *Perspective of Morality*. I pick Jean Porter because, I think, she has brought to light the theological framework more than others in a way that shows that we cannot have the Christian values of natural law without Christ.

31. Porter, "Catholic Social Thought and the Natural Law Tradition," quoted by Coleman, "Future of Catholic Social Thought," 530.

based on non-religious reason and must be held apart from Scripture has led "to the ultimately fruitless attempt to separate a purely rational natural law from what are seen as its scriptural and theological accretions."[32] Porter, in contrast, wishes to revive the theologically informed medieval notion of natural law rather than its modern, semiautonomous, rational variant.[33] Such a Catholic natural law

> is not an exclusively or distinctly Christian tradition. Many of its elements are clearly pre-Christian in origin. Jews, secularists, and Muslims have espoused their own variants of natural law. Yet the natural law was adopted by early Christian thinkers for specifically theological reasons and transformed by its appropriation into a distinctively Christian variant of the doctrine. Thus, this Christian tradition of natural law cannot be said to generate a universally valid morality which would be instantly recognized as such by all rational persons. But neither is it so fundamentally tradition-bound as to be unintelligible to non-believers or those in other traditions.[34]

These words really resonate with me. Since the beginning of my academic career, I strove to present Christian values on secular terms. By this I mean that I was convinced that it was possible to know the moral order without mentioning God, that natural law was accessible to reason alone, that human rights were an adequate instrument for a naturally moral social order. I was moved by the wish to achieve greater communication with and acceptance by non-believers, and, honestly, by fear of exclusion and ridicule. I now think that this path is insufficient. We have been trying to present authentically Christian values, like human dignity, freedom, and equality on secular terms. I now think that in order to preserve these values as secular ones that shape secular society, we need to make their Christian origins explicit for both Christians and our secular interlocutors. This does not mean that I desire a confessional state or, even worse, an exclusion of non-Christians from the fruition of these universal humanist values. Such an exclusion would be a self-contradictory negation of the Gospel, anti-evangelization. What I mean is that the Christian values of dignity, equality, and freedom, as they exist in Western legal systems, have their roots in Christian faith. They are authentically Christian and originate in the combination of Biblical

32. Porter, *Natural and Divine Law*, 141.
33. See Coleman, "Future," 530.
34. Coleman, "Future," 530.

values with Roman law institutions. Affirming this clearly, affirming the Christian matrix of liberal political and economic institutions could win back conservatives who have become increasingly anti/post-liberal and Catholics who seem to have become discouraged from seeing modern institutions as places in which they can work for the common good.[35] In the face of abortion, transgenderism, the dissolution of marriage between man and woman as the basis of family life, and other contradictions to Christian anthropology, some Catholics are skeptical about the capacity of liberalism to heal itself and overcome its crisis.[36] The temptation is great to abandon liberalism, to align with the radical right rather than with the social encyclicals, and to fall into a dystopian world of autocracies. The question is whether we can preserve the social achievements of the Enlightenment from their self-destruction due to the exclusion of Christian revelation inherent in the scientific and philosophical models of the Enlightenment. I am convinced it is possible by reviving the Catholic social and intellectual tradition from which the notions of dignity, equality, and freedom stem.

I am aware of the fact that the modern secular values did not and do not emanate from Christian faith in an automatic fashion, as fruit would grow on a tree. In other words, Christian faith alone is not enough to produce a decent humane society. It is, I believe, a necessary but not sufficient cause. As Hans Joas[37] and Charles Taylor[38] have convincingly shown, the historical process that brought about modernity was complicated, contingent, and implied a series of transformations that frequently occurred against the power structures of the established church. This process required effort and great personal sacrifice.

The Western polities and societies have inherited the values of Christian humanism from the past, but the well whence they stem has been sealed for various reasons that originate from the culture of exclusive humanism and secularism that characterizes much of modernity. The consequence is that we are culturally running out of the Christian sap that has hitherto kept the big social principles and values alive and formative in our societies. What ensues is comparable to a soccer field

---

35. One of the merits of the book by Reilly, *America on Trial* is that it shows the implicit, perhaps accidental, Catholicism of the American Founding in contrast with the explicitly anti-Catholic French Revolution.

36. See, e.g., Deneen, *Why Liberalism Failed*; Milbank and Pabst, *Politics of Virtue*.

37. See Joas, *Sakralität der Person* (English: *Sacredness of the Person*).

38. Especially in Taylor, *Secular Age*.

from which someone has removed the goals. For some time, the players remember where they were; the rules still make sense to them. Later generations, however, forget or never knew that there were once goals; and then the rules become incomprehensible. Something similar can happen to human intellectual life, culture, and society when faith as such is excluded from the public sphere on principle. Openness to the possibility of transcendence and the unknown keeps the mind open to discover further truth—we are never at an end of knowledge. Just as faith without reason can easily become fanatic, through the explicit rejection of faith culture can turn ideological.[39]

There is very little empirical evidence for my statements because we have no example of a past godless society. Godlessness is a modern phenomenon. Cultures that chose that path either already ended in catastrophe (like the Communist countries in the East) or are about to if they do not reform (like North Korea and China). Probably, cultures without faith in God are evolutionary dead-ends: these societies do not survive. There is no reason for my life if there is nothing greater than my life that inspires me because it is true, good, and beautiful. Without truth there is no hope, without beauty no love.

Conclusion

Since the encyclical *Quadragesimo Anno*, at least, the papal magisterium has used expressions like social justice and social charity, solidarity, and integral human development to describe its vision of a just and humane society structured by "relational liberalism."[40] Recent documents speak of fraternity and social friendship,[41] integral ecology,[42] and a new solidary humanism[43] that includes the whole planet. In the ebb and flow of the social movements characterized by the I-We-I curve, the Catholic Church

---

39. See Benedict XVI, "Meeting with the Representatives of British Society."

40. John Coleman uses the expression "communitarian liberalism," characterized by "a particular set of shared understandings about the human person, social goods, and their distributive arrangements." He rightly points out that "social Catholicism cannot survive without the discovery or creation of a new bearer of that tradition." Coleman, "Future," 527. We have tried to present our vision of relational liberalism in Schlag and Maspero, *After Liberalism?*

41. See Francis, *Fratelli Tutti*.

42. See Francis, *Laudato Si'*.

43. See Francis, *Laudato Si'*, nos. 141, 181.

has consistently upheld the need for social concern and compassion. Right at the zenith of community spirit, in the mid-1960s, the Second Vatican Council published its Pastoral Constitution *Gaudium et Spes*, and it does so too at the nadir we are experiencing by defending integral and solidary humanism. The twentieth century was characterized by the insurgence of atheist forms of humanism. Communism, National Socialism, anti-dogmatic liberalism in different ways glorified the human being without God. The twenty-first century, in contrast, seems to be the century of anti-humanism. Deep ecology, the rejection of "speciesism," the movement to grant legal personhood to animals, plants, and inanimate objects affect the moral and legal status of the human person. This movement could turn against man and woman by further confusing the notions of human rights and human dignity. A new Christian humanism that is built on human stewardship for our common home, not mere co-creationality, is necessary to adequately reflect the fact that only humans are endowed with reason and free will. Our spiritual soul is the seat of our unique dignity and responsibility as humans. It is the source of moral agency that is capable of discerning the moral considerability of animals, biodiversity, and the whole of God's creation with which we are in relation.

A revival of the tradition of Catholic social thought focused on addressing the key challenges of the day requires, I think, a new era of personal witness: a generation of Christians who live their faith in public unapologetically without, however, expecting recognition by the cultural and intellectual elites and without aspiring to power or domination over others.[44] This can be a lonely project. However, whoever embarks on this faith-driven mission of cultural transformation of a society can rest assured that reason illuminated by the Christian revelation is more reasonable than mere reason without faith. Faith, in the Christian understanding, is not opposed to reason in the sense of a contradiction or privation. The so-called strictly supernatural mysteries of Christian faith, like the Holy Trinity or the Incarnation of Christ, exceed what human reason can discover or know on its own, but that does not imply that they are meaningless or completely impenetrable. Quite to the contrary, they are unfathomable truths that human reason can never exhaust. We can derive more and more knowledge from them. Revelation is a light in human reason that cannot be "proven" in a scientific sense but shines in the

---

44. *Deus Caritas Est* makes the following important remark: "Catholic social doctrine . . . has no intention of giving the Church power over the State." See Francis, *Deus Caritas Est*, no. 28.

life of Christians. Christian ethics is the art of making Christ's redemption verifiable, visible, tangible for those who do not believe. Authentic Christian life is naturally attractive because grace does not destroy nature but heals, perfects, and elevates it. This attraction is what Pope Francis places at the center of his pastoral hermeneutic of evangelization. He does not want "proselytism," but attraction. In the skeptical and even hostile environment of modern Western societies, Christians need to be witnesses to faith who confess their personal belief that Christ is their Redeemer; that he lived, died, and rose from the dead for them; and that he is alive and active in their lives now. This life shows itself in charity and openness to others. Christ himself linked the notions of charity, unity, and credibility: "I pray not only for them, but also for those who will believe in me through their word, so that they may all be one, as you, Father, are in me and I in you, that they also may be in us, that the world may believe that you sent me."[45] These words define the proof of Christ's divine mission and tie it to our mutual love. In order to present Christ to the world, Christians need to be his true icon, not his caricature.

The Christian tradition of natural law can support this task on the intellectual level. One of its important principles is the goodness of creation, the *prima facie* assumption that what exists is good. This is compatible with the realism of knowing that human persons are sinful and social institutions are, at the least, ambiguous. They require constant maintenance not to become unjust or oppressive. The conviction of the goodness of creation and the ambiguity of social institutions constitutes the hermeneutic horizon that enables us to find God in the contemporary world, the society and culture of today. Christians who live in the world are constantly confronted with claims, proposals, and affirmations that either contradict or ignore Christian anthropology. Every spurious and wrong answer in our culture, however, is an answer to a real and true question. A Christian witness should not reject any of these answers a priori and in a knee-jerk reaction but should ask what the real underlying issue is and how Christian ethics could shed light on it. Diversity, equity, and inclusion, transgenderism, homosexuality, the legalization of drugs, and many others that already exist or will enter the scene in the future, are examples of challenges to Christian anthropology that we must address in a warm-hearted but clear and firm way. God is simultaneously

---

45. John 17:20–21.

truth and love,[46] a difficult and at times strained relationship. The big questions and challenges of our times, the signs of the times, are God knocking on our door, the door of modernity, waiting for us to let him in. Each one of us has their own path to follow. Theologically grounded arguments of natural law, expressed with the personal experience of believing in and loving God, could be a path worth reviving. Returning to the thinkers mentioned in the historical section of this chapter, the path trodden by John A. Ryan, not every step but the overall direction, seems to me to be the right one: reform not rejection of modernity on the basis of the Christian tradition of natural law.

Bibliography

Abell, Aaron I. *American Catholicism and Social Action: A Search for Social Justice, 1865–1950*. Garden City, NY: Hanover, 1960.

Alexander, Michelle. *The New Jim Crow: Mass Incarceration in the Age of Colorblindness*. 10th anniversary ed. New York: New, 2020.

Benedict XVI. "Address of His Holiness Benedict XVI to the Roman Curia Offering them his Christmas Greetings." https://www.vatican.va/content/benedict-xvi/en/speeches/2005/december/documents/hf_ben_xvi_spe_20051222_roman-curia.html.

———. *Deus Caritas Est: On Christian Love*. Vatican City: Libreria Editrice Vaticana, 2005.

———. "Meeting with the Representatives of British Society, Including the Diplomatic Corps, Politicians, Academics, and Business Leaders: Address of His Holiness Benedict XVI." https://www.vatican.va/content/benedict-xvi/en/speeches/2010/september/documents/hf_ben_xvi_spe_20100917_societa-civile.html.

Bowen, William G., and Derek Bok. *The Shape of the River: Long-Term Consequences of Considering Race in College and University Admissions*. 2nd ed. Princeton: Princeton University Press, 2000.

Boyle, Gregory. *Tattoos on the Heart: The Power of Boundless Compassion*. New York: Free, 2010.

Burke, Edmund. *Reflections on the Revolution in France*. Oxford: Oxford University Press, 2009.

Coleman, John A. "The Future of Catholic Social Thought." In *Modern Catholic Social Teaching: Commentaries and Interpretations*, edited Kenneth R. Himes, 522–44. Washington, DC: Georgetown University Press, 2005.

Curran, Charles E. *American Catholic Social Ethics: Twentieth-Century Approaches*. Notre Dame: University of Notre Dame Press, 1982.

———. *Catholic Social Teaching, 1891–Present: A Historical, Theological, and Ethical Analysis*. Washington, DC: Georgetown University Press, 2002.

Delgado, Mariano, and Michael Sievernich. "Zur Rezeption und Interpretation des Konzils der Metaphern." In *Die großen Metaphern des Zweiten Vatikanischen*

---

46. See John 14:6; 1 John 4:7–21.

Konzils: Ihre Bedeutung für heute, edited by Mariano Delgado and Michael Sievernich, 15–32. Freiburg: Herder, 2013.

Deneen, Patrick J. *Why Liberalism Failed*. New Haven: Yale University Press, 2018.

Ederer, Rupert J., ed. and trans. *Heinrich Pesch on Solidarist Economics: Excerpts from the Lehrbuch der Nationalökonomie*. Lanham, MD: University Press of America, 1998.

Engelen, William. "Social Reconstruction." *Central-Blatt and Social Justice* 17 (1924) 184–85.

———. "Social Reconstruction." *Central-Blatt and Social Justice* 18 (1922) 114–16.

———. "Social Reconstruction." *Central-Blatt and Social Justice* 19 (1926) 219–20.

Francis. "Address of His Holiness Pope Francis for the Opening of the Synod." https://www.vatican.va/content/francesco/en/speeches/2021/october/documents/20211009-apertura-camminosinodale.html.

———. *Amoris Laetitia: On Love in the Family*. Vatican City: Libreria Editrice Vaticana, 2016. https://www.vatican.va/content/dam/francesco/pdf/apost_exhortations/documents/papa-francesco_esortazione-ap_20160319_amoris-laetitia_en.pdf.

———. *Evangelii Gaudium: On the Proclamation of the Gospel in Today's World*. Vatican City: Libreria Editrice Vaticana, 2013. https://www.vatican.va/content/francesco/en/apost_exhortations/documents/papa-francesco_esortazione-ap_20131124_evangelii-gaudium.html.

———. *Fratelli Tutti: On Fraternity and Social Friendship*. Vatican City: Libreria Editrice Vaticana, 2020. https://www.vatican.va/content/francesco/en/encyclicals/documents/papa-francesco_20201003_enciclica-fratelli-tutti.html.

———. *Laudato Si': On the Climate Crisis*. Vatican City: Libreria Editrice Vaticana, 2015. https://www.vatican.va/content/francesco/en/encyclicals/documents/papa-francesco_20150524_enciclica-laudato-si.html.

Gleason, Philip. *The Conservative Reformers: German-American Catholics and the Social Order*. Notre Dame: University of Notre Dame Press, 1968.

Himes, Kenneth R., ed. *Modern Catholic Social Teaching: Commentaries and Interpretations*. Washington, DC: Georgetown University Press, 2005.

Joas, Hans. *The Sacredness of the Person: A New Genealogy of Human Rights*. Translated by Alex Skinner. Washington, DC: Georgetown University Press, 2013.

———. *Die Sakralität der Person. Eine neue Genealogie der Menschenrechte*. 3rd ed. Berlin: Suhrkamp, 2012.

Koslowski, Peter. *The Social Market Economy: Theory and Ethics of the Economic Order*. Berlin: Springer, 1998.

Lonergan, Bernard. "The Future of Thomism." In *The Collected Works of Bernard Lonergan*. Vol. 13, *A Second Collection*, edited Robert M. Doran and John D. Dadosky, 39–47. Toronto: Lonergan Research Institute, 2016.

———. "Theology in Its New Context." In *Collected Works of Bernard Lonergan*. Vol. 13, *A Second Collection*, edited by Robert M. Doran and John D. Dadosky, 48–59. Toronto: Lonergan Research Institute, 2016.

Maspero, Giulio, and Martin Schlag, eds. *After Liberalism? A Christian Confrontation on Politics and Economics*. Cham: Springer, 2021.

McWhorter, John. *Woke Racism: How a New Religion Has Betrayed Black America*. New York: Penguin, 2021.

Mering, Noelle. *Awake, Not Woke: A Christian Response to the Cult of Progressive Ideology*. Gastonia, NC: TAN, 2021.

Milbank, John, and Adrian Pabst. *The Politics of Virtue: Post-liberalism and the Human Future*. London: Rowman & Littlefield, 2016.

Paul VI. *Gaudium et Spes*. Vatican City: Libreria Editrice Vaticana, 1965. https://www.vatican.va/archive/hist_councils/ii_vatican_council/documents/vat-ii_const_19651207_gaudium-et-spes_en.html.

Porter, Jean. *Natural and Divine Law: Reclaiming the Tradition for Christian Ethics*. Grand Rapids: Eerdmans, 1999.

Putnam, Robert D., and Shaylyn Romney Garrett. *The Upswing: How America Came Together a Century Ago and How We Can Do It Again*. New York: Simon & Schuster, 2020.

Ratzinger, Joseph. "Church and Economy: Responsibility for the Future of the World Economy." *Communio* 13 (1986) 199–204.

———. "Europe in the Crisis of Cultures." *Communio* 32 (2005) 345–56.

———. "Kirche und Welt: Zur Frage der Rezeption des II. Vatikanischen Konzils." In *Theologische Prinzipienlehre: Bausteine zur Fundamentaltheologie*, 395–411. 2nd ed. Donauwoerth: Wewel, 2005.

Ratzinger, Joseph, and Vittorio Messori. *Ratzinger Report: An Exclusive Interview on the State of the Church*. Translated by Salvator Attanasio and Graham Harrison. San Francisco: Ignatius, 1985.

Reilly, Robert R. *America on Trial: A Defense of the Founding*. San Francisco: Ignatius, 2020.

Rhonheimer, Martin. *The Perspective of Morality: Philosophical Foundations of Thomistic Virtue Ethics*. Washington, DC: Catholic University of America Press, 2011.

Schlag, Martin, and Giulio Maspero, eds. *After Liberalism? A Christian Confrontation on Politics and Economics*. Cham: Springer, 2021.

Stevenson, Bryan. *Just Mercy: A Story of Justice and Redemption*. New York: Spiegel & Grau, 2014.

Taylor, Charles, *A Secular Age*. Cambridge: Belknap, 2007.

Zimring, Franklin E. *When Police Kill*. Cambridge: Harvard University Press, 2017.

5

The Social Formation of Msgr. John A. Ryan[1]

WILLIAM. F. MURPHY JR.,
INITIATIVE FOR SOCIAL CATHOLICISM

Abstract: This essay introduces what we might call the "social formation" of Msgr. John A. Ryan (1869–1945), who was arguably the most influential agent of social Catholicism in American history. In so doing, it seeks to offer not a comprehensive biography, but a brief narrative that illustrates some of the various factors that helped to prepare him for his social apostolate, many of which can function as material for an examination of conscience by especially American Catholics. These include the following: (i) a faith formation that rightly highlights the priority that the biblical and Catholic tradition places on justice regarding the common good; (ii) the exposure to others who demonstrate a commitment to this virtue over the individualistic neglect of it for personal advantage; (iii) the cultivation of an authentically Christian identity in fundamental solidarity with the oppressed and not with the wealthy and powerful; (iv) the development of a knowledge of—and solicitude for—the key questions of justice at stake; (v) a receptive stance toward the Social Doctrine

---

1. Originally published as "Formation for the Signs of Our Times" and is republished with permission.

of the Church and the discernment of the magisterium, including that regarding the "signs of the times"; (vi) a multidisciplinary openness to all sources of knowledge reflecting the Catholic harmony between faith and reason; (vii) the ability to learn from and collaborate with others working for justice despite disagreement on deeply held convictions; (viii) a deep awareness of how participation in market competition can be corrupted by ideologies and the temptation to "cut ethical corners" by engaging in corrupt practices; and (ix) an awareness of how work for justice and the common good must proceed based on a keen awareness of how the nexus between financial and political power manifests itself in a given time and place. This essay sketches the social formation of Ryan, not as an excursion into Catholic history, but specifically with an eye towards elucidating the kind of formation that can enable contemporary Catholics to reflect an authentically Catholic approach to social engagement and evangelization, a topic that will be treated explicitly in a subsequent contribution to this collection.[2]

Introduction

WITH AN EYE TOWARD the kind of formation that might foster a new social Catholicism and what Pope Francis calls "a better kind of politics," this essay introduces the social formation of Msgr. John A. Ryan who was arguably the most influential advocate of social Catholicism in American history. It does so in several steps considering his youth and early education, his seminary formation, his graduate training and ongoing learning before concluding with some brief remarks regarding his most important achievement and how we should strive to achieve something analogous in response to the polycrisis.

The "Signs of the Times"

As can be seen in Martin O'Malley's "Wilhelm von Ketteler: Nineteenth-Century Advocate for Catholic Social Thought," modern Catholic Social Teaching has been especially keen—from its beginning that is generally traced to Ketteler—to understand the signs of the times, the *Zeichen der*

---

2. This essay is a development of the first part of the endowed Paluch Lecture entitled "Formation for the Signs of Our Times." It was delivered at the University of St. Mary of the Lake, Mundelein Seminary, April 12, 2022.

Zeit for Ketteler. This solicitude for the requirements of justice in a given time and place has continued through the Pontificate of Francis, starting with his programmatic Apostolic Exhortation *Evangelii Gaudium: On the Joy of the Gospel*, and continuing through his encyclicals *Laudato Si': On Care for Our Common Home* and *Fratelli Tutti: On Fraternity and Social Friendship*, and his recent Apostolic Exhortation *Laudate Deum: On the Climate Crisis.*

To understand how Msgr. John A. Ryan's formation helped him to address the signs of his times, we need to note—at least briefly—some of the key social and economic challenges through which he lived. Although the industrial revolution had unfolded in the United States for several decades before the Civil War, it accelerated rapidly thereafter in the years surrounding Ryan's birth in 1869, the year that marked the completion of the first transcontinental railroad. His birth was amidst an influx of 14 million immigrants who arrived between 1860 and 1900, a time during which the United States surged ahead of Britain to become the world's leading industrial power. Ryan's birth also just preceded the start of what Mark Twain had dubbed the "Gilded Age (1877–1900)." This label signified the glitter of a thin gilding of gold—corresponding to the incredible wealth of the few—that seemingly covered over not just the political and economic corruption of the elites, but also the poverty and suffering among the masses of industrial workers and farmers. The challenges that workers faced during the industrial revolution included sustenance level wages, an average 100 hour work week in 1890 that made even Sunday worship difficult, hazardous working conditions, child labor, and a lack of the most fundamental benefits such as insurance for illness, accident, or old age.[3] For farm families like Ryan's, another challenge was reliance on the railroads, whose monopolistic position enabled them to "price gouge" farmers who were desperate to get their output to market.

The corruption and social inequities that accompanied this industrial transformation can be explained—at least to a significant degree—by the ideologies under which it unfolded, and by the lack of public institutions proportionate to the new economic, political and social realities. The reigning ideologies included economic liberalism, which strove for unregulated—or *laissez-faire*—capitalism, and social Darwinism, an application of survival of the fittest to the economic and social realms.[4]

---

3. See, for example, Lears, *Rebirth of a Nation*.

4. Even if these ideologies were present and the institutions to regulate the economy were absent, this does not mean that the government was absent from economic

This economic liberalism had unfolded in a context lacking the public institutions and regulations that would later be put in place to stave off the emerging threats of socialism on the left and oligarchic oppression on the right. Ryan would make his contribution by bringing the Catholic Church in the United States into fruitful collaboration with those working for a just form of political economy that avoided these extremes of the left and right.

Ryan's Youth and Early Formation for His Social Apostolate

Ryan was the first of 11 children born to devoutly practicing Catholic parents, both of whom had immigrated from Ireland before settling in Minnesota as farmers. John noted in his biography that his parents were both very virtuous. Ryan recalled how his father would go to great lengths to avoid committing an injustice. In one example, his father chose to take a significant financial burden upon himself rather than backing out of a financial obligation. The situation arose after his father had cosigned a loan with three others to help a neighbor in distress. When not only the original borrower but the other three cosigners did not fulfill their obligations, Ryan's father insisted on paying it back himself.[5] On the farm and seeing the daily example of his Catholic parents, young John not only developed the habits of living devoutly and working diligently; he also became well acquainted with the struggles of the working class, whether in the factory or on the farm.

Upon learning to read, Ryan became an increasingly voracious reader so that by fourth grade he would anxiously await Monday

---

development or that advocates of economic liberalism objected to what the government did. Quite the contrary, government intervention was essential to the development of the American economy and businesspersons benefitted greatly. This intervention occurred in many ways beginning even before the Declaration of Independence with the 1775 act establishing the postal system. Other early interventions to develop the economy during the first century of the nation included postal roads, other infrastructure such as a network of canals, protective tariffs, a national bank, investment in the development of machine tool manufacturing, facilitating the building of the intercontinental railroads (via bonds and land grants), the morally abhorrent appropriation of indigenous lands, the provision of land to settlers, and land grants to establish state colleges, among many other interventions.

5. Ryan, *Social Doctrine in Action*, 2.

mornings when he could be back at school.[6] He became alert to social issues from an early age through a monthly newspaper his father received that was called the *Irish World and American Industrial Liberator*, which was published out of New York under the editorship of Patrick Ford.[7] As suggested by the title, the paper both reported on matters of interest to Irish immigrants in America and focused on their liberation from the injustices of both agricultural and industrial work that so many of them were experiencing. The *Irish World* strongly supporting a labor union called the *Knights of Labor* which had been founded by a Catholic man named Terrance Powderly. This paper regularly reiterated the main struggles and injustices these Irish workers were enduring such that a gifted student and voracious reader like John Ryan can be assumed to have understood them well by his early teens. He later wrote that "One could not read the *Irish World* week after week without acquiring an interest in and love for economic justice, as well as political justice."[8] The *Irish World* also explicitly supported the *National Farmer's Alliance*, of which Ryan's father was a member.

Through such experiences Ryan learned to associate with those struggling under systemic injustices, which was natural in his case because they included his family and fellow Irish. Not surprisingly, such association of American Catholics with the marginalized seems to have become less of a natural occurrence as Catholics "came of age" and assumed positions of social prominence in the decades after the Second Vatican Council. The closest we have come in recent decades to a large number of contemporary Catholics associating with the most vulnerable is in the pro-life movement, but this has been within a context shaped more by the conservative movement and Republican politics than Catholic Social Teaching.[9] The potential for the emergence of a significant number of Catholics committed to a more comprehensive program of social reform in our day would seem to be proportionate to the development of greater understanding of and solidarity with those suffering from the broader range of contemporary systemic injustices including economic precarity, social marginalization and political disempowerment.

6. Broderick, *Right Reverend New Dealer*, 5.
7. Broderick, *Right Reverend New Dealer*, 3–4.
8. Ryan, *Social Doctrine in Action*, 8.
9. See chapter 8, "Liberalism, Conservatism, and Social Catholicism for the Twenty-First Century?" for a discussion of the tensions between American conservatism and Catholic Social Teaching.

Perhaps the development of a such a broader social solidarity among Catholics—most likely over the preservation and renewal of American democracy—could make a "happy fault" of the last several decades of declining middle class and growing social maladies.

Returning to our narrative of John Ryan, when he was eleven years old in 1880, the Farmer's Alliance and the *Irish World* were organizing protests against the monopolistic railroad system, which it denounced for defying laws, corrupting politics, and oppressing both producers and consumers.[10] By this young age, Ryan was already following political debates over parties and candidates based on issues of concern to the working class. He was also keenly alert to the machinations of the wealthy plutocrats of his day who effectively controlled the levers of political power through the politicians who served their interests. Contemporary American Catholics would do well to investigate whether similar dynamics are at play in our day.

In Ryan's early teens—that is, in 1882 or 1883—a neighbor recommended Henry George's *Progress and Poverty*. This work had been published in 1879 and was wildly popular, not only among workers but among many intellectual elites, especially because it offered an intriguing proposal of a "land tax" to address the injustice of rampant inequality. The neighbor lent his copy to the teenage Ryan, who read at least parts of it, which had the effect of both increasing his sympathy for the vulnerable classes and encouraging a lifelong deliberation about George's intriguing proposal of a land tax. Almost a decade before the 1891 publication of *Rerum Novarum: On Capital and Labor*, the first modern Catholic social encyclical, the teenage Ryan showed sufficient common sense to remain unconvinced of Henry George's proposal for a single tax on the value of privately held land.[11] Well into the twenty-first century, moreover, intellectual elites are often similarly intrigued by George's proposal, but have never been able to gain consensus for broad implementation of it.[12]

Ryan spent part of the academic year 1886–87 attending the Christian Brother's Cretin School in St. Paul for the equivalent of High School level course work, but by the fall of 1887 at the age of eighteen he had discerned a priestly vocation and transferred to St. Thomas Seminary.

---

10. Broderick, *Right Reverend New Dealer*, 8.

11. Ryan, *Social Doctrine in Action*, 9.

12. For a recent discussion about the ongoing interest in the feasibility of a land tax, see Neklason, "140-Year-Old Dream."

Ryan's Seminary Formation for Social Apostolate

After entering college seminary in 1887, Ryan spent the next five years at St. Thomas Seminary as a student of the classics, where he learned Greek, Latin, and German before graduating in 1892 as valedictorian. 1887 was also the year that James Cardinal Gibbons of Baltimore wrote the famous letter to Pope Leo XIII which brilliantly defended the *Knights of Labor* union against calls from five of the seventy-five American bishops for its condemnation. Because of this letter, Ryan credits Gibbons as providing "one of the first and also one of the most enduring contributions to [his] social education."[13] It is highly likely that Gibbons was assisted in writing this *tour de force* by his friend, and Ryan's ordinary, Archbishop John Ireland of St. Paul. While in Rome to present the letter, Cardinal Gibbons also encouraged Pope Leo to write on the labor question, which he finally did four years later with the publication of *Rerum Novarum*, which Ryan saw as strong confirmation of his discernment to devote himself to working for social justice.

By this time, Ryan's interest in questions of social justice had been further stimulated by the spellbinding Ignatius Donnelly, who lived in a neighboring township, occupied various state offices, and was the state orator for the Farmer's Alliance. Against the oligarchs and monopolists, Donnelly had organized the Anti-Monopoly Party back in 1870, several years before most scholars mark the beginning of the Gilded Age. Donnelly and his party were focused on fighting for what they called the "rights of man" against the "rights of the property" where the former were those of the broad population of farmers and wage laborers and the latter reflected the privilege of the tiny fraction of wealthy elites. Through moving and sometimes inflammatory rhetoric, Donnelly argued for generally reasonable policies such as the regulation of railroad rates, cheap water transportation for small scale businessmen, and direct and progressive taxation.[14] That is, those with higher disposable income should pay higher "marginal" tax rates as their income rose through the tax brackets. When the state legislature was in session, Ryan frequently took the short trolley ride from the seminary to watch the debates about the questions of the day and to enjoy the eloquence of Donnelly.[15] By the time Ryan completed his classics program at age twenty-three in 1892,

13. Ryan, *Social Doctrine in Action*, 18–20.
14. Ryan, *Social Doctrine in Action*, 14.
15. Ryan, *Right Reverend New Dealer*, 12.

the four-year era of the "populist" reform movement was just beginning. Ignatius Donnelly wrote the preamble to the platform of what was officially called the People's Party but was more commonly known as the Populist Party. Ryan, of course, was a strong and articulate supporter of the party, given that it had been formed through a joining of the Farmer's Alliance and the Knights of Labor,[16] both of which Ryan's family had followed and supported from his youth.

In 1892, Ryan cast his first vote in a presidential election for the Populist Party candidate, and through his later years he continued to hold that their platform was vindicated by subsequent developments, comparing Donnelly's assessment of the situation favorably with that of Pius XI's 1931 encyclical *Quadragesimo Anno*, written during the Great Depression.[17] Although the message of these populists was propagated through first rate oratory to mobilize the broad working class against the actual injustices of an oligarchic and plutocratic elite, this populism should be distinguished from analogous forms advanced by nationalist demagogues for the sake of illegitimate ends such as overthrowing democracy to gain autocratic power.[18]

During Ryan's college studies in Minnesota, a situation was emerging in which Catholics were increasingly embracing what were coming to be recognized as either "conservative" or "liberal" stances with respect to the surrounding American culture. German Catholics generally exemplified the conservative stance, which saw American culture as reflecting Protestant and secular influences which made it a threat to the integrity of the faith. Their focus, therefore, was on preserving the faith from cultural corruption, which is understandable. Irish Catholics, on the other hand, had been deeply shaped by their prior experience of the potato famine and exploitation by the British. They saw a unique opportunity to build a better life in America and tended toward what was called a "liberal" stance. This was characterized by a more sympathetic appreciation of the freedoms allowed by American culture and a corresponding desire to make it their home, which entailed building cordial relations

---

16. Ryan, *Social Doctrine in Action*, 15.

17. See Ryan, *Social Doctrine in Action*, 17–18.

18. In nos. 155–63 of his *Fratelli Tutti*, Pope Francis discusses the rise of populist leaders and notes the need for a "sound critique of demagoguery" (no. 157). He affirms the place of "popular" leaders who discern the needs of the people because he thinks the success of "long-term" projects of reform depends on their becoming "a collective aspiration" (no. 157).

with Protestant and secular culture.[19] The differences between these "conservative" and "liberal" Catholics centered, therefore, not in doctrine but in differing approaches to American society.[20] Since the last century of developments in Catholic Social Doctrine, on the other hand, I would argue that whether or not Catholics live out our Social Doctrine is a matter of doctrinal fidelity on which the health and unity of the Church and the future of human society depends.

Ryan's Archbishop, John Ireland of St. Paul, was the leader of the liberals and issued a rousing call in 1899 that embodied their perspective on American culture that then sophomore John Ryan took to heart. Ireland called upon the Church to "make America Catholic . . . to solve for the Church universal the all-absorbing problems with which religion is confronted in the present age." Ireland took on the conservatives directly.

> The conservatism which wishes to be safe is dry rot. . . . It is deplorable that Catholics grow timid, take refuge in sanctuary and cloister, and leave the bustling, throbbing world with its miseries and sins to the wiles of false friends and cunning practitioners. . . . These are the days for action, days of warfare. . . . Into the arena, priest and layman! Seek out social evils, and lead in movements that tend to rectify them. . . . [S]trive, by word and example, by enactment and enforcement of good laws, to correct them.[21]

Together with *Rerum Novarum*, these were the marching orders that would shape the rest of John Ryan's life. In a nutshell, it was a program of making America Catholic by confronting the "all-absorbing problems of the day," by enacting and enforcing good laws to correct them. From this example, we should note that a prerequisite to Ryan's bringing a Catholic social vision to bear in addressing the challenges of the industrial

19. Broderick, *Right Reverend New Dealer*, 14–15.

20. This is important to keep in mind because—as discussed in the introduction to this volume—many American Catholics link Catholic Social Teaching with the decades after the Second Vatican Council during which to embrace CST was largely seen to entail a disinterest in the doctrinal tradition. There is, however, absolutely no reason that a robust recovery of social Catholicism requires embracing what George Weigle frequently criticizes as the "Catholic lite" of the "silly seventies" or what Bishop Robert Barron calls the "beige" or "balloons-and-banners Catholicism," that is devoid of "metaphor, charm or beauty." As I discuss in the introduction, I see no defensible reason why the influential contemporary theologies that combine *ressourcement* and Thomistic thought, or the attractive presentations of the faith by Bishop Barron's *Word on Fire* should not go hand in hand with a new social Catholicism.

21. Broderick, *Right Reverend New Dealer*, 15.

revolution was a clear rejection of the defensive, inward-looking stance of the "conservatives" of his day, who focused on protecting against perceived outside threats. His alternative was a more missionary, apostolic and magnanimous posture of working for social reform to win others to Christ and the Church by the example of working virtuously for the common good.

As I see it, this is precisely the choice to which Pope Francis is calling contemporary Catholics, with the most influential, persistent and sometimes strident opposition coming from the United States. In his day, Ryan's evangelical choice prefigured the principled Christian humanism that the Church has consistently reflected in her Social Doctrine since especially the Second World War, building on the experience of earlier generations of social Catholics. This postwar embrace of Christian humanism entailed, moreover, a departure from the earlier integralist approach that had aligned the Church with the coercive power of the state to uphold doctrine and morals, an approach that aligned Catholics across Europe with the emerging fascist regimes in the interwar decades.[22] It is not hard to understand why many find the advocacy of contemporary conservative Catholics for integralism both naïve and frightening.

The missionary perspective of Archbishop John Ireland, Msgr. John A. Ryan, the social Catholics, and postwar Catholic Social Doctrine is grounded in confidence that Catholics can and should be fully engaged in addressing the great social challenges of their day, and that such efforts are integral to their broader evangelical mission. Ryan would have certainly considered anything less to manifest a failure in a variety of virtues including faith, hope, charity, justice, and courage, especially in the form of magnanimity.[23] The alternative of withdrawal inward in the face of the threat of a secular and Protestant culture would certainly and rightly have been seen as a manifestation of the vice of pusillanimity.

---

22. Yves Simon was an almost solitary voice among Catholics during these years. Simon, *Road to Vichy*. See chapter 6, "Maurice Blondel's Defense of Social Catholics."

23. We might also note that thoughtful American Catholics like Ireland and Ryan had already recognized by the early twentieth century that the great social challenges of the Industrial Revolution must be addressed through legislation, and thus through the building of public institutions. This recognition has been lost, however, in recent decades as the neoliberal economic paradigm was widely embraced by the early 1980s with a primary goal of undermining such institutions. As was mentioned in the Introduction and will be discussed further in the symposium on "New Economic Thinking after the Neoliberal Consensus," efforts toward a new paradigm are ongoing.

Although Archbishop Ireland was a great advocate of social reform, he was particularly concerned to foster cordial relations with the nation's political and industrial leaders and did not want to be associated with what he saw as the sometimes-demagogic rhetoric of people like Ignatius Donnelly or William Jennings Bryan even though Ireland was sympathetic with their desired reforms.[24] Ireland's own approach to civil society was laid out in an 1884 address on "The Church and Civil Society," given at the Third Plenary Council of Baltimore. This was fundamentally an encouragement to work for mutual understanding between the Church and American society. Ryan took an important lesson from his Archbishop's approach to social injustices. It was that—while recognizing the need to make compelling intellectual arguments, drawing upon all the relevant fields of knowledge—one should strive to employ moderate speech to avoid unnecessarily offending one's interlocutors, even when addressing matters of grave injustice, which is easier said than done.

Ryan's "clerical course" of studies at St. Paul's began in 1892 with two years of philosophy, which—at the insistence of Archbishop Ireland—included courses in sociology and economics to give his clergy the background to understand the socioeconomic context in which they would minister.[25] Ryan's personal journal indicates that he followed the populist movement over the next four years with great sympathy. His ongoing attention to the injustices following from an economy dominated by oligarchs is reflected in the following quote. "The money power is the real enemy of the people's prosperity; yet the people, misled by the hireling press and plutocratic orators, have voted to continue the power of Wall Street. . . . Great is the influence of Mammon and misrepresentation."[26] No doubt, he would say the same thing today about the influence of money and disinformation in politics but there is sadly little evidence to date that the main public voices representing American Catholics are aware of, or willing to acknowledge, these problems.

A decisive point in Ryan's education came in 1894 when he was given a class assignment to write a paper on Leo XIII's 1891 encyclical *Rerum Novarum: On Capital and Labor*. Having already read and

---

24. Ryan, *Social Doctrine in Action*, 21.

25. As far as I know, no contemporary seminary in the United States includes such courses in the required curriculum. The situation 130 years later—however—is considerably more complex, and the stakes proportionately higher, as I will discuss in chapter 13, "Formation for a New Social Catholicism."

26. Broderick, *Right Reverend New Dealer*, 15, 18.

thought about these questions from his youth, Ryan saw this encyclical as a confirmation of his life's mission of addressing "the social question" from a Catholic perspective. He focused his paper on the role of the state in rectifying injustices according to *Rerum Novarum*. This topic was a crucial breakthrough for Catholics of his day as it opposed the regnant doctrine of *laissez-faire* or "liberal" economics, thereby challenging the broad acquiesce of Catholics to the status quo and opening the way to work for justice through legislation on behalf of workers. Contemporary Catholics would do well to meditate on the contemporary relevance of the role of the state in rectifying injustices and fostering justice, and the corresponding role of the Church. Ryan then devoted the summer of 1894 to the study of economics, beginning with the broad overview provided by the Italian Jesuit Matteo Liberatore in his *Principles of Political Economy*, and building upon this with the works of English Catholic writer William Lilly.

Having been introduced to the basics of economics from trusted European Catholics, Ryan turned to the work of Richard T. Ely, the renowned founder of both the American Economic Association and the Christian Social Union. Ely was also in the forefront of the Progressive Reform and Social Gospel movements, both of which sought reforms along the lines encouraged by *Rerum Novarum*. In Ely's book *Socialism and Social Reform*,[27] the seminarian Ryan gained an appreciation of what a broad program of social reform in dialogue with the best of contemporary thought would look like. Rather than having to create from scratch, Ryan recognized that there were resources available in the contemporary scholarship upon which Catholics could draw, and persons with whom they could collaborate in their work for justice and the common good. With these foundations in place, Ryan got his written apostolate underway by publishing some short pieces on social questions in the local Catholic newspaper under a pseudonym.

Ryan's Graduate and Ongoing Studies

Following ordination in 1898, Ryan was assigned to a parish for the summer, but after a few months Archbishop Ireland sent him for graduate studies at the Catholic University of America. His primary instructor in moral theology was the Belgian Fr. Thomas J. Bouquillon, who was of

---

27. Broderick, *Right Reverend New Dealer*, 21.

international repute and would later be described by Ryan as the most erudite man he had ever met. This gave Ryan an appreciation for the world class Catholic scholarship of his day, but that would not be his personal focus. As part of his studies, Ryan also gained a further appreciation of the history of economics, although he never approached the expertise of a leading contemporary like the economist and social ethicist Richard T. Ely. He instead focused on learning what he needed to foster the cause of justice. As Ryan worked on his dissertation on the ethics of the living wage, he established a dialogue with Ely. The completion of the dissertation was delayed until 1905, however, as Archbishop Ireland called Ryan back to St. Paul to teach moral theology at his rapidly growing seminary.

Ely was delighted to write an introduction to the book version of Ryan's dissertation as he saw the burgeoning population of Catholics as key allies in building a political coalition for social reform. With the help of the attention that Ely's introduction brought to Ryan's study, it was widely reviewed in the U.S. and Europe giving the new Dr. Ryan an international reputation as a social ethicist bringing the Catholic Church in America into dialogue with the key questions and thinkers of the day. His ongoing learning focused on what he needed to know to participate intelligently in discussions about how best to address emerging challenges, which meant keeping on top of economic and social developments, on how these were impacting society, on reform policies being proposed or implemented in various states and countries, and on the efficacy of these policies. With the *gravitas* of a doctorate and international reputation, Ryan entered energetically into working for social reform, not just through his teaching, academic and popular writing, and public speaking, but also through participation in the political process.

Ryan's Greatest Achievement and a Challenge for Contemporary Catholics

Of Ryan's many achievements, I will highlight the one that would seem most important and most relevant to a new flourishing of social Catholicism. This was the central role he played in helping to shift American Catholics—and especially the United States Bishops—into constructive collaborations with those working for the reform of unjust social structures, first during the Progressive Era and then during the Great

Depression.[28] This entailed a shift from the defensive posture advocated by more conservative Catholics that emphasized protection from the dangers of a diverse and sometimes hostile culture to a magnanimous striving to "make America Catholic" precisely by moving Catholics into the forefront of efforts to solve the grave social problems of his day.

Although a defensive social posture can make sense in providing at least temporary protection from threats, a more missionary approach was required in Ryan's day to liberate the working and lower classes to the vicissitudes of a *laissez-faire* market rigged by the rich and powerful for their own benefit. The magnanimous approach that Ryan picked up from Archbishop Ireland and the broader tradition of social Catholicism,[29] made American Catholics an integral part of a broad consensus across political parties for a Keynesian mixed economy. According to this model, the dynamic power of the market was situated within the context of public institutions that sought to ensure stability and fair competition while providing the public goods that the market would not provide. This political-economic model resulted in the establishment of a broad middle class and a relatively high degree of social solidarity, at least among white Americans.

In my opinion, this primary achievement of Ryan is of great contemporary relevance because of the urgent need to renew American and other democracies and international institutions to meet the challenges of the polycrisis that have emerged after over four decades of globalization under a political-economic paradigm of market fundamentalism that had significantly sidelined social Catholicism. These grave and multifaceted challenges give good reason to fear that we face the threat of a dystopian future of failed or autocratic states on an increasingly

---

28. Related to this primary achievement are many others that enabled him to shape the direction of the U.S. Bishops for several decades and brought him into close collaboration with the administration of President Franklin Delano Roosevelt. Indeed, Ryan gave the benediction at two of Roosevelt's inaugurations and was nicknamed Right Reverend New Dealer. The appreciation of the Roosevelt administration for Catholic Social Teaching can be seen in the references to "social justice" in Roosevelt, "Address to the National Conference of Catholic Charities," given on October 4, 1933. In what was understood as an allusion to the emphasis on "social justice" in 1931 social encyclical *Quadragessimo Anno: On the Reconstruction of the Social Order*, Roosevelt explained "that humanity is moving forward to the practical application of the teachings of Christianity as they affect the individual lives of men and women everywhere."

29. Ireland was well aware of the European social Catholics and sought to benefit from their experiences, visiting France—for example—to learn from those defended by Maurice Blondel.

uninhabitable planet, and the resulting domestic and international instability, nihilism and deaths of despair illustrate the depths of the crisis.

The Catholic faith, however, provides us with the opportunity to deepen our trust in God, to renew our hope in the Divine help, and to participate more deeply in the pattern of redemptive love for God and neighbor. Amidst contemporary polarization into warring tribes, the Catholic faith also provides us with a vision of the Church as an efficacious sign of the unity of the human family, as a pilgrim people walking with Jesus in the way of missionary discipleship, and with a body of Social Doctrine regarding how to live the life of charity in the modern world. For those imagining how that might be done in the face of the polycrisis, the life and work of Msgr. John A. Ryan provides an example worthy of prayerful consideration.

Bibliography

Broderick, Francis L. *Right Reverend New Dealer: John A. Ryan*. New York: Macmillan 1963.

Francis. *Evangelii Gaudium: The Joy of the Gospel*. Vatican City: Libreria Editrice Vaticana, 2020. https://www.vatican.va/content/francesco/en/encyclicals/documents/papa-francesco_20201003_enciclica-fratelli-tutti.html.

———. *Fratelli Tutti: On Fraternity and Social Friendship*. Vatican City: Libreria Editrice Vaticana, 2020. https://www.vatican.va/content/francesco/en/encyclicals/documents/papa-francesco_20201003_enciclica-fratelli-tutti.html.

———. *Laudate Deum: On the Climate Crisis*. Vatican City: Libreria Editrice Vaticana, 2023.

———. *Laudato Si': On Care for Our Common Home*. Vatican City: Libreria Editrice Vaticana, 2015. https://www.vatican.va/content/francesco/en/encyclicals/documents/papa-francesco_20150524_enciclica-laudato-si.html.

Lears, Jackson. *Rebirth of a Nation: The Making of Modern America, 1877–1920*. New York: Harper, 2010.

Murphy, William F., Jr. "Formation for the Signs of Our Times: The Example of Msgr. John A. Ryan and the Renewal of Contemporary Democracy." *Chicago Studies* 61 (2023). Forthcoming.

Neklason, Annika. "The 140-Year-Old Dream of 'Government without Taxation.'" *The Atlantic*, April 15, 2019. https://www.theatlantic.com/national/archive/2019/04/henry-georges-single-tax-could-combat-inequality/587197/.

Roosevelt, Franklin Delano. "Address to the National Conference of Catholic Charities" https://www.religioninamerica.org/rahp_objects/address-to-the-national-conference-of-catholic-charities/.

Ryan, John A. *Social Doctrine in Action: A Personal History*. New York: Harper and Brothers, 1941.

Simon, Yves. *La Grande Crise de la République Française*. Montreal: Editions de l'Arbre, 1941.
———. *The Road to Vichy: 1918–1938*. Translated by James Corbett and George J. McMorrow. New York: Sheed & Ward, 1942.

6

Maurice Blondel's Defense of the Social Catholics and His Enduring Critique of Catholic Integralism

Peter J. Bernardi, SJ

Abstract: This essay offers a case study of an incisive diagnosis of the mentalities of French Catholics who were deeply divided over what strategy to adopt to re-Christianize society in the early decades of the twentieth century. In the wake of the first modern social encyclical *Rerum Novarum: On Capital and Labor* (1891), Maurice Blondel (1861–1949) defended the social Catholics of the nascent *Semaine sociale* organization who were open to collaboration with anti-clerical republicans to secure justice for the workers. On the other hand, Blondel sharply criticized Catholic collaboration with the politico-cultural movement of *Action Française* (AF) that sought an integralist restoration of "altar and throne" to defeat the dominant secular liberalism, pernicious fruit of the French Revolution. Blondel identified epistemological, ontological, and theological presuppositions at play, especially different understandings of the natural-supernatural relationship. Hans Urs von Balthasar (1905–88) claimed that Maurice Blondel's "Testis" articles were the unsurpassed treatment of the symptoms and diagnosis of the integralist mentality, a recurrent temptation for militant Catholics. Blondel's insights are pertinent to contemporary debates regarding liberal, democratic institutions and Catholic integralism.

THE CONTEMPORARY CRISIS OF liberal, democratic institutions poses a challenge to every conscientious citizen.[1] One particular threat to our national well-being is an aggressive secular liberalism that promotes individual "rights" in ways that undermine the common good.[2] In pluralist societies increasingly characterized by polarization and alienation, what strategy should people of faith adopt to safeguard respect for life and the common good? For those who view modern secular liberalism as the arch enemy of Christian faith, there is a temptation to embrace an authoritarian "integralism" that instrumentalizes Christian churches to bring about the "social reign of Christ," often empowered by the scapegoating of "alien" minorities.[3] To be sure, integralism is not a univocal phenomenon; it assumes different forms in different national contexts. Christian nationalism among Protestants is a related phenomenon in the American context that is characterized by a constitutional separation of Church and State. American Catholic integralists can serve as convenient political allies for them. In traditionally Catholic countries, such as France and Spain, with authoritarian traditions that closely linked Church and State, there have been sharp political and religious divisions among Catholics over how to respond to secular liberalism. This essay will offer a case study of an incisive diagnosis of the mentalities of early twentieth century French Catholics who were deeply divided over whether to collaborate with the political, cultural movement of *Action Française* that sought a restoration of "altar and throne" to defeat the dominant secular liberalism, pernicious fruit of the French Revolution.

In the early decades of the twentieth century, French Catholics were sharply divided over what strategy the Church should adopt to re-christianize society. In the wake of the abrogation of the concordat by the secularizing Third Republic, Catholic integralists sought to restore the

---

1. Kloppenberg, "Coming Apart?"

2. Alexander Stern argues, however, that economic oligarchs pose a bigger threat to liberal, democratic institutions. Stern, "Centrist Illusions."

3. David C. Schindler remarks: "In Catholic circles above all, there is a rising enthusiasm for 'integralism,' the cooperation between throne and altar that would not have been conceivable even five years ago." Schindler, "What Is Liberalism?," 4. For a counter to Schindler's anti-liberalism, see Riordan, *Human Dignity and Liberal Politics*.

institutional prerogatives of the Roman Catholic Church, even by way of an alliance with the agnostic, anti-Christian ideologist Charles Maurras and his neo-monarchist political movement of AF. In contrast, social Catholics, associated with the nascent *Semaines sociales*, rejected a top-down, authoritarian imposition of Catholicism in favor of a democratic strategy that viewed the aspirations of the working class for justice as an implicit cry for the Kingdom of God.

At the height of the Modernist Crisis (1909–12), French Catholic lay philosopher Maurice Blondel (1861–1949) engaged in a polemical exchange with the French Jesuit philosopher Pedro Descoqs (1877–1946) that still has relevance for understanding contemporary political-ecclesial controversies.[4] Blondel defended the sociopolitical, democratic strategy of the *Semaine Sociale* Catholics. In contrast, Descoqs offered a qualified defense of the *Action Française* Catholic integralists. I will introduce Blondel and Descoqs, describe their exchange, and set out the underlying philosophical and theological factors that continue to be relevant for understanding contemporary arguments over Christian sociopolitical engagements. Blondel contended that different understandings of the nature-grace relationship were at work in the different sociopolitical positions that Catholics adopted. Ironically, given Blondel's trenchant criticisms of the integralist mentality, his philosophy of the nature-grace relationship has been appealed to by contemporary integralists in support of their position. This issue will be addressed in the conclusion.

In a series of articles that appeared in the periodical *Études*, Jesuit Pedro Descoqs composed a qualified defense of a Catholic alliance with the proto-fascist, monarchist movement *Action Française*. Born in the wake of the infamous Dreyfus Affair, AF, under the intellectual leadership of Charles Maurras (1868–1952), promised to restore the historic union between the Roman Catholic Church and the French State that had been abrogated in 1905 by the anti-clerical Third Republic (1870–1940). AF's anti-liberal ideology was very appealing to a generation of Catholics who were alarmed by the Third Republic's secularizing policies.

In contrast, Maurice Blondel was appalled by Catholic-AF collaboration which he considered lethal to the Christian spirit. He defended collaboration between the democratic, social Catholics and the republican government to bring about justice for the workers. When these social Catholics were accused of "social modernism," Blondel published

---

4. For a book length treatment of this dispute, see Bernardi, *Maurice Blondel*.

a series of articles under the pseudonym "Testis," Latin for "witness." At the height of the Modernist Crisis, whose epicenter was France, Blondel sought to "witness" to the authentic Christian spirit that he considered under threat by the Catholic Maurrassians defended by Descoqs.

Maurice Blondel

Maurice Blondel has been called the most important Catholic philosopher of the last two centuries. Born in Dijon in 1861, even as an adolescent, Maurice Blondel had a keen sense of the cultural crisis and intellectual malaise that was gripping his society. He felt called to serve as a philosophical apologist for Christian truth that was disparaged by the university and cultural intelligentsia. Having matriculated at the prestigious *École Normale Supérieure*, Blondel conceived of a strictly philosophical project that would show the illegitimacy of the reigning "separated" philosophy, which considered the spiritual Transcendent as utterly superfluous to self-sufficient reason's claim to understand reality. This project came to fruition in his doctoral dissertation *L'Action* (in English, *Action*).[5]

Blondel's seminal insight was to conceive of "action" as the link between thought and being. The term "action" was not even an entry in the standard philosophical dictionary of the period. Blondel's genius was to elaborate a meticulous phenomenology that set out the "logic of action" in human life so as to disclose its ultimate insufficiency. In studying action, Blondel addressed the problem which dominates all human existence: "Yes or no, does life have a meaning and does man have a destiny?"[6] Michael Kerlin explains:

> [Blondel] wants to show that our acts themselves imply the solution. We cannot avoid acting, and every attempt to limit the scope and interpretation of our actions will push us beyond itself until finally we are faced with the question of the supernatural, a question that we can neither properly pose nor answer without going beyond our own resources.[7]

Blondel grounded the progressive and ineluctable expansion of action in the dialectic of human willing that futilely seeks to equate its specific and

5. Blondel, *Action*.
6. Blondel, *Action*, 3.
7. Kerwin, "Blondel," 104.

concrete expressions with its inexhaustible, aboriginal élan. This dialectic is the expression of the inevitable disproportion between what Blondel termed the "willing will" (*volonté voulante*) and the "willed will" (*volonté voulue*). The "willing will" is the inexhaustible aspiration to attain the infinite that is never fully quenched by the "willed will," namely, the specific, concrete instances of willing. James Le Grys epitomized Blondel's primordial insight: "The life of action is marked by the constant struggle to equal ourselves caused by the presence of the infinite within us, not the serenity of an emancipation through speculation."[8] Blondel argued that fidelity to the logic of action must lead to this "doubly imperious conclusion":

> It is impossible not to recognize the insufficiency of the natural order in its totality and not to feel an ulterior need; it is impossible to find within oneself something to satisfy this religious need. *It is necessary*; and *it is impracticable.*[9]

The "it" refers to the supernatural that Blondel's secular university contemporaries dismissed.

> Absolutely impossible and absolutely necessary for man, that is properly the notion of the supernatural. Man's action goes beyond man; and all the effort of his reason is to see that he cannot, that he must not restrict himself to it. A deeply felt expectation of an unknown messiah; a baptism of desire, which human science lacks the power to evoke, because this need itself is a gift. Science can show its necessity, it cannot give it birth.[10]

Having disclosed the necessity of a supernatural completion of the natural order, Blondel's "transcendental" analysis claimed to show that only the option for what he termed the "one thing necessary" (*Unique nécessaire*) could give ultimate meaning and coherence to the human project.[11]

---

8. LeGrys, "Christianization of Modern Philosophy," 480.

9. Blondel, *Action*, 297.

10. Blondel, *Action*, 357.

11. Blondel's analysis is "transcendental" in the sense that he discloses the necessary conditions for the possibility of human fulfillment. He establishes the necessity of the option for God, the "*Unique nécessaire*" in Part Four of *Action*; in Part Five (most of which was added for the sale version), he argued that only an option for the specifically Christian revelation fulfills human action. See Bouillard, *Blondel and Christianity*. The phrase "*Unique nécessaire*" is an implicit reference to the Lucan gospel story about Jesus' visit to the home of Martha and Mary. Jesus says to the preoccupied Martha: "There is need of only one thing" (Luke 10:42 RSV).

Charles Taylor's magisterial study of modernity *A Secular Age* limns the cultural background for Blondel's philosophical project.[12] Taylor clarifies why unbelief has become so prevalent in modern western culture. He analyzes what he terms the "immanent frame" that characterizes the modern age and the associated rise of an exclusive humanism that dismisses the reality of the supernatural order to which Christian faith attests. Blondel aimed to construct a compelling philosophical argument to show that the immanent order is not self-sufficient and that it requires the supernatural order for its completion.

Pedro Descoqs

Born in Normandy, France, Pedro Descoqs entered the Paris Province of the Society of Jesus in 1895.[13] His generation was forced to complete their studies outside of France because of measures enacted by the anti-clerical Third Republic. Descoqs was schooled in the Baroque scholastic philosophy of Francisco Suárez, SJ, considered the normative interpreter of St. Thomas Aquinas within the Jesuit order. He is remembered as an indefatigable worker and an ardent polemicist, who waged an incessant battle against the new philosophical trends, including neo-Thomism, transcendental Thomism, and Blondel's philosophy of action. Having resided in Paris during the years of the Nazi occupation, Descoqs died of typhoid at Mongré, outside of Lyon, in 1946.

Descoqs has been called "the last great representative of the Suarezian tradition."[14] Francisco Suárez, SJ (1548–1617), played a central role in the revival of scholastic thought during the sixteenth and seventeenth centuries. Descoqs's defense of Catholic collaboration with *Action Française* drew on certain basic Suarezian positions, that were largely shared with other scholastics. Suárez held that while the Church and State are distinct societies, the Church in the person of the Pope has indirect power over civil authority.[15] "There may occur a clash between the spiritual good and temporal convenience or expediency, and on such occasions

---

12. Taylor, *Secular Age*, 539–93.

13. Among useful sources of information on Descoqs, see the sympathetic, but candid obituary composed by fellow Suarezian and Jersey colleague Gabriel Picard, SJ. Picard, "In Memoriam." The name "Descoqs" is pronounced De-ko; his family named him "Pedro" to distinguish him from an uncle named "Pierre."

14. Coreth, *Christliche Philosophie*, 2:400.

15. Coreth, *Christliche Philosophie*, 2:402–3.

the temporal sovereign must yield to the spiritual."[16] The Church has this right because it serves a higher end, the human being's eternal salvation. Also, in contrast with Blondel, Suárez made a sharp distinction between the natural and supernatural orders; he gleaned from St. Thomas Aquinas the notion of an essential "pure nature" that he judged necessary for securing the gratuity of the supernatural gift.

Most French Jesuits of Descoq's generation favored a restoration of the monarchy.[17] They had good reason to feel alienated from the Third Republic because a series of fiercely anti-clerical administrations had effectively annulled the Society of Jesus as a corporate presence in France. Most notably, their extensive school system was suppressed.[18] In 1901, another flare-up of anti-clericalism resulted in a complete ban of "unapproved" religious congregations, among whom the Society of Jesus was a primary target. Forced entries, plundering of property, and expulsions were the order of the day. Catholic disaffection grew as the radical-republican coalitions holding sway pressed their agenda. Laicization of education, liberalization of divorce laws, and a variety of other secularizing measures were constant reminders of the "de-christianizing" of France. The anti-clerical tide reached its peak in 1905 when the Law of Separation was enacted that unilaterally abrogated the Concordat between the French State and the Roman Catholic Church. Many Catholics felt that grave harm had been inflicted on the Church and her interests. Catholic "liberals," however, tended to view the separation of Church and State as a progressive step. From Rome, Pope Pius X issued *Vehementer Nos* (February 11, 1906) which resolutely refused all accommodation to the Law of Separation and the humiliating measures it entailed. At this low ebb in the Church's institutional fortunes, Charles Maurras opportunely presented himself as her staunch defender.

As early as 1898, Maurras had invited Catholics to make common cause for the salvation of France. The enemy was the socially corrosive, egoistic individualism and liberalism that had its sources in the ideals of the French Revolution and the Protestant Reformation. The goal was the

---

16. Coreth, *Christliche Philosophie*, 2:403.

17. Belgian Church historian Roger Aubert estimated that perhaps three-fourth of the pre-First World War era Jesuits had monarchist sympathies. See Aubert, "*La discordance.*"

18. Anti-Jesuit animus played a special role in the republican politics of the era. See Cubitt, *Jesuit Myth*. For an overview of the Jesuits in France during the nineteenth and twentieth centuries, see Fouilloux, *Jésuites à Lyon*, 247–64.

defeat of the Third Republic and the restoration of the union of altar and throne. This was an assessment that was bound to appeal to the intransigent Catholics who refused all compromise with political liberalism. As we shall see, however, Maurras's appreciation of the Catholic Church scandalously eviscerated her biblically based prophetic mission.

In a five part series of articles published in the periodical *Études*,[19] Descoqs culminated his exposition of Maurras's system with this "most important" question: "In his blueprint [for social reconstruction] has Maurras reserved any place for Catholicism, and, if so, what is this place?"[20] Though recognizing that this "Catholic atheist" does not recognize the supernatural constitution of the Church, Descoqs lauds Maurras's esteem for the Church as "the rampart of order" to which he assigns a privileged position in his reconstituted state.[21]

Yet Descoqs did not deceive himself regarding the limits of Maurras's appreciation of the Church. "The Church appears to him, from his relativist perspective, both as the guarantee of civilization and the guardian of nationality."[22] Being a consistent positivist, Maurras justified the Church's privileged role in his monarchist State by adducing her historical role in maintaining social order and cohesiveness. Thus, in contrast with the anti-clerical "barbarians" who deposed the Church from its official public role, Maurras proudly calls himself "Roman" and champions the cause of the Catholic Church as the historic bulwark of social order.

> Against all those who take umbrage at the Church of Rome, against all these "barbarians" who only seem born to destroy, he declares himself "Roman." There lies his true faith, and this faith he expresses in a "symbol," known to all, that he intends to

---

19. These five articles were published between August and December of 1909 under the same title, namely "*À travers l'oeuvre de M. Ch. Maurras*." They are listed separately in the bibliography for this essay with the addition of a bracketed number from one to five and will be referenced below by short form including the bracketed number, such as "Descoqs, *À travers l'oeuvre* [2]." These articles were subsequently published as multiple editions of a monograph under the same title. In a pointed response to Blondel, Descoqs published "*Monophorisme et Action Française* (1910)" and *Monophorisme et Action Française* (1913).

20. Descoqs, "*À travers l'oeuvre* [2]," 339, 343.

21. Descoqs, "*À travers l'oeuvre* [2]," 344.

22. Descoqs, "*À travers l'oeuvre* [2]," 340–41. Descoqs was citing from Maurras's preface to *Le Dilemme de Marc Sangnier*. The "symbol" to which he refers was Maurras's rhetorical tour de force in which he repeatedly claimed "I am Roman" (*Je suis romain*). Descoqs felt no need to cite the "symbol" because it had been so widely reproduced in the press.

be above all a hymn of praise to the Church, guardian of order: "Order, tradition, discipline, hierarchy, authority, continuity, unity, work, family, corporation, decentralization, autonomy, labor organization," she alone has known how to preserve for societies the elements, [and] for intelligence the ideas, that found their life.[23]

Here Descoqs registers a significant caveat. He cautioned that "in the thought of M. Maurras, the term 'Roman' is not to be confused with the term 'Catholic.'"[24] Indeed, Maurras's use of the term "Catholic" was not to be confused with the term "Christian." His appreciation of the "true spirit" of the Church, was to say the least, peculiar. And he seemed to oppose the spirit of the "Roman" Church to the spirit of her founder. Maurras had expressed contempt for the spirit of the biblical prophets and even Jesus in certain of his early works. These passages were a scandal to any Christian who might contemplate an alliance with Maurras's movement. This was the second major impediment that Descoqs had to address if a collaboration between Catholics and Maurrassian positivists was to be deemed acceptable.

On the one hand, Descoqs extenuated the incriminating passages in which Maurras expressed his loathing for the "tumultuous sentences of the prophets" and the "venom" of the Magnificat. Maurras was simply castigating the "exegetical extravagances" of the Reformation that "revolutionaries and democrats" have employed to sanction their ruinous programs of social equality.[25] On the other hand, after conceding to Maurras that the gospel can give rise to "dangerous interpretations," and benevolently inferring from Maurras's praise of Rome an argument for the necessity of a magisterium to guard against "every fantastical interpretation," Descoqs firmly repudiated any suggestion of a dichotomy between the Church and her founder that Maurras's writings might suggest.

Apart from "these fundamental divergences" between Maurras's views and the Church's dogma, Descoqs opined that Maurras gave the impression of being "almost one of her sons."[26] Descoqs found it inexplicable why this "Catholic atheist" stopped short at the threshold, refusing to enter the Temple whose lines he so much admired.[27] Descoqs evidently

23. Descoqs, "À travers l'oeuvre [2]," 340n1.
24. Descoqs, "À travers l'oeuvre [2]," 336.
25. Descoqs, "À travers l'oeuvre [2]," 345.
26. Descoqs, "À travers l'oeuvre [2]," 334–35.
27. Descoqs, "À travers l'oeuvre [3]," 612.

hoped that Maurras would one day cross the threshold and return to the formative institution of his childhood. The Jesuit found no insuperable impediment in Maurras's positions that precluded his reconciliation with the Church.

Descoqs vigorously defended the soundness of Maurras's conclusions apropos of the "natural" order, while lamenting his religious and philosophical "deficiencies" that prevented "any positive accord on dogmatic terrain."[28] Descoqs defended Maurras's capacity to arrive at the truths because the political and social order has its own autonomy and right reason can legitimately arrive at valid conclusions without recourse to supernatural revelation as their necessary source or sanction. The fundamental issue, then, was the relationship between the natural and supernatural orders.

What were Descoqs's main lines of his case for collaboration? First, Descoqs argued that a union for the sake of results in the natural order, viz., social prosperity, is valid even though the "*ontological* value of these results" is regarded differently by the collaborating parties. Second, he stated that though the natural and supernatural orders are intimately related, nevertheless, "the end of the natural order can be pursued in a very large measure independently of the supernatural end." Third, though Maurras has a woefully "deficient" understanding of metaphysics and the Church, his own positivist principles lead him not to interfere with her activity; furthermore, the valid social and political truths of his system are open to and, indeed, require completion by the *philosophia perennis*. Just as deficiencies in Aristotle's philosophy had not prevented Aquinas from incorporating Aristotle's valid insights into a Christian synthesis, so Descoqs viewed his own apologetic efforts in relation to Maurras's system. I shall now show how Descoqs clarified each of these points.

Since Catholics and neo-monarchists are able to agree on the "means for realizing the temporal prosperity of the community," expedients that "the experimental method" confirms, they are able to work together for this very determinate end.[29] In making his case, Descoqs employed a helpful analogy that contrasted two sorts of working collaborations to illustrate the difference between permissible and impermissible coalitions.[30] On the one hand, consider two groups, made up of believers and

---

28. Descoqs, "À travers l'oeuvre [3]," 612.
29. Descoqs, *Monophorisme et Action Française* (1913), 60–61.
30. Descoqs, *Monophorisme et Action Française* (1913), 61–62.

unbelievers respectively, working together to transport heavy beams to Notre Dame Cathedral to erect a scaffolding. The believers intend to repair the sanctuary. The unbelievers intend to construct a pyre to destroy the Cathedral. Though the two groups agree on an immediate, "bare" (*brut*) end, i.e., the transport of the beams, their intentions are so contradictory that their joint venture must be unreservedly condemned as immoral.[31] On the other hand, imagine that these same two groups agree to transport the beams for the common goal of repairing the Church. The believers, motivated by a spirit of faith, want to give glory to God. The unbelievers simply want to safeguard an artistic marvel that is a legacy of French culture. Where would be the injustice or immorality of the collaboration of these two groups in hauling the beams since both propose to cooperate on the same good work?[32]

The collaboration between Catholics and unbelieving positivists is precisely akin to the second example. It is not a case of these groups having absolutely no idea in common. Catholics can collaborate with positivists because "these latter have very just, though incomplete and 'deficient' ideas on several points: order, authority, [and] tradition."[33] These truths "are from God . . . and ascend to God." Both parties "pursue a genuine good, the common, temporal good, which, according to rational philosophy and Christian doctrine, is the proper end of civil society."[34] Sufficient to found a legitimate collaboration, "this has nothing analogous to the immoral accord on the results considered above and the negation of a personal God; *a fortiori*, the sole fact of not knowing God will not necessarily render all accord illegitimate."[35] There is a realm of truth equally accessible to a Catholic and an unbeliever. If, in the order of being, God is the supreme principle and goal, in the order of logic, God is not the first object nor the first principle.[36] To require an explicit appeal to God to validate truths in the natural order is to embrace the errors "of the traditionalists and the ontologists."[37] Catholics and neo-monarchists

31. Descoqs, *Monophorisme et Action Française* (1913), 61.
32. Descoqs, *Monophorisme et Action Française* (1913), 61–62.
33. Descoqs, *Monophorisme et Action Française* (1913), 62.
34. Descoqs, *Monophorisme et Action Française* (1913), 62.
35. Descoqs, *Monophorisme et Action Française* (1913), 62–63.
36. Descoqs, *Monophorisme et Action Française* (1913), 74n1.
37. Descoqs, *Monophorisme et Action Française* (1913), 74. For the historical background of Descoqs's charge, see McCool, *Quest for a Unitary Method*. 37–58, and 113–28.

base their political constructions "on facts of experience that do not stem of themselves from any theory."[38] The natural order has "its proper value and relative independence."[39] Descoqs insisted on maintaining the "essential distinction . . . between purely political and economic questions and moral and religious questions."[40]

> The remote orientation [that the political and economic order] receives from the supernatural end does not change its proper object [nor] modify its laws. The supernatural corrects nature, extends its domain, completes it; it does not suppress it nor volatize it.[41]

The Jesuit recalled that Popes Leo XIII and Pius X had reaffirmed the just liberty for Catholics in the political order. Catholics do not have to renounce their principles to cooperate with Maurras on a plan of "immediately political reforms."[42]

The *Semaines sociales*[43]

What were the *Semaines sociales*? Literally, "social weeks," the *Semaines sociales* were a sort of peripatetic university (*"universite sociale ambulante"*) that were founded in 1904 by Marius Gonin, director of the *Chronique des comites du Sud-Est*, and Adéodat Boissard, Maurice Blondel's brother-in-law and professor at the School of Social and Political Sciences at the Catholic University of Lille. Seeking to propagate Catholic social teaching beyond the urban centers of Paris and Lille, the *Semaines sociales* brought together for a week in a different city each summer, a varied group of professionals, workers, clergy, and students. As many as two thousand participants followed courses given by experts on the Church's social doctrine and practice. Specific proposals for improving the workers' lot were shared and discussed. From its inaugural assembly in Lyon, these annual gatherings generated an enormous enthusiasm and energy. Veteran social Catholic Henri Lorin served as the first president. He defined their aim at their 1905 assembly: "To perfect the knowledge

38. Descoqs, *Monophorisme et Action Française* (1913), 73.
39. Descoqs, *Monophorisme et Action Française* (1913), 73.
40. Descoqs, *Monophorisme et Action Française* (1913), 80.
41. Descoqs, *Monophorisme et Action Française* (1913), 81.
42. Descoqs, *Monophorisme et Action Française* (1913), 82.
43. See Bernardi, "Social Modernism."

of Christian morality in our own consciences and to prepare us to make the social importance of Christian dogmas better known to people outside: this is our objective."[44]

Implied in this program are both a method and a spirit. The method was distinctive for the two sources it employed: "the fundamental moral teachings of Catholicism and the observation of facts, the science of sociology in the proper sense." The spirit was characterized by simple obedience to Christian conscience and a "disinterested attitude" reflected in their "concern to place themselves outside existing groups, whatever they may be."[45] Evidence of this disinterested attitude can be seen in the composition of its founding "patronage committee" and in the variety of its professors. The *Semaines sociales* received a broad range of support among leading social Catholics, including Albert de Mun and Marc Sangnier, and among clergy, especially several prominent democratic *abbés*. For example, though Christian democrats predominated among the leadership of the *Semaines sociales*, Gonin and Boissard turned down an invitation to join Marc Sangnier's national democratic political movement *le plus grand Sillon*.[46] Furthermore, the directors of the *Semaines sociales* invited Fr. Georges de Pascal, OP, an AF sympathizer, to give lessons in its early years. The leading social Catholic monarchist René de La Tour du Pin also lent his support. The *Semaines sociales* sought to bridge the rancorous political divisions among French Catholics.

Blondel's "Testis" Articles

During the pontificate of Pius X (1903–14), the perception of a crisis within the Church over the understanding and living of the faith grew sharper in Blondel. He especially deplored a certain Catholic reaction to the Law of Separation that sought to achieve "the triumph of political theocracy and the scholastic synthesis."[47] Responding to a national survey in 1907, Blondel articulated his sense of the "present crisis":

44. Lorin, "*Semaine sociale*," 267.

45. From a prospectus published in advance of the 1909 Bordeaux Semaine sociale, "Archives Chronique sociale de France," malle 1.

46. Sangnier's "greater" *Sillon* was condemned by the Vatican in 1910. See Pius X, *Notre Charge Apostolique*.

47. Blondel and Wehrlé, *Correspondance*, 2:375. Johannès Wehrlé, a diocesan priest, was a dear friend, confidant, and spiritual advisor of Blondel; they had been students together at the École Normale.

> Unprecedented perhaps in depth and extent—for it is at the same time scientific, metaphysical, moral, social and political—[the crisis] is not a "dissolution" [for the spirit of faith does not die], nor even an "evolution" [for the spirit of faith does not change], it is a *purification* of the religious sense, and an *integration* of Catholic truth.[48]

In 1907, Pope Pius X promulgated the anti-modernist encyclical *Pascendi* which procribed "Modernism" as "the synthesis of all heresies."[49] This papal document, however, was not the "purification" and "integration" of Catholic truth for which Blondel yearned. He thought that the condemnation in no way touched his own positions and, therefore, he had nothing to retract. Nevertheless, given the prevailing circumstances, he felt that he should keep silent. There were underlying reasons for the persistent incomprehension of his positions.

Approximately two years after the publication of *Pascendi*, Blondel decided to end his silence. Requested to offer a defense of the social Catholics of the *Semaines sociales*, he gave his "witness" against a pervasive and insidious "extrinsicist" mentality, which he labelled "monophorist" ["one-way street"] that, boasting of its orthodoxy, threatened "the very understanding of the moral destiny and the religious conscience."[50] Blondel disclaimed the intention to refute the specific charges brought against the social Catholics and suggested a larger purpose for the "Testis" series.[51] The underlying issues "transcend the horizon of the present controversies and . . . concern the entire future of Catholicism itself among us."[52]

In the "Testis" articles, Blondel contrasted two mentalities according to three fundamental orientations. The three orientations concerned epistemology: the relation of our thoughts to reality; ontology: the

---

48. Cited by Dru, "From the *Action Française* to the Second Vatican Council," 226. Blondel composed these lines as part of a response to an "international survey on the religious question" that was published by the *Mercure de France* in June 1907.

49. Pius X, *Pascendi*, no. 39. Pius X, *Lamentabili*, preceded *Pascendi*. Blondel was relieved that its sixty-five propositions contained no reference to the philosophy of action or the "new apologetics."

50. Blondel, *Catholicisme Social et Monophorisme*, 71. This volume is a reprint of Blondel's "Testis" essays that originally appeared in *Annales de philosophie chrétienne* between October 1909 and May 1910 bearing the title "*La 'Semaine sociale' de Bordeaux: Testis*." The facsimile reprint was published as Blondel, *Une alliance contre nature*.

51. Blondel, *Catholicisme Social et Monophorisme*, 4.

52. Blondel, *Catholicisme Social et Monophorisme*, 18.

relationships among the different orders of reality; and theology: the nature-supernatural relationship. Blondel used these articles to clarify his "philosophy of action." The contrasting positions that he limned, he attributed to the Maurrassian Catholics. Both mentalities were anti-modernist; they were nevertheless on a collision course.

The first thesis concerns "the problem of knowledge and the relations of thought with action."[53] This thesis is the philosophical crux of the other two.

> Actions are not simply the putting into practice of logically defined ideas and of geometrically shaped theories; and everything is not decided in the domain of abstractions, as if human beings were only pure intellects, as if concepts were the adequate substitute of things and the sole motivation of the will, as if we governed ourselves by them and them alone. In individual and social practice, there is always something more and different than in the speculative systems that appear to inspire it. That is why the ideas that determine actions do not prevent actions from prompting new ideas that, even setting out from inexact and mutilating theses, can become liberating and healing. The life of human beings and of peoples obeys a more complex logic than that of abstract thought; what one does is often better or worse than what one thinks.[54]

On the other hand, extrinsicist monophorists like the Catholic Maurrassians embrace an epistemological essentialism, a notional realism, that claims that our concepts grasp reality, independently of any consideration of human subjectivity and historicity. In short, there is a tendency to separate theory and practice and to regard our clear and distinct ideas as giving an adequate grasp on reality.

The second thesis formulated the particular ontology that corresponded to "this dynamic philosophy of thought and action." This conception of being recognizes the "solidarity and continuity" among its different orders "without failing to recognize the distinction of beings and the hierarchy of different orders."[55] Reality is an interconnected whole in which no order of being is absolutely enclosed in itself. In contrast with every "exclusive ideology" that compartmentalizes the world in accord with its mental habit of "isolating ideas like intellectual atoms

---

53. Blondel, *Catholicisme Social et Monophorisme*, 26.
54. Blondel, *Catholicisme Social et Monophorisme*, 26–27, 32.
55. Blondel, *Catholicisme Social et Monophorisme*, 30.

and logical blocks," reality is a continuum where "there is action from the top down and from the bottom up."[56]

This philosophy of the interconnectedness of the various levels of reality counters classical economics and philosophical rationalism that effect a "murderous vivisection" on the unity of the human being and the world.[57] In a negative allusion to the influential social doctrine of Auguste Comte, which Charles Maurras had adopted, Blondel declared "deceptive and myopic, that social physics that desires to suffice for scientifically regulating public and private interests from a positivist point of view."[58] Reality is not a series of "water-tight" compartments that are totally self-contained.

The third fundamental orientation concerned the understanding of the nature-supernatural relationship. Blondel declared this thesis to be "the most delicate of the disputed points, that which dominates the entire debate."[59] While insisting that the supernatural order is "entirely gratuitous and absolutely transcendent," Blondel contended that this order is not only "superimposed," but it is also "supposed and presupposed" by the natural order. Carefully stating that the supernatural order "is never able to be *naturalized*," he continued:

> [The supernatural order] is destined to penetrate and to assume [the natural order] in itself without becoming confused with it. And at the same time that it is proposed from on high by Revelation, the Incarnation and the Redemption, which substantially constitute it and which are not simply facts to observe and mysteries to believe, but reach souls invisibly by the effulgence of the grace of which they are the source, act upon all human beings so to speak from below to enable them to break out of all the enclosures in which they would like to confine themselves, to raise them above themselves, to burst every merely natural equilibrium, to put them on a level, and require them to be in accord, with the plan of providence.[60]

---

56. Blondel, *Catholicisme Social et Monophorisme*, 30–31, 33.

57. Blondel, *Catholicisme Social et Monophorisme*, 31.

58. Blondel, *Catholicisme Social et Monophorisme*, 31. Auguste Comte (1798–1857) was the founder of "positivism," an anti-metaphysical social philosophy that metamorphosed into a "religion of humanity." Considered to be among the greatest post-revolution philosophers, Comte's bust was gloriously enshrined at the Sorbonne in 1902; two years later his remains were solemnly interred in the Pantheon.

59. Blondel, *Catholicisme Social et Monophorisme*, 31.

60. Blondel, *Catholicisme Social et Monophorisme*, 33.

Blondel maintained that the human person can only be understood in his actual, concrete historical circumstances, and not by a putative state of "pure nature." This open-ended anthropology recognizes that human striving can never be satisfactorily explained or fulfilled in sheerly positivist terms. The social Catholics look to specifically "Christian solutions" to socioeconomic problems because, contrary to the prevalent economic liberalism and sociological positivism, they recognize that a self-contained socioeconomic order is an abstraction that falsifies the actual supernatural destiny of the concrete person.[61] In contrast, the Catholic Maurrassians separate the natural and supernatural orders, so that the supernatural is treated as an external overlay. The supernatural order is a gratuitous superimposition by purely extrinsic command that relates to a purely passive obediential potency, without the external gift being able or having to entail the help of an interior contribution . . . [specifically supernatural truths] are only supernatural in the measure that they are defined, named, and expressly imposed by way of authority.[62]

Blondel termed the ensemble of philosophical and theological positions to which he subscribed "integral realism."[63] "Monophorism" was Blondel's term for a reigning clerical authoritarianism which on principle refused to recognize that grace can be at work from below. Extrinsicist monophorism, claiming that nature is sufficient unto itself or, at most, possesses a "suitability" with respect to the supernatural, unavoidably presents the supernatural as a "sort of counter-nature" and presents Christianity as "a law of fear and constraint, as an instrument of domination."[64] Blondel blamed the "manualist theology" for this perversion of the tradition.

The social Catholics and the philosophers of action have done the most to show "the essential heterogeneity and real continuity of the two orders" of the natural and the supernatural.[65] As will be explained below, by their openness to collaborating with anti-clerical republicans on programs and legislation to bring about social justice, the *Semaine sociale* Catholics effectively appropriated Blondel's non-dualist understanding of the nature-grace relationship. The Second Vatican Council will vindicate this understanding of the value of human efforts to promote a just

61. Blondel, *Catholicisme Social et Monophorisme*, 31–32.
62. Blondel, *Catholicisme Social et Monophorisme*, 34–35; emphasis added.
63. Blondel, *Catholicisme Social et Monophorisme*, 34–35.
64. Blondel, *Catholicisme Social et Monophorisme*, 67.
65. Blondel, *Catholicisme Social et Monophorisme*, 68.

social order in relationship to the Kingdom of God, which relationship is a consequence of the unitary destiny of the human person.[66]

Monophorists, on the other hand, juxtapose "an exclusively extrinsicist and authoritarian supernaturalism" to an all-sufficient nature. In contrast to the social Catholics who are attentive to "[the] stammerings, the complaints, [the] griefs" that arise from the people, the monophorists treat the people as a "perpetual child," demanding "a passive docility" and presenting Christianity not "as a liberation and a expansion for our being" but "as a new subjection, as an oppression weighing upon a nature already full, solid, and sufficient, and crushing it under the mystery and under the divine power."[67] In the face of this radical "denaturing" of the "Good News," Blondel poignantly asked: "Apart from the Catholic truth, is not the very meaning of the moral destiny and the human religious conscience misconstrued?"[68]

Poisonous Fruits of Monophorism

Blondel judged Catholic collaboration with Maurras to be the most scandalous fruit of extrinsicist monophorism. Exposing the nature of the alliance between Catholics and the Maurrassian positivists was the decisive point to make his case that this mentality killed the Christian spirit. He indicated a sinister explanation for the attraction of intransigent Catholics to a political alliance with pagans:

> It is their *a-Christianity* and even *anti-Christianity* that you love and assist in them, and, dare I say, that which is systematically irreligious. That is the terrible observation that we are going to make.[69]

Blondel maintained that Catholic monophorists and Maurrassian positivists shared a common conception of authority that suppressed "interiority" (*le fait intérieur*). For both types of authoritarians, "the enemy is the liberty of souls and the initiative of spirit."[70] Blondel viewed Descoqs's apology for Maurras as a logically consistent but fatally flawed approach to the fundamental problem of the Christian renewal of society.

---

66. See Paul VI, *Gaudium et Spes*.
67. Blondel, *Catholicisme Social et Monophorisme*, 71; emphasis added.
68. Blondel, *Catholicisme Social et Monophorisme*, 71.
69. Blondel, *Catholicisme Social et Monophorisme*, 139.
70. Blondel, *Catholicisme Social et Monophorisme*, 137–38.

Furthermore, Maurras's philosophy was patently anti-Christian and efforts to extenuate its true character were hardly worthy of refutation. Blondel did not engage in a meticulous, point by point refutation of the Jesuit's qualified case on behalf of Maurras. Rather, he addressed certain axial assertions and criticized them in the light of the flawed monophorist positions that he had already expounded.

The monophorist system followed a logic of three stages: first, the confiscation of civic liberty, and the domestication and mobilization of the Catholic faithful for a crusade under the banner of religion; second, the organization not only of an exclusively religious politics, but of a political religion; and third, the pursuit of the dream of a temporal Empire, spiritually elevated, against the secular power.[71] Blondel viewed this state of affairs with great alarm: "It is a matter of interests so serious that we will be pardoned for expressing here our fears . . . whether one likes it or not, whether it is known or not, this is the theological enormity and political insanity to which certain minds are headed in the present crisis."[72]

The monophorist philosophy of nature at work here separates the different levels of reality, denying to the lower levels "any spontaneity, any suppleness, any solidarity" in their subjection to the higher levels; "legality and formal literalness reign."[73] The monophorist system depends on linking the supernatural to a "solid" natural order by means of "logical principles and external data." "Reason only exists to obey and to proclaim reasonable the agnosticism that is imposed on it."[74] Though reason is championed, it remains captive within its enclosure.

Disclaiming an attack on persons or motives, Blondel strongly reproached the collaboration between Catholics and Maurrassians for which Descoqs had offered a qualified, "theoretical" endorsement. He asserted that this "demoralizing and de-Christianizing" solution proved worse than the harmful liberal alternative. It turns Catholicism into a "war machine, an instrument of earthly reign" under cover of admiring a notion of "order" that suppresses "the spontaneous movement of souls."[75]

---

71. Blondel, *Catholicisme Social et Monophorisme*, 99–100.
72. Blondel, *Catholicisme Social et Monophorisme*, 100.
73. Blondel, *Catholicisme Social et Monophorisme*, 95.
74. Blondel, *Catholicisme Social et Monophorisme*, 95.
75. Blondel, *Catholicisme Social et Monophorisme*, 124.

Assessing the Fundamental Issues

The exchange between Blondel and Descoqs was messy. It was marked by misunderstandings, accusations, and what the French term a *"procès de tendances"* (conflict of mentalities). At a certain point, each admitted that his adversary's positions could be given an acceptable interpretation. Nevertheless, even after the condemnation of Action Française in 1926, Descoqs continued to insist that Blondel's approach to the problem betrayed a dangerous confusion of the natural and supernatural orders. In my assessment, I will focus on the central theological issue: the different understandings of the nature-supernatural relationship.

The complexity and interconnectedness of their epistemological, ontological, and theological positions can be illuminated by three different images that give concrete expression to three contrasting ways of understanding the relationship between nature and the supernatural that figured in the dispute between Blondel and Descoqs. Blondel's own position that emphasized that reality is a "continuum" in which there are no perfectly self-contained "airtight compartments," and in which there is an exigence for the supernatural, could be imaged by the structure of the Pantheon.[76] In the architectural design of this ancient Roman building, the lines of force of the circular walls converge on the open space above, the primary source of light. Standing within the windowless building, one notices that no part of the cavernous interior is "compartmentalized," but the eye is directed upwards to the incoming light. Though the lower part of the structure has solidity, it has no self-contained status. There are no "walls of separation" that divide one section from another. Furthermore, without the light that descends from above, it would be impossible to take adequate account of the lower levels.

No analogy is problem free, but I think this image wonderfully captures Blondel's view of the nature-supernatural relationship, both in its positive and defective aspects. On the positive side, it does translate Blondel's sense of the *élan* of the human spirit (and the whole created order) that is nowhere *chez lui* "at home"), but whose dialectical movement requires the supernatural to make ultimate sense. There is movement from below upward, and from on high downward. It also conveys the

---

76. I am indebted to Elizabeth A. Johnson for her reference to the Pantheon as an image to gain insight into a specific type of theological anthropology. Johnson, *Consider Jesus*, 24. Johnson does not explicitly relate this image to Blondel's philosophy of the supernatural, nor does she develop the image in such a detailed fashion.

ambiguity of Blondel's understanding of an "exigence" for the supernatural, i.e., the necessity that the supernatural be given in order for the lower levels to make sense. Indeed, the architectural design of the Pantheon translates Descoqs's accusation that Blondel's defective view of conceptual knowledge results in an undermining of the proper autonomy of the natural order. Imagine that the sole source of light in the Pantheon comes from the opening above—the oculus—at which the structural lines from below converge. Is this not analogous to Descoqs's charge that Blondel seemed to imply that humans can only attain certitude in their knowing by means of the experience of the supernatural? And that "without this light pouring in from up above," human understanding cannot attain a certain grasp of the truth? It seems that for Blondel the experience of grace was a *sine qua non* for arriving at truth.

The second image illuminates the understanding of the nature-supernatural relationship that Blondel ascribed to "extrinsicist monophorism," and thus to Descoqs. Imagine a two-story house with a ground floor that is partitioned into several rooms. This floor is completely furnished and fully livable. The windows provide sufficient light to carry on the tasks of daily life. The family residing on the ground floor has no real need of an upper floor. However, there does exist a second floor to which access is gained when trapdoors are opened from above and portable staircases let down. Only then does the family come to know of the existence of this upper level of which they had no previous inkling. They are told, furthermore, that a superior life awaits them above and that they must choose to ascend to the second floor under threat of being thrown out of the house altogether.

The ground floor is comparable to a supposed "pure nature" that has its own, self-contained consistency and fulfillment. The partitioning of the rooms corresponds to the divisions among the various sciences that are only externally connected with each other. By God's gift, a supernatural destiny (the second floor) has been added and staircases have been let down from above (God's salvific plan actualized in the sacramental ministry of the Church) by which the ground floor inhabitants gain access to supernatural life. There seems, however, to be nothing in their native experience that would make such a move to a higher, supernatural life a compelling necessity except for the fact that a summons, a revelation "from above," has been issued.

Such an image of "extrinsicist monophorism" in which the supernatural is regarded as a superimposition on a self-sufficient nature, characterized by a mere non-repugnancy for the supernatural, corresponds to the notion that Blondel derided. He ascribed this understanding to those whom he labeled as "monophorists." For Blondel, this conception of an adventitious, extrinsic relationship of the supernatural to nature explained why these monophorists accused him of undermining the claims of the natural order. Such monophorists would never admit of an "exigence" that would connect the two orders. Descoqs, however, rejected Blondel's imputation that he denied any exchange between the natural and supernatural orders and that he viewed grace as only a veneer, imposed by intellectual dialectic and authority. Descoqs rejected both of these understandings of the nature-supernatural relationship that have been pictured by the Pantheon and the two-story house.

A third image presents a significant variation on the second image and seems to correspond to Descoqs's understanding of the nature-supernatural relationship. This image also consists of a two-story house, but the inhabitants are no longer fully content to live on the ground floor but feel a longing ("attractions") for a possible second floor, the existence and nature of which they are incapable of ascertaining by reason alone. Once they have received the revelation by "external word" of the existence of and summons to an upper floor promising supernatural life, they experience an efficacious, positive desire ("grace") to dwell there. This positive desire, however, does not utterly cancel out the legitimate functions of the first floor. The first floor is inhabitable and is not dependent on the upper floor for its purpose and meaning. Even though, in the light of an explicit revelation, life on the second floor is shown to be infinitely superior to life on the first floor, the first floor continues to serve as a necessary support to life on the second floor and does not lose that function even after the occupants gain access to the upper level.

I want to suggest another image that addresses the concerns of Descoqs and Blondel, respectively, regarding the nature-grace relationship. Imagine an A-Frame cottage where the first floor has a certain solidity, but this living space is not completely separated off from an upper region which completes the structure. In this architectural analogy, the quasi-integrity of the ground floor corresponds to Descoqs's insistence that human reason can attain certain truths unaided by supernatural grace. The ground floor, however, is not absolutely self-contained and has an orientation to supernatural completion, symbolized by the upper level to which it is open and which is not extrinsically imposed on the lower level. This architectural image of a "natural" ground level that is not complete in itself but whose construction from the get-go opens to an upper-level captures the inherent dynamism towards supernatural fulfillment for which Blondel's philosophy of action contended.

Conclusion

Blondel's defense of the *Semaine sociale* Catholics over against their Catholic integralist opponents was buttressed by his philosophy of action that sought to overcome the pernicious extrinsicism that resulted from the modern scholastic separation of the natural order from the supernatural order.[77] He repeatedly and emphatically stressed the "fundamental error" that poisoned both the integralist Maurrassians and their monophorist apologists: "the failure to recognize the inner working of the divine gift, the doubly religious spontaneity of souls that are under the action of both grace and liberty."[78] Blondel's analysis of "monophorism" received high praise from the twentieth century's most distinguished theologians. Hans Urs von Balthasar (1905–88) claimed that Maurice Blondel's "Testis" articles were the unsurpassed treatment of the symptoms and diagnosis of the "integralist" mentality.[79] Balthasar's nephew Peter Henrici, SJ (1928–2023), described the "Testis" essays as "the most penetrating analysis of [what is called] Catholic integralism [*integrisme*] that ... represents an ever recurrent temptation for militant Catholics."[80] Balthasar described the nature of this Catholic integralism:

> From Blondel's investigations and beyond their situational contingency, [integralism] can be simply defined: integralism prevails wherever revelation is presented *primarily* as a system of true propositions to be believed from above and where, *as a result*, form is placed above content, power above the cross. The integralist strives by all means, visible and hidden, public and secret, *first* to gain political and social power for the church, and then to proclaim the Sermon on the Mount and Golgotha from this secured citadel and pulpit. This seemingly purely tactical

---

77. Henri de Lubac, SJ (1896–1991), gave Blondel primary credit for helping overcome the extrinsicist mentality that crippled Christian thought. See Lubac, *Brief Catechesis*, 37–38. As for the *Semaines sociales de France*, they continue to meet annually, bringing Catholic social teaching to bear upon contemporary social problems. For their annual program, see their website at https://www.ssf-fr.org/page/453326-accueil.

78. Blondel, *Catholicisme Social et Monophorisme*, 124; emphasis added.

79. See Balthasar, "Integralismus."

80. Blondel, *Une alliance contre nature*, viii.

"first" inherently contains, consciously or unconsciously, a higher value. The end value, for whose sake first and foremost the money, earthly power, and organization is collected, hoarded, and launched, inevitably gets caught in the tow of the putative value of the means, if the end value is just the humiliated lamb, the crucified love.[81]

Charles Hughes Huff and Anne Carpenter, the translators of Balthasar's essay, observe:

> In the US today, integralism is back with explicit adherents. Post-liberal Catholics in positions of distinct cultural power advance many of the same sorts of claims that Balthasar analyzes and rejects in this article. One example will suffice: Adrian Vermuele, of Harvard Law School, describes the necessity of political power: "One cannot argue a man out of an illusion with mere words; one has to make him see that it is wrong, to change his angle of vision. In some cases, the most obstinate cases, the liberal cannot be persuaded, but only defeated and reconciled." This type of rhetoric well fits Blondel's analysis of integralism as a political system that takes up worldly power to enforce "right concepts," using such coercion to "move the world rightly."[82]

Ironically, British Anglican theologian John Milbank has also appealed to Blondel's philosophy of action in support of his integralist position.[83] Milbank apparently interprets Blondel's philosophy of the natural-supernatural relationship according to the first image described above whereby "the experience of grace [is] a *sine qua non* for arriving at truth." While expressing admiration for Milbank's "breath-taking book . . . [and] breadth of intellectual culture," Aidan Nichols, among other critics, has pointedly described Milbank's thought as "hermetic" and "theocratic."[84] "For Milbank there can be no such thing as an intellectual indebtedness of the Church to natural wisdom."[85] Nichols acknowledges, with Milbank, that Blondel's philosophy sought to "supernaturalize the natural," but disagrees that Blondel, or de Lubac or Balthasar, "rejected any formal

---

81. Balthasar, "Integralismus," para. 7.

82. Carpenter and Huff, "Against Integralism," para. 11. See also Blakely, "Integralism of Adrian Vermuele."

83. "It [Blondel's philosophy] is, perhaps, the boldest exercise in Christian thought in modern times." Milbank, *Theology and Social Theory*, 219.

84. Nichols, "Milbank's Suasion to Orthodoxy," 326. See also the review by Kerr, "Simplicity Itself."

85. Nichols, "Milbank's Suasion to Orthodoxy," 327.

distinction of nature from the supernatural."[86] As described above, however, there was a certain ambiguity in Blondel's original work regarding the natural-supernatural relationship that Blondel sought to clarify in his mature work.[87]

Blondel's diagnosis has lost none its relevance at a time of increase of Christian nationalist movements that seek alliances with Christian institutions to attain political power. The case he made to justify the initiatives of the *Semaines sociales* Catholics who were open to collaboration with anti-clerical liberal republicans to achieve justice, on the one hand, and his incisive criticism of Catholic integralism, on the other, resonates with Pope Francis's refusal of "religious integralisms and nationalisms of exclusion."[88] The Blondelian legacy, especially the renewed understanding of the nature-grace relationship, is still pertinent to contemporary politico-theological debates.

Bibliography

Aubert, Roger. "La discordance (1880–1918)." In *Les jésuites et la société Française*, edited by Dominic Avon and Philippe Rocher, 81–120. Paris: Éditions Privat, 2001.

Balthasar, Hans Urs von. "Integralismus." Translated by Charles Huff and Anne Carpenter. *Theology and Society*. https://theologyandsociety.com/integralismus/.

Bernardi, Peter J. *Maurice Blondel, Social Catholicism, and Action Française: The Clash over the Church's Role in Society during the Modernist Era*. Washington, DC: Catholic University of America Press, 2009.

———. "Social Modernism: The Case of the *Semaines sociales*." In *Catholicism Contending with Modernity: Roman Catholic Modernism and Anti-Modernism in Historical Context*, edited by Darrell Jodock, 277–307. Cambridge: Cambridge University Press, 2000.

Blakely, Jason. "Not Catholic Enough: The Integralism of Adrian Vermeule." *Commonweal* 147 (2020) 34–37.

Blondel, Maurice. *Action: Essay on a Critique of Life and a Science of Practice*. Translated by Oliva Blanchette. Notre Dame: University of Notre Dame Press, 1984.

---

86. Nichols, "Milbank's Suasion to Orthodoxy," 328.

87. In his mature work, published in the 1930s and 1940s, Blondel was at pains to clarify ambiguities found in his 1893 dissertation *Action* regarding the natural order and its dynamic relationship to supernatural fulfillment. For example, Blondel wrote in his 1944 two-volume *La Philosophie et L'Esprit Chrétien*: "Loin donc de surnaturaliser d'emblée, de façon confuse ou présomptueuse et pervertissante, l'élan spirituel de la conscience proprement humaine, nous chercherons et trouverons toujours dans l'activité de la raison un fonds positif et solide à mettre en culture" (1:xiin1). Also see the correspondence between Blondel and de Lubac in Russo, *Henri de Lubac*, 177–200.

88. See Lind, "Maurice Blondel et le pape François."

---. *L'Action: Essai d'une critique de la vie et d'une science de la pratique.* Paris: Presses universitaires de France, 1950.
---. *Catholicisme Social et Monophorisme: Controverses sur les Méthodes et les Doctrines.* Paris: Bloud, 1910.
---. *La Philosophie et L'Esprit Chrétien.* 2 vols. Paris: Presses Universitaires de France, 1944.
---. "La 'Semaine sociale' de Bordeaux: Testis." *Annales de philosophie chrétienne* 159 (October 1909) 5–21; 159 (November 1909) 163–84; 159 (December 1909) 245–78; 159 (January 1910) 372–92; 159 (February 1910) 449–71; 159 (March 1910) 561–92; 160 (May 1910) 127–62.
---. *Une alliance contre nature: catholicisme et intégrisme: La Semaine sociale de Bordeaux 1910.* Bruxelles: Éditions Lessius, 2000.
Blondel, Maurice, and Johannes Wehrlé. *Correspondance.* 2 vols. Paris: Aubier-Montaigne, 1969.
Bouillard, Henri. *Blondel and Christianity.* Translated by James M. Somerville. Washington, DC: Corpus, 1969.
Carpenter, Anne, and Charles Hughes Huff. "Against Integralism." *Theology and Society.* https://theologyandsociety.com/against-integralism/.
Coreth, Emerich. *Christliche Philosophie in Katholischen Denken des 19. und 20. Jahrhunderts.* Band 2. Köln: Styra, 1988.
Cubitt, Geoffrey. *The Jesuit Myth: Conspiracy Theory and Politics in Nineteenth-Century France.* Oxford: Clarendon, 1993.
Descoqs, Pedro. "À travers l'oeuvre de M. Ch. Maurras [1]." *Études* 120 (July 1909) 153–86.
---. "À travers l'oeuvre de M. Ch. Maurras [2]." *Études* 120 (August 1909) 330–346.
---. "À travers l'oeuvre de M. Ch. Maurras [3]." *Études* 120 (September 1909) 593–628.
---. "À travers l'oeuvre de M. Ch. Maurras [4]." *Études* 121 (December 1909) 602–28.
---. "À travers l'oeuvre de M. Ch. Maurras [5]." *Études* 121 (December 1909) 773–86.
---. *À travers l'oeuvre de M. Ch. Maurras.* Paris: Beauchesne, 1911.
---. *À travers l'oeuvre de M. Ch. Maurras.* 3rd ed. Paris: Beauchesne, 1913.
---. "Monophorisme et Action Française." *Annales de philosophie chrétienne* 160 (1910) 225–51.
---. *Monophorisme et Action Française.* 3rd ed. Paris: Beauchesne, 1913.
Dru, A. "From the *Action Française* to the Second Vatican Council: Blondel's 'La Semaine sociale de Bordeaux.'" *Downside Review* 81 (1963) 226–45.
Fouilloux, Étienne. *Les jésuites à Lyon XVI–XX siècle. Sous la direction de Étienne Fouilloux et Bernard Hours.* Lyon: ENS Éditions, 2005.
Johnson, Elizabeth. *Consider Jesus.* New York: Crossroad, 1990.
Kerr, Fergus. "Simplicity Itself: Milbank's Thesis." *New Blackfriars* 73 (1992) 305–10.
Kerwin, Michael. "Blondel, Maurice." In *Augustine through the Ages: An Encyclopedia*, edited by Allan D. Fitzgerald, 103–5. Grand Rapids: Eerdmans, 1999.
Kloppenberg, James. "Is American Democracy Coming Apart?" *Commonweal* 150 (2023) 16–27.
Le Grys, James. "The Christianization of Modern Philosophy according to Maurice Blondel." *Theological Studies* 54 (1993) 455–84.
Lind, Andreas. "Maurice Blondel et le pape François: une pensée parallèle sur le refus des intégrismes et des nationalismes." *La Croix*, November 29, 2019. https://

doc-catho.la-croix.com/Urbi-et-Orbi/Documentation-catholique/Eglise-en-France/Maurice-Blondel-pape-Francois-pensee-parallele-refus-integrismes-nationalismes-conference-dAndreas-Lind-2019-11-29-1201063481.

Lorin, M. H. "La *Semaine sociale*: son caractère—son objectif—sa méthode, declaration faite par M. H. Lorin." Semaine sociale de France: Deuxième Session des Cours de Doctrine et de Pratique sociales, Orléans, 31 juillet—6 août. Compte-rendu. Lyons: Chronique du Sud–Est, 1905.

Lubac, Henri de. *A Brief Catechesis on Nature and Grace*. Translated by Richard Arnandez. San Francisco: Ignatius, 1984.

Maurras, Charles. "Preface." In *Le Dilemme de Marc Sangnier: essai sur la démocratie religieuse in La Démocratie Religieuse*, 17–29. Paris: Nouvelle Librairie Nationale, 1921.

McCool, Gerald A. *Catholic Theology in the Nineteenth Century: The Quest for a Unitary Method*. New York: Crossroad, 1977.

Milbank, John. *Theology and Social Theory: Beyond Secular Reason*. 2nd ed. Malden, MA: Blackwell, 2006.

Nicols, Aidan. "'*Non tali auxilio*': John Milbank's Suasion to Orthodoxy." *New Blackfriars* 73 (1992) 326–32.

Paul VI. *Gaudium et Spes: Pastoral Constitution on the Church in the Modern World*. Vatican City: Libreria Editrice Vaticana, 1965. https://www.vatican.va/archive/hist_councils/ii_vatican_council/documents/vat-ii_const_19651207_gaudium-et-spes_en.html.

Picard, Gabriel. "In Memoriam: Le Père Pedro Descoqs." *Archives de philosophie* 18 (1949) 129–35.

Pius X. *Encyclical Letter (Pascendi) of His Holiness Pope Pius X on the Doctrines of the Modernists to Which Is Added the Decree (Lamentabili) of July 4, 1907, on Modernist Errors*. London: Catholic Truth Society, 1907.

———. *Lamentabili sine exitu*. https://www.papalencyclicals.net/pius10/p10lamen.htm.

———. *Notre Charge Apostolique*. https://www.papalencyclicals.net/pius10/p10notre.htm.

———. *Pascendi dominici gregis*. https://www.papalencyclicals.net/pius10/p10pasce.htm.

———. *Vehementer Nos*. https://www.papalencyclicals.net/pius10/p10law.htm.

Riordan, Patrick. *Human Dignity and Liberal Politics: Catholic Possibilities for the Common Good*. Washington, DC: Georgetown University Press, 2023.

Russo, Antonio. *Henri de Lubac: Teologia e Dogma nella storia*. Rome: Edizioni Studium, 1990.

Schindler, David C. "What Is Liberalism?" In *The Politics of the Real: The Church between Liberalism and Integralism*, 3–40. Steubenville, OH: New Polity, 2021.

Stern, Alexander. "Centrist Illusions." *Commonweal* 150 (2023) 36–41.

Taylor, Charles. *A Secular Age*. Cambridge: Harvard University, 2007.

7

The Gospel and Human Dignity
Catholicism and Liberalism in Dialogue

DREW CHRISTIANSEN, SJ, GEORGETOWN UNIVERSITY (†)

Abstract: This essay illustrates how the discernment of the Magisterium—through its Social Doctrine—demonstrates a fruitful dialogue and collaboration between Catholicism and the key principles of the liberal political tradition, especially in its Anglo-American forms. The fecundity of this encounter was especially evident as the Church and world sought to respond to not only the experience of Fascism—with which many Catholics were entangled—but also the Second World War that grew out of it. In working to build a postwar order consistent with a robust account of the common good, this essay traces how the social encyclicals of Pope St. John XXIII mark the first ample embrace of the key tenets of liberalism including human rights, constitutional and democratic government, the equal dignity of every human person. It continues with a survey of how this fruitful dialogue with liberal principles continues through the teachings of the Second Vatican Council and through the subsequent social Magisterium of Popes St. Paul VI, St. John Paul II, Benedict XVI, and Francis all of whom presume a universal scope of the common good giving our social tradition a cosmopolitan perspective. The essay also notes the obvious fact that these convictions of Catholic social doctrine "are at odds in recent years with illiberal populist movements and overly zealous advocates of religious liberty."

The Gospel and Human Dignity—CHRISTIANSEN

> By no human law can the personal dignity and liberty of [human beings] be so aptly safeguarded as by the Gospel of Christ which has been entrusted to the Church. For this Gospel announces and proclaims the freedom of the [children] of God, and repudiates all the bondage which ultimately results from sin (cf. Rom. 8:14–17); it has a sacred reverence for the dignity of conscience and its freedom of choice.[1]

ON APRIL 11, 1963, with the publication of Pope Saint John XXIII's encyclical letter *Pacem in Terris: Peace on Earth*, the curtain came down on Catholicism's "long nineteenth century."[2] While Leo XIII's *Rerum Novarum: The Condition of Labor* is commonly regarded as the first social encyclical of the modern era, *Pacem in Terris* was the first encyclical to amply embrace modernity and in particular to subscribe to several tenets of Liberalism: human rights, constitutional government, democratic participation, the self-determination of peoples, and the equality of persons, especially women. Pius IX had condemned many of these propositions in his 1864 *Syllabus of Errors*, the epitome of Catholicism's long nineteenth century—long because it reached right up to the early 1960s.

While Syllabus declared that the pope would not reconcile with "progress, liberalism and modern civilization," John XXIII acclaimed the qualities that characterize "the present age" without criticism and praised those who labored and sacrificed to realize these goals within their societies and across the world. He also defined the proper work of government as "the recognition, respect, safeguarding and promotion of the rights of the human person."[3] Indeed, according to the encyclical, the cardinal principle of Catholic social thought, the common good, consists in citizens' enjoyment of these rights and government's protective activities on their behalf.

---

1. Paul VI, *Gaudium et Spes*, no. 41.

2. Historiographers attribute the first use of the phrase "long nineteenth century" for the period between the French Revolution (1789) and World War I (1914) to the British Marxist historian Eric Hobsbwam. In his *What Happened*, O'Malley extended the term to refer to Catholic Church history from the French Revolution to the death of Pius XII (1958).

3. John XXIII, *Pacem in Terris*, no. 139.

A Rapprochement with Liberalism

Pacem in Terris (PT) stands as the threshold between the church of the long nineteenth century, the church that defined itself by its alliance to the *ancien* régime, and the church as a community of faith in dialogue with the modern world, the post-Vatican II church. PT, however, is more than the threshold; it is also a master plan for the church's engagement with the world in which human rights advocacy has played a leading part. PT is the foundational text of modern Catholic political theology. Besides elaborating a doctrine of human rights, it presents a model of responsible, limited political authority, articulates for the first time the architectonic political norm of the universal common good, offers a new vision of the role of the church in politics and society, and embraces its call to be an instrument of peace for the one human family.[4]

Post-War Context

Though it is seldom noted, *Pacem in Terris* represented a rapprochement between Catholicism and Liberalism, both the Anglo-American political tradition with its stress on ordered liberty and democratic participation, and, perhaps to a lesser degree, with continental Liberalism due to its aggressive secularism and anti-clericalism. Both streams embraced human rights, but they differed in the degree to which they relied on state intervention and in how they conceived the relation of church and state.

In the post-war era, American support for Christian Democracy brought about greater congruence between Catholicism and the Anglo-American stream of the Liberal Tradition. The anti-fascist struggles of Catholic intellectuals like Jacques Maritain and Pietro Pavan, both of whom contributed to an appreciation of human rights and democracy among Catholics, also enforced this rapprochement. Among their admiring readers were Angelo Roncalli (Pope John XXIII) and Giovanni Batitsta Montini (Pope Paul VI). These liberal Catholic intellectuals had significant influence on the later development of the Church's social doctrine, Maritain indirectly, but Pavan directly, since he was the principal drafter of John XXIII's social encyclicals, Mater et *magistra* and *Pacem in Terris*. In addition, the founders of what became the European Union which consolidated liberal values within the European system—Robert

---

4. See my commentary *"Pacem in Terris,"* 217–43, especially 223–36 for the treatment of rights, governance, and international affairs.

Schuman, Jean Monnet, Konrad Adenauer, and Alcide de Gasperi—were all educated in Catholic Social Teaching and embraced European unity as a means of securing peace along the lines Pius XII projected during World War II.[5]

Pope John XXIII and Pope Paul VI as young priests had been active in Catholic Action, and they continued their contacts with the movement throughout their careers. As nuncio to Paris, John had encouraged the French jurist René Cassin in the drafting of the Universal Declaration of Human Rights. As pope, moreover, he endeavored to disengage the Vatican and the Italian bishops from direct (and compromising) involvement in Italian politics to adopt a more pastoral style in public affairs. John himself wrote the passage distinguishing between ideology and person that justified collaboration between Catholics and their ideological opponents, namely, Marxists, even while opposing their beliefs.[6]

In PT, John XXIII upheld a set of liberal values including "human dignity, freedom, equality and solidarity" along with limited government.[7] At the time, the most controversial of these values was freedom, explicitly condemned by Pio Nono in the Syllabus. John's conservative consultants objected to its inclusion, believing freedom conflicts with acknowledgment of the truth. For example, George Jarlot, a theologian at the Gregorian University and a Vatican consultant, balked at freedom as an "unsure guide" in public affairs.[8] Others, however, saw it as essential to John's approach to social teaching. Prophetically, John Courtney Murray found that John's "method of freedom" provided the basis for a complete unitary Catholic doctrine of Church and State capable of prudent application in the political and religious conditions of our times."[9] Murray, of course, whose life work focused on religious liberty and the church's acceptance of the American experiment had led to his censure by Roman

---

5. On Pius's plans for a post-war peace, see Riebling, *Church of Spies*.

6. The passage reads: "One must never confuse error and the person who errs. . . . The person who errs is always and above all a human being, and he retains in every case his dignity as a human person . . . [in whom] there is a need that is congenital to his nature and never extinguished, compelling him to break through the error and open his mind to the knowledge of the truth." John XXIII, *Pacem in Terris*, no. 158.

7. Here I will principally discuss the liberal political and juridical values the church beginning with John XXIII endorsed. I will leave the more complicated relation between Catholicism and liberal or neoliberal economics for another time. On those matters, Catholic social teaching has, on the whole, been far more critical, and in return conservative Catholic theorists have been prone to dissent from Church teaching.

8. Cited in Zizola, *Utopia of John XXIII*, 20.

9. Murray, "Things Old and New," 251–52.

officials, within two years would be one of the principal drafters of *Dignitatis Humanae*, the council's Declaration on Religious Liberty.[10]

Religion in Public Life

Many years later Pope Emeritus Benedict XVI, who lost his bid to include a reference to the continent's Christian heritage in the new European constitution, gave tribute to the Anglo-American tradition. In an exchange with the Laicist president of the Italian Senate Marcello Pera, Benedict acknowledged Catholics and liberal secularists like Pera open to Christianity shared many values.[11] There exists, he posited, "a Christian civil religion" in secular Europe. Appealing to the tree in the Parable of the Mustard Seed (Matt 13:31–32), he allowed, "the tree of the Kingdom of God reaches beyond the branches of the visible Church,"[12] and "seekers and believers in the dense thicket of branches filled with many birds, must move toward one another with greater openness."[13]

With reference to the American political tradition, Benedict argued, its conception of religious liberty "allow(s) religion to be itself."[14] In America unlike Europe, Benedict acknowledged, the separation of church and state permits religion and an array of private institutions, including universities, to flourish independent of the central government. "American society is built on a separation of church and state that is determined and indeed demanded by religion," he wrote, "(a separation whose motivation and configuration could not be more different from the conflictual separation of church and state imposed by the French Revolution and the systems that followed it.)"[15] In America, Benedict observed, "the private sphere has an absolutely public character."[16] In short,

---

10. On Murray's struggles and eventual vindication, see Huddock, *Struggle, Condemnation, Vindication*. For Murray's essays on the American Experiment, see *We Hold These Truths*.

11. See Ratzinger and Pera, *Without Roots*. At the time of this exchange of speeches and letters with Marcello Pera, Benedict was still Cardinal Josef Ratzinger, prefect of the Congregation of the Doctrine of the Faith. By the time it was published, he had become pope.

12. Ratzinger and Pera, *Without Roots*, 121.

13. Ratzinger and Pera, *Without Roots*, 123.

14. Ratzinger and Pera, *Without Roots*, 111.

15. Ratzinger and Pera, *Without Roots*, 110.

16. Ratzinger and Pera, *Without Roots*, 111.

American liberalism, while it separates state from the church, nonetheless, allows space for faith in political and social life.

While Benedict, operating within Vatican II's understanding of religion in public life, found common ground with Pera and others who share the Christian civil religion, a number of American and English Catholics have been rejecting the American experiment, proposing alternative ways to live their faith in an increasingly secular society. Patrick Deneen, Rod Dreher and John Milbank, drawing on Alasdair MacIntyre and Stanley Hauerwas, hope to foster intentional Christian communities in a post-Christian world branding this proposal "the Benedict Option" (named for the father of western monasticism, not the pope emeritus).[17] This inclination to simplicity of life lived in community is consistent with Gospel models of holiness and church renewal as in the Franciscan movement and today's lay ecclesial communities.[18] In some respects, it is also coherent with certain themes in contemporary papal teaching. The ecological accents in some of these reflect John Paul II's calls for human ecology,[19] and Pope Francis' concern for indigenous communities and his vision of communities of faith as healers of the cleft between the environment, culture and community, which are also major concerns of these critics.[20] At the same time, however, Francis warns of the escapist sectarianism that turns its back on a sorely afflicted world, especially evident in Dreher's version of the Benedict Option.[21] On the whole, the Church's integral ecology is inconsistent with today's anti liberal Christian movements.[22] Without serious re-working to oppose exclusivism, nationalism, and their ecclesial equivalent, sectarianism, the quest for small communities may not come to cohere with the political-moral expression of Catholicism,

---

17. "The Benedict Option" takes its name from the final suggestive chapter of Alasdair MacIntyre's *After Virtue* and especially its elaboration in Ron Dreher's countercultural Christian manifesto *The Benedict Option*. Perhaps the most formidable of the texts in this school is John Milbank's *Theology and Social Theory*, remarkable for its historical commentary and dialectical criticism but disappointing in its constructive ecclesiology.

18. On Francis, see Boff, *Saint Francis*, and on contemporary lay movements, see Leahy, *Ecclesial Movements and Communities*.

19. John Paul II, "Peace with God, Peace with All Creation," no. 14.

20. Francis, *Laudato Si'*, nos. 110–12, 144–46.

21. Francis, *Laudato Si'*, nos. 126, 149. For Dreher's proposal, see n17 [X-REF] above.

22. On integral ecology, see Francis, *Laudato Si'*, especially nos. 137–62.

namely, cosmopolitanism, its sense of responsibility to the world community and to the institutions needed to serve humanity at a global level.[23]

Cosmopolitanism, Community, and Culture

Catholic Cosmopolitanism namely, the conviction that Christians must act as citizens of the world as well as of a particular state and that political authorities everywhere have duties to defend the rights of persons anywhere is only partially shared with the Anglo-American Liberal Tradition. Generally, cosmopolitanism is a theory of international affairs that focuses on the realization of human rights across borders rather than state interests. Briefly put, in Catholic social teaching as in other cosmopolitan theories of justice, humanity trumps nationality.[24]

The Liberal International Order of the late twentieth century was based on the expansion of democracy, human rights and the rule of law outside the North Atlantic/Mediterranean Basins. In its first forty-five years, however, those tendencies were subordinate to the interests of the Cold War rivalry between the U.S. and USSR, epitomized in the Kirkpatrick Doctrine according to which the U.S. supported traditional authoritarian regimes when they shared U.S. foreign policy aims, but opposed revolutionary, that is Communist and left-leaning, autocracies.[25] Following the collapse of the Soviet Union the rights-based view of the international order was again eclipsed by, and arguably conflated with, economic globalization. Before the collapse of Communism, Pope Saint John Paul II condemned this "logic of blocs" scandalized neoconservative thinkers, who charged him with "moral equivalence."[26] Later, in *Car-*

---

23. John XXIII, *Pacem in Terris*, nos. 136–41. It is significant that from the start, the universal common good entails institutions to effect it. On the institutional duties correlative to rights, see Shue, *Basic Rights*, 166–73.

24. Martha Nussbaum, one of America's leading moral and political philosophers, has wrestled with finding a balance between global and local responsibilities. She argued first for a strong theory vindicating rights across borders in her essay "Patriotism and Cosmopolitanism." Then she argued for a more limited version, giving more weight to the nation-state's role in *The Cosmopolitan Tradition*. Miller, *National Responsibility*, explores both weak and strong forms of cosmopolitanism, opting against global egalitarianism but for "a split-level view of agents' responsibilities" on the grounds that it entails a more adequate conception of moral agency and responsibility.

25. Later U.S. Ambassador Jeane Kirkpatrick first rationalized double standards in a 1979 *Commentary* essay "Dictatorship and Double Standards." As Ronald Reagan's ambassador to the United Nations, she made the double standard U.S. foreign policy.

26. John Paul II, *Sollicitudo Rei Socialis*, nos. 22–39.

itas in Veritate ("Love in Truth"), Pope Emeritus Benedict would level a strenuous critique of the global financial system at the heart of economic globalization;[27] and Pope Francis in *Fratelli Tutti* proposes re-envisaging the social role of property with rights and duties beyond borders.[28]

To a degree, the disparity between Catholic Social Teaching and the Anglo-American Tradition on international justice is visible in the development of late-twentieth-century American political philosophy. The premier American essay on justice in the last third of the century was John Rawls' *Theory of Justice* (1971), but under the constraint of Rawls' method its referent was a moderately liberal society generated in a thought experiments unaffected by the historical conditions that have affected the evolution of Catholic Social Teaching.[29] While Charles R. Beitz built on Rawls' theory to elaborate a cosmopolitan theory of justice in his 1979 book *Political Theory and International Relations*, only in 1999 did Rawls release his own book-length study of international justice, *The Law of Peoples*. Beitz's cosmopolitanism with its emphasis on the rights of persons across borders, however, comes closer to Catholic Social Teaching than Rawls, but on the whole, in theory and practice, the Anglo-American political tradition places more weight on national interests than personal or minority group rights.

Catholicism's cosmopolitanism has biblical roots, particularly the dominical command, "You shall be my witnesses in Jerusalem and in all Judea and Samaria and to the ends of the earth" (Acts 1:8).[30] It continues with the Church's expansion across the Roman world and beyond, with the reach of the early ecumenical councils, and after the European discovery of the New World in the missionary expansion of Christianity to

---

27. Benedict XVI, *Caritas in Veritate*, nos. 33–36. The Pontifical Council for Justice and Peace later released a more technical examination of the issue, "Towards Reforming the International Financial and Monetary Systems."

28. Francis, *Fratelli Tutti*, nos. 118–27.

29. Even though it enjoys a substrate of principled political philosophy rooted in the Scholastic tradition, the development of Catholic Social Teaching, even before Pope John XXIII and Vatican II introduced the "Signs of the Times" method and was deeply affected by evolving historical conditions. In this respect, it is far different from Rawls' historically neutral theories. Of course, they presume their persuasiveness to a basically liberal society.

30. Interestingly, Orthodox Jewish rabbis have recognized a providential role for Christianity in spreading knowledge of the One God and the moral law to the ends of the earth, thereby sharing in the Jewish vocation to witness to divine revelation. See Center for Jewish–Christian Understanding and Cooperation, "To Do the Will of Our Father in Heaven."

Asia and the Americas. Today the Church's cosmopolitanism is a function of its international presence and the relations of solidarity fostered by Vatican II's mandating of what today is known as the Dicastery for Integral Human Development, "for the worldwide promotion of justice for the poor . . . to foster programs in needy regions, and social justice on the international scene."[31]

Gaudium et Spes also introduced a distinctively Catholic take on what would come to be called globalization but was then described as "growing interdependence."[32] Drawing on the Thomist conception of the social and political nature of human persons, the Council saw as one of the signs of the times a phenomenon it called "socialization," a growth and complexification of social ties.[33] The Council wrote,

> In our era for various reasons, reciprocal ties and mutual dependencies increase day by day and give rise to a variety of associations and organizations, both public and private.

Thus, the modern magisterium, while alert to its dangers, nonetheless has looked positively on globalization. For the Council, the communitarian character of human nature comes to fruition in the virtue of solidarity exemplified in the Jesus, the Word Incarnate.[34] In that spirit, the Council urged that citizens of all states "must look simultaneously to the welfare of the whole human family, which is tied together in manifold bonds linking races, peoples and nations."[35]

The Institutional Principle

Solidarity is a moral virtue that gives rise at the level of the *polis* to political institutions. In *Pacem in Terris*, Pope Saint John XXIII had introduced the concept of the universal common good with the concomitant political requirement of a global public authority "in a position to operate in an effective manner on a worldwide basis."[36] The concern for institution building is characteristic of the Catholic social tradition. "This is the institutional path—we might also call it the political path—of charity," Pope

31. Paul VI, *Gaudium et Spes*, no. 90.
32. Paul VI, *Gaudium et Spes*, no. 23.
33. Paul VI, *Gaudium et Spes*, no. 6.
34. Paul VI, *Gaudium et Spes*, no. 32.
35. Paul VI, *Gaudium et Spes*, no. 75.
36. See John XXIII, *Pacem in Terris*, no. 137.

Benedict wrote in *Caritas in Veritate*, "no less excellent and effective than the kind of charity which encounters the neighbor directly, outside the institutional mediation of the *polis*. ... In an increasingly globalized society," he added, "the common good and the effort to obtain it cannot fail to assume the dimensions of the whole human family, that is to say, the community of peoples and nations, in such a way as to shape the *earthly city* in unity and peace, rendering it to some degree an anticipation and a prefiguration of the undivided *city of God*."[37]

At the global level, the institutional principle reached its fullest expression in Pope Benedict's call for a global public authority. Writing in the wake of the 2008 global financial crisis, Benedict wrote:

> To manage the global economy; to revive economies hit by the [financial] crisis; to avoid any deterioration of the present crisis and the greater imbalances that would result; to bring about integral and timely disarmament, food security and peace; to guarantee the protection of the environment and to regulate migration: for all this, there is urgent need of a true world political authority.[38]

In advancing the idea of a global public authority, moreover, Benedict also advocates "giving poorer nations an effective voice in shared decision-making."[39] More recently, Pope Francis, in the encyclical *Fratelli Tutti*, renewed the call for "a juridical, political and economic order" with respect particularly to development and migration.[40] Thus, the modern Roman magisterium, while affirming states as an integral to political life, in response to the limits and failures of a world of nation-states, has repeatedly called for the establishment of "a public and universal authority."[41]

---

37. Benedict XVI, *Caritas in Veritate*, no. 7.

38. Benedict XVI, *Caritas in Veritate*, nos. 67, 149.

39. Benedict XVI, *Caritas in Veritate*, no. 67. Likewise, Thomas Pogge argues that inequalities in participation in international institutions is an underlying source of poverty and human rights abuses in the developing world. See Pogge, *World Poverty and Human Rights*. *Caritas in Veritate* is also notable for its praise of economic experiments that consciously aim at serving the common good even as they make profit (nos. 37–38).

40. Francis, *Fratelli Tutti*, no. 138 on development, and no. 132 on migration. For Pope Francis' general endorsement of an international political authority, see *Fratelli Tutti*, nos. 170–73, 177.

41. John XXIII, *Pacem in Terris*, no. 139.

Globalism and Local Culture

In the late twentieth century, neoconservative critics challenged the Church's appeal to a universal public authority as statist, inferring it aimed at a unitary world government. In response, Catholic social teaching repeatedly appealed to the principle of subsidiarity, emphasizing that global institutions are meant to supply for the limits of private sector arrangements and national governments and to support families, intermediate associations and other levels of political authority in fulfilling their responsibilities to the common good.[42] In recent years, however, pushback has come from theorists like Patrick Deneen, who favor small community, local culture and embodiment in place.[43] These critics properly fault liberalism for its destructive impact on community and failure to supply meaning. (I would point out that this is particularly true of the U.S., where an especially aggressive form of neoliberal capitalism is less regulated than in other liberal western societies.) While theologians, and particularly social ethicists like myself of an earlier generation, have little noted it, culture has been a major theme of modern papal and conciliar teaching.[44] Pope Francis has been particularly attentive to the destructive effects of globalization on culture, the need to balance the local and universal, and the role of culture in building a new society in a post-pandemic world.[45] "Universal fraternity and social friendship" in local communities," he writes, "are thus two inseparable and equally vital poles in every society."[46] He adds,

> We need to sink our roots deeper into the fertile soil and history of our native place, which is a gift of God. We can work on a small scale, in our own neighborhood, but with a larger perspective.

A global outlook, he argues, helps us, appreciate our own culture as one gem in the beauty of universal community.

---

42. On subsidiarity, see *Pacem in Terris*, nos. 138–41; *Caritas in Veritate*, no. 67; and particularly, c.3. "An Authority on Globalization" in Pontifical Council for Justice and Peace, "Towards Reforming."

43. See Deneen, *Why Liberalism Failed*.

44. Vatican II's Pastoral Constitution *Gaudium et Spes* devoted an entire chapter to faith and culture, nos. 53–63. Also, see Gremillion, *Gospel of Culture*, for extensive documentation of church teaching on culture.

45. Francis, *Fratelli Tutti*, nos. 142–353, esp. 214–21.

46. Francis, *Fratelli Tutti*, no. 142.

Culture has played an important role in Pope Francis' thinking as it has in the Theology of the People from which he has drawn inspiration.[47] *Evangelii Gaudium* put emphasis on how each people receives the Gospel in its own culture, giving rise to a distinctive synthesis.[48] The pope's Latin American experience led him to regard "the foundational cultural synthesis of Latin America" as the interweaving of Indian, black and European substrates."[49] To the bishops of CELAM in Bogota in 2015, he spoke of "our mestizo soul." A flourishing culture whether in the church or in the world, he holds, is one in which men and women encounter people of other cultures. In *Fratelli Tutti*, he writes, "A country flourishes when constructive dialogue occurs among its many rich cultural components: popular culture, university culture, youth culture, artistic culture, technological culture, economic culture, family culture and media culture."[50] The way to build a new society, he proposes, is to promote "a culture of encounter" where people meet one another, learn about one another and appreciate one another's cultures. It is opposed to a situation in which "one part of society would pacify the rest."[51] For that reason, while resonating with the desire for community and culture, Francis' social vision is not a sectarian one of a people in flight from the world. "The ability to recognize other people's right to be themselves and to be different . . . makes possible," he says, "the creation of a social covenant."[52]

With an implicit recognition, perhaps, of the difficulty of realizing such a culture of encounter, Pope Francis appeals for a renewal of the virtue of kindness. Like his frequent invocation of tenderness, the pope's invocation of kindness responds not just to the hardness that economic liberalism has brought to modern life, but also to the coarseness that has in recent decades attended various identity-centered liberation movements.[53] Behind Francis' belief in a culture united in diversity lies a profound faith in the power of the Holy Spirit working in the world as

---

47. On the Theology of the People, see Ivereigh, *Great Reformer*, esp. 111–13, 172–73.

48. On the role of culture in evangelization, see Francis, *Evangelii Gaudium*, nos. 61–75.

49. Quoted in Ivereigh, *Wounded Shepherd*, 237.

50. Francis, *Fratelli Tutti*, no. 199, quoting a 2013 address to Brazilian political, economic, and cultural leaders.

51. Francis, *Fratelli Tutti*, no. 216.

52. Francis, *Fratelli Tutti*, no. 218.

53. On kindness, see Francis, *Fratelli Tutti*, nos. 222–24.

well as in the church to "harmonize every diversity. It overcomes every conflict by creating a new and promising synthesis."[54] He explains,

> Diversity is a beautiful thing when it can constantly enter into a process of reconciliation and seal a sort of cultural covenant resulting in a "reconciled diversity." As the bishops of the Congo have put it: "Our ethnic diversity is our wealth. . . . It is only in unity, through conversion of hearts and reconciliation that we will be able to help our country to develop on all levels."[55]

Post-Vatican II Catholicism, then, does not see a forced choice between globalism, on the one hand, and native culture and local community, on the other. As in so many matters, it is a Catholic "both-and": Both global and local citizenship; universal solidarity and patriotism to community and nation too.

Human Rights and Religious Liberty

The embrace of liberal values first sketched out in *Pacem in Terris* was solidified by the Second Vatican Council in its Pastoral Constitution on the Church and the Modern World and Declaration on Religious Liberty. While the Pastoral Constitution is in many respects forward-looking, it is also a culmination of the Church's reckoning with its legacy in the struggle with Fascism and the lessons of the Second World War. *Gaudium et Spes* short chapter 4, "The Life of the Political Community," affirms the same rights-based approach to government found in *Pacem in Terris*. It cites as a sign of the times, "a keener awareness of human dignity" from which there arises a desire in many parts of the world for a political-juridical order in which personal rights can gain better protection."[56] Among these rights, it lists "the right of free assembly, of common action, of expressing personal opinions, and of professing a religion both privately and publicly." It affirms efforts to honor the rights of national minorities" and "respect [for] the opinions and religious beliefs of others."[57] These convictions are at odds in recent years with illiberal populist movements and overly zealous advocates of religious liberty.

---

54. Francis, *Evangelii Gaudium*, no. 230.
55. Francis, *Evangelii Gaudium*, no. 23.
56. Paul VI, *Gaudium et Spes*, no 73.
57. Paul VI, *Gaudium et Spes*, no 73.

When it comes to government, the Council allowed that "Individuals, families, and various groups," that is, intermediate associations, "are aware of their own insufficiency in the matter of fully human conditions of life."[58] Politics develops and government are instituted to secure these conditions. Given the increasing complexity of modern societies, however, the Council believed, increased government intervention may be required to bring about "conditions more likely to help citizens and groups more freely attain to complete human fulfillment with greater effect."[59] The Pastoral Constitution enjoins citizens' obedience to lawful political authorities who labor for the common good, but, when government "oversteps its competence and oppresses the people," they are permitted "to defend their own rights and those of their fellow citizens."[60]

A little more than two years after *Pacem in Terris* appeared, the Council in the Pastoral Constitution on The Church in the Modern World would identify the promotion of human rights as a principal way in which the Church serves the world.[61] In contrast, moreover, to tendencies of some contemporary advocates of religious freedom who see conflicts between religious freedom and other rights, the Council declared that "in the divine arrangement itself, the rightful autonomy of the creature, and particularly of [the human person], is not withdrawn, but is rather re-established in its own dignity and strengthened in it."[62]

Likewise, *Dignitatis Humanae*, the Council's Declaration On Religious Liberty, insisted on the principal of personal autonomy even in moral conflicts. It affirms, "In the exercise of their rights, individual men and social groups are bound by the moral law to have respect both for the rights of others and for their own duties toward others and for the common welfare of all."[63] The declaration explains, "no one is to be forced to act in a manner contrary to his own beliefs, whether privately or publicly, whether alone or in association with others, within due limits."[64] Thus, religious freedom, though essential, is not a super-right, but like all rights is open to balancing with the rights of others and with the common good. From the perspective of the human person, such judgments are matters of

58. Paul VI, *Gaudium et Spes*, no. 74.
59. Paul VI, *Gaudium et Spes*, no. 74.
60. Paul VI, *Gaudium et Spes*, no. 74.
61. Paul VI, *Gaudium et Spes*, no. 41. See epigram at the head of this article.
62. Paul VI, *Gaudium et Spes*, no. 41.
63. Paul VI, *Dignitatis Humanae*, no. 7.
64. Paul VI, *Dignitatis Humanae*, no. 2.

conscience;[65] and the Council admonished, "[People] are to deal with their fellows in justice and civility."[66] From the side of the political community, governments are responsible to "guard against abuses committed on the pretext of freedom of religion" and to effectively safeguard "the rights of all citizens and [secure] the peaceful settlement of conflicts of rights."[67]

Ecclesiological Context[68]

These principles for the adjudication of rights are important reminders, because critics of the Church's embrace of Liberalism seem either to believe that Church teaching on the morality ought always to be inscribed in public law, or that in accord with the imperial church model of late antiquity and the high Middle Ages, the spiritual authority of the Church is and ought to be superior to that of secular political authority. Critics seem to ignore the Council's instruction that the Dogmatic Constitution on the Church must be read in conjunction with the Declaration on Religious Liberty, the Decree on Ecumenism (*Unitatis Redintegratio*) and the Decree on Non-Christian Religions (*Nostra Aetate*). Together the four texts constitute a single conciliar teaching on ecclesiology, which demonstrates the respect Catholics should show to other communities of faith and those with other conscientious convictions, and the corresponding responsibility of government to "safeguard the rights of all citizens."

Likewise, critics seem attached to the institutional model of the church, rooted in the seventeenth century juridical paradigm of the church as "a perfect society," a model from the age of monarchial absolutism. They ignore the Council's abandonment of a single template for the notion of the Church as a mystery, only partially discernible through images that capture the reality of the Church in limited ways.[69] For *Lumen Gentium*, Vatican II's Dogmatic Constitution on the Church, the primary image is the Church as Sacrament.[70] For the Pastoral Constitution, the

---

65. Paul VI, *Dignitatis Humanae*, no. 11.
66. Paul VI, *Dignitatis Humanae*, no. 7.
67. Paul VI, *Dignitatis Humanae*, no. 7.
68. On the ecclesiological context of the Church's social praxis beginning with Vatican II, see Gaillardetz, "Ecclesiological Foundations," 72–98.
69. On the mystery of the Church revealed through images, see Paul VI, *Lumen Gentium*, no. 6.
70. Paul VI, *Lumen Gentium*, no. 1.

underlying image is Church as Servant, the servant of humanity.[71] These two images, Church as Sacrament and Church as Servant, provide the keys to discerning the future of Catholicism's engagement with the world and with the Liberal political tradition.

Richard Gaillardetz writes, "It is the cultural matter of this community (e.g., institutions, social conventions, and practices) that becomes within the Church, not just a set of cultural constructions but the means through which the Church can become a sign and instrument of God's saving offer to the world." He adds, "There is, in other words, implicit in any claim to the Church's own sacramentality, a necessary affirmation of the potential goodness of the social, political and economic communities that constitute human society."[72] In the Catholic social tradition, and particularly in the post-Vatican II era, that society embraces all levels and types of association from local community to cosmopolis.

As a Servant Church, the community of faith serves individual and groups under the inspiration of the Spirit by fostering human rights, freedom and liberty of conscience.[73] It serves the human family by promoting social unity through affirming processes of socialization that bring people together in a union of hearts and minds across "diverse human communities and nations" and "overcoming all strife between nations and races in the spirit of God's children."[74] She serves as "a leaven and a kind of a soul" for humanity, breathing life into both local communities and global society, contributing thereby to the full development of the one human family. Two decades into the 21st century, as the Church continues to cultivate human dignity in freedom and fosters global solidarity, her exchange of gifts with the Liberal Tradition continues into the foreseeable future.

---

71. See Paul VI, *Gaudium et Spes*, nos. 40–44, where the Council discusses how it accompanies humanity and, in particular, identifies two ways in which the Church serves the world in the defense of human rights (no. 41) and the promotion of unity (no. 42).

72. Gaillardetz, "Ecclesiological Foundations," 79–80.

73. Paul VI, *Gaudium et Spes*, no. 41.

74. Paul VI, *Gaudium et Spes*, no. 42.

Bibliography

Benedict XVI. *Caritas in Veritate: On Integral Development in Charity and Truth*. Vatican City: Libreria Editrice Vaticana, 2009. https://www.vatican.va/content/benedict-xvi/en/encyclicals/documents/hf_ben-xvi_enc_20090629_caritas-in-veritate.html#_ednref112.

Boff, Leonardo. *Saint Francis: Model of Human Liberation*. New York: Crossroads, 1982.

Center for Jewish–Christian Understanding and Cooperation. "To Do the Will of Our Father in Heaven: Toward a Partnership between Jews and Christians." In *From Confrontation to Covenantal Partnership: Jews and Christians Reflect on the Orthodox Rabbinic Statement of "To Do the Will of Our Father in Heaven,"* edited by Jehoschua Ahrens et al., 1–3. Jerusalem: Urim, 2021.

Christiansen, Drew. "Pacem in Terris." In *Modern Catholic Social Teaching: Commentaries and Interpretations*, edited by Kenneth Himes et al., 217–43. Washington, DC: Georgetown University Press, 2005.

Deneen, Patrick J. *Why Liberalism Failed*. New Haven: Yale University Press, 2018.

Dreher, Rod. *The Benedict Option: A Strategy for Christians in a Post-Christian Nation*. New York: Sentinel, 2017.

Francis. *Evangelii Gaudium: On the Proclamation of the Gospel in Today's World*. Vatican City: Libreria Editrice Vaticana, 2020. https://www.vatican.va/content/francesco/en/apost_exhortations/documents/papa-francesco_esortazione-ap_20131124_evangelii-gaudium.html.

———. *Fratelli Tutti: On Fraternity and Social Friendship*. Vatican City: Libreria Editrice Vaticana, 2020. https://www.vatican.va/content/francesco/en/encyclicals/documents/papa-francesco_20201003_enciclica-fratelli-tutti.html.

———. *Laudato Si': On Care of Our Common Home*. Vatican City: Libreria Editrice Vaticana, 2015. https://www.vatican.va/content/francesco/en/encyclicals/documents/papa-francesco_20150524_enciclica-laudato-si.html.

Gaillardetz, Richard. "Ecclesiological Foundations of Modern Catholic Social Teaching." In *Modern Catholic Social Teaching: Commentaries and Interpretations*, edited by Kenneth R. Himes et al., 72–98. Washington, DC: Georgetown University Press, 2005.

Gremillion, Joseph. *The Gospel of Culture after Vatican II*. Maryknoll, NY: Orbis, 1987.

Huddock, Barry. *Struggle, Condemnation, Vindication: John Courtney Murray's Journey Toward Vatican II*. Collegeville, MN: Liturgical, 2015.

Ivereigh, Austen. *The Great Reformer: Francis and the Making of a Radical Pope*. New York: Picador, 2014.

———. *Wounded Shepherd: Pope Francis and His Struggle to Convert the Catholic Church*. New York: Holt, 2019.

John Paul II. "Peace with God, Peace with All Creation." Vatican City: Libreria Editrice Vaticana, 1990. https://www.vatican.va/content/john-paul-ii/en/messages/peace/documents/hf_jp-ii_mes_19891208_xxiii-world-day-for-peace.html.

———. *Sollicitudo Rei Socialis: On Social Concern*. Vatican City: Libreria Editrice Vaticana, 1987. https://www.vatican.va/content/john-paul-ii/en/encyclicals/documents/hf_jp.ii_enc_30121987_sollicitudo-rei-socialis.html.

John XXIII. *Pacem in Terris: Peace on Earth*. Vatican City: Libreria Editrice Vaticana, 1963. https://www.vatican.va/content/john-xxiii/en/encyclicals/documents/hf_j-xxiii_enc_11041963_pacem.html.

Kirkpatrick, Jeane. "Dictatorship and Double Standards." *Commentary* 68 (1979) 35–45.
Leahy, Brendan. *Ecclesial Movements and Communities: Origins, Significance, and Issues*. Hyde Park, NY: New City, 2011.
MacIntyre, Alasdair. *After Virtue: A Study in Moral Theory*. Notre Dame: University of Notre Dame Press, 1981.
Milbank, John. *Theology and Social Theory: Beyond Secular Reason*. New York: Wiley, 2006.
Miller, David. *National Responsibility and Global Justice*. Oxford Political Theory. Oxford: Oxford University Press, 2012.
Murray, John Courtney. "Things Old and New in *Pacem in Terris*." In *Bridging the Sacred and the Secular*, edited by J. Leon Hooper, 215–52. Washington, DC: Georgetown University Press, 1994.
———. *We Hold These Truths: Reflections on the American Proposition*. Lanham, MD: Sheed and Ward, 2005.
Nussbaum, Martha. *The Cosmopolitan Tradition: A Noble but Flawed Idea*. Cambridge: Belknap, 2019.
———. "Patriotism and Cosmopolitanism." In *For Love of Country: Debating the Limits of Patriotism*, edited by Joshua Cohen, 21–54. New York: Beacon, 1996.
O'Malley, John W. *What Happened at Vatican II?* Cambridge: Harvard University Press, 2008.
Paul VI. *Dignitatis Humanae: Declaration on Religious Freedom*. Vatican City: Libreria Editrice Vaticana, 1965. https://www.vatican.va/archive/hist_councils/ii_vatican_council/documents/vat-ii_decl_19651207_dignitatis-humanae_en.html.
———. *Gaudium et Spes: Pastoral Constitution on the Church in the Modern World*. Vatican City: Libreria Editrice Vaticana, 1965. https://www.vatican.va/archive/hist_councils/ii_vatican_council/documents/vat-ii_const_19651207_gaudium-et-spes_en.html.
———. *Lumen Gentium: Dogmatic Constitution on the Church*. Vatican City: Libreria Editrice Vaticana, 1964. https://www.vatican.va/archive/hist_councils/ii_vatican_council/documents/vat-ii_const_19641121_lumen-gentium_en.html.
Pogge, Thomas. *World Poverty and Human Rights*. New York: Polity, 2008.
Pontifical Council for Justice and Peace. "Towards Reforming the International Financial and Monetary Systems." https://www.vatican.va/roman_curia/pontifical_councils/justpeace/documents/rc_pc_justpeace_doc_20111024_nota_en.html.
Ratzinger, Joseph, and Marcello Pera. *Without Roots: The West, Relativism, Christianity, Islam*. Translated by Michael F. Moore. New York: Basic, 2006.
Riebling, Mark. *Church of Spies: The Pope's Secret War against Hitler*. New York: Basic, 2015.
Shue, Henry. *Basic Rights: Subsistence, Affluence, and U.S. Foreign Policy*. 2nd ed. Princeton: Princeton University Press, 1996.
Zizola, Giancarlo. *The Utopia of John XXIII*. Translated by Helen Barolini. New York: Doubleday, 1985.

8

Liberalism, Conservatism, and Social Catholicism for the Twenty-First Century?

WILLIAM. F. MURPHY JR.,
INITIATIVE FOR SOCIAL CATHOLICISM

Abstract: Between a brief introduction and conclusion, this essay sketches a historical narrative of how especially American Catholics can understand the contemporary state of both liberalism and conservatism in relation to a proposed renewal of social Catholicism to foster a "better kind of politics" to address the challenges facing the human family. The first half focuses on liberalism, tracing it from its remote roots, through the American founding, through key nineteenth century developments, through twentieth-century reforms in rough alignment with the development of modern Catholic Social Teaching leading to the postwar "liberal consensus," and later to the so-called "end of history" followed by decades of globalization according to a market fundamentalist form of neoliberalism that has now broken down, with a resulting rise of populism, illiberalism, and postliberal integralism. The second half similarly traces the rise of conservatism rooted in a widespread and understandable disposition to moderate change. A narrative of conservatism is traced through its modern founding in the thought of Edmund Burke, through the so-called "fusion conservativism" of the Reagan era, through the neoconservative era, and through the rise of radical forms of right-wing illiberalism. It argues that while Catholics informed by our social tradition will reflect the best insights of the conservative tradition, the authentic living out of their faith will make them active and indispensable participants in the continual renewal of our constitutional democracies to meet the challenges of the polycrisis while eschewing the illiberal excesses of the left and right.[1]

Introduction

As DREW CHRISTIANSEN, SJ, explained in the previous contribution to this collection, Catholic Social Teaching since John XXIII has been marked by an "ample embrace" of modernity that is seen in the "fruitful dialogue" and collaboration with key tenets of liberalism including "human rights, constitutional government, democratic participation, the self-determination of peoples, and the equality of persons, especially women." He also noted that the convictions of Catholic social doctrine "are at odds in recent years with illiberal populist movements." These claims can be disconcerting to many American Catholics, however, because much of the institutional infrastructure of the Church in the United States—and thus the broader Catholic population—has come to identify as conservative as distinguished from liberal since roughly the Pontificate of St. John Paul II. As I discuss at further length in the introduction to this collection, this increasing identification of Catholics as conservative traces to several causes. These have included a renewed "postliberal" embrace of the doctrinal tradition after a de-emphasis on doctrine during the more liberal postconciliar decades, a reaction against the excesses of the illiberal left, and the significant financial investment by economic conservatives in promoting a generally conservative worldview which includes cultivating a hostility toward liberalism. Our identities, moreover, have a significant impact on how we interpret reality and ecclesial matters, so the increasing identification of American Catholics as conservative has significant implications, especially in raising obstacles to the reception of Catholic Social

---

1. An earlier version of this text was delivered as the Chester and Margaret Paluch Chair lecture at The University of St. Mary of the Lake, Mundelein Seminary on October 21, 2020 under the title of "Liberalism, Conservatism, and Social Catholicism for the Twenty-First Century?" It was subsequently published in *Chicago Studies* under the same title and published here in a later form with permission. Although some sections overlap with other contributions to this collection, they are maintained to retain the integrity of the narrative of this essay.

Teaching, which raises further obstacles to our ability to understand how we got into the polycrisis, and what is needed to manage it.

As is widely understood, historical narratives are particularly important in not only helping us to grasp fields of intellectual inquiry like political philosophy, but in forming our identities. The following essay, therefore, proposes a narrative through which Catholics can not only understand the development of liberalism and conservatism in relation to Catholic Social Teaching, but also cultivate a properly Catholic sense of identity for carrying out the mission of Christ in the twenty first century. In what follows I will, therefore, offer a brief engagement with key aspects of liberalism and conservatism with an eye to how they relate to CST, in the hope of illumining some of the key issues at stake in our day.

In the first of these parts, therefore, I will outline what seem to me the decisive points regarding the "liberalism" that had gained a broad consensus in the post World War II era into which I was born in 1962. In so doing, I will note the perhaps surprising degree of harmony that seemed to exist between this "liberal world order" and post Conciliar CST, especially since a century before Pius IX's *Syllabus of Errors* was understood to have excluded any reconciliation between liberalism and Catholicism. By the time the evolving liberal world order had triumphed over its main rival with the end of the Cold War in 1989, an influential public intellectual like Francis Fukuyama could famously raise the question of whether we had reached the "end of history" regarding political forms with liberalism as the only plausible option.

In the second part, I will similarly treat what seem to me the most important considerations regarding the conservatism that was coming into prominence with the Reagan Administration when I initially entered the professional workforce in 1984, as a newly minted Computer Systems Engineer with IBM. I will focus not only on some of the foundational insights of the conservative tradition that continues to make it attractive to religious believers and others in a time of accelerating change, but some of the developments that have led to a frightening return of especially right-wing nationalism and illiberalism, while also noting some of what I think are more promising initiatives from the right of center. I will conclude that Catholics should strive to adopt a more properly Catholic identity—which implies maintaining a critical distance in relation to ideologies and political parties—as we live out their missionary discipleship while striving for holiness and working for the common good. Such understanding can remove obstacles to living out a new social Catholicism through which a reinvigorated Church draws everyone closer to Christ by the witness of working in solidarity to solve the grave challenges that threaten a dystopian future, thereby manifesting her nature as "salt and light" and as an efficacious sign of unity and incarnation of divine love.

I. The Past Development, Apparent Triumph, and Present Peril of Liberalism

How should we understand liberalism? Why does it often have such bad connotations in our day, especially in the American context? And didn't Pope Pius IX, in his 1864 *Syllabus of Errors*, anathematize anyone who said the Church could be reconciled with it? And didn't too many Catholics become naïve about it after the Second Vatican Council? And don't we need to be concerned about persecution from the illiberal left if they get political power? In this first part, my goal is to shed sufficient light on the notion of liberalism to illumine both its past triumphs—including a perhaps surprising degree of alignment with Catholic Social Teaching—and its present peril. This will provide a narrative framework for understanding how it has related to different aspects of the conservative tradition, and how it relates to Catholic Social Doctrine and the embodiment of that in social Catholicism.

To do so, I will attempt to sketch the most relevant points in each of six stages in the tradition of liberalism. These include the following: (1) the proto-liberalism of the American founding; (2) the "refounding" of American liberalism after the civil war but bearing fruit only in the twentieth century; (3) post World War II liberal consensus into which I was born; (4) the emerging cleavage between liberalism and Catholicism; and (5) the apparent triumph of liberalism with the apparent "the end of history" following the Cold War; and (6) the present peril of liberalism in alienation from conservative Catholics.[2]

---

2. Among the many sources that influence my narrative, the most influential is Traub, *What Was Liberalism?*, which has the advantage of being written in recent years during which the survival of liberalism has been put in doubt by developments since the 2008 financial crisis. An even more recent work that could be drawn upon to enrich my narrative is Fukuyama, *Liberalism and Its Discontents*. A still current and comprehensive resource is Fawcett, *Liberalism*.

1. The Proto-liberalism of the American Founding and the French Revolution

The remote roots of modern liberalism—or perhaps better, constitutional democracy—can be traced back to Greco-Roman republican theory, to medieval understandings of mixed regimes, to the early roots of English constitutionalism such as the *Magna Carta*, and to the social contract theory and popular sovereignty of Thomas Hobbes and John Locke. An argument can be made, however, for starting with the American founders, who drew on these earlier sources but also made the significant advances needed to establish a constitutional government of sufficient stability to not only endure over centuries but to inspire much of the world to emulate it. Although these American founders did not use the word liberal to describe the government they created, the enduring success of the so called "American experiment in ordered liberty" was foundational for the widespread proliferation of what would subsequently be called liberal states. The famous prologue to the Declaration of Independence reflects three of the most important principles of this incipient or proto-liberalism, namely human equality, human rights and popular sovereignty. The key text reads as follows: "We hold these truths to be self-evident, that all men are created equal, that they are endowed by their Creator with certain unalienable Rights, that among these are Life, Liberty and the pursuit of Happiness. . . . That to secure these rights, Governments are instituted among Men, deriving their just powers from the consent of the governed."[3]

Whether we consider the original American Articles of Confederation or the Constitution that was adopted in 1787 and subsequently amended and interpreted by the Supreme Court, these three principles of the prologue to the declaration would seem to indicate some of the most fundamental aspects of the liberal tradition that will develop over time, namely human equality, human rights and popular sovereignty.[4] The American founders tended to describe what they had created as a federalist form of republic in which the national government had supremacy over the states, while its powers were limited by various checks and balances.[5] The success of this revolution helped to inspire the French

---

3. Jefferson et al., "Declaration of Independence."
4. In this section, I am drawing on Traub, *Liberalism*, ch. 1.
5. Whereas Alexander Hamilton saw a strong national government as essential for competing economically with European powers, James Madison—who was the

Revolution of 1789. Because it tragically descended into the murderous terror of the guillotine, it helped to alienate Catholicism from "liberalism" for well over a century. We should note, however, that the word liberal was only introduced into the discussion in 1797 by Frenchman Benjamin Constant.[6] Whereas the Catholic Church was alienated from the liberalism of the French Revolution, it later came to flourish under more religiously neutral liberalism of the American Revolution.

The American constitution of 1787 provided the foundation for a more stable form of popular sovereignty than could have been expected by past human experience. As spelled out in *Federalist 1* by Alexander Hamilton, one of the primary concerns of the founders was to design a form of republic that would not fall into tyranny through the election of a demagogue, a politician who gains power by deceptively appealing to the prejudices and desires of the people. The Constitution also included many flaws, the most serious of which was its toleration of the institution of slavery.

---

primary architect and defender of the constitution conceived a strong national government as necessary to defend the rights of citizens. As he famously argued in *Federalist 51*, the separation and balance of powers between the three branches of the national government, along with the sharing of power between federal, state, and local jurisdictions was the best way to protect citizens from the encroachment of their rights by not just government entities but also other citizens. Rather than a state guided by a knowable public good, Madison thus crafted a state to be guided by a clash between competing interests. In so doing, he sought to foster a balance between the equality implied by popular sovereignty and the liberty from coercion that was so important to the early generations of Americans. As Traub discussed, they had been influenced by the writings of Thomas Paine.

6. As discussed by Traub, *What Was Liberalism?*, 28, Constant did so especially with his 1797 essay "Of Political Reactions." In opposition to arbitrary rule and echoing the American founders, Constant used the word liberal to describe a strong constitutional, republican government grounded in the principles such as the famous "liberty, equality, and fraternity" of the Revolution. In light of the ancient understanding of the civic liberty of the citizen that included a subjection of the individual to the community, Constant wrote with some trepidation of how modern men increasingly saw liberty as "the enjoyment of security in private pleasures" and "the right to be left alone." Whereas the ancient tendency could lead to violation of rights and subjection to oppressive regimes, the modern could lead to behaviors that undermine personal and communal flourishing.

2. The Refounding of American Liberalism after the Civil War, Realized in the Twentieth Century

With the 1865 conclusion of the Civil War and the ratification of the three reconstruction-era constitutional amendments by 1870,[7] it would seem that the decisive pieces were in place for a refounding of American liberalism—or constitutional democracy—that better aligned with the profession of belief in the equal creation, unalienable rights, self-governance of "all men" that Thomas Jefferson had articulated so artfully in the prologue to the Declaration of Independence.

The realization of this refounding was delayed, however, with developments that began under the Presidency of Andrew Johnson who assumed office after the assassination of Abraham Lincoln. Being a former slaveholder from the South, Johnson sought a prompt restoration of seceded states to the Union without taking steps to protect the newly liberated and formerly enslaved persons. Conflicts over this reconstruction policy led to his impeachment and near removal in 1868. Struggles over reconstruction continued through the disputed 1876 election, which was settled through a "backroom deal" that gave the required electoral votes to Rutherford B. Hayes in exchange for withdrawing federal troops from the South. This effectively ended reconstruction and opened the way for the regime of so-called Jim Crow laws that disenfranchised most blacks and a lesser percentage of poor whites.

The long era of minority rule by the wealthier whites during the Jim Crow era followed a philosophy articulated earlier in the nineteenth century by South Carolina politician and political theorist John C. Calhoun (1782–1850). Although initially a modernizer and proponent of a strong national government, Calhoun became a proponent of "state's rights," limited government and "minority rule" in order to protect the social order in the American South, especially the institution of slavery,

---

7. For this section, I am relying mostly on Wikipedia, s.v. "Reconstruction Amendments," https://en.wikipedia.org/wiki/Reconstruction_Amendments, although the literature is abundant. The Thirteenth Amendment abolishing slavery was ratified by the states and adopted in 1865. The subsequent Civil Rights Act of 1866 was vetoed by President Johnson, but the veto was overridden by both chambers of Congress to become law. The Fourteenth Amendment was crafted to ensure the disputed constitutionality of this act. It was adopted in 1868 to define citizenship, protect privileges and immunities of citizens, and articulate their rights to due process and equal protection under law. With the adoption of the Fifteenth Amendment in 1870, the denial of the right to vote was prohibited.

which he defended as a "positive good." We will hear more of Calhoun's influence in the twentieth century and to the present day.

The end of the Reconstruction era in 1877 coincided with the beginning of the so-called "Gilded Age," a name that suggested a thin layer of gold gilding that masked grave social disorder. This was the era in which the industrial revolution took hold in the United States, spurred on by the growth of railroads and related industries including steel, and coal. This industrial boom took place during a time when there was no precedent for government oversight of business, when the views of both industrialists and political leaders were influenced by a "social Darwinist" understanding of the survival of the fittest along with a theory of laissez-faire unregulated capitalism.[8] The great business interests were organized into "trusts," which were said to have purchased the U.S. Senate as depicted in political cartoons of the day. These so called "Fat Cats" lived in splendor and "called the shots" politically while the masses worked in conditions approaching slavery and struggled to survive. In Europe, these conditions resulted in insurrections in various cities, threatening social stability.

In response similar developments in Europe, we saw in chapter 2 that a movement of "social Catholics"—a collaboration of laity and clergy—emerged through the example of Bishop Wilhelm Emmanual von Ketteler who would come to be considered the father of social Catholicism. These Catholics worked for solutions to what was called "the social question" regarding the plight of industrial workers. They did so through dialogue with the main alternatives of the day which were the socialists, on the one side, and the so-called "economic liberals," on the other. In the United States, the priests and bishops were slow to respond to the plight of workers throughout most of the nineteenth century. Although the workers had many reasons to join unions like the Knights of Labor, and many Catholics did, the clergy often opposed such organizations because of the mixed membership and fears of socialism. As we saw in chapter 5, the Knights of Labor had been founded in 1869 by a Catholic named Terrance Powderly. It soon had seven hundred thousand members just in the United States but was opposed by some bishops who were concerned about its secrecy and fears of socialism. In Canada, members of this union were even excommunicated, greatly undermining it. Cardinal Gibbons of Baltimore, on the other hand, saw the plight of the workers

---

8. Hofstadter, *Social Darwinism*.

and the value of the Knights of Labor and traveled to Rome in 1887 to prevent the condemnation that some of his fellow bishops had sought. His letter was a tour de force, providing compelling reasons why the condemnation was neither merited nor necessary nor prudent, but would instead be dangerous, inefficacious, self-defeating, and cruel. In addition, he asked Leo XIII to write on the ethical aspects of the conflict between capital and labor.

These efforts resulted in a series of reform proposals that were reflected in the first modern Catholic Social encyclical *Rerum Novarum: On the Condition of Workers*, which was published in 1891 by Pope Leo XIII. It built on classic principles of Catholic morality like justice and the common good and offered judgments about what is to be accepted and rejected in the positions of the disputing parties. Against the ideology of socialism Leo rejected their teaching on the communal ownership of the means of production and while upholding a right to possess private property, although with St. Thomas Aquinas, he limited this right by a duty to use property consistent with the universal destination of goods. Against the ideologies of economic liberalism, or *laissez-faire* capitalism, and social Darwinism, Leo called for state intervention to uphold the rights of workers, and specifically affirms their right to unionize, to receive a just wage, to have safe working conditions and to enjoy Sunday rest. In so doing, he therefore provided principles to guide a broad movement of Catholics to work for a more just society consistent with the common good. By not only affirming the need for government intervention against grave injustices but also articulating a broad notion of the common good,[9] *Rerum Novarum* opened the way for a deepening tradition of modern social encyclicals.

---

9. Leo XIII, *Rerum Novarum* no. 32. The discussion of the common good continues: "The foremost duty, therefore, of the rulers of the State should be to make sure that *the laws and institutions, the general character and administration of the commonwealth, shall be such as of themselves to realize public well-being and private prosperity. This is the proper scope of wise statesmanship and is the work of the rulers.* Now a State chiefly prospers and thrives through moral rule, well-regulated family life, respect for religion and justice, the moderation and fair imposing of public taxes, the progress of the arts and of trade, the abundant yield of the land-through *everything, in fact, which makes the citizens better and happier.* Hereby, then, *it lies in the power of a ruler to benefit every class in the State, and amongst the rest to promote to the utmost the interests of the poor; and this in virtue of his office, and without being open to suspicion of undue interference—since it is the province of the commonwealth to serve the common good. And the more that is done for the benefit of the working classes by the general laws of the country,* the less need will there be to seek for special means to relieve them" (emphasis added).

In the United States during the years immediately following the promulgation of *Rerum Novarum*, many similar social reforms were articulated by the so-called progressive movement (1890–1920). This movement was made up of especially the emerging urban and educated professional class and was rooted in the Republican party under the leadership of President Theodore Roosevelt (1901–9). Although the Republican party after Abraham Lincoln came to align with the business interests and industrialists of the Gilded Age, the Republican Teddy Roosevelt was distinguished by his efforts to break up the monopolistic industrial trusts, and to establish the national park system.[10] To keep a pledge that he had imprudently made, Roosevelt declined to run for a new term in the 1908 election, basically leaving the office to his former Vice President William Howard Taft, whose policies were more favorable to the business interests. When Roosevelt's third-party campaign to unseat Taft split the vote in the 1912 election, the beneficiary was Woodrow Wilson.

A few words about Wilson are important to our discussion of liberalism. He was a Southerner by way of his birth in Virginia and his early years in Georgia.[11] As an accomplished scholar of political philosophy and history, President of Princeton University and Governor of New Jersey, Wilson had a broad perspective within which he appropriated the central aspects of the progressive social reform that was advanced especially in the journal *The New Republic*. His own thought went far beyond the progressive reformers, looking to build international institutions—a liberal internationalism inspired by Immanuel Kant—to foster cooperation and discourage war, and foreseeing the national institutions of the welfare state. Because he placed the comprehensive reform agenda under which he ran under the heading of "New Freedom,"[12] the terminology of "liberal" came to edge out that of "progressive," aided by the fact that

---

10. For a helpful history of the Republican Party, see Richardson, *To Make Men Free*.

11. This section draws on Traub, *What Was Liberalism?*, ch. 3. As a Southern Democrat before the civil rights era, he was a segregationist and thus a racist. He did appoint, however, the first Roman Catholic and Jew to the Princeton faculty, although he excluded African American students.

12. Wikipedia, s.v. "Woodrow Wilson," https://en.wikipedia.org/wiki/Woodrow_Wilson. His domestic agenda focused on tariff reductions to reduce benefits to special interests at the expense of citizens, banking reform centered in the creation of the Federal Reserve system, trust regulation as realized by the Clayton AntiTrust Act of 1914 and the creation of the Federal Trade Commission, and the conservation of natural resources.

American had a long tradition of liberal "rugged individualism" that Wilson also wanted to attract.[13]

In parallel to and in dialogue with these progressive and liberal reforms was the work of Msgr. John A. Ryan. As we saw in chapter 5, Ryan became known for his work in advocating for a living wage while teaching at St. Paul Seminary in Minnesota.[14] While there, he also published in 1909 his "A Program of Social Reform by Legislation," meaning the reforms he thought needed to be implemented through public policy. Ryan's influence expanded considerably following his appointment in 1915 as a professor of moral theology at the Catholic University of America, where his ethical analysis was deeply informed by scholarship and teaching in economics and sociology. Inspired by *Rerum Novarum* and in dialogue with progressive reform, he argued in his scholarship—and lobbied in his public life—for the role of government in fostering justice and the common good through a variety of practical reforms. Among these reforms and programs advocated by Ryan were minimum wages, an eight-hour workday, the protection of women and children, the protection of organized labor, regulation of monopolies and stock exchanges, medical and unemployment insurance, social security, public housing for the homeless, taxation of not only income, but of inheritance and the increased value of land. All these reforms reflected his rejection of unregulated free-market capitalism, which he saw as contrary to sound economics and sound ethics.

Ryan was the primary author of "The 1919 Bishops' Program of Social Reform," and the guiding light for the conference on social ethics through the 1930s, setting the trajectory for the social teaching and outreach of the U.S. Bishops for generations, at least until the more conservative turn that gained momentum through the 1980s.[15] Ryan's work promoting trade unions and social legislation put him at odds with the Republican administrations during the "roaring" 1920s, which forsook progressive reform for more *laissez-faire* or unregulated free market

---

13. Traub, *What Was Liberalism?*, ch. 3.

14. For this section, see chapter 5: Murphy, "Social Formation of John A. Ryan," which draws on Broderick, *Right Reverend New Dealer*, and Ryan, *Social Doctrine in Action*.

15. Murphy, "Social Formation of John A. Ryan." The National Catholic War Council was formed in 1917; it was renamed the National Catholic Welfare Council in 1919. Bishops O'Connell of Boston and Dougherty of Philadelphia sought to have it suppressed in 1922, seeing it as a manifestation of Americanism. But most other bishops agreed about the need for the organization, so they petitioned the Pope.

policies. Ryan's efforts, on the other hand, greatly endeared him to the new administration of Franklin Delano Roosevelt during the Great Depression. The closeness between Ryan's work and the Roosevelt administration can be seen not only in the policy priorities noted above, but in Ryan's prominent role giving the benediction for two of Roosevelt's inaugurations, and through his nickname of Right Reverend New Dealer.

In response to the massive unemployment, poverty and suffering brought on by the Great Depression, President Franklin Delano Roosevelt advanced a series of programs under the heading of the New Deal.[16] These programs were experimental, so it is not surprising that several of them failed. Many others were more successful including the Securities and Exchange Commission, the Federal Deposit Insurance Corporation, the Social Security Administration, the Federal Housing Administration, the Public Works Administration, the Works Progress Administration, the Food and Drug Administration, the Tennessee Valley Association, and the Civilian Conservation Corps. After some experimentation and missteps, the administration increasingly aligned with the economic thought of John Maynard Keynes, who advocated what came to be called a "mixed economy" that affirmed both market activity and government institutions and services, providing regulation, oversight, and a social safety net. Roosevelt's broader vision was captured in his "Four Freedoms" Speech of 1941, where he distinguished the freedoms of speech, of worship, from want, and from fear. The freedom from want pointed toward a right to at least a subsistence. Freedom from fear would later be addressed through a further development of the liberal internationalism advanced by Woodrow Wilson, which Roosevelt updated with advocacy for the United Nations System that would help foster democracy and a rule based international order to secure peace and prosperity. Catholics should recognize in Roosevelt's vision for a more just and peaceful postwar world his many years of substantial alignment with Catholic Social Teaching.

As the Second World War moved toward completion in December of 1944, Pope Pius XII gave a Christmas address that is important for understanding the evolving position of the Catholic Church regarding the liberal order that was being planned as an outgrowth of the allied nations. In this Christmas address, Pius notes the broad yearning for

---

16. Kelly, "Top 10 New Deal Programs."

democratic rule as the allies struggled to defeat fascism.[17] He recalls, however, the traditional concern about the vulnerability of democracies to "the masses"[18] as distinguished from "the people." He is especially concerned about leaders of depraved moral character who might be empowered by the masses and subvert democracy with what he calls "state absolutism,"[19] which today we would call autocracy. This concern is fresh for him because Hitler had come to power democratically in 1930s Weimar Germany, before bending the democratic institutions to his will. Similarly, amidst political chaos of which he was a significant cause, Mussolini said only he could bring order to the country and was basically allowed to seize power. The lessons that contemporary American Catholics should draw from this in 2024 should not need to be spelled out. In his Christmas message, Pius XII further grants that the liberal

---

17. Pius XII, "Radio Message": "Taught by bitter experience, they are more aggressive in opposing the concentration of dictatorial power that cannot be censured or touched, and call for a system of government more in keeping with the dignity and liberty of the citizens. These multitudes, uneasy, stirred by the war to their innermost depths, are today firmly convinced—at first, perhaps, in a vague and confused way, but already unyieldingly—that had there been the possibility of censuring and correcting the actions of public authority, the world would not have been dragged into the vortex of a disastrous war, and that to avoid for the future the repetition of such a catastrophe, we must vest efficient guarantees in the people itself" (no. 12). "In such a psychological atmosphere, is it to be wondered at if the tendency towards democracy is capturing the peoples and winning a large measure of consent and support from those who hope to play a more efficient part in the destinies of individuals and of society?" (no. 13).

18. Pius XII, "Radio Message": "The masses, on the contrary, wait for the impulse from outside, an easy plaything in the hands of anyone who exploits their instincts and impressions; ready to follow in turn, today this flag, tomorrow another" (no. 24). "Hence follows clearly another conclusion: the masses—as we have just defined them—are the capital enemy of true democracy and of its ideal of liberty and equality" (no. 27).

19. In the "Radio Message," Pius XII discusses how democratic leaders should be of "Christian convictions, straight and steady judgment, with a sense of the practical and equitable, true to themselves in all circumstances; men of clear and sound principles, with sound and clear-cut proposals to make; men above all capable, in virtue of the authority that emanates from their untarnished consciences and radiates widely from them, to be leaders and heads especially in times when the pressing needs of the moment excite the people's impressionability unduly . . . of clear views, kindly interest, a justice equally sympathetic to all, and a bias towards national unity and concord in a sincere spirit of brotherhood" (no. 44). On the other hand, Pius is concerned about "mandatories of a mob, whose interests are often unfortunately made to prevail over the true needs of the common good" (no. 44), those who "take their places in order to make politics serve their ambition, and be a quick road to profit for themselves, their caste and their class, while the race after private interests makes them lose sight of completely and jeopardize the true common good" (no. 45).

democratic model offers best hope for postwar peace and prosperity and encourages the formation on international institutions to foster peace.[20] Throughout the war and after it, Pius worked to foster European integration, which eventually led to the founding of the United Nations, and the European Union. He was clear in his Christmas message, however, that the success of a democratic future is inseparable from "the religion of Christ and his Church."[21] Considering our contemporary situation with a major war raging on the European continent and another in the Middle East, we can no longer presume the postwar Pax Americana and should recognize that our futures are inseparable from the struggle for the future of democracy at home and abroad.

Not everyone, however, agreed with the emergence of Keynesian "mixed economy" that had gained credibility during the Great Depression, especially those who formed the Mount Pellerin Society (1947). These included the Austrian-British Friedrich von Hayek, and the Americans James McGill Buchanan and Milton Friedman. During the midst of the Great Depression, Hayek rose to prominence for his defense of the importance of market mechanisms against some who had advocated to go beyond Keynesian intervention and adopt a planned economy after the example of the Soviet Union.[22] His most famous work, *The Road to Serfdom* (1944) offers many valuable insights. It basically suggests, however, that government involvement leads to socialism; the subsequent experience of Western Europe and elsewhere, however, would seem to refute this alarming and influential assertion that was foundational to the rise of market fundamentalism in the United States. Economic

20. Pius XII, "Radio Message." "The decisions already published by international commissions permit one to conclude that an essential point in any future international arrangement would be the formation of an organ for the maintenance of peace, of an organ invested by common consent with supreme power to whose office it would also pertain to smother in its germinal state any threat of isolated or collective aggression" (no. 62).

21. Pius XII, "Radio Message": "If the future is to belong to democracy, an essential part in its achievement will have to belong to the religion of Christ and to the Church, the messenger of our Redeemer's word which is to continue His mission of saving men. For she teaches and defends supernatural truths and communicates the supernatural helps of grace in order to actuate the divinely-established order of beings and ends which is the ultimate foundation and directive norm of every democracy" (no. 82).

22. Muller, *Mind and the Market*. His work should be credited with helping to steer western thinkers from the temptation of centrally planned economies. Serious scholars, moreover, have argued that forms of neoliberalism are compatible with Catholic Social Teaching, and that the Keynesian model that the social encyclicals have reflected since John XXIII should not be considered Catholic teaching.

developments since especially the 2008 financial crisis, moreover, offer serious challenges to such views.

Buchanan, on the other hand, is known especially for his work in founding the branch of economic study called public choice theory, which critically scrutinizes government interventions in the economy seeking to discredit them. His work in founding the Virginia School of Political Economy is under renewed scrutiny for its reliance on the work of John C. Calhoun, the South Carolina politician and political theoretician of white minority rule in the South before the Civil War.[23] Also in the United States, Milton Friedman was perhaps the leading public intellectual for decades, and the leading figure of the "Chicago School" of free market economics that shaped the U.S. economy and the unfolding of globalization after the fall of the Soviet bloc.

3. Post World War II Liberal Consensus

Although I obviously did not realize it at the time, I was born in 1962 into an era of a considerable postwar consensus regarding American liberalism, and among Catholics in America, who were coming into prominence through various key figures and institutions.[24] Then as now, one of the more publicly visible institutions was the Notre Dame Football team. The most known and respected Catholics included Fulton Sheen as intellectual and churchman, Thomas Merton as man of the world turned monk, Dorothy Day as social conscience, and President John F. Kennedy as symbol that Catholics had assumed the highest positions of leadership in the free world. Kennedy's support by about 80 percent of American Catholics in the 1960 election was a highpoint of political consensus among them.

Political consensus could be seen in the continuities between the Democratic Kennedy Administration and the preceding one of Republican Dwight Eisenhower, who had accepted the New Deal institutions and programs from his Democratic predecessors. He also oversaw a massive public works program reminiscent of the New Deal, that built a significant portion of the interstate highway system. As Democratic presidents would after him, Eisenhower was also focused on the problem of civil rights in America, and appointed Fr. Theodore Hesburgh of the

23. MacLean, *Democracy in Chains*.
24. Massa, *Catholics and American Culture*.

University of Notre Dame to his new civil rights commission that would be continued by Kennedy. Hesburgh's contributions would prove indispensable, moreover, to the commission's ability to reach consensus which was unconceivable until he helped to foster the crucial relationships between Northerners and Southerners through his organization of a fishing trip. At the time of my birth, therefore, to be "liberal" in America did not have the derogatory connotations of recent decades. It instead meant to accept a free society, a constitutional democratic state with a broad distribution of powers. The postwar liberal consensus embraced a so-called "mixed economy" that was powered by vibrant free/liberal markets that were embedded within a broader context of public institutions. According to this arrangement, the government provided services like defense, law and order, infrastructure, research and development, the Federal Reserve System, the Postal Service, education, consumer safety, and a social safety net. Liberal simply meant a free society conducive to human flourishing as opposed to the totalitarianism of Soviet communism. It meant the governmental model of the free world, and the rule-based international order that promised not just to prevent great power conflict but to foster a peaceful and prosperous future.

At the more global level as well, the Catholic Church was not merely tolerant of this postwar liberal order but a significant force behind its coming into prominence, as was suggested by the above discussion of the 1944 Christmas message of Pope Pius XII and his early encouragement of European integration. Also crucial to this formation of postwar Europe were statesmen informed by Catholic social teaching including Conrad Adenauer of West Germany, Robert Schuman of France and Alcide de Gasperi who formed the Christian Democracy Party in Italy.

Catholic thought was also influential in the formation of the 1948 Universal Declaration on Human Rights, which was shepherded through drafting and adoption by Eleanor Roosevelt, the wife of the late President who had an appreciation for Catholic Social Teaching through the collaboration with Msgr. John Ryan.[25] The writings of the Catholic philosopher Jacques Maritain, moreover, helped to prepare the way for the Declaration among Catholics and more broadly.[26] Catholics

---

25. For a discussion of the origins of the declaration, see Glendon, *World Made New*. Regarding the fruitful new scholarship on the central role of Catholics in the twentieth century human rights movement, see vol. 2, chapter 16: Cajka, "Historians, the Catholic Church, and Human Rights."

26. Wood, *When Personalism Met Planning*. Wood discusses, for example, the

who contributed in different ways to the crafting of the Declaration included Maritain, whose writings influenced many and who served on a preparatory committee, and Papal nuncio to Paris, Angelo Roncalli—the future Pope John XXIII—who is said to have provided "discreet personal encouragements."[27] After some early foreign policy disasters in his attempts to establish a position of greater strength from which to negotiate with the Soviet Union—namely deploying nuclear missiles in Turkey and launching the failed Bay of Pigs invasion of Cuba—President Kennedy later shifted to an approach closer to that laid out in John XXIII's 1963 encyclical *Pacem in Terris: Peace on Earth*, which sought peace through the establishment of, and respect for, human rights. This shift was reflected especially in Kennedy's 1963 "Peace Speech."[28]

As he assumed office following the assassination of President Kennedy on November 23, 1963, President Lyndon Johnson was focused first on achieving passage of the civil rights and voting rights acts which finally brought an end to Jim Crow subjugation of African Americans in the South, but also opened a fissure between the Democratic Party and especially southern white Christians who resented the prospects of forced desegregation. The primary goal of Johnson's early presidency was to address the grinding poverty and social inequality that still existed among significant portions of the population, especially—but not exclusively—among African Americans who had continued to suffer discrimination of various forms. To achieve this goal, he launched series of domestic programs under the heading of The Great Society, which included a War on Poverty, which became a focus of socially-oriented politicians including the Catholic Robert F. Kennedy, who made a famous poverty tour. These programs addressed areas such as health and welfare, education, poverty, and consumer and environmental protection.[29]

---

fruitful dialogue between Maritain and a mostly Protestant group of British intellectuals throughout the 1930s and 1940s.

27. Christiansen, "*Pacem in Terris,*" 245. An Orthodox Lebanese statesman named Charles Malik, who was a student of CST, was also influential.

28. Sachs, *To Move the World*.

29. Although a number of these Great Society programs were well-conceived and promised to lift many out of poverty, others were ineffective. The effort was quickly undermined through a combination of the disastrous Vietnam war, the related loss of domestic funding in light of war expenses, the impatience of African Americans with their social situation (including their disproportionate representation in Vietnam) and the Watts riots in Los Angeles, the rise of the new left, the drug culture, and the antiwar protests along with the sexual revolution. These various aspects of social disruption opened the way for a conservative resurgence led by Richard M. Nixon under

The conciliar era Catholic Social Teaching of Popes St. John XXIII and St. Paul VI, therefore, should be understood as encouraging Catholics to pursue holiness within this emerging Liberal World Order, which required the witness of personal example, dialogue and working collaboratively for the common good. As becomes especially clear through Paul VI in the more turbulent times of the early 1970s, this social teaching should be understood as a non-ideological and non-partisan collaboration guided by principles including the dignity of every human person, justice, human rights as the basis for peace,[30] the common good including its global scope,[31] the solidarity of the human family, integral human development, the subsidiary distribution of power, etc. Under this teaching, Catholics move into the forefront of global efforts to promote human rights. The social legacy of John XXIII and Paul VI was robustly embraced by Pope St. John Paul II, under whose leadership the Catholic Church become world's foremost institutional defender of human dignity and rights.[32]

This discussion of a relative consensus about a certain compatibility between Catholicism and postwar liberalism helps to explain how earlier generations of Catholic clergy in the United States were mostly Democrats, well into the 1990s.[33] But what happened to this post war

---

the counsel of the Catholic traditionalist Patrick J. Buchanan. The new playbook emphasized "law and order," and the "Southern Strategy" of winning white voters through "racial dog whistles," all facilitated by an unprecedented campaign of political "dirty tricks" against his opponents carried out by operatives including "the plumbers" who committed the Watergate burglaries and the young insurgent Roger Stone, who had an image of Nixon tattooed on his back.

30. John XXIII *Pacem in Terris* (1963) presents a comprehensive political ethic centered in the defense of human rights.

31. John XXIII *Mater et Magistra* (1961) resituates the Church in a positive, collaborative relationship to new social institutions. The social encyclicals of Pope John XXIII would encourage Catholics to a positive engagement in efforts toward the common good, which he defined very broadly as "all those social conditions which favor the full development of human personality" (no. 65), a definition that is foreshadowed as far back as *Rerum Novarum* no. 32. This common good for John XXIII concerns not just one's community but extends to the national and global (nos. 79–81) levels. While assigning "the first place" in economic affairs to private initiative (no. 51), he sees public authorities as having a special responsibility for the common good (54), with the roles of public and private entities in fostering this good varying according to changing times (57).

32. I seem to remember getting this from George Weigel.

33. Socially and politically, the experience of several decades had suggested a much better alignment between a Democratic party that associated with working people, on the one hand, and a social and political vision grounded in the principles of CST as articulated in the post Conciliar era, on the other hand.

liberal consensus in America and the significant Catholic alignment with it? Of course, differing views were always present. One that would be particularly influential regarding Catholic Social Teaching could be seen as early as 1961, when the *National Review* under the editorship of conservative Catholic William F. Buckley Jr. responded to John XXIII's new social encyclical *Mater et Magistra: Christianity and Social Progress* with an editorial entitled "Mater Si, Magistra No." Such critical reception of Social Encyclicals by American conservatives would continue until the present day. John Paul II's 1991 *Centesimus Annus: On the Hundredth Anniversary of Rerum Novarum* enjoyed a much warmer reception, but this was at the expense of some significant distortions, especially by Catholic neoconservatives who presented it as an endorsement of the American economic model whereas it reflected a view much closer to European social democracy.

4. An Emerging Cleavage between American Liberalism and Catholicism

The implementation of Johnson's Great Society reforms fell victim to the Vietnam war, which we stumbled into through some decisions by Presidents Kennedy and Johnson that seemed reasonable at the time but turned out to be disastrous.[34] The war not only discredited Johnson as sponsor of the Great Society, but starved his domestic programs of their funding, and divided the country in a way that undermined such shared goals. The escalating protests against the Vietnam war fostered a climate in which a variety of social developments—like the efforts for women's and gay rights—tended to become radicalized, so that their merits were not easy to separate from their excesses.

Through the 1960s, the focus in human rights activism shifted from raising those who needed help to a modest standard of living to enhancing the freedoms and rights of groups that were often already middle-class. This is understandable but it also provided an opening for those who would demonize the word liberal, largely to undermine the mixed economy to allow domination by wealthy businessmen seeking wealth and political power. Women, who had been hindered from education

---

34. One way of describing the error was that, under the pressure of Cold War communist expansion, these Democrats tried to expand the liberal order when the military and political conditions were not sufficiently favorable, analogous to what the George W. Bush Administration will later try in Iraq.

and employment by hundreds of discriminatory laws, rightly wanted the freedom and right to study and work. With the availability of modern contraceptives, both women and men exercised a new freedom from traditional norms of sexual behavior. The ensuing increase of sex outside of marriage not surprisingly led to the desire for readily available abortion services and no-fault divorces. Those who had been under societal pressures to keep their homosexual practices "in the closet," moreover, wanted to be free to live as they saw fit; with the "Gay Pride" movement emerging by the late 1960s, they also demanded that their dignity be respected. As movements to secure these new rights grew out of the civil rights efforts that were more associated with the Democratic party, their advocates naturally congregated there, while the right took advantage of the opportunity to demonize the Democrats as godless degenerates.

These tendencies growing out of the so-called sexual revolution were disconcerting to many Catholics, who were often members of the Democratic party, because the Catholic tradition has always upheld a demanding sexual ethic to help people develop the virtuous integration of their sexuality, and to protect the stability of families so they can raise virtuous children who are well prepared to live fruitful lives in service to the common good.[35]

Tragically, considering the fruitful relation that had existed for generations between Catholics and the Democratic party that had aligned with so much of Catholic Social Teaching, disagreements regarding how to address desires for new rights resulted in increasing alienation. Such alienation only increased as the Democratic party embraced more

---

35. With the 1973 Roe v. Wade decision of the Supreme Court that effectively legalized elective abortions throughout the country, the issue that would most alienate Catholics from the Democratic party moved to the forefront. The Democratic party was on a trajectory toward extreme positions that would increasingly alienate Catholics, including insisting on abortion as a fundamental right, to be paid for by taxpayers. By the late 1980s, it had become the central concern of Supreme Court nominations, with Democrats going to great lengths to exclude anyone who might overturn Roe. By the time of the Bill Clinton presidency in 1992, it was to be promoted abroad through the state department and our delegation to the United Nations. Catholics were similarly alienated when the Democratic party supported policies allowing the destruction of embryonic stem cell and human embryos. Pro-life Catholics were increasingly denied the ability to run on Democratic tickets. After the reversal of Roe, however, the prospects for a consensus regarding abortion policy seem as remote as ever as pro-life advocates push for state and national restrictions, as the variety of medical complexities illustrate the difficulty of crafting policies, as the Republican party increasingly manifests authoritarian and anti-democratic means and ends, and as even red state voters overwhelmingly vote for abortion rights.

extreme policies such as supporting partial birth abortions or allowing the destruction of or experimentation on human embryos or excluding dissenting Catholics from positions of leadership. One of the most famous examples of the party's marginalization of Catholics over abortion was when Pennsylvania Governor Bob Casey was denied the right to speak at the 1992 Democratic Convention in favor of adding a minority plank in the party's platform acknowledging the place of pro-life Democrats. If the hallmarks of liberal tradition had included free exchange of ideas, and protections for the rights of the most vulnerable from the exploitation by the strong, it is not surprising that these Catholics saw an emerging illiberalism of the left, a departure from key principles of the liberal tradition under leftist ideologies. Less well-understood is the extent to which especially conservative Catholic political operatives in the Republican Party weaponized the support of the Democratic party for at least toleration of these departures from traditional morality to not only present the latter as the party of godless liberals, but the former as the home for Christian family values.

Through the 1970s and 80s, the main—if not only—group of Catholics who were rejecting the twentieth century Magisterial embrace of liberalism (in the form of constitutional democratic states and the postwar liberal world order) had been the schismatic Society of Saint Pius X (SSPX) founded by traditionalist Bishop Lefebvre. By the 1990s, however, serious Catholic scholars were beginning to argue that liberalism was radically—that is, from its very roots—opposed to Catholicism, though they proposed no serious proposals for an alternative polity. Within a quarter century, a conservative Catholicism had formed in the United States that tends toward what could be called an antiliberalism, postliberalism, or illiberalism of the right. But before discussing that, we need to consider the apparent triumph of liberalism with the conclusion of the Cold War in 1989.

5. The Apparent Triumph of Liberalism with "the End of History" following the Cold War (1989)

After the collapse of the Soviet bloc in the late 1980s, there was no serious political-economic rival to the liberal world order that had been built under the leadership of the United States and its allies since the Second World War. This seems to have contributed to an overconfidence in the form of it that was ascendent at the time, namely a market fundamentalism form of neoliberalism that rejected the economic rights of the 1948 Universal Declaration on Human Rights.[36] One of the most frequently cited discussions of this historical moment was Francis Fukuyama's *The End of History and the Last Man*, which asked the question of whether the history of man's ideological evolution had ended with the universalization of Western liberal democracy. The removal of the Soviet threat—and the discrediting of communist or socialist alternatives to capitalism—opened the way for an accelerated globalization according to the prevailing political-economic wisdom of the day. This wisdom, following the neoliberal model that had been gaining consensus since the late 1970s, heavily favored the allegedly self-regulatory capacities of the market and distrusted the possibility of shaping of globalization through national or international policy.[37] In the United States, there was bipartisan support for allowing market forces—driven by the logic of efficiency as measured by the maximization of profits—to shape the emerging global market and society. In 1996, even Democratic President Bill Clinton declared that "the era of big government is over"[38] as he agreed with Republicans to cut funding for social programs and regulations. Although China was a highly repressive single party society, it was even hoped that welcoming them into the World Trade Association would somehow foster a transition to liberal democracy through participation in market activity. By the time of the 2008 financial crisis, these hopes in what Ronald Reagan had frequently called "the magic of the market" were proving to be tragically mistaken, with economic crisis, rampant inequality and rising discontent with democracies that are becoming oligarchies.

---

36. Samuel Moyn argues that the neoliberal era coexisted with that of human rights in a situation that was "not enough." The "not enough" refers not merely the at best weak realization of social and economic rights, but also to the fact that a broader framework than rights is needed, along with a global movement working for human solidarity and flourishing. Moyn, *Not Enough*. The Catholic social tradition would align with that assessment in accepting human rights within a broader set of principles, accompanied by a proven methodology, within a broader worldview and global community who it would have working in solidarity out of love for God and neighbor.

37. Following the publication of the 1975 report of The Trilateral Commission on *The Crisis of Democracy*, the United States promoted an increasingly neoliberal economics through its foreign policy, which undermined the prospects of policies ordered toward the social and economic rights that had been part of the 1948 UDHR. Crozier, *Crisis of Democracy*.

38. Clinton, "State of the Union."

6. The Present Peril of Liberalism in Alienation from Conservative Catholics

Although a fuller consideration of the present perilous state of liberal democracy makes more sense after treating the evolution of conservatism in part II below, I will offer just a few points now in anticipation of what follows. The first is to reiterate that by liberalism I primarily mean constitutional democratic states—including the support of human rights—with market economies of some sort, and the rule-based international order that was designed to foster the fruitful coexistence of free societies. Despite its overlap with some illiberal tendencies of the left that we have already noted and will further discuss below, this liberal world order has been central to the prevention of great power conflict for three quarters of a century, which is an unprecedented historical achievement upon which the survival of humanity likely depends in an age of widespread proliferation of nuclear weapons. Speaking as someone who was a registered Republican for almost twenty-five years—partially over respect for life issues—but have been an independent for several years, my second point is that both American constitutional government and the liberal world order are in a state that can be described as "teetering on the brink," or "on life support," to put it mildly.

My third point is that this perilous situation has many causes, which need to be carefully considered if we are to be part of the solution as distinguished from part of the problem. Some of these have been indicated above in what Catholics—under the influence of conservative think tanks and media—increasingly saw as an emerging illiberalism of the left. The most problematic tendencies of the left have continued in subsequent years to include identity politics, "cancel culture" and "wokeism," which have contemporary conservatives claiming that the great threat is an illiberalism or—as Rod Dreher puts it—"a soft totalitarianism of the left," about which he was warning us up until the January 6 insurrection. Much more plausible in the short term, however, is an illiberalism of the right as discussed in multiple contributions to this collection. Permeating most of the left and right since at least the Clinton Administration in the 1990s, moreover, was a neoliberal economic model that enriched and politically empowered the elites, while leaving many behind such that large percentages of the populations think—with good reason—the system is rigged against them and are open to populist and demagogic leaders. My fourth point is that the alienation of Catholics from liberalism is a grave threat to the institutions and freedoms of constitutional democratic states, to social cohesion, to the rule based international order and to the ability of the human race to meet the existential challenges of the twenty-first century like global warming, as I discussed in the introduction.

II. The Origins, Development, and Present Crisis of Conservatism

In this second part, my goal is analogous to that of the first part. That is, I seek to offer a sufficient sketch of the conservative tradition to support my proposal that especially the Church in the United States needs to embrace a new era of social Catholicism that appropriates from conservatism what is valuable and compatible with Catholicism—including Catholic Social Teaching—and rejects what is not, namely the tendencies of the illiberal right toward exactly the dangers in democracy against which Pope Pius XII had warned in his 1944 Christmas message, which led to the breakdown of democracies into the fascist states that gave us the Second World War.

I will proceed in the following five steps: (1) the early conservatism of Edmund Burke and his successors; (2) the fusion conservatism of the Reagan era (1980–2008); (3) the more radical conservatism ushered in by Newt Gingrich and conservative media; (4) the neoconservatism of the George W. Bush administration in collaboration with the Catholic Neo/theoconservatives; and (5) the crisis of contemporary conservatism and the need for a center right party that accepts democracy.

1. The Early Conservatism of Edmund Burke and His Successors

As a preliminary definition, we can understand conservatism as a basic disposition to preserve valued institutions, traditions, or social conditions. It can be seen to arise naturally from human wariness regarding the uncertainty that accompanies change and has been occasioned by the increasing rapidity of social disruption that has followed since the unfolding of industrialization in the late eighteenth century, and through recent decades of globalization.[39]

---

39. For a related twentieth-century list of conservative principles that has been influential in the United States, see Kirk, "Ten Conservative Principles." These principles include reference to an enduring moral order, guidance by prudence, an appreciation

Edmund Burke (1729–97), the Irish born member of British Parliament, is often seen as the founder of the conservative intellectual tradition. Although he was a lifelong Anglican, Burke had a Catholic mother and thus an appreciation for the Catholic tradition. Although he was open to the social change that economic development was starting to drive, Burke sought to correct what he saw as the excessive trust in reason and corresponding dismissal of tradition that characterized Enlightenment thinkers of the seventeenth and eighteenth centuries. In both these ways Burke's thought is amenable to Catholic sensibilities, although Catholicism will also reject potentially related excesses in the form of either a traditionalist ideology that tends to insist on something just because it existed at some point in the past, or in the tendency to denigrate the power of human reason in policy making that we will see among more recent conservatives, like those who resist the overwhelming scientific consensus regarding global warming or the effectiveness of vaccines. Burke's early work on the sublime and the beautiful[40] was central, however, to his worthwhile efforts to correct these Enlightenment tendencies to dismiss the legitimate insights transmitted through tradition or to put excessive confidence in reason.

Whereas the Enlightenment political philosophy of Thomas Hobbes (1588–1679) and John Locke (1632–1704) built upon "thought experiments" about a hypothetical "state of nature," Burke argued that such experiments led to neglecting the natural bases of actual human societies.[41] These actual societies, he cogently argued, result from the union of mothers and fathers in the natural institution of the family, whereas the thought experiments of social contract theorists typically led one to neglect this reality and to embrace a false, individualist anthropology that denied the communal nature of human existence. Similarly, Burke insists that societies, therefore, need to be understood more as living organisms than as the collection of isolated individuals that arose from these thought experiments. On all these points, the Catholic tradition has strong affinities with the early conservatism of Burke, although—as we have seen—magisterial social teaching does not reject but favors the

---

of variety, a recognition of human imperfectability, an understanding of close links between freedom and property, a defense of voluntary community over collectivism, the need for prudent constraints on power and passions, and the need to reconcile permanence and change.

40. Burke, *Our Ideas of the Sublime and Beautiful*.
41. Levin, *Great Debate*.

liberal political forms that had evolved by the mid twentieth century, with roots in these thought experiments of social contract theory.

Burke's conservatism included, therefore, a presupposition in favor of preserving existing institutions including not just the family but the Church and the aristocracy, the latter of which he saw as providing an invaluable force in moderating social change. Based on these intellectual foundations, he wrote his *Reflections on the Revolution in France* (1790), in which he predicted that the growing hostility of revolutionaries to these institutions would destabilize the society and lead to disaster. When his predictions were quickly realized, considerable credibility and fame as social commentator ensued, ensuring his foundational place in the subsequent conservative tradition in Britain.

Whereas Burke was justifiably looking to preserve basic institutions like the family and Church, and more disputably the British aristocracy, subsequent conservatives can be identified precisely by the primary institutions and social conditions they sought to conserve, usually under the pressure of social change driven by the unfolding of market activity. As the industrial revolution progressed through the nineteenth century, businessmen typically wanted to preserve the situation in which they could successfully run their businesses without government intervention or taxation. Those in more rural settings, on the other hand, wanted to preserve the more communal and familial values that migration to cities was undermining. In the American South, property holding whites wished to preserve the many privileges they enjoyed, including minority rule, social prestige, and the ability to minimize labor costs and maximize profits through slave labor. A constant refrain from those who thought and wrote about these social changes driven by evolving economic developments was that they tended to erode the virtues upon which society depended.[42]

2. The Fusion Conservatism of the Reagan Era: Late 1970s and Subsequent Conservativisms

Given that so many of us who make up what we might call the "institutional infrastructure" of the Church—the clergy, the academics, media, committed laity—came of age and thus were shaped by the conservatism

---

42. For an intellectual history of attempts to think through the impacts of market activity on societies, see Muller, *Mind and the Market*, and of the tradition of thinkers seeking to moderate or resist that impact, see Muller, *Conservatism*.

that came into prominence in this era, it is vital that we understand how it emerged, what were its main characteristics, and how it relates to what has followed.

Several developments from the mid-1960s through the 1970s led to the impression that the country was on the wrong path economically, internationally, and socially and set the stage for the solidification of a new conservative coalition by the early 1980s during the Presidency of Ronald Reagan. Regarding the economy, those of us with a sufficient proportion of grey hair will remember the so-called economic stagflation that plagued several of the leading market economies from 1973 through 1982.[43] Regarding international relations and national security, the country was dispirited by a sense of decline and fear following the loss of the war in Vietnam and Southeast Asia, and by Soviet military aggression in Afghanistan and covert activities in many countries, topped off by a failed attempt to rescue Americans who were being held hostage by Islamic revolutionaries at the embassy in Tehran, Iran. Regarding changes in American culture, there was a widespread concern among more traditionally-minded Americans about various cultural developments including the rising divorce rates and breakdown of the traditional family unit, the drug culture, the ongoing sexual revolution, the legalization and proliferation of elective abortion, and the movements for women's and gay rights. All of these were weaponized in political campaigns by Republicans against Democrats, most prominently by Evangelical Protestants like Jerry Fallwell, the leader of the Moral Majority.

These social changes and their weaponization in a politics that shifted from questions of economics and justice to these culture war issues, which mostly benefitted the business interests who funded the culture warriors.[44] This enabled Republicans to appeal to especially white

---

43. This term stagflation referred to the combination of economic stagnation, or poor growth, and high inflation which meant increasing prices and interest rates. It was triggered by a steep rise in oil prices compounded by some failed economic policies including wage and price controls, along with increasing economic competition from Japan and Germany. Because this kind of economic downturn was not remedied by the government stimulus that had been used successfully since the adoption of Keynesian economic theory during the great depression, this opened the way for alternative economic approaches.

44. As I discussed in the introduction, Alexander Stern has argued that fostering this shift to the cultural realm is a long-established strategy of oligarchs to distract voters from the essentially political questions about property, justice, and power. Stern, "Centrist Delusions." As I discuss in chapter 14, this is similar to the "dead cat tactic" of populists like Boris Johnson.

citizens against the implementation of civil rights reforms, such as the forced school busing that had been implemented across the country, which led to the so-called "white flight" from urban neighborhoods to the suburbs. This strategy was articulated in 1969 by Republican operative Kevin P. Phillips in a famous book called *The Emerging Republican Majority*, and was followed by Richard M. Nixon through his "southern strategy" and "dog-whistle" appeals to "law and order."[45] These developments indeed provided the opportunity for the establishment of a new governing majority from the various strands of conservatism that existed in the country, and this opportunity was seized by leading operatives including the Catholic William F. Buckley Jr. who edited the *The National Review*. This new conservative majority—what was subsequently called "fusion conservatism"—resulted from the joining of economic, national defense, and social conservatives, and a public distancing from extreme elements such as the white nationalists and the conspiracy theorists of the John Birch Society.

Regarding economics, this new conservative coalition advanced approaches that relied more heavily on the allegedly self-regulatory capacities of the market and sought to reduce the role of the government, whether in social programs, regulation or taxes. The various terminology used to describe this new conservative economics included supply-side, market-oriented, libertarian, neoconservative, and—ironically—neoliberal, referring to the laissez-faire approach that dominated in the era of social Darwinist ideology before the progressive reforms of the early twentieth century and the rise of the Keynesian mixed economy. This new economic direction was the fruit of decades of work among opponents of the postwar Keynesian mixed economy, most famously the Mount Pellerin society led by thinkers including Fredrick von Hayek, James Buchanan and Milton Friedman, all of whom would have a significant impact in shaping especially the American economy over the last several decades.

Various Catholic intellectuals including Michael Novak who were both skeptical of the Keynesian mixed economy that the Catholic Social encyclicals seemed to presume, and advocates of this more market-oriented direction, made influential arguments in support of their views. By the time the U.S. Bishops published their pastoral letter on "Economic Justice for All" in 1986, its focus on building a just economy and society

---

45. Phillips, *Emerging Republican Majority*.

that benefits everyone sounded obsolete to those who were enjoying a period of increasing economic prosperity that was being attributed to having freed the market from government interference through reductions in regulations, taxes and social programs. It would be over twenty years before objections to this new economics are taken seriously, after decades of deregulation and cuts to the social safety net have contributed not only to the Great Recession following the 2008 financial crash, but to a massive shift of wealth to the top earners, and an accompanying growth in poverty and ensuing social decay that has internally destabilized Western democracies and made them vulnerable by growing threats from an alliance of autocracies led by Russia and China.

Regarding foreign policy, this fusion conservatism of the Reagan era embraced a significant increase in military spending and a policy of more firmly opposing Soviet expansionism. Key interventions included the deployment of battlefield nuclear weapons to Europe, supplying arms to anti-communist forces in Nicaragua, and anti-aircraft missiles to Afghan forces opposing the Soviet occupation. Compared to a contemporary rise of "America First" isolationism, this fusionist "conservative" foreign policy of the late Cold War still presupposed the importance of the international institutions of the post war liberal order, including the NATO alliance that had deterred Soviet aggression in Europe, and the United Nations system, which greatly expanded American soft power through a global array of allies who benefitted from different aspects of the rule based international order and international institutions. Also integral to the conservatism of the Reagan era was the promotion of human rights; in this it overlapped with a key aspect of Catholic Social Teaching, which saw the promotion of human rights as conducive to peace and order.

Regarding the socially conservative component of the fusion conservatism that solidified in the 1980s, this was centered in an emerging coalition of Catholics and Evangelical Protestants. Although Catholics had been primarily aligned with the Democratic party since the progressive era reforms for industrial workers and New Deal provision of a social safety net, they were becoming increasingly alienated from it especially as the Democratic coalition came to increasingly support initiatives to advance personal and sexual freedoms that Catholics tended to see as corrosive of the natural foundations of society in stable family units. With the 1973 "Roe v. Wade" decision of the U.S. Supreme Court, which essentially legalized elective abortions throughout the entire nine months of pregnancy, the decisive issue around which this Evangelical and Catholic coalition would form was in place. In the early years following the decision, however, the primary opposition was voiced by Catholics whereas a broad range of Protestants, including Southern Baptists, had supported Roe v. Wade.

By the late 1970s, however, Southern Baptist pastor Jerry Falwell was encouraged and supported by some Republican political operatives to form an organization called the "Moral Majority," the purpose of which was to mobilize conservative, and especially Southern, Christians to influence politics.[46] These operatives included Paul Weyrich,[47] the co-founder of the Heritage Foundation think tank and other allied organizations.[48] Interestingly, Weyrich was a former Roman Rite Catholic who switched to the Melkite Greek Catholic Church, largely because he thought the Catholic Church had become too liberal, especially in bishops inspired by Catholic Social Teaching speaking about temporal affairs.[49] Whereas the primary political concern for Southern conservatives like Falwell was on some court cases that threatened the tax exempt status of southern Evangelical schools that practiced racial segregation,[50] Weyrich helped them to see that forging a political alliance with conservative Catholics centered on the issue of abortion would be the most effective means for gaining a degree of political power that he foresaw "could well exceed our wildest dreams."[51] I point this out not to question

---

46. This happened in the wake of the "southern strategy" of President Richard Nixon, that apparently had been devised by conservative Catholic Patrick J. Buchanan to attract white southerners to the Republican party after their disaffection from the Democrats due to civil rights legislation of the 1960s. See Courson, "Document."

47. The name "moral majority" was immediately adopted by Falwell after Weyrich used the phrase in conversation. See Stewart, *Power Worshippers*, 62–63.

48. Another of the key operatives was Richard Viguerie, who was also a conservative Catholic and was instrumental in building the conservative movement through direct mail appeals for funding. For a first-hand account, see Viguerie and Martin, *Takeover*. Yet another of these Catholic conservative operatives was John Terrance (Terry) Dolan, who was the founder of the National Conservative Political Action Committee, a proponent of family values, and a closeted homosexual who died of AIDS at thirty-six years.

49. Keeley emphasizes that Paul Weyrich—who was advancing the Republican Latin American policy centered on serving business interests—objected to the engagement in temporal political discussions by the U.S. Bishops. Keeley, *Reagan's Gun-Toting Nuns*, 133.

50. Bob Jones University, in particular, had lost its nonprofit status in 1976 due to its segregationist policies.

51. According to historian Randall Balmer, "In fact, it wasn't until 1979—a full six years after Roe—that evangelical leaders, at the behest of conservative activist

the motivations of many in the pro-life movement who sought to protect the most vulnerable, but to point out some of the moral ambiguities in the very foundations of the alliance of social conservatives centered on the issue of abortion. These ambiguities concern not only the original segregationist motivations of the "moral majority," but those of operatives like Paul Weyrich, whose political views conflicted with especially post conciliar Catholic Social Teaching that had endorsed the postwar mixed economy with its social safety net.

With the completion of the Reagan Presidency in January of 1989, followed quickly by the collapse of the Soviet Union and prompt end of the Cold War under his former Vice President, George H. W. Bush, those of us who had come to identify as conservative Republicans were confident in our politics, in the future, and in the prospects for a new flourishing of Catholicism under the inspirational leadership of Pope John Paul II. A book that captured the spirit of the time was *The Catholic Moment: The Parodox of the Church in the Postmodern World* (1987) by a recent convert named Fr. Richard John Neuhaus. As suggested by the title, the book makes a winsome case for how Catholicism, drawing on the achievements of the Second Vatican Council and the leadership of John Paul II, together with his lead collaborator Joseph Ratzinger, was uniquely positioned to provide a leading role in fostering not only a more united and interreligiously attuned Christianity, but what Neuhaus called "a religiously informed public philosophy" with great relevance for an era in which the global consensus for liberal—that is, constitutional democratic—government was reaching new highs.

The conversion of Richard John Neuhaus to Catholicism, and his subsequent founding of the journal *First Things*, were crystalizing events in the rise of fusion era conservatism, precisely by fostering the growing alliance of religious and especially social conservatives, including not just Catholics and Evangelicals, but also Jews. Aided by the attention that Neuhaus's cultural commentary was attracting, this journal quickly became an intellectual point of reference for a conservative movement that was growing in not just prominence but political influence. *First Things* was also a home for initiatives like Evangelicals and Catholics together, which deepened the connections between these traditions. Neuhaus's so

---

Paul Weyrich, seized on abortion not for moral reasons, but as a rallying-cry to deny President Jimmy Carter a second term. Why? Because the anti-abortion crusade was more palatable than the religious right's real motive: protecting segregated schools." See Balmer, "Real Origins."

called "neoconservative" or "theoconservative" Catholic collaborators, especially Michael Novak and George Weigel advanced the cultural and political project. Novak focused on promoting the merits of market-oriented economics in the years of accelerated globalization following the end of the cold war, traveling extensively throughout Latin America and newly liberated Eastern Europe to spread his message of free market economics. Weigel, on the other hand, supported the more assertive military posture of the Republicans with a 1987 book that criticized the directions of the Papal Magisterium regarding peace and war since John XXIII, and especially the 1983 pastoral letter by the U.S. Bishops, "The Challenge of Peace: God's Promise and Our Response."[52]

After having appreciated the economic growth of the Reagan era, the vastly improved international situation after the Cold War, and seeing the potential for some social stabilization after the disruption of the 1960s, many Catholic social conservatives were angry if not distraught with the results of the 1992 Presidential election. Running with the disadvantages of both a recession and the third-party candidacy of populist Ross Perot,[53] sitting President George Herbert Walker Bush, whose approval ratings had previously exceeded 80 percent, lost his bid for reelection to Democrat Bill Clinton. Whereas Bush was widely respected for his military and government service, and as a last representative of the White Anglo Saxon Protestant (WASP) elite who had led the nation for generations and to victory in the Cold War, Clinton was broadly seen by social conservatives as unworthy due to his draft-dodging, pot smoking, womanizing, fast talking and looseness with the truth, to say nothing of his wife Hillary, who was an outspoken feminist and advocate for abortion rights. Clinton's election was quickly followed by the rapid expansion of conservative talk radio and a rapid growth in those who saw themselves as conservative, especially in what we would now call the red states, where talk radio is especially popular.

---

52. Weigel, *Tranquillitas Ordinis*.

53. Perot's populism reflected themes that would reemerge with Donald Trump, including an isolationist rejection of the first Gulf War and opposition to the North American Free Trade Agreement (NAFTA).

3. The Rise of Radical Conservatism: Newt Gingrich and the Rise of Conservative Media

A corresponding, and equally important, development that crystalized during the early 1990s was the emergence of a more radical form of conservatism, especially under the influence of Newt Gingrich as is described in a detailed 2018 piece published by McKay Coppins in *The Atlantic*.[54] As Gingrich explained to Coppins, his approach to politics traces back to his fascination with animals, and the ferocity of the struggle for existence as seen in one of his favorite books, *Chimpanzee Politics: Power and Sex among Apes* by Frans de Waal. This book develops the thesis that human politics is a development of the brutality and ugliness seen in the rivalries among communities of chimps. On this basis Coppins describes how Gingrich "pioneered a style of partisan combat—replete with name-calling, conspiracy theories, and strategic obstructionism—that poisoned America's political culture and plunged Washington into permanent dysfunction."[55] Although many of his Republican colleagues had valued an earlier era of relative bipartisan comity to do the nation's business, the fact that his tactics were effective in gaining political power eventually won the day among Republicans. One of the most important aspects of Gingrich's program was the way he also taught his colleagues how to implement his approach. To do so, Frank Lunz and the GOPAC group Gingrich headed developed and distributed a pamphlet entitled "Language: A Key Mechanism of Control," which trained Republicans "how to talk like Newt."[56] This meant to use a lexicon of positive words for their themselves and their initiatives—like freedom, liberty, prosperity, moral, principled, responsible—and negative ones for their opponents including "liberal" (which became almost an expletive), pathetic, sick, shallow, radical, self-serving, traitorous, corrupt, obsolete, incompetent, failed, greedy, or bizarre. This led to a Republican debating style centered in attacking early and never backing down. Coppins describes Gingrich's 2018 view of the current wreckage of modern politics as "gleeful," because he approves of the fact that "The old order is dying.... [T]he system isn't working."[57]

Having appreciated the apparent gains of the Reagan-Bush years, and having been troubled by some of the policies of the Clinton

---

54. Coppins, "Man Who Broke Politics."
55. Coppins, "Man Who Broke Politics," para. 14.
56. Wikipedia, s.v. "GOPAC," https://en.wikipedia.org/wiki/GOPAC.
57. Coppins, "Man Who Broke Politics," para. 17.

Administration during its first two years—like the promotion of abortion as a human right through the state department and United Nations—many conservatives were sympathetic to the resistance led by Gingrich, although few understood his tactics, or what they would do to the legislative branch of government and broader political climate. Many of us Catholic conservatives during the Reagan-era were similarly sympathetic to the rise of conservative media, especially given the biased way the mainstream media covered cultural debates like that surrounding abortion. The growth of conservative media was facilitated by the Reagan Administration's 1987 removal of the Federal Communications Commission's (FCC) "fairness doctrine" that had been instituted in 1949 to foster equitable and balanced broadcasting regarding controversial topics. Few, however, could have envisioned the radicalization of especially right-wing media that would follow,[58] or the threat this would pose to American democracy and the global common good.

Under the minority party opposition of the House Republicans led by Gingrich, with support of the sprawling conservative media ecosystem of talk radio, the liberal agenda of Clinton's first two years led—through the 1994 midterm elections—to the loss of the House to the Republicans with Gingrich becoming Speaker. Under the leadership of Gingrich, one of the primary characteristics of the new congress was an inclination to deconstruct what Newt called the "warshington [sic] bureaucracy." One strategy to do so was the ploy of shutting down the government to force budget cuts to social programs during Democratic administrations while running up the deficit through tax cuts during Republican ones.[59] For our purposes, another important result was the way a weakened Clinton pivoted to cut deals with the Republicans. These included not just "welfare reform," but a more market-oriented or neoliberal economic and trade policy, as seen especially in the North American Free Trade

---

58. Although I recognize that partisan and ideological bias also occurs on the left, I think it is obvious that the problems are not symmetrical between contemporary left and right media. Left-leaning mainstream media such as CNN or even MSNBC still affirms traditional standards of journalism as demonstrated by the fact that they will issue corrections when they get the facts wrong, whereas Fox News does not. As the electronic correspondence released during the Dominion Voting Systems trial clearly demonstrated, "Fox News" is much more a profit center and arm of the Republican Party than a traditional news outlet.

59. This tactic builds on the "Two Santas" strategy of Republican operative Jude Wanniski through which the Republicans give tax breaks to counter the popular social programs that Democrats advance, and then call for austerity against the social programs when the Democrats are in power.

Agreement (NAFTA), which will later be widely criticized for offshoring manufacturing and other businesses, and would ultimately break the bonds between the working class and the Democratic Party. By the end of Clinton's two terms in the year 2000, however, he had survived being impeached for an affair with an intern, the economy was booming, the budget was balanced, and the country was at peace. The impeachment had been orchestrated by Gingrich, who was a serial philanderer himself, and soon found a home within Conservative Catholicism, before being driven from office by the chaos agents he had brought into the House of Representatives.[60]

4. The Neoconservative Presidency of George W. Bush in alliance with Catholic Neo/theoconservatives

With the election of Republican George W. Bush in the year 2000, an administration was formed that was profoundly shaped by the neoconservative movement that had been growing in strength during the Clinton years, whether in the burgeoning conservative think tanks or in lesser office. As of this time, there was still a strong consensus for the tripartite fusion conservatism of the Reagan era: an emphasis on freeing market activity from regulatory or tax burdens, on an assertive defense posture, and on an alliance with religious and social conservatives, especially on issues like abortion. Regarding the first, a neoliberal model of market-oriented globalization was spreading rapidly, with free movement of capital and labor and the rise of the Asian economies, including China.

Regarding foreign policy, neoconservative thinkers who congregated in think tanks—like the Project for the New American Century—during the Clinton Administration had been considering policy options for when the Republicans were back in power. They planned considering the fact that the United States was the world's sole superpower following the collapse of the Soviet Union and given the fact that there were areas of instability in the world—especially the Middle East—that threatened the prospects for peace and prosperity in the new century. Since the United States had unrivaled military power, would it not make sense to impress order on the Middle East, starting with one country like Iraq, and then

60. The next four Republican speakers would suffer the same fate until the 2023 election of Mike Johnson, who worked closely with Donald Trump to overturn the 2020 election and organized the efforts of the house Republicans against certifying the election of Joe Biden, which earned him Trump's endorsement for speaker.

spreading democracy throughout the region? The attacks on the World trade center towers would provide an occasion to carry out these plans.

Through his international bestseller *Witness to Hope: The Biography of Pope John Paul II* (1999) George Weigel had gained a high level of credibility as a Vatican insider who could authoritatively mediate the meaning of this dynamic Pontificate to the Church in the United States, which he did through widespread speaking engagements and a column published in many diocesan newspapers. Weigel continued to help align conservative Christians with the more assertive foreign policy stance of fusion conservatism. Against Pope John XXIII's emphasis on working to extend human rights to build a just order and thereby remove the conditions that might lead to war, Weigel had championed and understanding of "war as an instrument of statecraft." Against the repeated pleadings of St. John Paul II that the neoconservative George W. Bush Administration refrain from their threatened 2003 invasion Iraq, which the Pope knew would destabilize the region and harm ancient Christian communities, Weigel published a series of articles in *First Things* building support among religious conservatives for what would become arguably the worst foreign policy blunder in American history.[61]

By the end of 2008, the neoconservative administration of President George W. Bush was enduring some of the lowest presidential approval ratings in history despite having Fox News acting as a de facto arm of the Republican Party. Not only had what was clearly an elective war against Iraq proven to be a disaster, but the deregulatory policies of neoliberal globalization had contributed significantly to a financial crisis that threatened to collapse the global economy. Besides this, public opinion had turned increasingly against social conservatism, as evidenced in the growing support for gay marriage, especially among younger Americans. Thus, all three pillars of fusion conservatism had apparently collapsed, which also left the Catholic theoconservatives in disarray as Barack Obama assumed office in 2009, shortly after the passing of Fr. Richard John Neuhaus of *First Things*.

---

61. See, for example, Weigel, "Moral Clarity in a Time of War."

5. The Present Crisis of Conservatism: Some Promising Initiatives

In this section, I will first offer some brief remarks on the evolution of the American right after the collapse of both Republican neoconservatism and the adjacent Catholic theoconservatism, after which the American right has been entertaining a variety of populist, anti-institutional, nationalist, integralist, and authoritarian directions that are more reactionary than conservative. I will also briefly sketch an argument that the failure of Catholic theoconservatism is readily explained by its departures from an authentic social Catholicism, an explanation that illumines the path for contemporary Catholics to become agents of societal renewal and reconciliation. This explanation is an alternative to accepting a radically antiliberal or postliberal stance that—as far as I can tell—would align Catholics with the anti-democratic right, which in my opinion would be a tragic mistake along the lines of that made by Catholics during the rise of twentieth century fascism as discussed by Yves Simon.[62] I also indicate some recent initiatives on the center right with which a new generation of social Catholics could collaborate given the way they would subordinate ideology and partisanship to the integral and solidary humanism of Catholic Social Doctrine.

After the collapse of the neoconservatism of the Republican George W. Bush Administration, there was an inconclusive period of reevaluation within the party and in the adjacent theoconservative movement centered around the journal *First Things*. Since the ascendance of Donald Trump in 2015, the party has been increasingly transformed by MAGA populism, demagoguery, contempt for the rule of law, authoritarianism and neofascist leanings in encouraging political violence through stochastic terrorism.[63] As Rep. Matt Gaetz—who deposed Speaker Kevin McCarthy—subsequently proclaimed on Steve Bannon's War Room,

---

62. Simon, *Road to Vichy*.

63. Stochastic terrorism is the employment of the media by public figures to intimidate opponents by indicating to followers that these opponents are legitimate targets for attack. Corn, "Donald Trump, Stochastic Terrorist." In his recent biography of Mitt Romney, McKay Coppins discusses how—since the January 2021 insurrection—Senator Romney has paid $5,000 per day for security services for himself and his family. He also discusses how many of Romney's colleagues vote with the MAGA wing because of the at least implicit but often explicit threats against them and their families, and the fact that many of them don't have the financial resources to employ the security services that would be needed if they went against Trump and the MAGA movement. Coppins, *Romney*.

the election of Mike Johnson as Speaker of the House makes clear that "MAGA is ascendent"[64] in the Republican party. This is clearly the case as the remaining "moderates" who long for the conservatism of the fusion era are largely marginalized, especially in the House.

The crisis of Catholic theoconservatism amidst the collapse of the Bush Administration does raise a crucial question. During the pontificates of St. John Paul II and Benedict XVI, *First Things* under the editorship of Fr. Neuhaus had been a locus of support for what he called the liberalism of the American Revolution. Neuhaus argued that Catholics should contend—through participation in the political process—for the version of American liberalism most compatible with the fullness of Catholic truth, thereby realizing the promise of the previously mentioned "Catholic Moment." He did so in a long running debate with David L. Schindler who had argued that liberalism was radically—that is, from its metaphysical roots—flawed because it was not grounded in the very foundations of truth in Trinitarian love. The implication seems to be that efforts to work for the common good through the political process would be significantly undermined—if not futile—given the flawed metaphysics of liberalism. The crucial question is whether Neuhaus's program of contending for a version of American liberalism most compatible with the fullness of Catholic truth failed because of the flawed metaphysical roots of liberalism or for other reasons?

I think other reasons go a long way to explaining why the Catholic theoconservative program failed, all of which can be seen as departures from Catholic Social Teaching. These reasons reflect the fact that their program was shaped too much by the conservativism and Republican party politics of the day and too little by CST. According to the three pillars of fusion conservatism, I will briefly summarize the most important departures from Catholic Social Teaching that I think explain the failure of their project, at least to a significant degree. First, regarding economics, the theoconservatives were closely aligned with the market fundamentalism that was being advanced first by the Republican Party, and later at least partially by Democrats including President Bill Clinton. This market fundamentalism was explicitly opposed to the "mixed economy" or "embedded liberalism" that was presupposed in recent generations of social teaching, as will be discussed in our symposium on "Social Catholicism and New Economic Thinking after the Neoliberal Consensus."

---

64. Bertman, "'MAGA Is Ascendant.'"

Second, regarding foreign policy, the theoconservatives supported the militarism of the Bush Administration against the emphasis of CST on working to establish justice and peace to prevent war; their advocacy for the Iraq war went directly against the strenuous objections of St. John Paul II, moreover, who understood well the disaster that would follow. Third, I would argue that the socially conservative alliance with Evangelical Protestants fostered by party operatives and focused on "culture war" and "wedge issues" like abortion deserves much of the blame for the polarization that has not only degraded the nation, but communities and families. It is a stark alternative to the "integral and solidary humanism" and social friendship of CST, and its appeals to the irascible passions of fear and anger have led to the societal degradation that one would expect.

While I strive to understand, live and teach a Catholic understanding of human sexuality, marriage and respect for life, moreover, I think these are best advanced through personal example, through dialogue, through the democratic process, and within an authentic Catholic social vision. I think American Catholic conservatives, on the other hand, have not only insisted at key times on positions that were "more Catholic than the Pope,"[65] but have increasingly tried to impose moral teachings through the political process as if we were still living in the age of Christendom.[66] Other departures from CST that were deep flaws in the theoconservative project were the anti-institutionalism, the explicit partisanship, and the alignment with the rich and powerful over the vulnerable. Rather than realign to a posture better informed by Catholic Social Teaching, *First Things* during the age of Trump has been a platform for antiliberalism, and generally encouraged their audience of conservative Republicans in retaining a focus on the culture war issues while exploring a variety of increasingly antidemocratic ideas including those discussed by Julian Waller in chapter 11 and Matt McManus in chapter 12.

Behind the scenes of Republican politics, moreover, the business wing of the party is still dominated by libertarian donor networks who are happy to go along with a largely Trumpian agenda of culture wars and opposition to abortion as long as the party still delivers on their goals of low taxes and deregulation, and as long as they maintain a Supreme

---

65. Murphy, "Ethics of Life, Synodality, and Untying Knots"; Murphy "Reflections on Fundamental Morality."

66. For a discussion of the end of Christendom, and how the Church might adopt a new Marian stance in relation to our new situation, see Bauerschmidt, "Christendom and the Marian Path."

Court supermajority that largely serves their agenda. This court has, for example, given the wealthy the ability to pour unlimited money into dominating the political process, while weakening voting rights so Republicans can suppress voting in Democratic leaning districts, radically gerrymander "Red States," and continue to "deconstruct the administrative state" so it is impotent to hinder an oligarchic multiplication of profits and political power while our slide toward climate catastrophe accelerates. Although this assessment may sound partisan, it comes from a long-time former Republican who has never belonged to another party, who appreciates key insights of Burkean conservatism, who thinks the illiberal and identitarian elements of the left are intellectually misguided and politically self-destructive, who recognizes the need for a healthy center-right party, and who affirms the Republican Party's vital contributions to the nation under Abraham Lincoln, Theodore Roosevelt and Dwight D. Eisenhower.[67]

Although my assessment may also sound exaggerated, I would argue that the dire situation is manifest daily in many ways, including by the expressions of alarm by those who led the Republican Party before the Trump era, which they articulate through an ongoing deluge of books, articles and television interviews. The severity of the situation is also plain in ongoing attempts of the Justice Department to reestablish the rule of law. Many former insiders are sounding the alarm of the tragedy that awaits us in the upcoming 2024 election if the Republican Party as it currently exists secures political power. Among the most notable works in the weeks of this writing are *Romney: A Reckoning* by McKay Coppins, which is an authorized biography of the current Senator and former Republican presidential candidate Mitt Romney. It is based on free access to Romney's contemporary diaries, emails, and text messages, plus months of interviews with him, his family and his staff. It reflects Romney's desire to alert the public about how his Republican colleagues have come to the place that they not only fostered the insurrection of January 6, 2021, but have continued to pursue minority rule, posing a grave threat to American Democracy. Consistent with Romney's epigraph that exalts conscience over political success and fame, Coppins presents

---

67. See Richardson, *To Make Men Free*, for a discussion of the ideological oscillation of the party from its founding to promote economic opportunity and justice for all through the Civil War, to its co-option by industrialists after the Civil War, to its return to egalitarianism under Theodore Roosevelt, to its capture by business interests during the 1920s, to its acceptance of the New Deal during the 1950s under Eisenhower, to its recapture by business interests leading to the current crisis.

Romney's political career as a morality tale in which he compromised his principles to be the party's standard bearer, for example by playing to the populist base while running for President while not believing what he had to say. He compromised less so than others, however, while opting more strongly for conscience in recent years as the threat posed by the party grows and he transitions to a retirement amidst a loving family, and great wealth. Romney's morality tale should be taken as a warning to all of us—including those working in the Church—about how the passions of political struggle and dubious ideological and partisan affinities can entangle us in a web of compromises that blind us to what should be obvious questions of justice and the common good.

Also hot off the press is *The Conspiracy to End America: Five Ways My Old Party Is Driving Our Democracy to Autocracy* by Stuart Stevens, who has been called the most successful Republican political operative of his generation. After working mostly behind the scenes, Stevens became more widely known during the 2020 election cycle for his work with *The Lincoln Project*. The book discusses the five elements the Republican party is now employing to establish single party rule and autocracy in America, which are a development of the strategies that were employed during Stevens' days as party operative. These five elements start with (1) the financiers and include (2) the propagandists like Fox News, (3) the party machinery, (4) the legal theorists and advocates at places like the Claremont Institute who both legitimize and help to effect the takeover, and (5) the "shock troops" exemplified by the "dirty trickster" Roger Stone. This book can be seen as a follow-up to Stevens' prior effort at making amends for his complicity in the crisis facing our country, namely *It Was All a Lie: How the Republican Party Became Donald Trump*. In it, Stewart emphasizes the centrality of racial "dog whistle" politics to the success of the party, but he also discusses, for example, how the party emphasis on "family values" was embraced largely for its utility in attacking, defining and "othering" Democrats, on the one hand, and courting conservative white Evangelical Protestants and Catholics, on the other.

This is not the place for a further discussion of the present crisis of American conservatism and the Republican Party,[68] a predicament of

---

68. Those familiar with the history and current state of the Democratic and Republican will recognize that the former is almost universally represented by those who see government service as serious business and public institutions to be nurtured as integral to the common good and whereas the latter have increasingly gone to Washington to shrink, obstruct or deconstruct it. For a detailed recent study of the qualifications of representatives, see Podhorzer, "Hiding in Plain Sight," who marshals evidence

great importance to the Catholic Church in the United States, especially given that so many who make up our "institutional infrastructure"—including clergy, intellectuals and other influential persons—have been formed in recent decades of conservative ascendance. Although the experience of several nations over the last two centuries indicates that a healthy center right party that accepts democracy is required if democracy is to survive, let alone thrive,[69] given that the House Republicans just voted unanimously for someone who has not only long denied the results of the 2020 presidential election, but led the legal efforts of his conference to oppose certifying the results of that election, it is difficult to envision how that party can be entrusted with political power in the foreseeable future. If the party in its current form takes national power through the 2024 elections, and if Donald Trump becomes President, he has been promising at his rallies to purge public institutions of career professionals, to fill them with loyalists, and to use the powers of the government to punish his opponents.

To balance out this discussion and end on a more positive note, I will briefly introduce some promising initiatives on the center right that could be part of future collaboration with the left. Among the more promising of today's conservative scholars in my opinion is Yuval Levin. His book on *The Great Debate*, for example, offers insight into the origins of conservative thought in Edmund Burke, who was in a lively debate with Thomas Paine, one of the more radical figures in the American Revolution, who went on to support the French Revolution. Levin's latest book argues persuasively for conservatives to gain a new appreciation of institutions, and not just those of family and Church, that are typically lauded by conservatives, but also public institutions. The title indicates the scope and timeliness, namely *A Time to Build: From Family and Community to Congress and the Campus, How Recommitting to Our Institutions Can Revive the American Dream*. Levin's focus on institutions offers a point of contact within conservatism for the project of renewing

---

regarding the experience and qualifications that the current MAGA dominated Republican Party. Besides just choosing an election denier to be the least experienced speaker in 140 years, he documents that the GOP house "is the least qualified, least experienced majority caucus since at least the end of World War II." He concludes that it can be understood as a kakistocracy, a government by the worst, or least qualified. At the time of the polycrisis and after Roe v. Wade has already been struck down, to imply that Catholics should support such people because they claim to be against abortion is difficult to defend, in my opinion.

69. This need is demonstrated at great length in Fawcett, *Conservatism*.

American democracy that I argued in the introduction should be the immediate focus of Catholics if the "nuclear reactor" of the polycrisis is to be managed.

Regarding economics, the American Compass web portal provides a home to ongoing efforts of young conservatives who are breaking from the "market fundamentalism" that has marked the Republican Party for decades. Regarding Foreign Policy, the Catholic Conservative Andrew Bechevich offers a compelling break from the militarism of the neoconservative Catholics of past decades. Regarding local efforts to rebuild our social fabric, *New York Times* columnist David Brooks is involved in a nationwide project he calls the weavers, who are those working locally to address social problems and build community. Although he is more of a centrist, Brooks still considers himself a conservative, and remains appreciative of his mentor Bill Buckley. Although they are perhaps more closely aligned with the social conservatism of recent decades than I would be, I think Robert George's Witherspoon Institute at Princeton makes excellent contributions, including through their online journal *Public Discourse*. One can find good material there, for example, to illustrate some of the best arguments against the radical antiliberalism embraced by so many contemporary Catholics.

In my opinion, such initiatives are perhaps the most promising advanced by self-identified conservatives with the potential for broad collaboration among those working to rebuild our social fabric and democracy.

III. Conclusion: A New Social Catholicism for the Twenty-First Century?

From the perspective of the Catholic social tradition, this essay sketched a narrative of how we might understand the evolution and current state of both liberalism—or perhaps better, constitutional democracy—and conservatism in relation to the argument of this collection for a contemporary renewal of social Catholicism and a better kind of politics to build a future worthy of the human family. Although the word liberal has been made into almost an explicative due to both illiberal excess on the left and effective propaganda from the right,[70] I have tried to show that the key

---

70. Oreskes and Conway, *Big Myth*; Mayer *Dark Money*; MacLean, *Democracy in Chains*; Richardson, *How the South Won the Civil War*.

tenets of what we might call the tradition of political liberalism have been amply embraced in the authoritative documents of the last six decades of Catholic Social Teaching, such that the Catholic Church clearly favors an understanding of the political community that includes constitutional and democratic government, human rights, the equal human dignity of every person, free and fair elections and the distribution of powers. Catholics, therefore, should not accept a radical antiliberalism, postliberalism, or conservatism that makes them vulnerable to the sophisticated propaganda and corrupt ends of the increasingly radical right, including oligarchs and their agents. We should instead employ proper distinctions so we can support the good in constitutional democracy that has been recognized by the Catholic tradition and sound reasoning.

I have also argued that, on the one hand, some of the foundational insights of the conservative tradition align nicely with the tradition-mindedness of Catholicism. On the other hand, I have argued that much of what is presented as conservative in today's right-wing media and in the contemporary Republican party is instead something quite contrary to the best of the conservative tradition, to Catholic Social Doctrine, to the promise of American democracy, and to the hope for managing what can be managed in the global polycrisis. Although the illiberal left appeared to provide the greater threat to the common good in earlier generations, today the illiberal right poses precisely the kind of threat against which Pope Pius XII warned the Church in his 1944 Christmas address, through which he pointed the Church toward participation in the postwar plans for building a liberal democratic order, which he warned would not succeed without the Church. Consistent with other essays in this collection, I have highlighted this contemporary crisis of liberal democracy and "conservatism" as an urgent threat requiring the vigorous efforts of Catholics, working together with all of goodwill to realize the promise of constitutional democracy and fend off the very real and proximate threat of a new authoritarian dystopia at a time of unprecedented geopolitical and climactic peril. I have also noted some of the more promising initiatives from the contemporary center right that could be part of fruitful conversations about the common good.

The integral and solidary humanism of Catholic Social Doctrine provides a tested set of principles, a winsome and realistic methodology of dialogue and participation, a long history of responding to different historical situations, a tradition of both institution building and grass roots action, along with the needed spiritual foundations for a perhaps decisive contribution to addressing the great challenge of our times. I do not think it is an exaggeration to say that the future of the Church, of American democracy, of the human family and of the planet will be significantly shaped by whether contemporary Catholics make a more positive contribution to the common good through a robust appropriation of our social tradition.

Bibliography

Balmer, Randall. "The Real Origins of the Religious Right." *Politico Magazine*, May 27, 2014. https://www.politico.com/magazine/story/2014/05/religious-right-real-origins-107133.

Benedict XVI. *Caritas in Veritate: On Integral Development in Charity and Truth*. Vatican City: Libreria Editrice Vaticana, 2009. https://www.vatican.va/content/benedict-xvi/en/encyclicals/documents/hf_ben-xvi_enc_20090629_caritas-in-veritate.html#_ednref112.

Bertman, Christopher. "'MAGA Is Ascendant': Gaetz Comments on Speaker Johnson's Election." https://gaetz.house.gov/media/in-the-news/maga-ascendant-gaetz-comments-speaker-johnsons-election.

Broderick, Francis L. *Right Reverend New Dealer: John A. Ryan*. New York: Macmillan Company 1963.

Burke, Edmund. *A Philosophical Enquiry into the Origin of Our Ideas of the Sublime and Beautiful*. London: Dodsley, 1757.

———. *Reflections on the Revolution in France: A Critical Edition*. Edited by J. C. D. Clark. Stanford: Stanford University Press, 2001.

Clinton, William J. "State of the Union." https://clintonwhitehouse4.archives.gov/WH/New/other/sotu.html#:.

Chappel, James. *Catholic Modern: The Challenge of Totalitarianism and the Remaking of the Church*. Cambridge: Harvard University Press, 2018.

Christiansen, Drew. "Pacem in Terris." In *Modern Catholic Social Teaching: Commentaries and Interpretations*, edited by Kenneth Himes et al., 217–43. Washington, DC: Georgetown University Press, 2005.

Constant, Benjamin. *Des Reactions Politiques*. Whitefish, MT: Kessinger, 2010.

Coppins, McKay. "The Man Who Broke Politics." *The Atlantic*, November 2018. https://www.theatlantic.com/magazine/archive/2018/11/newt-gingrich-says-youre-welcome/570832/.

———. *Romney: A Reckoning*. New York: Scribner, 2023.

Corn, David. "Donald Trump, Stochastic Terrorist: He Demonizes His Foes—and That Makes Them Possible Targets of Violence." *Mother Jones*, September 29, 2023. https://www.motherjones.com/politics/2023/09/donald-trump-stochastic-terrori-milley-violence-muskst/.

Courson, Paul. "Document: Nixon Campaign Strategists Considered Racial Strategy." *CNN*, January 11, 2010. https://www.cnn.com/2010/POLITICS/01/11/nixon.racial.strategy/index.html.

Crozier, Michael J., et al. *The Crisis of Democracy: Report on the Governability of Democracies to the Trilateral Commission*. New York: New York University

Press, 1975. https://ia800305.us.archive.org/29/items/TheCrisisOfDemocracy-TrilateralCommission-1975/crisis_of_democracy_text.pdf.

Fawcett, Edmund. *Conservatism: The Fight for a Tradition*. Princeton: Princeton University Press, 2020.

———. *Liberalism: The Life of an Idea*. 2nd ed. Princeton: Princeton University Press, 2018.

Francis. *Fratelli Tutti: On Fraternity and Social Friendship*. Vatican City: Libreria Editrice Vaticana, 2020. https://www.vatican.va/content/francesco/en/encyclicals/documents/papa-francesco_20201003_enciclica-fratelli-tutti.html.

———. *Laudate Deum: On the Climate Crisis*. Vatican City: Libreria Editrice Vaticana, 2023. https://www.vatican.va/content/francesco/en/apost_exhortations/documents/20231004-laudate-deum.html.

———. *Laudato Si': On Care for Our Common Home*. Vatican City: Libreria Editrice Vaticana, 2015. https://www.vatican.va/content/francesco/en/encyclicals/documents/papa-francesco_20150524_enciclica-laudato-si.html.

Fukuyama, Francis. *The End of History and the Last Man*. New York: Free, 1992.

———. *Liberalism and Its Discontents*. New York: Farrar, Strauss, and Giroux, 2022.

Glendon, Mary Ann. *A World Made New: Eleanor Roosevelt and the Universal Declaration of Human Rights*. New York: Random House, 2001.

Hamilton, Alexander. "Federalist no. 1: General Introduction." In *The Federalist Papers*, edited by Bob Blaisdell, 1–4. Mineola, NY: Dover, 2016.

Hayek, Friedrich A. *The Road to Serfdom*. Chicago: University of Chicago, 1944.

Hofstadter, Richard. *Social Darwinism in American Thought*. Reprint ed. Boston: Beacon, 1992.

Jefferson, Thomas, et al. "Declaration of Independence." https://www.archives.gov/founding-docs/declaration-transcript.

John XXIII. *Mater et Magistra: On Christianity and Social Progress*. Libreria Editrice Vaticana, 1961. https://www.vatican.va/content/john-xxiii/en/encyclicals/documents/hf_j-xxiii_enc_15051961_mater.html.

———. *Pacem in Terris: Peace on Earth*. Vatican City: Libreria Editrice Vaticana, 1963. https://www.vatican.va/content/john-xxiii/en/encyclicals/documents/hf_j-xxiii_enc_11041963_pacem.html.

John Paul II. *Centesimus Annus: On the Hundredth Anniversary of Rerum Novarum*. Vatican City: Libreria Editrice Vaticana, 1991. https://www.vatican.va/content/john-paul-ii/en/encyclicals/documents/hf_jp-ii_enc_01051991_centesimus-annus.html.

Keeley, Theresa. *Reagan's Gun-Toting Nuns: The Catholic Conflict over Cold War Human Rights Policy in Central America*. Ithaca, NY: Cornell University Press, 2020.

Kelly, Martin. "Top 10 New Deal Programs of the 1930s." *ThoughtCo*, April 7, 2020. https://www.thoughtco.com/top-new-deal-programs-104687.

Kirk, Russell. "Ten Conservative Principles." https://kirkcenter.org/conservatism/ten-conservative-principles/.

Leo XIII. *Rerum Novarum: On the Condition of Workers*. Vatican City: Libreria Editrice Vaticana, 1891. https://www.vatican.va/content/leo-xiii/en/encyclicals/documents/hf_l-xiii_enc_15051891_rerum-novarum.html.

Levin, Yuval. *The Great Debate: Edmund Burke, Thomas Paine, and the Birth of Right and Left*. New York: Basic, 2014.

———. *A Time to Build: From Family and Community to Congress and the Campus: How Recommitting to Our Institutions Can Revive the American Dream*. New York: Hachette, 2020.
Lilla, Mark. *The Once and Future Liberal: After Identity Politics*. New York: Harper, 2018.
Mayer, Jane. *Dark Money: The Hidden History of the Billionaires behind the Rise of the Radical Right*. New York: Doubleday, 2016.
MacLean, Nancy. *Democracy in Chains: The Deep History of the Radical Right's Stealth Plan for America*. New York: Penguin, 2018.
Massa, Mark. *Catholics and American Culture: Fulton Sheen, Dorothy Day, and the Notre Dame Football*. New York: Herder & Herder: 2001.
Moyn, Samuel. *Not Enough: Human Rights in an Unequal World*. Cambridge: Belknap, 2018.
Muller, Jerry Z. *Conservatism: An Anthology of Social and Political Thought from David Hume to the Present*. Princeton: Princeton University Press, 1997.
———. *The Mind and the Market: Capitalism in Western Thought*. New York: Anchor, 2002.
Murphy, William F. Jr. "Ethics of Life, Synodality, and Untying Knots in Moral Theology." *Where Peter Is*, September 26, 2022. https://wherepeteris.com/ethics-of-life-synodality-and-untying-knots-in-moral-theology/.
———. "Reflections on Fundamental Morality, Conscience, Norms, and Discernment (nos. 109–33)." In *Etica Teologica della Vita: Scrittura, tradizione, sfide pratiche: Atti Seminario Studio Promosso Dalla Pontificia Accademia Per La Vita*, edited by Vincenzo Paglia, 217–43. Vatican City: Libreria Editrice Vaticana, 2022.
Neuhaus, Richard John. *The Catholic Moment: The Paradox of the Church in the Postmodern World*. New York: HarperCollins, 1987.
Oreskes, Naomi, and Erik M. Conway. *The Big Myth: How Business Taught us to Loath Government and Love the Free Market*. New York: Bloomsbury, 2023.
Phillips, Kevin P. *The Emerging Republican Majority*. New Rochelle, NY: Arlington House, 1969.
Pius IX. *Syllabus of Errors*. https://www.papalencyclicals.net/pius09/p9syll.htm.
Pius XII. "Radio Message of His Holiness Pius XII to the People of the Entire World." Vatican City: Libreria Editrice Vaticana, 1944. https://www.vatican.va/content/pius-xii/en/speeches/1944/documents/hf_p-xii_spe_19441224_natale.html.
Podhorzer, Michael. "Hiding in Plain Sight: The Sources of MAGA Madness and Congressional Kakistocracy." *Weekend Reading*, October 29, 2023. https://www.weekendreading.net/p/hiding-in-plain-sight-the-sources.
Pontifical Council for Justice and Peace. *Compendium of the Social Doctrine of the Church*. Washington, DC: USCCB, 2005. https://www.vatican.va/roman_curia/pontifical_councils/justpeace/documents/rc_pc_justpeace_doc_20060526_compendio-dott-soc_en.html.
Richardson, Heather Cox. *How the South Won the Civil War: Oligarchy, Democracy, and the Continuing Fight for the Soul of America*. Oxford: Oxford University Press, 2020.
———. *To Make Men Free: A History of the Republican Party*. New York: Basic, 2014.
Ryan, John A. "A Program of Social Reform by Legislation." *Catholic World* 89 (1909) 433–44. https://cuomeka.wrlc.org/files/original/8accf1a4c93197b5be22da86e574b318.pdf.

———. *Social Doctrine in Action: A Personal History*. New York: Harper and Brothers, 1941.

Sachs, Jeffrey D. *To Move the World: JFK's Quest for Peace*. New York: Random House, 2013.

Simon, Yves. *La Grande Crise de la République Française*. Montreal: Editions de l'Arbre, 1941.

———. *The Road to Vichy: 1918–1938*. Translated by James Corbett and George J. McMorrow. New York: Sheed & Ward, 1942.

Stern, Alexander. "Centrist Illusions: How Not to Defend Liberalism." *Commonweal* 150 (2023) 36–41.

Stevens, Stuart. *The Conspiracy to End America: Five Ways My Old Party Is Driving Our Democracy to Autocracy*. New York: 12 Twelve, 2023.

———. *It Was All a Lie: How the Republican Party Became Donald Trump*. New York: Random House, 2020.

Stewart, Katherine. *The Power Worshippers: Inside the Dangerous Rise of Religious Nationalism*. New York: Bloomsbury, 2019.

Traub, James. *What Was Liberalism? The Past, Present, and Promise of a Noble Idea*. New York: Hachette, 2019.

United States Conference of Catholic Bishops. "The Challenge of Peace: God's Promise and Our Response." Washington, DC: USCCB, 1983. https://www.usccb.org/upload/challenge-peace-gods-promise-our-response-1983.pdf.

Waal, Frans de. *Chimpanzee Politics: Power and Sex among Apes*. New York: Harper & Row, 1982.

Weigel, George. "Moral Clarity in a Time of War." *First Things*, January 2003. https://www.firstthings.com/article/2003/01/001-moral-clarity-in-a-time-of-war.

———. *Tranquillitas Ordinis: The Present Failure and Future Promise of American Catholic Thought on War and Peace*. New York: Oxford University Press, 1987.

———. *Witness to Hope: The Biography of Pope John Paul II*. New York: Cliff Street, 1999.

Wood, John Carter. "When Personalism Met Planning: Jacques Maritain and a British Christian Intellectual Circle, 1937–49." In *How Neo-Thomism Helped Shape the Twentieth Century*, edited by Rajesh Heynickx and Stéphane Symons, 77–108. Berlin: de Gruyter, 2017.

Viguerie, Richard, and Jenny Beth Martin. *Takeover: The 100-Year War for the Soul of the GOP and How Conservatives Can Finally Win It*. Washington, DC: WND, 2014.

9

Metaphysics, Ethics, Politics, and Theology
Can Natural Lawyers Embrace Liberalism?

Thomas Howes, Princeton University

Abstract: Often the disagreements among natural law theorists about politics are not a result of disagreements about moral principles, but because of differences in how they understand the relationship between ethics and politics. For some, differences in outlook even come down to how they understand the relationship between metaphysics and ethics or politics. In this article, I present what I see as a sound way of thinking about the relationships among these domains, especially with reference to the work of Martin Rhonheimer. Finally, I close with a few thoughts about how to understand the relationship between politics and theology (with reference to Joseph Ratzinger), which allow us to make sense of, and embrace the novelties in political theology of the Second Vatican Council and postconciliar documents.

Natural law theory can be divided into two main types. One is a neo-scholastic variety that is more inclined to downplay the distinction between speculative and practical reason.[1] Advocates of this variety also tend to emphasize a primacy of metaphysics in relation to ethics. The other kind—what I call neoclassical natural law theories, an umbrella term that covers New Natural Law theory, the rational virtue ethics of Martin Rhonheimer, and adjacent accounts—focuses more on philosophical reflection that is grounded in the first-personal perspective of practical reason. This is the perspective of the deliberating person who is moved by practical inclinations and by the rational goods grasped in those same inclinations.[2]

Although in practice, advocates of both neo-scholastic and neoclassical natural law theories tend to reach similar conclusions about personal morality, the political viewpoints associated with each appear to have become more divergent in recent years.[3] With the rise of postliberalism and integralism among Catholic scholars, it is perhaps easy to associate natural law theory with these political philosophies. But most authors working from one of the neoclassical natural law theories, and even some proponents of neo-scholastic theories,[4] still defend the basic political culture behind modern constitutional democracies. Although some of the variance in tendencies between the two perspectives is cultural, much of it can be understood in terms of the different ways advocates of these two kinds of natural law theory view the relationship between metaphysics, ethics, and politics.

---

1. See, for instance, Rommen, *Natural Law*; McInerny, *Ethica Thomistica*; Hittinger, *Critique of the New Natural Law Theory*; see also Feser, "Role of Nature in Sexual Ethics."

2. What I call neoclassical natural law theories can be defined as natural law perspectives that are first personal and practical and are in closer continuity with classical ethics, especially the Aristotelean variety. I would include among neoclassical natural law theories: (1) the New Natural Law perspective (Grisez, Finnis, and their collaborator, Joseph Boyle); as well as the rational virtue ethics of the Swiss philosopher and theologian Martin Rhonheimer, and those who embrace it such as Angel Rodríguez-Luño and the late Italian ethicist Giuseppe Abbà; (2) those working with a "Basic Goods" models, such as David S. Oderberg and Alfonso Gómez-Lobo; (3) along with some natural lawyers whose positions are more independent, such as R. J. Snell, Mark C. Murphy, V. Bradley Lewis, and Christopher Kaczor. For some of the important similarities and differences between New Natural Law and rational virtue ethics, see Rhonheimer, "Practical Reason, Human Nature, and the Epistemology of Ethics."

3. It is worth noting that Heinrich Rommen and Russell Hittinger are both defenders of modern constitutional democracy. On the other hand, Giuseppe Abbà, whom I included among contemporary natural law theorists, had political views more in line with the postliberals; see Abbà, *Le virtù per la felicità*, ch. 1.

4. See, for instance, Rooney, "Illiberalism Will Not Secure the Common Good."

Metaphysics, Ethics, and Politics

A common misunderstanding about neoclassical natural law perspectives is that they try to do away with metaphysical considerations. In truth, neoclassical natural lawyers believe that they are using better methods for arriving at and explaining ethical claims that appeal to metaphysics and philosophical anthropology. They believe that our understanding of the latter depends on practical experience, practical insight, and practical reasoning. Therefore, they reverse the methodological order favored by neo-scholastic natural lawyers, without denying the ethical relevance of either metaphysics or philosophical anthropology. Even when appealing to metaphysical or anthropological facts, ethical claims must also feature at least some reference to practical principles.

Neo-scholastic and neoclassical natural lawyers agree that there are moral facts (murder is wrong, friendship is good, etc.) and that there are also moral truths that go beyond common knowledge, and which can be grasped by wise people and defended philosophically.[5] They sometimes differ in how they explain these truths. An example of a more neo-scholastic natural law mentality is that of Heinrich A. Rommen, who starts from a metaphysics that holds that the "essential being" (*esse essentiae*) of the human being is the norm of morality.[6] Martin Rhonheimer, for one example, does not think that this way of speaking is particularly helpful.[7] When metaphysicians like Aristotle or Thomas Aquinas speak of the essence or form of a living thing as its end or telos, this concerns its development as an organism from the womb to adulthood. Moreover, for Aristotle, and for Thomas, virtue does not follow spontaneously from nature, but is a sort of second nature: "Neither by nature, then, nor contrary to nature do the virtues arise in us; rather we are adapted by nature to receive them, and are made perfect by habit."[8]

For both Aquinas and Aristotle, it is instead *reason* that is the proximate norm of morality.[9] Yet reason is natural to the human being, and therefore, in that sense to act according to reason is natural. But to recognize reason as the dominant faculty of the human person, and to

---

5. See Aquinas, *ST* I–II, q. 100, a. 1.
6. See Rommen, *Natural Law*, 141.
7. Rhonheimer, *Natural Law and Practical Reason*, 18.
8. Aristotle, *Nicomachean Ethics*, bk. II, ch. 1, 1103a, pp. 24–26. See Aquinas, *In II Ethic*, lect. 1, nos. 248–50.
9. See the classic of Lehu, *Raison règle*.

recognize what is reasonable, and therefore most natural to the person, cannot be gleaned completely from the outside. To know what is reasonable, to know what constitutes virtuous behavior, requires instead taking the "perspective of the acting person."[10] It is thus from the standpoint of first-personal practical experience that we gain necessary material for any metaphysical or philosophical-anthropological knowledge that is ethically relevant. We can then refer to that metaphysical and anthropological knowledge in ethical reflection. The relationship is therefore reciprocal, with the first-personal perspective of practical reason being primary. We would not know friendship or knowledge as genuine human goods, and thus as perfective of our nature, if not for our practical experience of these goods. But it is also legitimate to say that human beings by nature require friendship and knowledge for their fulfillment. Similarly, through reflection we can come to insights about the relationship between morality and more anthropological and even metaphysical concepts like intentionality, freedom, personhood, etc. But again our understanding of these things has already been informed by our practical experience.

What about the relationship between metaphysics and politics? It turns out that how we understand this relationship will also affect how we think about politics. D. C. Schindler, for instance, a metaphysician who adopts something that at least resembles a neo-scholastic natural law perspective, creatively attempts to draw political conclusions directly from metaphysics.[11] Although it is sensible to posit that one's metaphysical understanding of things will influence one's ethics and one's politics, Schindler is unique in that he bases his critique of modern liberalism explicitly and predominantly on metaphysical considerations. In fact, his central argument is that modern liberal regimes like that of the United States reflect a faulty metaphysics because they implicitly deny the "primacy of actuality" over potency,[12] which in Thomas Aquinas's metaphysics can mean several things. It may refer to the fact that prior to all potencies or capacities in nature, there must be some actuality that serves as a fundamental explanation for how anything is actual at all, that is, there must be a pure Act, namely, God, upon which all things that exist rely for their existence; this is based on the principle that "nothing can be reduced from potentiality to actuality, except by something in a

10. John Paul II, *Veritatis Splendor*, no. 78. See Rhonheimer, *Natural Law and Practical Reason*, 425–37.

11. See Schindler, *Politics of the Real*.

12. Schindler, *Politics of the Real*, ch. 2.

state of actuality."[13] Or it might refer to Aristotle's observations that the perfection of anything resides in its act,[14] or in Thomas's claim that "act is always more perfect than potency."[15] For example, to act virtuously is more perfect than to be virtuous yet inactive. In fact, Thomas equates *act* with perfection, especially the "act of all acts," the act of existence (*actus essendi* or simply *esse*).[16]

Schindler uses the metaphysical principle of the primacy of actuality to make various, not always closely related, arguments. One of these arguments is that modern liberal regimes like the United States, which are limited to framework conditions that secure liberty, justice, peace, and other *political* ethical values—and which are supposed to be neutral about *non-political* substantive matters of personal morality and religion—form an artificial mechanism that divorces the polity from the fecundity of a natural reality.[17] As Aristotle says in his *Politics*,

> Therefore, if the earlier forms of society are natural, so is the state, for it is the end of them, and the nature of a thing is its end. For what each thing is when fully developed, we call its nature, whether we are speaking of a man, a horse, or a family.[18]

There is thus an artificial limitation, Schindler thinks, that prevents these regimes from achieving their natural end or telos.

In other places, Schindler discusses the problem in terms of wholes and parts. Natural lawyers more friendly with modern constitutional democracies tend to make a distinction between what they call the "political common good"—which constitutes the common good insofar as it is the legitimate object of political activity—and the "integral common good" (the more complete fulfillment of the community and

---

13. Aquinas, *ST* I, q. 2, a. 3, corp., "Prima autem et manifestior via" (The First Way).
14. See Aristotle, *Nicomachean Ethics*, bk. 1, chs. 5 and 7.
15. Aquinas, *De Potentia*, q. 7, a. 2, ad 9: "actus est semper perfectior potentia."
16. Aquinas, *De Potentia*, q. 7, a. 2, ad 9: "esse est actualitas omnium actuum." In this regard, at least, Schindler evades the essentialism of Rommen, who thought, following a certain trend in scholastic Thomism, that the fundamental metaphysical distinction for Thomas Aquinas was between the mere fact of existence and the essence or essential being (*esse essentiae*), and not that between the *act* of existence and essence. See Rommen, *Natural Law*, 142. See by contrast, Wippel, *Metaphysical Thought of Thomas Aquinas*; Clarke, *One and the Many*; and for older, but still very relevant, accounts of Thomas Aquinas's metaphysics according to this interpretation, see Fabro, *Nozione metaphysica*; Fabro, *Partecipazione e causalità*; Gilson, *Being and Some Philosophers*.
17. Schindler, *Politics of the Real*, ch. 2.
18. Aristotle, *Politics*, bk. I, ch. 2, 1252b, 30–34, p. 1129.

its members).[19] As Schindler sees it, with this more liberal conception, the "political common good" relates to the "integral common good" as a part to a whole. But the liberal order, the object of the political common good—he argues—explicitly avoids any specific reference to the integral common good, and therefore as a part it cannot be integrated into the whole.[20] It is thus purportedly divorced from the actuality of the whole as a disparate part—and perhaps this would be like an organ separated from the organism that gives it life. Even if we consider this according to the analogy of an organism, which seems a natural interpretation, we might say that laws and political authority are like one organ, say the lungs, that serves the body in a specific way, whereas individuals, families, Churches, etc., are like the other organs that depend on the function of the lungs, but also serve the body in ways that lungs do not. The deeper issue, however, is taking such analogies too far. Political regimes are social realities to which the metaphysical analysis of natural realities only has limited relevance.

Deceptive Analogies

There are thus certain disputable metaphysical assumptions in these types of arguments. Sometimes modern politics is treated as a top-down construction, as inorganic and mechanical, and a more organic model of politics is favored. And there is some value to this analogy. Indeed, left to their own devices, people tend to form political regimes almost spontaneously, based on strong human need for an authority to establish, adjudicate, and enforce rules necessary for human coexistence.[21] But the "organic" analogy can blind us to the fact this emergence involves the free interactions of individuals acting on *reasons*—or often, less pleasantly, it involves a violent struggle, the dominance of one group, or a negotiation between different groups at the expense of the rest.[22]

19. I prefer to distinguish between the social common good, the political common good, and the integral common good, with the first two representing common practical goods and the third constituting more a regulative ideal than a practical good.

20. Schindler, *Politics of the Real*, ch. 3.

21. See Finnis, *Natural Law and Natural Rights*, ch. IX.

22. Following research from Harvard polymath Joseph Henrich (see *The WEIRDest People in the World*), economist Jonathan F. Schulz has argued, with empirical support, that the Catholic Church's reforms of marriage law, preventing the marriage of cousins, reducing kinship bonds in the Middle Ages, had the effect of leading to more self-government and participatory institutions in western Europe, as opposed to excessive

When it comes to matters of conflict within social arrangements, there is often deliberation (if violence is to be avoided) that more explicitly concerns the social arrangement itself, such as deliberations about changes in the law, or changes in regime. If we are going to use the term "organic" analogously here, then the persistence of such explicit reasoning about the regime and its laws should also be seen as "natural" to human societies. And to evaluate any regime that emerges from this process involves us already in ethical considerations. In the case of a political regime with its coercive laws, we would have to evaluate these laws based on their fairness to individuals and their common benefit to those communities—or other communities and individuals affected by them.

Furthermore, there are other important disanalogies between human communities and other organic realities. As James V. Schall points out, a political regime is not a substance with its own substantial unity—e.g., it is not a human being, a cat, a tree, or a carbon atom.[23] It is not therefore a substantial unity but only a unity of order, dependent upon the way in which people relate to one another and to the natural world. To speak then of the good of the whole community cannot be separated from consideration of the benefit of the parts, that is, persons and their relations.[24] To speak otherwise, we would run the risk of collectivism, which, in practice, always masks benefits to those in power at the expense of everyone else, as is evident in socialist and fascist countries. There is indeed no human community independent of persons and their relations. And this is the motivation for a more limited political common good, because too aggressive state interference in people's lives does more harm than good to persons in the community. It interferes with important aspects of human fulfilment, such as personal responsibility and authenticity, and is thus opposed to the principle of subsidiarity.

An ontology of properly human realities would be helpful here.[25] Many human realities, such as money or tools, are defined in terms of

---

control by a ruling elite. See Schulz, "Kin Networks and Institutional Development," 2578–613.

23. Schall, *Politics of Heaven and Hell*, 237.

24. Heinrich Rommen is very clear about this; see *The State in Catholic Thought*, 44, 138–39.

25. What I call human realities, Francisco Suárez calls moral entities; see his *De bonitate et militia humanorum actuum*, d. 1.3. See Schwartz, "Francisco Suárez on Consent and Political Obligation," 66–67. This also relates to the four orders Aquinas discusses towards the beginning of his commentary on Aristotle's *Nicomachean Ethics*, particularly the second, third, and fourth orders; see *In Eth*. I, 1, 14–24, "Ordo autem

how people relate to natural objects or to one another. The scholastics had a term, *esse obiectivum*, sometimes translated as "objective being," which only "is" insofar as it is an object of the mind (e.g., the number four).[26] Such realities are not even real relations but pure *relata*. They occupy a realm of mere formal and final causality, without their own material causality and without any capacity for efficient causality. Some call such intellectual relata, mental beings.[27] Relatedly, there is what might be called "social" being, following Heinrich Rommen's terminology, such as money or contracts.[28] Indeed, gold and paper are *real*, but insofar as they are *money*, they are only so because of how people relate to them and to one another. That is, *as money*, they lack any proper act of existence, even the existence of a real "accident" (e.g., a feature such as a dog's weight, or my relation to my friend).

Most of what we discuss in political philosophy concerns either persons, their relations, or these social phenomena that emerge from the relations that persons have to one another and to the natural world. It is thus helpful to recognize that we are discussing phenomena occurring within what some phenomenologists have called the "life world,"

---

quadrupliciter..." (Leon. 47.1.4), as well as the commentary that follows which qualifies the part-whole relationship between citizens and society.

26. See Minerd, "Beyond Non-Being," 353–79; Minerd, "Thomism and the Formal Object of Logic," 411–44. Technically all things that exist substantially have *esse obiectivum* (along with their *esse subiectivum*), because they can also be objects of thought, will, sense, imagination, etc., but I am discussing here what has only *esse obiectivum*, the being of which is merely to be an object of all those forms of intentionality.

27. See Clarke, *One and the Many*, 29. Thomas Aquinas understood that *entia rationis* were distinct from Aristotle's ten categories of real being, because he distinguished them from both substances and accidents: "In the fourth grade of beings are the nine kinds of accidents. The fifth grade is those which are not in the nature of things, *but only in cognition*, which are called *beings of reason*, such as genus, species, opinion and so forth" ("In quarto gradu entium, sunt accidentia quae sunt in novem generibus. Quintus gradus est eorum quae non sunt in rerum natura, *sed in sola cogitatione*, quae dicuntur *entia rationis*, ut genus, species, opinio et huiusmodi"); Aquinas, *In De divinis nominibus*, ch. 5, l. 2 (Marietti, 1950, p. 246, my translation); see also: "And a being in an unqualified sense is a substance, whereas a being in a certain respect is an accident, *or even a being of reason*" ("Ens autem simpliciter est substantia, sed ens secundum quid est accidens, *vel etiam ens rationis*"), ST I-II, q. 17, a. 4, corp., in Aquinas, *Treatise on Happiness*, 150.

28. See Rommen, "Social Being," in *The State in Catholic Thought*, 33–56. From the standpoint of neoclassical natural law, Rommen represents a more naturalistic school of natural law. Yet he has a sophisticated understanding of social ontology, and this serves as a good foundation for his political thought.

the world of human realities.[29] One needs to be careful in applying the metaphysical analysis of substances to the life world, because morally relevant differences of human behavior are inexplicable when we apply that lens alone. For example, someone who has never seen or heard of a surgical operation could walk into a room in which a surgery is taking place and have no idea that the surgeons there were carrying out a morally licit surgery and not a morally abhorrent mutilation. The physical behavior would be the same. The moral relations among the persons would differ, but we only know this by reference to the object of their intentional choice. Similarly, from the standpoint of the order of nature (*genus naturae*) Nazi Germany had as much *actuality* (or *esse*) as other perfectly livable and decent countries; whereas from the standpoint of the order of morality (*genus moris*), it was a hellscape.[30]

Therefore, it is inappropriate to rely solely on a metaphysical analysis of natural realities for evaluating political arrangements. Political regimes and political communities are not substances. The relations that form political communities are real, as are the relating persons, but in referring to the political common good, we are dealing, first, with a state of affairs within the life world, a world characterized by persons and their relations to one another and to the natural world; and, secondly, we are concerned with that human state of affairs insofar as it is a good or end shared by the community and binding on its members.

Focusing specifically on the common good as a goal, one can abstract the element that concerns the aim of the political community insofar as it applies the coercive arm of the state to promote the common good. That practical end need not be incorporated into anything, it just must imply a sound assessment of what the appropriate use of state power is for serving the common good. There are plenty of other self-directing persons in the community who can serve the common good in other ways, such as through charity or hard work.

Other More Promising Connections between Metaphysics and Politics

In addition to articulating a sound ontology of human realities, there are other ways that metaphysics can be relevant to politics. For instance, if

---

29. See Sokolowski, *Introduction to Phenomenology*, 146.
30. See Aquinas, *ST* I-II, q. 20, a. 6, corp.

it is the case that people developed a more capricious understanding of God in the late Middle Ages, as some postliberals like Schindler argue, then it would be more intuitive to connect this idea to absolutist, theocratic states rather than modern liberalism.[31] After all, the idea of divinity as capricious was not a medieval invention; it has been present in many times and places, and it is usually associated with fundamentalist regimes that impose beliefs on everyone without arguing the reasonability of those beliefs. When people think God is eminently reasonable, reason itself becomes a norm accessible to all, and it is recognized as having divine authority. Robert Reilly, in fact, argues that the Anglo-American response to modern absolutism was a return to a primacy of reason over caprice, and was thus a return to the best in medieval politics against the abuses of the Early Modern Period.[32] Whether this narrative of a voluntaristic zeitgeist is historically accurate, I am unsure, this indirect association between voluntarism and political absolutism is at least *prima facie* plausible.[33]

A similarly plausible application of metaphysical considerations to politics would be the point made by Joseph Ratzinger, influenced by Augustine's *City of God*, that belief in transcendence lends itself to a healthy recognition of the limits of politics. As Joseph Ratzinger says,

> Marx taught us that we must depart from transcendence so that mankind, saved from false consolations, may at last build the perfect world. Today we know that man needs transcendence so that he may shape his world that will always be imperfect in such a way that people can live in it in a manner keeping with human dignity.[34]

But note that this example and that which preceded it are more about how metaphysical ideas can indirectly influence our political thinking, and not cases of drawing political conclusions directly from metaphysical principles. For Ratzinger, the latter was the mistake of Eusebius of Caesarea (for example), and it ultimately leads, he thinks, to the loss of freedom. Ratzinger thinks it is more fruitful to follow Aristotle and Aquinas, who instead make arguments about politics based on ethical

31. See Schindler, *Politics of the Real*, ch. 1.

32. Reilly, *America on Trial*, chs. 5–9.

33. James Wilson, the Founding Father, connected voluntarism with the theory of the divine right of kings, rejecting both; see Hall and Hall, *Collected Works of James Wilson*, 494. For discussion on this, see Rosenthal, *Crown under Law*, 259–63.

34. Ratzinger, "Christian Orientation in a Pluralist Democracy?" in *Church, Ecumenism, and Politics*, 211. See also Schall, *Politics of Heaven and Hell*, esp. ch. 3.

considerations.³⁵ Along with a proper social ontology to inform our political and ethical analysis, there are thus ways that other metaphysical considerations might indirectly affect how we think about politics, but they cannot determine it precisely.

Natural Law and Political Ethics

Leaving aside the relationship between metaphysics and politics, we can now consider more closely the proper relationship between ethics and politics, which is also a source of contention among natural lawyers. For those who support a limited political common good, this cannot mean a mere reduction of politics to personal ethics, even if it involves a certain kind of application of ethical principles to the political realm. Ángel Rodríguez Luño clarifies the relationship, arguing that while "personal ethics regulates the use of freedom, political ethics regulates the use of coercion."³⁶ From this perspective, political philosophy is nothing else but "fundamental political ethics,"³⁷ as Martin Rhonheimer calls it, without being a mere codification of personal ethics.

Thomistic natural law theory includes what are called first and common principles of natural law, along with additional secondary principles and norms which, in light of further experience (often the moral experience of good faith efforts at improvement, and thus involving inchoate prudence, are recognized as following from those first and more common principles of natural law). Some of these norms and principles are obvious (e.g., prohibitions against murder and assault), while others are recognized only by the wise and taught to the community (e.g., the norm

---

35. Ratzinger, *Politik und Erlösung*, 20.

36. Rodríguez Luño, *Introducción a la Ética Política*, 15. See also the comments of Murray, *We Hold These Truths*, 61–62, in which he clarifies Pope Pius XII's point about how the repression of error is often not obligatory if it is for the sake of a greater good: "The Pope makes a clear distinction between the abstract order of ethics or theology, where it is a question of qualifying doctrines or practices as true or false, right or wrong, and the concrete order of jurisprudence, where it is a question of using or not using the coercive instrument of law in favor of the true and good, against the false and wrong. In this latter order the highest and most general norm is the public peace, the common good in its various aspects. This is altogether a moral norm."

37. Rhonheimer, "Why Is Political Philosophy Necessary?," in *The Common Good of Constitutional Democracy*, 2. The articles in this volume are collections of original articles written in German, Italian, and English. See William F. Murphy Jr., "Introduction," in Rhonheimer, *Common Good of Constitutional Democracy*, xxiii–xxxvii, for the original publication information.

of monogamy in marriage). Nonetheless, these natural law principles and norms are not specialized knowledge per se, they are discoverable by all healthy persons with the moral experience that comes from good-faith efforts at the moral improvement that is everyone's concern. That is, they do not depend on specialized knowledge like that of a surgeon, astronaut, physicist, or economist. When it comes to general ethical principles, much of sound politics involves applying those principles through political prudence. Nonetheless, political prudence itself can still make use of general principles from other areas of knowledge, such as political theory, economics, or other forms of institutional analysis. For example, political philosophers like Aristotle, Montesquieu, and James Madison looked to historical constitutions to find realistic principles of politics. Although all three favored natural law either explicitly or implicitly (Aristotle did not use the term but affirmed natural justice and the natural knowledge of human ends), they all looked for principles outside ethics to apply to politics.

In sum, the application of ethical principles to politics inevitably means applying ethical principles to contingent contexts, and this entails coming to political-ethical judgments that are often mediated by empirical knowledge, both specialized knowledge (whether it be political, historical, sociological, or economic) and general knowledge, with such general knowledge sometimes an achievement of historical experience. This mediation in our political-ethical judgments of politically relevant empirical knowledge, acquired historically or by specialization, explains a good deal of the disagreement among people on matters of politics even when they substantially agree about personal morality. For example, one's thoughts on the economic effects of certain policies (e.g., price controls) will affect whether one considers them justified or not. And one's understanding of the nature of wealth and how it comes about will mediate one's judgment about its just distribution. Furthermore, certain events of the past centuries have led to a general sociological and political awareness that has influenced our ethical evaluation of the use of coercion in religious matters, without any radical change in ethical principles.

Martin Rhonheimer defends on historical grounds the modern political ethos of secular constitutional democracy as an arrangement that better achieves ethical values like peaceful coexistence and justice.[38] Thus,

---

38. Rhonheimer, "The Political Ethos of Constitutional Democracy and the Place of Natural Law in Public Reason: Rawls's 'Political Liberalism' Revisited," in *The Common Good of Constitutional Democracy*, 191–264, esp., 248–64. For John Rawls's later

like many other contemporary natural lawyers, he proposes a political ethics that is more limited in scope than personal ethics. His account is noteworthy because of his rejection of what he sees as a false understanding of neutrality in some forms of liberal theory.[39] For Rhonheimer, in fact, absolute neutrality is impossible.[40] We cannot set aside our "comprehensive vision" (Rawls's term), or our views about morality, when making political determinations, even if we accept an obligation to argue the public and politically relevant quality of any legislation we promote.

Nonetheless, there are good kinds of neutrality that Rhonheimer recognizes as part of the political culture of modern constitutionalism, such as the neutrality of impartial democratic procedures.[41] We could also include as a good kind of neutrality the substantive and juridical disestablishment of religion in modern constitutional democracies—compatible with toothless establishments like the United Kingdom—as well as neutrality regarding other matters beyond the government's competence and legitimacy. Joseph Ratzinger implicitly affirms such "good" neutrality in his criticism of the "bad" form of secularity, secularism, which he says "no longer has that element of *neutrality*, which opens space for the liberty of all. It begins to be transformed into an ideology . . . which presents itself as if it were the only voice of rationality."[42] If one wants to argue against the ethos of modern secular constitutional democracies, it is not enough to deny, as postliberals and integralists do, the plausibility or feasibility of perfect neutrality in a state. One must argue against the partial and functional neutrality that has traditionally been the aim of these political cultures, even if it has always been imperfectly realized.[43]

---

position on these matters, see Rawls, *Political Liberalism*; Rawls, "The Idea of Public Reason Revisited," in *The Law of Peoples*.

39. See Rhonheimer, "Political Ethos of Constitutional Democracy," 260–64; see also Rhonheimer, "Democratic Constitutional State and the Common Good," in *The Common Good of Constitutional Democracy*, 72–141, at 118–20, along with another article from that volume: "The Liberal Image of Man and the Concept of Autonomy: Beyond the Debate between Liberals and Communitarians," 36–71.

40. Rhonheimer, "Liberal Image of Man," 61.

41. Rhonheimer "Democratic Constitutional State and the Common Good," 119.

42. Ratzinger, "Il laicismo nuova ideologia, l'Europa non emargini Dio" (my translation).

43. For the argument, partly implied, that liberal regimes cannot be perfectly neutral, and thus we should abandon the ideal, see Deneen, *Why Liberalism Failed*, 34. Although he does not spend much time on the theme, it seems Deneen shares Rhonheimer's criticism of bad notions of neutrality without affirming the positive sort that is also affirmed by both Rhonheimer and Ratzinger.

Furthermore, Rhonheimer sees the limited political common good as embodying certain political but nevertheless substantive values,[44] along with framework conditions for the pursuit of other substantive goods. He shares Rawls's concern for treating our fellow citizens fairly in our use of coercive law the need to account for disagreement, and he affirms that part of our inherited ethos is an obligation to justify our use of coercive law with arguments that it is being used for a public, politically relevant, and non-sectarian purpose, while respecting impartial democratic procedure. It is, nonetheless, politically legitimate to make natural law arguments, or moral arguments in general, when we are promoting political reform, so long as we also argue that our moral arguments have political relevance, such as when we defend the juridical protection of marriage.[45] Against Rawls specifically, he argues that such moral facts as those concerning marriage and family qualify as objects of a wide consensus just as well as anything Rawls would consider part of an overlapping consensus. And for more controversial matters, if they are politically relevant, we must convince our fellow citizens, remaining faithful to democratic processes.[46]

Nevertheless, postliberals are unlikely to be convinced by any of this without a proper response to the practical reservations they have about modern secular regimes. Some of the difficulty stems from the tendency of such thinkers to have unrealistic expectations because they are prone to compare current political realities to the ideals of classical thinkers

---

44. Responding to Alasdair MacIntyre's claim that "modern politics is civil war carried on by other means" (*After Virtue*, 253), Rhonheimer states the following: "Modern politics in constitutional democracies is not civil war at all, but a means of overcoming and preventing civil war by political culture, a conflictive political culture, of course, but a culture that precisely endures such conflict by avoiding the *summum malum* that is civil war, and maintain peaceful coexistence and mutually advantageous cooperation of citizens over time. This is the basis of a culture of liberty and personal freedom. Political conflict in constitutional democracy is part of a highly differentiated political ethos that does not simply appeal to the virtues of citizens . . . but first of all is an institutional ethos, which is not only procedural but also includes *substantive*, although political, *values*. As a set, these values—peaceful coexistence, individual liberty, justice as equality of liberty—formulate a common good and work as a shared moral principle of politics and public reason" (Rhonheimer, "Political Ethos of Constitutional Democracy," 257; emphasis mine).

45. Rhonheimer, "Political Ethos of Constitutional Democracy," 239.

46. Rhonheimer, "Political Ethos of Constitutional Democracy," 247. I would include with democratic processes, not just majoritarian and super-majoritarian principles which might better correspond to prudence handling such matters, but principles of federalism and the use of freedom of exit at more local levels as a principle of showing more respect to political minorities in our use of coercive law and to mitigate conflict.

instead of comparing the ideals of today's thinkers to classical thinkers, or current political realities to ancient ones.[47] Because of this, they tend to greatly overrate past conditions, as if ancient Greece was a better place to live than today's United States. Still, there are really issues today, many of which are unique to our own time, and it is important to address them.

Catholic integralists, moreover, will claim that we erred by thinking the Church could carry on its mission just fine in a modern liberal regime. They tend to believe that modern politics inevitably leads to atheism and moral relativism. Therefore, to convince them that the Church does not need such political support, I would like to draw attention to the Catholic Church in the nineteenth-century United States to show that many of the problems they see are mostly recent problems and are not to be blamed on the essential elements of modern political culture.

It has long been recognized that the experience of Catholics in the United States changed the way the Church viewed the relationship between Church and State. Nineteenth-century popes, caught up in battles with the *laïcité* or *laicismo* movements in France and Italy were for decades unaware of the full significance of what was going on in the U.S., but gradually, as Pope Benedict XVI points out:

> People came to realize that the American Revolution was offering a model of a modern State that differed from the theoretical model with radical tendencies that had emerged during the second phase of the French Revolution.[48]

Pope Benedict XVI sees this as a step leading to the Second Vatican Council's declaration on religious liberty, *Dignitatis Humanae*, which, he says, recovered "the deepest patrimony of the Church."[49] It is remarkable, in fact, how the Church thrived and grew in a mostly Protestant nation under secular governance. This was not lost on many Catholics at the time. Cardinal James Gibbons of Baltimore even went so far as to attribute the American founding to divine providence: "We consider the establishment of our country's independence, the shaping of its liberties

---

47. Robert A. Dahl points out this tendency in the writing of Alasdair MacIntyre (*Democracy and Its Critics*, 200–300). Rhonheimer recognizes the same tendency in Patrick Deneen's *Why Liberalism Failed*; see Rhonheimer, "Has Liberalism Failed?," 5.

48. Benedict XVI, "Address to the Roman Curia Offering Christmas Greetings."

49. Benedict XVI, "Address to the Roman Curia Offering Christmas Greetings."

and laws, as a work of special Providence, its framers 'building wiser than they knew,' the Almighty's hand guiding them."[50]

Later, respected European Catholic intellectuals like G. K. Chesterton[51] and Jacques Maritain[52] would also express their fondness for America upon visiting it. For the first 185 years of U.S. history, in fact, it would have been difficult for American Catholics to have viewed its secular character, or its robust religious liberty, as anything but a blessing.

The Rise of American Catholicism

It is well-known that the latter half of the nineteenth century featured an influx of Catholic immigrants, changing the religious demography of the country. This growth is recorded, along with the growth of the Methodist and Baptist churches, in *The Churching of America: 1776–2005* by Roger Finke and Rodney Starke.[53] These authors argue, however, that the rise of the Catholic Church in the United States cannot be explained solely in terms of immigration, even if that played a necessary role. Any explanation of its growth must also account for the Church's fruitful and energetic mission relative to the missions in European countries, with the Church in America building a vast network of Catholic schools and effective parish missions. Very often, these authors argue, the immigrants from Catholic countries were in serious need of catechesis or even evangelization:

> In his insightful history of American Jesuits in middle America, Garraghan noted "a curious feature of these early parish missions was the large number of adults who made their first holy communion on such occasions. This delay in receiving the sacrament was due in most cases to neglect on the part of the parents." And we have ample testimony that this neglect was the common "Catholic heritage" of the vast majority of immigrants as they came down the gangplanks.[54]

Those who idealize a Catholic state officially endorsing and favoring Catholic culture should note these findings of Finke and Stark: "the

---

50. Gibbons, "Pastoral Letter of the Archbishops and Bishops of the United States Assembled in the Third Plenary Council of Baltimore," in *Memorial Volume*, 20. Note the odd pagination in the volume. This text is found near the end of the book.
51. Chesterton, *What I Saw in America*.
52. Maritain, *Reflections on America*.
53. Finke and Starke, *Churching of America*, 121.
54. Finke and Starke, *Churching of America*, 130.

great majority of people in 'Catholic' nations . . . seldom attend mass, rarely participate in the sacraments, and do not contribute money to the church."[55] That is, they lack the "vigorous participation we have come to associate with American Catholicism."[56] Nineteenth-century immigrants to the U.S. from Catholic countries often found in America a vital Church that went far beyond the cultural Catholicism they knew in their native countries. This fact is, at very least, in tension with the narrative pushed by postliberals who favor *state* support for "cultural Christianity."[57]

It is notable that even recently, a Pew Research survey on religiosity indicates that Americans have far greater religiosity than their European counterparts. The differences are rather shocking: in 2014, 68 percent of American Christians reported praying daily, in comparison to only 18 percent of Western European Christians. Seventy-six percent believed in God with absolute certainty, in comparison to only 23 percent of Western European Christians, and 68 percent of American Christians say religion is very important in their lives, in comparison to 14 percent of European Christians. Even the religiously unaffiliated Americans are much more religious than their European counterparts.[58]

In a mostly Protestant country, it is obvious that religious freedom made Catholicism's quick rise possible, and there seems to be something to the Tocquevillian idea that its independence from state authority strengthened its perceived legitimacy. Moreover, it made it easier for people to make the faith their own. As Tocqueville says,

> Religion sees in civil freedom a noble exercise of the faculties of man; in the political world, a field left by the Creator to the efforts of intelligence. Free and powerful in its sphere, satisfied with the place that is reserved for it, it knows that its empire is all the better established when it reigns by its own strength alone and dominates over hearts without support.[59]

---

55. Finke and Starke, *Churching of America*, 117.
56. Finke and Starke, *Churching of America*, 117.
57. See Ahmari et al., "In Defense of Cultural Christianity."
58. Evans, "U.S. Adults Are More Religious Than Western Europeans."
59. Tocqueville, *Democracy in America*, ch. 2.

Modern Secularization

Many think that modern secular governments are inherently secularizing. And if that were the case, an argument could be made they were promoting just another sect, no different than religious establishments. Yet for a long time this secularizing tendency was strong only in Europe. What explains this? Certainly, the longstanding religious conflicts did not help, nor did its brand of aggressive secularism. In addition, Peter Berger theorizes that this problem was made worse by Europe's centralized education systems, which crowded out parochial schools and allowed the secular elite to influence the masses.[60]

I would add that public administration of education in a secular nation, especially when it is centralized, has an inherent tendency to inculcate a relativization of any moral claims that go beyond the political-moral values of peace and justice (or related values like diversity, equality, and inclusion).[61] Truth claims about revealed religion are especially susceptible to such relativization. This happens almost naturally because of the felt need to not promote any claims that are seen as sectarian. An environment emerges in which such values proper to personal morality are seen as relative, or at least of lesser importance than the political-moral values legitimated and fully incorporated into the curriculum and classroom culture. Nothing, however, prevents such political-moral values from being absolutized in an intolerant and illiberal way. The U.S. escaped the worst effects of this secularizing and "liberalizing" effect of public education for a long time because administration of public schools was localized in small districts, where concern for pluralism could be handled prudentially.

Nevertheless, this tendency was there in some form from the beginning. As early as the nineteenth century, Archbishop John Hughes of New York called the compromised moral doctrine taught in public schools "nothingarianism," a popular term at the time.[62] In response, he pleaded unsuccessfully for public educational funds to be shared with religious schools. From then on, the nothingarian problem became only more significant as districts got larger, and then the states and eventually federal government came to exercise more influence and control. If Catholic postliberals want to know how the secular hegemony arose, I

---

60. Berger et al., *Religious America, Secular Europe?*, 19–20.
61. See Howes, "Public Education and Liberal Neutrality."
62. Patterson, "Catholic Republicanism in America," 2.

suggest they first look first at the education system, not the political arrangement that allowed the U.S. Catholic Church to grow and thrive in a mostly Protestant country.

Therefore, if something like a non-sectarian state can create a functionally level playing field for the various sects in society to compete for cultural influence, as seems to be case given American history, then it becomes less tenable to argue that we might as well embrace a religiously sectarian government because sectarianism is inevitable. What is needed is not absolute neutrality, but as I interpret Rhonheimer to argue, the functional neutrality of modern constitutional democracy, based in legitimate moral values such as justice and peace. Moreover, a pluralistic education system, rather than a falsely neutral one, would be more in keeping with this functional neutrality.

Politics and Theology: Responding to Catholic Postliberals and Integralists

Another thing that is surely on the minds of Catholic postliberals is how to make sense of the Catholic Church's rather late acceptance of modern religious liberty. I will close with a few thoughts, leaving it to the theologians to delve further. Catholics should be attentive to the fact that the Church's application of moral principles in political matters is always mediated by beliefs about the world that go beyond revealed doctrine. When applying perennial moral principles in politics, one cannot forgo relevant political, sociological, economic, and historical considerations, as if Revelation or natural law gave us ready-made answers to every political question. In the case of religious liberty, certain general beliefs about political possibilities have changed over the years, and that affects how we assess the necessity, and therefore the fairness, of applying state coercion in religious matters; that is, the basic principles do not change, but their application in the light of new information does.

As Pope Benedict XVI puts it, in the context of explaining how the Church's doctrine of religious liberty in *Dignitatis Humanae* relates to what came before it, "the Church's decisions on contingent matters . . . should necessarily be contingent themselves."[63] He further elabo-

---

63. Benedict XVI, "Address to the Roman Curia Offering Christmas Greetings." It is a strategy of some postliberals and integralists to minimize the doctrine of *Dignitatis Humanae* by appealing to the document's statement that it "leaves untouched traditional Catholic doctrine on the moral duty of men and societies toward the true religion and

rates on this theme in the first volume of his *Jesus of Nazareth*, speaking not as Pope but as theologian. There, in the context of discussing how the Law of Moses relates to the Law of Christ, and how the latter can be viewed as a fulfillment of the former, Benedict appeals to a distinction some biblical scholars have identified between two different types of law in the Torah, between the laws that are casuistic and those that are apodictic. Casuistic law, he says,

> stipulates legal arrangements for very specific juridical issues.... These juridical norms emerged from practice and they form a practically oriented legal corpus that serves to build up a realistic social order, *corresponding to the concrete possibilities of a society in a particular historical and cultural situation*. In this respect, the body of law in question is also historically conditioned and entirely open to criticism, often—at least from our ethical perspective—actually in need of it. . . .These casuistic provisions . . . are nonetheless not directly divine law, but are developed from the underlying deposit of divine law, and are therefore subject to further development and correction.[64]

Pope Benedict continues:

> And the fact of the matter is that social order has to be capable of development. It must address changing historical situations *within the limits of the possible*, but without ever losing sight of the ethical standard as such.[65]

He then notes how even in the Old Testament the prophets, and later Jesus, had to contradict these casuistic laws to preserve the more fundamental

---

toward the one Church of Christ" (Paul VI, *Dignitatis Humanae*, no. 1). However, one must read the whole sentence and the sentence that precedes it: "Religious freedom, in turn, which men demand as necessary to fulfill their duty to worship God, has to do with immunity from coercion in civil society. *Therefore* it leaves untouched traditional Catholic doctrine on the moral duty of men and societies toward the true religion and toward the one Church of Christ" (emphasis mine). In other words, why does it leave untouched the moral duty of men and societies, etc.? Because it only concerns "immunity from coercion in civil society." Thus, the aspect it leaves untouched is not the matter of immunity from coercion, but the specifically moral duties of individuals and society in relation to true religion. Since the latter cannot, by the logic of these two sentences, refer to immunity from coercion, it likely refers to something like the prior statement that "all men are bound to seek the truth, especially in what concerns God and His Church, and to embrace the truth they come to know, and to hold fast to it" (Paul VI, *Dignitatis Humanae*, no. 1).

64. Benedict XVI, *Jesus of Nazareth*, 1:123–24.
65. Benedict XVI, *Jesus of Nazareth*, 1:124 (emphasis mine).

ethical principles of the Torah, which Ratzinger calls apodictic laws.⁶⁶ And here comes the part most relevant for my purposes:

> Consequently, *Christianity constantly has to reshape and reformulate social structures and "Christian social teaching."* There will always be new developments to correct what has gone before. In the inner structure of the Torah, in its further development under the critique of the Prophets, and in Jesus' message, which takes up both elements, Christianity finds the wide scope for necessary historical evolution as well as the solid ground that guarantees the dignity of man by rooting it in the dignity of God.⁶⁷

This makes better sense of *Dignitatis Humanae*'s relationship to what precedes it and to other matters of the Church's social teaching in which perennial moral principles must be applied in light of new contexts and new possibilities.⁶⁸

According to the old political theology, it was believed that the basic demand of civic order would only legitimate religious coercion if the state were itself directed by the pope's indirect authority in temporal matters. Certainly, religious coercion that acted against the orthodox faith could not be justified in the eyes of the Church. Hence, the origin of the theory that only the Church could use the state to impose civil penalties for ecclesial ends. Once it becomes apparent, however, that such coercive law for sectarian/ecclesial ends was not necessary either for civil order or for the Church's own freedom, and that its absence does not in any way entail indifference to the truth—and once it is recognized that while error has no rights (Pope Pius IX), the human person does (*Dignitatis Humanae*)—then it becomes much more difficult to square with moral principles the Church affirms, such as regard conscience, faith, and human dignity. What would have previously been an understandable application of principles becomes, in light of a new awareness of political possibilities, unnecessary coercion that now constitutes an injustice to those people harmed by it and a failure of reciprocity in relation to other members of the political community.

Based on these considerations, applying Pope Benedict's hermeneutic principles that the Church's decisions on contingent matters are

---

66. Benedict XVI, *Jesus of Nazareth*, 1:126.

67. Benedict XVI, *Jesus of Nazareth*, 1:126–27 (emphasis mine).

68. Finnis, "Radical Critique of Catholic Social Teaching," in Bradley and Brugger, *Catholic Social Teaching*, 548–84.

themselves contingent, and that social doctrine always involves mutable and perfectible applications of perennial ethical principles, there is no theological reason to reject the political philosophy implied in the *Dignitatis Humanae*, *Gaudium et Spes*, or other later ecclesial documents, even if admittedly they differ from previous papal treatments of these matters.[69] It must be said that revelation contains no political philosophy, just as it contains no atomic theory or astronomy. Nonetheless, the political philosophy implied in these conciliar and postconciliar documents is an indispensable tool with which the Church can apply perennial principles of natural law in light of newly discovered political possibilities that have made the old political theology untenable.

Conclusion

Catholic postliberals and integralists are perfectly within their rights to question the political philosophy assumed by these documents. Nonetheless, for reasons mentioned, and other reasons still, I argue that their criticisms of this political philosophy are misguided. The biggest issues we face today are not necessary consequences of the American experiment; they can and must be addressed, imperfectly of course, without abandoning the conditions for free, humane, and peaceful coexistence in a pluralistic world. To show this, however, it was first necessary to elucidate the relationships among metaphysics, ethics, politics, and theology, and in dialogue with others who are sympathetic to natural law theory.

Bibliography

Abbà, Giuseppe. *Le virtù per la felicità*. Rome: Editrice LAS, 2018.

Ahmari, Sohrab, et al. "In Defense of Cultural Christianity." *The American Conservative*, November 9, 2021. https://www.theamericanconservative.com/articles/in-defense-of-cultural-christianity/.

Aquinas, Thomas. In *De divinis nominibus*. In *Librum Beati Dionysii De Divinis Nominibus Expositio*, edited by C. Pera. Turin: Marietti, 1950.

———. *De Potentia: Quaestiones disputatae de Potentia*. In vol. 2 of *Quaestiones disputate*, edited by P. Baazzi et al. 10th ed. Turin: Marietti, 1965.

———. In *Ethic (Commentary on Aristotle's Nicomachean Ethics)*. In *Decem libros Ethicorum Aristotelis ad Nichomachum expositio*, edited by R. M. Spiazzi. 3rd ed. Turin: Marietti, 1964.

---

69. For instance, the papal encyclical of John Paul II, *Centessimus Annus*, or the Congregation for the Doctrine of Faith's "Doctrinal Note on Some Questions Regarding the Participation of Catholics in Political Life."

———. *Summa Theologiae*. Translated by the Fathers of the English Dominican Province. 2nd ed. London: Burns Oates & Washbourne, 1920. www.newadvent.org/summa.

———. *The Treatise on Happiness—The Treatise on Human Acts: Summa Theologiae I–II 1–21*. Translated by Thomas Williams. Indianapolis: Hackett, 2016.

Aristotle. *The Basic Works of Aristotle*. Edited by Richard McKeon. New York: Random House, 2001.

———. *The Nicomachean Ethics*. Translated by David Ross. Revised by Lesley Brown. Oxford: Oxford University Press, 2009.

Benedict XVI. "Address of His Holiness Benedict XVI to the Roman Curia Offering Them His Christmas Greetings." https://www.vatican.va/content/benedict-xvi/en/speeches/2005/december/documents/hf_ben_xvi_spe_20051222_roman-curia.html#

———. *Jesus of Nazareth*. 3 vols. New York: Doubleday, 2007.

Berger, Peter, et al. *Religious America, Secular Europe? A Theme and Variations*. Burlington, VT: Ashgate, 2008.

Bradley, G., and E. Brugger, eds. *Catholic Social Teaching: A Volume of Scholarly Essays*. Cambridge: Cambridge University Press, 2019.

Chesterton, G. K. *What I Saw in America*. London: Anthem, 2009.

Clarke, W. Norris. *The One and the Many*. Notre Dame: University of Notre Dame Press, 2001.

Congregation for the Doctrine of the Faith. "Doctrinal Note on Some Questions Regarding the Participation of Catholics in Political Life." November 24, 2002. https://www.vatican.va/roman_curia/congregations/cfaith/documents/rc_con_cfaith_doc_20021124_politica_en.html.

Dahl, Robert A. *Democracy and Its Critics*. New Haven: Yale University Press, 1989.

Deneen, Patrick. *Why Liberalism Failed*. New Haven: Yale University Press, 2018.

Evans, Jonathan. "U.S. Adults Are More Religious Than Western Europeans." *Pew Research Center*, September 5, 2018. https://www.pewresearch.org/fact-tank/2018/09/05/u-s-adults-are-more-religious-than-western-europeans/.

Fabro, Cornelio. *La nozione metaphysica di partecipazione secondo S. Thommaso d'Aquino*. Milan: Edivi, 1939.

———. *Partecipazione e causalità*. Turin: Società Editrice Internazionale, 1960.

Feser, Edward. "The Role of Nature in Sexual Ethics." *The National Catholic Bioethics Quarterly* 13 (2013) 69–76.

Finke, Roger, and Rodney Starke. *The Churching of America: 1776–2005*. Rev. ed. New Brunswick, NJ: Rutgers University Press, 2005.

Finnis, John. *Fundamentals of Ethics*. Washington, DC: Georgetown University Press, 1983.

———. *Natural Law and Natural Rights*. Oxford: Oxford University Press, 1980.

Gibbons, James. *The Memorial Volume: A History of the Third Plenary Council of Baltimore, November 9—December 7, 1884*. Baltimore: Baltimore, 1885.

Gilson, Étienne. *Being and Some Philosophers*. Toronto: Pontifical Institute of Mediaeval Studies, 1949.

Grisez, Germain. "First Principle of Practical Reason: A Commentary on the *Summa Theologiae* 1–2, q. 94, a. 2." *Natural Law Forum* 10 (1965) 168–201.

Hall, Kermit, and Mark David Hall, eds. *The Collected Works of James Wilson*. Indianapolis: Liberty Fund, 2007.

Henrich, Joseph. *The WEIRDest People in the World: How the West Became Psychologically Peculiar and Particularly Prosperous.* New York: Picador, 2021.

Hittinger, Russell. *A Critique of the New Natural Law Theory.* Notre Dame: University of Notre Dame Press, 1987.

Howes, Thomas D. "Public Education and Liberal Neutrality." *Public Discourse*, September 28, 2021. https://www.thepublicdiscourse.com/2021/09/78148/.

John Paul II. *Centesimus Annus.* May 1, 1991. https://www.vatican.va/content/john-paul-ii/en/encyclicals/documents/hf_jp-ii_enc_01051991_centesimus-annus.html.

———. *Veritatis Splendor.* August 6, 1993. https://www.vatican.va/content/john-paul-ii/en/encyclicals/documents/hf_jp-ii_enc_06081993_veritatis-splendor.html.

Lehu, Léonard. *La raison règle de la moralité d'après saint Thomas.* Paris: Librairie Lecoffre, 1930.

MacIntyre, Alasdair. *After Virtue: A Study in Moral Theory.* 2nd ed. Notre Dame: University of Notre Dame Press, 1984.

Maritain, Jacques. *Reflections on America.* New York: Image, 1974.

McInerny, Ralph. *Ethica Thomistica: The Moral Philosophy of Thomas Aquinas.* Rev. ed. Washington, DC: The Catholic University of America Press, 1997.

Minerd, Matthew K. "Beyond Non-Being." *American Catholic Philosophical Quarterly* 91 (2017) 353–79.

———. "Thomism and the Formal Object of Logic." *American Catholic Philosophical Quarterly* 93 (2019) 411–44.

Murray, John Courtney. *We Hold These Truths: Catholic Reflections on the American Proposition.* New York: Sheed and Ward, 1960.

Patterson, James. "Catholic Republicanism in America." *Perspectives on Political Science* 52 (2022) 1–13.

Paul VI. *Dignitatis Humanae.* December 7, 1965. https://www.vatican.va/archive/hist_councils/ii_vatican_council/documents/vat-ii_decl_19651207_dignitatis-humanae_en.html.

Ratzinger, Joseph. *Church, Ecumenism, and Politics: New Essays in Ecclesiology.* New York: Crossroad, 1988.

———. "Il laicismo nuova ideologia, l'Europa non emargini Dio." *La Repubblica*, November 19, 2004. https://www.ratzinger.us/Il-laicismo-nuova-ideologia-lEuropa-non-emargini-Dio/.

———. *Politik und Erlösung: Zum Verhaltnis von Glaube, Rationalitat und Irrationalem in der sogenannten Theologie der Befreiung.* Opladen: Westdeutscher Verlag, 1986.

Rawls, John. *The Law of Peoples.* Cambridge: Harvard University Press, 1999.

———. *Political Liberalism.* New York: Columbia University Press, 1996.

Reilly, Robert. *America on Trial: A Defense of the Founding.* San Francisco: Ignatius, 2020.

Rhonheimer, Martin. *The Common Good of Constitutional Democracy.* Edited by William F. Murphy Jr. Washington, DC: The Catholic University of America Press, 2012.

———. "Has Liberalism Failed? Patrick Deneen's Populist Anti-Liberalism: A Catholic Classical Liberal's Response." *Austrian Institute*, November 7, 2020. https://austrian-institute.org/en/blog/has-liberalism-failed-patrick-deneens-populist-anti-liberalism-a-catholic-classical-liberals-response/.

———. "Practical Reason, Human Nature, and the Epistemology of Ethics: John Finnis's Contribution to the Rediscovery of Aristotelian Ethical Methodology in Aquinas's Moral Philosophy: A Personal Account." *Villanova Law Review* 57 (2012) 873–88.

———. *Natural Law and Practical Reason: A Thomist View of Moral Autonomy.* Translated by Gerald Malsbary. New York: Fordham University Press, 2000.

Rodríguez Luño, Ángel. *Introducción a la Ética Política.* Madrid: Ediciones Rialp, 2021.

Rommen, Heinrich A. *The Natural Law: A Study in Legal and Social History and Philosophy.* Translated by Thomas R. Hanley. Indianapolis: Liberty Fund, 1998.

———. *The State in Catholic Thought: A Treatise in Political Theology.* St. Louis, MO: Herder, 1945.

Rooney, James Dominic. "Illiberalism Will Not Secure the Common Good." *Law & Liberty*, April 12, 2022. https://lawliberty.org/illiberalism-will-not-secure-the-common-good/.

Rosenthal, Alexander S. *Crown under Law: Richard Hooker, John Locke, and the Ascent of Modern Constitutionalism.* Lanham, MD: Lexington, 2008.

Schall, James V. *The Politics of Heaven and Hell.* San Francisco: Ignatius, 2020.

Schindler, D. C. *The Politics of the Real: The Church between Liberalism and Integralism.* Steubenville, OH: New Polity, 2021.

Schulz, Jonathan F. "Kin Networks and Institutional Development." *Economic Journal* 132 (2022) 2578–613.

Schwartz, Daniel. "Francisco Suárez on Consent and Political Obligation." *Vivarium* 48 (2008) 59–81.

Simon, Yves R. *Philosophy of Democratic Government.* Chicago: University of Chicago Press, 1951.

Sokolowski, Robert. *Introduction to Phenomenology.* Cambridge: Cambridge University Press, 2000.

Suárez, Francisco. *De bonitate et militia humanorum actuum.* In *Opera Omnia*, 4:277–454. Paris: Vivès. 1856.

Tocqueville, Alexis de. *Democracy in America.* Chicago: University of Chicago Press, 2000.

Wilken, Robert Louis. *Liberty in the Things of God: The Christian Origins of Religious Freedom.* New Haven: Yale University Press, 2019.

Wippel, John F. *The Metaphysical Thought of Thomas Aquinas: From Finite Being to Uncreated Being.* Washington, DC: The Catholic University of America Press, 2000.

10

The Boundaries and Authority of Catholic Social Teaching

A Reply to John Finnis

Bernard G. Prusak, John Carroll University

Abstract: This chapter submits that getting clearer on the complexity of practical reasoning is crucial for clarifying the relationship between Catholic social teaching (CST) and what is commonly understood as Catholic moral teaching. The chapter engages as its principal interlocutor the philosopher and legal theorist John Finnis, who contributed three chapters to the recent, monumental *Catholic Social Teaching: A Volume of Scholarly Essays*. It is argued that practical reasoning is more complex than Finnis allows and accordingly that a hard distinction between "authoritative moral teachings" and "matters of prudential judgment" cannot be sustained. Against Finnis's deflationary view of the authority of CST, reducing it to a set of principles of indeterminate application, the chapter concludes by proposing that there is no one, overarching answer to the question of the authority of CST for the faithful Catholic. Instead, different social teachings, on diverse topics (e.g., the rights of labor), will be found and come to have varying authority as the faithful receive, examine, and prayerfully consider them.

Social Catholicism for the Twenty-First Century?—Volume 1

IN JUNE 2015, WHEN it was still plausible that someone other than Donald J. Trump would be the Republican Party's nominee for president in the 2016 election cycle, former Florida governor Jeb Bush made news by preemptively distancing himself from Pope Francis's encyclical *Laudato Si'*, scheduled for publication in the coming days.[1] "I don't get economic policy from my bishops or my cardinals or my pope," Bush declared. "I think religion ought to be about making us better as people and less about things that end up getting in the political realm."[2] The pundit Rod Dreher pounced with a brief column entitled "Jeb Bush, Cafeteria Catholic." "Jeb Bush, as a Catholic," Dreher intoned, "is not free to discard the social teaching of the Catholic Church ... because it doesn't suit his personal beliefs."[3] Dreher acknowledged that bishops are neither "policy wonks" nor "experts at dictating economic policy," but he underlined that "Catholic Christianity is not focused only on personal piety, but has a broad social dimension as well." Bush's statement, Dreher concluded, made it clear that he was "no better than liberal Catholics who reject the Church's teaching on abortion, marriage, and other areas that inconvenience their consciences."

This chapter concerns the boundaries between Catholic social teaching (hereafter CST), such as Pope Francis's *Laudato Si'*,[4] and Catholic moral teaching, commonly identified with the magisterium's condemnation of such practices as abortion, contraception, and euthanasia. In his haste to lump Bush with "liberal Catholics," Dreher ran roughshod over any boundary, but his reluctant acknowledgment that bishops are neither "policy wonks" nor "experts at dictating economic policy" suggests that there is more to say. This chapter also addresses, though more briefly, the related question of how to understand the authority of CST for faithful Catholics. Is the faithful Catholic, as Dreher seems to imply, obliged to assent and defer to each and every social teaching of the Church, just the same as to its teaching on abortion, contraception, and the like?

---

1. A leaked copy was published on June 15, 2015 in *L'Espresso*; Bush was reacting to early reports. *Laudato Si'* appeared officially on June 18, 2015.

2. Stern, "Jeb Bush Rejects His Church's Teachings on Climate Change," para. 1. The full quotation is less dismissive: Bush also says, "I'd like to see what [Pope Francis] says as it relates to climate change and how that connects to these broader, deeper issues before I pass judgment."

3. Dreher, "Jeb Bush, Cafeteria Catholic," para. 2.

4. Francis explicitly describes *Laudato Si'* as belonging to "the body of the Church's social teaching." See *Laudato Si'*, no. 15.

Of course, this chapter's inquiries hardly proceed in a vacuum. Distinguished scholars have spoken to these questions,[5] and there are relevant magisterial texts and theological commentaries.[6] I take as this chapter's principal interlocutor one such distinguished scholar, the philosopher and legal theorist John Finnis, who contributed three chapters to the recent, monumental *Catholic Social Teaching: A Volume of Scholarly Essays*, edited by Gerard V. Bradley and E. Christian Brugger.[7] That volume's closing chapter, Finnis's "A Radical Critique of Catholic Social Teaching," stakes out provocative positions on the authority of CST. In chapters of their own, Bradley and Brugger also take positions along the same lines as Finnis's. Accordingly, this chapter begins by presenting and commenting on Bradley's, Brugger's, and Finnis's arguments. The chapter then turns to a critical discussion of the account of practical reasoning that Finnis uses to support the contrast between teachings that apply negative moral norms with teachings that apply affirmative or positive moral norms. Here I draw on work by the moral theologian Jean Porter, in particular her book *Moral Action and Christian Ethics*. This part of the chapter argues that practical reasoning is more complex than Finnis allows and that the contrast that he, Brugger, and Bradley draw between the teachings in question is overly sharp. Finally, the chapter considers the implications of that conclusion for the authority of CST.

Catholic Moral Teaching, *Si*; Catholic Social Teaching, *No*

In the introduction to their volume, Bradley and Brugger present CST as "an expression—indeed a branch—of moral theology."[8] CST is not, in other words, an altogether separate body of doctrine from the Church's other moral teachings. Instead, there is a common root, so to speak. More fully, guided by both divine revelation and natural reason, CST "reflects upon issues and events *in history* in the light of moral principles and offers

---

5. See, for example, Curran, "Catholic Social and Sexual Teaching." Compare, more recently, Salzman and Lawler, "*Amoris Laetitia*."

6. See, for example, the instruction *Donum Veritatis*, esp. no. 24; Dulles, *Craft of Theology*, ch. 7, "Magisterium and Theological Dissent," 105–18; Sullivan, *Creative Fidelity*, esp. 21–44.

7. See my review in *Commonweal*, 54–55.

8. Bradley and Brugger, "Introduction," 2.

guidance for living a Christian life."⁹ Yet CST to date exhibits, according to the editors, several "weaknesses." These include "ambiguity about its scope or subject-matter, insufficient attention to the dependence upon empirical and other factors inherent in any justice consideration, [and] inappropriate assumptions about who it is that has primary responsibility for undertaking such considerations."¹⁰ Nonetheless, against unnamed Catholic theologians characterized as engaged "in radical theological dissent against the authoritative teaching of the Church," Bradley and Brugger affirm that the magisterium's

> authoritative *moral* teachings . . . can and do include the excluding of certain moral objects as always and everywhere wrongful to choose . . . and that the propositions asserted in these latter teachings are practically prior to matters of prudential judgment that men and women of good faith can and do disagree upon without any fallacy in their thinking or objective disorders in their willing.¹¹

Note the inchoate distinction between "authoritative *moral* teachings" and "matters of prudential judgment."

The editors' respective chapters reiterate and amplify these themes. Bradley states that CST is "really applied moral teaching."¹² He also notes that "according to a sound understanding of the laity's apostolate," as expounded in Vatican II and post-conciliar documents, "one can critically judge a particular pastoral intervention as inappropriate, for it might impose obligations of assent and deference upon the laity that in truth they should not be made to bear."¹³ For example, "Matters of sociological, economic, demographic, and scientific fact—including the patterns of earth's temperatures and the human responsibility for any sharp deviations from expected patterns—are not within the bishops' distinctive competence."¹⁴ As Dreher reluctantly acknowledged, bishops are not "policy wonks." From this perspective, Bush was within his rights, as a lay politician, not simply to defer to *Laudato Si'*. It belongs to the laity,

---

9. Bradley and Brugger, "Introduction," 2.
10. Bradley and Brugger, "Introduction," 4.
11. Bradley and Brugger, "Introduction," 7–8.
12. Bradley, "How Bishops Should Teach Catholic Social Doctrine," 528.
13. Bradley, "How Bishops Should Teach Catholic Social Doctrine," 532.
14. Bradley, "How Bishops Should Teach Catholic Social Doctrine," 537.

Bradley writes, "to judge for themselves contingent matters of fact" and to "weigh prudential considerations."[15]

Brugger has much more to say about the relationship of CST and what he calls the "'moral documents,' texts not ordinarily associated with the CST corpus," such as Pope Paul VI's encyclical *Humanae Vitae*.[16] According to Brugger, "CST *is just* Catholic moral teaching with emphasis upon the political and economic realms."[17] He thus rejects as "harmful and indeed nonsensical" the "bifurcation . . . between the Church's commitment to 'social justice' on the one hand and her teachings on the Fifth and Sixth Commandments of the Decalogue on the other" (roughly, killing and sex).[18] He acknowledges, however, a difference in "the nature of obligation" according to whether what is in question "is an affirmative law (a positive norm) or a prohibitive law (a negative norm)."[19] All moral norms impose obligation, but "positive norms do not bind absolutely."[20] Instead, circumstances make a difference. For example (not Brugger's), what is commonly called the duty to rescue does not normally bind when the act of rescue would imperil the rescuer's own life, the determination of which involves an assessment of facts and likelihoods.[21] By contrast, "Negative norms . . . bind absolutely—always and in every instance (*semper et pro semper*); they require that we always refrain from—*not* perform—the kind of action they proscribe," on which point Brugger cites Pope John Paul II's encyclical *Veritatis Splendor*.[22]

Brugger uses this distinction between how negative and positive norms bind in order to say more about the "harmful bifurcation" between CST and magisterial teaching bearing on abortion, contraception, and so forth.[23] Admittedly, there is a bifurcation—after all, the editors' introduction, as quoted above, presents CST as a "branch . . . of moral

---

15. Bradley, "How Bishops Should Teach Catholic Social Doctrine," 532.
16. Brugger, "Catholic Social Teaching Is Catholic Moral Teaching," 511.
17. Brugger, "Catholic Social Teaching Is Catholic Moral Teaching," 510.
18. Brugger, "Catholic Social Teaching Is Catholic Moral Teaching," 510–11.
19. Brugger, "Catholic Social Teaching Is Catholic Moral Teaching," 513.
20. Brugger, "Catholic Social Teaching Is Catholic Moral Teaching," 513.
21. Parents might hold themselves to a higher standard.
22. Brugger, "Catholic Social Teaching Is Catholic Moral Teaching," 513–14. See John Paul II, *Veritatis Splendor*, nos. 52, 82.
23. See Brugger, "Catholic Social Teaching Is Catholic Moral Teaching," 514: "This distinction is important for assessing the harmful bifurcation spoken about above." I am reading Brugger charitably on whether there is a bifurcation or not. If CST is "a branch . . . of moral theology," then bifurcation there must be.

theology"—but the apparent divergence of CST from other moral teachings is put in proper perspective once we change the metaphor and see "positive norms and exceptionless negative norms as two sides, as it were, of the same moral coin, namely, the field of rational guidance toward integral human fulfillment."[24] What is potentially harmful about the bifurcation, we might say, is thereby taken out of circulation. According to Brugger, our view of CST must be widened so that we see exceptionless negative norms as belonging to CST inasmuch as respecting them "is an absolutely minimal demand of social justice and an essential first step on the way to that perfection in Christian charity called for by the Gospel."[25] Going forward, Brugger advises, magisterial "documents should be careful to communicate the differences in the ways that negative norms and nonabsolute positive norms bind (*semper et pro semper* vs. *semper sed non pro semper* [always and in every case vs. always but not in every case or all circumstances]), and [the documents] should solicitously avoid the common mistake of formulating their teachings of positive norms in overly absolutist ways."[26] As he observes regarding economic justice, "'Don't defraud the poor' is . . . straightforward. 'Help them overcome their poverty' is not."[27] The magisterium oversteps its competence if it claims expertise in the policies that politicians must enact.

Notwithstanding, Brugger acknowledges that, since "the competency of the magisterium to teach authoritatively extends . . . to what pertains to good morals," it follows that "the magisterium rightly addresses social issues bearing upon human good."[28] His position is not that the magisterium should cease issuing social teachings (though he does suggest significantly "shortening the length" of the documents),[29] but that "Church leaders should be mindful to remain within their proper competencies while doing so."[30] In his view, the "concrete positive application" of norms of justice regarding, say, the economy or the environment exceeds the magisterium's ken.[31] By contrast, "If . . . some behavior is

---

24. Brugger, "Catholic Social Teaching Is Catholic Moral Teaching," 523.
25. Brugger, "Catholic Social Teaching Is Catholic Moral Teaching," 522.
26. Brugger, "Catholic Social Teaching Is Catholic Moral Teaching," 524.
27. Brugger, "Catholic Social Teaching Is Catholic Moral Teaching," 514.
28. Brugger, "Catholic Social Teaching Is Catholic Moral Teaching," 525.
29. Brugger, "Catholic Social Teaching Is Catholic Moral Teaching," 526.
30. Brugger, "Catholic Social Teaching Is Catholic Moral Teaching," 525.
31. Brugger, "Catholic Social Teaching Is Catholic Moral Teaching," 525. See further 526: "Members of the hierarchy may, of course, express what opinions they have,

rightly identified as an instance of the kind singled out by an exceptionless negative norm, Church leaders rightly oppose every social initiative aimed at shielding that behavior or securing liberties to carry it out."[32]

The first clause of that last sentence ("If . . . some behavior . . .") suggests an account of practical reasoning and thus leads into Finnis's "Radical Critique of Catholic Social Teaching," where such an account is made explicit.[33] To begin with, Finnis agrees with Bradley and Brugger that "CST is part of Catholic moral teaching and cannot be well studied or taught without a clear grasp of its dependence upon, and integration within, that moral teaching as a whole."[34] Finnis also affirms "the basic division between the two kinds of norms (affirmative and negative) that the Church, like common morality, teaches."[35] As he writes:

> Negative moral norms bind always and in relation to every instance of the kind of act they pick out; affirmative moral norms, however, although they are to be borne in mind as general guidance, do not bind *specifically* except in appropriate circumstances. The application of affirmative moral norms of justice is always dependent, therefore, on assessment of the circumstances, an assessment that, though morally guided, always involves some judgment about facts and likelihoods.[36]

Finnis uses this distinction just as Brugger does: namely, to contrast magisterial teaching that applies affirmative (positive) norms with magisterial teaching that applies negative norms. In Finnis's words again:

---

but they should ensure that the faithful do not take those opinions as the teaching of the Catholic Church."

32. Brugger, "Catholic Social Teaching Is Catholic Moral Teaching," 525.

33. Note that the sentence's second clause, claiming that "Church leaders rightly oppose," etc., may be more controversial than it at first appears, depending on what is taken to follow from it. Imagine that the "social initiative" in question is a law protecting abortion rights. Are Catholic politicians bound in conscience to follow the lead of the magisterium in opposing such a law? More to the point, does the magisterium have the competence to dictate what good law is in a particular society? Is good law always the same as legally enforcing sound morality? See for discussion Kaveny, "Toward a Thomistic Perspective on Abortion"; Kaveny, *Law's Virtues*.

34. Finnis, "Radical Critique of Catholic Social Teaching," 556. See also 575: "It is artificial and hazardous to separate the Church's teaching in the way that has become institutionalized in the Roman Curia's separate organs for marriage (and family), and for justice (and peace and development)."

35. Finnis, "Radical Critique of Catholic Social Teaching," 564.

36. Finnis, "Radical Critique of Catholic Social Teaching," 557.

> Pastors and laity alike should constantly remind themselves ... that, *because* the diagnosing of causalities, effects and side-effects, risks and probabilities is an inherently difficult and often uncertain matter, it is entirely possible for informed and well-catechized Catholics in good faith to hold *diametrically opposed views on, say, climate change, migration policy, sentencing policy, healthcare policy, the organization of employment, laws of inheritance and taxation*, and so on, while respecting all relevant moral principles and norms.[37]

The case is different when it comes to "the teaching of *negative* responsibilities and norms": according to Finnis, "In this domain, stable and specific teaching can rightly be proposed as certain on a good many matters."[38]

The account of practical reasoning that supports this contrast is straightforward and seemingly incontrovertible:

> All practical reasoning includes premises of two kinds: one (or more) *evaluative* premise(s), about what is desirable, good, appropriate, permissible, and so forth; and at least one *factual* premise about what behavior would be involved in the proposed action, and what good and bad effects are likely to result from that behavior in the circumstances as they actually are or are likely to be.[39]

Finnis concedes that "even the application of exceptionless negative moral norms, such as the norm excluding the intent to kill a person or persons, can sometimes involve difficult assessments of complex facts," but he insists that "the application of affirmative moral norms is inherently even more—much more—relative to assessment of circumstances."[40]

The claim that the application of affirmative moral norms depends on the assessment of circumstances is familiar by now: Bradley, Brugger, and Finnis make this claim time and again. What is new is Finnis's concession that "even the application of exceptionless negative moral norms ... can sometimes involve difficult assessments of complex facts." This concession warrants attention, despite or perhaps all the more because of Finnis's

---

37. Finnis, "Radical Critique of Catholic Social Teaching," 573.

38. Finnis, "Radical Critique of Catholic Social Teaching," 558.

39. Finnis, "Radical Critique of Catholic Social Teaching," 556. Compare, interestingly, Hare, *Language of Morals*, 56, though for Hare we choose our principles, whereas for Finnis they are given by our nature. See for discussion MacIntyre, *Short History of Ethics*, 260–61.

40. Finnis, "Radical Critique of Catholic Social Teaching," 556.

seeming attempt to diminish it by claiming that the point holds "even more" and "much more" for the application of affirmative norms.

Recall that Finnis also writes that "negative moral norms bind always and in relation to every instance of the kind of act they pick out."[41] A simple point to note is that norms do not themselves "pick out" acts. People identify particular actions as kinds of actions. Moreover, people sometimes disagree about how to describe the "object" of an action: that is, the generic concept in terms of which it is correctly described.

Take the well-known case of Captain Lawrence Oates, who died, in 1912, in an expedition to the South Pole. Suffering from gangrene and frostbite and estimating that his condition was jeopardizing the survival of his three remaining companions, who had refused to leave him behind, Oates walked out from his tent into a blizzard, thereby sacrificing his life. Joseph Boyle, a onetime frequent collaborator with Finnis, claims that "actions like that of Captain Oates need not be suicide, but can be described as a side effect of choices to do other things (e.g., removing oneself from the group), which have death as a predictable result."[42] That description of what Captain Oates did is dubious. Are we to agree that Oates's "close-in intention," to use Finnis's terminology,[43] was simply to remove himself from the group, with death as a predictable "side effect"? It is more plausible to say that Oates intended to sacrifice himself for the sake of his companions; that is why he walked out from his tent into the blizzard. Whether his action is correctly described as suicide, however, seems to be a further question. There is, of course, a traditional rule, though disputed in some quarters, against suicide as a kind of wrongful killing. Even if we say that Oates intended to die (rather than simply remove himself from the group), is what he did correctly described as "suicide"? At the very least, Oates's action is hardly a paradigmatic example of suicide, and it is also hard to see it as contravening the rationale or point of the rule against suicide, namely (though roughly), that human life should not be treated as cheap.

An observation of Jean Porter's is to the point: "a knowledge of facts is not sufficient to resolve the question of classification, since our

---

41. Finnis, "Radical Critique of Catholic Social Teaching," 557. Compare Brugger, "Catholic Social Teaching Is Catholic Moral Teaching," 525: "If, for example, some behavior is rightly identified as an instance of the kind singled out by an exceptionless negative norm." Norms also do not themselves "single out" kinds of behavior.

42. Boyle, "Sanctity of Life and Suicide," 233.

43. Finnis, "Radical Critique of Catholic Social Teaching," 558.

difficulty lies precisely in determining what significance we ought to give the facts that we know."[44] Further, "the distinction between description and evaluation . . . is seen to be a misplaced distinction," as the choice of how to describe what Oates did is bound up with our evaluation of what he did.[45] But if that claim is right, then practical reasoning is more complex than Finnis allows. More precisely and fully, practical reasoning involving the application of negative norms is not simply a matter of applying an evaluative premise to a factual premise. Instead, at least in difficult cases (the kind that occupy "casuists"), practical reasoning involving the application of negative norms requires us to reckon with not only the correct description of a particular action, but also the proper interpretation and scope of a rule.[46]

Blurring the Line

Getting clearer on the complexity of practical reasoning is crucial for clarifying the relationship between CST and Catholic moral teaching (Brugger's "moral documents," such as *Humanae Vitae*). Porter serves as an insightful guide.

Porter's *Moral Action and Christian Ethics* is focused on the question: "how are we to move from concepts of generic kinds of action to correct descriptions of specific actions?"[47] More simply put, "how do we arrive at moral judgments?"—which, she observes, is "equivalent to asking for an account of moral rationality."[48] The basic problem is evident in the case of Captain Oates. There is a traditional rule against suicide. If pressed, many people likely could provide paradigmatic examples of the violation of this rule, and they could articulate its rationale or point. But it is not clear whether what Oates did should count as suicide. He certainly did not show wanton disregard for the value of human life in sacrificing his life for the sake of his companions. Was the "object" of his action nonetheless suicide? Did he do evil so that good might come, against Paul's letter to the Romans (3:8)? Was his action an intrinsic evil,

---

44. Porter, *Moral Action and Christian Ethics*, 29.

45. Porter, *Moral Action and Christian Ethics* 37. As Julius Kovesi remarked, "We always evaluate under a certain description." See Kovesi, *Moral Notions*, 151.

46. See further Kovesi, *Moral Notions*, 110–11: "once we know what is the morally relevant description of our act we do not need a major premise to come to a conclusion."

47. Porter, *Moral Action and Christian Ethics*, 4.

48. Porter, *Moral Action and Christian Ethics*, 5.

the kind of action that can never be made right or good by motive or circumstances or consequences? Aristotle gives the examples of adultery, theft, and murder: "There is ... never any possibility of getting anything right about them, but one always goes astray, nor is there doing anything well or not well about such things [say] by committing adultery with the right woman and when and in the way one ought, but simply doing any of these things is to go wrong."[49]

The concept of an intrinsic evil is relevant for present purposes. Pope John Paul II's *Veritatis Splendor*, amply cited by Brugger and Finnis, quotes *Gaudium et Spes* in listing, to begin with, "homicide, genocide, abortion, euthanasia, and voluntary suicide" as examples of intrinsic evils.[50] As Porter observes elsewhere, however, "*Veritatis Splendor* does not appear to acknowledge the indeterminacy of moral concepts, and the correlative necessity for judgment in their application."[51] It is one thing to hold that suicide, for example, is an intrinsic evil, never to be made right by motive or circumstances or consequences; but it is another thing to judge that a particular action, such as Oates's, is suicide. Like all generic concepts in a natural language, 'suicide' has an open texture. There is a core of paradigmatic examples that many people would call suicide, but there is also a measure of indeterminacy. In other words, it is not always obvious whether a particular action, like Oates's, that might be classified and condemned as suicide is properly described in that way. How to describe what Oates did involves, in Porter's words, an "irreducible element of discretion."[52] We must make a judgment, based on our understanding of the rationale of the rule against suicide. That judgment in turn deepens our understanding of the rule. Clearly, there is room for reasonable disagreement about both the appropriate judgment and the understanding of the rule.

Moral Action and Christian Ethics may be characterized as a polemic against a Kantian understanding of practical reason, according to which, in Porter's words, moral rules function to "determine the uniquely correct answer to any moral question that may arise, in a way that is compelling

---

49. Aristotle, *Nicomachean Ethics*, book 2, ch. 6, p. 30, 1107a. It is worth noting here both that calling an act intrinsically evil "does not, by itself, say anything about the comparative gravity (or seriousness) of the act" and that recognizing that an act is intrinsically evil "does not necessarily mean that it is a grave evil." See Kaveny, "Intrinsic Evil and Political Responsibility," 127, 129.

50. John Paul II, *Veritatis Splendor*, no. 80, quoting *Gaudium et Spes*, no. 27.

51. Porter, "Moral Reasoning," 208.

52. Porter, *Moral Action and Christian Ethics*, 31.

to any impartial, rational individual."[53] The book's thesis in that regard is that "moral rules logically cannot function in the way that the Kantian account would suggest."[54] The primary reason is because of the nature of generic moral concepts: a moral rule against suicide, or against adultery or abortion or theft,[55] to vary the examples, is indeterminate to the same extent that those concepts are.

The example of adultery may remind readers of the controversy over Pope Francis's apostolic exhortation *Amoris Laetitia*, released April 2016 following the 2014 and 2015 synods on the family in Rome.[56] In September 2016, four retired cardinals sent him five *dubia* raising questions about chapter 8 of the exhortation, in particular whether it was to be understood as reversing, in several instances, "the teaching of St. John Paul II's encyclical *Veritatis Splendor* . . . based on sacred Scripture and the Tradition of the Church."[57] In a much-discussed footnote in chapter 8, Francis suggests that people "living in 'irregular' situations," such as divorced and remarried without an annulment, might, in some cases, be permitted to receive the sacraments.[58] He goes on, in the same note, to quote his apostolic exhortation *Evangelii Gaudium*, reminding priests "that the confessional must not be a torture chamber, but rather an encounter with the Lord's mercy" and that the Eucharist "is not a prize for the perfect, but a powerful medicine and nourishment for the weak."[59]

One of the *dubia* asks whether, after *Amoris Laetetia*, "one still need[s] to regard as valid the teaching of St. John Paul II's encyclical *Veritatis Splendor*, no. 79, based on sacred Scripture and on the Tradition

---

53. Porter, *Moral Action and Christian Ethics*, 8. Similarly, Joseph Boyle claims against Kantians that "the notion of 'respecting rational nature as an end in itself' is simply too vague to be decisively predicated . . . except perhaps in a few uncontroversial kinds of acts, like slavery and rape. Disagreements about what kinds of acts are properly described as acts of respecting rational nature or failing to respect it cannot, it seems to me, be settled except by compromise, intuition, or decision." See Boyle, "Aquinas, Kant, and Donagan on Moral Principles," 407.

54. Porter, *Moral Action and Christian Ethics*, 34.

55. See Aquinas, *Summa Theologiae* II-II, q. 66, a. 7 on theft in cases of urgent need—not, properly speaking, theft at all.

56. For further discussion of the controversy, see my paper "Regarding Silence," 195–201.

57. See Brandmüller et al., "Full Text and Explanatory Notes." The authors of the *dubia* are Cardinals Walter Brandmüller, Raymond Burke, Carlo Caffarra, and Joachim Meisner.

58. Francis, *Amoris Laetitia*, no. 305n351.

59. See Francis, *Evangelii Gaudium*, nos. 44, 47.

of the Church, on the existence of absolute moral norms that prohibit intrinsically evil acts and that are binding without exceptions." An interesting question to ask in this regard is whether it makes sense to say that a person who is divorced and remarried commits *adultery* against his or her first spouse when having sex with his or her second spouse.[60] Each sexual act in the second marriage might be seen as an ongoing and accumulating betrayal of the first marriage (in a word, adultery even years later). Or we might consider the first marriage effectively over (though not canonically dissolved), with the consequence that the former spouses just can no longer be either faithful or faithless toward one another. From this perspective, the possibility of their committing adultery toward one another has passed.

Or take the story of Susanna in chapter 13 of the Greek version of the book of Daniel.[61] Susanna refuses to submit to the wishes of two unjust judges who threaten to have her condemned to death if she does not have sex with them. *Veritatis Splendor* presents her as an "admirable witness[] of fidelity to the holy law of God even to the point of a voluntary acceptance of death."[62] The encyclical goes on: "Susanna . . . bears witness not only to her faith and trust in God but also to her obedience to the truth and to the absoluteness of the moral order. By her readiness to die a martyr, she proclaims that it is not right to do what God's law qualifies as evil in order to draw some good from it." But imagine that Susanna had submitted to having sex lest she be killed (also change the story so that she is threatened with imminent death, not a trial in which she might be rescued by the likes of Daniel). Although she is a married woman, would what she does count as "adultery"? Is that the correct description here? Such a judgment is hardly plausible—it seems, instead, grotesque—but *Veritatis Splendor* apparently takes for granted that Susanna would have been guilty of adultery, and of doing evil so that good might come of it, had she not chosen likely death.

We might also consider more complicated examples, such as cases of so-called vital maternal-fetal conflict, or more complicated rules, such as the so-called doctrine or principle of double effect.[63] The point, how-

---

60. I paraphrase here Kaveny, *Ethics at the Edges of Law*, 198. See also Cloutier and Koerpel, "Beyond the Law-Conscience Binary," 187–91.

61. I follow Porter in considering this story; see my "Moral Reasoning," 210–11.

62. John Paul II, *Veritatis Splendor*, no. 91.

63. For an extended discussion of both the notorious case of an abortion at St. Joseph's Hospital in Phoenix, Arizona in 2009 and the doctrine or principle of double

ever, should be clear by now: moral rules do not and cannot "determine a uniquely correct solution to every moral dilemma";[64] practical reasoning is accordingly more complex than applying an evaluative premise to a factual premise. At the same time, it would be a mistake to conclude that practical reasoning is thus irrational or arbitrary, a mere exercise of will. To the contrary, reasons can be given for judging that, for example, what Captain Oates did should not count as suicide, or that a married woman who submits to unwanted sex lest she be killed does not thereby commit adultery. The moral traditions to which we belong—in Alasdair MacIntyre's oft-quoted sense of historically embedded, socially embodied arguments over what goods to pursue and evils to shun[65]—give us plenty of material to work with as we seek to deepen and refine our grasp of a rule. That said, the judgments we make in difficult cases will not be dictated by the rule; our judgments will be under-determined, so to speak, by the rule as it was handed down to us. It is noteworthy that Brugger, as quoted above, presents respecting exceptionless negative norms as "an absolutely minimal demand of social justice and an essential *first step* on the way to that perfection in Christian charity called for by the Gospel."[66] Arguably, a demand of justice is that it be informed by charity and mercy *from the start*. To paraphrase an observation of Porter's, if the moral law is not interpreted in a spirit of genuine empathy and concern for neighbor, it risks inflicting injustice, for example on the woman who is a victim of sexual violence.[67] Francis's reminder "that the confessional must not be a torture chamber, but rather an encounter with the Lord's mercy" also seems germane.

---

effect, see my *Catholic Moral Philosophy in Practice and Theory*, 41–72. For the record, I agree with Porter that "the insight expressed by the Pauline principle [that evil is not to be done so that good may come], or the doctrine of double effect, is better understood as a reflection of . . . general assumptions about the limits and the extent of human responsibility, than as a decision procedure . . . for resolving any and all moral dilemmas." See Porter, *Moral Action and Christian Ethics*, 71; compare Botros, "Error about the Doctrine of Double Effect"; Keenan, "Function of the Principle of Double Effect."

64. Porter, *Moral Action and Christian Ethics*, 74.

65. MacIntyre, *After Virtue*, 222.

66. Brugger, "Catholic Social Teaching Is Catholic Moral Teaching," 522 (emphasis added).

67. Porter, "Moral Reasoning," 215. See also Porter, *Moral Action and Christian Ethics*, 195: "After two centuries of Kantian moral theory, we need to emphasize again how critically important it is that justice be tempered with mercy, even from the standpoint of justice itself."

Two objections should be anticipated before turning to the import of this line of argument for the contrast that Finnis, Brugger, and Bradley draw between CST and Catholic moral teaching. The first objection is that the moral theory that Finnis helped develop together with Joseph Boyle and Germain Grisez is not Kantian and accordingly not vulnerable to Porter's polemic against a Kantian understanding of practical reason. Finnis, Boyle, and Grisez sought to recover natural law from centuries of misunderstanding. Whether they did so, or instead invented a new form of natural law (the so-called new natural law), is notoriously subject to debate,[68] but it is indisputable that they intended to displace the Kantian imperative to respect persons in favor of a Thomistic imperative to respect the goods of persons. The second objection is that the "object" of an action is not so indeterminate as I have claimed it to be. To the contrary, as Pope John Paul II writes in *Veritatis Splendor*:

> In order to be able to grasp the object of an act which specifies that act morally, it is . . . necessary to place oneself *in the perspective of the acting person*. . . . By the object of a given moral act, then, one cannot mean a process or an event of the merely physical order. . . . Rather, that object is the proximate end of a deliberate decision which determines the act of willing on the part of the acting person.[69]

In Finnis's words, "for moral assessment and judgment, the act is just what it is . . . as intended, i.e. under the description it has in the proposal which the agent adopts by choice."[70]

The response to the first objection is that the new natural law (whether in the sense that it is renewed or that it is novel) is Kantian in the way that matters for present purposes. In fact, the new natural lawyers recommend their theory in part because, according to them, the Thomistic imperative to respect the goods of persons provides firmer guidelines and more "absolutes" than the Kantian imperative to respect persons.[71] This chapter is not the place to summarize the new natural

---

68. See, for example, McInerney, "Principles of Natural Law."
69. John Paul II, *Veritatis Splendor*, no. 78.
70. Finnis, "Object and Intention in Moral Judgments," 18.
71. See Gómez-Lobo, *Morality and the Human Goods*, 129. Compare Boyle, "Aquinas, Kant, and Donagan on Moral Principles," 408; Boyle, "Sanctity of Life and Suicide," 234–35, 246–47. Boyle writes at 235 in the latter paper: "[Kantian] procedures allow for far too few moral absolutes."

law.[72] Suffice it to say, its basic rule is that "what one should do is to promote and never violate" the basic goods of human life, such as life itself, knowledge, and friendship, among others.[73] The theory also requires us to believe, however, not only that there are such basic goods evident to all upon reflection, but that we grasp them with enough content that they can be action-guiding.

Porter is again an insightful guide. She allows that "the claim that these goods are self-evidently manifest as such as soon as they are experienced is indeed plausible with respect to some of these, such as life or knowledge," but she goes on to note that, "even with respect to such goods . . . , [the new natural lawyers] find it necessary to qualify what these goods comprise in order to show how certain moral conclusions flow from them."[74] Her example is how the good of life "is expanded to include procreation, in order to justify the claim that the use of contraception involves 'acting against' the good of life."[75] What is difficult to see is how our practical knowledge that life is a basic good "can yield specific moral conclusions" all on its own, without question-begging stipulations.[76] Putting contraception aside, consider Captain Oates again. Was his wandering away from his companions an attack on the good of life? The answer is hardly obvious. Or, to consider other goods, just how to specify the key ingredients of, say, the good of family, and to determine what counts as an attack against this good? Must a family comprise "mothering and fathering"?[77] Would allowing gay couples to adopt children violate, or promote, the good of family life? And so forth. The point is that indeterminacy is endemic to the new natural law, not eliminated by it.

The response to the second objection is twofold. First, a purely first-person account of human action appears indefensible.[78] It is a mistake to reduce the object of an action to what is physically done—John Paul II is right in *Veritatis Splendor* that "the object of a given moral act" is not just "a process or an event of the merely physical order"—but it is

72. See, for a beginning, my *Catholic Moral Philosophy in Practice and Theory*, 181–87.
73. Boyle, "Aquinas, Kant, and Donagan on Moral Principles," 407.
74. Porter, *Nature as Reason*, 128.
75. Porter, *Nature as Reason*, 128.
76. Porter, *Nature as Reason*, 129.
77. Compare Gómez-Lobo, *Morality and the Human Goods*, 14.
78. I take this wording from Tollefsen, "Is a Purely First Person Account of Human Action Defensible?"

equally a mistake to reduce the object of an action to what the agent proposes to do, as if the specification of the object depended solely on the agent's purpose. Yet this is just what the new natural lawyers do. Recall Finnis's claim, quoted above, that "for moral assessment and judgment, the act is just what it is ... as intended, i.e. under the description it has in the proposal which the agent adopts by choice."[79] The upshot is that, for example, as Finnis, Grisez, and Boyle claim, "when someone chooses to do a craniotomy on a baby to save his or her mother's life in an obstetrical predicament, the morally relevant description of the act would not include killing the baby."[80]

The problem here is that, in the words of a critic of the new natural law, "the object of the will is constituted *both* by the choice of the acting person *and* by the physical structure of the act"—not just its physical/material component, but also not just the acting person's purpose.[81] In other words, *what* one can say one intends is constrained by *what* it is one is physically doing, that is, the physical structure of the action.[82] One cannot reasonably and intelligibly say that, in choosing to set in motion a process or event that one knows constitutes killing, what one is doing is not killing because one does not intend to kill and has some other object in mind instead. As Elizabeth Anscombe remarks, "Circumstances, and the immediate facts about the means you are choosing to your ends, dictate what descriptions of your intention you must admit."[83]

Second, however, concede for the sake of argument that a purely first-person account of human action is defensible. The indeterminacy of the "object" of an action—that is, the generic concept in terms of which it is correctly described—is not thereby eliminated. If how to describe an action is not always clear to third-person observers, why should we suppose it is always clear from the first-person perspective? Otherwise put, why should we *not* suppose that the acting person is sometimes beset with the same problem as observers? Do agents always just know, perspicaciously and infallibly, under what description they propose to act or have

---

79. Finnis, "Object and Intention in Moral Judgments," 18.
80. Finnis et al., "'Direct' and 'Indirect,'" 29.
81. Austriaco, "Abortion in a Case of Pulmonary Arterial Hypertension," 514.
82. Compare Murphy, "Principle of Double Effect," 200: "The intention with which the agent acts is constrained by the structure or design or nature of the act-type"; and Jensen, "Getting Inside the Acting Person," 468: "Causal structures are the material conditions out of which intentions are made."
83. Anscombe, "Action, Intention, and 'Double Effect,'" 23.

acted? For example, would how to describe Oates's action be resolved if only we could query him? The literary example of Huckleberry Finn suggests that the first-person perspective may not be at any advantage. To the contrary, time and again, the words at Huck's disposal—the "deep conceptual attitudes," to take a phrase from Iris Murdoch, that constitute the moral vision of the slaveholding society in which he was born and raised—limit what he can grasp and articulate and thus work against the development of his own point of view.[84]

Here is the upshot. If practical reasoning is more complex than Finnis allows—which it surely is—then a hard distinction between "authoritative *moral* teachings" and "matters of prudential judgment" cannot be sustained. In other words, the line between CST and Catholic moral teaching on abortion, contraception, euthanasia, and so forth is blurrier than Finnis, Brugger, and Bradley allow.

To recall, Bradley and Brugger affirm that the magisterium's

> authoritative *moral* teachings . . . can and do include the excluding of certain moral objects as always and everywhere wrongful to choose . . . ; and that the propositions asserted in these latter teachings are practically prior to matters of prudential judgment that men and women of good faith can and do disagree upon without any fallacy in their thinking or objective disorders in their willing.[85]

As we also have seen, Brugger and Finnis make much of the difference between how negative moral norms and affirmative moral norms bind: *semper et pro semper* vs. *semper sed non pro semper*. As Finnis goes on to observe, "The application of affirmative moral norms of justice is always dependent, therefore, on assessment of the circumstances, an assessment that, though morally guided, always involves some judgment about facts and likelihoods,"[86] which all three authors are quick to note does not fall within the special competence of the magisterium. Instead, following Vatican II, they emphasize, in Finnis's words, "the lay role of forming reasonable judgments about the facts, causalities, trends, and consequences at stake in applications of all the affirmative responsibilities commanded by the Lord and taught by the Church."[87]

---

84. For discussion, see my paper "When Words Fail Us." See also Murdoch, "Vision and Choice in Morality," 43.
85. Bradley and Brugger, "Introduction," 7–8.
86. Finnis, "Radical Critique of Catholic Social Teaching," 557.
87. Finnis, "Radical Critique of Catholic Social Teaching," 577.

Resisting "overly absolutist" prescriptions about what justice demands—for example, the rejection of markets in carbon credits, as Francis has suggested[88]—does seem well-warranted. But here Finnis, Brugger, and Bradley are simply in agreement with moral theologians whom they in other regards dismiss. Charles Curran, for example, observes that modern Catholic social teaching changed over the twentieth century to recognize "significant gray areas" with respect to the proper resolution of social ills.[89] By contrast, Curran also observes that "contemporary official Catholic teaching on sexual ethics" admits "very little gray area."[90] Typically, "Something is either forbidden or permitted," whatever its complexity.[91]

Finnis, Brugger, and Bradley seem to think that this contrast is just as it should be, following from the difference between how negative moral norms and affirmative moral norms bind. In light of the indeterminacy of moral rules, however, this chapter has pointed out gray areas around adultery and suicide, only as examples. No doubt other examples could be multiplied. To be clear, the difference between how negative moral norms and affirmative moral norms bind—*semper et pro semper* vs. *semper sed non pro semper*—does indeed generally distinguish CST from Catholic moral teaching. But it is not the case that only CST admits reasonable disagreement; Catholic moral teaching does as well. I leave it open to debate whether Finnis is right that, as I quoted him above,

> *because* the diagnosing of causalities, effects and side-effects, risks and probabilities is an inherently difficult and often uncertain matter, it is entirely possible for informed and well-catechized Catholics in good faith to hold *diametrically opposed* views on, say, climate change, migration policy, sentencing policy, healthcare policy, the organization of employment, laws of inheritance and taxation, and so on, while respecting all relevant moral principles and norms.[92]

Perhaps the philosopher protests too much, though that would be the subject for a different paper. What this chapter has argued is that there is an ineliminable gray area—on account of there being, in Porter's words,

---

88. Francis, *Laudato Si'*, no. 171. But see further Peñalver, "Carbon Trading and the Morality of Markets in *Laudato Si'*."
89. Curran, "Catholic Social and Sexual Teaching," 439.
90. Curran, "Catholic Social and Sexual Teaching," 440, 439.
91. Curran, "Catholic Social and Sexual Teaching," 440.
92. Finnis, "Radical Critique of Catholic Social Teaching," 573.

"an ineliminable element of judgment"[93]—in the application of *negative* norms. It follows, *pace* the apocalyptic language accompanying some magisterial moral teaching,[94] that not every disagreement on neuralgic moral issues is a sign of the degeneracy and corruption of the modern world.[95] Instead, given the complexity of the issues, disagreement is to be expected both among people of good will and even among faithful Catholics.

Questioning the Premises

As we have seen, Finnis, Brugger, and Bradley take a deflationary view of the authority of CST. Finnis goes the furthest of the three. According to him:

> *Popes and other pastors should generally state only [CST's] timeless moral norms and general moral principles; if they teach anything beyond these as CST, it should always be in* **hypothetical** *form. Pastors should generally not propose even hypothetical CST teachings without first having every disputable question of economic causality, other social consequences, or natural-scientific facts, carefully and even-handedly* **debated** *in their presence by competent lay Catholics who hold opposing positions about those matters.*[96]

Moreover, "The Church's pastors should more or less completely abandon attempts to *teach* diagnoses of the current causes of the evils that afflict their societies and humanity as a whole, and attempts to teach that the Church has 'solutions' to those supposed causes."[97] More modestly (and sounding remarkably like Pope Francis), "In the field of CST, pastors' primary concern should be to *inform* and *animate* the consciences of the faithful."[98]

This deflationary view of the authority of CST seems to depend, however, on the juxtaposition of CST with Catholic moral teaching. In that juxtaposition, Catholic moral teaching is free from reasonable

---

93. Porter, "Moral Reasoning," 216.

94. See, for example, Pope John Paul II's encyclical *Evangelium Vitae*, no. 28: "We are facing an enormous and dramatic clash between good and evil, death and life, the 'culture of death' and the 'culture of life.'"

95. See further Porter, "Moral Reasoning," 216–19.

96. Finnis, "Radical Critique of Catholic Social Teaching," 572.

97. Finnis, "Radical Critique of Catholic Social Teaching," 572.

98. Finnis, "Radical Critique of Catholic Social Teaching," 574. Compare Francis, *Amoris Laetitia*, no. 37: "We have been called to form consciences, not to replace them."

disagreement; CST is rife if not overrun with it. In syllogistic form, the logic seems to be, roughly:

> If a teaching admits reasonable disagreement, its authority is limited.
> CST admits reasonable disagreement.
> Therefore, CST's authority is limited.

But what follows for the authority of CST once it is acknowledged that Catholic moral teaching, too, admits reasonable disagreement? Does the same logic hold for Catholic moral teaching, or do we have reason instead to question the premises and formulate them anew?

This chapter's interest is the authority of CST, not the authority of magisterial moral teaching on abortion, contraception, and so forth. With respect to the teachings of the ordinary, non-definitive magisterium, I take it for granted that the faithful Catholic, whether lay or clergy, is enjoined to what has traditionally been called *obsequium religiosum*, which appears as well in the documents of Vatican II.[99] Just what *obsequium* means, however, is a matter of some controversy.[100] Helpfully for present purposes, the distinguished canon lawyer Ladislas Orsy proposes that "the discussion whether [*obsequium*] means precisely 'respect' or 'submission' works on a wrong assumption, which is that the Council indeed meant it in a specific and precise way."[101] According to Orsy, what is called for in all cases is an attitude of "love of God and love of His Church," which will be in need of specification in every concrete case. Sometimes submission could be called for, sometimes respect, "depending on the progress which the Church has made in clarifying its own beliefs."[102]

Following Orsy, here, then, is a closing suggestion: there is no one, overarching answer to the question of the authority of CST for the faithful Catholic. Instead, different social teachings, on diverse topics (e.g., the rights of labor), will be found and come to have varying authority as the faithful receive, examine, and prayerfully consider them.[103] By contrast, Finnis seems to want to raze the *tradition* of Catholic social teaching: more precisely, to reduce it to a set of principles of indeterminate

99. See, for example, Paul VI, *Lumen Gentium*, no. 25.

100. See Bretzke, *Handbook of Roman Catholic Moral Terms*, 163–64.

101. Orsy, "Magisterium," 490. Compare Dulles, *Craft of Theology*, 110–11; Sullivan, *Creative Fidelity*, 23–24.

102. Orsy, "Magisterium," 490. Orsy does not specify what he means by 'Church.' Perhaps he would reply that there is no one definite sense, but it is noteworthy that he speaks more than once in his paper of "the whole Church" (e.g., 483, 484, 487).

103. Compare Bersnak, "Magisterium and Social Doctrine," esp. 327–30.

application. Another observation of Curran's is to the point: "The unofficial canon of Catholic social teaching today"—the documents, or parts of documents, that are remembered and invoked and discussed, as opposed to the many that have fallen into oblivion—"has been brought about by the reception of the church itself and by subsequent popes." In other words, "The whole church has played a role in what is viewed today as constituting the body of official Catholic social teaching."[104] From this perspective, we can understand why Jeb Bush's seeming dismissiveness toward *Laudato Si'* was inappropriate—it did not exhibit an attitude of "love of God and love of His Church"—while Dreher's insistence that Bush must be submissive was also off the mark. Bush would not have been wrong to want to read the document and to examine and consider its teachings with the rest of the Church; to the contrary, the affirmative norms of love of God and love of Church enjoin just such use of critical intelligence. Moreover, it may be that what calls for consideration in a document like *Laudato Si'* are not only or even primarily the normative claims that it makes, but the faith-filled vision it presents of human beings' relationship with creation and with one another. *Laudato Si'* at least, if not also other CST encyclicals and magisterial documents, seeks to shape its readers' ways of seeing the world.[105] That aspect of CST goes missing in analyses focused on principles and policies.[106]

Bibliography

Anscombe, Elizabeth. "Action, Intention, and 'Double Effect.'" *Proceedings of the American Catholic Philosophical Association* 56 (1982) 12–25.

Aristotle. *Nicomachean Ethics*. Translated by Joe Sachs. Newburyport, MA: Focus, 2002.

Austriaco, Nicanor Pier Giorgio. "Abortion in a Case of Pulmonary Arterial Hypertension: A Test Case for Two Rival Theories of Human Action." *National Catholic Bioethics Quarterly* 11 (2011) 503–18.

Bersnak, P. Bracy. "The Magisterium and Social Doctrine: Weighing and Interpreting the Documents." *Journal of Catholic Social Thought* 19 (2022) 321–40.

Botros, Sophie. "An Error about the Doctrine of Double Effect." *Philosophy* 74 (1999) 71–83.

---

104. Curran, "Catholic Social and Sexual Teaching," 426.

105. On this point, see Miller, "Higher Education and the Ecological Crisis," esp. 134–37.

106. I thank Kathleen Maas Weigert, Jennifer Reed-Bouley, and M. Therese Lysaught for comments on drafts of this chapter. Thanks also to Bill Murphy for inviting me to write it.

Boyle, Joseph M., Jr. "Aquinas, Kant, and Donagan on Moral Principles." *New Scholasticism* 58 (1984) 391–408.

———. "Sanctity of Life and Suicide: Tensions and Developments within Common Morality." In *Suicide and Euthanasia: Historical and Contemporary Themes*, edited by Baruch Brody, 221–50. Dordrecht: Kluwer, 1989.

Bradley, Gerard V. "How Bishops Should Teach Catholic Social Doctrine." In *Catholic Social Teaching: A Volume of Scholarly Essays*, edited by Gerard V. Bradley and E. Christian Brugger, 528–47. Cambridge: Cambridge University Press, 2019.

Bradley, Gerard V., and E. Christian Brugger, eds. *Catholic Social Teaching: A Volume of Scholarly Essays*. Cambridge: Cambridge University Press, 2019.

———. "Introduction: Contingency, Continuity, Development, and Change in Modern Catholic Social Teaching." In *Catholic Social Teaching: A Volume of Scholarly Essays*, edited by Gerard V. Bradley and E. Christian Brugger, 1–8. Cambridge: Cambridge University Press, 2019.

Brandmüller, Walter, et al. "Full Text and Explanatory Notes of Cardinals' Questions on 'Amoris Laetitia.'" *National Catholic Register*, November 14, 2016. https://www.ncregister.com/blog/full-text-and-explanatory-notes-of-cardinals-questions-on-amoris-laetitia.

Bretzke, James T. *Handbook of Roman Catholic Moral Terms*. Washington, DC: Georgetown University Press, 2013.

Brugger, E. Christian. "Catholic Social Teaching Is Catholic Moral Teaching." In *Catholic Social Teaching: A Volume of Scholarly Essays*, edited by Gerard V. Bradley and E. Christian Brugger, 509–27. Cambridge: Cambridge University Press, 2019.

Cloutier, David, and Robert Koerpel. "Beyond the Law-Conscience Binary in Catholic Moral Thought." *Journal of Moral Theology* 10 (2021) 160–93.

Congregation for the Doctrine of the Faith. *Donum Veritatis: On the Ecclesial Vocation of the Theologian*. May 24, 1990. https://www.vatican.va/roman_curia/congregations/cfaith/documents/rc_con_cfaith_doc_19900524_theologian-vocation_en.html.

Curran, Charles E. "Catholic Social and Sexual Teaching: A Methodological Comparison." *Theology Today* 44 (1988) 425–40.

Dreher, Rod. "Jeb Bush, Cafeteria Catholic." *American Conservative*, June 16, 2015. https://www.theamericanconservative.com/jeb-bush-cafeteria-catholic/.

Dulles, Avery. *The Craft of Theology: From Symbol to System*. New York: Crossroad, 1992.

Finnis, John. "Object and Intention in Moral Judgments according to Aquinas." *Thomist* 55 (1991) 1–27.

———. "A Radical Critique of Catholic Social Teaching." In *Catholic Social Teaching: A Volume of Scholarly Essays*, edited by Gerard V. Bradley and E. Christian Brugger, 548–84. Cambridge: Cambridge University Press, 2019.

Finnis, John, et al. "'Direct' and 'Indirect': A Reply to Critics of Our Action Theory." *Thomist* 65 (2001) 1–44.

Francis. *Amoris Laetitia: On Love in the Family*. Vatican City: Libreria Editrice Vaticana, 2016. https://www.vatican.va/content/dam/francesco/pdf/apost_exhortations/documents/papa-francesco_esortazione-ap_20160319_amoris-laetitia_en.pdf.

———. *Evangelii Gaudium: On the Proclamation of the Gospel in Today's World*. Vatican City: Libreria Editrice Vaticana, 2013. https://www.vatican.va/content/francesco/en/apost_exhortations/documents/papa-francesco_esortazione-ap_20131124_evangelii-gaudium.html.

———. *Laudato Si': On the Climate Crisis*. Vatican City: Libreria Editrice Vaticana, 2015. https://www.vatican.va/content/francesco/en/encyclicals/documents/papa-francesco_20150524_enciclica-laudato-si.html.

Gómez-Lobo, Alfonso. *Morality and the Human Goods: An Introduction to Natural Law Ethics*. Washington, DC: Georgetown University Press, 2002.

Hare, R. M. *The Language of Morals*. Oxford: Oxford University Press, 1952.

Jensen, Steven J. "Getting Inside the Acting Person." *International Philosophical Quarterly* 50 (2010) 461–71.

John Paul II. *Evangelium Vitae: The Gospel of Life*. Vatican City: Libreria Editrice Vaticana, 1995. https://www.vatican.va/content/john-paul-ii/en/encyclicals/documents/hf_jp-ii_enc_25031995_evangelium-vitae.html.

———. *Veritatis Splendor: The Splendor of the Truth*. Vatican City: Libreria Editrice Vaticana, 1993. https://www.vatican.va/content/john-paul-ii/en/encyclicals/documents/hf_jp-ii_enc_06081993_veritatis-splendor.html.

Kaveny, Cathleen. *Ethics at the Edges of Law: Christian Moralists and American Legal Thought*. Oxford: Oxford University Press, 2018.

———. "Intrinsic Evil and Political Responsibility: Is the Concept of Intrinsic Evil Helpful to the Catholic Voter?" In *Voting and Holiness: Catholic Perspectives on Political Participation*, edited by Nicholas P. Cafardi, 126–34. New York: Paulist, 2012.

———. *Law's Virtues: Fostering Autonomy and Solidarity in American Society*. Washington, DC: Georgetown University Press, 2012.

———. "Toward a Thomistic Perspective on Abortion and the Law in Contemporary America." *Thomist* 55 (1991) 343–96.

Keenan, James F. "The Function of the Principle of Double Effect." *Theological Studies* 54 (1993) 294–315.

Kovesi, Julius. *Moral Notions*. London: Routledge, 1967.

MacIntyre, Alsadair. *After Virtue: A Study in Moral Theory*. 2nd ed. Notre Dame: University of Notre Dame Press, 1984.

———. *A Short History of Ethics*. 2nd ed. Notre Dame: University of Notre Dame Press, 1998.

McInerney, Ralph. "The Principles of Natural Law." *American Journal of Jurisprudence* 25 (1980) 1–15.

Miller, Vincent. "Higher Education and the Ecological Crisis: Integral Ecology as a Catalyst for Critical and Creative Transdisciplinary Engagement." In *Catholic Higher Education and Catholic Social Thought*, edited by Bernard G. Prusak and Jennifer Reed-Bouley, 126–45. New York: Paulist, 2023.

Murdoch, Iris. "Vision and Choice in Morality." *Proceedings of the Aristotelian Society, Supplementary Volume* 30 (1956) 32–58.

Murphy, James G. "The Principle of Double Effect: Act-Types and Intentions." *International Philosophical Quarterly* 53 (2013) 189–205.

Orsy, Ladislas. "Magisterium: Assent and Dissent." *Theological Studies* 48 (1987) 473–97.

Paul VI. *Lumen Gentium: Dogmatic Constitution on the Church*. Vatican City: Libreria Editrice Vaticana, 1964. https://www.vatican.va/archive/hist_councils/ii_vatican_council/documents/vat-ii_const_19641121_lumen-gentium_en.html.

Peñalver, Eduardo M. "Carbon Trading and the Morality of Markets in *Laudato Si'*." In *Care for the World: Laudato Si' and Catholic Social Thought in an Era of Climate Crisis*, edited by Frank Pasquale, 41–55. Cambridge: Cambridge University Press, 2019.

Porter, Jean. *Moral Action and Christian Ethics*. Cambridge: Cambridge University Press, 1995.

———. "Moral Reasoning, Authority, and Community in *Veritatis Splendor*." *Annual of the Society of Christian Ethics* 15 (1995) 201–19.

———. *Nature as Reason: A Thomistic Theory of the Natural Law*. Grand Rapids: Eerdmans, 2005.

Prusak, Bernard G. *Catholic Moral Philosophy in Practice and Theory: An Introduction*. New York: Paulist, 2016.

———. "Regarding Silence: Ethics and Ecclesiology in Two Recent Controversies." In *One Bread, One Body, One Church: Essays on the Ecclesia of Christ Today in Honor of Bernard P. Prusak*, edited by Christopher Cimorelli and Daniel Minch, 191–208. Leuven: Peeters, 2021.

———. Review of *Catholic Social Teaching: A Volume of Scholarly Essays*, edited by Gerard V. Bradley and E. Christian Brugger. *Commonweal*, September 2020.

———. "When Words Fail Us: Reexamining the Conscience of Huckleberry Finn." *Journal of Aesthetic Education* 45 (2011) 1–22.

Salzman, Todd A., and Michael Lawler. "*Amoris Laetitia*: Toward a Methodological and Anthropological Integration of Catholic Social and Sexual Ethics." *Theological Studies* 79 (2018) 634–52.

Stern, Mark Joseph. "Jeb Bush Rejects His Church's Teachings on Climate Change. Why Not on Marriage Equality?" *Slate*, June 17, 2015. https://slate.com/human-interest/2015/06/jeb-bush-rejects-the-popes-climate-change-teachings-why-not-marriage-equality.html.

Sullivan, Francis A. *Creative Fidelity: Weighing and Interpreting Documents of the Magisterium*. New York: Paulist, 1996.

Tollefsen, Christopher. "Is a Purely First Person Account of Human Action Defensible?" *Ethical Theory and Moral Practice* 9 (2006) 441–60.

11

Integralism, Political Catholicism, and Democracy in the Modern West

JULIAN G. WALLER, GEORGE WASHINGTON UNIVERSITY

Abstract: The emergence of a strain of contemporary Catholic thought known as "integralism," (also termed "neo-integralism") has engendered a fierce backlash among intellectuals, political commentators, and policy-oriented writers in the United States. While the focus for many scholars has been on integralism's theological-political claims or its relevance as a suspected "Trojan Horse" for political authoritarianism, less has been made of its position as an ideational project in specific dialogue with other forms of illiberal political thought, as well as an intellectual reaction to secularization and twenty-first-century "post-Christian" politics. This chapter briefly reviews the current intellectual ecosystem of integralist thought in the Anglo-American context, and then identifies and illustrates the ways in which contemporary integralism fits into the broader pattern of "postliberal" ideological ferment, especially in the Catholic context. Finally, the chapter suggests the issue-areas and schools of thought to which this intellectual movement is likely to find most purchase and cross-pollination within the structures of actually-existing democracies today, a regime-type to which its relationship remains sharply debated.

Introduction

THE EMERGENCE OF A strain of Catholic thought known as "integralism," or "neo-integralism" among a small set of theologians, philosophers, and political thinkers in the Western world has engendered a fierce backlash by both Catholic and non-Catholic intellectuals and commentators, starting in the late 2010s.[1] Both scholarly and public engagement has focused largely on either integralism's primary theological and ecclesiastical claims or engaged with assertions about its plausibility as a "Trojan Horse" for outright political authoritarianism.[2] In this sense, integralism has most often been discussed either as a philosophical or a barefaced political project headed by a curious set of contrarian, conservative Catholic academics.[3] From a place of considerable obscurity, the idea—or looming "specter," depending on one's point of view—of integralism has captured the imaginations of thinkers across the Anglophone world.[4]

Given the dominance of these framings, somewhat less has been made of integralism's position as an *ideational project* in specific dialogue with other forms of "illiberal" political thought, as well as an unexpected, but genuine, intellectual reaction to processes of secularization and post-Christian politics in the modern West.[5] That is, there remains many analytical vantage-points from which to approach integralism that are

---

1. For a selection of academic critiques with reviews of the relevant scholarly and commentary literature, see Ménard and Su, "Liberalism, Catholic Integralism, and the Question of Religious Freedom"; Frohnen, "Common Good Constitutionalism and the Problem of Administrative Absolutism"; Schwartzman and Wilson, "Unreasonableness of Catholic Integralism."

2. For prior critiques of integralism as it relates to political regime, see, for example, Waller, "Quirks in the Neo-Integralist Vision"; Barnes and Jones, "Decision against Carl Schmitt"; Barnes, "Ahmari, Vermeule, and Burying Liberalism for Good"; Patterson, "After Republican Virtue"; Patterson, "Why Integralism Is an Ideology of Despair."

3. Rooney, "Illiberal Integralist Elites"; Patterson, "No to Neo-Integralism."

4. On the usage of the "specter of integralism" as either a danger or a promise see, for example, Storck, "What Is Integralism?"; Turowsky, "Appeal and Danger of Integralism."

5. For conceptual discussions of "illiberalism," see Waller, "Distinctions with a Difference"; Laruelle, "Illiberalism." A working definition of the concept is "a modern ideational (or ideological) family that perceives itself in reaction and opposition to philosophical liberalism, distrusts checking or minoritarian political institutions formed by apolitical experts, and promotes a variety of collective, hierarchical, majoritarian, national-level, and/or culturally-integrative approaches to contemporary political society," taken from Waller, "Distinctions with a Difference."

neither simply theological nor purely political disputes, but rather approach its broader place within a critical, illiberal intellectual ecosystem developing alongside and in dialogue with it, both in the United States and elsewhere.[6] This is a particularly vital task, as it confronts directly the question of relevance—for whom and in what ways does it matter to even know what integralism is and entails, if one is not a theologian, speculative philosopher, or someone with a curious interest in anachronistic monarchism and other hypothetical flavors of ideal-typed political regime.[7]

For evident reasons, this sort of assessment is therefore a regrettable lacuna prominent in scholarly discussions of integralism today. There remain very few integralist thinkers proper, and its prospects as a mass movement in modern Western societies are negligible over the short-term to medium-term. Yet in many ways, the fact that there is only a narrow field of intellectuals and theorists that fully embrace integralism today is largely beside the point. Integralism is part of a broader intellectual movement of political reaction that cross-pollinates with diverse streams of ideational thought discontented with the contemporary social and political order found in the West and can be understood in these terms with greater analytic leverage when placed in an appropriate, ideological context.[8]

The phenomenon of integralism as both an ideology and a framing worldview has important theoretical, theological, philosophical, elite behavioral, and symbolic components, all of which can and should be studied and discussed directly, even if the fullest expression of integralism in real-world politics is unlikely to come to pass in the near future.[9]

---

6. On developing contemporary illiberal intellectual ecosystems see, for example, Waller, "Illiberalism and Postliberalism"; Addison, "Fusionism Relitigated"; Buzogány and Varga, "Illiberal Thought Collectives and Policy Networks in Hungary and Poland"; Varga and Buzogány, "Two Faces of the 'Global Right'"; Johnston, "Rise of Illiberal Conservatism."

7. Monarchism, "clerico-fascism," and other descriptors of authoritarian political regimes are sometimes used to describe integralist political visions, although many of these claims rely on extrapolation and historical argument rather than evidence from integralists themselves, with some exceptions. For a discussion of integralism and how it may or may not fit within modern conceptions of representative government and democracy, see Waller, "Quirks in the Neo-Integralist Vision." For discussions of classical political forms that have been a point of interest among integralist or integralist-adjacent writers, see Deneen, *Regime Change*; Waller, "Classical Political Forms, the Mixed Regime, and the State of Emergency—Roman, Byzantine, Muscovite?"

8. Waller, "Illiberalism and Postliberalism"; Addison, "Fusionism Relitigated."

9. Patterson, "An Awkward Alliance."

Indeed, integralism itself is no longer confined to low-viewership online blogs, but is widely commented on by others within a diverse ecosystem of illiberal right-wing, "dissident," and "postliberal" political thought, especially in the United States and Great Britain.[10] A raft of recent publications, taking a broadly postliberal approach to critique, while engaging with or informed by deeper integralist thought, has emerged since the early 2020s.[11] Focusing on those who are in full agreement with either the personal politics and goals of integralists specifically, or the broader philosophical framework in general, misses a much more dynamic ideational space in which integralist ideas are simply one element of a broader environment.

Indeed, integralism *qua* Catholic political thought (or a specific form thereof) also works in a more holistic and entrepreneurial manner, acting as a constructive moral or political imperative for new thinkers seeking coherence in a still-inchoate environment innovating illiberal ideas and aspirations within modern liberal democracies.[12] That is, integralism should not simply be ignored due to its more radical ideological and political-theological claims. To the concern of some, and the interest of others, it has found special purchase among illiberal elites pushing the boundaries of the politically-possible and generating new ideas for a far wider spectrum of viewpoints about 21st century politics, law, and society.[13] Indeed, the liberal political philosopher Kevin Vallier has noted much the same thing, arguing that integralism is in important ways, "the most intellectually sophisticated and long-standing Christian anti-liberalism."[14]

This chapter is organized to provide the reader with a practical view of integralism as an illiberal political ideology, its position in the broader milieu of critical "postliberal" thought, and its place as a guiding force for more substantive engagement with contemporary politics and society as a version of modern elite "political Catholicism." It first briskly reviews the current intellectual ecosystem of explicitly integralist thought in the

---

10. See, for example: Waller, "Illiberal Right Moves beyond Critique"; Harrington, "Am I Really a Threat to Democracy?"; Roussinos, "Tories against Democracy"; Reno, "Return of the Strong Gods."

11. For a collection of recent postliberal monographs, see Ahmari, *Tyranny, Inc.*; Rufo, *America's Cultural Revolution*; Deneen, *Regime Change*; Harrington, *Feminism against Progress*; Vermeule, *Common Good Constitutionalism.*

12. Laruelle, "Illiberalism"; Varga and Buzogány, "Family Tree of Illiberalism."

13. Waller, "Quirks in the Neo-Integralist Vision."

14. Vallier, "Fairness Argument against Catholic Integralism."

Anglo-American world and what is meant by the term. It then identifies and illustrates the ways in which contemporary integralism fits within the broader array of postliberal ideological ferment. Finally, it suggests the ways in which this intellectual movement is likely to find the most purchase and cross-pollination within the structures of actually-existing democracies today.

Perhaps surprisingly, given the rather confined set of thinkers promoting integralism as a full-fledged approach to politics and society, this ideological framework has a great deal of impact when understood in the broader context of general illiberal and postliberal thought.[15] This is especially the case for those seeking to revive a form of elite political Catholicism in American circles that goes beyond critiques and diagnoses of modern societal problems. This is true even as the fullest claims of the integralist viewpoint are very likely to be well beyond probable reach for real politics in real modern societies.

Summarizing Integralism

It is not difficult to find extensive summaries and genealogies of contemporary integralist thought, both from proponents and detractors.[16] The purpose of this chapter is not to rehash these excellent overview efforts, but it is relevant to provide a definitional baseline for unfamiliar readers. The specific contours of what modern integralism consists of remain debated by several groups of scholars and theorists, and the degrees and ways in which it speaks to specific academic and theoretical disciplines are still contested or uncertain.[17] Despite this, we can with reasonable clarity provide an initial assessment of what forms the unifying features of this political-theological framework, as well as where it has been most influential thus far.

---

15. Sajó et al., *Routledge Handbook of Illiberalism*.

16. For a small selection of review articles see, for example, MacDougald, "Catholic Debate over Liberalism"; Patterson, "After Republican Virtue"; Pinkoski, "How Not to Challenge the Integralists"; Maas, "Coming Anti-Catholicism."

17. For a review from a political theory perspective, see Vallier, *All the Kingdoms of the World*; Vallier, "Political Liberals vs. Integralists."

Assessing Core Definitions

The core of integralist thought can be identified in the writings of a small subset of theologians and philosophers, including Fr. Thomas Crean, Alan Fimister, Thomas Pink, Fr. Edmund Waldstein and a small but active set of online writers at *The Josias* online publication.[18] Elaborations of integralism's legal and political application and ramifications have, in turn, been broadly promoted by the constitutional law scholar Adrian Vermeule, the political scientist Gladden Pappin, and the legal scholar Patrick Smith. Outside of this group, a closely-related group of scholars that are associated with the integralist project—but do not necessarily assume the label—include postliberal philosophers such as Chad Pecknold, Patrick Deneen, and others.[19]

A separate group agreeing to some elements of primary integralist claims (especially in regards to theology), while rejecting others (primarily in terms of its orientation to politics), include those tied to the *New Polity* journal such as D. C. Schindler, Marc Barnes, Andrew Willard Jones, and others.[20] This group, which is related to the "*Communio*" strand of conservative Catholic thought, has sometimes described itself as integralist, other times as postliberals, and both in opposition to the former sets of writers around the project at *The Josias*.[21] Finally, an integralist-associated movement in the legal field, spearheaded by Vermeule and his coauthor, the Irish legal scholar Conor Casey, have put forward a "common-good constitutional" or "common-good conservative" approach to contemporary politics in the Anglo-American world that has found quick purchase beyond the confines of integralism and its metaphysical and theological claims proper.[22]

Major statements on the core precepts of integralism are not difficult to find, although they differ in degree. For example, *The Josias* web publication attempts a curt definition of "Catholic integralism" as "a tradition of thought that rejects the liberal separation of politics from concern with the end of human life, holding that political rule must order

---

18. See https://thejosias.com/.
19. See https://postliberalorder.substack.com/.
20. See https://newpolity.com/.
21. Hanby, "Are We Postliberal Yet?"; Barnes, "Ahmari, Vermeule, and Burying Liberalism for Good."
22. Vermeule, *Common Good Constitutionalism*; Casey and Vermeule, "Myths of Common Good Constitutionalism."

man to his final goal. Since, however, man has both a temporal and an eternal end, integralism holds that there are two powers that rule him: a temporal power and a spiritual power. And since man's temporal end is subordinated to his eternal end, the temporal power must be subordinated to the spiritual power."[23] This also is the definition followed in a published volume of essays edited by *The Josias* contributors Fr. Waldstein and Peter Kwasniewski.[24]

A second definition comes from a recent "manual" publication by Fr. Crean and Fimister. They state that integralism is: "the application to the temporal, political order of the full implications of the revelation of man's supernatural end in Christ and of the divinely established means by which it is to be attained. These implications are identified by means of the *philosophia perennis* exemplified in the fundamental principles of Saint Thomas Aquinas. Since the first principle in moral philosophy is the last end, and man's last end cannot be known except by revelation, it is only by accepting the role of handmaid of theology that political philosophy can be adequately constituted."[25]

Elsewhere, they write that "in an ecclesiastical context the term Integralism (and its variant Integrism) is . . . used to denote an uncompromising adherence to the Social Kingship of Christ, that is, an insistence upon the moral duty of men and societies toward the true religion and toward the one Church of Christ . . . [and] is applied to the tendency to see Scholasticism, and more specifically Thomism, no less than the imperishable Patristic Age, as a completed and indispensable stage in Catholic thought which must be assimilated and appropriated as one's own by any authentically ecclesiastical writer of a later age."[26]

A third definition comes from Thomas Storck, a Catholic theorist of distributism, who writes in 2022 that:

> Integralism is essentially nothing but adherence to all the teachings of the Catholic Church on faith and morals, something which, as Catholics, we are always obliged to do. Specifically, integralism is distinguished by three chief points: (1) adherence to the Church's teaching on the social order and, in particular, to the restatement of that teaching by Pope Leo XIII in the late 19th century; (2) recognition that religion is not merely a private

---

23. For reference, see Waldstein, "Integralism in Three Sentences."
24. Waldstein and Kwasniewski, *Integralism and the Common Good*.
25. Crean and Fimister, *Integralism*, sec. Back Cover.
26. Crean and Fimister, *Integralism*, 5–6.

matter, and so discourse about God, good and evil, and the ultimate purpose of human life needs to take place at the level of society itself; and (3) as a result of the first two points, opposition to liberalism in all its forms.[27]

Importantly, although integralism may be ostensibly policed as a nascent (or rediscovered) philosophy by a few particular figures writing in online publications and personal blogs, these voices are trebled in influence and widened with a clear, networked relation to others working in the conservative legal field, in online conservative or "reactionary" politics and postliberal writing, and in the broader world of right-wing political Catholicism.[28]

Given this, we can say that the burgeoning contemporary political philosophy that is modern integralism and its familial ideologies is at a minimum a political-theological program that seeks to reorient political and state power towards a (Catholic) conception of the common good and away from the assumptions and practices of political liberalism in Western societies.

This claim, taken seriously, forces a reassessment of political institutions, legal frameworks, and sociocultural emphases by elite actors which often fall outside the assumptions of post-Cold War Western societies. In short, it is the attempt to make government, the political actors who inhabit it, and the policies it promotes, to be outwardly and explicitly Catholic. We may see this as a *de facto* "actually-existing integralism," instead of the narrower, formal definition preferred by some of its core proponents. In this sense, integralism provides a coherent, justifying framework for making political and social claims that are more both more radical and more traditionalist vis-à-vis the assumptions of contemporary liberal democracies, especially in the American context.

Integralism as a Program of Action

The evolving integralist program seeks to achieve its goals in a few ways, although given the relatively early stage of what amounts to an ideological thought experiment, it is not always clear what exactly the most common lines of debate are. In the more forthright positions of some integralist proponents, this takes the form of raising the Catholic Church

27. Storck, "What Is Integralism?"
28. Dueck, "New Traditionalists"; Culbreath, "Catholic Integralism after Liberalism."

as an authority superior to secular law and promoting an avowedly confessional state, sometimes with implicit monarchical goals.[29] In others, it takes on more expanded and ecumenical critiques of the professional-managerial class and the libertarian capture of conservative institutions in support of the actual, presumed socially conservative and communitarian concerns of traditional working-class constituencies.[30] The latter constitutes integralism in its social-diagnostic form, the former in its political and structural emphases.

Furthermore, both emphasize a deep illiberal tradition as their basis, taking a general, political theory-derived depiction of modern political liberalism—most popularly outlined by Patrick Deneen of the University of Notre Dame—as secretly coercive, fundamentally incoherent, and ultimately destructive of a variety of community and spiritual goods that undergird properly organized societies that contribute to true human flourishing.[31] The special motivation is that not only is liberalism a false bill of goods, but it is rapacious and cannot help itself due to its own "theological" character—and thus must be actively opposed by conscious illiberals.[32]

The difference here is partially in emphasis, but partially in goal. Whereas the more theological cast of integralist thinkers, as well as those interested primarily in the reorientation of the state towards community-based illiberalism, speak widely in terms of liberal "regimes," the spiritually destructive nature of autonomous individualism and so on, the more legally-oriented seek specific policy-redress and the safeguarding of conservative principles by reformulating or reinterpreting actually-existing systems of governance, decision-making, and rule.

The wide variety of views percolating among integralist circles today is notable, furthered by open-ended discussions and interactions online and enriched (or corrupted, depending upon one's preference)

---

29. It should be noted that some might describe this orientation as 'theocratic' in generic usage. Yet widespread hesitance of integralists or historical political Catholicism to support rule by clerics suggests that other descriptors, such as 'fundamentalist' (admittedly a pejorative in normal usage) or 'confessional,' are definitionally more appropriate. See, for example, Vermeule, "Christian Strategy"; Trabbic, "Catholic Church, the State, and Liberalism."

30. Frost, "Characterless Opportunism of the Managerial Class"; Lind, *New Class War*; Bothur, "Workingman's Case for Integralism."

31. Vermeule, "All Human Conflict Is Ultimately Theological"; Deneen, *Why Liberalism Failed*; Shadle, "Paradoxes of Postmodern Integralism."

32. Vermeule, "All Human Conflict Is Ultimately Theological."

by engagement with more unabashedly reactionary or more liberal-friendly thinkers at other points within the contemporary right's wider intellectual constellation. Yet these two specific and assuredly, if quietly, overlapping strands of thought are most common at present, and most often encountered both when reading integralists as well as referenced by their antagonists.

As noted above, the first is that of a more holistic, radical, and complete philosophy and program of neo-integralism, one that both encompasses Fr. Waldstein's particular vision of integralism as well as related forms of Catholic social corporatism and organic, distributist, and illiberal visions of the properly ordered society against the atomizing destruction of modern hegemonic liberalism.[33] This is a more international variant, undergirded by online epistemic communities on social media and based in a shared Catholicism.[34]

Integralism in Relation to the Developing Illiberal Ecosystem

The specific claims of integralism are in some ways less relevant than the ideational company with which it has found itself in during the ideological turbulent period stretching from the 2010s to the present day. Integralist thinkers have recognized this, and some have sought to broaden the framework to fit in dialogue with a variety of "postliberal" intellectual projects that have also emerged at the same time. To some degree, this is due to a shared overarching criticism of modern liberalism and the evolution of Western liberal democratic societies since the turn of the millennium.

Most of these critiques take the broad, and ill-defined label of "postliberalism." Postliberalism is a term initially developed in the United Kingdom by former left-wing and neoliberal writers who have become disenchanted with the atomization, secularism, and materialism dominant in the wake of the Cold War.[35] As a label with far less baggage than conservatism and other traditional terms to define right-wing thought, it

33. Smith, "Brick through the Window."
34. Sanchez, "Other Illiberal Catholicism."
35. See, for example, Waller, "Illiberalism and Postliberalism"; Pabst, *Demons of Liberal Democracy*. Note that "postliberalism" also refers to strain of critique in theology, although it is more narrowly specified relative to the current critical approach of many self-described postliberals. See, for example Milbank and Pabst, *Politics of Virtue*; Milbank et al., *Radical Orthodoxy*.

has been eagerly seized on by proponents—especially given the recognition that the field of critique holds far greater unanimity than a positive program *per se*.

Scholarship has labeled this discontent as a variety of "illiberalism," which conceptually delimits a wide swathe of reactive ideological development against the perceived hegemony of modern liberalism.[36] This has its own problems, as liberalism is of course a vague and contested term itself.[37] Indeed, illiberalism is distinct from simple social conservatism or traditionalism, insofar as it describes political reaction against the experience of living under economic and political liberal regimes.[38] Discontent with the core of liberalism's claims for the proper society—preferencing the perceived good of the autonomous individual raised above communal or societal goods—is the core motivation for illiberal movements and the philosophies that buttress them.[39]

Integralism thus fits nicely within a much broader frame of resistance to the encroachment of liberal ways of organizing and ordering social and political life, which have many starting points sometimes quite distinct from the Catholic ecclesial approach fundamental to the integralist project.[40] Most importantly, integralism acts as a kind of *locus referens* for Catholic variations on illiberal reaction more broadly. It provides an encompassing framework and justification for how to think about the modern world, and to give substance to why discontent with liberalism is not simply grievance, but a symptom of a path that does not need to be taken from a Christian perspective.[41]

As the demand signal for alternatives to progressive liberalism is large and growing in many parts of the Western world, the integralist approach—which forms a full denunciation of and alternative program to liberal assumptions about society—has become valuable as it meets this demand with an entire philosophical architecture, one that also asserts full orthodoxy and fittingness with the Catholic Church.

---

36. Waller, "Distinctions with a Difference"; Laruelle, "Illiberalism."
37. See, for example, Bell, "What Is Liberalism?"
38. Laruelle, "Illiberalism."
39. Waller, "Distinctions with a Difference."
40. Varga and Buzogány, "Family Tree of Illiberalism"; Hendrikse, "Rise of Neo-Illiberalism."
41. Pappin, "Contemporary Christian Criticism of Liberalism."

The Rise of Integralist-Adjacent Academic Projects

The easiest translation from integralism to other intellectual projects is through the postliberal movement among conservative philosophers. Postliberalism accepts all the critiques of liberalism offered by the integralist approach, and then asks "what next" in a more ecumenical way. For some, this remains in close alignment with the Catholic Church but is couched in less explicit terms. For others, the postliberal project transforms the critique into a list of policies and preferred political arrangements undergirded by a shared diagnosis.[42]

One example comes from the integralist/postliberal political scientist Gladden Pappin, who has worked hard at developing concrete proposals for family policy and corporate restructuring that are designed to be neutral as to religious background and easy to plug into the political and societal platforms of conservative, traditional, and center-right political actors.[43] Another effort from the philosopher Chad Pecknold seeks to identify core points of societal and collective civic worship, derived in part from research on Classical polities by Fustel de Coulanges.[44] He argues that as all societies have *de facto* state religions or quasi-religious cults, it is important to identify the civic "altars" that are inevitably raised up in any community, to promote those that lead to human flourishing and to "crush" those that are "foul" and antihuman.[45] This fits as well with arguments from Adrian Vermeule that have discussed liberalism in sacramental terms, re-enacting a "founding Festival" of Reason liturgically, complete with compulsory rituals, doctrinal loyalty, and an ersatz eschatological motivation.[46]

Postliberalism has adherents farther afield than Catholic writers seeking answers to opposing the accelerating liberalism of modern Western societies, as well. Across the Atlantic, British writers who accept the label have taken on the integralist diagnosis of society, as well as the Catholic postliberal conception of a society that will, one way or another, choose something to worship.[47] The "reactionary feminist" writer Mary

---

42. Pappin, "Return to Normalcy."

43. Pappin, "Family Policy Imperative"; Pappin, "Corporatism for the Twenty-First Century."

44. Coulanges, *Ancient City*.

45. Speech at "Restoring a Nation" Conference, October 2022.

46. Vermeule, "Liturgy of Liberalism."

47. Waller, "Illiberalism and Postliberalism."

Harrington playfully uses the term integralism as both a descriptor of a full sociopolitical regime and as a bogeyman concept. She has argued that modern progressive liberalism is itself a form of integralism, merging state and society in an atomizing whole to which state coercion is applied at the level of action and thought to conform populations to the shibboleths and assertions of radical culturally progressive modes of life.[48]

Harrington is intentionally provocative and mixes ideological frames with ease, writing that, "we are already living under integralism," just an integralism of radical gender theory, oikophobic self-hatred, and conceptions of race and ethnicity derived from imported American academic concepts.[49] The idea of a "liberal integralism," and thus integralism as a shorthand for comprehensive sociopolitical order has also been noted by the American political writer R. R. Reno.[50] Reno edits *First Things*, the premier conservative Catholic magazine read widely in the United States.

Another British writer, Aris Roussinos, has taken to calling the recently enthroned King Charles III as the United Kingdom's "post-liberal monarch," which he means in an ecumenical sense of rejecting "the marketisation of ever more aspects of human life" and one that promotes a sort of paternalistic stewardship of state and society in opposition to market liberalism and cultural atomization.[51] Adrian Pabst, the British postliberal political philosopher who has written on both the problems of "liberal democracy" as well as the promise of "Blue Labour" (that is, a culturally conservative, societally-unitive political project with left economic underpinnings) also fits in this mold, albeit at a less symbolic register.[52]

British postliberalism is far less theologically-derived than its American variant, and there is some distance between the religious inflection and decentralized localism that characterizes Deneen and Pecknold (at least in earlier writings), and the openly statist politics of Roussinos or Pabst. Roussinos describes the difference, regarding intra-British political debates in 2022, as one between:

> A harder-edged, American postliberal ... vision of the Catholic-administrative state [which is used by some] to condemn British

---

48. Harrington, *Feminism against Progress*; Harrington, "Blasphemy Is Dead."
49. Palladium Podcast, "Palladium Podcast 31."
50. Reno, "Liberal Integralism."
51. Roussinos, "Liz Truss Has Betrayed Conservatism"; Roussinos, "Mythic Power of King Charles III."
52. Pabst, "Keir Starmer Finally Goes Blue Labour"; Pabst, *Demons of Liberal Democracy*.

postliberalism, which is in truth a conservative variant of socialism, infused with a traditionalist Tory discomfort with modernity, and drawn from our nation's distinct historical path. British Postliberals, like other social democrats, do indeed believe that the nation's good as well as prosperity would be enhanced if everyone were to be given support by the state to settle down, form families and own their own homes: this is, or was, a very basic tenet of Toryism, too. But this is quite a different thing from state compulsion: there will be no roaming squads of tweed-jacketed postliberals forcing otherwise happy singletons to marry, and frogmarching them into suburban semis.[53]

Yet despite these differences, all share the concern with active state investment in and promotion of "things that are good," such as family policy *per* Pappin, and most agree with the criticism of liberalism as a cultic altar to destructive cultural tendencies, per Pecknold or Harrington.[54] Pappin takes an especially broad approach, and in many ways summarizes the key threads from which the more Catholic-inflected forms of postliberalism appeal to in an essay on the "return to normalcy" desired by postliberals in its more widened ambit of thought:

> Postliberalism looks for a different source of the elements of good governance. Instead of bespoke concoctions like originalism or libertarianism, it turns to the tradition of classical jurisprudence, the *jus commune* and Roman law. It looks to Catholic social teaching, the *ragion di stato* tradition as well as successful examples of modern governance in both West and East. On this basis, it seeks to make practical recommendations for good rule in present circumstances, while also adverting to the picture of good governance implied by the classical approaches.[55]

This is a grand mix of approaches, but shares not only an outlook and a diagnosis, but a sense of what should motivate a postliberal politics and notes explicitly what it is not (for the American context: "originalism" and "libertarianism"). Indeed, as we will see in the next subsection, a concern with a renewed framing of just politics as being pervaded by a sense of the national or communal "common-good" in juridical and legal terms is shared by both sides of the Anglo-American postliberal milieu as well.

53. Roussinos, "Liz Truss Has Betrayed Conservatism," para. 13.

54. For a critical account from the British perspective on the postliberalism debate, see Whyte, "Taking Liberties."

55. Pappin, "Return to Normalcy," para. 17.

The Practical Promise of a "Common-Good" Framework

As noted earlier, the first direct, practical outflow from integralist thought has centered on the legal world, where it has informed new approaches to renewing the classical legal tradition and the natural law in the Anglo-American context. This project, termed "common-good constitutionalism" by Vermeule, does not make integralist theological arguments proper, but relies on the same tradition of Roman and medieval Catholic legal theory to provide its undergirding justifications and baseline frameworks.[56]

This approach takes the form of careful distinctions between concepts of *ius* and *lex*, an appreciation of *iustitium* as a classical form of the state of exception, the role of the state in promoting and conceptualizing the common good, and the ways and means of legal interpretation derived from natural law authorities above positivist and textualist understandings of jurisprudence.[57] Throughout, it is asserted that the classical legal tradition from which common-good constitutionalism derives is in fact a native component of the American jurisprudential tradition, but one that was obscured or thrown off only as late as the mid-twentieth century.[58]

Undeniably, an important reason for both the popularization of integralism as well as the curious intermixing with narrower disputes among American legal scholars about the federal judiciary is the result of the articulate and prolific writing of Vermeule. A noted conservative scholar of administrative law, he has been a font of creative academic writing on integralism, showcased in *Church-Life Journal*, *First Things*, *Ius et Iustitium*, and *Mirror of Justice*, as well as writing concretely on the empowerment of the American executive presidency, the promotion of administrative state power as a proper form for winning conservative battles in American politics, and the undermining of the judicial oligarchy that powerfully impacts U.S. policymaking today, as found

---

56. Vermeule, *Common Good Constitutionalism*. See also Waldstein, "Primacy of the Common Good."

57. Casey and Vermeule, "Myths of Common Good Constitutionalism"; Waller, "Classical Political Forms."

58. Vermeule, *Common Good Constitutionalism*; Casey and Vermeule, "Myths of Common Good Constitutionalism"; Helmholz, "Origins of the Privilege against Self-Incrimination."

in his academic research, as well as popular essays in *The Atlantic, The Washington Post, The New York Times,* and elsewhere.[59]

This is fundamentally an American debate within the conservative legal field about remaking the federal judiciary and executive, although one that most observers understand to be informed by Vermeule's integralist background.[60] The common-good vision derived from Vermeule's work would see these institutions recrafted as assertive, conservative institutions that explicitly seek to block the presumed destructive proclivities of liberal elites and deny further victories through deceptive, "value-neutral" procedural formats that are believed to *de facto* systematically favor liberal ideologies.[61]

Significant criticism has quickly emerged from some corners of the legal establishment. One set of legal academics describes Vermeule's key book on the subject as a "manifesto" rather than an outline of an alternative to American originalist jurisprudential frameworks.[62] Amusingly, Vermeule has termed this line of attack as one by the "Bourbons of Jurisprudence," who fail to understand the degree to which their own legal framework is far from the consensus they depict and thus they have both "learned nothing and forgotten nothing" when faced with an alternative framework.[63] Others claim that this project, rather than producing a theory of achieving the common good, rather leads to an "uncommonly bad" constitutionalism instead.[64] Still others are more sanguine about the prospects of the framework, especially for those who believe that a natural law approach to American constitutionalism is possible, but are concerned that in Vermeule's application it overly denies the American constitutional inheritance from the founding as a tradition unto itself or leads to an overwhelming reliance on administrative authority.[65]

Vermeule's split-persona, a "common-good" conservative legal scholar promoting a form of administrative-oriented statism as well as

---

59. For Vermeule's full publications, see Harvard University Faculty Bibliography, "Adrian Vermeule."

60. Vermeule, "Beyond Originalism."

61. Patten, "Liberal Neutrality"; Kekes, "Incompatibility of Liberalism and Pluralism."

62. Baude and Sachs, "'Common-Good' Manifesto."

63. Vermeule, "Bourbons of Jurisprudence."

64. Patterson, "Uncommonly Bad Constitutionalism."

65. Pojanowski and Walsh, "Recovering Classical Legal Constitutionalism"; Frohnen, "Common Good Constitutionalism."

an open integralist promoting the superiority of the Catholic Church and spiritual authority over secular authority, has undoubtedly cast strong shadows on the debates that currently rage online and in right-leaning publications.[66] That Vermeule spends a good deal of time pointing out Schmittian concepts of the inherent political antagonism baked into society and the desultory and unjust nature of the current liberal "regime" bleeds into all corners.[67] This framing by such a prominent integralist is all the more influential given the otherwise often-skeptical views of the modern state taken by theorists like Fr. Waldstein or Deneen.[68] The rather specific entangling of executive and administrative statist supremacism with clear background whispers of what kind of morality would in fact be enforced provides sufficient worries for pluralists and liberals to cry authoritarianism.

Yet the common-good constitutionalism project is formally distinct from integralism, and its promoters see it as a capable vehicle through which preferred outcomes can be achieved within the context of the American legal system. One early, good-faith academic exploration of its practical outcomes has focused on environmental jurisprudence, which highlights its empowerment of administrative instruments as a potential boon for environmental advocacy groups.[69] Another has looked at the project's possibility as a framework to promote "equal dignity" in line with classical continental law, although with major questions for dominant liberal-constitutional approaches.[70] Indeed, for Conor Casey, another theorist of common-good constitutionalism, in many ways the project is more a reminder of the strong potential utility of continental legal traditions—which hew closer to the classical legal tradition—than a "Trojan Horse" for integralism proper.[71]

---

66. Vermeule, *Law's Abnegation*.

67. Blakely, "Integralism of Adrian Vermeule"; Posner and Vermeule, "Demystifying Schmitt"; Vermeule, "Our Schmittian Administrative Law."

68. "Many of the criticisms that people raise against integralism come from a misunderstanding of what we mean by the 'common good'. The common good is not the good of an abstract individual known as 'the state,' but rather the true good of the persons who make up a complete society." Twitter (@sancrucensis), April 22, 2020, https://twitter.com/sancrucensis/status/1252987056671907840; see also Deneen, "Community AND Liberty OR Individualism AND Statism."

69. Quigley, "Common Good Constitutionalism."

70. Foran, "Rights, Common Good, and the Separation of Powers"; Foran, "Equal Dignity and the Common Good."

71. Casey, "'Common Good Constitutionalism.'"

Integralism as Elite Political Catholicism

Integralist ideas have moved far beyond their initial confines, and now sit amidst a diffuse but very real illiberal ideational ecosystem that includes a wide and disparate range of thinkers and viewpoints. Despite its small group of full adherents, arguments derived from integralist approaches to philosophy, to understanding and structuring an encompassing view of modern state and society, and situating the place of the Catholic Church and her faithful are now integrated into much broader conversations about what the twenty-first century means for those discontented with its trajectory. As the field of possible illiberal interpretations of the new century is rather large, integralism acts in a particular way—as a touchstone for a new generation of "political Catholicism" confronting the challenges of the age. Why is this so?

We should understand political Catholicism in its historical sense— the modern phenomenon of lay Catholics advocating for increased Catholic influence on the societies in which they live.[72] The integralist variant of this approach is potentially extreme in its prescriptions and does not constitute the whole vantage of possibilities for Catholic political life in modern democracies. Yet it benefits from the clarity of its charges against secularization, liberalism, and increasingly atomized populations. It also benefits from a lack of alternative supply at the level of intellectuals. This poses the key challenge to other Catholics looking to combine faith and public life in the contemporary West.

Political Catholicism in the prewar era was dominated by "Catholic Action" groups, which were influential in historically-Catholic countries with anti-clerical regimes in the nineteenth and pre-WWII twentieth century.[73] Indeed, this legacy has both authoritarian and anti-fascist roots, as in the *Ständestaat* of Interwar Austria, where *Katholische Aktion* institutions worked as the only cohesive political organization distinct from the statist-authoritarian Fatherland Front. The historian Laura Gellott noted that in this role, such political Catholic groups were "eventually a means by which to resist certain programs and goals of the Fatherland Front," that were otherwise entirely foreclosed by the regime.[74] Others

---

72. Wolkenstein, "Hans Kelsen on Political Catholicism and Christian Democracy"; Woods, *Church Confronts Modernity*; Conway, *Catholic Politics in Europe*.

73. Denny and Connolly, *Empowering the People of God*; Woods, *Church Confronts Modernity*; Moloney, *American Catholic Lay Groups*; Conway, *Catholic Politics in Europe*; Truman, *Catholic Action and Politics*.

74. Gellott, "Defending Catholic Interests in the Christian State," 578.

can point to more fascist origins as well, such as in France where the *Action Française* worked towards nationalist-monarchist goals.[75]

Political Catholicism in the immediate post-Vatican II era centered around questions of life and human dignity, providing an underlying foundation for both human rights advocacy against communism abroad and pro-life movements in domestic politics.[76] Saint John-Paul II is in many ways the key intellectual and ecclesiastic link between lay-supported political Catholicism and the Church for that period.[77] Additionally, the Church was more fully reconciled to electoral democracy over the course of this period, which allowed for the full expression of political regime fitting into compatibility with the ecclesial worldview.[78] Yet this inheritance has been fundamentally undermined by scandal within, seeing a nadir in the prospects of politics taking guidance from Church institutions seen as corrupt or predatory.

Further, many Catholic institutions are seen by conservatives as coopted or undermined by progressive liberal assumptions that strike at the core of Church dogma. Indeed, the traditional reaction among lay faithful has been towards *de facto* schism and non-compliance, found most notably among so-called "sedevacantist" sectarians. This in itself is a large topic for scholars writing about Catholicism today, which see these sorts of groups as both a threat to Church unity as well as a negative influence on otherwise faithful communities within her broad expanse.[79]

Critically, integralism provides a Church-compliant alternative to breakaway insubordination that is attractive to some elite, conservative Catholics. The integralist emphasis on the vitality of Church hierarchy and authority undercuts claims that the only answer is schismatic traditionalism and is at pains to show that their own philosophical views are not only deeply drawn from Leonine and Neo-Thomistic thought, but that adherence to the institutional reforms of the post-conciliar

---

75. Nolte, *Three Faces of Fascism*.
76. Denny and Connolly, *Empowering the People of God*.
77. Weigel, *Witness to Hope*.
78. Fleet and Smith, *Catholic Church and Democracy in Chile and Peru*; Kalyvas and van Kersbergen, "Christian Democracy"; Corrin, *Catholic Intellectuals and the Challenges of Democracy*; Conway, "Democracy in Postwar Western Europe"; Eberts, "Roman Catholic Church and Democracy in Poland."
79. See, for example, Cavadini et al., "Way Forward from the Theological Concerns with the TLM Movement"; Cavadini et al., "Papal Responses to the Emergence of the TLM Movement"; Doherty, "Immolated Victim"; Pawelec, "Sedewakantyzm"; Allitt, "Traditionalist vs. Tradition."

Church is also proper and open to those of a traditionalist orientation.[80] Moreover, that this is simply what the Church has always taught and thus that the faithful are already "read-in" to the core motivations and tenets described and promoted by integralists.[81]

The prospect of integralism as providing answers for Catholics looking to engage in the temporal world while not jettisoning the Church itself, either institutionally or in doctrinal terms, cannot be underestimated. Indeed, there is evidence that among high-education Catholics in the United States, the choice set has become either to look towards the integralist program with interest (if not agreement) or to move further on the path of semi-schism. Self-described conservative or traditionalist Catholic writers in periodicals that once supported "fusionist" politics now use integralism as a broad term to encompass what amounts to conservative Catholicism itself, even if its ideological and philosophical claims are far deeper and more radical than that anodyne description. And others point to "soft," "moderate," and "hard" forms of integralism, suggesting that its *de facto* evolution towards a broad term encompassing conservative forms of Catholic politics is well on its way.[82]

Is this the only possibility on option? Not at all. Indeed, there are many distinct elements of society, from Traditional Latin Mass communities to Catholic "hipster" online groups to thriving local parishes that can provide this sort of structure without recourse to integralism itself, either philosophically or in political or social terms. Yet the draw of a unifying framework which combines descriptions of society as-is and society as it could be is naturally enticing, especially when a concrete political program is on offer alongside social critique and support.[83]

---

80. One example comes from Fr. Waldstein, in a long essay whose central assertion is that "[while] integralism has fallen out of fashion since the teaching Church ostensibly abandoned it at Vatican II, and opinion is now divided among various alternative positions. I shall argue, however, that Vatican II did not and could not abandon the essence of integralism." See Waldstein, "Integralism and Gelasian Dyarchy."

81. Toner, "Core of Integralism."

82. Brungardt, "Question of Catholic Integralism."

83. For a discussion of recent developments and the turn towards practical politics by some integralist advocates, see Liedl, "Showdown over American Catholic Political Engagement."

Integralism and Democracy in the West

It is impossible to avoid the question of integralism's relationship to political structure and political regime, not least because many of its fiercest critics are particularly keyed into this exact question.[84] The fullest expressions of integralism, found in the writings of Fr. Waldstein and in the manual of Fr. Crean and Fimister, provides reasonable evidence for this concern among defenders of modern forms of representative democracy. The assertion of natural hierarchies in state and society, the theological superiority of the Church's claims over human societies, and the questioning of the place of non-Catholics within the ideal, integralist society lends credence to beliefs that integralism, if fully accepted by a political society, would lead to a sort of authoritarian regime.[85]

This is further underlined by the positions on political authority given by integralism's premier constitutional legal scholar, Adrian Vermeule. His writing on the power and legitimacy of the administrative state and his stated doubts about the relevance of both judicial checks on executive authority as well as the role of legislative institutions is carefully worded but makes for an easy target.[86] The reliance on analogies to Catholic monarchy and Roman imperium as core political forms to be admired furthers this belief.[87]

Given all this, it is not always clear what the integralist position on governance is, especially in the American context, where no monarchical background history exists, and republican government is a longstanding political tradition and an unbroken constitutional framework. Furthermore, an obvious difficulty lies with the demographic characteristics of the United States, which is overwhelmingly non-denominational protestant or *de facto* secular, relative to its Catholic population.

The integralist vision is a direct challenge to liberal-pluralist interpretations of democratic governance. Yet no "authoritarian theory" of actualizing on an integralist state, or an integralist-infused politics in the

---

84. Patterson, "After Republican Virtue."

85. For critics that make this claim and emphasize citizenship and status concerns, see, for example, Vallier, *All the Kingdoms of the World*; Patterson, "No to Neo-Integralism."

86. Vermeule, *Law's Abnegation*.

87. For an example of analogizing Roman Imperial forms of governance as a justification for administrative power and the supremacy of an (elected) executive, see Vermeule, "Constitution of Imperium," as well as the follow-on working paper: Vermeule, "Many and the Few."

real-world thus far exists.[88] It is common in comprehensive ideological worldviews to propose permanent solutions, or ideal-typical regime formats, that conflict with the on-the-ground realities of plural, democratic politics—a problem encountered by theorists of progressive deliberative democracy, liberal theories of minoritarian technocracy, and democratic socialism as well, to take left and liberal examples.[89] "Thicker" conceptions of democracy—what we would describe as the ideal-typical liberal democracy of the twenty-first century—require degrees of secularism, pluralism, individual-rights preferences, and even speech codes that would certainly collide with integralist goals.[90] "Thinner" or minimalist conceptions of democracy, which we tend to call electoral democracy, and which consider procedural-constitutional elements the core substance of democratic political regimes, are less inhospitable to integralism, at least in theory.[91] The latter understanding of democracy allows for less strict secular liberalism to be the *de facto* state ideology and traditionally allows much more leeway for cultural and religious preferences that can be divorced from regime-type.

That does not mean that integralists are really "small-d" democrats, however. The manualist approach in integralist writing, lauds the mixed regime found in Aristotelian-Thomistic thought, but is certainly ambivalent about whether the ideal mixed regime would be recognizable as a modern electoral democracy. Fimister wrote in a response to a review of the *Integralism* manual, saying:

> There is no suggestion in the book that democracy, either in the sense of pure democracy or a mixed polity with a democratic element, is contrary to natural and/or divine law. In fact, insofar as Integralism does propose a constitutional form as superior in the abstract, it is a mixed polity with a democratic element. . . . Historically, the attempt to shackle integralism to one particular form of government, contrary to the teaching of Leo XIII and to its own principles, has done great harm. . . . *Integralism: A Manual of Political Philosophy* is in no way a royalist text. It fully

---

88. Waller, "Intellectual Entrepreneurs against Democracy."

89. Tushnet, *New Fourth Branch*; Vergara, *Systemic Corruption*; Mouffe, *For a Left Populism*; Mounk, *People vs. Democracy*.

90. Coppedge et al., *Varieties of Democracy*; Dahl, *On Democracy*; Dahl, *Polyarchy*.

91. Przeworski, *Democracy and the Limits of Self-Government*; Przeworski, "Minimalist Conception of Democracy"; Rustow, "Transitions to Democracy."

recognises the multiformity of the temporal order and recognises that multiformity as a good.[92]

He affirms that integralists can agree to the United States as "a well-ordered Republic," citing Pope Leo XIII and provides a thought-experiment for the United Kingdom:

> We may distinguish two levels in which Integralism may be fulfilled. On the shallow level in, e.g., (the English portion of) the United Kingdom, the elimination of those legislative instruments which conflict with natural law and the replacement of Anglicanism by Catholicism, as the religion of the civil order, would immediately fulfil the requirements of the Social Kingship of Christ. On the deeper level, the attainment by Catholicism of the position in the civil order enjoyed by Anglicanism in the opening decades of the nineteenth century would accomplish the full soul-body union of the spiritual and the temporal demanded by the social teaching of Pope Leo XIII. Whether the condemnation of a law or the deposition of a ruler, by the supreme spiritual power, would have a recognised effect in the civil order (in the manner of EU law "setting aside" national legislation) or would need to be given effect by the submission of the sovereign elements of a given polity through the ordinary mechanisms of public law is a question of technique indifferent in itself.[93]

This statement may not represent all integralists and may indeed be doubted by skeptics as occlusion or misdirection. Questions of suffrage for non-Catholics have been raised in regard to Fr. Crean and Fimister's work in particular, although that debate remains unresolved. It is undoubted that a fully integralist political regime would not be a secular, Western-style liberal democracy, but whether it satisfies minimalist electoral democratic criteria is more open. Although, again, given the paucity of evidence for mass support of integralism either among the public or even among large segments of a given state's political elite, the question is academic and speculative.

Integralism's relationship with actually-existing democracies is trickier, in some ways. The legacy of political Catholicism in the late nineteenth and early twentieth centuries in Europe and Latin America would suggest interest in engaging with electoral politics, building local-level civil society institutions, and broadly acting as an active bulwark

---

92. Fimister, "Make Disciples of All Nations," paras. 1, 4, 9.
93. Fimister, "Make Disciples of All Nations, para. 7.

against secular, liberalizing, and anti-clerical (today, more likely state-enforced areligiosity) politics. Historically, this has taken the form of Church-affiliated political parties, such as *Zentrum* in Germany during the *Kulturkampf* of the Bismarck era, or Christian Social and Christian-Democratic parties found throughout Europe into the twentieth century.[94] These parties have had different approaches to democracy, with some fully engaging with pluralist, parliamentary democracies and others taking a more skeptical view.[95] The European Union and its earlier incarnations represent the postwar integration of Christian-Democratic politics with forms of European democracy, of course.[96]

Integralist thought aligns with some of these party legacies fairly clearly, especially more clericalist movements found in Germany and Austria. At the same time, at present it would be naïve to make a clear connection to the most explicitly pluralist-democratic forms of political Catholicism in Europe in the twentieth century. Democratic states can indeed hold to ideological values, yet meshing integralism's core claims for the Church to be afforded formal respect and authority in temporal politics is no small matter.

Integralism also suffers from terminological association with more nakedly authoritarian political Catholic movements in European and Latin American history. The *Action Française* of Charles Maurras represents one form of *integrisme* which was explicitly authoritarian, as well as the experience of Brazilian *integrismo* in the interwar period.[97] Both avowed a far more nationalist and religiously-instrumental approach to politics than anything offered by existing integralist accounts today, and indeed are sometimes categorized as fascist in terms of political ideology.[98] Other variations that were less "fascist" and more traditionalist existed in Iberia and parts of Latin America during the pre-WWII era as well.[99] This represents a clear challenge for modern integralists when engaging with politics, as some of the prior bearers of the name

94. Kalyvas, *Rise of Christian Democracy in Europe*; Kaiser, *Christian Democracy and the Origins of European Union*.

95. Ziblatt, *Conservative Parties and the Birth of Democracy*.

96. Kaiser, *Christian Democracy and the Origins of European Union*.

97. See, for example, Gonçalves and Neto, *Fascism in Brazil*; Lima Grecco, "Samba with Fascism"; Bernardi, *Maurice Blondel, Social Catholicism, and Action Française*; Arnal, *Ambivalent Alliance*; Nolte, *Three Faces of Fascism*.

98. Blatt, "Relatives and Rivals."

99. Spektorowski, "Joseph de Maistre, Donoso Cortés, and Argentina's Catholic Right"; Vakil, "Representations of the 'Discoveries.'"

undoubtedly sit outside the accepted bounds of electoral democracy.[100] This is a complication, even if integralists may (rightly) claim that their project shares little to no substantive relation to the authoritarian nationalism of prewar French, Brazilian, Argentinian, or Spanish "integrists."[101]

What has made the situation for measured assessment of what integralism actually *means* for organizing a given polity especially difficult is the often radically earnest illiberals and faithful priests that comment in online fora or wax poetic in theoretical works on avowedly illiberal state models of prior centuries. It is in fact quite difficult to spend any time reading tweets or blog-posts by integralists without running across references to the monarchical splendor and ordered rule of Saint Louis IX's thirteenth-century France, to papal encyclicals from the nineteenth and early twentieth centuries expressing grave doubts about liberal democracy, or to Salazar's Estado Novo, *Franquism* in Spain, and other interwar authoritarian regimes.[102]

This represents a key challenge for integralists, and for others who work in related illiberal ideational fields. The question of adherence to democracy, or at least its twenty-first-century liberal-democratic variant that is dominant across the West today will not go away. The fullest expression of integralism likely involves tutelary-theocratic mechanisms, but its more practical form as a type of motivating political Catholicism likely does not. Whether a rejection of liberal democracy simply means rejecting the former part of the term, rather than the latter, already varies across thinkers. The Church's midcentury peace with democratic forms of government also looms large in and around integralist debates, and what this means substantively in partisan politics or as regards constitutional and structural questions will be a longstanding point of interest.

Conclusion

The place of integralism in the broader political world remains uncertain, even as its theological and philosophical relevance to discussions within and without the Church are ongoing—and will do so for the foreseeable future. This chapter has overviewed some of the basic political-theological

100. Medhurst, "Spanish Conservative Politics."

101. González and Ferran, "Antiliberal Political Traditionalism"; Bernardi, *Maurice Blondel, Social Catholicism, and Action Française*; Arnal, *Ambivalent Alliance*.

102. Jones, *Before Church and State*; Sanchez, "Illiberal Catholicism One Year On"; Kurth, "For Whom the Bell Tolls."

claims of this framework and identified the concrete ways in which it has moved beyond online writing into substantive projects.

Integralism can certainly be understood primarily for its theological or its perceived political claims, but richer fruit can also be identified in the ways it fits within a much larger illiberal ideational ecosystem. Its key strengths—the inheritance of the Church's teachings on modernity, the wealth of thought accumulated over two millennia to which it can turn to justify its own position on twenty-first century life, and its ability to speak to discontents beyond particularly Catholic debates cannot be discounted. Integralism itself remains marginal and is accepted by only a few core thinkers writing at the periphery of contemporary debates. But it has been easily integrated into larger conversations, and full acceptance of its largest claims will not stop ideological borrowing from other sources.

Three primary takeaways are relevant given this short overview account. First, integralism has proved to be able to move beyond its more esoteric origins, attracting interest well beyond the remit of traditionalist Catholic intellectual circles, although it nonetheless remains as merely one of several points of interest within those groups. Second, its growth is in part because it speaks to both intra-Catholic and broader intra-conservative debates about the place of Church and the state within modern society, which feeds into the burgeoning postliberal strain of political thinking that continues to attract interested parties, if not full adherents. Third, it benefits from a *prima facie* orthodox interpretation of what the institutional Church still is, most relevantly in regard to core issues such as the legitimacy of the Papacy and the Vatican II documents, thus resisting the call of schism even as it brings forward a tremendous challenge to current trajectories within the faith.[103]

For these reasons, integralism should be understood in a measured way. It is very far from gathering a mass following (indeed, many other flavors of Catholic traditionalism have much larger sets of supporters numerically), but rather works at the level of intellectuals, scholars, and high-information political thinkers. In substantive ways, integralism will thus likely stay in this arena for the foreseeable future. Yet even so, within

---

103. It should be noted that other currents in the Church might object to claims of an unimpeachable integralist fidelity to modern interpretations of Church teaching, although this is a separate discussion requiring a full treatment not available here. That integralists maintain they are within the ambit of the contemporary Church and its hierarchy remains relevant, especially in comparative context with other movements on the more traditional side of debates within global Catholicism.

a few short years it has moved from online pages to mainstream publications, even if only as either a pejorative or positive term of art to be used in ongoing debates about society in the twenty-first century. Concerns over the relationship between integralism and actually-existing democracies in the West remain perfectly valid, although its place as an elite intellectual movement and the diversity of historical patterns to which it can find reference points means that more democratic—if not liberal-secular—options are not foreclosed. The new century is unlikely to be the century of integralism, but it is very likely to be one of new forms of political Catholicism, to which integralism may end up speaking more effectively than some expect.

Author's Note: My grateful thanks to Joe Barnas and Bill Murphy for thoughtful comments on a prior draft of this chapter.

Bibliography

Addison, Daniel. "Fusionism Relitigated." *Postliberal America*, February 2023. https://www.illiberalism.org/fusionism-relitigated/.

Ahmari, Sohrab. *Tyranny, Inc.: How Private Power Crushed American Liberty—and What to Do about It*. New York: Forum, 2023.

Allitt, Patrick. "Traditionalist vs. Tradition." Edited by Michael W. Cuneo. *CrossCurrents* 48 (1998) 265–68.

Arnal, Oscar L. *Ambivalent Alliance: The Catholic Church and the Action Française, 1899–1939*. Pittsburgh: University of Pittsburgh Press, 1985.

Barnes, Marc. "Ahmari, Vermeule, and Burying Liberalism for Good." *New Polity*, July 2020. https://newpolity.com/blog/burying-liberalism-for-good.

Barnes, Marc, and Andrew Willard Jones. "The Decision against Carl Schmitt." *New Polity*, July 6, 2021. https://newpolity.com/blog/against-schmitt.

Baude, William, and Stephen E. Sachs. "The 'Common-Good' Manifesto." *Harvard Law Review* 136 (2023) 861–906.

Bell, Duncan. "What Is Liberalism?" *Political Theory* 42 (2014) 682–715. https://doi.org/10.1177/0090591714535103.

Bernardi, Peter J. *Maurice Blondel, Social Catholicism, and Action Française: The Clash Over the Church's Role in Society During the Modernist Era*. Washington, DC: The Catholic University of America Press, 2009.

Blakely, Jason. "The Integralism of Adrian Vermeule." *Commonweal Magazine*, October 2020. https://www.commonwealmagazine.org/not-catholic-enough.

Blatt, Joel. "Relatives and Rivals: The Responses of the Action Française to Italian Fascism, 1919–26." *European Studies Review* 11 (1981) 263–92.

Bothur, Ian. "A Workingman's Case for Integralism." *American Conservative*, April 30, 2020. https://www.theamericanconservative.com/a-workingmans-case-for-integralism/.

Brungardt, John G. "The Question of Catholic Integralism: An Internet Genealogy." *The Josias* (blog), May 29, 2020. https://thejosias.com/2020/05/29/the-question-of-catholic-integralism-an-internet-genealogy/.

Buzogány, Aron, and Mihai Varga. "Illiberal Thought Collectives and Policy Networks in Hungary and Poland." *European Politics and Society* 24 (2021) 1–19. https://doi.org/10.1080/23745118.2021.1956238.

Casey, Conor. "'Common Good Constitutionalism' and the New Debate over Constitutional Interpretation in the United States." SSRN Scholarly Paper, November 4, 2020. https://doi.org/10.2139/ssrn.3725068.

Casey, Conor, and Adrian Vermeule. "Myths of Common Good Constitutionalism." *Harvard Journal of Law and Public Policy* 45 (2022) 103–46.

Cavadini, John, et al. "Papal Responses to the Emergence of the TLM Movement." *Church Life Journal*, November 2022. https://churchlifejournal.nd.edu/articles/papal-responses-to-the-emergence-of-the-tlm-movement/.

———. "The Way Forward from the Theological Concerns with the TLM Movement." *Church Life Journal*, November 2022. https://churchlifejournal.nd.edu/articles/the-way-forward-from-the-theological-concerns-with-the-tlm-movement/.

Conway, Martin. *Catholic Politics in Europe, 1918–1945*. New York: Routledge, 1997.

———. "Democracy in Postwar Western Europe: The Triumph of a Political Model." *European History Quarterly* 32 (2002) 59–84. https://doi.org/10.1177/0269141420032001562.

Coppedge, Michael, et al. *Varieties of Democracy: Measuring Two Centuries of Political Change*. Cambridge: Cambridge University Press, 2020.

Corrin, Jay P. *Catholic Intellectuals and the Challenges of Democracy*. Notre Dame: University of Notre Dame Press, 2010.

Coulanges, Numa Denis Fustel de. *The Ancient City*. Baldwin City, KS: Imperium, 2020.

Crean, Thomas, and Alan Fimister. *Integralism: A Manual of Political Philosophy*. Neunkirchen-Seelscheid: Editiones Scholasticae, 2020.

Culbreath, Jonathan. "Catholic Integralism after Liberalism." *Medium* (blog), June 9, 2019. https://maestrojmc.medium.com/catholic-integralism-after-liberalism-952f/98/3e06.

Dahl, Robert A. *On Democracy*. New Haven: Yale University Press, 2020.

———. *Polyarchy: Participation and Opposition*. New Haven: Yale University Press, 1971.

Deneen, Patrick J. "Community AND Liberty OR Individualism AND Statism." *Front Porch Republic* (blog), July 29, 2011. https://www.frontporchrepublic.com/2011/07/community-and-liberty-or-individualism-and-statism/.

———. *Regime Change: Toward a Postliberal Future*. New York: Sentinel, 2023.

———. *Why Liberalism Failed*. New Haven: Yale University Press, 2018.

Denny, Christopher D., and Mary Beth Fraser Connolly. *Empowering the People of God: Catholic Action before and after Vatican II*. New York: Fordham University Press, 2013.

Doherty, Bernard. "The Immolated Victim: Traditionalist Roman Catholicism and Mel Gibson's 'the Passion of the Christ.'" *St Mark's Review* 234 (2015) 77–101. https://doi.org/10.3316/informit.811004203963225.

Dueck, Colin. "The New Traditionalists." *AEI Reports*, May 29, 2020.

Eberts, Mirella W. "The Roman Catholic Church and Democracy in Poland." *Europe-Asia Studies* 50 (1998) 817–42. https://doi.org/10.1080/09668139808412567.

Fimister, Alan. "Make Disciples of All Nations." *Reality*, July 9, 2020. https://realityjournal.org/2020/07/09/make-disciples-of-all-nations/.

Fleet, Michael, and Brian H. Smith. *The Catholic Church and Democracy in Chile and Peru*. Notre Dame: University of Notre Dame Press, 2015.

Foran, Michael P. "Equal Dignity and the Common Good." SSRN Scholarly Paper, October 21, 2022. https://papers.ssrn.com/abstract=4254952.
———. "Rights, Common Good, and the Separation of Powers." *Modern Law Review* 86 (2023) 599–628. https://doi.org/10.1111/1468-2230.12769.
Frohnen, Bruce P. "Common Good Constitutionalism and the Problem of Administrative Absolutism." *Catholic Social Science Review* 27 (2022) 81–96. https://doi.org/10.5840/cssr20222722.
Frost, Amber A'Lee. "The Characterless Opportunism of the Managerial Class." *American Affairs* 3 (2019) 126–39.
Gellott, Laura. "Defending Catholic Interests in the Christian State: The Role of Catholic Action in Austria, 1933–1938." *Catholic Historical Review* 74 (1988) 571–89.
Gonçalves, Leandro Pereira, and Odilon Caldeira Neto. *Fascism in Brazil: From Integralism to Bolsonarism*. New York: Routledge, 2022.
González, Toledano, and Lluís Ferran. "Antiliberal Political Traditionalism: The Catalan Carlists." *Catalan Historical Review* 14 (2021) 69–88. https://doi.org/10.2436/chr.voi14.149377.
Hanby, Michael. "Are We Postliberal Yet?" *New Polity*, Summer 2022. https://newpolity.com/blog/are-we-postliberal-yet.
Harrington, Mary. "Am I Really a Threat to Democracy?" *UnHerd*, September 6, 2022. https://unherd.com/2022/09/am-i-really-a-threat-to-democracy/.
———. "Blasphemy Is Dead. Long Live Blasphemy." *Reactionary Feminist*, October 26, 2022. https://reactionaryfeminist.substack.com/p/blasphemy-is-dead-long-live-blasphemy?sd=pf.
———. *Feminism against Progress*. Washington, DC: Regnery, 2023.
Harvard University Faculty Bibliography. "Adrian Vermeule." https://hls.harvard.edu/bibliography/?instructor_reverse=Vermeule%2C%20Adrian.
Helmholz, R. H. "Origins of the Privilege against Self-Incrimination: The Role of the European Ius Commune." *New York University Law Review* 65 (1990) 962–91.
Hendrikse, Reijer. "The Rise of Neo-Illiberalism." *Krisis: Journal for Contemporary Philosophy* 41 (2021) 65–93. https://doi.org/10.21827/krisis.40.2.37158.
Johnston, Savannah Eccles. "The Rise of Illiberal Conservatism: Immigration and Nationhood at National Review." *American Political Thought* 10 (2021) 190–216. https://doi.org/10.1086/713668.
Jones, Andrew Willard. *Before Church and State: A Study of Social Order in the Sacramental Kingdom of St. Louis IX*. Steubenville, OH: Emmaus Academic, 2017.
Kaiser, Wolfram. *Christian Democracy and the Origins of European Union*. New Studies in European History. Cambridge: Cambridge University Press, 2007.
Kalyvas, Stathis N. *The Rise of Christian Democracy in Europe*. The Rise of Christian Democracy in Europe. Cornell University Press, 2018. https://doi.org/10.7591/9781501731419.
Kalyvas, Stathis N., and Kees van Kersbergen. "Christian Democracy." *Annual Review of Political Science* 13 (2010) 183–209. https://doi.org/10.1146/annurev.polisci.11.021406.172506.
Kekes, John. "The Incompatibility of Liberalism and Pluralism." *American Philosophical Quarterly* 29 (1992) 141–51.
Kurth, James. "For Whom the Bell Tolls: The Franco Regime and Contemporary Spain." *Modern Age* 55 (2013) 27–36.
Laruelle, Marlene. "Illiberalism: A Conceptual Introduction." *East European Politics* 38 (2022) 303–27. https://doi.org/10.1080/21599165.2022.2037079.

Liedl, Jonathan L. "Showdown over American Catholic Political Engagement Entered New Phase in 2022." *National Catholic Register*, December 30, 2022. https://www.ncregister.com/news/showdown-over-american-catholic-political-engagement-entered-new-phase-in-2022.

Lima Grecco, Gabriela de. "Samba with Fascism: Ação Integralista Brasileira and Its Relations with the New State of Getúlio Vargas." *Journal of Iberian and Latin American Studies* 27 (2021) 133–49. https://doi.org/10.1080/14701847.2021.1939528.

Lind, Michael. *The New Class War: Saving Democracy from the Managerial Elite*. New York: Penguin Random House, 2020.

Maas, Korey D. "The Coming Anti-Catholicism." *Public Discourse*, May 1, 2019. https://www.thepublicdiscourse.com/2019/05/51277/.

MacDougald, Park. "A Catholic Debate over Liberalism." *City Journal*, Winter 2020. https://www.city-journal.org/article/a-catholic-debate-over-liberalism/.

Medhurst, Kenneth. "Spanish Conservative Politics." In *Conservative Politics in Western Europe*, edited by Zig Layton-Henry, 292–317. New York: St. Martin's, 1982. https://doi.org/10.1007/978-71-349-16252-9_13.

Ménard, Xavier Foccroulle, and Anna Su. "Liberalism, Catholic Integralism, and the Question of Religious Freedom." *BYU Law Review* 47 (2022) 1171–218.

Milbank, John, and Adrian Pabst. *The Politics of Virtue: Post-Liberalism and the Human Future*. New York: Rowman & Littlefield, 2016.

Milbank, John, et al., eds. *Radical Orthodoxy: A New Theology*. New York: Routledge, 1998.

Moloney, Deirdre M. *American Catholic Lay Groups and Transatlantic Social Reform in the Progressive Era*. Chapel Hill, NC: University of North Carolina Press, 2003.

Mouffe, Chantal. *For a Left Populism*. New York: Verso, 2018.

Mounk, Yascha. *The People vs. Democracy: Why Our Freedom Is in Danger and How to Save It*. Cambridge: Harvard University Press, 2018.

Nolte, Ernst. *Three Faces of Fascism: Action Francaise, Italian Fascism, National Socialism*. Translated by Leila Vennnewitz. New York: Holt, Rinehart, and Winston, 1969.

Pabst, Adrian. *The Demons of Liberal Democracy*. Cambridge: Polity, 2019.

———. "Keir Starmer Finally Goes Blue Labour." *UnHerd*, September 28, 2022. https://unherd.com/thepost/keir-starmer-finally-goes-blue-labour/.

Palladium Podcast. "Palladium Podcast 31: Towards a Healthy Postmodernism with Mary Harrington." *Palladium*, April 9, 2020. https://www.palladiummag.com/2020/04/09/palladium-podcast-31-towards-a-healthy-postmodernism-with-mary-harrington/.

Pappin, Gladden. "Contemporary Christian Criticism of Liberalism." In *Routledge Handbook of Illiberalism*, edited by András Sajó et al., 43–59. London: Routledge, 2021.

———. "Corporatism for the Twenty-First Century." *American Affairs* 4 (2020) 89–113.

———. "The Family Policy Imperative." *Public Discourse*, April 17, 2021. https://www.thepublicdiscourse.com/2021/04/75329/.

———. "Return to Normalcy." *The Postliberal Order*, October 27, 2022. https://postliberalorder.substack.com/p/return-to-normalcy.

Patten, Alan. "Liberal Neutrality: A Reinterpretation and Defense*." *Journal of Political Philosophy* 20 (2012) 249–72. https://doi.org/10.1111/j.1467-9760.2011.00406.x.

Patterson, James M. "After Republican Virtue." *Law & Liberty*, April 22, 2020. https://lawliberty.org/after-republican-virtue/.

———. "An Awkward Alliance: Neo-Integralism and National Conservatism." *Religion & Liberty*, April 11, 2022. https://www.acton.org/religion-liberty/volume-35-number-1-2/awkward-alliance-neo-integralism-and-national-conservatism.

———. "No to Neo-Integralism." *National Review*, January 6, 2023. https://www.nationalreview.com/magazine/2023/01/23/no-to-neo-integralism/.

———. "Uncommonly Bad Constitutionalism." *Law & Liberty*, April 28, 2022. https://lawliberty.org/book-review/uncommonly-bad-constitutionalism/.

———. "Why Integralism Is an Ideology of Despair." *Law & Liberty*, November 28, 2018. https://lawliberty.org/why-integralism-is-an-ideology-of-despair/.

Pawelec, Przemysław. "Sedewakantyzm: wybrane zagadnienia." *Resovia Sacra. Studia Teologiczno-Filozoficzne Diecezji Rzeszowskiej* 16 (2009) 321–35.

Pinkoski, Nathan. "How Not to Challenge the Integralists." *Law & Liberty*, April 30, 2020. https://lawliberty.org/how-not-to-challenge-the-integralists/.

Pojanowski, Jeffrey, and Kevin Walsh. "Recovering Classical Legal Constitutionalism: A Critique of Professor Vermeule's New Theory." *Notre Dame Law Review* 98 (2022) 403.

Posner, Eric, and Adrian Vermeule. "Demystifying Schmitt." In *The Oxford Handbook of Carl Schmitt*, edited by Jens Meierhenrich and Oliver Simons, 612–26. Oxford: Oxford University Press, 2017.

Przeworski, Adam. *Democracy and the Limits of Self-Government*. New York: Cambridge University Press, 2010.

———. "Minimalist Conception of Democracy: A Defense." In *Democracy's Value*, edited by Ian Shapiro and Casiano Hacker-Cordon, 23–55. Cambridge: Cambridge University Press, 1999.

Quigley, Brian. "Common Good Constitutionalism and the Future of Environmental Law." *Vermont Journal of Environmental Law* 23 (2022) 349–73.

Reno, R. R. "Liberal Integralism." *First Things*, March 2018. https://www.firstthings.com/web-exclusives/2018/03/liberal-integralism.

———. "Return of the Strong Gods." *First Things*, May 2017. https://www.firstthings.com/article/2017/05/return-of-the-strong-gods.

Rooney, James Dominic. "Illiberal Integralist Elites." *Law & Liberty*, January 3, 2023. https://lawliberty.org/illiberal-integralist-elites/.

Roussinos, Aris. "Liz Truss Has Betrayed Conservatism." *UnHerd*, October 2, 2022. https://unherd.com/2022/10/liz-truss-has-betrayed-conservatism/.

———. "The Mythic Power of King Charles III." *UnHerd*, September 11, 2022. https://unherd.com/2022/09/the-mythic-power-of-king-charles-iii/.

———. "The Tories against Democracy." *UnHerd*, November 11, 2020. https://unherd.com/2020/11/the-tories-against-democracy/.

Rufo, Christopher F. *America's Cultural Revolution: How the Radical Left Conquered Everything*. New York: Broadside, 2023.

Rustow, Dankwart A. "Transitions to Democracy: Toward a Dynamic Model." *Comparative Politics* 2 (1970) 337. https://doi.org/10.2307/421307.

Sajó, András, Renáta Uitz, and Stephen Holmes, eds. *Routledge Handbook of Illiberalism*. New York: Routledge, 2021. https://doi.org/10.4324/9780367260569.

Sanchez, Gabriel S. "Illiberal Catholicism One Year On." *Front Porch Republic* (blog), January 26, 2015. https://www.frontporchrepublic.com/2015/01/illiberal-catholicism-one-year/.

———. "The Other Illiberal Catholicism." *Opus Publicum*, July 10, 2014. https://opuspublicum.com/the-other-illiberal-catholicism/.

Schwartzman, Micah, and Jocelyn Wilson. "The Unreasonableness of Catholic Integralism." *San Diego Law Review* 56 (2019) 1039–68.

Shadle, Matthew. "The Paradoxes of Postmodern Integralism." *Political Theology Network*, March 6, 2015. https://politicaltheology.com/the-paradoxes-of-postmodern-integralism/.

Smith, Patrick. "The Brick through the Window." *Semiduplex* (blog), May 8, 2019. https://semiduplex.com/2019/05/08/the-brick-through-the-window/.

Spektorowski, Alberto. "Joseph de Maistre, Donoso Cortés, and Argentina's Catholic Right: The Integralist Rebellion against Modernity." *Totalitarian Movements and Political Religions* 9 (2008) 455–74. https://doi.org/10.1080/14690760802436084.

Storck, Thomas. "What Is Integralism?" *New Oxford Review*, September 2022. https://www.newoxfordreview.org/documents/what-is-integralism/.

Toner, James H. "The Core of Integralism." *Crisis Magazine*, February 8, 2022. https://www.crisismagazine.com/2022/the-core-of-integralism.

Trabbic, Joseph G. "The Catholic Church, the State, and Liberalism." *Public Discourse*, May 2018. https://www.thepublicdiscourse.com/2018/05/21405/.

Truman, Tom. *Catholic Action and Politics*. Melbourne: Georgian, 1959.

Turowsky, Nathan. "The Appeal and Danger of Integralism." *Where Peter Is* (blog), September 20, 2020. https://wherepeteris.com/the-appeal-and-danger-of-integralism/.

Tushnet, Mark. *The New Fourth Branch: Institutions for Protecting Constitutional Democracy*. Cambridge: Cambridge University Press, 2021.

Vakil, Abdoolkarim. "Representations of the 'Discoveries' and the Imaginary of the Nation in Portuguese Integralism." *Portuguese Studies* 11 (1995) 133–67.

Vallier, Kevin. *All the Kingdoms of the World: On Radical Religious Alternatives to Liberalism*. New York: Oxford University Press, 2023.

———. "The Fairness Argument against Catholic Integralism." *Law, Culture and the Humanities*, October 2021. https://doi.org/10.1177/17438721211054187.

———. "Political Liberals vs. Integralists: Where the Conflict Really Lies." *Reconciled* (blog), October 30, 2020. https://www.kevinvallier.com/reconciled/political-liberals-vs-integralists-where-the-conflict-really-lies/.

Varga, Mihai, and Aron Buzogány. "The Family Tree of Illiberalism: Lineages and Alignments." *Illiberalism Studies Program Working Papers* 5 (2021) 1–5.

———. "The Two Faces of the 'Global Right': Revolutionary Conservatives and National-Conservatives." *Critical Sociology*, December 2021. https://doi.org/10.1177/08969205211057020.

Vergara, Camila. *Systemic Corruption: Constitutional Ideas for an Anti-Oligarchic Republic*. Princeton: Princeton University Press, 2020.

Vermeule, Adrian. "All Human Conflict Is Ultimately Theological." *Church Life Journal*, July 26, 2019. https://churchlifejournal.nd.edu/articles/all-human-conflict-is-ultimately-theological/.

———. "Beyond Originalism." *Atlantic*, March 2020. https://www.theatlantic.com/ideas/archive/2020/03/common-good-constitutionalism/609037/.

———. "The Bourbons of Jurisprudence." *Ius & Iustitium* (blog), August 15, 2022. https://iusetiustitium.com/the-bourbons-of-jurisprudence/.

———. "A Christian Strategy." *First Things*, November 2017. https://www.firstthings.com/article/2017/11/a-christian-strategy.

———. *Common Good Constitutionalism*. Medford: Polity, 2022.

———. "The Constitution of Imperium." Speech presented at the Restoring a Nation Conference, Steubenville, Ohio, October 7, 2022.

———. *Law's Abnegation: From Law's Empire to the Administrative State*. Cambridge: Harvard University Press, 2016.

———. "Liturgy of Liberalism." *First Things*, January 2017. https://www.firstthings.com/article/2017/01/liturgy-of-liberalism.

———. "Our Schmittian Administrative Law." *Harvard Law Revue* 122 (2009) 1095–148.

———. "The Many and the Few: On the American Lex Regia." SSRN Scholarly Paper. https://papers.ssrn.com/abstract=4321671.

Waldstein, Edmund. "Integralism and Gelasian Dyarchy." *The Josias* (blog), March 3, 2016. https://thejosias.com/2016/03/03/integralism-and-gelasian-dyarchy/.

———. "Integralism in Three Sentences." *The Josias* (blog), October 17, 2016. https://thejosias.com/2016/10/17/integralism-in-three-sentences/.

———. "The Primacy of the Common Good." *The Josias* (blog), June 19, 2023. https://thejosias.com/2023/06/19/the-primacy-of-the-common-good/.

Waldstein, Edmund, and Peter A. Kwasniewski, eds. *Integralism and the Common Good: Selected Essays from The Josias*. Brooklyn: Angelico, 2021.

Waller, Julian G. "Classical Political Forms, the Mixed Regime, and the State of Emergency—Roman, Byzantine, Muscovite?" *Ius & Iustitium*, October 27, 2022. https://iusetiustitium.com/classical-political-forms-the-mixed-regime-and-the-state-of-emergency-roman-byzantine-muscovite/.

———. "Distinctions with a Difference: Illiberalism and Authoritarianism in Scholarly Study." *Political Studies Review*, March 2023. https://doi.org/10.1177/14789299231159253.

———. "Illiberalism and Postliberalism: Comparing Ideological Ferment in Eastern Europe and the Anglo-American World." Research Paper. Postliberal America. https://www.illiberalism.org/illiberalism-and-postliberalism-comparing-ideological-ferment-in-eastern-europe-and-the-anglo-american-world/.

———. "The Illiberal Right Moves beyond Critique." Research Paper. Postliberal America. https://www.illiberalism.org/the-illiberal-right-moves-beyond-critique/.

———. "Intellectual Entrepreneurs against Democracy: Theorizing Authoritarian Futures in America." SSRN Scholarly Paper. https://papers.ssrn.com/abstract=4117901.

———. "Quirks in the Neo-Integralist Vision." *Church Life Journal*, February 4, 2021. https://churchlifejournal.nd.edu/articles/quirks-in-the-neo-integralist-vision/.

Weigel, George. *Witness to Hope: The Biography of Pope John Paul II*. New York: Harper Perennial, 2020.

Whyte, Jamie. "Taking Liberties: Why Postliberals Are Wrong about Personal Freedom." Discussion Paper. Institute of Economic Affairs. https://iea.org.uk/publications/taking-liberties-why-postliberals-are-wrong-about-personal-freedom/.

Wolkenstein, Fabio. "Hans Kelsen on Political Catholicism and Christian Democracy." *European Journal of Political Theory*, July 2, 2023. https://doi.org/10.1177/14748851231184999.

Woods, Thomas E. *The Church Confronts Modernity: Catholic Intellectuals and the Progressive Era*. New York: Columbia University Press, 2004.

Ziblatt, Daniel. *Conservative Parties and the Birth of Democracy*. New York: Cambridge University Press, 2017.

12

The World out of Joint
The Hard Right and Postliberalism in Twenty-First Century American Politics

MATT MCMANUS, UNIVERSITY OF MICHIGAN[1]

Abstract: The hard right has resurfaced in many parts of the world. While it has yet to achieve lasting success of the sort predicted by the "wave" of victories from 2016–18, the ebbing tide has by no means rolled all the way back. This paper will examine different strands of American hard right ideology and explore their prospects in an increasingly fertile political plain, focusing especially on postliberalism. The paper will be broken into three parts. The first will examine what has been called the "hard right," dividing it into three separate ideologies: the Nietzschean right, national conservatism, and postliberalism. The second part of the paper will summarize some of the basic features of postliberalism, including its critique of liberalism and the endorsement of "common good conservatism" and constitutionalism. The third section will discuss how postliberalism both differs from and overlaps with other species of modern hard right thinking, especially national conservatism. It will argue that a "fusionism"

---

[1]. Currently a Lecturer in the Department of Political Science, University of Michigan (Ann Arbor).

of national conservatism and postliberalism is most likely, and would have a genuine shot at appealing to many on the American hard right. The paper will conclude with a brief discussion of why liberal socialism and not postliberalism is the political ideology which deserves a real shot at the future.

Introduction: The Right Is Back

IN HIS LATE EIGHTEENTH century polemic "Against Rousseau," the conservative, Catholic thinker Joseph de Maistre wrote, "Human reason reduced to its own resources is perfectly worthless, not only for creating but also for preserving any political or religious association, because it only produces disputes, and, to conduct himself well, man needs not problems but beliefs. His cradle should be surrounded by dogmas, and when his reason is awakened, it should find all his opinions ready-made, at least all those relating to his conduct. Nothing is so important to him as prejudices, Let us not take this word in a bad sense. It does not necessarily mean false ideas, but only, in the strict sense of the word, opinions adopted before any examination. Now these sorts of opinions are man's greatest need, the true elements of his happiness, and the Palladium of empires. Without them, there can be neither worship, nor morality, nor government."[2]

For our sins we liberals have been cursed with our own version of the eternal recurrence of the same. That is, the "hard"[3] right will always try again no matter how many times it triumphantly emerges, fails miserably, brings shame upon itself and everyone it touches and slinks back into obscurity. In some ways this is to be welcomed since an end to history, as Fukuyama himself acknowledged, would probably be a very dull time and its liberalism a very uninspiring[4] liberalism.[5] Bereft of any

---

2. De Maistre, *Against Rousseau*, 87.

3. I use the term "hard right" in Fawcett's sense, as designating a very right-wing movement that has nonetheless achieved sufficient mainstream appeal to no longer warrant the designation "far right." As he puts it the hard right is a "segment of conservatism that rejects one or more core elements of the liberal-democratic status quo. An unstable alliance of free-market hyper-liberals and popular anti-liberals, the hard right claims to speak for "the people" against "the elites." It is called "hard," not "new," because its themes are old; and "hard," not "far" or "extreme," because since 1980, it has drawn off votes from the center right to join the mainstream. See Fawcett, *Conservatism*, 420.

4. See Fukuyama, "End of History?," 18.

5. If we're being honest, uninspiring is one of the politest words for the system

serious historical alternatives, Fukuyama warned that the end of history would be a very dull time peopled by Nietzsche's "last men" focused on willing nothing much in particular. By contrast we live in an era where exotic possibilities seem commonplace, and where old world seems to be straining while the new one has yet to be born. This has engendered a number of novel or resuscitated political ideologies competing for oxygen in an increasingly competitive circuit where much seems up for grabs. One of the most intriguing of these new ideologies is postliberalism.

This paper will break into three parts. The first will examine the state of the hard right today, offering a brief survey of some of the movement and characters that have taken up a lot of political oxygen and MSNBC's attention since 2016. The second will summarize some of the basic features of postliberalism. And the third concluding section will discuss how postliberalism differs and overlaps with other species of modern hard right thinking. I will also briefly discuss why I think liberal socialism and not postliberalism is the political ideology which deserves our attention.[6]

The State of the Hard Right Today

Postliberalism is a problematic name for an appropriately problematic doctrine. The label suggests postliberals are defined primarily by their negations rather than a shared political programme. And depending on how expansively one conceives of postliberalism, this may or may not be true. For the purposes of this essay I will refer to anti-liberalism to describe the wide swathe of rightist ideologies committed to rejecting liberal principles and the institutions of liberal democracy, and postliberalism to describe a more specific doctrine. Since coming out of the closet in 2016 the anti-liberal right includes a huge swathe of very different figures and movements. At the (influential) fringes one finds everything from unabashed fascists and "white identitarians," to Eurasianists after the model of "Putin's Brain" Aleksandr Dugin, traditionalists in the mode of the postwar Italian Julius Evola, outright Catholic integralists, and alt-right nihilists who just want to see liberalism burn and everything in between.[7]

---

of neoliberal governance that was hegemonic through the end of the century, and which is responsible for many of the same symptoms of resistance many neoliberals now decry. See McManus, *Rise of Post-Modern Conservatism*; McManus, *Emergence of Postmodernity*.

6. See my forthcoming McManus, *Political Theory of Liberal Socialism*.
7. See Sedgwick, *Key Thinkers of the Radical Right*.

In the United States there are three anti-liberal ideologies which have gained significant traction, to the point of being able to openly influence the mainstream.

The first and (for now) smallest is a growing cadre of Carlyean and Nietzschean inspired reactionary modernists who combine a heady mixture of antiquarian appeals with more trollish kinds of ultra-masculism and assertions of natural hierarchy and domination. Often secular, these figures see liberal democracy as embodying a degenerate and effeminate kind of egalitarianism which has none the less erected itself as a force of totalitarian oppression.[8] In particular liberal democracy establishes a kind of hegemonic culture, embodied by ominous neologisms like the "cathedral" or "the longhouse," which both abets anarchistic libertinism and constrains the liberty to dominate of the most rarefied and coconut oil lathered specimens.[9] Or as Lom3Z (yes you read that right) put it in his *First Things* debut, the "longhouse" of technocratic governance and "wokeness" constrain the "drive to assert oneself on the world, to strike out for conquest and expansion. Male competition and the hierarchies that drive it are unwelcome. Even constructive expressions of these instincts are deemed toxic, patriarchal, or even racist."[10] Whether such perennially glued to their screen online influencers could in fact become roided up "super-duper" men cosplaying as Conan the Barbarian is a "big political problem for this doctrine it has yet to answer.[11]" Both in the figurative sense of being problematic and the literal sense of typically nebbish online rightists getting jacked and leaving the basement to baste themselves in tanning lotion.

Irresolvable dialectical tensions aside, it is important not to underestimate the influence and potential power of secular authoritarians in the United States. Figures like Bronze Age Pervert and Curtis Yarvin have gathered considerable followings. This includes in the auspicious halls of power as the *Bronze Age Mindset* had a cult following amongst younger Trump aides[12] and Yarvin receives laudatory references by Chris Rufo—responsible for reshaping Florida's post-secondary curriculum—and is

---

8. Authors like Curtis Yarvin, Bronze Age Pervert, and LOM3Z cater to this demographic, and have gained a disturbing level of mainstream credibility.
9. See Bronze Age Pervert. *Bronze Age Mindset*, 149.
10. See Lom3Z, "Longhouse."
11. See Ganz, "Super-Duper Men."
12. See Gray, "How Bronze Age Pervert Built."

financed by billionaire Peter Thiel.[13] More comfortable with ironically and sincerely deploying the language of racism, sexism, and even eugenics these figures have tapped into a sincere animosity towards liberal norms of egalitarian toleration. Whether they could move from tin-foil ruminations about Cathedrals and totalitarian "huemen" to offer a concrete programme capable of enticing political support outside the hard core of the Republican party is another story. What its future could be in an increasingly diverse country, where a majority of voters are usually women, is another again.

Less extreme and more respectable than the secular Nietzschean right are "national conservatives." Once upon a time conflated with postliberals, there are in fact considerable differences between postliberalism and national conservatism. A national conservative, according to amiable and erudite philosopher and lead spokesman Yoram Hazony, is "a person who works to recover, restore, and build up the traditions of his forefathers and to pass them onto future generations."[14] At its philosophical heart, national conservatism repeats the counter-Revolutionary objection that liberalism is an airy "rationalist" creed which is unable to conjure sufficient human affections and loyalties. Predicated on abstract universal principles like liberty and equality for all, it should be replaced by a "historical empiricism" which reverences the national traditions, practices, and of course hierarchies into which we are born.

These ironically abstract epistemological questions aside, national conservatism is distinct in having a relatively clear political programme. For Hazony, rejecting "liberal democracy" would entail rejecting liberal ideas about the moral equality of all human beings. This is because the people of one's own "nation" will always be entitled to a higher degree of moral concern. And also because it is beneficent for individuals to submit to traditional hierarchies as the "ability to give honor to a superior in an unchosen hierarchical relationship is the one capacity on which all other gains in knowledge, wisdom, skills, and capacities depends."[15] Cashed out, Hazony argues that this national conservative deference to hierarchical tradition would best be administered by a "conservative" democracy. This conservative democracy would differ from its liberal counterparts in unabashedly embodying the identity and traditions of the dominant national tradition while rejecting deep pluralism at the

---

13. See Sedgwick, *Key Thinkers of the Radical Right*.
14. See Hazony, *Conservatism*, 1.
15. See Hazony, *Conservatism*, 131.

domestic level.[16] As a nationalist Hazony naturally rejects cosmopolitanism and internationalism, insisting that the nation is the most general imagined community to which we can commit ourselves. He is critical of cosmopolitan internationalists for their allegedly "imperialist" insistence on imposing their moral principles on independent nations.[17]

Interestingly, while Hazony rejects deep pluralism at the national level-calling for restrictive immigration policies and rejecting liberal rights for minorities in favor of "carve outs"[18]—it respects and even mandates a kind of deeply pluralistic international community. He has even gone so far as to adopt Millsian language in defending the existence of different nation states as "experiments" which should be left to run. Though even here Hazony is clear that this doesn't mean *all* experiments, since some nations aren't necessarily[19] entitled to a state.[20] Never the less Hazony's appeal to ever popular conservative nationalism and the elastic nature of his pluralistic internationalism has ensured that his doctrine has found a wide audience. This includes in the United States where there is now an annual "National Conservatism" (or NATCON as its called) conference and prominent conservatives like Marjorie Taylor Greene[21] and Trump[22] describe themselves as nationalists of Christian nationalist. National conservatism has also found receptive ears in other countries, with Hungarian autocrat Victor Orban attending the 2020 National Conservatism conference in Rome[23] and conferences in the United Kingdom featuring a prominent array of British conservatives.

Ironically, national conservatism echoes the Nietzschean right in containing a considerable volume of modernist ideas and principles. Hazony's "historical empiricism" may emphasize ancient traditions, but its traditionalism is very vulnerable to the classic Straussian objection that it is ultimately a form of historicism which distances itself from appeals to transcendent truth through appeal to crude empirical facts. Hazony himself has been eager to rebut this charge, though this has been

16. See Hazony, "Conservative Democracy."
17. See Hazony, *Virtue of Nationalism*.
18. See Hazony, "Why National Conservatism?"
19. As an Israeli nationalist one can make a pretty good guess about why Hazony adopts this line. Gives himself a bit of an ideological carve out as it were.
20. See Hazony, *Virtue of Nationalism*.
21. See Tyler, "Marjorie Taylor Greene's Words."
22. See Forgey, "Trump."
23. See NATCON Rome, "Prime Minister Viktor Orbán."

at the theoretically extreme cost of having to bake very unempirical transcendent entities like God and indeed the "nation" into his philosophy.[24] Nevertheless, no matter how much political theorists resent it, strict consistency has never been a metric for how popular a political ideology will become. If that were the case the political right would have buried itself generations ago through endless attacks on rationalism. Given these precedents, my hunch is that national conservatism has the best shot at being a "big tent" for the hard right since it is both internationally pluralist and, to a degree, can incorporate both secularists and true believers in a way the Nietzschean and postliberal right cannot.

What Is Postliberalism?

This brings us to our third anti-liberal ideology which has been gaining steam on the hard right: postliberalism itself. An ambitious genealogy of postliberalism could of course go all the way back to pre-liberal thinkers such as Aristotle and Aquinas. More recent intellectual antecedents include the cultural critique of T. S. Eliot and his calls for a "Christian society,"[25] the critique of modernity pioneered by Leo Strauss and Eric Voegelin,[26] John Finnis' sophisticated defense of natural law and good ol' fashioned homophobia,[27] the MacIntyrean critique of liberal atomism and nihilism,[28] and most disconcertingly the political theology and decisionist legal theories of the fascist jurist Carl Schmitt.[29] At a less academically rarefied level, within the United States there were prominent outlets which served as incubators for postliberal philosophy. Without a

---

24. See Hazony, *Conservatism*, 290–296.

25. See Eliot, *Christianity and Culture*. The debt to Eliot is often unsubtle and sometimes borders on the hagiographic. For instance, R. R. Reno "pulling a Netflix" and giving us an unasked for late sequel to Eliot's minor classic. See Reno. *Resurrecting*.

26. See McAllister, *Revolt Against Modernity*; Strauss, *Natural Right and History*. Note the reference to a "postliberal order" in McAllister's work.

27. See Finnis, "Law, Morality, and Sexual Orientation"; Finnis, *Natural Law and Natural Rights*.

28. For the most part, excepting Deneen, of course ignoring MacIntyre's persistent Marxism. See MacIntyre. *After Virtue*; MacIntyre, *Marxism and Christianity*.

29. Adrian Vermeule, the chief legal theorist amongst the postliberals, isn't shy about affirming his debt to Schmittian decisionism and political theology. See Vermeule. "All Human Conflict Is Ultimately Theological," and for a more extensive treatment, Vermeule, *Common Good Constitutionalism*. For Schmitt's own work, see Schmitt, *Concept of the Political*; Schmitt, *Constitutional Theory*, and perhaps most importantly, Schmitt, *Political Theology*.

doubt the most important is the magazine *First Things*, which has published virtually all the significant postliberal thinkers and activists.[30] But its only been recently that postliberalism has a broader cultural cache, both among young right wing activists[31] and within the conservative legal movement.[32]

So what then is postliberalism? Much like the earlier hard right movements we looked at, its proponents don't speak with one voice. But as their name suggests they look forward to a time after liberalism where, after sufficient time spent time dozing through the Latin Mass, we achieve a deeper sense of solidarity and meaning as individuals and a community.[33] This has often entailed being very critical of liberalism for its atomizing and distintegrationist qualities; always upending the conventions of moral order through force in the name of emancipating the people from ignorance. Or as Vermeule put it the "good liberal should always be able to say, "We have made progress, but there is still much to do." This is why the triumph of same-sex marriage actually happened *too suddenly and too completely*. Something else was needed to animate liberalism, and transgenderism has quickly filled the gap, defining new forces of reaction and thus enabling new iterations and celebrations of the Festival [of Reason]."[34]

Without a doubt the most extensive, comprehensive and rich articulation of postliberal thinking is given by Patrick Deneen. Because I have already discussed his views in considerable detail elsewhere, and for reasons of space, I'll be brief.[35] Deneen holds that the real basis of liberalism is in the materialist ontology pioneered by Francis Bacon and

---

30. See Deneen. "Unsustainable Liberalism"; Reno, "End of Christendom?"; Vermeule, "Liturgy of Liberalism."

31. See Adler-Bell, "Radical Young Intellectuals." See especially the reference to "postliberal" localists, in the vein of Patrick Deneen, who wrote *Why Liberalism Failed*, and Rod Dreher, the irascible Eastern Orthodox blogger and author of *The Benedict Option*, a spirited argument for Christian retreat from the turpitude of public life into virtuous communal separatism. And others are Roman Catholic integralists, aspiring to a theologically ordered politics: Harvard Law professor Vermeule and University of Dallas politics professor and *American Affairs* editor Gladden Pappin are their touchstones.

32. See Ward, "Critics Call It Theocratic and Authoritarian."

33. Not coincidentally the writings of Peter Lawler have been an influence on postliberals. Lawler called for a "post-modern conservatism" which was intended to reject modernity. See Lawler, *American Heresies*; Lawler, *Postmodernism Rightly Understood*.

34. See Vermeule, "Liturgy of Liberalism."

35. See McManus. *Political Right and Equality*, 176–83.

other early advocates of the scientific method. This metaphysics rejected the Scholastic view of a teleological universe in favor of one which conceived nature as mere matter in motion. The normative takeaway from this is the only good in human life was the pursuit of hedonic pleasure, giving rise to the classical liberal worldview centered around securing rights for the individual to maximize their utility without interference from the state or civil society. As time went on classical liberalism gave way to "progressive" liberals like J. S. Mill and John Rawls, who argued that the state must in fact actively facilitate the individual's "experiments" in living through various welfarist programs while insulating them from condemnation by socially conservative groups eager to retain the antiquarian notion of the good.[36] This led to the emergence of a technocratic liberal "power" elite instantiating a "perverse combination of the new and older forms of tyranny; neither raw imposition of power of few resulting in the misery of many, nor the soft despotism of a paternalistic state that keeps its citizens in a state of permanent childishness, but the forced imposition of radical expressivism upon the population by the Power Elite."[37]

Deneen follows Hazony in also having an alternative at hand to replace liberalism through enacting a "regime change." This would be what he calls a "mixed regime" of aristopopulism which would enforce an ideology of "common good conservatism."[38] This would entail ending the tyranny of the liberal "power" elite by replacing it with a conservative "power" elite." A new boss which I suppose will be much different from the old boss. Interestingly, Deneen makes some gestures towards political and economic populism. For instance by taking measures to "mix" classes in the federal government through increasing the number of political representatives[39] and the "development of national economic policies that will displace the primacy of economic wealth-creation for a small number of elites, instead with a concern for the national distribution of productive work, expectation of a family supportive wage for at least one member of a family, and the redistribution of social capital." However, much like other right-wing "anti-capitalist" programmes which are not

---

36. See Deneen, *Why Liberalism Failed*.

37. Deneen, *Regime Change*, 60.

38. The language of the "common good" appears to be the more positive label post-liberals are gravitating towards to cease being defined purely by their negations. See also Vermeule, *Common Good Constitutionalism*.

39. See Deneen, *Regime Change*, 171.

in fact anti-capital, Deneen's economics will not involve the extensive "redistribution of wealth" since such policies have historically led to "extensive damage to the broader economic order while leaving in place the institutions and attitudes that divide the elite from the people."[40]

Finally, and most importantly, common good conservatism would implement extensive socially conservative measures designed to reintegrate the community. These range from potentially reintroducing the draft, turning a skeptical eye on liberal and progressives modes of analysis like critical race theory, encouraging heterosexual family formation and eroding the separation of the Church and state which Deneen characterizes as "totalitarian."[41] Unsurprisingly, autocratic Hungary is often pointed to as a potential model for emulation.[42] Common good conservatives would also very likely reject liberal notions of the rule of law and legal neutrality, including those embodied by originalism, and transforming the judiciary with judges more willing to make transparently normative judgements in the name of common good constitutionalism. Judges oriented by common good constitutionalism would take a dim view of rights for the queer population, on abortion, and potentially even democracy where democratization abets liberal or libertine values.[43] As Vermeule chillingly puts it, when it comes to implementing the common good "democracy, in the modern sense of mass electoral democracy, has no special privilege in this regard. A democracy, in that sense, may or may not be oriented to the common good; one has to see whether it is, and the answer will depend on circumstances."[44]

One or another of these transformations might not constitute a "regime change" but taken together we can accept Deneen's word that enough would qualitatively change to warrant the label. The question then becomes where postliberalism lands on the hard right, and what its future prospects happen to be.

---

40. See Deneen, *Regime Change*, 166.
41. See Deneen, *Regime Change*, 228.
42. For a discussion of Hungary's "illiberal" democracy, see Lendvai. *Orban*.
43. As discussed in Vermeule, *Common Good Constitutionalism*.
44. See Vermeule, *Common Good Constitutionalism*, 47.

Conclusion: Where on the Hard Right to Situate Postliberalism?

As one might expect postliberals have expressed a deep wariness bordering on hostility towards the burgeoning Nietzschean right in the United States.[45] This is to their credit. Not only do postliberals reject the Nietzschean right's condemnation of Christianity and muscular atheism, they express considerable hostility towards its often overt racism[46] and glorification of Homeric militarism.[47] In the MacIntyrean choice between Aristotle and Nietzsche, the postliberals are emphatically with the defender of natural slavery *plus* polis.

Things get more complex when it comes to the relationship between national conservatism and postliberalism. Here there is a far deeper elective affinity between their concrete aspirations, even if the theoretical underpinnings of national conservatism and postliberalism are quite different. For instance Hazony has been sharply critical of the universalist aspirations of the Catholic Church which is the spiritual home of many postliberals. His rhetoric often portrays it as precursor of the kind of global cosmopolitan order he opposes.[48] This of course relates back to his selective endorsement of pluralism flowing from a historical empiricist metaphysics. Firing back, postliberals like Deneen have been sharply critical of nationalism as an effectively modernist doctrine which emerged with the French revolution and locates the site of communitarian integration in thinly defended tradition. As Deneen puts it, in "the heat generated by contemporary divides, it is unsurprising that the liberal origins and progressive commitment to nationalism have been altogether forgotten or suppressed by the various parties."[49] He in turn chastises American conservatives for putting their highest faith in the national ideal, appealing to Pope Francis to call for a wider sense of membership

---

45. I say "bordering" since *First Things* magazine has published some Nietzschean rightists such as Lom3Z and Michael Millerman's defense of Duginism.

46. This isn't to say the postliberals are enthusiasts about ending racism where this takes on a progressive connotation. Deneen is typical in endorsing an end to racism while condemning critical race theory for enacting a "separation" rather than an integration of peoples. One is tempted to fire back that the real source of racial "separation" in the United States might have been the systems of slavery and segregation and then ghettoization enacted through the country's history. You know, the kinds of things the critical race theorists criticize. The debate goes on. See Deneen, *Regime Change*, 200.

47. See the conclusion in Rose, *World after Liberalism*, 136–257.

48. See Hazony, *Virtue of Nationalism*.

49. Deneen, *Regime Change*, 219.

that eventually includes "the whole of humanity."[50] Interestingly,[51] this standpoint reflects the humanist and egalitarian ethos underpinning Christianity which Nietzsche amongst others was so correct to associate with liberalism, democracy, and socialism.[52]

In the long run this would likely mean that an idealized postliberal regime would be friendlier to at least some Christian cosmopolitan institutions and universalist aspirations than national conservatism. But in the short run its likely to be a cosmetic difference since so many of the concrete domestic ambitions of national conservatism and postliberalism overlap. This explains why major figures like Hazony and Deneen have been far more comfortable dialoguing with one another, and why postliberals like Rod Dreher have happily attended National Conservatism conferences and discussions. They also share a deep admiration for states like Hungary and Poland which readily combine Christian and Burkean nationalist anti-liberalism.[53] And of course this is by no means an idiosyncratic conservative approach in theory of practice.[54]

Speculating on the future is always dangerous for any political theorist, and both postliberalism and national conservatism has steep hills to climb on the route to success. While populist forms of postliberalism and national conservatism have enjoyed influence in the GOP, their more populist and authoritarian ventures remain checked by the still considerable influence of well funded neoliberal and ordered liberal actors. While hardly occupying the hegemonic space in U.S. politics they once did, neo and ordered liberty liberals also have the benefit of presenting a moderate face to a potentially liberalizing American electorate where majorities have voted Democrat in seven of the last eight Presidential elections. But its as safe a bet as any that if the hard right manages to fully overcome the neoliberal and ordered liberty conservatives in the Republican party, it will likely be through some vague alliance between national conservatives and postliberals. Perhaps operating on a new fusionist basis by labelling

---

50. Deneen, *Regime Change*, 226.

51. A more nuanced and less immanently critical approach to liberalism and socialism might take this Nietzschean insight about their origins in Christian thought seriously. For example see Taylor, *Secular Age*.

52. See my discussion in McManus, "Nietzsche's Critique of Egalitarian Post-Christianity."

53. See Dreher, "What Conservatives Must Learn From Orban's Hungary."

54. See Devlin, *Enforcement of Morals*.

themselves overt "Christian nationalists" to the outrage of liberal pundits.[55] This Christian nationalism would almost certainly have to reject Hazony's moderate internationalist pluralism to lean into the language of divinely ordained American exceptionalism,[56] while on the other end postliberals would probably have to cede some of their economic demands to the traditionalist emphasis on the market "liberty." Deneen's lukewarm, comparatively unenthusiastic analysis of economic "populism" amounts to nothing more than a return to the economics of the Eisenhower administration when the United States established a famously mediocre welfare state. This doesn't suggest the loss of economic populism would be all that significant for postliberals eager above all to enact a socially conservative agenda, and who will be plenty occupied censoring rainbows wherever they appear. Taken together this new Christian nationalist fusion, whether going by that name or not, would be a very potent force, especially in white America. It could potentially complete the overturning of neoliberal conservatism ala Paul Ryan and Matthew Continetti and move the party in a permanently more populist direction.[57]

But a Christian nationalist fusion would be very vulnerable to other, more comprehensively democratic and egalitarian forms of liberalism. The most potent response would likely be to actually lean in on liberal economic populism and egalitarian social policies while continuing to endorse the expressive individualism of Mill and Rawls. One thing rarely discussed by postliberals is the unexpected rise of Bernie Sanders and democratic socialism in the United States, which has been the other beneficiary of dissatisfaction with neoliberal governance. A liberal socialist politics wouldn't constitute a kind of regime change of the sort postliberals are talking about, but instead a fulfillment of the Jeffersonian promise to create a country where all of us who are created equal genuinely have an equal opportunity to lead a good life. Liberal socialism, not postliberalism, is a politics which actually deserves a future.

55. See Tyler, "Marjorie Taylor Greene's Words."

56. This evangelizing approach to American nationalism would hardly be novel in the United States. No less a figure than Ronald Reagan mastered it through the 1980s. It was also present in considerably mutated form within Trumpism. See Winston, *Righting the American Dream*.

57. See Continetti, *Right*.

Bibliography

Adler-Bell, Sam. "The Radical Young Intellectuals Who Want To Take Over the American Right." *New Republic*, December 2, 2021.

Bronze Age Pervert. *Bronze Age Mindset*. Independently Published, 2018.

Continetti, Matthew. *The Right: The Hundred Year War for American Conservatism*. New York: Basic, 2022.

De Maistre, Joseph. *Against Rousseau: On the State of Nature and On the Sovereignty of the People*. Translated and edited by Richard A. Lebrun. Kingston: McGill-Queen's, 1996).

Deneen, Patrick J. "After Liberalism: Can We Imagine a Humane, Post-Liberal Future?" *Religion and Ethics*, December 11, 2014. https://www.abc.net.au/religion/after-liberalism-can-we-imagine-a-humane-post-liberal-future/10098770.

———. *Conserving America: Essays on Present Discontents*. South Bend, IN: St. Augustine's, 2016.

———. *Democratic Faith*. Princeton: Princeton University Press, 2005.

———. "How Will Future Historians Treat Same-Sex Marriage." *Public Discourse*, July 10, 2013. https://www.thepublicdiscourse.com/2013/07/10513/.

———. *Regime Change: Toward a Postliberal Future*. New York: Sentinel, 2023.

———. "Unsustainable Liberalism." *First Things*, August 2012. https://www.firstthings.com/article/2012/08/unsustainable-liberalism.

———. *Why Liberalism Failed*. New Haven: Yale University Press, 2018.

Devlin, Patrick. *The Enforcement of Morals*. Maccabean Lecture in Jurisprudence, 1959. Oxford: Oxford University Press, 1959.

Dreher, Rod. *The Benedict Option: A Strategy for Christians in a Post-Christian Nation*. New York: Sentinel, 2017.

———. "What Conservatives Must Learn from Orban's Hungary." *YouTube*, November 2, 2021. https://www.youtube.com/watch?v=BEB7FdogGS4.

Eliot, T. S. *Christianity and Culture: The Idea of a Christian Society and Notes Towards the Definition of Culture*. New York: Harvest, 1949.

———. *Selected Prose*. Edited by John Hayward. London: Penguin, 1953.

Fawcett, Edmund. *Conservatism: The Fight for a Tradition*. Princeton: Princeton University Press, 2020.

Finnis, John. "Law, Morality, and Sexual Orientation." In *Same Sex: Debating the Ethics, Science, and Culture of Homosexuality*, edited by John Corvino, 31–43. Lanham, MD: Rowman and Littlefield, 1997.

———. *Natural Law and Natural Rights*. 2nd ed. Oxford: Oxford University Press, 2011.

Forgey, Quint. "Trump: I'm a Nationalist." *Politico*, October 22, 2018. https://www.politico.com/story/2018/10/22/trump-nationalist-926745.

Fukuyama, Francis. "The End of History?" *The National Interest* 16 (1989) 3–18.

Ganz, John. "The Super-Duper Men." *Unpopular Front*, February 20, 2023. https://www.unpopularfront.news/p/the-super-duper-men.

Gray, Rosie. "How Bronze Age Pervert Built and Online Following and Injected Anti-Democracy, Pro-Men Ideas into the GOP." *Politico*, July 16, 2023. https://www.politico.com/news/magazine/2023/07/16/bronze-age-pervert-masculinity-00105427.

Hazony, Yoram. *Conservatism: A Rediscovery*. Washington, DC: Regnery, 2022.

———. "Conservative Democracy: Liberal Principles Have Brought Us a Dead End." *First Things*, January 2019. https://www.firstthings.com/article/2019/01/conservative-democracy.

———. "The Challenge of Marxism." *Quillette*, August 16, 2020. https://quillette.com/2020/08/16/the-challenge-of-marxism/.

———. *The Virtue of Nationalism*. New York: Basic, 2018.

———. "Why National Conservatism?" *National Conservatism*, July 15, 2019. https://www.youtube.com/watch?v=4cpyd1OqHJU&t=1725s.

Hendricks, Obery. *Christians against Christianity: How Right Wing Evangelicals Are Destroying Our Nation and Our Faith*. Boston: Beacon, 2021.

———. *The Politics of Jesus: Rediscovering the True Revolutionary Nature of Jesus' Teachings and How They Have Been Corrupted*. New York: Three Leaves, 2006.

Lawler, Peter Augustine. *American Heresies and Higher Education*. South Bend, IN: St. Augustine's, 2016.

———. "Conservative Postmodernism, Postmodern Conservatism." *Intercollegiate Institute*, October 8, 2014. https://isi.org/intercollegiate-review/conservative-postmodernism-postmodern-conservatism/.

———. *Postmodernism Rightly Understood: The Return to Realism in American Thought*. Lanham, MD: Rowman and Littlefield, 1992.

Lendvai, Paul. *Orban: Hungary's Strongman*. Oxford: Oxford University Press, 2018.

Lom3Z. "The Longhouse." *First Things*, February 16, 2023. https://www.firstthings.com/web-exclusives/2023/02/what-is-the-longhouse.

MacIntyre, Alasdair. *After Virtue: A Study in Moral Theory*. 3rd ed. Notre Dame: University of Notre Dame Press, 2007.

———. *Marcuse*. London: Fontana, 1970.

———. *Marxism and Christianity*. Notre Dame: University of Notre Dame Press, 2003.

———. "The Virtues, the Unity of a Human Life, and the Concept of a Tradition." In *Liberalism and Its Critics*, edited by Michael Sandel. New York: New York University Press, 1984.

———. *Whose Justice, Which Rationality?* Notre Dame: University of Notre Dame Press, 1989.

Maistre, Joseph De. *Considerations on France*. Translated by Richard A. Lebrun. New York: Cambridge University Press, 1994.

———. *Essay on the Generative Principle of Political Constitutions*. Translated by Renata Czekalska. Krakow: New Direction, 2019.

———. *The Generative Principle of Political Constitutions: Studies on Sovereignty, Religion, and Enlightenment*. Edited and Translated by Jack Lively. London: Routledge, 1965.

———. *St. Petersburg Dialogues*. Translated by Richard A. Lebrun. Montreal: McGill-Queens University Press, 1993.

McAllister, Ted V. *Revolt Against Modernity: Leo Strauss, Eric Voegelin, and the Search for a Postliberal Order*. Lawrence, KS: University of Kansas Press, 1995.

McManus, Matthew. *The Emergence of Postmodernity at the Intersection of Liberalism, Capitalism, and Secularism: The Center Cannot Hold*. Palgrave Studies in Classical Liberalism. Cham: Palgrave MacMillan, 2022.

McManus, Matthew. "Nietzsche's Critique of Egalitarian Post-Christianity." In *Nietzsche and the Politics of Reaction: Essays on Liberalism, Socialism, and Aristocratic Radicalism*, edited by Matthew McManus, 9–23. Palgrave Studies in Classical Liberalism. Cham: Palgrave McMillian, 2023.

———. *The Political Right and Equality: Turning Back the Tide of Egalitarian Modernity*. New York: Routledge, 2024.

———. *The Rise of Post-Modern Conservatism: Neoliberalism, Post-Modern Culture, and Reactionary Politics*. Cham: Palgrave MacMillan, 2019.

NATCON Rome. "Prime Minister Viktor Orbán: Interview with Chris DeMuth | NatCon Rome 2020." *YouTube*, February 10, 2020. https://www.youtube.com/watch?v=9WP8xzxH7YY.

Reno, R. R. "The End of Christendom?" *First Things*, April 2022. https://www.firstthings.com/article/2022/04/the-end-of-christendom.

———. *Resurrecting the Idea of Christian Society*. Washington, DC: Regnery Faith, 2016.

———. *Return of the Strong Gods: Nationalism, Populism, and the Future of the West*. Washington, DC: Regnery Faith, 2019.

Rose, Matthew. *A World after Liberalism: Philosophers of the Radical Right*. New Haven: Yale University Press, 2021.

Sedgwick, Mark. *Key Thinkers of the Radical Right: Behind the New Threat to Liberal Democracy*. Oxford: Oxford University Press, 2019.

Schmitt, Carl. *The Concept of the Political*. Chicago: University of Chicago Press, 1996.

———. *The Concept of the Political: Expanded Edition*. Chicago: University of Chicago Press, 2007.

———. *Constitutional Theory*. Translated by Jeffrey Seitzer. Durham: Duke University Press, 2008.

———. *Legality and Legitimacy*. Translated by Jeffrey Seitzer. Chicago: University of Chicago Press, 2004.

———. *The Leviathan in the State Theory of Thomas Hobbes*. Chicago: University of Chicago Press, 2008.

———. *The Nomos of the Earth in the International Law of Jus Publicum Europeaum*. Candor, NY: Telos, 2006.

———. *Political Theology*. Chicago: University of Chicago Press, 2005.

Strauss, Leo. *Natural Right and History*. Chicago: University of Chicago Press, 1953.

Taylor, Charles. *A Secular Age*. Cambridge: Harvard University Press, 2007.

Tyler, Amanda. "Marjorie Taylor Greene's Words on Christian Nationalism Are a Wake Up Call." *CNN*, July 22, 2022. https://www.cnn.com/2022/07/27/opinions/christian-nationalism-marjorie-taylor-greene-tyler/index.html.

Vermeule, Adrian. "All Human Conflict Is Ultimately Theological." *Church Life Journal*, July 26, 2019. https://churchlifejournal.nd.edu/articles/all-human-conflict-is-ultimately-theological/.

———. *Common Good Constitutionalism: Recovering the Classical Legal Tradition*. Cambridge: Polity, 2022.

———. "The Liturgy of Liberalism." *First Things*, January 2017. https://www.firstthings.com/article/2017/01/liturgy-of-liberalism.

Ward, Ian. "Critics Call It Theocratic and Authoritarian. Young Conservatives Call It an Exciting New Legal Theory." *Politico*, December 9, 2022. https://www.politico.com/news/magazine/2022/12/09/revolutionary-conservative-legal-philosophy-courts-00069201.

Winston, Diane. *Righting the American Dream: How the Media Mainstreamed Reagan's Evangelical Vision*. Chicago: University of Chicago Press, 2023.

13

Formation for a New Social Catholicism[1]

WILLIAM. F. MURPHY JR.,
INITIATIVE FOR SOCIAL CATHOLICISM

Abstract: Presupposing our consideration in chapter 5 of the formation of Msgr. John A. Ryan that prepared him to foster an era of social Catholicism in the United States during the first half of the twentieth century, this essay proposes ten theses regarding the primarily intellectual formation needed to enable something similar so Catholics can do their part in addressing the great challenges of the twenty-first-century polycrisis. These begin with the need for a properly theological methodology and hermeneutic, and the cultivation of a distinctively Catholic identity that keeps critical distance from ideological and partisan commitments and gives due attention to the discernment of the magisterium. They include an understanding of our place in a multifaceted historical narrative addressing at least the following dimensions: the relation between Christianity and the state; the reception of the Second Vatican Council; different understandings of liberalism and constitutional democracy; Catholicism in American history, especially since postconciliar era; economic history, American Catholic history, and the history of American politics. Another thesis

---

1. This chapter is the development of a part of an essay published in *Chicago Studies* and is republished with permission.

concerns the need to strive for an economy and society that works for everyone and is environmentally sustainable. Yet another concerns the need to understand and avoid risks of ideological extremes. In addition, we must learn to respond wisely to today's propaganda, disinformation and post truth, to recognize the contemporary struggle between democracy and autocracy, and make a firm commitment to the renewal of constitutional democracy, supporting or opposing political parties based especially on their support for democracy and their opposition to autocracy. The final thesis is that a new social Catholicism must foster a global, and Catholic perspective.

Introduction

IN WHAT FOLLOWS, MY goal is to outline the key aspects of especially intellectual formation that can help well-disposed Catholics to appreciate not only the challenges we face but the potentially decisive resources that our tradition can offer to a world that too often despairs of the future. It outlines a path to develop what St. Thomas Aquinas calls the "confidence" or "preparedness of mind" so we can magnanimously—that is, with greatness of soul—play our indispensable part in building a future worthy of the human family. In citing various sources, my goal is to indicate the abundance of literature available to those who want to understand the challenges so they can join in the struggle to address them by drawing on the principles and methodology of our social tradition, while incorporating the discernment of the magisterium. Such an approach enables us to work in a spirit of faithful trust in God, hope in the divine promise of assistance—especially in addressing the grave challenges that lead many to despair—and according to the rationality of charity which reflects the marks of social friendship in working for the common good.

In focusing on the formation of intellectual virtues in the context of the theological virtues, I am in no way denying the need for a broader formation in all the virtues. On the contrary, a renewed social apostolate will require the full configuration of cardinal and moral virtues. This will include, for example, the virtue of prudence to put the light of right reason into our actions, which will require a deep understanding of the relevant principles, the benefit of experience and the openness to take counsel and learn from the insights of others. Agents of a new social Catholicism will need to cultivate a burning hunger and thirst for justice, especially on behalf of those who have been disadvantaged or left behind, which is more difficult than in John Ryan's day as many contemporary Catholics are of higher social status and more associated with wealth and power than poverty and disadvantage. We need to make special efforts, therefore, to empathize with the underprivileged: those who have been left behind by rising economic inequality, those who have suffered from the denial of their rights and human dignity, and those who have been oppressed by systemic injustices including—for example—the widespread gerrymandering of election districts, and the disproportionate influence of money on politics. In our day, moreover, we need to be especially alert to questions of intergenerational justice given the crises we are leaving to the young, such as the climate catastrophe, a polarized and degraded democracy, and massive debt.

These new social Catholics—including those of us who are older and have enjoyed the advantages of our generation—will need the virtue of courage, and the gifts of the Holy Spirit to address what are often systemic injustices that have been put in place to benefit entrenched interests. They will also need the virtues of patience and perseverance because these systemic injustices permeate the various structures of power, including political parties, lobbying organizations, donor networks, thinktanks, and universities. They will also need the full configuration of virtues for the challenges they will meet within the Church, where views that are not easily reconcilable with our social tradition are widespread, firmly held and institutionalized.

Nor does my focus on intellectual formation deny the need to engage in practical action, and to reform and build institutions which will be essential to a new social Catholicism. These practical tasks, however, will lack direction and be ineffective if they are not grounded in a robust conversation about the problems and how our tradition might be brought into contemporary dialogue about how to address them. I have organized my remarks around ten theses about the intellectual formation that will be needed to foster a new social Catholicism, some of which have been touched upon previously but are brought together here to foster conversation and efforts toward social formation.

1: We Must Cultivate a Properly Catholic Theological Methodology and Hermeneutic

Given what I think must be recognized as the significant non-reception of Catholic Social Doctrine in the United States over at least the last forty years, one way we can begin to appreciate this doctrine anew is to reconsider it in light of some of the most fundamental principles of Catholic theological methodology and hermeneutics.

The key point regarding theological methodology concerns the place of magisterial teaching, which—I would argue—provides an indispensable aid to discernment in Catholic theology. According to the Second Vatican Council's *Dei Verbum: Dogmatic Constitution on Divine Revelation*, although the fullness of truth is revealed in Christ,[2] the Church endeavors throughout her history to gain deeper insights into this fullness. In this striving to grasp God's revelation, a fundamental principle is the inseparability of Scripture, Tradition, and the teaching office of the Church.[3] This text offers a doctrinally weighty statement of the alignment of properly Catholic theology with the discernment of the magisterium, which was enthusiastically affirmed by conservative American Catholics during the Pontificates of St. John Paul II and Benedict XVI when it was employed to affirm traditional teachings. This magisterial discernment has been more selectively accepted, however, regarding certain moral teachings and especially the social teaching of these Popes, whereas the latter of Pope Francis has received scant attention at best and often been at least indirectly opposed, despite the fact that his teaching reflects an organic development of the preceding tradition.

Regarding theological hermeneutics, the essential principle was most famously articulated by Pope Benedict XVI in his 2005 Christmas Address to the Roman Curia, but it is at least implicit in the tradition of social encyclicals. In this Christmas Address, Benedict addressed the vital topic of how contemporary Catholics should understand the Second Vatican Council, a key part of which was to bring the Church into a less confrontational and more incarnational relation with the modern world marked by natural sciences and constitutional democratic states supporting human rights, including freedom of religion. As his test case for this hermeneutic, Benedict took the Council's *Dignitatis Humanae: The*

---

2. Paul VI, *Dei Verbum*, no. 2.
3. Paul VI, *Dei Verbum*, no. 10.

Declaration of Religious Liberty.[4] Against a hermeneutic of rupture and discontinuity, on the one hand, and one of strict continuity on the other, he proposed a hermeneutic of reform and renewal in the continuity of the life of the one Church.[5] This approach allows for elements of both continuity and discontinuity with past, with continuity in the key principles and the possibility of discontinuity in contingent matters, such as how the principles apply in a particular historical context. In particular, the approach considers how the Church came to prefer the secular democratic state after the Second World War, reversing the nineteenth-century judgment of Pius IX as typically cited from his *Syllabus of Errors*. With this hermeneutic, for example, the Church is able to recover the original separation between Christianity and the state after preferring a Catholic state for centuries. She can do so by—on the one hand—upholding in continuity principles such as (i) that Divine Revelation has been entrusted to the Church, (ii) that we must seek the truth and adhere to it when found, and (iii) that the act of faith must be made freely. This hermeneutic allows discontinuity—on the other hand—in the contingent judgments that the nineteenth century Church could reject the liberalism of the French revolution while the twentieth century Church can accept secular states in their postwar form.

Regarding key contemporary discussions among Catholics, these mutually complementary theological and hermeneutical principles would strongly incline one toward the Church's preference for a political community of constitutional democratic states. On the other hand, it would militate against the claims of contemporary "postliberals" that one advances a Catholic perspective when advancing a new "integralism" in which the Church would align with an autocrat, for example, to gain some alleged temporal advantages such as state assistance in coercing people to follow Catholic teachings of sexual and life ethics.

2: We Must Foster Distinctively Catholic Identities

The vital importance of identity has become increasingly evident in recent decades, whether in the proliferation of various forms of identity politics, or in the resurgence of ethno-nationalisms over the last decade,

---

4. Paul VI, *Dignitatis Humanae*.

5. This principle of reform and renewal within the life of the Church is at least implicit in all the modern social encyclicals. See, for example, the introductory section of John Paul II, *Solicitudo Rei Socialis*.

or in various studies in the sociology of knowledge regarding how much of our reasoning is motivated to defend our identity, or in the exploration of the way we are wired from the deepest recesses of our "lizard brains" to react positively to those we identify as "us" and negatively to those we see as "them."[6] Because human behavior is so grounded in identity, the prospects for a new social Catholicism are proportionate to the extent that Catholics appropriate identities informed by a Catholic faith that includes our social doctrine, which means reshaping identities that are deficient to it.

The bad news, however, is that the ideologies dominant in particular cultures can militate against a properly Catholic identity. For example, one of the most distinctive characteristics of American culture is the "individualism" according to which we seek personal goods without due concern for the common good, neglecting the relational dimensions of human existence. We naturally cling, moreover, to our identities and consider challenges to them as personal attacks, which complicates the task of trying to help others develop a more properly Catholic sense of self. Closely aligned with individualism, many and influential American Catholics in recent decades have come to think that it is legitimate to interpret the Catholic faith through a commitment to a conservative identity and conservative principles, whereas our social tradition wisely warns against the ambiguities of ideologies. The *Compendium of the Social Doctrine of the Church*, moreover, blames the failure to build a culture of "civil friendship" and "fraternity" precisely on "the influence of individualistic and collectivistic ideologies."[7]

The good news includes the fact that more robust and adequate identities can be appropriated, and that Catholics seeking holiness should be open to such growth, especially those in formation for ordination to priestly ministry or for other apostolates. The goodness, truth and beauty of appropriating a fundamentally Catholic identity, moreover, should be naturally attractive. I would argue, however, that the shape of especially American Catholicism has been and is being and deliberately shaped by the investment of massive amounts of money to serve ideological and partisan ends.

Various works of recent scholarship can also be invaluable in reflecting upon identity and its formation, such as Francis Fukuyama's

---

6. Sapolsky, *Behave*.
7. Pontifical Council for Justice and Peace, *Compendium*, no. 390.

2018 book *Identity: The Demand for Dignity and the Politics of Resentment*. This work can help us to understand, for example, that the human demand for affirmation of our identity reflects the inherent dignity of the human person. Fukuyama also provides valuable insights into how we can develop a multifaceted sense of identity for life in a diverse but interdependent world. Thus, for example, I could see myself most fundamentally as a Catholic Christian, but also a husband, a son, a brother, a colleague, an American, a member of the human family, a defender of human rights and dignity, a Fan of Fighting Irish football, an appreciator of Edmund Burke's early conservatism, a former Republican, a political independent, and someone who wants to work collaboratively with those of good will for the common good.

3: The Need for a Multifaceted Historical Narrative

The power of narratives to shape identity and motivate action has been recognized for millennia, and I am convinced that the resources are available to articulate a compelling narrative that can inform a new movement of social Catholicism. Such a narrative will include multiple dimensions or sub-narratives. One of these would tell the long story of Christianity and the secular state, and how the original Christian separation between Church and state was lost for at least several centuries before being recovered with the Second Vatican Council.[8] As distinguished from the liberalism of the French Revolution, it will include the significant influence of the constitutional democracy or "liberalism" of the American revolution, precisely in the mid-twentieth century form of the Keynesian mixed economy, which was predominant at the time of the Council.[9]

A second sub-narrative would treat American history, and the long struggle to realize the three founding principles, namely human equality, human rights and popular sovereignty as told by Jill Lepore in her 2018 work *These Truths: A History of the United States*. This second sub-narrative would also include a discussion of the oligarchic ideology that has persisted since the American founding: that is, the idea that some people are better than others and deserve to rule. This idea is intertwined with the ongoing problem of racism, with the individualism that militates

---

8. Rhonheimer, "Christianity and Secularity," 342–428.

9. For a sober discussion of liberalism in the sense of constitutional democracy, see Traub, *What Was Liberalism?* More recently, see Fukuyama, *Liberalism and Its Discontents*.

against the common good, and with the libertarian donor networks that buy near oligarchic control of the political process. The idea that some deserve to rule also seems present in the postliberal integralism through which many American Catholics are willing to forgo democracy and employ the coercive power of an illiberal democracy to impose an interpretation of Catholic morality upon their fellow citizens. Regarding the American original sin of racism, this narrative of oligarchy would include its full manifestation in the antebellum slavery in the South followed by its continuation in the Jim Crow era. It would also include a sober assessment of today's blatant voter suppression and gerrymandering. This historical thread of oligarchy is skillfully narrated by Heather Cox Richardson in her *How the South Won the Civil War*.[10] If we are to approach the understanding that the young John Ryan had of the crony capitalism and plutocracy of his day, moreover, our narrative would benefit from works like Jane Mayer's *Dark Money: The Hidden History of the Billionaires Behind the Rise of the Radical Right*. I will save the economic thread of this narrative for the next thesis.

A third sub-narrative would treat the history of social Catholicism, especially in the United States, including the story of Msgr. John A. Ryan as sketched in chapter 5. The historical dimension of some of the additional theses discussed below can further support these narratives.

4: We Must Strive to Foster an Economy that Works for Everyone

This fourth thesis is that, if there is to be a new era of social Catholicism to address the great challenges of our century, Catholics will need to be sufficiently engaged in questions of what we might call political economy to contribute to the building of a system that works for everyone. I distinguish such an era of reform from recent decades in which income and wealth have shifted decisively to the wealthiest members of society, making the relative security of middle-class existence increasingly unattainable. With this shift of wealth has followed the effective capture of political power by economic and corporate elites, and the widespread perception that the system is rigged. This contributes to a subsequent breakdown of societal cohesion, of democratic norms and institutions, along with other crises including unsustainable environmental degradation.

---

10. See also her Substack, "Letters from An American."

Such a broader engagement of Catholics in efforts toward a more just and sustainable economic model would entail a broadening of the narrative supporting social Catholicism to include yet another sub-narrative addressing the history of political economy. This would have to make sense of the transition from the postwar consensus for the Keynesian mixed economy that saw a broad sharing in economic growth into the era of what is commonly called a "neoliberal" consensus that emerged through the nineteen eighties in response to the economic challenges of the nineteen seventies, which had undermined confidence in Keynesianism. The subsequent shift to a neoliberal paradigm created great wealth but distributed it especially to the top earners, while devastating the natural environment, before this consensus ended during the 2008 financial crisis and subsequent Great Recession.

This economic sub-narrative would continue into the last decade or so of rethinking economics[11] in the wake of this lost neoliberal consensus.[12] Globally, and in the context of the possible renewal of liberal democracies and international institutions, it would seriously consider the argumentation of scholars like Samuel Moyn who claim that this failure has much to do with ignoring economic rights along the lines of those articulated in the 1948 UDHR.[13] In the United States, this rethinking has been pursued primarily on the political left, with at least one prominent initiative on the right[14] without a significant change of direction until perhaps the last few years. Early signs of a change include the bipartisan Keynesian style relief and stimulus during the pandemic, and the

---

11. This broad rethinking is reflected in institutions such as the Institute for New Economic Thinking at the Oxford Martin School at the University of Oxford. https://www.inet.ox.ac.uk/.

12. It would need to address how the magisterium came to prefer constitutional democracy in the postwar era during which there as a consensus for a Keynesian "mixed economy" that aligns roughly with European style social democracy. In the United States and elsewhere during the postwar decades, such arrangements resulted in broadly shared prosperity, a growing middle class, and relatively high levels of social harmony. As we moved through the 1980s, the more market fundamentalist form of neoliberal economics came to prevail in the United States and beyond, which emphasized deregulation, tax cuts, and the shrinking of social safety nets. The same philosophy had informed American foreign policy since the implementation of the 1975 report of the Trilateral Commission, which promoted neoliberal economic development without the social supports needed to foster a broadly shared prosperity. Crozier et al., *Crisis of Democracy*.

13. Moyn, *Not Enough*.

14. I am thinking of *The American Compass* led by Oren Cass at https://americancompass.org/.

rebellion of the financial markets against the "skinny budget" prosed by short lived UK Prime Minister Liz Truss whose failure to recognize the changed economic context was seen as disqualifying.[15] Potentially lasting signs of a shift would include the broad consensus in the Democratic Party for a new "middle out"—in contrast to a "trickle-down"—economic paradigm through organizations such as the Roosevelt Institute in close collaboration with the Biden Administration.[16] It should go without saying, moreover, that our economic model needs to be sustainable to address the multifaceted climate crisis, although the dark money being distributed by fossil fuel interests has purchased many voices of disinformation. Given the importance of the topic, the second volume of this collection includes a four-part symposium on New Economic Thinking after the Neoliberal Consensus.

5: We Must Avoid Ideological Extremes: Illiberalisms, Traditionalism, and the Far Right

Because I would argue that the whole tradition of modern Catholic social teaching can be understood as seeking a Thomistic understanding the rational mean between the extremes—that is, what reason judges to be best—in different historical contexts, the rejection of contemporary ideological extremes follows naturally. Through the conciliar era, the social encyclicals primarily rejected the extremes of socialism on the left and laissez-faire capitalism on the right, but by the time of Paul VI's *Octogesima Adveniens* in 1971, what I am calling the seeking of a rational mean broadens into a warning about the ambiguous nature and inadequacy of ideologies. This widening of the scope of the warning allows it to address extremes of the day such as the left-wing utopianism of that era and the post-War radical right-wing traditionalism of Julian Evola. The warnings against ideologies multiply in social teachings of Popes St. John Paul II, Benedict XVI and Francis, although the term ideology is underdeveloped.[17]

---

15. For an informed discussion, see the interview of Tooze, "Is the British Economy in a Doom Loop?"

16. See, for example, the report by Strickland and Wong, "New Paradigm for Justice and Democracy"; Wong, *Emerging Worldview*.

17. The reference to ideology in the Catholic social documents certainly contains strongly negative connotations but is not clearly defined. For a serious contribution toward a more adequate understanding of ideology, see Blakely, *Lost in Ideology*.

I would say the contemporary message we should take from this rejection of extremes and ideologies would start with the proper use of philosophy within theology, as discussed in John Paul II's 1998 encyclical *Fides et Ratio: On Faith and Reason*, which gives a rich account of the Catholic understanding of the harmony between faith and reason as mentioned under our first thesis as essential for a properly Catholic theological method. Regarding the social realm, I would argue that this harmony of faith and reason would put Catholic Social Teaching in friendly but critical[18] dialogue with all relevant fields of study, including the tradition of political philosophy, as in Martin Rhonheimer's *The Common Good of Constitutional Democracy: Essays in Political Philosophy and On Catholic Social Teaching*. It offers a valuable resource for Catholics interested in the relation between political philosophy and Catholic Social Teaching, but that hasn't recently seemed to be what our age seeks, as I will discuss below. A key takeaway is that a proper appreciation of the harmony of faith and reason would rule out the illiberalisms of both the left and the right, supporting the achievements and institutions of constitutional democracy as part of the common good, and working for a political and economic paradigm that allows us to address contemporary challenges.

In the decades following the rise of the new left in the late sixties through the ascent of postmodern relativism into the 2000s, it seemed to many of us that the illiberalism of the left was the greatest threat to the common good. Because few in my primary intended audience in the current institutional infrastructure of the Church are tempted by forms of left-wing illiberalism such as political correctness, cancel culture, speech codes, wokeness, or the coercive imposition of nonbinary pronouns,[19] I will focus on the illiberalism of the right, which I think—as will become evident—poses the most urgent threats in both the short and medium terms.[20]

---

18. By the addition of critical, I'm indicating a recognition that the social sciences should not be seen according to an older naturalistic interpretation that would see them grasping human realities the way natural sciences explain the natural world. Instead, Blakely and Bevir argue that "the study of human behavior—and thus all social sciences—ought to be historical, employing narratives as explanations, and not neglecting the meanings and beliefs of the relevant agents." Bevir and Blakely, *Interpretive Social Science*, 9. See also Blakely, *Alasdair MacIntyre, Charles Taylor, and the Demise*.

19. Some of the most helpful critiques of the illiberal left come from those of the left. See, for example, Rauch, *Constitution of Knowledge*, ch. 7, "Cancelling: Despotism of the Few." Similarly, see Goldberg, "Left's Fever Is Breaking."

20. Although some commentators of the right like Rod Dreher present themselves as preferring liberal democracy if the threat of an illiberal pink police state of the left

The long history of the illiberalism of the right can be seen in the last two centuries of conservatism, as traced by Edmund Fawcett in his 2020 volume *Conservatism: The Fight for a Tradition*. Fawcett illustrates in detail how constitutional democracies can flourish where the conservative parties take a more moderating role that accepts the legitimacy of democracy, but such polities become unstable and fail if a moderate conservative party that accepts democratic norms and institutions is lacking. After the Second World War, the Republican Party of President Dwight D. Eisenhower exemplified such a moderate conservatism as treated by David Stebenne in his *Modern Republican: Arthur Larson and the Eisenhower Years*. Unfortunately, it is currently hard to envision how such a modern Republicanism will arise in the United States given the radicalization of the party over the last several years, such that it has been described as extreme, radically antiliberal, radical hard or far right.

I will next focus on the broader international revival of the far-right. Recent decades have witnessed a global resurgence of what is often called the radical right, but which often goes under the heading of Traditionalism. This is to be distinguished from the Traditionalism we know within Catholicism, which is often identified with a preference for the Traditional Latin Mass. This broader movement of far-right Traditionalism builds on thinkers tracing back to at least the nineteenth century. They are treated in a range of recent works including Mark Sedgwick's *Key Thinkers of the Radical Right: Behind the New Threat to Democracy*, and Matthew Rose's *A World after Liberalism: The Philosophers of the Radical Right*. These thinkers of the radical right are generally defined by their opposition to liberal society and democracy, especially its universality, and its understanding of human rights and equality. They instead emphasize things like human inequality, hierarchy, and authoritarianism. Although the intellectual leaders and others of the radical right affirm a kind of spirituality, and they are often well versed in Christian theology, they often despise Christianity for initiating what they see as the destruction of Western Civilization by affirming the dignity of every person, of their consequent human rights, especially their applicability to what they consider to be lesser races, especially those with darker skin.

---

hadn't rendered that impossible, I discussed in "Three Alternatives to Social Catholicism" why I think Dreher clearly is more of a gifted propagandist for right-wing illiberalism than a trustworthy guide for Catholics. This is clear from his paid service to Victor Orbán's "illiberal Democracy."

The Church and Western world encountered some of the early fruits of such thinkers through their influence on the rise of fascism in the nineteen twenties and thirties. Sadly, a great many Catholics throughout Europe supported or at least acquiesced to these authoritarian regimes, at least as they initially came into power, after which it is too late. Perhaps the most notorious case was how Catholics in Vichy France came to collaborate with the Nazis, an early account of which was provided by Catholic philosopher Yves Simon in his 1942 book *The Road to Vichy: 1918–1938*. As James Chappel treats in his 2018 study *Catholic Modern: The Challenge of Totalitarianism and the Remaking of the Church*, the Catholic Church learned a hard lesson from having taken a paternalistic approach to social ethics in aligning with—or at least insufficiently opposing—fascists in the decades leading to the Second World War.[21] After the horrors perpetrated by these regimes, the Church instead and wisely adopted a fraternal approach of collaborative and dialogical participation in democratic societies, which has been integral to Catholic social teaching ever since.

This humanistic social teaching has been largely opposed by many Catholics in the United States since at least the famous response of "*Mater Si, Magistra No*" in William F. Buckley's *National Review* in response Pope John XXIII's 1961 encyclical *Mater et Magistra: Christianity and Social Progress*. That is, Buckley's flagship journal of the conservative movement admits the Church as our mother, but not our teacher, especially given the alignment of the Church with the postwar Keynesian "mixed economy" and with international efforts toward development. Matthew Rose concludes his previously noted study of the radical right with a discussion of "The Christian Question." This movement, which understands the essence of Christianity to lie in its belief in human dignity and rights, despises the faith for precisely this reason, while ironically sharing a radical illiberalism in common with contemporary influential Catholics. In presenting a vigorous alternative vision of life against what they see as a weak and sterile Christianity, Rose sees the radical right as challenging Christians to live the drama of cruciform love.

We might also mention Benjamin R. Teitelbaum's 2020 *The War for Eternity: Inside Bannon's Far-Right Circle of Global Power Brokers*. Teitelbaum's book is based on his close access to various members of the radical right, especially Steven K. Bannon, who served for a time as Chief

---

21. In this approach, the Church accepted such states as long as they allowed the Church to carry out her mission, and as long as they upheld key teachings of the natural law, such as those concerning sexuality and marriage.

Strategist for President Donald Trump. Bannon—a Catholic of sorts—has not only been deeply immersed in the key thinkers of radical right for decades, but he brought their agenda to the White House, and worked for years to implement it, including after he left the White House. This agenda was multifaceted but centered in undermining American liberal democracy by deconstructing our public institutions and international alliances, and especially NATO, the North Atlantic Treaty Organization that protected Europe from Soviet aggression during the Cold War.

Inspired by the apocalyptic vision of the radical right, Bannon delighted in the opportunity to usher in a new era of turmoil analogous to the 1930s, which is reminiscent of the way the convert to conservative Catholicism Newt Gingrich delights in the havoc he wrought in grinding congress to a halt by propagating a vicious style of partisan combat as I discussed in chapter 8. After leaving the White House, Bannon worked to build alliances with other thinkers of the radical right, including Alexander Dugin, who is the intellectual architect behind Vladimir Putin's goal of establishing a Eurasian Empire that spans from Dublin, Ireland to Vladivostok. Authors including Teitelbaum document how Bannon also worked to undermine democracy and foster autocracy in Europe, Latin America or wherever the opportunity arose. He continues to push his agenda of ushering in a postliberal age, especially through his "War Room" broadcasts, which he conducts before an image of the Sacred Heard of Jesus. If Bannon and Trump had made more progress in undermining NATO before Vladimir Putin's invasion of Ukraine, it is frightening to think of how far the Russian invasion of their Western neighbors would have progressed.

As I discussed in chapter 8, the Republican Party has become increasingly radicalized and antagonistic toward constitutional democracy since at least Newt Gingrich's term as Speaker of the House in the 1990s. Given the global phenomenon of democratic backsliding, there is ample literature on how this tends to unfold. Among the most respected works in this regard is the 2018 book *How Democracies Die* by Steven Livitsky and Daniel Ziblatt,[22] which explains how this usually happens through a gradual slide from democracy into authoritarianism. This democratic backsliding progresses through obstructing the legislature, packing the courts, gerrymandering the voting districts, corrupting the voting process, attacking the press and sowing propaganda and disinformation. Is there any need to even ask whether such tendencies can be reconciled

22. Levitsky and Ziblatt, *How Democracies Die.*

with the Catholic social tradition of principled and solidary humanism, or whether the Republican Party is well down the path of implementing this illiberal playbook?

As Daron Acemoglu and James A. Robinson have argued convincingly in their *Why Nations Fail: The Origins of Power, Prosperity, and Poverty* and *The Narrow Corridor,* open and inclusive political institutions are the decisive factor for flourishing societies. The corruption that prevents or undermines these political institutions, on the other hand, leads to failed states and widespread misery. At a time when the illiberalism of the right threatens to destroy the institutions of American democracy and plunge much of the world into dystopia, Catholics need to reject these illiberal tendencies and work in a spirit of "integral and solidary humanism" to renew and reinvigorate our institutions. I take it for granted that Catholics should equally reject any illiberal tendencies of the left, but I don't think there is any question that the threats from the illiberal left are more cultural than political and are not as urgent.

6: We Must Respond Wisely to Today's Propaganda, Disinformation, and Post Truth

Whereas the word "propaganda" originally had positive connotations about communicating the truth as in the Vatican Society for the *Propaganda Fidei,* it developed strongly negative ones during the First World War when efforts to deceive the enemy were developed and deployed. In 1925, Edward Bernays published his influential book *Propaganda* that sought to channel the lessons that had been learned about persuasion during the war toward commercial purposes, out of which grew the twentieth century advertising industry. During the Second World War and the Cold War, these techniques were further perfected, and subsequently channeled into controlling populations, both by governments—as in the American campaigns to sell the Vietnam war and the 2003 Invasion of Iraq—and by businesses. They concur in employing the evolving tools of mass media as treated in Noam Chomsky's 2002 *Media Control: The Spectacular Achievements of Propaganda.* My main point for the present context is that propaganda of various forms profoundly influences the twenty first century social and political context that we are called to infuse with the spirit of the Gospel. If a new generation of social Catholics are to avoid being "easy marks" for manipulation by these powerful forces, we need to be well-informed about them, about how they are being deployed, about the vision they seek to advance, and how to advance an alternative vision consistent with a defensible account of the common good.

Although this is not the place to make a detailed argument, I would argue that a primary reason why the actual Social Teaching of the Church has been rendered so impotent in the United States in the last several decades—as compared to the *previous* several starting with Msgr. John A. Ryan—is largely because of a massive campaign of propaganda to advance an alternative social vision. The long history of this persuasion can be gleaned by many historical works, especially the two I mentioned in the introduction by Erik M. Conway and Naomi Oreskes, namely their 2023 *The Big Myth: How Business Taught us to Loath Government and Love the Free Market* and their 2010 *Merchants of Doubt: How a Handful of Scientists Obscured the Truth on Issues from Tobacco Smoke to Global Warming*. In a nutshell, this campaign succeeded by the 1980s, when Ronald Reagan—consistent with his famous line about how government was not the solution but the problem—effected the transition from the so-called "postwar liberal consensus" for a "Keynesian mixed economy" to a market fundamentalist form of the neoliberal economic paradigm that lowered tax rates, cut regulations, shrunk the social safety net and channeled wealth and power upward.

It also shrewdly enlisted religious conservatives by dragging them into culture war politics. This campaign succeeded not just because the economic malaise of the 1970s provided an opportunity to promote an alternative socioeconomic paradigm. It also succeeded through related propaganda employing fearmongering and exaggeration to gain political power, such as Richard Nixon's "Southern" and "law and order" strategies, which "dog whistles" to appeal to white voters who resented civil rights legislation. This strategy evolved into the more inflammatory "culture war" politics advanced by figures including the traditionalist Catholic Patrick J. Buchanan and Newt Gingrich. Since the founding of Fox News in 1996, the promotion of an increasingly radical right-wing—that is, one that employs appeals to emotion and lies to overthrow democratic norms and institutions—continues to be advanced through similar propagandistic techniques. Although I would expect that almost everyone thinks they are competent to avoid being manipulated by propaganda, I think it is closer to the truth to say that most of us are more influenced by it than we would think, including highly educated Catholics with advanced degrees.

The second point is that the contemporary challenge of propaganda and disinformation is a multifaceted one with national and international dimensions that gravely threaten the common good. Internationally, the most aggressive forms of disinformation have been employed by Vladimir Putin, with the asymmetric war of disinformation he has waged for several years in preparation for his military aggression. This disinformation has been focused on not only Ukraine but also the United States as the center of the "liberal world order," but it has been employed more broadly to foster chaos wherever possible. Rather than present a narrative to persuade as does traditional propaganda, this disinformation seeks to disorient us so that we give up on trying to separate truth from fiction and become cynical, disengaging in frustration after being convinced that everyone is corrupt. According to *This Is Not Propaganda: Adventures in the War against Reality* by the Ukrainian author Peter Pomerantsev, this disinformation strategy is based on the work of the Soviet KGB that came to fruition just before the Soviet Union fell. It is highly effective, especially when propagated to the masses via social media. It has been widely deployed against liberal democracies, especially the United States, and recent developments in artificial intelligence ensure that the upcoming election season will see an accelerated campaign of disinformation.

Within the United States, this disinformation has already gravely undermined social solidarity. In the words of Steve Bannon, who has been among its pioneers, the strategy is simple, namely to "flood the zone with excrement," only he used the four-letter word rhyming with "hit." The strategy is well understood by Donald Trump, who has been described as a "super-spreader of disinformation" by Anne Applebaum,[23] the Pulitzer-prize winning historian and co-director of the Program on Disinformation and Twenty-First-Century Propaganda at the Johns Hopkins School of Advanced International Studies. The Tucker Carlson show was masterful in purveying propaganda and disinformation, especially in support of Kremlin talking points. He is so effective at this that Kremlin memos obtained and published by American media were directing Russian media to frequently rebroadcast excerpts from his show, which they have been doing for years.[24]

My basic point is that a new era of sociopolitical engagement by Catholics needs to be alert to the contemporary context that has been

---

23. Applebaum, "Trump Is a Super-Spreader."
24. Pengelly, "Russian Media to Use Tucker Carlson."

shaped by not only sophisticated propaganda, but propaganda that is influenced by radical right-wing ideology that is often presented as compatible with Catholicism.[25]

Thesis 7: We Must Understand the Struggle Between Democracy and the New Autocracy

My last two theses have discussed how a resurgence of the radical right has built upon a robust body of thought that is diametrically opposed to the liberal postwar order of constitutional democracies. This sophisticated body of antidemocratic thought has also been promulgated by the propaganda and disinformation discussed above. Under this seventh thesis, I will simply build upon my reference to the 2018 book *How Democracies Die* by Steven Livitsky and Daniel Ziblatt by introducing two complementary works connecting the decline of democracies with the rise of autocracy.

The first is 2022 book *The Revenge of Power: How Autocrats are Reinventing Politics for the Twenty-First Century* by Moisés Naím. In it, Naím offers a fascinating explanation for the frightening proliferation of autocratic leaders in the last several years. After the 1989 fall of communism, democratic governments were seen as the only legitimate form of polity, but these governments were weakened by the shift of power to corporations with globalization, and with their apparent inability to deal with the aftermath of the Great Recession that followed the 2008 financial crisis. This inability had to do with fact that the still dominant neoliberal economic paradigm demanded austerity programs for everyone but the banks, which left governments unable to assist "main street" after having generously bailed out "wall street."

In this climate, would be autocrats developed a new and very effective playbook for gaining power based on the 3Ps of Populism, Polarization and Post Truth. This strategy starts with *populism*, blaming socioeconomic problems on the "liberal elites" in government and presenting themselves as outsiders defending "the people." The 3P strategy continues by *polarizing* the population by siding with the majority and demonizing not just the elites but vulnerable groups, such as minorities—including sexual minorities—and immigrants. It concludes with

---

25. For a recent discussion of how certain forms of Catholicism are drawing converts from at least the fringes of the radical right, see Weiss, "Conversion to Catholicism Shouldn't Be a Right-Wing Power Play."

post truth, the propagation of disinformation, which disorients the population, discourages the opposition, and allows the seizure of power, after which democratic safeguards of checks and balances are undermined as described in *How Democracies Die*. With this strategy, people soon realize they are living under an autocrat, with all that entails regarding the loss of rights and a degradation of society. These autocracies are almost always kleptocracies, that is, criminal or gangster states.

A second resource is Jason Stanley's *How Fascism Works: The Politics of Us and Them*, which explains not a particular fascist regime such as those of the 30s, but the basic tactics of authoritarian politics, which echoes what one would find in *The Revenge of Power* or *How Democracies Die*. We have seen many of these tactics employed in Western democracies in recent years.

8: We Must Support Constitutional Democracy as Integral to the Common Good

Because influential contemporary Catholic intellectuals are asserting the failure and radical opposition between "liberalism" and Catholicism, I would instead argue that the institutions of constitutional democracy should be recognized as integral to the common good in the contemporary world and that Catholics should be working collaboratively to renew and strengthen democracy. This follows clearly from the 2003 *Compendium of the Social Doctrine of the Church*, especially the eighth chapter on "The Political Community." That these public institutions are integral to the common good can be seen especially in the ones that uphold particular aspects of that good, such as those for national defense, law enforcement and the judicial system, infrastructure and public transportation, health care, education, social services, public administration, etc. A broader argument along these lines can be found in the previously mentioned book on *The Common Good of Constitutional Democracy*.

Among the social encyclicals, I would argue that this recognition about public institutions being integral to the common good is implicit in many of them, but it is most explicit in Benedict XVI's 2009 *Caritas in Veritate: On Love in Truth*, as also highlighted in the introductory essay to this collection. In the seventh section, Benedict encourages Catholics to "take a stand for the common good" by being solicitous of "that complex of institutions that give structure to the life of society, juridically, civilly, politically, and culturally." He continues, "this is the institutional path—we might also call it the political path—of charity, no less excellent than the kind of charity that encounters the neighbor directly." I think that Benedict XVI offers a message of great urgency in our day when especially American Catholics are too often in the forefront of attacking constitutional democracy, or otherwise discouraging fruitful participation in it, rather than working for renewal. As extensively documented in the previously cited works by Acemoglu and Robinson, there is compelling evidence that such efforts to renew our institutions instead of attacking and undermining them can be expected to make the difference between flourishing societies offering a future worthy of the human person, on the one hand, and dystopia on the other.

9: Support for Political Parties Should Be in Proportion to Their Potential to Renew Democracy

Consistent with what I think are the wise warnings of the Catholic tradition regarding the limitations of ideologies and dangers of falling into partisanship, I will not elaborate this thesis at any length. Looking back to the example of Msgr. John A. Ryan, however, we already saw that he supported whichever party he judged would best serve the common good by employing the powers of the government to address the challenges of the time, shifting his support between Populists, Republicans and Democrats as the circumstances indicated. Similarly, I would argue that contemporary Catholics would do well to support candidates and parties that best align with the principles and methodology of Catholic Social Teaching in working for a future worthy of the human person. Besides this perhaps obvious point, I would add that there is a profound need to find ways to foster a more informed conversation about the common good among Catholics. To achieve this, we will need to get beyond the weaponization of the question of abortion, so Catholics treat it as part of a broader conversation about the common good shaped by our social doctrine.

10: We Foster a Global and Comprehensive Catholic Perspective

Since chapter 27 offers a robust discussion of how Catholic Social Teaching addresses the global human family, I will let this thesis speak largely for itself, only adding that many of our recent challenges illustrate the Catholic understanding that the common good needs to be understood at the global level due to the unity and interdependence of the human family. This interdependence could be seen in the global financial crisis, in the COVID-19 pandemic, in the weakening of the postwar security architecture, and in climate crisis. Given the way that the radical right denies the unity of the human family and the equal rights and dignity of every human person, and given the way influential leaders of anti-democratic movements claim to hold the authentic Catholic position, the Church will need regain its authentic and prophetic voice on these matters if it is to prevent cooption by the radical right. Of course, that the same caution would apply to the illiberal left if there were a serious danger of that corrupting the faith and life of the Church.

Conclusion

Building upon the previous consideration in chapter 5 of how the social formation of Msgr. John A. Ryan prepared him to lead the Church in the United States in fruitful responses to the challenges of the Industrial Revolution and Great Depression, this chapter proposed several theses regarding a social formation that would help contemporary Catholics respond effectively to the challenges of what global leaders have come to call the polycrisis, corresponding to the "dark clouds" about which the social teaching of Pope Francis has warned us with increasing urgency.

Although an authentically Christian and Catholic response to the social conditions of a given time and place will be marked most fundamentally by trust in God, hope in the divine power to assist us, and the labor of love, it must be grounded in a realistic assessment of the challenges to be addressed, and it is not often clear from much of contemporary Catholic leadership or media that such a realistic assessment is operative. So that Catholics might build a more adequate and shared foundation for appropriate action, this essay has proposed these theses.

The second volume of this collection subtitled *New Hope for Ecclesial and Societal Renewal* turns more toward the future to consider key themes and topics that will be important if we are to realize a new social Catholicism and a better kind of politics. My hope and prayer is that many Catholics are given the Grace to see this magnanimous task of working collaboratively for the common good as integral to their high calling in Christ and their vocation to what St. Paul calls "the ministry of reconciliation" (2 Cor 5:18). In this way, the Church can show herself to be "a sign and instrument both of . . . union with God and of the unity of the whole human race" spoken of by the Fathers of the Second Vatican Council in the opening number of the *Dogmatic Constitution of the Church: Lumen Gentium*.

Bibliography

Acemoglu, Daron, and James A. Robinson. *The Narrow Corridor: States, Societies, and the Fate of Liberty*. New York: Penguin, 2019.

———. *Why Nations Fail: The Origins of Power, Prosperity, and Poverty*. New York: Crown, 2012.

Applebaum, Anne. "Trump Is a Super-Spreader of Disinformation." *Atlantic*, October 3, 2020. https://www.theatlantic.com/ideas/archive/2020/10/trump-super-spreader-disinformation/616604/.

Benedict XVI. "Address of His Holiness Benedict XVI to Roman Curia Offering Them His Christmas Greetings." https://www.vatican.va/content/benedict-xvi/en/speeches/2005/december/documents/hf_ben_xvi_spe_20051222_roman-curia.html#.

———. *Caritas in Veritate: On Integral Development in Charity and Truth*. Vatican City: Libreria Editrice Vaticana, 2009. https://www.vatican.va/content/benedict-xvi/en/encyclicals/documents/hf_ben-xvi_enc_20090629_caritas-in-veritate.html#_ednref112.

Bernays, Edward. *Propaganda*. Brooklyn: Ig, 2004.

Bevir, Mark, and Jason Blakely. *Interpretive Social Science: An Anti-Naturalist Approach*. Oxford: Oxford University Press, 2018.

Blakely, Jason. *Alasdair MacIntyre, Charles Taylor, and the Demise of Naturalism*. Notre Dame: University of Notre Dame Press, 2016.

———. *Lost in Ideology: Interpreting Modern Political Life*. Newcastle upon Tyne: Agenda, 2024.

Chappel, James. *Catholic Modern: The Challenge of Totalitarianism and the Remaking of the Church*. Cambridge: Harvard University Press, 2018.

Chomsky, Noam. *Media Control: The Spectacular Achievements of Propaganda*. 2nd ed. New York: Seven Stories, 2011.

Crozier, Michael J. et al. *The Crisis of Democracy: Report on the Governability of Democracies to the Trilateral Commission*. New York: New York University Press, 1975. https://ia800305.us.archive.org/29/items/TheCrisisOfDemocracy-TrilateralCommission-1975/crisis_of_democracy_text.pdf.

Fawcett, Edmund. *Conservatism: The Fight for a Tradition*. Princeton: Princeton University Press, 2020.

Fukuyama, Francis. *Identity: The Demand for Dignity and the Politics of Resentment*. New York: Farrar, Straus, and Giroux, 2018.

———. *Liberalism and Its Discontents*. New York: Farrar, Straus, and Giroux, 2022.

Goldberg, Michelle. "The Left's Fever Is Breaking." *New York Times*, December 16, 2022. https://www.nytimes.com/2022/12/16/opinion/left-activism.html.

Social Catholicism for the Twenty-First Century?—Volume 1

John XXIII. *Mater et Magistra: Christianity and Social Progress*. Vatican City: Libreria Editrice Vaticana, 1963. https://www.vatican.va/content/john-xxiii/en/encyclicals/documents/hf_j-xxiii_enc_15051961_mater.html.

———. *Pacem in Terris: Peace on Earth*. Vatican City: Libreria Editrice Vaticana, 1963. https://www.vatican.va/content/john-xxiii/en/encyclicals/documents/hf_j-xxiii_enc_11041963_pacem.html.

John Paul II. *Fides et Ratio: On Faith and Reason*. Vatican City: Libreria Editrice Vaticana, 1998. https://www.vatican.va/content/john-paul-ii/en/encyclicals/documents/hf_jp-ii_enc_14091998_fides-et-ratio.html.

———. *Solicitudo Rei Socialis: On Social Concern*. Vatican City: *Libreria Editrice Vatica*na, 1987. https://www.vatican.va/content/john-paul-ii/en/encyclicals/documents/hf_jp-ii_enc_30121987_sollicitudo-rei-socialis.html.

Lepore, Jill. *These Truths: A History of the United States*. New York: Norton, 2018.

Levitsky, Steven, and Daniel Ziblatt. *How Democracies Die*. New York: Broadway, 2018.

———. *Tyranny of the Minority: Why American Democracy Reached the Breaking Point*. New York: Crown, 2023.

Mayer, Jane. *Dark Money: The Hidden History of the Billionaires behind the Rise of the Radical Right*. New York: Doubleday, 2016.

Moyn, Samuel. *Not Enough: Human Rights in an Unequal World*. Cambridge: Belknap, 2018.

Murphy, William F., Jr. "Formation for Social Catholicism: The Example of Msgr. John A. Ryan (1945†) and the Renewal of Constitutional Democracy." *Chicago Studies* 61 (2023). Forthcoming.

———. "Three Contemporary Alternatives to Social Catholicism." *Chicago Studies* 61 (2023). Forthcoming.

Naím, Moisés. *The End of Power: From Boardrooms to Battlefields and Churches to States, Why Being in Charge Isn't What It Used to Be*. New York: Basic, 2013.

———. *The Revenge of Power: How Autocrats are Reinventing Politics for the 21st Century*. New York: St. Martin's, 2022.

Paul VI. *Dei Verbum: Dogmatic Constitution on Divine Revelation*. Vatican City: Libreria Editrice Vaticana, 1965. https://www.vatican.va/archive/hist_councils/ii_vatican_council/documents/vat-ii_const_19651118_dei-verbum_en.html.

———. *Dignitatis Humanae: Declaration on Religious Freedom*. Vatican City: Libreria Editrice Vaticana, 1965.

———. *Octogesima Adveniens: A Call to Action*. Vatican City: Libreria Editrice Vaticana, 1967. https://www.vatican.va/content/paul-vi/en/apost_letters/documents/hf_p-vi_apl_19710514_octogesima-adveniens.html.

———. *Lumen Gentium: Dogmatic Constitution on the Church*. Vatican City: Libreria Editrice Vaticana, 1964. https://www.vatican.va/archive/hist_councils/ii_vatican_council/documents/vat-ii_const_19641121_lumen-gentium_en.html.

Pengelly, Martin. "Kremlin Memos Urged Russian Media to Use Tucker Carlson Clips—Report." *Guardian*, March 14, 2022. https://www.theguardian.com/media/2022/mar/14/kremlin-memos-russian-media-tucker-carlson-fox-news-mother-jones.

Pomerantsev, Peter. *This Is Not Propaganda: Adventures in the War against Reality*. New York: Hatchette, 2020.

Pontifical Council for Justice and Peace. *Compendium of the Social Doctrine of the Church*. Washington, DC: USCCB, 2005.

Rausch, Jonathan. *The Constitution of Knowledge: A Defense of Truth*. Washington, DC: Brookings, 2021.

Rhonheimer, Martin. "Christianity and Secularity: Past and Present of a Complex Relationship." In *The Common Good of Constitutional Democracy: Essays in Political Philosophy and on Catholic Social Teaching*, edited by William F. Murphy Jr. Washington, DC: The Catholic University of America Press, 2013.

———. *The Common Good of Constitutional Democracy: Essays in Political Philosophy and on Catholic Social Teaching*. Edited by William F. Murphy Jr. Washington, DC: The Catholic University of America Press, 2012.

Richardson, Heather Cox. *How the South Won the Civil War: Oligarchy, Democracy, and the Continuing Fight for the Soul of America*. Oxford: Oxford University Press, 2020.

Rose, Matthew. *A World after Liberalism: The Philosophers of the Radical Right*. New Haven: Yale University Press, 2021.

Roosevelt, Franklin Delano. "Address to the National Conference of Catholic Charities." https://www.religioninamerica.org/rahp_objects/address-to-the-national-conference-of-catholic-charities/.

Sapolsky, Robert. *Behave: The Biology of Humans at Our Best and Worst*. New York: Penguin, 2017.

Sedgwick, Mark. *Key Thinkers of the Radical Right: Behind the New Threat to Democracy*. New York: Oxford University Press, 2019.

Simon, Yves. *La Grande Crise de la République Française*. Montreal: Editions de l'Arbre, 1941.

———. *The Road to Vichy: 1918–1938*. Translated by James Corbett and George J. McMorrow. New York: Sheed & Ward, 1942.

Stanley, Jason. *How Fascism Works: The Politics of Us and Them*. New York: Penguin Random House, 2018.

Stebenne, David. *Modern Republican: Arthur Larson and the Eisenhower Years*. Bloomington: Indiana University Press, 2006.

Strickland, Kyle, and Felicia Wong. "A New Paradigm for Justice and Democracy: Moving beyond the Twin Failures of Neoliberalism and Racial Liberalism." A Roosevelt Institute Report. https://rooseveltinstitute.org/wp-content/uploads/2021/11/RI_A-New-Paradigm-for-Justice-and-Democracy_Report_202111-11.pdf.

Teitelbaum, Benjamin R. *The War for Eternity: Inside Bannon's Far-Right Circle of Global Power Brokers*. New York: HarperCollins, 2020.

Tooze, Adam. "Is the British Economy in a Doom Loop?" *Foreign Policy*, September 30, 2022 https://foreignpolicy.com/2022/09/30/british-economy-liz-truss-budget-currency-pound/.

Traub, James. *What Was Liberalism: The Past, Present, and Future of a Noble Idea*. New York: Hatchette, 2019.

Weiss, Rebecca Bratten. "Conversion to Catholicism Shouldn't Be a Right-Wing Power Play." *National Catholic Reporter*, December 19, 2022. https://www.ncronline.org/opinion/guest-voices/conversion-catholicism-shouldnt-be-right-wing-power-play.

Wong, Felicia. *The Emerging Worldview: How New Progressivism Is Moving beyond Neoliberalism—A Landscape Analysis*. https://rooseveltinstitute.org/wp-content/uploads/2020/07/RI_EmergingWorldview_report-202001-1.pdf.

Subject Index

abortion, 15, 20, 21, 24n68, 45, 49, 61,
    61n139, 66, 67, 154, 241n35,
    242, 248, 250–52, 251–52n51,
    253, 260, 296, 299, 312, 363, 389
  as human right, 255
  as intrinsic evil, 305
  see also pro-life movement
absolutism, 30, 130–31, 233
action, objects of, 311–12
Action Française, 62, 177, 178, 179, 338
*Ad Theologiam Promovendam: To
    Advance Theology* (ATP), 10–11
Adenauer, Konrad, 207, 237
adultery, 305–8, 313
Affordable Care Act, 148
Afghanistan, 248, 250
America First, 250
American Compass, 264
American Constitution, 226, 227
  First Amendment, 145
  Fourteenth Amendment, 145
  reconstruction-era amendments, 228
American Economic Association, 172
American exceptionalism, 366
American Revolution, 226–27
Americanists, 145
Amoris Laetitia, 306
anthropology
  Christian, 141, 154, 157
  individualist, 246
  philosophical, 272–73
  theological, 196n76

anti-capitalism, 362–63
anti-clericalism, 183, 206
anti-fascism, 337
antiliberalism, 30–31, 59, 62n142, 65,
    242, 260, 264, 265, 357
  Christian, 323
  nationalist, 365
  see also conservatism, national;
    liberalism; Nietzschean right;
    postliberalism
Anti-Monopoly Party, 167
Aquinas. *See* Thomas Aquinas
Argentina, 344
aristopopulism, 362
Aristotle, xviii, 51n127, 186, 260, 272,
    274, 279, 281, 305, 360
artificial intelligence, 12n41, 49, 386
associationism, 148
atheism, 83, 140, 284
  Catholic, 184, 185
  humanist, 138, 156
  muscular, 364
atomization, 329, 332, 337
ATP (*Ad Theologiam Promovendam: To
    Advance Theology*), 10–11
Augustine of Hippo, 98, 126, 279
  City of God, 279
Austria, 337
authoritarianism, 258, 320, 321, 336,
    340, 358, 381
autocracy, 18, 154, 168, 210, 233, 250,
    262, 363, 371, 374, 383, 387–88

Subject Index

Benedict Option, 209
Benedict XVI, Pope
    address to the Roman Curia, 139, 151
    Caritas in Veritate: On Love in Truth, xvii, 5n13, 35, 210–11, 213, 388–89
    Christmas address (1944), 373
    on the common good, 35–36
    Deus Caritas Est, 103n2
    on economy and the environment, xviii, 51n128, 58
    on hermeneutic of continuity, 31
    on Law of Moses vs. Law of Christ, 289–90
    liberalism of, 63, 208–9, 259, 284
    on modernity, 139
    political teachings of, xix, 51n128, 58
    pontificate of, 23
    on religious liberty, 208–9, 288
    social teaching of, 60, 204, 373, 379
    see also Ratzinger, Joseph Cardinal
Berlin University, 108
Bernardin, Joseph, 41
Biden Administration, 20n57, 54
Bismarck, Otto von, 103, 110, 113, 343
Blondel, Maurice, 179, 180–82, 199–201
    on "action," 180–81, 191
    vs. Descoqs, 195–99
    "Testis" articles, 180, 189–94, 199
Blue Labour, 332
Bob Jones University, 251n50
Bolivar, Simon, 84
Brazil, 344
Bronze Age Mindset, 357
Bryan, William Jennings, 171
Buchanan, James McGill, 235, 236, 249
Buchanan, Patrick J., 238–39n29, 251n46, 385
Bush, George H. W., 252, 253
Bush, George W., 256–57
Bush (George W.) Administration, 240n34, 257, 258, 260
Bush, Jeb, 296, 316

Caballero, José Augustín, 77
Calhoun, John C., 228, 236
cancel culture, 45, 244

capitalism, 140, 143, 146–47
    alternatives to, 243
    crony, 377
    free-market, 232
    laissez faire, 163, 230, 232
    neoliberal, 214
    technocratic, 5n14
    unregulated, 229, 232
Caritas in Veritate: On Integral Development in Charity and Truth, xvii, 5n13, 35, 210–11, 213, 388–89
Carlson, Tucker, 386
Carroll, James, 81
Carter, James "Jimmy," 251–52n51
Casey, Bob, 242
Cassin, René, 207
casuists, 304
Catholic Action, 207, 337
Catholic Church, 1n1
    and American society, 171
    authority of, 218, 327–28, 336
    and democracy, 18n53
    in Europe, 122
    expansion of, 211–12
    in France, 179, 183–84
    in Germany, 123, 131
    institutional infrastructure of, 40, 63, 196, 247
    long nineteenth century, 205, 206
    Melkite Greek, 251
    mission and emphasis, 10–11
    and modernity, 345
    as Mystical Body of Christ, 143
    and the postwar liberal consensus, 4–7
    reform and renewal for, 374
    and the Republican party, 24n68
    rights of, 122–23, 131
    as Sacrament, 218–19
    as "salt and light," 36n96, 225
    as Servant, 24, 219
    social role of, 3
    sovereignty of, 123
    unity of, xx
    in the U. S., 9, 23, 145–49, 284, 288, 390

Subject Index

U.S. Bishops, 20, 21, 174n28, 232, 249, 253
  see also Catholicism
Catholic Enlightenment, 88, 94
Catholic moral teaching, 297–304
  see also moral teaching
Catholic Social Doctrine (CSD), xix–xx, xxii, 3, 9, 15, 24, 45–46, 69, 169, 375
  and American democracy, 55
  Benedict's presentation of, xvii–xviii
  commitment to, 7
  conditions conducive to the reception of (or not), 23–24
  defined, 2n4
  Francis's emphasis on, 10
  humanism of, 13, 258, 265
  and liberalism, 225
  locating within the broader tradition, 55–56
  marginalization of, 25
  missionary perspective of, 170
  opposition to, 34
  poor reception of, 19–23, 373
  reasons for embracing, 18
  Ryan's view of, 161–62
Catholic Social Teaching (CST), 8, 11, 29, 39, 43, 165, 210, 222, 237, 245, 380, 385, 389
  vs. the Anglo-American Tradition on international justice, 211
  boundaries and authority of, 295–316
  vs. Catholic moral teaching, 313
  and Christian humanism, 3–4n7
  and conservatism, 223–24, 240, 250
  course on, xvi, 10–11
  defined, 2n4
  and the Democratic Party, 241–42
  departures from, 259–60
  and European unity, 207
  as expression of the Gospel, 46–47n120, 47–48
  and Ketteler, 103
  and liberalism, 223–24, 265
  methodology for, 51
  modern, 47
  and natural law, 148–49
  opposition to, 251, 252, 297–304
  opposition to evil, 66
  and the principle of subsidiarity, 214
  and Roosevelt's vision, 233
  and the *Semaines sociales*, 188–89
  and the signs of the times, 162–63
  understanding of, 316
  weaknesses of, 298
  see also moral theology
Catholic social tradition, 6–7n18, 9, 34, 40, 52, 148–49, 371
  defined, 2n4
  grounded in truth, 48–49
Catholicism
  American, xvi, 284–86, 370, 375
  atheist, 184, 185
  conservative, 67, 256
  Cuban, 82
  and fascism, 27n76, 43n117, 59, 63, 204, 216, 258, 382
  in France, 227, 284
  in Italy, 284
  and liberalism, 45, 204–19, 227, 236–42, 259, 388
  liberalism and, 259
  political, 67, 323–24, 337–38, 337–39, 342–43, 346
  post-Vatican II, 216
  and social, political, and cultural life, 17
  Traditionalist, 381
  see also Catholic Church; Christianity; social Catholicism
Catholics
  American, 8, 11, 15, 19, 25n70, 44, 62, 145, 165–66, 168–71, 173–74, 209, 223, 236, 260, 285, 373, 376–77
  collaboration with Evangelicals, 21, 252–53
  collaboration with unbelievers, 183–88, 194, 195, 207
  conservative, 8, 60, 61, 67, 223, 240, 242, 244–45, 253, 260, 373
  conservative drift, 21
  conservative vs. liberal, 40, 168–70
  decline in number of, 23–24
  educated, 385

Subject Index

Catholics (*cont.*)
  English, 209
  European, 170
  French, 62, 177, 183–84, 382
  German, 103, 110, 118, 168
  German-American, 57–58, 142–45
  as immigrants, 57–58
  institutions of mutuality and support, 145
  Irish, 57–58, 168
  liberal, 125, 145, 168
  marginalization of, 242
  militant, 63
  postliberal, 32, 36, 200, 287–88
  pro-life, 34
  and the renewal of democracy, 18–24
  response to polycrisis, 14–18
  as social conservatives, 28
  see also Christians
causality, 277
Centesimus Annus, 240
charity, xvii–xviii, 16, 18, 48, 51, 51n127, 60, 106, 170, 175, 212, 308, 371
  social, 155
Charles III (King of England), 332
Chicago School, 236
child labor, 163
Child Labor Amendment, 143
China, 243, 250, 256
Christ. *See* Jesus Christ
Christian Democracy Party (Italy), 237
Christian democrats, 189
Christian Liberation Movement, 97
Christian Social Union, 172
Christianity
  cultural, 286
  egalitarianism of, 365
  humanism of, 365
  mysteries of, 156
  and the Nietzschean right, 364
  and the state, 370, 374, 376–77
  values of, 153–54
  see also Catholicism; Protestantism
Christians
  American, 286
  duties of, 138
  Western European, 286
  see also Catholics; Protestants

Church. *See* Catholic Church
Church of the Transfiguration (New York), 78
Church-Life Journal, 334
Cicero, 81, 97
City of God, 213
civil friendship, 6
civil law, 28–29, 45, 66
civil rights movement, 236–37, 249
Claremont Institute, 262
class struggle, 53n129
clerico-fascism, 322n7
climate crisis, 44, 52, 66, 245, 313, 372, 379, 390
Clinton, Hillary, 253
Clinton, William Jefferson "Bill," 21n59, 241n35, 243, 253, 255–56, 259
Clinton Administration, 21, 244, 254–55, 256
co-creationality, 156
Cold War, 210, 240n34, 250, 252, 253, 383
collectivism, 6–7, 276
Cologne Conflict, 110, 123
common good, xviii, xix, 11, 19, 22, 29, 30, 45, 49, 56, 57, 67, 196, 206, 224, 230, 371, 375–76
  and constitutional democracy, 52, 388–89
  and economic policy, 54
  as framework, 334–36
  as goal, 278
  and illiberalism, 265
  vs. individual rights, 178
  justice and, 161
  Ketteler's approach to, 102, 105, 130
  political, 278
  political vs. integral, 274–75, 275n19
  and property rights, 50
  public institutions as, 388
  social, 275n19
  and social justice, 85
  threats to, 134, 386
  universal, 206, 210n23, 212
  work for, 46, 162
communism, 156
  collapse of, 210, 236, 242, 252, 256
communitarianism, 364

Subject Index

communities of faith, 209
Compendium of the Social Doctrine of the Church, xviii, 2n4, 6, 6–7n18, 9, 16, 24, 38, 45, 47, 48, 49, 51, 55, 65, 66, 375, 388
confessional, 306, 308
Configuration for the Evangelization of Peoples (*Propaganda Fidei*), 384
congregationalism, 148
conjugal morality, 17
conscience, 98n60, 161, 290
conservatism, xv–xvi, 2n3, 7, 7n20, 13, 25n70, 28n77, 45, 60
   among Catholics, 168
   of Burke, 245–47, 261, 376
   and Catholic Social Teaching, 223–24, 250
   and Catholicism, 143–45
   common good, 354, 362–63
   cultural, 15
   development of, 60, 245–64
   economic, 249
   far right, 379–84
   fusion, 21, 222, 247–53, 257, 259, 339, 354–55, 365–66
   German, 132
   hard right, 67, 354, 355n3, 356–60
   illiberal, 66
   MAGA, 259
   in the media, 24n68
   national, 67, 354–55, 358–60, 364–65
   national defense, 249
   new right, 43
   neoliberal, 366
   and the Nietzschean right, 354, 357–58, 364
   present crisis of, 258–64
   radical, 254–56
   radical right, 382, 390
   social, 66, 249, 253, 264, 330
   and social Catholicism, 222, 264
   see also neoconservativism; theoconservatism
Conservative Political Action Committee (CPAC), 32
conspiracy theories/theorists, 249, 254
constitutional originalism, 29
   see also originalism

constitutionalism, 282, 335, 354
   common good, 33, 334, 336, 363
   democratic, 77, 96
   English, 226
consumerism, 12
contraception, 67, 146, 241, 296, 299, 310, 312
corduroy roads, 102, 105
corruption, 53, 163, 168, 314, 384
Cortes of Càdiz, 78
cosmopolitanism, 210–12, 359
COVID-19 pandemic, 390
CPAC (Conservative Political Action Committee), 32
creation, stewardship of, 50, 55
critical race theory, 363, 364n46
CSD. *See* Catholic Social Doctrine (CSD)
CST. *See* Catholic Social Teaching (CST)
Cuba, 56, 75–78, 82–84, 95–97, 238
culture, local, 214–16
culture wars, xix, 15, 21, 24n68, 41, 50–51n126, 61, 248, 260, 385

dark money, 379
Day, Dorothy, 236
de Mun, Albert, 189
decisionism, 360
Declaration of Independence, 226, 228
Decree on the Apostolate of the Laity: Apostolicam Actuositatem, 5
deep ecology, 156
deep fakes, 12n41, 49
DEI (diversity, equity, and inclusion), 141, 157, 287
Dei Verbum: Dogmatic Constitution on Divine Revelation, 6, 373
democracy
   American, xvi, xx, xxii, 15–16n49, 37, 44, 55, 61, 140, 266
   American liberal, xvi
   authentic, 18n53
   authoritarian, 5n14
   vs. autocracy, 371, 387–88
   Christian, 206
   and Christianity, 365
   and the Church, 18n53
   and the common good, 363, 388–89
   conservative, 358

Subject Index

democracy (*cont.*)
    constitutional, xix, 8, 16, 17, 19, 25, 52, 53, 56, 57, 59, 63, 65, 67, 68, 205, 223, 226, 228, 244, 252, 264, 265, 271, 288, 370, 371, 373, 374, 378n12, 387, 388–89
    contemporary, 25
    dangers in, 245
    electoral, 338, 341, 342, 344, 363
    in Europe, 383
    European social, 240
    expansion of, 210
    illiberal, 44, 64, 68, 377
    and integralism, 340–44
    liberal, xvi, 17, 45, 60, 243, 244, 265, 323, 329, 332, 342, 344, 356, 357, 358, 363, 381, 386
    and the masses, 233
    need to uphold, 60
    polarized, 372
    progressive deliberative, 341
    renewal of, 19, 389
    representative, 340
    secular, 374
    social, 3, 22, 53–54, 54, 58, 147
    "thicker" vs. "thinner" concepts of, 341
    Western, 243, 342
Democratic Party, and Catholic Social Teaching, 241–42
Democrats, pro-life, 242
DeSantis, Ron, 43
desegregation, 238
Deus Caritas Est, 103n2
Dicastery for the Promotion of Integral Human Development, 66, 212
digital communication, 12
Dignitatis Humanae: The Declaration on Religious Liberty, 31, 31–32n86, 140, 208, 216, 217, 288, 290, 291, 373–74
dignity
    shared, 49
    see also human dignity
disinformation, 49, 52, 171, 379, 383, 384–87
distributism, 326
diversity, 215–16

diversity, equity, and inclusion (DEI), 141, 157, 287
division of powers, 140, 144
divorce, 306–7
Dobbs decision, 2n3, 61n139
Dogmatic Constitution of the Church: Lumen Gentium, 4, 218–19, 391
Dogmatic Constitution on Divine Revelation: Dei Verbum, 6, 373
Dolan, Terrance (Terry), 251n48
Dominican House of Studies, xv
Donnelly, Ignatius, 167–68, 171
double effect (doctrine/principle of), 307
Droste zu Vischering, Clemens August Baron von, 110–11, 116

ecclesiology, 218–19
eclecticism, 93
Economic Justice for All: Pastoral Letter on Catholic Social Teaching and the U.S. Economy (U.S. Bishops), 21, 249
economics
    American system of, 142–43
    conservative, 20–21
    disruptions in, 13
    free market, 29, 236, 253
    global, 53n130
    industrial market, 132
    Keynesian, 20, 22, 68, 174, 233, 235, 249, 376, 378n12, 382, 385
    laissez faire, 57, 172, 174
    liberal, 17, 172
    libertarian, 30, 249
    macro-, 17–18
    market-oriented, 17–18, 20, 22, 147, 162, 232, 243, 249
    "middle-out," 20n57, 54, 379
    mixed, 3, 22, 53, 54, 68, 174, 233, 235, 237, 240, 249, 259, 376, 378n12, 382, 385
    neoconservative, 249
    neoliberal, 29, 44, 53, 249
    political, 377–79
    under Reagan, 20–21n58
    supply-side, 249
    sustainable, 17
    "trickle-down," 20n57, 54, 379

Subject Index

ecumenism, 145
Edmundite Initiative for Human Dignity, xxi
education
　public, 287
　religious, 287–88
egalitarianism, 357, 365
Eichhorn, Karl Friedrich, 108
Eisenhower, Dwight D., 236, 261, 381
Eisenhower administration, 366
empiricism, 358, 359, 364
England, 133
　see also Europe
Enlightenment, 117, 118–19, 140, 154, 246
entrepreneurship, 17
environmental advocacy, 336
environmental crisis, 8, 17, 19, 50–51n126, 53, 377
epistemology, 190, 196
equality
　economic, 148
　of persons, 205, 223, 226
　see also inequality
Espada, José Díaz de, 77
Estado Novo, 344
ethics
　business, 141
　Christian, 144–45, 157
　cultural, 47
　economic, 47
　legal, 47
　life, 27, 28, 65–66, 374
　marital, 27, 28
　medical, 66
　and metaphysics, 271, 272–78, 280–85
　personal, 280, 282
　political, 47, 270, 274, 280–85, 282
　sexual, 27, 28, 65–66, 241, 313, 374
　social, xv, xix, 47, 49, 52, 64, 66, 142, 144–45, 145, 149, 173
　virtue, 271
ethno-nationalism, 374
Eucharist, 306
eugenics, 358
Europe
　autocracy in, 383

Catholics in, xx, 91, 93, 96, 122, 125, 170, 172, 173, 285, 382
church/state relationship in, 132
Eastern, 253
fascism in, 59
Ketteler in, 103
and NATO, 250, 383
New World exploration by, 211
political Catholicism in, 342–43
religion in, 286
revolutions in, 118
secular, 208, 287
social Catholicism in, 229
social democracy in 58, 240
unity of, 207, 235, 237
see also England; France; Germany; Italy; Spain
European Union, 206, 235, 343
Eusebius of Caesarea, 279
euthanasia, 305, 312
evangelical mission, 24
Evangelii Gaudium: On the Joy of the Gospel, 163, 215, 306–7
evangelization, 32, 40–41, 44, 54, 58, 150, 157, 162, 170
　and postliberal ressourcement Thomism, 44–46
evil
　avoiding, 28, 308
　intrinsic, 48n112, 65, 66, 304, 305, 307
　liberalism as, 64, 89
　preventing, 110
　social, 6–7n18, 169
exclusivism, 209
expansionism, Soviet, 250
expressivism, radical, 362
extremism, 12, 86

fairness doctrine, 255
faith, 290, 374
　and reason, 48, 162
Falwell, Jerry, 60, 248, 251
family policy, 331
family unit, 142, 146, 154, 196, 248, 250, 310, 363
　and the sexual revolution, 241
　see also marriage

Subject Index

family values, 242, 251n48
fanaticism, 86, 95
Farmer's Alliance, 167
fascism, 32, 33n91, 234, 276, 388
   and Catholicism, 27n76, 43n117,
     59, 63, 204, 216, 382
   clerico-, 322n7
   neo-, 258
Federal Communications Commission
   (FCC), 255
Federal Reserve System, 20, 237
federalism, 143, 144
Federalist (Hamilton and Madison),
   227, 226–27n5
feminism, 253, 331
Ferdinand VII (King of Spain), 78
Fides et Ratio: On Faith and Reason, 380
financial crisis, 53
First Things, xvi, 8, 252, 257–60, 332,
   334, 357, 361, 364n45
First Vatican Council, 122, 131
Ford, Patrick, 165
Fordham University, 94
foreign policy, 243n37, 250, 256–57,
   260, 264
France, 78, 95, 133, 178, 180–83, 237,
   247, 284, 338, 344, 382
   see also Europe; French Revolution
Francis, Pope
   Amoris Laetitia, 306
   on "a better kind of politics," xx, 3,
     13, 15, 16, 18–19, 25, 36, 52,
     54–55, 60, 61, 65, 68, 69, 162,
     222, 264, 390
   on the confessional, 308
   on the "dark clouds," 45
   on the demands of justice, 313
   discernment of, 19
   on economics and politics, 364, 379
   emphasis on Social Doctrine, 10,
     15, 18
   Evangelii Gaudium, 163, 215, 306–7
   on evangelization, 150, 157
   *Fratelli Tutti: On Fraternity and
     Social Friendship*, 11–13, 19, 45,
     163, 211, 213, 215
   on globalization, 214
   on human dignity, 204, 209
   Laudate Deum, 10, 19, 52, 163
   *Laudato Si': On Care for Our
     Common Home*, 12, 19, 52, 296,
     298, 316
   on politics, 36n98
   pontificate of, xvii, 6, 38, 65
   priorities of, 13–14
   on the signs of the times, 11–13, 49,
     52, 163
   on social friendship, xx, 2n4, 9n25,
     11, 13, 16, 51, 52, 64, 163, 214
   social vision of, 9, 10, 41, 58, 69,
     170, 314, 373
   warning of "dark clouds," 9n24,
     11–12, 15, 45, 46, 390
Frankfurt Parliament, 118, 121
Franqism, 344
*Fratelli Tutti: On Fraternity and Social
   Friendship*, 11–13, 19, 45, 163,
   211, 213, 215
Frederick William III (king of Prussia),
   110
Frederick William IV (king of Prussia),
   118, 121
freedom, 127–28, 207, 273
   and religion, 119, 286
   Roosevelt's "four freedoms," 233
French Revolution, 226–27, 364, 374,
   376
Friedman, Milton, 235, 236, 249
fundamentalism, 279
   market, 22, 23, 30, 36, 51n128, 53,
     53n130, 174, 243, 259, 264
fusionism, 60
   see also conservatism, fusion

Gaetz, Mattt, 258
Gangs of New York, The (film), 98n62
Gasperi, Alcide De, 207, 237
Gaudium et Spes, 4–5, 5n11, 138, 140,
   156, 212, 216–17, 291, 305
Gay Pride movement, 241
gay rights, 21, 248, 257, 310, 363
genocide, 305
geopolitics, 13
Georgetown University, 93
German Romanticism, 102, 108, 112

Subject Index

Germany, 56, 90, 103-4, 105, 111, 113, 123, 124, 130-33, 146-47, 150, 234, 237, 278, 343
  see also Europe; Prussia
gerrymandering, 372, 377, 383
Gilded Age, 148, 163, 229
global humanism, 3
global public authority, 213-14
global warming. See climate crisis
globalism and local culture, 214-16
globalization, 7, 12, 174, 211, 212, 236, 243, 245
godlessness, 155
Gonin, Marius, 188-89
GOPAC, 254
Görres, Guido, 112
Görres circle (Görreskreis), 106, 112, 113
Göttingen University, 107-8
grace, 114, 157, 179, 192, 193, 197-200, 201, 390
Great Depression, 233, 235, 390
Great Recession, xvii, xviii, xix, 250, 378, 387
Great Society, 238, 240
Greene, Marjorie Taylor, 359
Gregory XVI, Pope, 110
guilds, 143
Gulf Wars, 253n53
gun violence, 44

happiness, 134
Hayes, Rutherford B., 228
Heidelberg University, 108
Heritage Foundation, 61, 251
hermeneutics
  Catholic theological, 373-74
  of continuity, 31
  of evangelization, 58, 150, 157
  historical, 149
  philosophical, 151
  of reform and renewal, 31
Hesburgh, Theodore, 236-37
"hipster" online groups, 339
historical consciousness, 149
historicism, 359
Hitler, Adolf, 233
Holy Trinity, 156

homicide. See murder
homophobia, 360
homosexuality, 157, 241, 248
  see also gay rights
hope, 139, 155, 170, 371, 390
human dignity, 49, 57, 60, 61, 156, 239, 265, 290, 338, 376
  and DEI initiatives, 141
  and the Gospel, 204-19
  Ketteler's approach to, 102, 105, 129
  of migrants, 12
  protection of, 104, 126
  of sexual minorities, 44
  solidary, 155
human ecology, 209
human flourishing, 26, 27n75, 28, 47, 50, 63, 65, 129, 227n6, 237, 243n36, 328, 331, 384, 389
human life, defense of, 2n3, 8, 48, 303
human realities, 276-77, 278
human rights, xix, 12, 49, 57, 59, 67, 140, 156, 205, 206, 226, 239, 243n36
  and abortion, 255
  expansion of, 210
  and liberalism, 126, 223
  in *Pacem in Terris*, 238
  and religious liberty, 216-19
  scholarship on, 69
  support for, 63, 104, 240, 244, 373
  violation of, 63
Humanae Vitae, 299
humanism, 365, 382
  anti-, 156
  atheist, 138, 156
  of Catholic Social Doctrine, 13, 23, 258, 265
  Christian, xviii, 3-4n7, 4, 58, 69, 140-41, 154, 156
  global, 3
  integral and solidary, xviii, 13, 16, 23, 38, 46, 51, 61n139, 64n145, 66, 156, 258, 260, 265, 384
Hungary, 32-33, 363, 365
hyperbole, 12

Iberia, 343
  see also Spain

Subject Index

identitarians, white, 356
identity politics, 374
Ignatius of Loyola, Saint, 114
illiberalism, 34, 50–51n126, 204, 222, 244, 330, 344, 379–84
   and the common good, 265
   and the ecosystem, 329–39
   of the left, 60, 242
   of the right, 25, 60, 64, 223, 323, 380–84
immigrants, 12, 52, 66, 163, 387
   Catholic, 285
   German, 142–43
   Irish, 78, 164–65
immigration, 313
imperialism, 359
indigenous communities, 209
individualism, 7n20, 12, 53, 143, 146, 148, 161, 232, 246, 375, 376
   autonomous, 328
   economic, 7
   expressive, 366
Industrial Revolution, xx, 53, 55–57, 59, 163, 170n23, 229, 247, 390
industrialization, 245
inequality, 66, 381
   economic, 18, 52, 372
   political, 18
   social, 163
   see also equality
infallibility, doctrine of, 131
injustice, 372
   social, 117, 171
   systemic, 165, 372
   see also justice
integral realism, 193
integralism, 59, 64, 67, 170, 178, 258, 271, 282, 291, 320, 374
   adjacent academic projects, 331–33
   assessment of, 321–24, 344–46
   Catholic, 66, 199–201, 325
   core definitions, 325–27
   critique of, 179
   and democracy in the West, 340–44
   and the developing illiberal ecosystem, 329–39
   as elite political Catholicism, 337–39
   as ideational project, 321
   liberal, 332
   neo-, 329
   postliberal, 15, 17, 25–36, 45, 222, 377
   preconciliar, 64, 68
   as program of action, 327–29
   response to, 288–91
   summarizing, 324–29
integration, 249
Intellectual Dark Web, 43
intentionality, 273
Intercollegiate Studies Institute, 7n20
interconnection, 10, 12, 50, 132, 191, 192, 196
internationalism, 359
interstate highway system, 236
Iran hostages, 248
Iraq War, 240n34, 256–57, 260, 384
isolationism, 250, 253n53
Italy, 94, 133, 237, 284
   see also Europe
Ius et Iustitium, 334

Jesuit order, 106, 111, 114, 115, 127, 183
Jesus Christ
   Incarnation of, 156
   Law of, 289
   as Redeemer, 157
   Resurrection of, 46n118
   right of, 126
   as Word Incarnate, 212
Jim Crow laws, 228, 238, 377
John Birch Society, 249
John Paul II, Pope/Saint
   Centesimus Annus, 240
   in Cuba, 79, 80
   Fides et Ratio: On Faith and Reason, 380
   leadership of, 252
   peace agenda of, 257, 260
   and political Catholicism, 210, 338
   pontificate of, xvii, xix, 6, 23, 63, 204, 259
   and the signs of the times, 11
   social teaching of, xviii, 38–39, 42, 47, 209, 373, 379

Subject Index

Veritatis Splendor: The Splendor of Truth, xvi, xvii, xviii, 299, 305, 306, 307, 309, 310
John XXIII, Pope/Saint
  Discernment of, 5n13
  Mater et Magistra: Christianity and Social Progress, 206, 240, 382
  Pacem in Terris: Peace on Earth, 31–32n86, 205, 206, 207, 212, 216, 217, 238
  peace agenda of, 257
  social teachings of, 204, 205, 206, 207, 239
Johnson, Andrew, 228
Johnson, Lyndon, 238, 240
Johnson, Mike, 259
Josias, The (online publication), 325–26
justice, 16, 45, 49, 55, 63, 170, 230, 239, 281, 287, 288
  advocacy for, 56, 61, 104, 162
  and Catholicism, 76, 86, 124–25
  and the common good, 161
  demands of, 313
  economic, 165, 300
  hunger and thirst for, 371
  for industrial workers, 62
  informed by charity and mercy, 308
  intergenerational, 372
  international, 211
  key questions of, 161
  for laborers, 130
  political, 165
  racial, 44
  and the role of the state, 172
  theories of, 80–88, 210
  virtues that inform, 94, 125
  see also injustice; social justice
justice and peace ministry, 39

Kennedy, John F., 236, 237, 240
  "Peace Speech," 238
Kennedy, Robert F., 238
Ketteler, Clemens von, 107
Ketteler, Friedrich von, 107
Ketteler, Wilhelm Emmanuel von, 102–34
  Advent Sermons, 120–21, 127, 132
  background, 103–7

  as Bishop of Mainz, 103, 121–22
  on church, state, and religious freedom, 122–30
  education, 104, 107–9
  on human dignity, 129
  Leichenrede, 119–20
  and the Prussian legal system, 109–11
  on the role of the Church, 130–32
  sermons on the social question, 118–21
  and the signs of the times, 162–63
  and social Catholicism, 229
  transition to clerical life, 113–18
  vocational discernment, 106, 111–13
Keynesianism, 378
kindness, 215
Kingdom of God, 194
Kirkpatrick Doctrine, 210
kleptocracies, 388
Knights of Labor, 165, 167, 229–30
Kulturkampf, 104, 110, 113, 343

La Tour du Pin, René de, 189
labor unions, 146, 165, 167, 230, 232
laicismo, 284
laïcité, 284
laissez faire, 53, 57, 163, 172, 174, 230, 232
Lathroop, Rose Hawthorne, 86n23
Latin America, 48n122, 76, 78, 83–84, 87, 96, 97, 139, 215, 251n49, 253, 342, 343, 383
Laudate Deum: On the Climate Crisis, 10, 19, 52, 163
Laudato Si': On Care for Our Common Home, 12, 19, 52, 296, 298, 316
law/Law
  apodictic, 290
  casuistic, 289–90
  of Christ, 289
  cultural, 125
  human, 134
  moral, 28–29, 65
  of Moses, 289
  positive, 134
  of Separation, 183, 189
  see also natural law

Subject Index

Leo XIII, Pope, 103, 104, 138, 167, 171, 188, 205, 230, 326, 341–42
Rerum Novarum: On Capital and Labor, 94, 103, 104, 122, 166, 167, 169, 171–72, 205, 230
Liberal International Order, 210
liberal rights theory, 133
liberal world order, 224, 239, 242, 244, 386
liberalism
    Anglo-American, 59, 68, 206, 210, 228–36
    anti-dogmatic, 156
    Catholic, 88
    and the Catholic social tradition, 59–60, 222, 223–24, 225, 264, 265
    and Catholicism, 168, 204–19, 236–42, 259, 388
    and Christianity, 64n143, 126, 365
    classical, 17–18, 362
    communitarian, 155n40
    continental, 206
    criticism of, 64, 64n143, 64n144, 65, 214, 273, 333, 337
    debates about, 63
    development of, 225–45
    economic, 53, 57–58, 140, 163–64n4, 164, 215, 229
    embedded, 3, 22, 259
    evolution of, 60
    excesses of, 45
    fear of, 123
    of the French Revolution, 374, 376
    German, 124, 128, 132, 133
    hegemonic, 329–30
    and human rights, 126
    key tenets of, 223
    market, 332
    modern, 279, 329–30
    ordered liberty, 365
    political, 57–58, 140, 265, 328
    post–World War II, 236–40
    postliberal attack on, 35
    progressive, 332, 362
    proto-, 225–27
    radical flaws of, 29–30
    rejection of, 62
    relational, 155
    skepticism regarding, 154
    secular, 177–78
    understandings of, 370
    uninspiring, 355
    see also antiliberalism; postliberalism
liberation movements, 215
libertarianism, 21, 24n68, 30, 36, 260, 333, 377
life world, 277–78
Lincoln, Abraham, 58, 261
localism, 332
Louis IX, Saint, 344
love
    Christian, 13
    cruciform, 382
    divine, 24, 46, 157–58
    of God and His Church, 315, 316
    for our neighbors, 55
    Trinitarian, 259
Lumen Gentium: Dogmatic Constitution on the Church, 4, 218–19, 391

Maceo, Antonio, 84
macroeconomics, 17–18
marriage, 146, 154, 260, 281
    mixed, 110
    remarriage, 306–7
    same-sex, 67, 257, 361
    see also family unit
Martí, José, 79
Marxists, 207
Mater et Magistra: Christianity and Social Progress, 206, 240, 382
materialism, 53n129, 90, 329, 361
Maurrassians, 180, 185, 191, 193–95, 199
McCarthy, Kevin, 258
media
    Catholic, 12
    conservative, 24n68, 253, 254–56, 257
    Fox News, 262, 385
    left-leaning, 255n58
    propaganda in, 262
    Russian, 386
media manipulation, 6–7n18
Melina, Livio, xvi
mental health, 13
Merton, Thomas, 236

Subject Index

Meštrović, Ivan, 98–99
metaphysics, xvi, xix, 62, 64, 270, 362
    empiricist, 364
    and ethics, 271, 272–78, 280–85
    and natural law, 272
    and politics, 273–85
Michelangelo, 98–99
migrants. *See* immigrants
militarism, 260, 364
minimum wage, 67, 146, 232
Mirror of Justice, 334
modernism, 179, 190, 357, 359, 364
modernity, 138–39, 140, 154, 158, 223, 345, 360
monarchism, 322n7
Monnet, Jean, 207
monophorism, 190, 193, 194, 194–95, 195
    extrinsicist, 193, 194, 197–98
monopolies, 163, 231
Montini, Giovanni Batista. *See* Paul VI (Pope/Saint)
moral agency, 156
moral entities, 276–77n25
Moral Majority, 60, 248, 251, 252
moral norms, 313
    obligations of, 299
    positive vs. negative, 300–304, 312–14
moral teaching
    authoritative, 66, 295, 298, 312
    Catholic, 189, 260, 295–301, 304, 309, 312, 313–15
    magisterial, 314, 315, 373
    see also Catholic Social Teaching (CST)
moral theology, 18, 24, 55, 61n139, 66, 93, 172–73, 232, 297, 313
moral theory, xvii, 133
moral truths, 272
Mount Pellerin Society, 235, 249
Mundelein Seminary, xx, 42
Munich University, 108, 109
murder, 118, 227, 272, 280, 305
Mussolini, Benito, 233

NAFTA (North American Free Trade Agreement), 253n53, 255–56

Napoleon (Bonaparte), 107
National Catholic Welfare Council, 143
National Conservatism (NATCOM), 359
National Conservative Political Action Committee, 251n48
national park system, 231
nationalism, xx, 209, 258, 359, 364, 365
    American, 366n45
    authoritarian, 344
    Christian, 67, 178, 366
    ethno-, 374
NATO (North Atlantic Treaty Organization), 250, 383
natural environment, 13
natural law, 81, 105, 120, 128, 132, 134, 149–55, 291, 309, 360
    Catholic, 152–53
    and Catholic Social Teaching, 148–49
    Christian, 157–58
    classical, 133–34
    and moral judgment, 152
    neo-scholastic tradition, 149
    and political ethics, 280–85
    Ratzinger's approach to, 137–38
natural law theory, 97–98, 270–71, 271n2, 291
    neo-scholastic vs. neoclassical, 271, 272
    New, 65, 271, 309–10
    Thomistic, 280
nature-grace relationship, 179, 193, 198, 201
neoconservatism, xvi, 210, 214, 222, 253, 256–57
    in the market, 249
    and the Republican party, 256–58
    see also conservatism
neofascism, 258
neo-integralism, 321, 329
    see also integralism
neoliberalism, 18, 20n57, 21, 53, 53n130, 69, 243, 365, 378
    economic, xix
    fundamentalist, 36
    market fundamentalist, 36
    see also liberalism

Subject Index

Neo-pragmatism, 98
neo-scholasticism, 112, 149
Neo-Thomism, 67, 182, 338
New Deal, 20, 22, 24, 57, 59, 146, 147, 233, 236, 250
new evangelization, 23
New Natural Law theory, 65, 271, 309–10
New Polity journal, 325
new right, 43
Nicaragua, 250
Nietzschean right, 354, 357–58, 364
nihilism, 175, 356
Nixon, Richard M., 238–39n29, 249, 251n46, 385
North American Free Trade Agreement (NAFTA), 253n53, 255–56
North Atlantic Treaty Organization (NATO), 250, 383
Nostra Aetate: Decree on Non-Christian Religions, 218
Notre Dame University, 94
nuclear weapons, 244, 250

Oates, Lawrence, 303–4, 305, 308, 310, 312
Obama, Barack, 257
objective beings, 277
obsequium religiosum, 315
obstructionism, 254
Octogesima Adveniens: A Call to Action, 5, 379
O'Gavan, Juan Bernardo, 77
oligarchs and oligarchies, xx, 18, 22, 29, 30, 33, 35, 36, 49, 53, 164, 167, 168, 171, 178, 243, 248n44, 261, 265, 376–77
  judicial, 334
ontology, 190–91, 196
  of human realities, 276–77, 278
  materialist, 361
  social, 280
Orbán, Victor, 32, 64, 68, 359
originalism, 29, 333, 363

Pacem in Terris: Peace on Earth, 31–32n86, 205, 206, 207, 212, 216, 217, 238

pandemics, 12
Papacy
  infallibility of, 131
  legitimacy of, 345
Pascal, Georges de, 189
Pascendi, 190
Pastoral Constitution on the Church in the Modern World: Gaudium et Spes, 4–5, 5n11, 138, 140, 156, 212, 216–17, 291, 305
paternalism, 332, 362, 382
patriarchy, 128, 357
patriotism, 87–88
  false, 87
Paul of Tarsus, Saint, 391
Paul VI, Pope/Saint, 5, 204, 206, 207
  Humanae Vitae, 299
  Lumen gentium, 4, 218–19, 391
  Octogesima Adveniens: A Call to Action, 5, 379
  social legacy of, 239
Payá, Oswaldo, 97
Payá, Rosa María, 97
Peace of Westphalia, 123
Perot, Ross, 253, 253n53
personal goods, 134
personhood, 156, 273
phenomenology, 277–78
philosophy
  of action, 191
  anthropology of, 272–73
  hermeneutic, 151
  Kantian, 111
  moral, xviii
  moralist-realist, 134
  political, 64, 211, 224, 277–78, 291, 326, 380
  postliberal, 360
  Stoic, 152
  and theology, 380
Pius VIII, Pope, 110, 116
Pius IX, Pope, 94, 131, 205
  Syllabus of Errors, 122, 124, 205, 207, 224, 225, 290, 374
Pius X, Pope, 183, 188, 189–90
  Pascendi, 190
  Vehementer Nos, 183

Subject Index

Pius XI, Pope, 168
Pius XII, Pope, 207
    Christmas address (1944), 233–35, 237, 245, 265
Platonism, 92
Platt Amendment, 84
pluralism, 358, 359, 364
    internationalist, 366
plutocracy, 146, 168, 377
Poland, 365
polarization, 12, 69, 148, 175, 372, 387
    tribal, 36
politics
    American, 370
    Catholic, 339
    Classical, 331
    common-good constitutional/conservative, 325
    deceptive analogies, 275–78
    democratic, 341
    disruptions in, 13
    and ethics, 272–78, 280–85
    fusionist, 339
    identity, 244, 374
    influence of money on, 372
    medieval, 279
    and metaphysics, 273–85
    moral principles in, 288
    post-Christian, 321
    and theology, 270, 288–91
polycrisis, xvii, 23, 25, 34, 48, 57, 60, 61, 68–69, 174, 175, 223, 224, 264, 265, 370, 390
    management of, 19
    response to, 13–18
Pontifical College Josephinum, xv
Pontifical Council for Justice and Peace, 2n4, 47
    see also *Compendium of the Social Doctrine of the Church*
Pontifical John Paul II Institute for Studies on Marriage and Family, xv, xvi, 37n99, 62
popular sovereignty, 94, 140, 226, 227
populism, xix, 8, 60, 69, 168, 204, 222, 253, 258, 387, 389
    cultural, 17
    economic, 33, 67, 366
    illiberal, 223
    MAGA, 258
    and postliberalism, 365
    right-wing, 36
    socially conservative, 67
Populist Party, 168
positivism, 192n58
post truth, 384–88
postliberalism, 17, 18, 25, 59, 65, 66, 67, 68, 242, 265, 271, 279, 282, 283, 291, 320, 323, 329, 331, 354–55, 356, 374
    American Catholic, 28–31
    and American illiberal democracy, 32–34
    British, 332–33
    Catholic, 36, 287–88, 331
    and Catholic Social Teaching, 31–32
    defined, 360–63
    and evangelization, 31–32
    and the hard right, 354–66
    populist, 365
    response to, 288–91
    roots and development of, 26–27
Powderly, Terrance, 165, 229
power distribution, 50
Power Elite, 362
practical reason, xvi
privatization, 148
    of religion, 105
probabilism, 98n60
Program on Disinformation and Twenty-First-Century Propaganda, 386
Progressive Era, 146, 148, 173
Progressive Reform movement, 24, 172
progressives and progressivism, 142–43, 146, 231
pro-life movement, xvi, 61n139, 165, 252
    see also abortion
"Promise of Peace, The: God's Promise and Our Response" (U.S. Bishops), 249
propaganda, 18, 49, 262, 264–65, 383, 384–87
Propaganda Fidei, 384
property rights, 50, 53, 127, 130, 211, 230
Protestant Reformation, 117

Subject Index

Protestant Social Gospel, 48n122
Protestantism
    in America, 286
    Anglican, 246
    Baptist, 285
    and Christian nationalism, 178
    Evangelical, 21, 24n68, 54n133, 61, 248, 252, 262
    in Germany and Austria, 130
    liberal, 40, 45
    Methodist, 285
    respect for, 119–20
    Southern Baptist, 251
    see also Christianity
Prussia, 107–13, 116–18, 121, 122, 130–31
psychology, social, 13
public goods, 53n130, 174
public spirit, 56, 75, 81–82
Puritanism, 82
Putin, Vladimir, 383, 386

Quadragesimo Anno, 155, 168
Quanta Cura, 122, 131

racial justice, 44
racism, 69, 358, 364, 364n46, 376, 377, 381
radical gender theory, 332
radicalism, 118
rationalism, 133, 134, 358, 360
Ratzinger, Joseph Cardinal, xvii, 252, 270, 279, 282, 290
    on modernity, 139–40
    and natural law, 137–38
    see also Benedict XVI, Pope
Reagan, Ronald, 243, 248, 252, 366n45, 385
Reagan Administration, 20, 21, 22, 224, 247–53, 255, 256
Reagan era, 60
realism, integral, 193
reason, 272–73, 331, 355
    critical theory, 141
    and critical thinking, 141
    faith and, 48, 162
    practical, 305
    right, 8

reconciliation, 9, 391
Reisach, Karl August Graf von, 114, 115–16
relativism, responsible, 98
religion
    and freedom, 286
    political, 195
    in public life, 208–10
    respect for others, 218–19
    state, 331
religious freedom, 31–32n86, 57, 60, 126–27, 131, 140, 149, 204, 207, 373
    and human rights, 216–19
    modern, 288
    protection of, 103
    and the Second Vatican Council, 284
religious tolerance, 95–97
Republican Party, xv–xvi, 60, 231
    crisis of, 262–63
    and the far right, 365
    and market fundamentalism, 259
    modern, 381
    and neoconservatism, 256–58
    and populism, 67
    positive contributions of, 261
    radicalization of, 61
Rerum Novarum: On Capital and Labor, 94, 103, 104, 122, 166, 167, 169, 171–72, 205, 230
ressourcement, xviii, 10, 15, 37, 37n99, 40, 59, 62, 63
revelation, 55, 156–57, 291, 373, 374
rights
    economic, 378
    gay, 21, 248, 257, 310, 363
    liberal, 133
    natural, 94, 95
    of man, 167, 290
    states', 57, 143–44, 228
    subjective, 104–5
    women's, 240–41, 248
Rodin, Auguste, 98–99
Roe v. Wade, 2n3, 45, 241n35, 250–51
Romney, Mitt, 258n63, 261–62
Roncalli, Angelo, 206, 238
    see also John XXIII, Pope/Saint

Subject Index

Roosevelt, Eleanor, 237
Roosevelt, Theodore, 58, 231, 261
rule of law, 29, 56, 75, 80, 210, 258, 261, 363
Russia, xix, 42, 250, 383, 386
   see also Soviet Union
Ryan, John A., 20, 24, 232–33, 237, 370, 377, 385, 389, 390
   achievements, 173–75
   background, 163–64
   and Catholic Social Doctrine, 161–62
   family and early years, 164–66
   graduate and ongoing studies, 172–73
   in seminary, 166–72
   social formation of, 161–75

Salazar, António di Oliveira, 344
San Martín, José de, 84
Sanders, Bernie, 366
Sangnier, Marc, 189
scholasticism, 109, 112, 152
school busing, 249
Schuman, Robert, 206–7, 237
Second Great Awakening, 96
Second Vatican Council
   Apostolicam actuositatem, 5
   Dei Verbum: Dogmatic Constitution on Divine Revelation, 6, 373
   Dignitatis Humanae: The Declaration on Religious Liberty, 31, 31–32n86, 140, 208, 216, 217, 288, 290, 291, 373–74
   on moral norms, 312
   Pastoral Constitution on the Church in the Modern World: Gaudium et Spes, 4–5, 5n11, 138, 140, 156, 212, 216–17, 291, 305
   on natural law, 149
   political theology of, 65, 270, 376
   reception of, xvii, xxiii, 24, 55, 345, 370
   on religious liberty, 126, 284
   social teachings of, 18, 140, 212, 298, 315
   understandings of, 373

sectarianism, 148, 209
sedevacantist, 338
secularism, 132, 206, 208
secularization, 63, 123, 127, 133, 287–88, 321, 329, 337
segregation, 58, 251, 364n46
self-determination, 205, 223
Semaine sociale, 177, 179, 188–89, 199, 201
sex abuse crisis, xvii, 42
sexism, 358
sexual minorities, 44, 387
sexual morality, 17
sexual revolution, 241, 248
sexuality, 260
Sheen, Fulton, 236
signs of the times, xxiii, 11–13, 43n116, 49, 50, 51, 52, 68, 103, 131, 132, 158, 162–64, 211n29, 212
skepticism, 89
slavery, 78, 80, 82, 144, 227, 228
social capital, 362
social Catholicism, xx, 15, 17, 37–38, 56, 58–59, 62, 68, 170, 174, 179, 229, 258, 372
   and Catholic identity, 374–76
   and conservatism, 264
   contemporary renewal of, xxii–xxiii
   defined, 2n4
   and democracy, 19
   guiding convictions for, 47–54
   history of, 76–80, 377
   and liberalism, 264
   new, 47–54
   postliberal, 15
   and social media, 69
   for the twenty-first century, 264–66
   of Varela, 75–99
social class, 105
social contract theory, 93, 226, 246–47
social corporatism, 329
social Darwinism, 53, 163, 229, 230, 249
social friendship, xx, 2n4, 3, 9n25, 11, 13, 16, 24, 34n92, 50–51n126, 51, 52, 55, 61n139, 64, 69, 148, 155, 163, 214, 260, 371
social Gospel (Protestant), 48n122

Subject Index

social justice, 41, 60, 66, 155, 167, 299, 300, 308
  and the Catholic Enlightenment, 94
  Thomistic approach to, 94
  Varela's theory of, 85
Social Kingship of Christ, 326
social media, 69
social modernism, 179
social movements, 2n4
social psychology, 13
social romanticists, 143
social sciences, 380n18
socialism, 53, 230, 243, 276
  bureaucratic, 5n14
  and Christianity, 126, 365
  democratic, 366
  liberal, 68, 355, 356
  national, 156
  objection to, 130
  threat of, 164
socialization, 212
Society for the Rule of Law, 29n79
Society of Jesus. See Jesuit order
Society of St. Pius X (SSPX), 242
solidarism, 142, 146–47
solidarity, 212
Soviet Union, 210, 235, 238, 252, 256
  see also Russia
Spain, 77–78, 83–84, 178, 344
  see also Europe
Spanish-American War, 84
speciesism, 156
Spiritual Exercises, 114
SSPX (Society of St. Pius X), 242
St. Edmund's Retreat Center, xxi
St. Mary's Seminary (Baltimore), 93
stagflation, 248
Ständestaat, 337
state of nature, 93, 246
statism, 335, 336
stewardship, 50, 55
Stockholm Resilience Centre, 53n131
Stoicism, 152
Stone, Roger, 238–39n29, 262
subsidiarity, principle of, 85, 126, 126–27, 214, 239, 276
suicide, 303, 304, 305, 306, 308

supernatural, 133, 156, 177, 180, 181–82, 183, 184, 186, 188, 191–201, 235n21, 326
Supreme Court, 260–61
Susanna (biblical), 307
sustainable development, 17, 50, 371
Syllabus of Errors, 122, 124, 205, 207, 224, 225, 374

Taft, William Howard, 231
teleology, 362
terrorism
  stochastic, 258
  World Trade Center, 257
theft, 305, 306
theoconservatism, xvi, 253, 256–60
theocracy, 279
theology, 191, 196
  Catholic, 111–12, 373
  Catholic academic, 111–12
  of liberation, 139
  Lonergan's view of, 150
  manualist, 193
  moral, 18, 66
  and philosophy, 380
  political, 65, 206, 270, 288–91, 360
  and political philosophy, 326
  vs. religion, 150–51
  of work, 69
Theology of the People, 215
Thiel, Peter, 358
Thomas Aquinas, Saint, xvi, xviii, 37n101, 81, 132–33, 230, 279, 360, 371
  and Aristotle, 186
  on charity, 51n127
  influence on Varela, 93
  and integralism, 326
  metaphysics of, 272, 273–74
  on pure nature, 183
  Summa Theologica, 105, 126, 133
  see also Thomism
Thomism, 63, 309
  in Kettler's theology, 125–26
  and natural law, 120, 128
  neo-, 182
  ressourcement, xviii, 15, 37–46

Subject Index

transcendental, 182
  in the U. S., 93–94
  of Varela, 93
  see also Thomas Aquinas
Thomistic ethics, xv
thought experiments, 211, 246–47, 327, 342
totalitarianism, 357, 358, 363
trade unions. See labor unions
Traditional Latin Mass communities, 339, 381
traditionalism, 330, 339, 345, 356, 379–84
transcendence, 45, 155, 192
transgenderism, 154, 157, 361
tribalism, 17, 39n105, 52, 69, 148, 175
Trilateral Commission, 378n12
Trump, Donald, 33, 36, 42, 253n53, 258, 260, 263, 296, 359, 383, 386
Truss, Liz, 379
truth
  and Catholic social tradition, 48–49
  fullness of, 373
  post-, 384–88
  seeking, 374
truth claims, 30, 32, 287
"Two Santas" strategy, 255n59

UDHR (Universal Declaration of Human Rights), 3, 207, 237, 243, 378
Ukraine, 383
ultra-masculinism, 357
unionization. See labor unions
Unitatis Redintegratio: Decree on Ecumenism, 218
United Kingdom, 133
  see also Europe
United Nations, 8n21, 233, 235, 255
United States
  Catholics in, 8, 11, 15, 19, 25n70, 44, 62, 145, 165–66, 168–71, 173–74, 209, 223, 236, 260, 285, 373, 376–77
  foreign policy of, 243n37, 250, 256–57, 260, 264
Universal Call to Holiness, 24

Universal Declaration of Human Rights (UDHR), 3, 207, 237, 243, 378
universalism, 364, 365
University of St. Mary of the Lake, xx
utopian thinking, 5
utopianism, 82, 119

Valdés, Dagoberto, 97
values, political ethical, 274
Varela, Félix
  background and career, 77–80
  Letters to Elpido, 82, 89, 95–97
  significance for today, 97–99
  on social Catholicism, 75–99
  social philosophy of, 88–94
  theory of justice, 80–88
Varela Project, 97
Vatican I, 122, 131
Vatican II. See Second Vatican Council
Vehementer Nos, 183
Veritatis Splendor: The Splendor of Truth, xvi, xvii, xviii, 299, 305, 306, 307, 309, 310
Vietnam War, 238–39n29, 240, 248, 384
Virginia School of Political Economy, 236
virtue
  cardinal, 371
  moral, 371
  as second nature, 272
  theological, 371–72
virtue ethics, 271
voluntarism, 279
voter suppression, 377

Wanniski, Jude, 255n59
War on Poverty, 238
Watergate burglaries, 238–39n29
wealth redistribution, 363
weavers, 264
WEF (World Economic Forum), 13, 19
welfare reform, 255
welfare state, 231, 366
Weyrich, Paul, 60–61, 251, 251n49, 251–52n51, 252
white nationalism, 249
Wilson, Woodrow, 231

Subject Index

Witherspoon Institute, 264
wokeism, 45, 244
women's rights, 240–41, 248
Word on Fire Institute, 43n116
Word on Fire ministry, 44, 169n20
World Economic Forum (WEF), 13, 19

World Trade Association, 243
World Trade Center, 257

xenophobia, xx, 96

Zentrum, 343

Author Index

Abbà, Giuseppe, 291
Abell, Aaron I., 145, 146, 158
Acemoglu, Daron, 69, 384, 389, 391
Addison, Daniel, 346
Adler-Bell, Sam, 367
Ahmari, Sohrab, 30, 34, 43, 69, 291, 346
Alexander, Michelle, 158
Allitt, Patrick, 346
Anscombe, Elizabeth, 311, 316
Applebaum, Anne, 386, 391
Aquinas. *See* Thomas Aquinas
Aristotle, 274, 292, 316
Arnal, Oscar L., 346
Arnhart, Larry, 69
Arnsdorf, Isaac, 69
Aubert, Roger, 201
Austriaco, Nicanor Pier Giorgio, 316

Bachem, Karl, 134
Bacon, Francis, 361
Balmer, Randall, 69, 266
Balthasar, Hans Urs von, 62–63, 177, 199, 200–201
Bannon, Steven K., 258, 382–83, 386
Barnes, Marc, 325, 346
Barron, Robert, 38, 40–44, 69
Baude, William, 346
Bechevich, Andrew, 264
Behr, Thomas C., 99
Beitz, Charles R., 211
Bell, Duncan, 346
Benedict XVI, 70, 158, 220, 266, 292, 391

Benitez, Juan Manuel Campos, 99
Berdahl, Robert M., 134
Berger, Peter, 99, 287, 292
Bernardi, Peter J., 201, 346
Bernays, Edward, 384, 391
Bersnak, P. Bracy, 316
Bertman, Christopher, 266
Bevir, Mark, 70, 391
Birke, Adolf M., 125–26, 130, 134
Blackbourn, David, 135
Blakely, Jason, 70, 201, 346, 391
Blakeslee, William Francis, 99
Blatt, Joel, 346
Blondel, Maurice, 62, 177–202
Boff, Leonardo, 220
Boissard, Adéodat, 188–89
Bok, Derek, 158
Bolten, Analouise Clissold, 116, 135
Bothur, Ian, 346
Botros, Sophie, 316
Bouie, Jamelle, 70
Bouillard, Henri, 202
Bouquillon, Thomas J., 172–73
Bowen, William G., 158
Boyle, Gregory, 158
Boyle, Joseph, 303, 309, 311, 317
Bradley, Gerard V., 70, 292, 297–99, 301–2, 309, 312–14, 317
Brandmüller, Walter, 317
Brennan Center, 70
Brentano, Clemens, 113
Bretzke, James T., 317

Author Index

Briggs, Kenneth A., 70
Broderick, Francis L., 175, 266
Bronze Age Pervert, 357, 367
Brooks, David, 264
Brugger, E. Christian, 70, 292, 297–302, 308–9, 312–14, 317
Brungardt, John G., 346
Buckley, William F. Jr., 7n20, 240, 249, 264, 382
Burghardt, Walter J., 70
Burke, Edmund, 81, 82, 128, 141, 158, 222, 245–47, 263, 266, 376
Buzogány, Aron, 347, 351

Cairns, Madoc, 41, 42, 70
Carpenter, Anne, 200, 202
Casarella, Peter, 56, 99
Casey, Conor, 325, 336, 347
Cavadini, John, 347
Center for Jewish-Christian Understanding and Cooperation, 220
Chappel, James, 70, 266, 382, 391
Chemerinsky, Erwin, 70
Chenu, Marie-Dominique, 149
Chesterton, G. K., 285, 292
Chomsky, Noam, 384, 391
Christiansen, Drew, 220, 266
Clarke, W. Norris, 292
Clinton, William J., 266
Cloutier, David, 317
Coleman, John A., 152, 158
Collinge, William J., 94, 99
Comte, Auguste, 191, 192, 192n58
Condorcet, 90
Congregation for the Doctrine of the Faith, 292, 317
Connolly, Mary Beth Fraser, 347
Constant, Benjamin, 227, 266
Continetti, Matthew, 366, 367
Conway, Erik M., 72, 268, 385
Conway, Martin, 347
Coppedge, Michael, 347
Coppins, McKay, 254, 261, 266
Coreth, Emerich, 202
Corn, David, 266
Corrin, Jay P., 347
Courson, Paul, 266

Craig, Gordon A., 135
Crean, Thomas, 325–26, 340, 342, 347
Crowe, Ian, 99
Crozier, Michael J., 266, 391
Cubitt, Geoffrey, 202
Culbreath, Jonathan, 347
Cummings, Kathleen Sprows, 99
Curran, Charles E., 144, 149, 158, 313, 317

Dahl, Robert A., 292, 347
de Condillac, Étienne Bonnot, 90, 92
De La Torre, Miguel, 99
De Maistre, Joseph, 355, 367, 368
de Mello, Anthony, 41
Del Duca, Gemma Marie, Sr., 99
Delgado, Mariano, 158
Deneen, Patrick J., 28, 33, 70, 159, 209, 214, 220, 292, 325, 328, 332, 336, 347, 361–67
Denny, Christopher D., 347
DeSantis, Ron, 43
Descartes, René, 88, 92
Descoqs, Pedro, 179, 180, 182–86, 188, 194–96, 198, 202
Destutt de Tracy, Antoine de, 90, 91
Devlin, Patrick, 367
Díaz-Stevens, Ana María, 100
Dietrich, Donald J., 135
Dilthey, Wilhelm, 151
Doer, John, 70
Doherty, Bernard, 347
Döllinger, Ignaz von, 116
Donahue, John R., 70
Dreher, Rod, 209, 220, 244, 296, 298, 316–17, 365, 367
Dru, A., 202
Dueck, Colin, 347
Dugin, Aleksandr, 356
Dulles, Avery, 317
Dupré, Louis, 90, 100
Dussel, Enrique, 90, 100

Eberts, Mirella W., 347
Ederer, Rupert J., 146–47
Elias, Norbert, 135
Eliot, T. S., 360, 367
Ely, Richard T., 172, 173

Author Index

Engelen, William, 142–43, 159
Engels, Friedrich, 121
Espín, Orlando, 100
Estévez, Felipe, 83, 89, 94, 100
Evans, Jonathan, 292
Evola, Julius, 70, 356

Fabro, Cornelio, 292
Faggioli, Massimo, 42, 70
Fawcett, Edmund, 267, 367, 381, 391
Feijóo y Montenegro, Benito Jerónimo, 88–89
Ferran, Lluís, 348
Feser, Edward, 292
Figueroa y Miranda, Manuel, 100
Fimister, Alan, 325, 326, 340–42, 347
Finke, Roger, 285, 292
Finnis, John, 65, 66, 81, 100, 292, 297, 301–3, 309, 311–15, 317, 360, 367
Fleet, Michael, 347
Fleming, James E., 70
Foran, Michael P., 348
Forgey, Quint, 367
Fornet-Betancourt, Raúl, 90
Foucault, Michel, 45
Fouilloux, Étienne, 202
Fox, Matthew, 41
Francis, Pope, 70–71, 159, 175, 220, 267, 317–18
Freedom House, 71
Frohnen, Bruce P., 348
Frost, Amber A'Lee, 348
Fukuyama, Francis, 224, 243, 267, 355–56, 367, 375–76, 391
Fustel de Coulanges, Numa Denis, 331, 347

Gadamer, Hans-Georg, 151
Gaillardetz, Richard, 219, 220
Ganz, John, 367
Garrett, Shaylyn Romney, 148, 160
Gellott, Laura, 337, 348
Gener, Tomás, 81
George, Henry, 166
George, Robert, 264
Gibbons, James, 167, 229–30, 284, 292
Gilson, Étienne, 292

Gingrich, Newt, 254–55, 383, 385
Gleason, Philip, 159
Glendon, Mary Ann, 267
Goldberg, Michelle, 391
Goldman, Ari L., 71
Gómez-Lobo, Alfonso, 318
Gonçalves, Leandro Pereira, 348
González, Toledano, 348
Görres, Johann Joseph, 106, 110, 112
Gray, Rosie, 367
Gregory XVI, 135
Gremillion, Joseph, 220
Grisez, Germain, 292, 309, 311
Grotius, Hugo, 140
Guriev, Sergei, 71

Habermas, Jürgen, 126, 135
Hall, Kermit, 292
Hall, Mark David, 292
Hamilton, Alexander, 227, 267
Hanby, Michael, 348
Hare, R. M., 318
Harrington, Mary, 331–33, 348
Harvard University Faculty Bibliography, 348
Hauerwas, Stanley, 209
Hayek, Friedrich A., 235–36, 249, 267
Hazony, Yoram, 358–59, 362, 364–68
Hegel, G. W. F., 90, 91, 108, 109
Heinrich, Joseph, 124, 293
Helmholz, R. H., 348
Hendricks, Obery, 368
Hendrikse, Reijer, 348
Henrici, Peter, 63, 199
Himes, Kenneth R., 159
Hittinger, Russell, 293
Hobbes, Thomas, 93, 226, 246
Hoffman, David E., 100
Hofstadter, Richard, 267
Hogan, William Edward, 135
Holmes, Stephen, 350
Howes, Thomas D., 293
Huddock, Barry, 220
Huff, Charles Hughes, 200, 202
Hughes, John, 287

Institute of Political Science and Sociology, 71

417

Author Index

Ireland, John, 24, 58, 145, 167, 169, 170–71, 173
Isasi-Díaz, Ada-María, 98
Ivereigh, Austen, 220

Jarlot, George, 207
Jefferson, Thomas, 87, 228, 267
Jensen, Steven J., 318
Joas, Hans, 154, 159
John Paul II, 71, 100, 220, 267, 293, 318, 392
John XXIII, 71, 220, 267, 392
Johnson, Elizabeth, 202
Johnston, Savannah Eccles, 348
Jones, Andrew Willard, 325, 346, 348

Kaiser, Wolfram, 348
Kalyvas, Stathis N., 348
Kant, Immanuel, 109, 231, 309
Kaplan, Grant, 135
Kaveny, Cathleen, 71, 318
Keeley, Theresa, 267
Keenan, James F., 318
Kekes, John, 348
Kelly, Martin, 267
Kenkel, Frederick P., 142, 143, 144
Kerlin, Michael, 180
Kerr, Fergus, 202
Kerwin, Michael, 202
Ketteler, Wilhelm Emmanuel von, 45, 102–35, 229
Keynes, John Maynard, 233
Kirk, Russell, 267
Kirkpatrick, Jeane, 221
Klee, Heinrich, 117
Kleutgen, Joseph, 93
Kloppenberg, James, 202
Koerpel, Robert, 317
Koslowski, Peter, 159
Kovesi, Julius, 318
Krieger, Leonard, 135
Kurth, James, 348
Kwasniewski, Peter A., 326, 352

Lamas, Carmen E., 100
Laruelle, Marlene, 348
Laursen, John Christian, 100
Lawler, Michael, 319

Lawler, Peter Augustine, 368
Lawrence, Michael, 71
Le Grys, James, 181, 202
Leahy, Brendan, 221
Lears, Jackson, 175
Lefebvre, Marcel, 31, 242
Lehner, Ulrich, 88, 100
Lehu, Léonard, 293
Leidl, Jonathan L., 349
Lendvai, Paul, 368
Leo XIII, 94, 267
Lepore, Jill, 376, 392
Levering, Matthew, 38, 40, 44, 71
Levin, Yuval, 263, 267–68
Levitsky, Steven, 71, 392
Liberatore, Matteo, 94, 172
Lilla, Mark, 268
Lilly, William, 172
Lima Grecco, Gabriela de, 349
Lind, Andreas, 202
Lind, Michael, 349
Lindbeck, George, 40
Livitsky, Steven, 383, 387
Locke, John, 90, 226, 246
Lom3Z, 357, 368
Lonergan, Bernard, 92, 149–50, 159
Lorin, M. H., 188–89, 203
Lubac, Henri de, 62, 63, 200, 203
Lunz, Frank, 254

Maas, Korey D., 349
MacDougald, Park, 349
MacIntyre, Alasdair, 152, 209, 221, 293, 308, 318, 368
MacLean, Nancy, 71, 268
Madison, James, 226–27n5, 281
Maritain, Jacques, 71, 133, 135, 237–38, 285, 293, 306
Martin, Jenny Beth, 269
Marx, Karl, 45, 90, 91, 103, 121, 279
Maspero, Giulio, 159, 160
Massa, Mark, 268
Maurras, Charles, 179, 183–86, 188, 191, 192, 194–95, 203, 343
Mayer, Jane, 71, 268, 377, 392
McAllister, Ted V., 368
McCadden, Helen M., 100
McCadden, Joseph, 100

Author Index

McCool, Gerald A., 135, 203
McInerny, Ralph, 293, 318
McManus, Matthew, 368–69
McWhorter, John, 159
Medhurst, Kenneth, 349
Medina, Vicente, 100
Ménard, Xavier Foccroulle, 349
Mering, Noelle, 159
Messori, Vittorio, 160
Milbank, John, 160, 200, 203, 209, 221, 349
Mill, John Stuart, 362, 366
Miller, David, 221
Miller, Vincent, 318
Minerd, Matthew K., 293
Misner, Paul, 135
Möhler, Johann Adam, 112
Molina, Luis de, 94
Moloney, Deirdre M., 349
Montaigne, Michel de, 82, 89
Monte, Domingo del, 97
Montesquieu, 81, 281
More, Thomas, 82
Mouffe, Chantal, 349
Mounk, Yascha, 349
Moyn, Samuel, 268, 378, 392
Muller, Jerry Z., 268
Murdoch, Iris, 312, 318
Murphy, James G., 318
Murphy, William F. Jr., 71–72, 175, 268, 392
Murray, John Courtney, 140, 207, 221, 293

Naím, Moisés, 387, 392
NATCON Rome, 369
Navia, Juan M., 100
Neklason, Annika, 175
Nell-Breuning, Oswald von, 94
Neto, Odilon Caldeira, 348
Neuhaus, Richard John, xvi, 252, 257, 259, 268
Newman, John Henry, 92
Nichols, Aidan, 200, 203
Nietzsche, Friedrich, 45, 356, 364–65
Nolte, Ernst, 349
Nono, Pio, 207
Novak, Michael, 249, 253

Nussbaum, Martha, 221

O'Brien, David J., 72
O'Malley, John W., 221
O'Malley, Martin J., 56, 135–36
O'Meara, Thomas F., 136
Oreskes, Naomi, 72, 268, 385
Orsy, Ladislas, 315, 318
Ozouf, Mona, 100

Pabst, Adrian, 160, 332, 349
Paine, Thomas, 263
Palladium Podcast, 349
Pappin, Gladden, 72, 325, 331, 333, 349
Patten, Alan, 350
Patterson, James M., 293, 350
Paul VI, 72, 160, 203, 221, 293, 318, 392
Pavan, Pietro, 306
Pawelec, Przemysław, 350
Pecknold, Chad C., 32, 64, 72, 325, 331–33
Peñalver, Eduardo M., 319
Pengelly, Martin, 392
Pepper, David, 72
Pera, Marcello, 208–9, 221
Pesch, Heinrich, 142, 146
Peterson, Jordan, 43
Pew Research Center, 72
Pfülf, Otto, 136
Phillips, George, 108, 116
Phillips, Kevin P., 249, 268
Picard, Gabriel, 203
Piccadori, Giovanni Battista, 93, 100
Pilkington, Philip, 29, 73
Pink, Thomas, 325
Pinkoski, Nathan, 350
Pintado-Murphy, Patricia, 73
Pius VIII, 136
Pius IX, 268
Pius X, 203
Pius XI, 101
Pius XII, 268
Podhorzer, Michael, 268
Pogge, Thomas, 221
Pojanowski, Jeffrey, 350
Pomerantsev, Peter, 386, 392
Pontifical Council for Justice and Peace, 73, 221, 268, 392

Author Index

Porter, Jean, 152, 160, 297, 303–5, 310, 313–14, 319
Portier-Young, Anathea E., 73
Posner, Eric, 350
Prusak, Bernard G., 319
Przeworski, Adam, 350
Putnam, Robert D., 148, 160

Quigley, Brian, 350

Rahner, Karl, 38, 39
Rand, Ayn, 22
Ratzinger, Joseph, 62, 65, 138–39, 160, 221, 252, 293
Rausch, Jonathan, 392
Rawls, John, 211, 282, 283, 293, 362, 366
Reich, Robert, 73
Reid, Thomas, 90
Reilly, Robert R., 160, 279, 293
Reimann, Mathias, 136
Reithmayr, Franz Xaver, 117
Reno, R. R., 332, 350, 369
Rhonheimer, Martin, xvi, xix, 65, 73, 160, 270–72, 280–83, 288, 293–94, 380, 393
Richardson, Heather Cox, 73, 268, 377, 393
Richardson, Katherine, 73
Riebling, Mark, 221
Riordan, Patrick, 203
Robinson, James A., 69, 384, 389, 391
Rodríguez Luño, Ángel, 280, 294
Rommen, Heinrich A., 272, 277, 294
Rooney, James Dominic, 294, 350
Roosevelt, Franklin Delano, 57, 58, 146, 174n28, 175, 233, 393
Rorty, Richard, 98
Rose, Matthew, 73, 369, 381, 382, 393
Rosenthal, Alexander S., 294
Rousseau, Jean-Jacques, 81, 93
Rousselot, Pierre, 92
Roussinos, Aris, 332, 350
Rufo, Christopher F., 43, 350, 357
Russell, Kerri, 73
Russo, Antonio, 203
Rustow, Dankwart A., 350

Ryan, John A., 142–46, 158, 161–75, 268–69, 372
Ryan, Paul, 366

Sachs, Jeffrey D., 269
Sachs, Stephen E., 346
Saco, José Antonio, 81
Sajó, András, 350
Salzman, Todd A., 319
Sanchez, Gabriel S., 351
Sapolsky, Robert, 393
Savigny, Friedrich Carl von, 108
Schall, James V., 276, 294
Schatz, Klaus, 122, 136
Scheppele, Kim Lane, 73
Schindler, D. C., 62–64, 73, 203, 259, 273–75, 279, 294, 325
Schlag, Martin, 159, 160
Schmidtlein, Eduard Joseph von, 108
Schmitt, Carl, 360, 369
Schuck, Michael J., 101
Schulz, Jonathan F., 294
Schwartz, Daniel, 294
Schwartzman, Micah, 351
Sedgwick, Mark, 369, 381, 393
Segovia, Fernando, 96, 101
Shadle, Matthew, 351
Shannon, Thomas A., 72
Sheehan, James J., 109, 136
Shue, Henry, 221
Sievernich, Michael, 158
Simon, Yves R., 176, 258, 269, 294, 382, 393
Smith, Adam, 140
Smith, Brian H., 347
Smith, Patrick, 325, 351
Smith, Talmon Joseph, 73
Society for the Rule of Law, 73
Sokolowski, Robert, 294
Spektorowski, Alberto, 351
Spinoza, Baruch, 88
Stadlbaur, Max von, 116
Stahl, Friedrich Julius, 136
Stanley, Jason, 388, 393
Starke, Rodney, 285, 292
Stebenne, David, 381, 393
Sterling, Gregory E., 73
Stern, Alexander, 73, 203, 269

Author Index

Stern, Mark Joseph, 319
Stevens, Stuart, 262, 269
Stevenson, Bryan, 160
Stewart, Katherine, 269
Storck, Thomas, 326, 351
Strauss, Leo, 360, 369
Strickland, Kyle, 73, 393
Su, Anna, 349
Suárez, Francisco, 182–83, 294
Sullivan, Francis A., 319

Taparelli, Luigi, 94
Taylor, Charles, 154, 160, 182, 203, 369
Teilhard de Chardin, Pierre, 41
Teitelbaum, Benjamin R., 382, 383, 393
Thibaut, Anton, 108
Thomas Aquinas, 134, 291–92
Tocqueville, Alexis de, 97, 286, 294
Tollefsen, Christopher, 319
Toner, James H., 351
Tooze, Adam, 13, 14, 16, 393
Torres-Cuevas, Eduardo, 101
Trabbic, Joseph G., 351
Traub, James, 269, 393
Treisman, Daniel, 71
Truman, Tom, 351
Turowsky, Nathan, 351
Tushnet, Mark, 351
Tyler, Amanda, 369

Uitz, Renáta, 350
United Nations General Assembly, 73
United States Conference of Catholic Bishops, 73, 269

Vaidyanathan, Brandon, 74
Vakil, Abdoolkarim, 351
Vallier, Kevin, 323, 351
van Kersbergen, Kees, 348
Vanden Heuvel, Jon, 136
Vander Schel, Kevin M., 135
Varela, Félix, 56, 75–99, 101
Varga, Mihai, 347, 351
Veiga González, Roberto, 101

Vergara, Camila, 351
Vermeule, Adrian, 28, 29, 33, 74, 325, 331, 334–36, 340, 350–352, 361, 363, 369
Vigener, Fritz, 106, 136
Viguerie, Richard, 269, 251n48
Vitier, Cintio, 101
Voegelin, Eric, 360
Voltaire, 97

Waal, Frans de, 254, 269
Waldstein, Edmund, 325, 326, 329, 336, 340, 352
Waller, Julian G., 352
Walsh, Kevin, 350
Ward, Ian, 369
Wehrlé, Johannes, 202
Weigel, George, 253, 257, 269, 352
Weiss, Rebecca Bratten, 393
Wessman, Aaron, 101
West, Cornell, 98
White, Christopher, 74
White, Thomas Joseph, 74
Whyte, Jamie, 352
Wieacker, Franz, 136
Wilken, Robert Louis, 294
Wilson, Jocelyn, 351
Windischmann, Friedrich, 117
Winston, Diane, 369
Wippel, John F., 294
Witt-Swanson, Lindsey, 74
Wolkenstein, Fabio, 353
Wong, Felicia, 73, 393
Wood, John Carter, 269
Wooden, Cindy, 74
Woods, Thomas E., 353
World Economic Forum, 74

Yarvin, Curtis, 357

Ziblatt, Daniel, 71, 353, 383, 387, 392
Zimring, Franklin E., 160
Zizola, Giancarlo, 221

www.ingramcontent.com/pod-product-compliance
Lightning Source LLC
Chambersburg PA
CBHW052049290426
44111CB00011B/1679